GREAT BORDEAUX WINES

GREAT BORDEAUX WINES

James Seely

Research by Christian Seely
Photographs by Charles Martin

SECKER & WARBURG·LONDON

In memory of Martin Bamford, M.W.
of Château Loudenne

First published in England 1986 by
Martin Secker & Warburg Limited
54 Poland Street, London W1V 3DF

Copyright © James Seely 1986

British Library Cataloguing in Publication Data

Seely, James
    Great Bordeaux wines.
    1. Wine and wine making——France——
    Bordeaux——History
    I. Title
    641.2'22'094471   TP553

    ISBN 0-436-44490-9

Set in Linotron Bembo by Tradespools Ltd.,
Frome, Somerset
Printed and bound by Butler & Tanner Ltd.,
Frome and London

Contents

Preface

The writing of this book is the fulfilment of an idea that has been germinating over a period of twenty-five years spent in the English wine trade. Of all the many great wines that are made in the world, it is the wine of Bordeaux which has given me the most pleasure, and, like countless Englishmen before me, I have always had a special fascination for this corner of south-western France; year after year I have found myself drawn back to the Gironde by the myriad of tiny threads, which, woven together, make up a rich tapestry depicting a love-affair between our two countries that has lasted over eight centuries, ever since Henry II married Eleanor of Aquitaine, thus acquiring Gascony and Bordeaux as her dowry.

The first and most difficult problem was the selection of the properties to be encompassed by the book. At first it was my intention to cover only the sixty-two red wine châteaux listed in the 1855 classification, which included only the great properties of the Médoc peninsula, plus Château Haut-Brion in the Graves. This, however, would have meant excluding the whole of St Emilion, Pomerol, the Graves, Sauternes and many excellent lesser growths of the Médoc. There are over three thousand châteaux producing wine in the Bordeaux area, and to treat them all in the manner I have adopted in this work would have filled some twenty-five volumes (quite apart from taking the rest of my life to complete, which might have been considerably shortened in the process by the sheer weight of Bordelais hospitality).

My final decision was to take as the base of my studies all the members of the Union des Grands Crus de Bordeaux, as well as those Crus Classés of the Médoc who, for varying reasons, are not members of this body, as well as three of my own personal favourites. The Union des Grands Crus de Bordeaux, under the able and dedicated presidency of Pierre Tari of Château Giscours, is a revitalised form of the Union des Grands Crus de la Gironde, which was established just after the 1855 classification under the leadership of the Marquis de Lur Saluces, great-uncle of the present owner of Château d'Yquem. On his death the organisation was disbanded, to be revived in 1973 by Pierre Tari and a group of some twenty other proprietors, under the slightly modified name. The standards for membership are strictly defined; member-properties may be from any of the great appellations, embracing the whole of the Médoc, Graves, Sauternes, St Emilion and Pomerol, and all are serious winemakers. The Union meets regularly in its office in the Maison du Vin in the Cours du XXX Juillet in Bordeaux, is dedicated to the maintenance of the standards of quality and reputation of the wines of Bordeaux, and is responsible for extensive promotional activities in France and many overseas countries. I am deeply indebted to the Union and all its members, and, in particular to Pierre Tari and Philippe Guyonnet-Dupérat, President and Director respectively, for their unflagging help and support throughout the years of visits and research that have culminated in the publication of this book.

On the broad canvas presented by this collection of 137 fine properties, I have endeavoured to paint a picture of the region, the history of its châteaux and their owners, and the elements of soil, climate, viticulture, vinification and people which combine to produce what is for me the noblest of wines. It has been a mammoth and, on occasions, gruelling task, but one which, thanks to the warmth and generous hospitality of the Bordelais, has given me some of the happiest months of my life. The object of this book is to share the joys of my romp through these Elysian fields, as well as a little of the knowledge that I gained during my many months of research, tastings and visits.

Of the many benefits I have derived from this work, perhaps the greatest is the number of new friendships formed and old ones cemented. My thanks are due to all the owners and their staff, too numerous to mention individually, but a special word of gratitude is due to two very good friends; firstly I must thank Hugues Lawton for all his many kindnesses, and for the wealth of information past and present that he gave me from his seemingly inexhaustible knowledge of Bordeaux; secondly I am profoundly grateful to Michel Tesseron, who so generously allowed me to live at Château Malescasse for the whole of my long sojourn in the Médoc, and whose only recompense was an introduction to the delights of the English breakfast and Indian cooking. At the same time I would be churlish to forget the saintly kindness of Monsieur and Madame Dufau of Malescasse, who came to my rescue on many an occasion during the dreadful freeze of January 1985.

Since this preface has become the platform for thanks, it is appropriate that I should close with a restrained, but no less heartfelt acknowledgement to someone who has given me his tireless and unstinting help throughout every stage of this book. My son, Christian, has been responsible not only for finding, chauffeuring and generally organ-ising our talented photographer, Charlie Martin, he has also done endless research and accompanied me on numerous sorties through the chais, tast-ing-rooms, dining-rooms and vineyards of Bor-deaux. His company has always been a joy and pleasure, and his rewards few, and it is typical of his modesty that he would not share my place on the spine of this book as co-author. When I met Odette Hallowes, the heroic Odette Churchill of the last war, I told her that I was writing a book with my son. 'If a father and son can work well together on such a project,' she said, 'that is a rare thing, and I think you are a lucky man.' She was dead right.

Introduction

The place

Just to the west of the Greenwich meridian line, on both sides of Latitude 45° North, there is a triangle of land which is my particular 'corner of a foreign field'; it is known as the Gironde, and within its 500-odd square kilometres are made some of the greatest wines in the world. To find this area on a map of France, take a line south-south-east from Le Verdon at the tip of the Médoc peninsula some 65 km to the village of Sauternes near Langon; from here the second leg of the triangle runs 22 km north-east, crossing the A62 Bordeaux–Toulouse autoroute, the Garonne river, then the Dordogne and terminating at the hilltop town of St Emilion; the third side, joining St Emilion to Le Verdon, is about 50 km long, and cuts through Pomerol and skirts the eastern edge of the Côtes de Blaye and Bourg.

Geology

The banks of the Gironde estuary, and the Isle, Dordogne and Garonne rivers in south-west France were geologically blessed during the latter part of the last five hundred million years of the earth's history, the quaternary period. It was during this time that the quartz-rich gravels, which are the *sine qua non* of every great vineyard in this area, were brought here by these rivers from the Massif Central to the east and the Pyrenees to the south. This was a classic blessing in disguise, for this soil that is so suited to the cultivation of the noble vines supports practically no other form of agriculture.

Climate

The second vital element in the making of fine wine is the weather, and here again the Gironde is admirably favoured. The maritime climate, influenced by the warm Atlantic waters of the Gulf Stream, gives generally mild and short winters followed by a balmy spring and a summer and autumn that are generally warm and sunny, with just the right amount of rainfall. Severe frosts are happily rare; in my lifetime there has been but one really disastrous winter, when the late February frosts of 1956 destroyed vast areas of vines. In January of 1985 there was the third heavy snowfall of the century in the Gironde, accompanied by night-time temperatures of $-17°C$; happily this was too early for the sap to have started to rise in the vines and, though at the time of writing it was too early to assess any damage, it was thought that only the previous year's plantings were at risk.

A separate mention should be made, while speaking of climate, of the very special conditions which apply in Sauternes. Here an individual microclimate exists, which allows and encourages the fungoid growth called *botrytis cinerea*, *pourriture noble* or noble rot. The spores of this fungus attack the skins of the grapes without penetrating them, shrivelling the berries to a raisin-like appearance. The juice is reduced and concentrated to an amazing degree of honeyed sweetness, allowing for the production of a *vin liquoreux* of wonderful complexity and richness. The conditions that work this miracle are a combination of early-morning mists, rising from the tiny Ciron river that flows through the parishes of the Sauternes district in to the Garonne, and fine sunny autumn days that often extend well into November. Apart from this tiny area, wines of this exquisite type can only be made naturally in two other places in the world, the Rhine and Moselle valleys and a small part of the Tokay vineyards in Hungary.

The vines

Having examined briefly the geology and climate of the Bordeaux region, the third vital ingredient is the raw material from which the wine is made, the grape. In the early days of winemaking little importance was attached to the variety of vine employed, so long as it produced sufficient quantities of juice with enough sugar to ferment satisfactorily – indeed it is less than four hundred years since the juices of both black and white grapes were mixed indiscriminately and vinified together. In the seventeenth century the knowledge of vinification and techniques of ageing began to improve, and the suitability of different varieties of *vitis vinifera* to different soil types began to assume some of their present significance. Viticultural studies of this type are of necessity a slow process, since a vine takes upwards of twenty years to reach optimum production, and it was not until the mid-nineteenth century that the classic varieties from which the best Bordeaux wine is made – and indeed must now by law be made – emerged in their present form.

For the red wine there are five varieties permitted, and I list them below, giving the characteristics they impart to the wine and the approximate proportions in which they appear in the various appellations of the Gironde.

(i) **Cabernet Sauvignon** The aristocrat of the Médoc vineyards, where it represents anywhere between 50% and 90% of the total *encépagement* of most Grand Cru vineyards. This variety gives colour, tannin and structure to the wine, and is largely responsible for long life. It is also the grape that gives the distinctive blackcurrant bouquet that typifies good Bordeaux red.

(ii) **Cabernet Franc** More productive and less distinguished than the Cabernet Sauvignon, this grape is present in lesser quantities in the Médoc, but is more widely favoured in St Emilion and Pomerol, where it is also known as the Bouchet. It gives a softer wine, more aromatic and less deep-coloured than the Cabernet Sauvignon, with less tannin and backbone, and ripens slightly earlier.

(iii) **Merlot** The predominant variety in St Emilion and Pomerol, it is also present to a greater or lesser degree in almost all the Médoc vineyards. It comes into flower earlier than the Cabernets, and is therefore prone to *coulure* – arrested growth and dropping off of the tiny buds at flowering time caused by rain, cold or high winds – as occurred in 1984. *Coulure* was wrongly referred to by the wine journalists as a malady of the vine, and 1984 was predicted as an off-vintage. The grapes that survive this accident of nature can be perfectly healthy, as was the case in 1984, and the resulting wine has every chance of being a good one, though small in terms of quantity. The Merlot ripens first of all the varieties by as much as ten days, and gives a wine high in alcohol, soft and fat, with less tannin and acidity than the Cabernets.

(iv) **Malbec** Now being used less and less throughout the region, though small quantities are still grown in many vineyards. The wine it produces is quite large in character and fairly tannic, though it tends to lack finesse.

(v) **Petit Verdot** Again an 'also-ran' variety, abandoned by many properties, the Petit Verdot still has its champions. The highest proportion of this I have seen is 15%, but it is more usually 10%, 5% or even less. It is difficult to grow, and ripens last of all, in some years not at all. It gives a very concentrated, tannic wine of great backbone and finesse and lends a consistent deep colour to the final blend. It is perhaps indicative of the type of wine produced that it has been dropped by Robert Dousson at de Pez and Jean Louis Charmolüe at Montrose, top growers in the commune of St Estèphe, where the vines are already tough and tannic enough.

The white wines of the area, whether dry or sweet, are all made from a combination of three varieties in varying proportions, and sometimes from only one of these to the exclusion of the other two.

(i) **Sauvignon Blanc** Basically a dry white wine grape, it is also found in varying proportions of from 5% to 30% in most of the great Sauternes vineyards. In the Graves, it is more predominant, varying from 100% at Château Malartic-Lagravière, where it gives a dry white of impeccable breeding with wonderful ageing qualities, down to a more usual average of between 40% and 60%. To the Sauternes wines it adds a distinctly refreshing quality, and does not 'take' the *pourriture noble* readily. It is essentially a 'grapey' grape, and gives a delicious crisp, dry wine with a beautiful clarity of style, and is also widely used in the Loire valley.

(ii) **Semillon** The dominant Sauternes variety, which gives alcohol, richness and suppleness to the wine; it is the grape which is most readily affected by the noble rot, and usually represents from 70% to 90% of the *encépagement* in Sauternes. It is also used in the production of dry white wine, though in far smaller quantities.

(iii) **Muscadelle** Grown in small proportions, mainly in the Sauternes and Barsac vineyards and occasionally in the Graves. Often confused with

the Muscat, it gives a faintly similar agreeable flavour to the wine. In Sauternes it usually appears in a proportion of from 1% to 10% of the *encépagement*, but more generally 5% or less.

As with the soil, so with the vine, greatness comes only from adversity and quality is only ever achieved at the expense of quantity. Pruning is severe, with the object of producing a low yield of grapes in optimum condition, which have drawn moisture, nourishment and trace elements from the roots, which reach down sometimes as far as thirty feet into the subsoil below. The pruning method adopted in the Gironde is an adaptation of the Guyot system. The vines are pruned between December and March, and one cane is left with anything from one to six buds for this year's growth, plus a shorter 'spur' with one bud for the following year; this is known as Guyot Simple, and is universally used in St Emilion and Pomerol, and only rarely in the Médoc. The Guyot Double, as the name suggests, leaves two long canes and two spurs, directed horizontally away on either side of the trunk pointing down the row of vines. This is the system almost universally employed in the Médoc. Both systems are used in the Graves, according to the preference of the owner or the suitability of local conditions. A third and even more drastic system of pruning is used, principally for the Semillon vines, in the Sauternes and Barsac vineyards; it is known as *à cot*, and only three, two or sometimes only one bud is left on one spur per vine.

The Human Element

We have looked at the three natural ingredients of weather, soil and grapes, and this brings us to the fourth – and vital – human element. Most of the Bordelais play down the importance of their role in the winemaking process with typical modesty, but without the love, care and control exercised by the owners and vignerons alike, the wine of Bordeaux could soon lose its very singular identity. One owner told me that the secret of making great wine was the capacity for taking endless trouble over hundreds of minor details; this is true enough, but there is more to it than that. The reputation and quality of the wines of Bordeaux has survived, and can only survive in the future in all its magic and majesty, through the dedication of those who make it. They have a special quality, these people, that transcends adversity. Through wars, revolution, religious strife, economic depression, disease and disaster, they have carried on the business of making and selling their great wines which give such joy to countless wine lovers the world over. It is partly a selfless work, for the temptations of short-term profits often have to be resisted. Computers are with us, and business efficiency experts, who will doubtless advocate changes in vinification to produce wines that mature quicker to give faster returns on capital invested; to keep Bordeaux where it has always been, in pride of place in the world's cellars and on the world's wine-lists, this rare breed of men will carry on, albeit using every modern technique of oenology and ampelology, making the traditional *grand vin* that can only be made in Bordeaux.

History

The potential afforded by the natural elements of soil and climate for the making of great wine in the Gironde was only realised comparatively recently: indeed the Médoc was regarded as a wild and infertile tract of scrub and marsh until as late as the seventeenth century, when a vast programme of drainage was carried out by Dutch engineers. Vines were certainly planted in the area round the limestone outcrop of St Emilion and other parts of the Gironde as early as the first century AD and were introduced by the Romans, but the wine that they and their successors made bore very little resemblance to the fine table wines that we know today. It was a thin and often bitter drink, and had to be drunk within a few months of being made, since nothing was known of ageing and keeping techniques until hundreds of years later.

The 'viticultural revolution' did not really take place until the late seventeenth century, when vinification in clean oak vats and ageing in wooden casks began to be widely adopted. It was about this time that people first began to understand the significance of different grape varieties and the all-important equation between quality and quantity. The real breakthrough in the production of claret as we know it today, with its extraordinary finesse and great longevity, was the technical ability to produce glass bottles of reasonable uniformity, in which, when closed with a cork stopper of good quality, the wine spends by far the greatest part of its long maturation; this was at the end of the eighteenth century.

The first autonomous Bordeaux wines, 'Grands Crus' or 'great growths' sold under the name of the proprietor or vineyard from which they came, were those of the Graves. The de Pontac family, owners of Château Haut-Brion in Pessac, exported their wine to England in the latter part of the seventeenth century; moreover they were sufficiently commercially-minded to open their own tavern, the Pontac's Head, in the city of London in 1666, where the wine of 'Ho Bryan' was available for the princely sum of seven shillings a bottle.

From that day until this, Bordeaux has enjoyed a healthy export market for its liquid gold in ever-widening circles across the surface of the globe. For nearly three centuries, however, the consumer was very much in the hands of middle-men. The provenance and quality of Bordeaux wine was entirely dependent on the knowledge and integrity of the négociants, or wine merchants, of Bordeaux through whom all the wine of the region was sold, and of the importing merchants. Until the 1920s bottling at the châteaux was the exception rather than the rule, even for the Premiers Crus, and the general practice was for the wine to be bought by the négociants in cask; it would then be delivered, still in cask, to the cellars of the buyer, usually on the Quai des Chartrons or the Quai de Bacalan in Bordeaux, where it would either be bottled after spending the requisite ageing period, or whence it would be shipped in cask for bottling by the importing merchant. It can be seen that between leaving the château of its birth and arriving on the table of the consumer, there was, under this system, ample opportunity for the wine to lose not only its original character, but even, at worst, its very identity. Out-and-out fraud was happily rare, though it would be silly to assume that the obvious temptations never proved

too much for the less scrupulous; the main danger for the proprietor who cherished the name and fame of his château lay in the care and bottling of his wine between its departure from his chai and its ultimate appreciation by the drinker. The best safeguard, both for the owner and the consumer, lies in the words 'mis en bouteille au château', which happily must now appear on the label of every Grand Cru claret or Sauternes.

The earliest advocate of château-bottling was Baron Philippe de Rothschild, who adopted the practice at Mouton very soon after his arrival in 1922. The first total château bottling of Mouton-Rothschild was in 1924, and the other First Growths, encouraged by the young baron, followed suit, though the practice did not become universal until as late as the 1970s.

It is perhaps, the order, discipline and reserve inherent in the making and the eventual character of Bordeaux wines that, for me at least, make their study and enjoyment such an endless fascination and pleasure. I shall have achieved my objective if, in the pages of this book, I have in some small way succeeded in showing the extraordinary blend of skills, patience, sacrifice and, above all, love of their work and product, that combine to make the Bordeaux winemakers a very special breed of men. I salute them.

Explanatory notes on the Technical Information Sections

General

Appellation

The law of 'Appellation d'Origine Contrôlée' is administered by the government body known as the Institut National des Appellations d'Origine, generally referred to as the INAO. The regulations embodied within the structure of this legislation are complex, but are basically successful in their intention – the protection of the quality and reputation of the wines of France.

Without going into too much detail, the basic concept of the AOC is a geographic one; it is a reasonably accurate rule of thumb to say that the smaller the area defined by the INAO, the more stringent are the regulations that apply to that particular appellation, and the higher will be the quality of the wine produced. Thus the appellation Pauillac is likely to produce a wine superior to the wider one of Haut-Médoc, which in turn tends to signify a better quality than the much broader area covered by the appellation of plain Bordeaux.

Within each appellation, apart from a strictly defined geographic location, the regulations cover such things as the grape varieties that may be used, pruning methods, cultivation, treatments of the vines, permissible fertilisers, vinification systems and the maximum yield allowed in hectolitres per hectare. INAO inspectors ensure adherence to these rules, and the system is undoubtedly beneficial to owner and consumer alike.

Classification

With the exception of Pomerol, all the main areas within the Bordeaux wine-producing region have been officially classified at various times. The first and best-known classification was of the wines of the Médoc and Sauternes, and was made in 1855 for the Great Exhibition in Paris of that year. The Bordeaux Chamber of Commerce produced this list, and it was based on quality and price as advised by the 'courtiers' of the period. The wines of the Médoc were divided into Grands Crus, subdivided into four Premiers, fifteen Deuxièmes, fourteen Troisièmes, ten Quatrièmes and eighteen Cinquièmes, followed by a small group of seven Crus Exceptionnels, which are followed by some two hundred Crus Bourgeois and Crus Artisans.

It should be borne in mind that to be classified as a Fifth Growth of the Médoc in no way indicates a fifth-rate or inferior wine; inclusion in the elevated ranks of the five dozen or so Crus Classés from among over 3,000 Bordeaux wine properties is an indication of the highest quality.

Obviously during the one hundred and thirty years since 1855, owners have changed, bits of land have been bought and sold, and many châteaux have had their ups and downs; there are also several properties of Cru Bourgeois status where wine is being made of Cru Classé standard, and many people and organisations within the Bordeaux wine trade have from time to time agitated for a re-classification. It is, nonetheless, surprising how accurate the 1855 listing still remains. Only one official change has been made to the original grouping, when Château Mouton-Rothschild was rightly elevated in 1973 from Second to First Growth status. It can be justifiably argued that an overhaul of the system of classification for the whole Bordeaux region is long overdue, but the bureaucratic and political problems entailed in such an exercise are legion and almost insurmountable.

The 1855 classification of the Sauternes vineyards showed one Premier Grand Cru – Château d'Yquem – nine Premiers and twelve Deuxièmes; the number of first growths shows the importance of Sauternes in the middle of the last century, since the same yardstick of price was applied to the wines of the Médoc, where only four Firsts were listed, including one, Château Haut-Brion, in the Graves.

The wines of the Graves were first classified in 1953 and this was revised in 1959. Since 1984 the wines of the Graves made around Pessac and Léognan have been entitled to include this information on their labels. Thirteen red wines are entitled to the words Grand Cru Classé and nine whites. Of the red wines classified, only two do not produce a white wine, and there is only one of the whites, Château Couhins, which is not produced by a red wine property.

Across the Dordogne in St Emilion, the first official listing was the classification of 1955, when the best vineyards were divided into twelve Premiers Grands Crus, of which two, Châteaux Ausone and Cheval-Blanc bear the suffix A, and the rest are known as Premiers Grands Crus Classés B, and no less than seventy-one Grands Crus. The rules for the classification are strict, and entitlement is subject to annual tasting. The classification is reviewed at regular intervals; the original intention was to revise the listing every ten years, but the enormity of the bureaucratic process have caused this period to be extended. Since 1955 there have been two revisions – one in 1958 and one in 1969 – and the third one is currently in progress.

The wines of Pomerol have never been officially classified, though various listings have been made by sundry organisations and experts. All are agreed that Château Petrus stands out in a class of its own, and would undoubtedly rank with the Premiers Crus in any wholesale re-classification of the wines of the Gironde. There is also a fairly unanimous agreement as to the hierarchy of the next dozen or so châteaux.

Area under vines

This indicates the total number of hectares under vines on a property that is entitled to the appellation; a proportion of this area may be taken up with newly planted vines, thus a property may have 60 hectares of AC vineyard, but only 55 may be in production at any given time.

Production

I have given the average production over a ten-year period, expressed in cases of twelve 75cl bottles. This will obviously vary considerably from vintage to vintage; to confuse the issue, some proprietors have a second label under which they sell the produce of younger vines and any wine not considered good enough for inclusion in the Grand Vin. This is sometimes included in the average production figure, but more often not.

Distribution of vines

I thought it interesting to include this information, since wines made on vineyards that are all in one piece tend to have a more uniform character from year to year, as opposed to those of vineyards that are widely scattered over a commune, and are therefore subject to microclimatic variations and their diverse effects on differing soil types.

Names of owners, directors, administrators, maîtres de chai, régisseurs, etc.

Frequently a château is owned by a company, and, where this the case, I have tried to show the name of the family or person with the controlling interest as well. Names of proprietors and their staff obviously change from time to time, and this information will be updated in subsequent editions.

Consultant Oenologist

Over the past fifteen years or so more and more châteaux have employed the services of these technocrats of the wine world. Professors Emile Peynaud and Pascal Ribereau-Gayon are the doyens of the oenological world, though the former is now semi-retired and much of this work is carried out by his pupil Jacques Boissenot. The knowledge and expertise of such pundits is unquestioned, but it is ultimately up to the proprietor to decide whether to follow their advice. A similar service, ranging through advice on encépagement, viticulture, vinification and the all-important blending of the assemblage, as well as the provision of chemical analyses of soils and wine samples, is also available from a number of oenological stations or laboratories throughout the region.

Viticulture

Geology

This is probably the single most important natural factor in determining the eventual quality and character of the wine produced on any property. With one or two exceptions, the most notable of which is Château Petrus, all the top growths have a high proportion of large, medium or fine gravel in the top layer of soil. This has the double advantage of reflecting the sun's rays to the underside of the bunches of grapes, and of retaining heat during the hours of darkness. Subsoils are of varying types from region to region, but the most essential quality is that the subsoil should be of a striated or fissured nature to allow for good drainage and deep penetration of the vine roots.

Grape varieties

The varieties most widely used and their contributions to the style of the wine have been covered in the introduction. It should also be emphasised that the percentage figures shown only indicate the numbers of vines grown at each property; obviously the different varieties fare differently from year to year, as they flower, ripen and mature at different rates. Thus in a year like 1984 the Merlot crop was virtually wiped out by coulure in St Emilion and Pomerol, and reduced by about 50% in the Médoc; so a wine like, for instance, Château la Conseillante in Pomerol, although it has 60% of its vineyard planted with Merlot, may have as little as 20% in the final assemblage of the 1984 vintage.

Pruning

The different systems employed are described in the introduction.

Rootstock

All the classic French vines are grafted on to American rootstocks; this practice has been adopted since late last century, when the American stocks were found to be resistant to the ravages of the *Phylloxera vastatrix*, a beetle which virtually destroyed the whole of France's vineyards in the 1870s. They are generally referred to by code numbers such as 3309, 101-14, SO4 or Riparia Gloire, which is, in fact, the 'parent' of most of the rootstocks employed in the region.

Vines per hectare

This figure is dependent on the width between the rows of vines and the space between the vines themselves. A planting system widely adopted is based on rows 1 metre apart and a space of 1 metre between the vines, giving 10,000 vines per hectare. Lower density is sometimes used, according to soil and drainage conditions, to achieve optimum growth.

Yield per hectare

Maximum yield in hectolitres per hectare is strictly laid down by the INAO, but considerably lower yields are often deliberately sought in pursuit of quality. The prime example of low yield/high quality is clearly illustrated in the vineyards of Sauternes and Barsac, where as little as one or two glasses of wine can ultimately come from one vine.

Replanting

Some properties employ a regular rotational system, replanting a certain percentage of the total vineyard every year; others use the *complantation* method, which involves grubbing up and replacing only individual vines as they pass their productive peak, no matter where they may be in the vineyard. All are agreed that a high average vine age is desirable, since the older the vine the greater the quality of the wine; production decreases in terms of volume with age, so a proper balance of young and old vines must be maintained.

Vinification

Added yeasts

Most of the top growths pride themselves on their 'natural' fermentation; this is to say that, given average conditions at vintage time, the native yeast strains present in the grapes are sufficient to start and complete the alcoholic and malolactic fermentations. The vagaries of nature are such, however, that the addition of 'imported' yeast strains is occasionally necessary to start the process. Recent important experiments, particularly at Château Rahoul in the Graves, are proving definite connections between taste and yeast strains, especially in the low-temperature fermentation of white wines.

Length of maceration

The maceration is the period during which the juice is left in contact with the skins and pips, and is of vital importance in the optimum extraction of colour and tannins of red wine. Maceration takes place in the vats or *cuves*, and the wine is usually run off the *marc*, or cap of skins, before the malolactic fermentation, after which, generally in December or January, it ages in oak casks for a period of between one and two-and-a-half years before bottling.

Temperature of fermentation

The ideal temperature for the first, alcoholic fermentation of red wine is generally held to be between 28 and 32°C; secondary, or malolactic fermentation, during which the malic acid in the wine is converted into lactic acid, normally takes place some time after the first fermentation at a lower temperature. It is only in recent years that the beneficial effect of this process has been fully understood and deliberately encouraged before the wine is transferred into cask for ageing.

Oenologists are now generally agreed that a slow, cool fermentation is most beneficial for the production of quality white wine, and a temperature of between 17 and 21°C is sought.

Control of fermentation

The temperatures referred to in the preceding note are rarely achieved under entirely natural conditions, and have to be attained by artificial raising or lowering of the temperature of the must or grape-juice. Raising the temperature is usually achieved by warming the *cuvier*, or vathouse, by the use of hot-air blowers; in very hot weather, however, mere ventilation of the vathouse is often insufficient to cool the overheating must, and other methods are used.

In the past, when all fermentation was in oak vats, cooling was often achieved by the submersion of large blocks of ice in the vats, but this was expensive and unsatisfactory; the same result can be and is still arrived at by passing the juice through a serpentine coil, which is cooled by cold running water. The general emergence of stainless steel as an alternative material for fermentation vats, in place of oak or concrete, has greatly facilitated this vital temperature-control; cold water can be run down the outside surface of the vat, thus quickly cooling the must within. Thermostatic control systems of varying complexity in the individual vats are frequently employed, and at some properties, such as Château Guiraud in Sauternes, temperatures are controlled by computer.

Type of vats

The traditional fermentation vat for Bordeaux is of oak, and these are still in use at many properties; three of the five Premiers Crus have resisted the temptations of the more easily regulated stainless steel, and the beautiful ranks of gleaming dark oak can still be seen at Lafite, Margaux and Mouton.

Concrete is widely used, lined with epoxy-resin or glass, as are metal tanks, also lined with a suitable hygienic material. Stainless steel is now seen more and more, and it has many obvious advantages; it is ideally suited for rapid cooling or warming of the must, as described in the preceding note, it is easy to clean, is a completely neutral material, can impart no bad flavours or elements to the wine,

and has a life of twenty to thirty years with a minimum of maintenance other than routine cleaning.

Champions of the traditional oak point out that it is the very neutrality of stainless steel that weighs against it, and that a properly-maintained oak *cuve* adds an essential part of the tannins to the wine during maceration. Eyebrows were raised when Haut-Brion and Latour installed stainless-steel vats in the early 1960s, but the wine does not appear to have lost anything in the process.

Vin de Presse

This is the wine made from the pressing of the residues after the regular wine has been made and run off. It is very concentrated and tannic, and varying proportions may be incorporated in the final *assemblage* of the Grand Vin, according to the character of the vintage. There is normally a series of two or three pressings, the resulting wine being progressively harsher and more tannic; usually only the first pressing is used, and in some years and at some properties it is not included at all.

Age of casks

The traditional *barriques bordelaises*, in which the wine of all 'Grands Crus' spends from 12 to 30 months before bottling, represent a heavy investment, costing, as they do now, around 1,700 French Francs apiece. Arguments rage as to the ideal proportion of new barrels used in any one vintage. The new wood adds tannin to the wine, but a wine that is not 'big' enough cannot support too much of this 'new oak' character. All the Premiers Crus, and one or two others, such as Cheval-Blanc, Figeac, Petrus and La Lagune, use 100% new casks every vintage; the average is normally between 25% and 50%, the rest being casks of one or two vintages. In former times almost all châteaux employed their own coopers, but now only Lafite-Rothschild and Margaux have this luxury; the most important bonus derived from making your own casks is the selection and proper ageing of the best oak.

Time in cask

This varies between 12 and 30 months at most red wine properties, while in Sauternes it can be a little longer; at Yquem, for instance, the wine spends a minimum of three years in wood. During the first year in cask, most châteaux keep the barrels loosely bunged, with the stopper uppermost; regular topping up or *ouillage* is carried out two or three times a week to replace wine lost by evaporation, and to avoid harmful contact with the air. For the last part of the wine's sojourn in wood, the casks are tightly stoppered, and kept with the bung to the side.

During its time in cask *soutirage*, or racking, takes place four times a year. This involves drawing the wine off the lees, and transferring it to a clean and sterilised cask.

Fining

This is the process of clarification of the wine by the addition of colloidal material, which carries any suspended particles floating in the wine to the bottom of the cask or vat. Traditional fining of Bordeaux red wine is carried out with the beaten whites of four or five eggs, which are poured into each 225-litre cask, mixed well and left to settle before the final racking. Many properties now use powdered egg albumen or gelatine, and fining is carried out in vat, thus ensuring a total and uniform clarification.

Filtration

Two forms of filtration are employed, though by no means at all properties; many purists are proud to declare that their wine is never filtered. The first filtration, if it is employed, is known as *sur terre*, when the wine is passed through a screen of powdered shells before going into casks for the first time. The second, more widely adopted, is the filtration *sur plaque*, when the wine is gently run through cellulose filters just before bottling to remove any remaining particles that may cloud the wine.

Type of bottle

This is almost invariably the traditional bordelaise shape, with its clearly defined shoulder, of great assistance when decanting an old wine away from its sediment. A few properties use a different shape, notably Haut-Brion with its distinctive Hollandaise bottle; until recent years, the house of Cordier also had a similar bottle, but they have now returned to the normal Bordeaux style. A number of properties, like Château Giscours for instance, personalise their bottles with embossed names or crests, and Giscours plan to emboss the vintage on future bottles, an excellent if costly idea.

Bottle sizes are normally either 75 cl, the 37.5 cl half-bottle or the 1.5 litre magnum, though double-magnums, six-bottle-size jeroboams and the

majestic Impériale, containing the equivalent of eight bottles, are still produced. As a general rule of thumb, the larger the bottle, the slower and better the wine will mature. Although it is not within the scope of this book, it should be noted that this is not the case with giant bottles of Champagne such as the Methuselah and mighty Salmanazar; they have been filled from ordinary bottles after the Champagne process, and should be drunk within months rather than years.

Commercial

Vente Directe

This is the sign frequently seen in all parts of the Bordeaux region, which indicates that the wine of the property is available for purchase by the bottle or case to passing motorists. It does not mean that the château will export wine on a direct basis.

Direct ordering from the château

This generally means that the proprietor welcomes enquiries for shipping orders from trade customers, and does not sell exclusively through the local négociants, as is the general practice with Grand Cru châteaux.

Exclusivities

Sometimes a proprietor opts to sell his wine, for family or commercial reasons, through only one or two négociants, and where possible I have given details.

Agents overseas

Occasionally a proprietor will appoint an agent overseas, who will represent his château on an exclusive or partly-exclusive basis. More often the wines of Bordeaux are widely disseminated throughout the world market through the medium of the négociants. If a private customer has difficulty in obtaining any particular wine, his best course is to write to the proprietor for information.

Sales through the négociants

The vast majority of the wine of Bordeaux is sold both in France and overseas by the négociants or merchants, who are based mainly in Bordeaux and Libourne. They buy from the châteaux, sell on to the world's wine merchants at a modest mark-up, and provide an excellent service to owners and buyers alike.

Visits

Most proprietors are pleased to receive visitors, and it is sometimes possible to taste the young wines and purchase a few bottles. Weekends and holidays should be avoided, and many châteaux close for their annual break during the month of August. The vintage and subsequent vinification period are the busiest time in the winemakers' calendar, and visits should generally be avoided between mid-September and the end of October; in any case it is usually advisable to telephone the property for an appointment.

Some notes on tasting

The first principle of critical tasting may equally be applied to the enjoyment of wine at the table – 'give the wine a fair chance'.

Firstly the temperature of the wine must be right; as a rule of thumb, I suggest red wines are best served at around 18°C and whites at around 7° to 10°. Secondly, always use a properly shaped glass of sufficient volume to hold at least 15 centilitres of wine when the glass is only one-third full; the best glass is of a tulip shape, and plain rather than cut, as the tulip shape allows you to swirl the wine around, releasing and retaining the bouquet. Thirdly, most red wines benefit from being opened an hour before tasting, unless they are very old, and claret of four or five years age and over is best decanted away from any sediment that has formed. Lastly, make sure that your palate is as clean as possible; it is manifestly unfair on the wine if your taste-buds are fatigued from a recent highly-flavoured meal, strong black coffee, sweets or heavy smoking. Equally the tasting-room should be free from strong smells of cooking, central-heating vapours, etc.

Three senses are employed in the tasting of wine – sight, smell and taste; if you would become a good taster, memory is also vitally important. Since few of us are gifted with a photographic palate-memory, it is essential to write notes on everything you taste; keep them, and refer back to them constantly. It is only by building up a dossier of tasting-notes that you will slowly increase your knowledge of tastes, smells and colours, and that they will gradually start to acquire meaning. Remember that tasting is a very personal business, and that your notes are for your own benefit; always write down exactly what the colour, smell and taste convey to you; it does not matter if you think it sounds unprofessional, as long as it serves as a meaningful reference point for future tastings.

As a general rule, when tasting several wines I prefer to taste white before red and young before old; as an exception to the latter, it is sometimes better to taste a lighter year before a greater one, even if it is older, as, for example, a 1980 or 1977 claret will be overpowered by tasting a 1982 before it. For the sake of accurate comparison, especially of the appearance of a wine, the glasses should be filled to the same level when tasting a series of vintages. The generally adopted procedure is first to look at the wine, then to smell it and finally to taste it. Let us look at these three stages of tasting, and try to enumerate some of the things to look for.

Visual appearance Wine is best looked at in natural daylight against a white background. Look for and note clarity and colour. Is the wine clear and bright, does it contain cloudy, suspended matter or other impurities? Colour is a good guide to age; red wines tend to be deeper, more bluey or purple when they are young, and become browner as they mellow into old age. White wines, on the other hand, are usually very light when young, and in extreme youth can be almost colourless; as they grow older, particularly in the case of Sauternes and Barsacs, they acquire an ever-deepening golden hue. The good, dry whites of the Graves keep their light, youthful colour for many years.

The presence of floating particles, crystals or sediment need not be detrimental to a wine; in a young wine they may well disappear with fining, racking or filtration, and in older wines they may merely indicate rough handling between cellar and tasting-room. Crystals in the bottom of a bottle of red or white wine are frequently wrongly identified as sugar; more often than not they result from the natural precipitation of tartrate at low temperatures, and this is beneficial to the wine.

Nose or Bouquet The smell of a wine is best appreciated by swirling the wine gently around the glass; for this reason it is best not to fill the glass more than a third full, as there is less risk of spillage, and it allows a space in the glass for the bouquet to collect. In white Bordeaux, look for freshness and fruit in younger wines; the crisp, grapey smell of the Sauvignon grape soon becomes clearly distinguished from the fatter, rounder smell of the Sémillon; in the vins liquoreux of Sauternes and Barsac you will also soon learn to detect the authentic, rich ripeness of the 'noble rot', as opposed to the simply 'rôti' smell of very ripe grapes, which can indicate a good, luscious dessert wine that will lack the essential qualities given by *pourriture noble*.

'Nosing' a red Bordeaux is a complex business. In cask the wine will tend to have a powerful nose of the grape, combined with the slightly vanilla-like smell imparted by new oak from the barrel. After bottling the bouquet will become closed, or fermé, not giving much scent for a period that varies with the quality of the vintage; generally speaking the bigger and harder the wine, the longer it takes to develop its bouquet. The smell that most typifies good red Bordeaux is that of cassis or blackcurrant, which stems mainly from the Cabernet grape. Margaux wines have a definitely softer nose than other red Bordeaux, often likened to violets; another typical red Bordeaux smell is cigar-box, or cedarwood, and I have often found this to a marked degree in some Pauillac wines, especially Château Lynch-Bages.

Taste Good wine should always taste clean and wholesome. The hard, bitter taste of young red wines comes from the tannin, the element most essential for good ageing; in youth there must be the proper proportion of tannin and fruit, otherwise the wine will not have the balance to develop into a gracious old age. A long aftertaste is also a good indicator of quality, provided of course, that it is a pleasing sensation. A slight prickle on the tongue often shows that the wine is still fermenting, and this is not necessarily a bad thing, provided that the wine is still very young and all the other elements are present. Good qualities to look for are suppleness, good fruit, roundness, power, finesse and elegance. It is never considered rude to spit out the wine at a tasting; indeed, if you are lucky enough to taste several wines in a morning, it is essential, to avoid the palate – and the brain – becoming fatigued and confused.

Some people have a gift for tasting, but for most of us it is a question of hard work and experience. The most important thing to remember is to taste as much as you can, and always make notes. If tasting 'blind', never be discouraged by mistakes. I have known people of thirty years' experience mistake Bordeaux for Burgundy and vice-versa!

MARGAUX

Margaux is the most southerly of the four major appellations of the Médoc, which are all contained in the more broadly defined area of the Haut-Médoc. The vineyards entitled to the Margaux appellation lie within a rectangular area, approximatly five kilometres wide by eight kilometres long; the southern base of this rectangle runs from the village of Arsac, below the boundary of Château Giscours to Château Dauzac near the estuary, and extends north-west on either side of the D2 to the village of Tayac.

As well as numerous excellent Crus Bourgeois and lesser properties, the Margaux appellation embraces one Premier Cru, Château Margaux itself, five Deuxièmes, ten Troisièmes, three Quatrièmes and two Cinquièmes Crus. This represents over a third of all the properties deemed worthy of classification in 1855, and only two of these Fifth Growths, a clear indication of the high quality of the wines of Margaux.

The wines of five separate communes, Margaux itself, Arsac, Cantenac, Labarde and Soussans have the right to the name of Margaux, provided that they follow all the regulations laid down by the INAO. A peculiarity of the vineyards of this appellation is their fragmented nature; a single property may have dozens of small parcels of vines, sometimes spread over two, three or even four of the communes. Although this makes for difficulties of transport of men, machinery and grapes, the locals will tell you that it also has advantages; different locations also mean different soils, different exposure to sun, wind and frost and consequently spread the risk of adverse weather conditions.

Margaux wines have a character quite distinct from the other Bordeaux appellations; they have a soft elegance and feminine charm that is seen at its apogee in the wine of its monarch, Château Margaux itself.

From the gastronomic point of view, the traveller in the Médoc finds himself in a comparative desert. For an area producing a huge volume of the world's finest wine, good restaurants are very thin on the ground. Margaux, however, is a relative oasis. In Labarde there is the Rendez-Vous des Chasseurs, where one may lunch or dine adequately in fairly basic surroundings. Further up the road, in the village of Margaux itself, is the

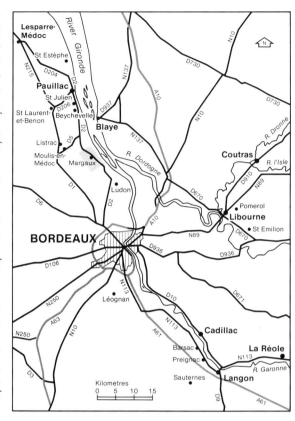

Auberge de Savoie, where the food is an excellent blend of traditional French cooking and *nouvelle cuisine*, supported by a heavily Médoc-orientated wine list; the ambience is very *sympathique*, and M. Fougeras presides in the kitchen while his wife takes care of the restaurant. Towards the northern edge of the Margaux appellation you will find the Restaurant Larigaudière in the village of Soussans, where you will find the regional dishes like lampreys, escargots bordelais, entrecôte cooked over vine twigs and, in season, delicious cèpes bordelaises.

I await with interest the opening of a new hotel and restaurant currently under construction near Ile Vincent on the banks of the Gironde; the services of a renowned Parisian chef have already been engaged, and great things are promised. Certainly there is room in the Médoc, particularly for accommodation of a high standard.

CHATEAU
D'Angludet
MARGAUX

As you enter Cantenac from the south on the D2, Château d'Angludet is signposted down a small road to the left, just before the church. Go under the railway bridge, pass between Pouget and Boyd-Cantenac, and the drive to Château d'Angludet is about 500 metres further on your left.

In the middle of the 12th century this was part of a large 'Seigneurie' belonging to the noble Chevalier d'Angludet, and remained in this family until one of his descendants, Guillaume de Donisson, sold it to a man called Rompriol in 1350. The estate stayed in this family's ownership, passing through the female line, until it was acquired in 1583 by an Englishman, or possibly a Scotsman, called Makanan, from whom it was confiscated in 1631 during the fierce religious war of that period. D'Angludet was then bought by M. Pommiers who sold it shortly afterwards to a family called de Mons or Demons.

At the time of the Revolution the property belonged to a Monsieur Legras, who prudently changed its name to 'La République'. On his death at the end of the 18th century, Legras was succeeded by his four children. Peter Sichel told me that foundations of another house have been found on the other side of the courtyard; the present château originally had two front doors, and it is reasonable to assume that all four families lived on the estate. In the late 18th and early 19th centuries, the wine of d'Angludet enjoyed the price and status of a Third or Fourth Cru, and it may be due to difficulties caused by the four-way split that the property was not included in the 1855 classification. By 1867 there were as many as five families, all descendants of Legras, living here – Henri Legras, MM. Dauglade and Bignon, and the widows Mouchu and Lalanne.

By the 1880s the vineyard had become divided into two distinct entities known as Domaine and Château d'Angludet, the former belonging to Jacques Promis, and the latter to Jules Jadouin. Jadouin became sole owner in 1892, and the two halves, thus reunited, reverted to their original name of Château d'Angludet.

Jadouin was followed by his son-in-law, Jacques Lebègue, who added considerably to the property, so that by 1922 it extended over 160 hectares, of which 55 were under vines. The quality of the wine improved during the inter-war years, and a firm demand was established, especially in the United Kingdom through Lebègue's London-based wine business. Just before the 1939–45 war, d'Angludet was bought by a Biarritz industrialist by the name of Paul Six, who appears from the régisseur's records to have been more interested in the eggs and butter from the farm than in the making of wine. Six's widow sold what had now become virtually a dairy-farm in 1953 to Mme. Rolland of Château Coutet, who bought it for her son by an earlier marriage, one M. Thomas. He replanted about 4 hectares of the vineyard, but the terrible frosts of 1956 wiped out all the young vines.

When the present owner, Peter Sichel, an Englishman, bought d'Angludet in 1961, the vineyard had to all intents ceased to exist – only three hundred cases of that magic vintage were made. Sichel only bought 80 hectares of the total estate, the vineyards on the Notton plateau being acquired by Lucien Lurton of Château Brane-Cantenac.

Now that the replanted vines are well established, Peter Sichel is making first-class wine at Angludet. It has wonderful depth of colour, and tends to be more robust and tannic than most Margaux, and was particularly good in the two lighter vintages of 1977 and 1980 that I tasted. 1981, 1982 and 1983 will be outstanding, all fairly typical of their vintages. The 1979 is already very good, with a lovely Cabernet 'blackcurrant' bouquet, and it is a wine which I shall always remember

3

with pleasure, since it was served at a dinner at Château Palmer for Peter's twin sons' twenty-first birthday celebrations. Sichel is also the major shareholder in Palmer. Château d'Angludet is marketed exclusively by Maison Sichel, the family wine business on the Quai de Bacalan in Bordeaux. The wine from young vines and the cuves excluded from the Grand Vin is sold under the name of Bory.

Peter and his wife, Diana, live at Château d'Angludet, where the atmosphere is one of hospitable warmth. The house is very much a home, with one or more of the six Sichel children continually coming and going. The drawing-room has a fine mural, painted on canvas, of the Spanish riding school in Vienna, copied from the original by the Austrian painter Reidinger.

TECHNICAL INFORMATION

General

Appellation:	Margaux
Area under vines:	32 hectares
Average production:	12,000 cases
Distribution of vines:	In one block
Owner:	Société Civile du Château d'Angludet
Director:	Mr Peter Sichel
Régisseur:	M. Chauvet
Consultant Oenologist:	M. Jacques Boissenot

Viticulture

Geology:	Deep gravel with some sand and clay
Grape varieties:	50% Cabernet Sauvignon, 15% Cabernet Franc, 5% Petit Verdot, 30% Merlot
Pruning:	Guyot Double
Rootstock:	Various
Vines per hectare:	6,666
Average yield per hectare:	36 hectolitres
Replanting:	As necessary

Vinification

Added yeasts:	Yes, to start first vat
Length of maceration:	2–3 weeks
Temperature of fermentation:	30°C

Control of fermentation:	By passing through water-cooled coil
Type of vat:	Concrete
Vin de presse:	Quantity for inclusion decided at the assemblage
Age of casks:	$\frac{1}{4}$ to $\frac{1}{3}$ new each vintage
Time in cask:	12 months
Fining:	Gelatine
Filtration:	Sur plaque, at bottling
Type of bottle:	Bordelaise lourde

Commercial

Sales:	All commercialisation through Maison Sichel, S.A., 19 Quai de Bacalan, 33300 Bordeaux Telephone: 56 39 35 29
Agents overseas:	Yes, contact office for information
Visits:	Yes, by appointment Telephone: 56 88 71 41 Hours: 0900–1130, 1400–1700 Monday to Friday Arrangements can occasionally be made at weekends

THE TASTING AT CHATEAU D'ANGLUDET, 15 January 1985
J.S., Peter Sichel

1983 Dense, almost black colour. Nose beginning to evolve, with fruit and new oak. Lots of fruit and quite hard tannin for '83 Margaux. Very long in mouth; will be a superb wine, but must be kept quite a long time.

1982 Same deep, inky colour. Nose still quite closed, but starting to be good. Very rounded and mouthfilling, full of power and lovely fruit. Already showing well.

1981 A shade lighter in colour. Bouquet good, but not yet giving much. Beautifully structured wine, with elegance and long, feminine legs. Fruit and tannin starting to harmonise, will soon be a fine bottle.

1980 Deep red for 1980. Lovely open nose, blackcur-

rant evident. Good instant fruit appeal, but has a lot of backbone for a 1980 and will stay well.

1979 Dark, dense bluey red. Nose very powerful and ripe. Generous and robust with lots of fruit and keeping qualities.

1978 A shade lighter than '79. Fine bouquet with lovely fruit, still a bit reserved. A good 1978, with complex fruit and good tannins. Long aftertaste, will develop well.

1977 Medium-dark colour, no browning. Nice nose, quite open and evolved. Clean, very slightly astringent on palate with nice flavour. A very successful 'petite année', which can be kept and will improve.

1976 Bright medium-to-dark colour. Open, ripe bouquet with good fruit. Not a complex wine; well-made, ready to drink now.

CHATEAU

Boyd-Cantenac

MARGAUX

As you travel north on the D2 towards Margaux, take the turning to your left just before the church in the village of Cantenac. There is a signpost pointing to Châteaux Boyd-Cantenac and Pouget. Go under the railway bridge, and you will find Boyd-Cantenac's chais and cuvier after about 1 km opposite Château Pouget.

In 1754 one 'Messire' Jacques Boyd, of Irish origin but a squire in the hierarchy of French nobility, bought, through the offices of Maîre Deyrem, notaire of Castelnau-de-Médoc, the lands of 'Sieur' Bernard Sainvincens, former treasurer of France and Bourgeois de Bordeaux. At this date the estate of Boyd-Cantenac came into being. On 28 August 1806 – 10th Fructidor of the year XIII in the revolutionary calendar – that interesting adventurer and reprobate from Cantenac-Brown, the Englishman John Lewis Brown, took over the management of Boyd-Cantenac. This gentleman did not stay in charge long, since he was shortly afterwards declared bankrupt, and lost all his properties.

Ownership then passed to Abel Laurent, and later to the Ginestet family. It is to Pierre Ginestet that Boyd-Cantenac owes a debt, for this great wine-maker did much to re-establish the name, fame and quality of this Third Growth Margaux. In the 1930s the Guillemet family, then, as now, owners of Château Pouget, became the proprietors. Today it is Pierre Guillemet who runs Château Boyd-Cantenac. He lives at Château Pouget, and the wine is vinified and aged in a separate complex of chai and cuvier adjoining Pouget. There is not, and never has been a château attached to this vineyard. The wine of Boyd-Cantenac, made from a classic encépagement of predominantly Cabernet grapes, tends to be of an appealing, soft, typically Margaux character; it benefits from the gravelly soil, a low average yield and the rigorous selection and care exercised by Pierre Guillemet.

I have been especially impressed with the 1971 and 1975 vintages. The former was one of the best Margaux of that vintage I tasted, being strong in fruit, but at the same time possessed of supple Margaux finesse, and with a lovely long finish; the 1975 was already becoming quite approachable, with a concentration of flavour, and a promise of long and successful evolution. I am grateful to Pierre Guillemet for the time and hospitality he gave me, for his willingness to produce endless samples for tasting and for the knowledge that he shared so freely.

TECHNICAL INFORMATION

General

Appellation:	Margaux
Area under vines:	18 hectares
Average production:	7,000 cases
Distribution of vines:	In three blocks of 8 hectares, 4 hectares and 6 hectares to the west of Château Pouget.
Owner:	Guillemet family – Groupement Foncier Agricole des Chx. Pouget et Boyd-Cantenac
Director and Régisseur:	M. Pierre Guillemet
Consultant Oenologist:	Professor Emile Peynaud

Viticulture

Geology:	Gravel and sand, on a clay/gravel subsoil
Grape varieties:	67% Cabernet Sauvignon, 7% Cabernet Franc, 20% Merlot, 6% Petit Verdot
Pruning:	Guyot Double
Rootstock:	101.14
Vines per hectare:	Part 10,000, part 6,000
Average yield per hectare:	35 hectolitres
Replanting:	When necessary

Vinification

Added yeasts:	No
Length of maceration:	15 days average
Temperature of fermentation:	25–30°C
Control of fermentation:	Water circulation
Type of vat:	Cement
Vin de presse:	Usually about 17% incorporated, depending on vintage
Age of casks:	30% new, the rest of one vintage
Time in cask:	About 2 years
Fining:	Albumen of egg
Filtration:	Sur plaque before bottling
Type of bottle:	Bordelaise lourde

Commercial

Vente Directe:	Yes
Direct Ordering from château:	Yes
Sold on Bordeaux market;	Yes
Visits:	Yes, telephone 56 88 30 58 Hours: 0800–1200, 1400–1800

THE TASTING AT BOYD-CANTENAC, IN THE CHAI, 14 November 1984
J.S., Pierre Guillemet

1984 Not finished malolactic fermentation, but colour and all indications excellent.

1983 Excellent deep blue-red. Nose good and forthcoming, some wood. Mouthfilling, with loads of fruit and quite hard tannin. Long. Will be superb in 10–20 years.

1982 Dense red. Nose already good, soft fruit. Big, fat wine with flesh and sinew. Tannins not aggressive. Will be ready relatively soon, but will go on a long while.

1980 Colour bright and quite a deep red for 1980. Soft, mellow bouquet, ripe. A good honest and well-balanced wine, perfectly nice to drink now, but will also keep.

1978 Good medium red. Nose a bit closed, but what there is is very good. Flavour complex, still shut in, but has good fruit and tannin. Promises to be a good wine in 3–5 years.

1975 Deep, brilliant red. Nose open and aromatic. Long, mouthfilling, with concentrated flavour. Quite evolved for 1975, but still has a long road ahead. Worth the journey!

1971 Colour still good, intense red with hardly any brown. Nose good, lovely ripe fruit – cassis. Plenty of fruit and tannin still, but has supple elegance of mature Margaux. Very good bottle, with plenty of life still.

CHATEAU

Brane-Cantenac

MARGAUX

As you drive north up the D2 towards Margaux, pass through the village of Cantenac; after about $1\frac{1}{2}$ km there is a small turning to your left; just before the village of Issan, signposted to Château Cantenac-Brown. Take this road, cross a level-crossing, and Château Brane-Cantenac is about 1 km further on your left.

Early history shows the land of Brane-Cantenac to have belonged to a family named Hosten, but its origins as an important vineyard start in the first part of the 18th century, when it passed into the hands of the Gorce family, by which name it was known for a hundred years. The last of the Gorces was an old lady by the name of Marie-Françoise, born in 1764, who succeeded to the estate when still a child, both her parents having died very young. According to the archives, the property was run during her minority by one Le Sieur Estèbe, a relation of her mother. During her long life the vineyard, now known as Château Gorce, grew in size and reputation; by the time of the French Revolution the wine of Gorce was grouped with a handful of Seconds that commanded prices only just below the Premiers Crus.

Marie-Françoise was married – and widowed – twice, and for a short time the property had the name of her second husband tacked on to it, becoming Gorce-Guy. In 1833 the merry widow sold her vineyard to the famous Napoléon des Vignes, Baron Hector de Branne, who had just sold Brane-Mouton (now Mouton-Rothschild) to Monsieur Thuret. Hector de Branne is an attractive character; as well as being a dedicated and successful winemaker and empire-builder, he was also something of a lady's man and an addicted gambler. There is a parcel of the vineyard known as the 'Champs de Bataille', so called, not as legend would have us believe from an ancient battle against the invading Saracens, but in commemoration of de Branne being soundly slapped for making a pass at one of his young lady-friends among the vines!

In spite of his amorous adventures and hours spent at the card tables, de Branne found time to extend the vineyard, double its production, and maintain and improve the already high reputation of its wine. In 1838 he changed the name of the property

to its present form of Brane-Cantenac, and was rewarded for his efforts by being placed among the Second Growths in the 1855 classification.

By 1866 the Baron's fortunes were at a low ebb, and he put the property on the market. The buyer was Gustave Roy, who purchased the property as an investment for a family trust, the principal beneficiaries of which were his wife, Marie-Anne and her two brothers Georges and Casimir Berger. Roy had bought Château d'Issan only a few days earlier for the same purpose, but loved the place so much that he decided to keep it as his personal property, and bought Brane-Cantenac for the trust instead. In his memoirs he speaks fondly of the Baron, who undertook to teach him all he knew to ensure the continuing renown of the vineyard to which he had given his name. He records that he never failed to visit the Baron on his frequent trips to the Médoc, though appointments were only possible in the afternoons, as the old fellow was a late sleeper, and the nights were taken up with his aforementioned pursuits! The price paid by Gustave Roy was high – 1,000,000 francs, plus a sum for fixtures and fittings – only marginally less than Baron James de Rothschild had paid for Mouton some thirteen years earlier.

The property stayed in the ownership of the Roys and the Bergers until 1919, when the heirs sold Brane-Cantenac to the grandiose-sounding Société des Grands Crus de France. This company was a consortium of négociants and wine-growers, who owned or had shares in many properties, including Châteaux Margaux, d'Issan, Lagrange, Giscours and Coutet. Lucien Lurton, the present owner, is the grandson of one of the shareholders in that company, Leonce Recapet. A few years later, Recapet and Lucien's father, François Lurton, acquired Brane-Cantenac on the break-up of the owning company.

The dynastic inheritance problems of a family as large as the Lurtons are complex to say the least, but a division of the properties was effected in the mid-fifties, and Lucien became the sole owner of Brane-Cantenac in the ill-fated year of 1956, when an enormous proportion of the vines were lost in the horrendous early spring frosts. Despite this

7

early setback, Lucien Lurton has steered Brane on a path of continuing success and quality.

It may be the air, the soil, the climate or the wines of this corner of Cantenac – more likely a combination of all four – that encourages proliferation. Lucien Lurton is a patriarch in the Victorian mould with his ten children and ten châteaux to match. Comparisons with de Branne are inevitable, and I like to think of him as a latter-day Napoléon des Vignes; his brother André controls another completely separate vineyard empire from the family house at Château Bonnet near Grezillac in the Entre-Deux-Mers, and the family also own the Premier Grand Cru Classé, Clos Fourtet in St Emilion.

Though only Lucien and his wife live permanently at the small, elegant Chartreuse château, one is left in no doubt as to the continued Lurton presence at Brane; his children and grandchildren appear and disappear with mind-boggling frequency, and I have still to be sure which one is which. The modest proportions of the house are surprising,

bearing in mind that Brane-Cantenac is one of the largest Crus Classés in terms of area under vine.

The wines of Brane-Cantenac are quintessentially Margaux in style, with great finesse, elegance and feminine charm, and present themselves well in youth. 1983, a classic, even great vintage for Bordeaux in general, was especially successful in Margaux, and Brane-Cantenac is no exception; it has more sinew and finesse than the soft and generous 1982, and will make a superb bottle in five to ten years. The wine from young vines and the vats not quite good enough to be included in the Grand Vin are sold under the name of Château Notton, which derives from the part of the vineyard bearing that name in the southern part of the property, near Arsac; it is interesting to note that a second wine was sold as long ago as the beginning of last century, surely one of the first instances of such a practice, and indicative of selection and attention to quality all too rare in those early days.

TECHNICAL INFORMATION

General

Appellation:	Margaux
Area under vines:	85 hectares
Average production:	30,000 cases
Distribution of vines:	5 blocks, mainly on the Cantenac plateau
Owner:	M. Lucien Lurton
Maître de Chai	M. Yves Blanchard
Chef de Culture:	M. Serge Branas
Consultant Oenologists:	Professor Emile Peynaud, M. Jacques Boissenot

Viticulture

Geology:	Deep gravel of the Gunzian and Mindelian period
Grape varieties:	70% Cabernet Sauvignon, 13% Cabernet Franc, 15% Merlot, 2% Petit Verdot
Pruning:	Guyot Double
Rootstock:	Riparia Gloire, 101-14, 3309
Vines per hectare:	6,666
Average yield per hectare:	35 hectolitres
Replanting:	Complantation

Vinification

Added yeasts:	No
Length of maceration:	Average 20 days
Temperature of fermentation:	28–30°C

Control of fermentation:	By serpentine coil, and by wetting the vats
Type of vat:	Stainless steel
Vin de presse:	From 7% to 10% included, according to vintage
Age of casks:	From 1 to 3 years old
Time in cask:	18 months
Fining:	Egg-white
Filtration:	Sur plaque
Type of bottle:	Bordelaise lourde

Commercial

Vente Directe:	No
Sales:	Through the négociants
Exclusivities:	None
Visits:	Yes, by appointment Telephone 56 88 70 20 Hours: 0900–1200, 1500–1700

THE TASTING AT THE CHATEAU,
28 January 1985
J.S., Christian Seely, Lucien Lurton, Brigitte Lurton, and another daughter of Lucien Lurton who is a qualified oenologist

1983 Lovely deep colour. Nose still quite closed, but beginning to show beautifully when aerated a while in the glass. Lovely rich, elegant Margaux flavour, full of charm and fruit, with backbone and tannin to make a good bottle in 5 years.
1982 Very dense colour, more black than '83. Nose cedary, but still a bit closed. Rounded, charming and already lovely, with a mass of fruit and non-aggressive tannin. Beautiful.
1981 Deep colour again, with lovely soft Margaux bouquet, cassis and violets. Elegant, structured wine with ladylike charm and finesse. Will be lovely in three or four years. Classic.

At lunch
1962 Medium colour, beginning to brown. Nose ripe, aromatic, slight cigar-box and fruit. Mature, ready now, finishes quite short. Elegant now, but not to keep for too long.

9

CHATEAU
Cantenac-Brown
MARGAUX

Driving northwards up the D2 in the direction of Pauillac, pass through the village of Cantenac, and just before you reach Issan there is a small turning on your left, which is signposted to Château Cantenac-Brown; almost immediately you will be able to see the red-brick, neo-Tudor pile of Château Cantenac-Brown, about 1 km away across the vines. Follow this small road, over a level crossing, and continue until you come to the driveway, clearly signposted, on your right.

The property was bought in the early 1800s by John Lewis Brown, the scion of an English family of négociants established in Bordeaux since the early 18th century. The previous owner was an Amsterdam wine merchant called François Coudac, who inherited the estate from a M. Louis Massac, also from Amsterdam. When Brown took over, the wines had a well-established following in Holland, where they were sold as plain Château Cantenac. As frequently happened in those times, Brown hastened to add his name to the property, and the wine was sold as Brown-Cantenac; confusion soon became rife, especially with overseas customers who could not master the subtleties of French pronunciation, so the names were soon reversed to Cantenac-Brown, thus avoiding possible mix-ups with the neighbouring, and slightly more illustrious, 2nd Growth Brane-Cantenac.

Brown was both an aesthete and an ambitious man of affairs. He was a painter of some skill, specialising in the sporting pictures so beloved of the French at that time, and was at his best when depicting horses and dogs. He was taught by Princeteau, and another of Princeteau's pupils, Henri de Toulouse-Lautrec, was a friend and frequent visitor, sharing the same predilection as his host for good wine and naughty young women. Brown's taste for the good life may have been his undoing, for in the mid-1800s he was declared bankrupt, and all his property was put on the market.

A banker by the name of Gromard then became the owner, but his interests lay in the world of finance rather than winemaking, for the property, somewhat neglected, was acquired soon afterwards in 1860 by Armand Lalande, a wealthy négociant, owner of Léoville-Poyferré and other wine properties. Lalande's daughter married Edward Lawton of the well-known Anglo-Irish Bordeaux family, and it was their son, Jean Lawton, who bought the estate from the Lalandes in 1935.

In 1968 Cantenac-Brown was purchased by the du Vivier family, who were also owners of the Bordeaux firm of A. de Luze et Fils. This company became part of the Cognac house of Rémy Martin in 1980, but the du Viviers retained Château Cantenac-Brown for themselves. Aymar du Vivier and his wife Marie-Ange now run the property, and there is every indication that with their combined energy, enthusiasm and expertise, the wine of this 3rd Growth château has already returned to its rightful place in the firmament of the Crus Classés.

The château, an extraordinary piece of Victorian neo-Stewart architecture, looks as if it would be far happier if it could be spirited away to some leafy garden in Surrey, or somewhere within reach of England's northern industrial cities, where any 19th-century industrial tycoon would have been proud to have built such a monster. Certainly it would need an army of servants to run it and at least a couple of ocean-going liners' boilers to heat it. For these reasons, it has not been lived in as one house for many years, but has been split up into apartments, and the ground floor was, until recently, used for receptions by the du Viviers. They have now regained the freehold of

10

the house, and have many plans for its future.

The wine of Cantenac-Brown is a traditional Bordeaux, a little more austere than many Margaux, though the later vintages, made under the auspices of Aymar du Vivier seem to have a slightly suppler style.

An excellent Bordeaux Supérieur, sold as Château Lamartine, is also vinified at Cantenac-Brown; it should be emphasised that this is in no way a 'deuxième vin', but is made from grapes grown in the 'palus' or marshland of Cantenac, entirely separate from the Margaux appellation vines. 9½ hectares are planted with 80% Cabernet Sauvignon and 20% Merlot grapes.

TECHNICAL INFORMATION

General

Appellation:	Margaux
Area under vines:	31 hectares
Production:	15,500 cases
Distribution of vines:	19 hectares in one piece around the château. The remainder in several parcels around Cantenac and Arsac, with 1 hectare at Soussans
Proprietor:	Société Civile du Château Cantenac-Brown
Director and Régisseur:	M. Aymar du Vivier
Maître de Chai:	M. Willy Przybyski
Consultant Oenologist:	M. Boissenot

Viticulture

Geology:	Deep gravel; ⅔ of the vineyard to a depth of over 15 metres
Grape varieties:	77% Cabernet Sauvignon, 6% Cabernet Franc, 17% Merlot
Pruning:	Guyot Double
Rootstock:	Various
Vines per hectare:	5 hectares at 6,500, 26 hectares at 10,000
Yield per hectare:	42 hectolitres
Replanting:	Complantation, according to necessity

Vinification

Added yeasts:	No
Length of maceration:	3 weeks minimum

Temperature of fermentation:	28°C
Method of control:	Cooling by serpentine, and by wetting down the cuves Warming by gas heater
Type of vat:	Steel, enamelled inside
Vin de presse:	Incorporated according to vintage
Age of casks:	⅓ new each vintage
Time in cask:	18 months
Fining:	Gelatine of egg
Filtration:	Sur terre before going in cask, sur plaque before bottling
Type of bottle:	Bordelaise lourde

Commercial

Exclusive contract in force up to the 1983 vintage with Maison de Luze. New arrangements are currently being made by the proprietor.

Visits:	Yes, by arrangement Telephone: 56 88 39 75 M. Aymar du Vivier

Château Lamartine

Appellation:	Bordeaux Supérieur
Area under vines:	9.5 hectares
Grape varieties:	80% Cabernet Sauvignon, 20% Merlot
Production:	4,000 cases
Distribution of vines:	In one piece in the palus of Cantenac
Density of planting:	6,500 vines per hectare.

THE TASTING HELD AT CHATEAU MALESCASSE, 31 January 1985

J.S., Christian Seely, Michel Tesseron

1983 Good red, not specially dark. Bouquet very closed. A good, delicate mouthful of Margaux, with fine fruit and good tannins. Some finesse, and long aftertaste, will be a winner.

1982 Much deeper colour than the '83. Nose fuller and more open. A fat, rounded wine with lots of 'puissance', fruit and tannin, still a little dumb, but will be a very good bottle.

1981 Medium depth of colour. Good nose. A medium-weight wine, with good fruit and some elegance, sound but not particularly thrilling.

1979 Deep colour. Quite a good bouquet. Respectable wine, a little dull, and lacks the body of some 1979s.

1978 Medium to light red. Not much on nose. Rather flat for 1978, and a bit lacking in character.

1976 Lightish in colour. Bouquet quite faded. Thin and uninteresting with not much body, and fading fruit; slightly bitter finish.

(N.B. The younger wines show clearly the improvements that have been made since Aymar and Marie-Ange du Vivier have been in charge.)

CHATEAU
Dauzac
MARGAUX

Take the D2e into the Médoc from Eysines, through Blanquefort; immediately after the level crossing at Labarde, take a hairpin right turn back down the D2 towards Macau, and Château Dauzac is less than a kilometre along on your left.

One of the oldest properties to have continuously produced wine, Château Dauzac owes its name to one Petrus d'Auzac, who was granted title to the property by Richard, Comte de Poitiers, son of Henry II of England and later to become Richard the Lionheart. The original deed is to be found in the archives at the Tower of London. The property, apart from owning extensive vineyards since the 12th century, also owned the right to extract a toll on every tonneau of wine that was shipped from the ancient port of Macau-en-Médoc.

Among the owners of Dauzac were those ubiquitous winemaking monks of the Abbaye de Sainte Croix, who also owned Château Carbonnieux in the Graves, along with other fine properties. The château, no longer lived in, was built in the early 1700s, and it was here in 1749 that the famous Comte Lynch, of Irish extraction, was born. Lynch was an able and dedicated winemaker, and owner of not only Dauzac but also Lynch Bages, Lynch-Moussas and Pontac-Lynch. It would seem that his dedication and loyalty was more constant with respect to his vineyards than to any particular régime or party, since his successful political career spanned the Revolution and the tricky post-revolutionary period, whilst his properties remained intact. It is almost certainly due to his work and care at Dauzac that the property was placed in the great classification of 1855.

Before the Lynch ownership, Dauzac was known as Château la Bastide, as well as Château de Labarde, the latter being the name now given to the second wine of Dauzac. The foundations of

the original château were discovered when the new cuvier was built in 1980.

From 1863 to 1920, Dauzac belonged to Nathaniel Johnston, who was also owner of Château Ducru-Beaucaillou in St Julien. During the terrible phylloxera-ravaged years at the end of last century, Dauzac must have owed much of its survival to the 100 hectares of vines on the lower 'palus' or tidal marshland. Though not part of the vignoble of Château Dauzac itself, these vines proved resistant to the dreaded beetle, and gave a steady yield of 1,000 tonneaux of good commercial wine right through the bad years.

It was by accident that one of the most important viticultural discoveries of the past century was made at Château Dauzac one hundred years ago, in June 1885. Nathaniel Johnston's régisseur, Ernest David, was much plagued by unauthorised vendangeurs, who kept helping themselves to bunches of grapes from the vines that bordered the road. As a deterrent, M. David sprayed the rows nearest to the road with a solution of water, copper sulphate and lime; this turned the leaves a sickly greenish-blue colour, and was most effective in putting off 'scrumpers'. It was only after a season or two that it became apparent that these vines did not suffer from mildew. After much testing and refinement with the help of Professor Millardet and Professor Ulysse Gayon, grandfather of Pascal Ribereau-Gayon, the final formula was evolved and officially approved for the famous 'Bouillie Bordelaise' or Bordeaux Mixture that is still in use today.

In 1897 the Société des Agriculteurs de France awarded Nathaniel Johnston a prize for his services to viticulture. In the 'attribution' setting out the reasons for this award, mention is made of his work at Dauzac, both in the cultivation and study

12

of the vine, and concerning the treatment of mildew with the 'Bouillie Bordelaise'.

The property was sadly neglected for many years, and when Alain Miailhe bought it in 1966, he took on a mighty task; unfortunately, due to inheritance problems that so often beset families in France, Alain Miailhe had to sell the property again in 1978, when it was bought by M.F. Chatellier, a dynamic businessman with many interests – he has just acquired the important Champagne house of Abel Lepitre.

Following the excellent advice of the redoubtable Professor Peynaud, Chatellier has done nothing to the old chai and cuvier, or indeed to the château itself; instead he has built a magnificent new cuvier with every modern aid to vinification, and an enormous and elegant air-conditioned and humidified new ageing cellar, holding over 1,000 casks on one level. The entire complex, which faces the road across a car-park flanked by flags of all nations, also houses modern offices and a large reception room.

The wine of Dauzac is only just beginning to return to its former glory as a result of all the recent work and investment.

TECHNICAL INFORMATION

General

Appellation:	Margaux
Area under vines:	45 hectares
Average production:	22,500 cases
Distribution of vines:	In one block
Owner:	S.A.F. Chatellier et Fils
Régisseur:	M. Michel Dufaure
Consultant Oenologists:	Professor Emile Peynaud and M. Jacques Boissenot

Viticulture

Geology:	Garonne gravel and silico-chalk
Grape varieties:	59% Cabernet Sauvignon, 35% Merlot, 3% Cabernet Franc, 3% Petit Verdot
Pruning:	Guyot Double
Rootstock:	Riparia 101.14, 3309, SO4
Vines per hectare:	60% 10,000, 40% 8,500
Average yield per hectare:	45 hectolitres
Replanting:	As necessary: 4 hectares are scheduled for 1985

Vinification

Added yeasts:	Yes
Length of maceration:	3–4 weeks

Temperature of fermentation:	28–30°C
Control of fermentation:	Cold water run on exterior of vats
Type of vat:	Stainless steel, with sloped bases to assist with removal of the marc and cleaning
Vin de presse:	Incorporated in Grand Vin, after one year separate ageing
Age of casks:	⅓ new each year
Time in cask:	16–18 months
Fining:	Albumen of egg
Filtration:	Sur plaque before bottling
Type of bottle:	Bordelaise lourde

Commercial

Vente Directe:	Yes
Direct trade ordering:	Yes
Exclusivities:	None
Agents overseas:	Yes, for further information contact: Château Dauzac Labarde 33460 Margaux
Visits:	Yes, for appointment telephone: 56 88 32 10 Telex: 550407 F Hours: 0900–1200, 1400–1700

THE TASTING AT CHATEAU DAUZAC,
22 October 1984
J.S., M. Chatellier, 2 representatives from Gault et Millau

1983 Very deep, bluey red. Fine bouquet with lots of new wood. Taste redolent of new wood and tannin, but fruit in plenty. Will take some years.
1982 Colour also deep blue red. Bouquet bigger and more fruity than 1983. Big mouthfilling wine, quite long in mouth, with muted tannins. Finishes a little dry.
1981 Good colour, bit lighter than '82. Nose finer, beginning to evolve. Well-structured wine, long in mouth, harmonious. Will be a good bottle in 2/3 years.
1980 Lighter, bricky red. Nice open nose with good fruit. Well made 1980, with some elegance. Finishes dry.
1979 (At dinner.) Good deep colour. Nose open, with good fruit. Well-made, if slightly austere for a Margaux.
1970 (At dinner.) Good colour, beginning to show brown. Nose good, with plenty of power still. Quite a forward 1970, but delicious now, if lacking some of the backbone of most 1970s.

CHATEAU

Desmirail

MARGAUX

There is no château attached to the vineyards of Desmirail, which are scattered around the commune of Cantenac; the largest part being known as Baudry-Notton

The vineyards of Château Desmirail originally formed part of the great estate of Pierre des Mesures de Rauzan, but were given away as a dowry to one of the young ladies of the family, Mademoiselle Rauzan du Ribail, when she married a legal gentleman named Jean Desmirail, from whom the name derives. Good wine was made there by Desmirail, and consistently fetched Third-Growth prices long before this rank was confirmed in the 1855 classification, when the owner was a M. Sipière, who was also manager of Château Margaux.

At the beginning of this century Desmirail was bought by a Berlin banker named Mendelssohn, a family that boasted among its number not only the great musician but, of more local interest, the less talented but prolific poet of the Médoc, Biarnez. Poor Mendelssohn lost the property when his estate was sequestered in the First World War, and Desmirail was acquired in 1923 by Monsieur Michel. This gentleman was nearly responsible for the complete disappearance of this

wine, and sold the buildings, the château and the vines separately in 1938. The château itself, built by Sipière in 1860, was bought by Paul Zuger, father of Jean-Claude of Marquis d'Alesme, which at that time had no house attached to the property, and is now known as Château Marquis d'Alesme. During the years following the Second World War, Lucien Lurton's family gradually bought back parcels of vines that formed the original property of Desmirail; finally, in 1980, Lucien effected an exchange with Château Palmer, fitting in the final two-hectare piece of the jigsaw puzzle and giving him the right to the use of the name. For the vinification and ageing of the wine, Lurton bought the fine 18th-century buildings of a property called Port-Aubin in the village of Cantenac and 1981 saw the first bottling of the phoenix-like Château Desmirail.

Lucien Lurton is making a classic Margaux out of Desmirail; the three vintages since the re-birth of this Troisième Cru all impressed me with their fine, deep colour, typically soft blackcurrant-and-violets bouquet, and their delicate structure of fruit and good tannin, all of which points to excellent ageing potential and a bright future for Château Desmirail.

14

TECHNICAL INFORMATION

General

Appellation:	Margaux
Area under vines:	18 hectares
Average production:	Around 5,000 cases
Distribution of vines:	Fragmented
Owner:	Lucien Lurton
Régisseur:	Brigitte Lurton
Maître de Chai:	Philippe Peschka
Consultant Oenologist:	Prof. Emile Peynaud

Viticulture

Geology:	Gravel
Grape varieties:	69% Cabernet Sauvignon, 7% Cabernet Franc, 23% Merlot, 1% Petit Verdot
Pruning:	Guyot Double Médocaine
Rootstock:	101.14, Riparia Gloire, 420A
Average yield per hectare:	25 hectolitres
Replanting:	As necessary

Vinification

Added yeasts:	No
Length of maceration:	20–27 days
Temperature of fermentation:	27–30°C
Control of fermentation:	Water cooling
Type of vat:	Steel and stainless steel
Vin de presse:	From 7% to 10% incorporated
Age of casks:	One quarter new each vintage
Time in cask:	20 months
Fining:	Egg whites
Filtration:	Sur plaque at bottling
Type of bottle:	Bordelaise lourde

Commercial

Vente Directe:	No
Sales:	Through the négociants
Visits:	No

THE TASTING AT CHATEAU BRANE-CANTENAC, 28 January 1985
J.S., Christian Seely, Lucien Lurton, Brigitte Lurton

1983 Deep red, almost black. Lovely fragrant nose – violets? A big mouthful of cassis fruit and good tannins. Has an excellent future.

1982 Quite bluish red. Soft, Margaux bouquet. Well-structured wine with plenty of good fruit and soft tannins; a rounded wine that will drink quite soon.

1981 Good medium red. Nice cassis smell. Has good flesh and a well-formed physique underneath. Nicely balanced, elegant, will be a good bottle.

CHATEAU
Durfort-Vivens
MARGAUX

As you enter the village of Margaux on the D2 heading north, the buildings are on your left, opposite the driveway to Château Margaux. Part of the vineyard is also opposite the buildings. The actual château is on the opposite side of the small left turning to Arsac, but no longer forms part of the property.

In the 15th century all the land in this area belonged to the powerful Durfort family, lords of Blanquefort, including la Noble Mothe de Margaux, on which Château Margaux itself now stands. Two hundred years later, the property was all one with the lands of the Chevalier de Lascombes, of whom I have written in the chapter on that château. From de Lascombes, Durfort passed in to the hands of the de Montbrisons and the de Vivens.

As early as 1785 the indefatigable Thomas Jefferson, future American President and noted wine-bibber, classed Durfort as one of only a handful of Second Growths, with Rozan (*sic*) and Léoville, an opinion confirmed in the 1855 classification. In 1824 the Vicomte de Vivens ousted his cousins, and became sole owner, changing the name of the property to Durfort-Vivens. In the famous document of 1855, the owner of Vivens-Durfort is shown as de Puységur, the Comte of that ilk having married the niece of the Vicomte de Vivens, and inherited the château and land.

In 1866 Puységur sold Durfort-Vivens for 500,000 francs – a high price for the times, since only about 30 hectares were under vines. It changed hands in 1882, and again in 1896, both times for less than the price achieved by the Puységurs, but these were difficult years in the Médoc, with mildew and phylloxera both rampant.

The buyers in 1896 were the Bordeaux négociant house of Delor. They bought more land around the area, but did not increase the size of the Durfort-Vivens vineyard. Despite their position as a leading Bordeaux market-house, Delor were forced to put their property on the market, like so many other Médoc owners, following the desperate years of the world slump and the atrociously bad vintages of the early thirties. It was in 1937 that the company that owned Château Margaux across the road, headed by the Ginestets, bought Durfort-Vivens from Delor: Lucien Lurton's grandfather, Monsieur Recapet, was one of the shareholders in the Société Civile du Château Margaux.

During the 24 years of the Ginestet ownership, the

16

vineyard was gradually reduced in size to 11 hectares. Thus when Lurton bought the vineyard and winemaking buildings from Pierre Ginestet in 1961, he had much to do to re-establish Durfort-Vivens in its rightful high-ranking position of Deuxième Cru Classé. Ginestet kept the château, which Lucien Lurton had no need of, since he was already installed at Brane-Cantenac.

His first priority at Durfort was the improvement and extension of the vineyards. In addition to the small plot among the Château Margaux vines, there are also three smaller parcels around the Brane-Cantenac vineyard, and the most recent acquisition is a piece of land between Margaux and Arsac. There is a large proportion (82%) of Cabernet Sauvignon in the encépagement of Durfort-Vivens, which is more than any other Margaux Cru Classé.

The soil and vinification of Durfort-Vivens are virtually identical with Brane-Cantenac, but the wines are of totally different character. Durfort has more backbone, and is much slower to yield its undoubted charms than the typically Margaux, soft and feminine wine of Château Brane-Cantenac. This may to some extent be due to the predominance of Cabernet Sauvignon and the comparative youth of many of the vines; it will be interesting to note the evolution of the Durfort-Vivens vintages of the early eighties.

Until 1975 the vinification of Durfort took place at Brane-Cantenac, but now the wine is fermented and aged in its own chai and cuvier. There is a second wine which sells as Domaine de Cure-bourse.

TECHNICAL INFORMATION

General

Appellation:	Margaux
Area under vines:	20 hectares
Average production:	6,000 cases
Distribution of vines:	Relatively fragmented
Owner:	M. Lucien Lurton
Director:	M. Lucien Lurton
Maître de Chai:	M. Guy Birot
Consultant Oenologist:	Professor Emile Peynaud and M. Jacques Boissenot

Viticulture

Geology:	Deep quaternian gravel
Grape varieties:	82% Cabernet Sauvignon, 10% Cabernet Franc, 8% Merlot
Pruning:	Guyot Double
Rootstock:	101-14, Riparia Gloire
Vines per hectare:	6,666
Average yield per hectare:	35 hectolitres
Replanting:	3% per annum

Vinification

Added yeasts:	No
Length of maceration:	20 days, and more according to vintage
Temperature of fermentation:	28–30°C
Control of fermentation:	By serpentine coil, and wetting exterior of vats
Type of vat:	Steel
Vin de presse:	7–10% according to vintage
Age of casks:	1–3 years
Time in cask:	18–20 months
Fining:	Egg whites
Filtration:	Sur plaque at bottling
Type of bottle:	Bordelaise lourde

Commercial

Vente Directe:	No
Direct Ordering from château:	Possible
Exclusivities:	None
Agents overseas:	None
Visits:	Yes, by appointment Telephone: 56 88 70 20

THE TASTING AT CHATEAU BRANE-CANTENAC, 28 January 1985
J.S., Christian Seely, Lucien Lurton, Brigitte Lurton

1983 Dark, purple colour. Bouquet soft and with good fruit, typical Margaux. More reserved and less immediate attraction than the '83 Brane-Cantenac, which we tasted at the same time. Tannins more punchy. Definitely a wine to lay down for several years.

1982 Fine, deep red. Nose delicious, with classic Cabernet blackcurrant. Rounded and relatively approachable, but with enough fruit and tannins to keep for a long time.

1981 Good, medium dark red. Good nose, still quite closed. Elegant with finesse and good fruit and tannin, long aftertaste. Will be a good, balanced wine for drinking in four or five years.

17

CHATEAU

Giscours

MARGAUX

Drive north up the D2, through Blanquefort towards Pauillac. Shortly after passing Macau-en-Médoc, a village that lies to the right of the road, you will see a sign on your right, pointing across the road to Château Giscours. Turn left, and take the private road through the vineyard, which is well signposted, to the château.

The estate of Château Giscours is at the southern entrance of the Margaux appellation, and extends into three communes, those of Arsac, Cantenac and Labarde. Apart from the two 'outposts' of Château la Lagune and Château Cantemerle, it is also the first Cru Classé that the traveller comes upon as he travels up the Médoc peninsula from the city of Bordeaux. Giscours is a fitting introduction to the Elysian fields of the Médoc vineyards. It is a model estate covering 370 hectares, consisting of parkland, agricultural and grazing land, three lakes and, of course, the vineyard of 80 hectares.

The vineyard, of which about 70 hectares are in production at any one time, is an excellent example of the ideal terroir for the noble vines which exists in the Médoc. It consists mainly of four large croupes or hillocks of gravel of large and medium size, on a subsoil of sand and coarse gravel. The topsoil gravel, deposited here in the Pleistocene period – between 400,000 and 1,200,000 years ago – was carried here from the Massif Central by the Ayout and Tarn rivers, from the Limousin mountains by the Isle and the Drône and from the Pyrenees by the Ariège and the Garonne; it is in these beds of gravel, sometimes 15 to 20 metres in depth, that the best vineyards of the Médoc are found.

The history of the Giscours estate is more interesting in the last 200 years, although documents exist proving its existence in 1330 as a fortified manorial castle, exercising feudal rights over all the adjoining parishes. There is a deed of sale dated 1552, when the purchaser was one Sieur Delhomme, who paid 1,000 livres for the property. The interesting part of this deed refers to the high quality of the vineyard at that early date. This is borne out a mere hundred years later, when according to Feret, the wine of Giscours was served to Louis XIV.

At the time of the French Revolution, Giscours belonged to the noble Saint-Simon family, from whom it was confiscated and designated a 'Bien National'. The Marquis Claude-Anne de Saint-Simon went into exile in Spain, where he took the pseudonym of Giscours – perhaps the only time an owner has taken the name of his château unto himself, rather than adopting the more usual practice of adding his own to that of the château!

After confiscation, Château Giscours was sold to an American who specialised in such acquisitions; his name was Michael Jacob, and he had two other Americans as partners – merchants by the name of John Gray and Jonathan Davis. In 1825, presumably having made a tidy profit, these gentlemen sold the property to Monsieur Marc Promis, a Bordeaux merchant whose family name is immortalised in Sauternes in the name of Château Rabaud-Promis. He did much to enhance the property, including improvements to the vineyard and the building of a château worthy of the name.

In 1847 Promis sold to a banker from Paris, le Comte de Pescatore, for 500,000 gold francs, and he it was who built the château in its present Renaissance style. The earlier effort, built by M. Promis, had been burnt to the ground, and Pescatore needed an imposing mansion in which to receive a visit from the Empress Eugénie de Montijo. Pescatore's nephew, who had succeeded him in 1855, sold Giscours in 1875 to Edouard Cruse for 1,000,000 francs. This sounds like a reasonable profit, but the construction of such an imposing residence must have cost a small fortune, even in those days of cheap labour.

The Cruse family did much to improve the reputation and standing of Giscours, including the building of the cuvier and ageing-chai. They sold to a M. Emile Grange, already a substantial proprietor in the Médoc, in 1913, and from that date until after the Second World War Giscours passed through several hands.

When M. Nicolas Tari, a pied noir from Algeria, bought the estate in 1952 it was in a sorry state. From 60 hectares of vines that existed under the Cruse ownership, the vineyard was reduced to a few hectares of worn-out vines of hybrid and unsuitable varieties, and the château, farm and

buildings were falling in ruins.

With half a century of experience, a large investment and a great deal of hard work, Nicolas set
about the slow task of replanting, repairing and
restoration that culminated in the beautiful property we see today.

Since 1970, Nicolas Tari has been aided in his
work by his eminently able son, Pierre, who is
perhaps one of the Médoc's most widely travelled
and enthusiastic ambassadors. As well as being
involved in local politics – he is Mayor of Labarde
– Pierre Tari holds a number of important posts in
the Bordeaux wine world. He is President, and
founder, of the Union des Grands Crus de Bordeaux, Vice-President and Founder of the Groupement d'Intérêt Economique des Vins du Médoc,
Secretary-General of the Association of the Crus
Classés of 1855, President of the Association for
the development of Agriculture in the Médoc,
Member of the Académie du Vin de Bordeaux and
a Commander of a Chapter of the Commanderie
du Bontemps de Médoc.

In his various guises, Tari jets all over the globe
promoting the Médoc in general and Château
Giscours in particular. Among countless public
relations exercises, the winners of the coveted
Gault et Millau 'Clé d'Or' award for outstanding
chefs were presented with their own weight in
bottles of Château Giscours. Pierre Tari, along
with like-minded fellow proprietor-members of
the Union des Grands Crus, thinks nothing of
going to New York, San Francisco, Tokyo, London and all the European capitals, where he
attends tastings, seminars, lunches and dinners by
the hundred. The net result is a file of press-
cuttings that would put many a film star in the
shade. Not content with the huge volume of good
publicity he engenders, he even publishes his own
newspaper, *Giscours Réalités*.

As if all this activity were not enough to occupy a
man, Tari devotes yet more of his seemingly
boundless energy to his other love, the game of
polo. He has his own team, a polo ground at
Giscours and a string of polo ponies. An annual
tournament is staged at the château in August,
which attracts the leading teams from all over the
world, and this again does no harm to the wines of
Giscours and Bordeaux in general.

If I have painted Pierre Tari as a French version of
Barnum and Bailey rolled into one, it is not the
whole picture; he is also an intellectual and a
philosopher, who would really like to have been a
poet. He is a great lover of the arts, and has
recently commissioned a very beautiful audio-
visual about Giscours which is well worth seeing.
If you are lucky enough to visit Giscours (and
some 15,000 visitors make the pilgrimage each
year) you will come away with a greater under-

19

standing of what the great wines of Bordeaux are all about.

The vines, 65% Cabernet Sauvignon, 15% Merlot and the remaining 20% a mixture of Cabernet Franc, Malbec and Petit Verdot, are grown on the four hills – Grand and Petit Pougeau to the south-west of the château, and Cantelaude and Belair to the east and north-east. The perfect soil-type, exposure and drainage of these hills, aided and abetted by the artificial lakes created to improve the microclimate of Giscours, combine to afford perfect growing conditions for the noble grapes.

Vinification is traditional; the cuvier, with its 42 enamelled steel vats, allows for separate fermentation and maceration of the different grape varieties and for the production from each sector of the vineyard. Ageing is in wooden casks over a period of 22 months, during which time the casks are topped up twice a week, racked four times a year and fining with fresh egg-whites takes place in January of the second year. Every stage of viticulture and winemaking is meticulously overseen by Lucien Guillemet, the young régisseur, whose father owns Châteaux Boyd-Cantenac and Pouget nearby.

The wine of Château Giscours is not really a typical Margaux, tending to have a more full and aggressive style than its neighbours. A rigorous selection process is adopted at Giscours in order to maintain quality; the 'rejected' cuves are always sold as 'generic' wines, since Tari does not agree with the practice of selling a second wine. This individualistic approach reflects in the commercialisation of the wines of Château Giscours; since 1974 Pierre Tari has had an exclusive distribution contract with Gilbey de Loudenne, the Bordeaux négociant arm of I.D.V., the giant English wines, spirits and hotel group, who distribute Giscours throughout the world. Tari believes that the traditional Bordeaux market puts a château's wine too much at the mercy of speculative buying, and feels that as long as he has an assured outlet for his wine at an agreed and sensible price, this leaves him the time to do what he is best qualified to do – making a great wine and carrying its name to all four corners of the globe. 'I like to play poker,' says Pierre, 'but with cards, not with wine.'

The Taris have also recreated an 18-hectare vineyard called La Houringue, which lies to the south of the property; this has been totally replanted in stages since 1982, and the wine, which has the appellation Haut-Médoc, will be in full production in 1986. They have recently acquired a large property in the Premières Côtes de Blaye called Château le Virou, which will eventually have an annual production of around 250,000 bottles of red and white wine. Château Branaire-Ducru in St Julien is also a family property.

TECHNICAL INFORMATION

General

Appellation:	Margaux
Area under vines:	81.53 hectares, 77 in production
Average production:	25,000 cases
Distribution of vines:	Principally in 2 blocks, east of the château on either side of the D2, and south-west of the château around the new lake
Owner:	G.F.A. du Château Giscours
Président-Directeur-General:	M. Pierre Tari
Régisseur and Oenologist:	M. Lucien Guillemet
Maître de Chai:	M. Gino Surani

Viticulture

Geology:	Gravel and sand
Grape varieties:	65% Cabernet Sauvignon, 25% Merlot, with some Cabernet Franc and a little Petit Verdot
Pruning:	Médocaine
Rootstock:	Riparia Gloire 3309, 101-14, Millardais 4
Vines per hectare:	8,000 and 10,000
Yield per hectare:	33.43 hectolitres (13-year average)
Replanting:	2.65 hectares per year (7-year average)

Vinification

Added yeasts:	None
Length of maceration:	15 days, average
Temperature of fermentation:	31°C
Control of fermentation:	By remontage, and use of heat-exchange equipment
Type of vat:	Concrete, epoxy-resin lined
Age of casks:	Up to 50% new each year, depending on vintage.
Time in cask:	20–34 months, depending on vintage
Fining:	Fresh egg-whites, sometimes powdered egg-whites used
Filtration:	Sur plaque, before bottling
Type of bottle:	Embossed with Giscours crest, also with vintage from 1983

Commercial

Vente Directe:	Very little
Sales:	Through Gilbey de Loudenne, S.A. Château Loudenne St Yzans-de-Médoc 33340 Lesparre
Agents overseas:	Yes: for information contact Gilbey de Loudenne S.A.
Visits:	Yes: telephone 56 88 34 02 or Gilbey de Loudenne, S.A. 56 41 15 03 Hours: 0800–1100, 1400–1700 Monday to Friday

THE TASTING AT CHATEAU GISCOURS, 7 November 1984

J.S., Mme. Nicole Heeter-Tari, Lucien Guillemet, Charles Eve, M.W., Miss Pamela Prior

1984 (From a cuve of Cabernet Sauvignon.) Intense, bluey purple. Nose very closed. Very hard, slight fermenting prickle. Very difficult stage at which to taste wine, but good fruit and tannin there.

1982 Good, deep red. Good, slightly peppery bouquet beginning to open up. Big mouthful, with lots of fruit and ripe tannin.

1981 Colour slightly bluer than 1982. Lovely, soft bouquet, cassis. Harmonious well-made wine with backbone and elegance. Will be an excellent bottle.

1980 Bright, medium red. Attractive open nose. Ready, pleasant 1980, good now but will keep a few years.

1979 Very dense, blackish red. Beautiful nose, powerful ripe cassis. Well structured, robust wine; complex flavour, with great length. A really outstanding 1979.

1978 Good, medium colour, just beginning to brown a little. Ripe bouquet, suggestion of wet vegetation. Complex flavour, quite forward, a bit flat. (Lucien Guillemet said this was not a good bottle.)

1977 Light, bricky red. Bouquet greenish, with a slight metallic tang. Light, fruity wine – a bit on the short side, but quite good for 1977. (No Merlot grapes in this vintage.)

1976 Deep, tawny colour. Nose ripe, but not very powerful. Distinct ripe strawberry flavour; good, not very long, with a slightly dry finish.

1975 Dense, dark colour. Bouquet good, but still very closed. Concentrated flavour, very long aftertaste. Will be superb.

1974 Excellent colour for the year. Pleasant nose. Ripe, easy on the palate. Ready now.

CHATEAU
D'Issan
MARGAUX

Take the D2 north from Blanquefort towards Pauillac, pass through the village of Labarde. After about 1 km you enter Cantenac; turn right opposite the garage, and you come to the gateway of Château d'Issan.

From the early history of Margaux, two estates have always dominated the parish, those of La Mothe-Margaux and La Mothe-Cantenac, currently Château Margaux and Château d'Issan. D'Issan prior to the 17th century was called Château Théobon, and was owned successively by the noble families of Ségur, Salignac and de la Vergne. In the early 17th century, the estate became the property of one Chevalier d'Essenault, and d'Issan is a contraction of his name. D'Essenault demolished the old castle that stood here, and built the château that stands today.

After the d'Essenaults, d'Issan passed into the hands of the powerful de Foix Candale family, seigneurs of the Château de Cadillac and other vast domaines, and d'Issan became known as Château de Candale. At the French Revolution all the Foix Candale properties were confiscated and let to local citizens.

In the early 19th century the Dulucs owned d'Issan, and they were followed by a family called Blanchy, who owned it at the time of the 1855 classification. In that historic document there were only five properties to have the word 'Château' preceding the name of the Cru; one of them was d'Issan, the others being Lafite, Latour, Margaux and Beychevelle.

The kind of hospitality offered to that indefatigable poet of the Médoc, Biarnez, by the Blanchy family at d'Issan intrigues me. He versifies eloquently on the beauty of the château, the copious and delicious wines, and then goes on to suggest that after supper the beautiful young châtelaines may offer other forms of delight. He then pulls himself up short in the last two lines, as though suddenly remembering Mme. Biarnez: 'But pleasure, alas, is ever ephemeral, and awakening disposes a sweet dream.'

The Blanchys sold d'Issan in 1866 to a Parisian entrepreneur by the name of Gustave Roy, and I am indebted to Lionel Cruse for the loan of interesting documents relating to this period. M.

Roy apparently came to Bordeaux from Paris, accompanied by his brothers-in-law, on family business. They were to purchase a Bordeaux wine château as an investment for a family trust. The original intention had been to buy Château Ducru-Beaucaillou, and they had made an offer of 1,000,000 francs which according to the memoirs had been accepted, only to find on arrival that they had been 'gazumped' by Nathaniel Johnston.

The next day they were called upon by a Bordeaux notaire, who had learned of their story by the Médoc bush telegraph (which still operates today). He was able to offer them the choice of two other Grands Crus, Château Brane-Cantenac and Château d'Issan. Appointments to view were fixed, and Gustave Roy first visited d'Issan; he came, saw and was conquered. A deal was struck at 800,000 Francs, which included the 1865 crop, 100 tonneaux of which were lying in the chai. There seemed little point in visiting Brane-Cantenac, but Roy's brother-in-law suggested that, since Gustave was so taken with d'Issan, he might like to keep it for himself and consider the other property for the family trust, and this was in fact what transpired. Roy visited the famous Baron Hector Branne, and the château was bought for 1,000,000 Francs, plus 25,000 for fixtures and fittings, on behalf of the héritiers Berger.

Gustave Roy's impressions of the great Napoléon des Vignes, Hector de Branne, in the twilight of his years are fascinating. He found him knowledgeable, charming and helpful, insisting that Roy should become his pupil and offering to teach him all he could about the running of the great wine property that now bore his name. Roy records his gratitude to this grand old man, saying that he never visited Bordeaux without calling on him, though this was not always easy, since the Baron was an inveterate gambler, and could only be drawn away from the tables during the afternoons. He also states that de Branne had a young mistress, and one is tempted to conclude that the lure of the green baize and the pursuit of fleshly pleasures may have been the cause of the sale.

There follows a detailed account of the work and investment involved at d'Issan. First a new cuvier was built in 1872, attached to the chai by a bridge over the moat. Roy then set about making the château habitable, as he was living at Brane-Cantenac, and naturally preferred the idea of living in his own property. He writes at length of the restoration, refurbishment and furnishing of the castle, culminating in a château with an 'assez grand air'. The only problem was the lack of water, which had to be brought in casks from the stockyard, and was always warm and tasted of wood. For a fee of 10,000 Francs, an artesian well was sunk to a depth of 108 metres, which gave a flow of 500 litres a minute of cool, sweet water; Roy then had built a 'château d'eau', and a system of pipes that fed the château itself, the cuvier, the chais and a washhouse. The surplus water was fed into the moat, and Roy records that from that time on there were no mosquitoes. The account goes on to describe how the consumption of Grands Vins was greatly diminished at that time, and how, thanks to the existence of some good palus or marshlands on the estate, Roy was able to create a vineyard, which he christened Moulin d'Issan, producing a lighter claret Bordeaux Supérieur A.C. (This appellation was as it were created on the palus of the Médoc in the 19th century, and the wines enjoyed great popularity throughout Northern Europe until the First World War.) Roy planted the vineyard almost entirely with Petit-Verdot vines, since this variety ripens much later than the Cabernet Sauvignon, and the harvest of the two vineyards would not interfere with each other. He later discovered that this grape produced a wine that was too hard, and added some Cabernets and a small proportion of other varieties. The other great advantage of the low-lying palus was that the phylloxera beetle, now just starting its ravages, could be combated by submersion of the vineyard. Gustave Roy's description of his Herculean labours encompasses every problem and disaster a winemaker can encounter, and the measures he took against them. It appears that it was on his instigation that the 'sulfateur à dos' was invented, enabling one man

to spray the vines against mildew with the newly discovered Bordeaux Mixture. He also invented a system for destroying the cochylis moth, whose eggs turn into grubs which attack the vines; this involved a series of oil-lamps, spread about the vineyard, set in wide pans of galvanised iron, filled with water. The moths, attracted to the light reflected in the water, flew to these traps and drowned by the thousand.

When he had completed all his work in the Grand Vin and Moulin d'Issan vineyards, Roy found his winemaking buildings totally inadequate for the vastly increased crops, and was forced in to yet more investment in the construction of two new cuviers and three more chais. He finished up with a model property, but concluded that it was the only venture he had ever undertaken that was not profitable. His heirs sold d'Issan just before the First World War.

After the Roy ownership, which had been of immeasurable benefit to d'Issan, the property went into a period of eclipse. It was with great courage that the much respected Emmanuel Cruse bought it in 1945. His son Lionel showed me the photographs taken in that year, and they tell a sorry tale. There were trees growing out of the château windows, and everywhere was ruin and decay. The entire crop of the 1945 vintage amounted to only six hogsheads. Cruse had the choice of buying either d'Issan or Giscours at that time; Giscours was in the same dilapidated state, and had the added attraction of having been a Cruse property in the past. However, common sense and economics prevailed, and he decided in favour of the smaller and more manageable d'Issan. What has been achieved here by the Cruses is plain for all to see – and to taste. The château has been restored and furnished with love and taste by Mme. Emmanuel Cruse, and the painstaking care that has gone into the gradual re-establishment of this fine vineyard is evident in the consistent high quality and finesse of its wines, especially in the lesser vintages. The Société Civile du Château d'Issan also owns a smaller vineyard of Haut-Médoc status called Château de Candale, which will produce a yearly average of 2,500 cases.

It is interesting to note that Gustave Roy found the ownership of the palus land such a saving factor in the economy of the estate, banishing from it his herd of 20 unproductive cows to create a vineyard of Bordeaux Supérieur status; some 80 years later, Emmanuel Cruse found this same land saved him during the difficult post-war years because he could derive an income from it as farmland, and now almost exactly 100 years after Roy's purchase, the wheel has come full circle, and Lionel

23

Cruse is replanting the palus with vines and re-establishing the name of 'Moulin d'Issan'. Plus ça change. . .

Every May, the 'Mai Musicale' of Bordeaux organizes two concerts which are always attended by a very large audience in the old 17th-century cellar.

D'Issan was a favourite wine of the Emperor Franz-Joseph of Austria, was sold to the Prince of Wales, later King George II of England, in 1723, and was reputed to have been served at the marriage feast of Eleanor of Aquitaine and Henry Plantagenet. Rightly then was the motto inscribed above the gateway 'Regum mensis arisque Deorum' – for the tables of Kings and the altars of the Gods.

TECHNICAL INFORMATION

General

Appellation:	Margaux (d'Issan)
	Haut-Médoc (Candale)
Area under vines:	28 hectares (d'Issan)
	5·50 (Candale)
Average production:	13,000 cases (d'Issan)
	2,500 cases (Candale)
Distribution of vines:	In one piece
Owner:	Société Civile du Château d'Issan
Director and Régisseur:	M. Lionel Cruse
Maître de Chai:	M. Arnaudin
Consultant Oenologist:	C.E.I. OE. Médoc et Haut-Médoc, Pauillac

Viticulture

Geology:	Fine gravel, with some chalk clay
Grape varieties:	75% Cabernet Sauvignon, 25% Merlot
Pruning:	Guyot Double
Rootstock:	Riparia Gloire 420A, 3309, 44/53 SO4
Vines per hectare:	8,300
Average yield per hectare:	45–50 hectolitres

Replanting:	By rotation every 35–40 years

Vinification

Added yeasts:	Yes
Length of maceration:	2–3 weeks
Temperature of fermentation:	25–28°C
Control of fermentation:	Cooling by cold water on outside of vats
Type of vat:	Stainless steel
Vin de presse:	Part incorporated, according to year
Age of casks:	$\frac{1}{4}$ to $\frac{1}{3}$ new each vintage
Time in cask:	18 months
Fining:	Albumen of egg
Filtration:	Light, before bottling
Type of bottle:	Bordelaise, Union des Grands Crus bottle

Commercial

Vente Directe:	No
Sales:	Sold through the Bordeaux négociants
Visits:	Telephone for appointment 56 44 94 45 (Office), 56 88 70 72 (Château)

TASTING OF CHATEAU D'ISSAN AT LIONEL CRUSE'S OFFICE, BORDEAUX, 16 December 1984
J.S., Lionel Cruse, Daniel Lawton

1983 Colour dark and almost black. Nose powerful, with touch of new oak. Big, mouthfilling and great length. Tannins, fruit and backbone all there. A great baby.

1982 Same depth and density of colour. Nose a little dumb, possibly due to the 'mise en bouteille' in September. Roundness and generosity dominate the non-aggressive tannins. A rich, long wine. Ready soon, but will last.

1981 Colour again very deep. Nose beginning to evolve, feminine, eloquent with good fruit and flowers. Elegant, fine, balanced and harmonious. Not a fat wine, but classic and attractive. Will be very good.

1980 Good deep, bluey red. Nose powerful with fruit and elegance. Delicious, harmonious and elegant, with enough fruit and tannin to support a good ageing.

1979 Colour very dark. Nose open, rich and fruity – Christmas pudding! Very big and fat, quite tannic. Will go on longer than some 1979s. Not very complicated, but good.

1978 Colour medium, slightly browner than 1974 or 1973. Nose good, touch of overripeness. Pleasant enough, touch of bitterness, but plenty of fruit. Good now.

1976 Colour browning a little, but dense. Nose of ripe fruit, hot-weather bouquet. Well-developed, ripe wine. Almost *à point*. Good '76 with some life.

1975 Good medium red. Nose open for 1975. One of the most approachable 1975s I have tasted, but quite complex, delicious and plenty of potential.

1974 Colour good for year. Nose ripe, but not over. Good for year, lots of fruit. Bit short, but very good for '74.

1973 Colour quite light, but not brown. Nose delicate and perfumed. Light, pleasing and elegant, perfect to drink now, with pleasant fresh aftertaste.

CHATEAU

Kirwan

MARGAUX

Driving north on the D2, pass through the village of Labarde, and as you enter the village of Cantenac, take the first turning left after the garage. The entrance to Château Kirwan is about 200 metres along on your right.

Fortunately for posterity, the history of Château Kirwan can be traced with accuracy, following the discovery of a comprehensive set of archives in a strongbox in the offices of the owners, Messrs. Schröder and Schÿler, only five years ago. The present head of the firm, M. Jean-Henri Schÿler, does not know how long the strongbox has remained unopened, but suspects that his father had no knowledge of its existence.

From as early as the 12th century wine has been made on the estate; the first recorded owners were the de Lassalle family, who owned the property, known then as Domaine de Lassalle, until the 17th century. In 1751, the domaine was bought by an English merchant in Bordeaux, Sir John Collingwood. Sir John had two daughters, one of whom married an Irishman from County Galway called Kirwan, and it was this worthy who succeeded to the property in 1781 on the death of his father-in-law, and changed the name to Château Kirwan. Though his name lives on, he lasted but a short while, losing both his head and his property in the Revolution.

His children, of whom there were eleven, no less, must have been possessed of some native Hibernian cunning, for they managed to regain possession of Château Kirwan very soon after 'the troubles', and in 1826 we find one of the Kirwan daughters, a spinster, still in charge. Further evidence of the Kirwan family's adaptability and instinct for survival can be deduced from their extensive improvement of the vineyard and the château during the difficult post-revolutionary years.

In 1827 the property was acquired by a M. Lanoix, who died soon after the purchase. His wife remarried a M. Deschryver, and it is his name that appears as owner at the time of the 1855 classification. M. Lanoix had a daughter who laid claim to the estate, and there was a long and complicated lawsuit, which resulted in the sale of Kirwan to a M. Godard from Castelnau, who was also a substantial landowner in the departement of Lot et Garonne. M. Godard's son, Camille, succeeded to the estate; he was rich, a passionate botanist, and a philanthropist and politician – he became deputy-mayor of Bordeaux. Camille died unmarried in 1881, and left Kirwan and the Parc Bordelais, where his statue now stands, to the city of Bordeaux. During his ownership, Camille Godard invested much of his fortune in the vineyard and grounds of Kirwan, planting many fine trees, which can be seen today in the gardens. The city of Bordeaux, albeit duly grateful for this unexpected bequest, did not see itself in the role of proprietor, and stopped all investments forthwith.

In 1902 Oscar Schÿler, great-grandfather of Jean-Henri, and the then head of Schröder and Schÿler, negotiated a contract with the city of Bordeaux for the sole distribution rights for the wines of Château Kirwan. The city finally decided to sell the property in 1907, and it was bought at auction by Daniel and Georges Guestier, who wanted it as a summer house for their very large family. It is curious that Schröder and Schÿler did not acquire the estate at this time, and Jean-Henri finds it quite inexplicable, particularly as it was his grandfather who snapped it up when next it came on the market in 1926. The exclusive contract negotiated in 1902 was respected during the Guestier ownership, so Kirwan has been continuously marketed world-wide by Schröder and Schÿler for over 80 years.

From 1926 until after the Second World War, Schröder and Schÿler, in common with many other proprietors, were not in a position to invest much capital in the property, and Kirwan had suffered from lack of cash injection ever since it was left to the city of Bordeaux back in 1881. It was not until the 1950s that Jean-Henri Schÿler was able to begin the massive replanting, refurbishment and modernisation that have put Château Kirwan back in its rightful place among the better Crus Classés of Margaux.

The vines now have an average age of 20 years, and up to half the casks are renewed each vintage. The wine has a beautiful depth of colour, is always elegant and flowery on the nose, and from the 1979 vintage onwards I found that Kirwan has gained considerably in backbone and finesse, probably due to the increased use of new casks. Château-bottling only began in 1967; prior to 1934 the wine was always sold without a vintage.

TECHNICAL INFORMATION

General

Appellation:	Margaux
Area under vines:	32 hectares
Production:	Between 8,000 and 20,000 cases, depending on vintage and selection
Distribution of vines:	One large parcel around the château, and several smaller parcels
Owner:	Schröder and Schÿler & Cie.
Director:	Jean-Henri Schÿler
Régisseur/Maitre de Chai:	Louis de Mezzo
Consultant Oenologist:	François Latapie

Viticulture

Geology:	Sand, chalky gravel
Grape varieties:	40% Cabernet Sauvignon, 30% Merlot, 20% Cabernet Franc, 10% Petit Verdot
Pruning:	Guyot Simple and Guyot Double
Rootstock:	420A: 5BB: SO4
Density of planting:	Variable from 6,500 to 10,000 vines per hectare
Yield per hectare:	30–45 hectolitres
Replanting:	15 hectares in 25 years

Vinification

Added yeasts:	None
Length of maceration:	20 days
Temperature of fermentation:	22–28°C
Control of fermentation:	Cooling by water circulation
Type of vat:	Cement and metal, epoxy-lined
Vin de presse:	Added to Grand Vin when possible
Age of casks:	25–50% new each year
Time in cask:	18–24 months
Fining:	Gelatine
Filtration:	Very light
Type of bottle:	Bordelaise

Commercial

Vente Directe:	No
Exclusivity:	Schröder and Schÿler & Cie 97 Quai des Chartrons 33300 Bordeaux
Agents abroad:	Sold in 65 different countries
Visits:	Yes, by appointment Telephone 56 81 24 10 or 56 88 71 42

THE TASTING, AT SCHRÖDER AND SCHÿLER'S OFFICE, 31 October 1984
J.S., J.H. Schÿler

1982 Lovely dark colour, almost black. Bouquet already very open and attractive. Taste also very open, with a mass of fruit and mute tannin. Will be drinkable quite soon, but will go on.

1981 Same beautiful deep colour. Bouquet good, fruit and flowers, quite complex. Lovely wine, well-made with good structure and finesse – harmonious. Will be a very good bottle.

1980 Excellent depth of colour. Elegant, perfumy nose of fruit, soft. Attractive, easy to drink, a *little* short, but an excellent 1980. Very Margaux in style.

1979 Again that depth of colour. Bouquet really good, generous with lots of fruit. Very well-made wine with fruit, backbone and very supple. A winner.

1978 Shade of brown in the colour. A little flat on the nose. Taste good at first, but finishes a bit short and lacks finesse. Jean-Henri Schÿler suggests that this is a result of late-ripening grapes.

1976 Good medium red, only very slight browning. Slight smell of wet wood. Still has good fruit, but a little short.

1974 Colour deep, but quite brown. Nose a bit cooked. A good 1974, a little over the top, but still very drinkable.

CHATEAU

Labégorce

MARGAUX

As you drive north on the D2 from Margaux towards Pauillac, you will come to a sign on your right after about 1 km, pointing to the château which lies well back from the road, screened by trees.

The three properties of similar-sounding name, Labégorce, Labégorce-Zédé and l'Abée Gorsce de Gorsce, were at one time a single estate. Château Labégorce boasts a fine château, built around 1830 in Louis XV style on the site of a former house, which was destroyed by fire. Among many owners, one of the earliest mentioned was Louis Gourdan de Genouillac, Baron de Bessan, who was the proprietor in 1611. In 1683 a M. de Beaucorps bought the estate for 16,950 livres, and was followed in 1728 by a family called de Mons, who took the title of Seigneur de La Bégorce. Just after the French Revolution, a series of proprietors are recorded in the 1868 edition of Feret, among them some apparently diverse nationalities; there is a Wettner, one Pierre Capelle, a gentleman named Valtapani and Marcelin Clauzel – surely an ancestor of the present owners of Château la Tour de Mons just up the road. At that time there were 68 hectares in production, so presumably the division had not yet taken place.

Jean-Robert Condom's parents bought Labégorce in 1965 from the Flemish Roorycks. The sound, consistent wine of Château Labégorce is made with a great deal of care and attention to detail. It is a very well-made and reliable wine, though not especially Margaux in style to my taste. The chai and cuvier are spotless, and the reception room with its walls of varnished case-ends, has an attractive view of the ageing-chai through a huge plate-glass wall.

Under the supervision of Jean-Robert Condom, who took over the management of the property in 1978, much is being done to maintain and improve the quality of Château Labégorce. He has installed a lot of new vinification equipment, including a new and revolutionary heat-exchange

27

apparatus for temperature control during fermentation, and has significantly increased the proportion of new barrels that are used each vintage. The château now has its own bottling line, whereas in the past this was done by a contractor.

Distribution before Jean-Robert took over was handled exclusively by Dourthe Frères; although they, or their parent company, CVGB at Parempuyre, are still the only négociant in Bordeaux to handle the wines of Château Labégorce, they no longer have an exclusivity, and a large proportion of the production is commercialised directly by Jean-Robert Condom. It is yet one more indicator of the personal attention that is being given to every aspect of Labégorce.

TECHNICAL INFORMATION

General

Appellation:	Margaux
Area under vines:	30 hectares
Average production:	13,500 cases
Distribution of vines:	Grouped around the château
Owner:	Jean-Robert Condom
Maître de Chai:	Michel Duboscq
Consultant Oenologist:	Professor Emile Peynaud

Viticulture

Geology:	Gravel
Grape varieties:	60% Cabernet Sauvignon, 5% Cabernet Franc, 35% Merlot
Pruning:	Guyot Double
Rootstock:	101-14, 3309 principally
Vines per hectare:	5,500 and 10,000
Yield per hectare:	45–48 hectolitres
Replanting:	Since 1965, only new ground has been planted

Vinification

Added yeasts:	Yes, the first vats – 10 kg per 110 hl
Length of maceration:	Minimum 20 days
Temperature of fermentation:	28°C
Control of fermentation:	Large heat-exchange pump
Type of vat:	Cement
Vin de presse:	Incorporated following tasting and analysis
Age of casks:	$\frac{1}{4}$ to $\frac{1}{3}$ new each vintage
Time in cask:	18 months
Fining:	Egg-whites
Filtration:	Light, before bottling
Type of bottle:	Bordelaise lourde

Commercial

Vente Directe:	Yes
Direct ordering from château:	Yes
Exclusivity:	Sole Bordeaux négociant, CVGB, Parempuyre
Visits:	Yes, telephone 56 88 71 32 Hours: 0800–1200, 1400–1800

THE TASTING AT CHATEAU LABEGORCE, 13 November 1984
J.S. and Jean-Robert Condom

1983 Very deep red. Bouquet already quite flowery. Elegant wine with lots of fruit and new wood. Will be good.

1982 Again good depth of colour. Nose good and fruity. Already rounded and supple, with good fruit and soft tannins. Does not have the sinew of 1983.

1981 Same consistent deep red. Good bouquet, slight undergrowth. Harmonious, long in the mouth. Forward, nearly ready.

1980 Colour excellent for 1980. Open, soft bouquet – blackcurrants. Pleasing and easy on the palate. Well-made 1980, with a good finish.

1979 Good deep, almost blue red. Nose soft and quite Margaux. Fruit there, but lacks backbone. Soft, slightly glycerine character. Ready and good to drink now.

1978 Good intense red. Bouquet powerful, but elegant. Well-made, fat wine. Balance excellent. Very drinkable now, but will evolve further.

CHATEAU
Lascombes
MARGAUX

Take the D2 northwards in the direction of Pauillac. As you enter the village of Margaux, there is a turning on your left, opposite the drive to Château Margaux, and Château Lascombes is clearly signposted from here through the back streets of the village.

In its early history, the lands of Château Lascombes were joined with those of Durfort-Vivens, and were the feudal property of the Ducs de Duras. The estate first acquired a separate identity when it was acquired by the Chevalier Antoine de Lascombes.

I have not been able to establish whether the present name of the château derives from Antoine de Lascombes, as there is another school of thought, namely that he may have taken his name from the property, which could have been called Lascote, in turn a corruption of La Cote; this referred to the rounded côte, or hill, on which the main part of the vineyard is situated. The de Lascombes family remained in possession until after the Revolution, when Anne de Lascombes sold the domaine to the ubiquitous Nathaniel Johnston; he did not keep it long, and was followed by a Monsieur Favre who in turn sold to Monsieur Loraigue in the 1820s. Loraigue sold Lascombes for 90,000 francs to M. Hue, whose daughter is shown as the owner in the classification of 1855. It was placed quite high – 4th of the Second Growths if you discount Mouton – and documents and price-lists of that era bear witness to the high quality of the wine, although the vineyard was very much smaller than today.

Mademoiselle Hue married a Monsieur Petit, and for a time the property was called Petit-Lascombes, a practice which I hope will not be followed by the daughter of the late M. Mentzelopoulos, Mme. Corinne Petit, who runs Château Margaux so ably – Château Petit-Margaux would not sound quite right! Gustave Chaix d'Est-Ange bought Lascombes from M. Petit; he was a politician of some note, Secretary to the Gironde Senate in 1867. His son, Jean-Jules Théophile, succeeded him on his death in 1887, a barrister of great renown; it was he who won the case for France in her dispute with the Egyptian government over the ownership of the Suez canal. In recognition of this patriotic service, Chaix d'Est-Ange received from a grateful Napoleon III a coffee service of Sèvres porcelain decorated with nubile portraits of Louis XIV's mistresses. The worthy litigant may not have had too much time to devote to Lascombes, for the vineyard had fallen to only 13 hectares, and in the early 20th century the wine did not enjoy a great reputation. In the twenties Chaix d'Est-Ange died, and Lascombes became the property of a company, the principal shareholders of which were the Ginestet family. Capable as they were, times in the Médoc were difficult in the thirties and through the war years, and they sold their share, having only partly

rebuilt the reputation of Lascombes, to General Brutinet, head of intelligence for the Allied armies for south-western France and Spain.

It was in 1952 that the colourful 'Pape des Vins', Alexis Lichine, already himself proprietor of Prieuré-Lichine, got together a consortium of American investors to buy Lascombes. Prior to the purchase, Lichine invited David Rockefeller, one of the participants in this venture, to stay in Margaux. During his visit, he met Pierre Ginestet, and asked his advice; Ginestet's reply was, 'Ownership of a vineyard will not make you very rich, but it is one of the only investments of which you can always taste the dividends.' In the twenty years of the Lichine consortium's owner-ship much was achieved; by 1971 the production had increased tenfold, and the reputation and quality of the wine was firmly re-established.

In 1967 Lichine sold his distribution company, Alexis Lichine and Co. in Bordeaux, to the Eng-lish brewing giant Bass Charrington. Lascombes had always been quite separate from this com-pany, being the property of Alexis Lichine and his group of investors, and they finally decided to sell Lascombes to the same English group in 1971, for a price reputed to be in the region of $2,000,000.

Since 1971, Bass Charrington have invested prodi-gious sums in improving and rebuilding the chais, cuvier and other buildings. The château, which owes more to the Victorian Scottish Baronial than any other recognisable architectural style, has acquired a number of comfortable guest suites for visiting executives and other guests, and there is an impressive Beverly Hills type swimming-pool. The vineyard has been extended, and there are now 94 hectares in production, making Las-combes the second largest Grand Cru in terms of productive vines after Château Brane-Cantenac. It is also probably the most fragmented vineyard in the Médoc, comprising literally hundreds of dif-ferent parcels of vines. Though this creates prob-lems when working the vineyard, it also gives, by its very atomisation, a broader spread of risk from the myriad problems of disease, infestation and vagaries of the capricious Médocain microclimate. Château Lascombes produces a thoroughly reli-able Margaux, which is more noticeably good in poor vintages; it has a tendency to mature relati-vely quickly, but at the same time has good ageing potential, and is inclined to gain rather than lose colour in bottle in the first five or ten years, a quirk which makes for difficulties when tasting it blind. Lascombes also produces a delicate, dry rosé from vines grown on the lower marshland, sold as Chevalier de Lascombes under the Bor deaux Supérieur appellation. The chapter on Las-combes must include mention of the 3rd Growth property, Château Ferrière. This is a tiny walled vineyard in the centre of Margaux, which is leased to Château Lascombes. The wine from its 4 hectares is vinified and aged at Lascombes, but is kept quite separate. Most of the production is sold to the French restaurant trade. It was the property of the Ferrière family from the 18th century until 1914, when it was sold to Armand Feuillerat, who owned Château Marquis de Terme nearby; the owner today is his daughter, Mme. Durand. The wine tends to be a little harder and less supple than that of Lascombes.

TECHNICAL INFORMATION

General

Appellation:	Margaux
Area under vines:	94 hectares
Production:	Between 25,000 and 50,000 cases depending on vintage
Distribution of vines:	Very fragmented
Owner:	Bass Charrington, London
President Director General:	M. Alain Maurel
Régisseur:	M. C. Gobinau
Maître de Chai:	M. R. Dupuy
Oenologist:	M. P. Léon

Viticulture

Geology:	Varied, but in principal deep gravel, on chalk/clay subsoil
Grape varieties:	65% Cabernet Sauvignon, 32% Merlot, 2% Petit Verdot, 1% Cot or Malbec
Pruning:	Guyot Double
Rootstock:	101.14, Riparia, 3309
Vines per hectare:	Part 7,000, part 9,000
Yield per hectare:	25–40 hectolitres
Replanting:	2 hectares per annum

Vinification

Added yeasts:	Yes, for first vat when necessary
Length of maceration:	15–20 days
Temperature of fermentation:	25–30°C
Type of vat:	Cement and stainless steel
Age of casks:	⅓ new each vintage
Time in cask:	14–20 months
Fining:	Fresh egg-whites
Type of bottle:	Bordelaise lourde, with 'Lascombes' engraved in the glass.

Commercial

Vente Directe:	Yes, to private customers in France
Agents in foreign countries:	U.K. Hedges and Butler Ltd.
General Sales:	By Alexis Lichine and Co., Bordeaux
Visits:	Yes: telephone 56 88 70 66 Hours: 0900–1200, 1400–1700 Monday to Friday

THE TASTING AT THE OFFICES OF ALEXIS LICHINE & CO., BORDEAUX,
8 November 1984
J.S. and M. Marc Quertinier

1983 Good bluey red. Nose good with fruit and new wood. Well structured, long with good fruit, tannins just right. Elegant.

1982 (Bottled late September.) Blackberry colour. Nose very good. Great richness of flavour, but tannins predominate. A big wine, suffering a little from the recent bottling.

1981 Bright medium red. Nose beginning to show well, soft with good fruit. First impressions of openness and maturity, but finish is quite hard. A very good bottle in two or three years.

1980 Colour quite light. Charming and open bouquet. Fresh, appealing flavour, with charm and some length. Good now, but will go on for a year or two.

1979 Quite deep, dense red. Fruit good on nose – fraises des bois? Lots of fruit, but quite aggressive. Finishes dry.

1978 Colour beginning to brown a little. Nose quite open, but more enclosed than the '79. Quite mature for 1978, finishes a bit short, but an elegant wine.

1977 Good colour for '77, very like the '78. Attractive bouquet, with good fruit. Quite a harmonious, well-made '77. Lightish, with hint of dryness on finish, but good for year.

1976 Colour quite brown. Nose ripe and a little oxidised. Shortish, though still has some fruit. A wine to drink now.

CHATEAU

Malescot-St Exupéry

MARGAUX

As you enter the village of Margaux, driving north on the D2, the road bends very sharply left. Château Malescot St Exupéry is to be found some 100 metres after the bend on your left.

In the 16th century, the as yet modest estate belonged to a family called Escoussès, who were notaries in Margaux. Only about 30 or 40 tonneaux of wine were produced then, but the records show that the various plots of the vineyard bore the same names then as they do today. The last Escoussès, a lady called Louise, sold the property to Maître Simon Malescot in 1697; this worthy was a man of some power and influence, being at the same time Public Prosecutor, and King's adviser in the Bordeaux parliament. He and his descendants remained proprietors for over a hundred years, surviving the vicissitudes of the Revolution. Under their ownership Malescot prospered – the vineyard was improved and extended, the chais enlarged and a château was built.

The next owner was Count Jean-Baptiste de Saint-Exupéry, who bought it in 1827 and added his name to that of Malescot; the property at this stage was more or less the same size as it is today. Saint-Exupéry sold in 1853 to a Monsieur Fourcaude, who ran it in partnership with his son-in-law, Monsieur de Boissac, and it was they who built the present château.

This was a golden period for Château Malescot-St Exupéry, as it was now known, and, two years after Fourcaude became the châtelain, he must have been proud to have it classified as a Third among the Great Growths in the classification of 1855.

Between 1880 and 1955 the history of this Margaux property has been a chequered one. Five owners, phylloxera, mildew, two world wars and economic slumps all took their toll. M. Paul Zuger, a Swiss of Alsatian origin, was managing the property for the last owners, an English subsidiary company of Seager Evans called William Chaplin and Sons Ltd. By the 1950s there were only 7 hectares under vines, and all the

buildings and the château were in ruins. In 1955 Zuger bought the property, and he and his sons set about the task of restoring the vineyard to its original size and rebuilding its reputation. Now, 30 years later, their success is there for all to see, both in the quality of the wine and the appearance of the property. Paul Zuger died in 1981, and it is his son Roger who lives in the beautifully restored château and runs the vineyard. He is President of the Syndicat Viticole de Margaux.

The vineyard is in five main blocks, all in the parish of Margaux, and they all enjoy a good depth of principally Pyreneean gravel. It is perhaps the rather high proportion of Merlot vines (35%) which gives the wine of Malescot-St Exupéry a slightly bigger and more robust style than some of its more feminine Margaux neighbours. An excellent deuxième vin is produced, and sold under the name 'Château Loyac'.

TECHNICAL INFORMATION

General

Appellation:	Margaux
Area under vines:	30 hectares
Average production:	14,000 cases
Distribution of vines:	In 5 blocks, all in Margaux appellation
Proprietors:	Société Civile du Château Malescot-St Exupéry
Director:	M. Roger Zuger
Maître de Chai:	M. J.-F. Miquau
Chef de Culture:	M. J.-C Durand
Consultant Oenologist:	M. Boissenot

Viticulture

Geology:	Deep gravel, mainly Pyrenean, on alios subsoil
Grape varieties:	50% Cabernet Sauvignon, 35% Merlot, 10% Cabernet Franc, 5% Petit Verdot
Pruning:	Guyot Double
Rootstock:	Various
Vines per hectare:	6,600 to 10,000
Average production per hectare:	45 hectolitres
Replanting:	As necessary to maintain average vine age of 30 years

Vinification

Added yeasts:	No
Length of maceration:	30 days
Temperature of fermentation:	30°C, with a 4–5 hour period at 34°C
Control of fermentation:	Cold water on exterior of cuves
Type of vat:	Stainless steel and concrete
Vin de presse:	Incorporated according to vintage
Age of casks:	$\frac{1}{5}$ new each vintage
Time in cask:	18 months
Fining:	Gelatine of egg-white
Filtration:	None
Type of bottle:	Bordelaise lourde

Commercial

Vente Directe:	Yes
Direct ordering from château:	Yes, for French private customers
Agents:	Consult château for details.
Visits:	Yes
	For appointment, telephone 56 88 70 68

THE TASTING AT CHATEAU MALESCOT-ST EXUPERY IN M. ROGER ZUGER'S KITCHEN, 10 January 1985
J.S., M. Roger Zuger

1983 Very dark red. Nose soft with good fruit. Quite hard and tannic, but with a mass of fruit and flesh.

1982 (Bottled July 1984.) Colour almost as dark as 1983. Nose good, but quite closed. Flavour very shut in, but all the elements are there. Quite hard and unapproachable for this vintage in Margaux and needs a lot of time.

1981 Again lovely deep colour. Elegant bouquet just beginning to develop. A wine just entering adolescence. Already has promising style and finesse, with a great deal of charm.

1979 Deep red. Nose powerful and rounded. Mouth-filling and long, with plenty of fruit and muscular body.

Not a complex wine, but already good, and will keep and improve.

1975 Colour just beginning to brown. Bouquet quite open. More advanced than many 1975s I have tasted. Pleasant, not too complicated, has some length, and will keep.

1973 Colour very pale brown. Nose maderised. Taste also maderised, over the hill and going down quite quickly.

1971 Good colour, no brown. Bouquet lovely, very Margaux, with fruit and violets. Fruit good, elegant and charming, with long aftertaste. Rounded and complete, perfect to drink now.

1970 Excellent depth of colour. Nose very strong, blackcurrant. Roger Zuger says this is typical of old style of Malescot-St Exupéry. Great concentration of fruity, flowery flavours – just beginning to evolve. Will be fine bottle for many years.

CHATEAU

Margaux

MARGAUX

Driving north on the D2, pass through the villages of Cantenac and Issan, and just before you enter Margaux itself, Château Margaux is signposted to your right down a private road through the vines.

The earliest recorded 'Seigneurs de la Mothe Margaux' were the d'Albrets in the 13th century. It is possible that the seigneurie may have belonged to the King of England, as Duke of Aquitaine, but this is by no means certain. In 1447 the property passed by marriage to the Baron François de Montferrand, who was later exiled after the battle of Castillon for his Anglophile tendencies. His successor was Thomas de Durfort, whose family name lives on in Château Durfort-Vivens, across the road from Margaux. Durfort sold the land in 1480 to a Bordeaux merchant called Gimel, whose daughter married into the Lory family.

The history of Margaux as an important vineyard, however, only begins in 1590 with Pierre de Lestonnac. This gentleman had begun assembling a large vineyard twenty years earlier, by buying and exchanging many small plots of vines in the area, and it was in 1590 that he was able to buy the 'Seigneurie du Noble Mothe de Margaux' from the Lorys.

Lestonnac descendants remained in possession at Margaux for two centuries, though the name disappeared as the property passed three times down the female line, first through the d'Aulèdes, then the de Fumels and finally the d'Hargicourts.

In 1694 the Marquis d'Aulède succeeded his father as owner of Margaux, and in the next fifty years rivalled Alexandre de Ségur, the Prince des Vignes, in the size of his vineyard holdings; not only had he inherited Margaux from his father, but he was also left Château de Pez and a half share in Château Haut-Brion by his mother. Under his regime at Margaux, the property was run by a pioneering régisseur named Berlon, who is credited with may innovations in the techniques of winemaking, not least of which was the separate vinification of red and white grapes. The learned Professor Pijassou has aptly dubbed him the Dom Pérignon of Bordeaux.

The Marquis d'Aulède died, childless, in 1746, and the property passed into the hands of the de Fumels, one of whom had married his sister. Joseph de Fumel, the new owner, was immensely rich; his one and only child, a girl named Marie-Louise Elisabeth, in spite of being sole heiress to his vast fortune, was not marked out by fate for happiness.

Alas for Marie-Louise Elisabeth, the avaricious eye of Madame duBarry had fallen upon her and her wealth. Her lover and protector Louis XV was clearly dying, and duBarry was fearful for her future. With the King's assistance, she put pressure on the luckless de Fumel heiress, and arranged a marriage between her and her brother-in-law, Monsieur du Barry. On the King's death, du Barry, not unnaturally, wished to change his name; the noble de Fumels were unwilling to let this adventurer assume theirs, so he took unto himself the title of Comte d'Hargicourt. It was this gallant who attracted the attention of Louis XVI by the brilliance of his court buttons. The King remarked upon them, taking them for huge diamonds, whereupon d'Hargicourt replied that they were the diamonds of his soil; they were, in fact, quartz pebbles, picked up in the Margaux vineyard.

When the Revolution came, this charmer promptly emigrated, abandoning the hapless Marie-Louise Elisabeth and his property; his departure was heartless, but prudent, since both she and her father were arrested and guillotined. Margaux was sequestrated as the property of an émigré, but was bought back by Laure Fumel, a cousin of the unfortunate Marie-Louise.

Laure Fumel married the famous Baron Hector de Branne, later to be known as the Napoléon des Vignes, but now in straitened circumstances. Soon after buying Margaux back, Laure was obliged to lease out the property, due to the unforeseen insistence of the revolutionary government that one-third of the re-purchase price had to be paid in gold rather than paper money. De Branne was forced to leave the country, and all his property was forfeit.

Laure managed to hang on to Margaux, as she had paid for it herself, but in 1802, now divorced and re-married, she sold Margaux, encumbered with debts and legal problems, to the Marquis de la

34

Colonilla for 650,000 francs, more than 300,000 francs less than she had paid six years previously.

Colonilla, a French merchant venturer who had won his title and fortune in Spain, was not greatly interested in winemaking, and the reputation of the vineyard declined under his ownership. The estate, however, has reason to be grateful to de la Colonilla, for it was he who commissioned the great Louis Combes to design the magnificent Palladian mansion and range of buildings at Margaux. By 1816 the work was all but finished, but sadly de la Colonilla died that year, having never lived in his dream house.

In 1836 Margaux was purchased from Colonilla's three children by the colourful and hugely successful banker Alexandre Aguado, Marquis de las Marismas del Guadalquivir, for a massive 1,350,000 francs. Unlike Colonilla, Aguado was a true Spaniard, and had made his fortune as a sort of 'financier royal' to the Spanish King. He was responsible for the organisation of Spain's national debt, and obtained his sonorous title from the King as an inducement to organise and fund the massive drainage scheme of the marshlands of the Guadalquivir river in Andalusia. Like many chancellors who have to raise money for their countries, although he was not an official one, Aguado was not the most popular man in Spanish society, and finding the cool disdain of the nobility hurtful, he turned his back on Spain and set up as a banker in France.

By the time he became a naturalised Frenchman, Margaux was just one of a handful of houses and estates owned by the banker in France and Spain. He continued his international financing activities from Paris, but the remaining fourteen years of his life were mainly devoted to the tasteful enjoyment of the vast fortune he had amassed. He was a patron of the arts – the composer Rossini was his protégé – and his collection of paintings, donated to the nation, serves as a memorial to Aguado; it can be seen today, hanging in, appropriately, the Aguado Gallery in the Louvre.

Aguado's eldest son, another Alexandre, inherited Margaux on his father's death in 1842. The second Alexandre's wife, a Scottish beauty, born Emily Macdonnell, was clearly a remarkable woman, and like Marie-Louise Elisabeth de Fumel before her, the role of châtelaine of Margaux did nothing to ameliorate a life of almost unremitting tragedy. Her husband died after a long period of insanity; she married his younger brother, the Vicomte Onesime Aguado, but it seems happiness was not for her; she lost in very quick succession her daughter, her two sons and finally her new husband. She was lady-in-waiting to the Empress Eugénie, to whom she was devoted, and followed her to England when the Emperor was kicked from the throne in 1870. Nine years later, with all hopes of restoration dashed by the death in battle of the Emperor's only son, Vicomtesse Aguado sold the Margaux estate to another Parisian banker, the Comte Pillet-Will, for 5,000,000 francs.

The price paid was a good one, and enabled Emily Aguado to stay with the Empress Eugénie free from financial worries. Things did not, however, work out well for the new owners; they bought into the Médoc at the worst possible time, for the last part of the 19th century was marked by a succession of disasters, including a world economic slump, oidium, mildew and phylloxera. When Comte Pillet-Will's son-in-law, the socialist Duc de Trémoille, sold Margaux in 1921, the

family not only incurred a capital loss of half a million francs, but had consistently lost money on the estate for forty years.

The new owners were a syndicate of investors from the Hérault, headed by the Bordeaux broker, Pierre Moreau, who had for some years concerned himself particularly with the sales of Château Margaux's wine. Moreau, backed by Albert Isenberg, a shipping magnate and the leader of the owning syndicate, did much to re-establish the estate and the quality of its wines. With the young Baron Philippe de Rothschild, he was the moving force behind the Union des Six Grands Crus Classés de la Gironde – Mouton, Margaux, Latour, Haut-Brion, Lafite and d'Yquem – who combined to protect the authenticity of their wine by total château-bottling. In the improvement of Margaux's wine, Moreau was greatly assisted by the appointment of the very able Marcellus Grangerou as maître de chai, a post successively held by his son Marcel, and his grandson Jean, the present cellarmaster. Despite the ability and energy of Moreau and his team, the resources of the Hérault backers were insufficient to weather the economic storm of the late '20s, followed by the disastrous vintages of '30, '31 and '32, and in 1934 the estate was put up for sale.

It was at this stage that the noble figure of Fernand Ginestet came to the rescue. Ginestet raised the necessary funds through the offices of the French Mayor of Saigon, Monsieur Boylandry, an adventurer who had built a fortune and a network of

wealthy connections in the Far East, mainly by acting as agent for French suppliers of luxury goods, of whom the Ginestets were one. Fernand Ginestet telegraphed an immensely long description of the financial complexities of the purchase to Saigon, and it is a mark of the trusting regard of Boylandry for Ginestet that he simply cabled back 'How much?', and that the funds were made instantly available.

The Ginestets were model proprietors at Margaux, gradually restoring the vineyard to its proper location and somewhat smaller proportions, constantly improving the wine and restoring the magnificent château, and exchanging the 40% holding of Lucien Lurton for the St Emilion Premier Grand Cru, Clos Fourtet. In the early 1970s, however, a combination of factors, headed by Ginestet's almost insanely honourable fulfilment of all their contracts with growers for the purchase of the virtually unsaleable vintages of 1973 and 1974 after the crash in fine wine prices, left them with insoluble cash-flow problems. The mountain of stock thus acquired for their négociant business was costing them 20,000 francs a day in interest, and the only option open to them was the sale of Château Margaux.

There followed almost four years of search for a satisfactory buyer. The Ginestets wanted three things: protection of their wine company's monopoly on the sale of Margaux wine, the assurance that their employees' jobs would be safeguarded and the right for Pierre Ginestet, now over seventy, to end his days living peacefully in the château for which he had done so much. A succession of potential purchasers either failed to meet these criteria, or were rejected by the French government on the grounds that they were not French, an attitude deeply and rightly resented by the Ginestets: had not Latour been allowed to pass into English hands only ten years before?

The agonies of Pierre Ginestet were finally resolved by the appearance, not of a Frenchman, but a Greek, in the person of André Mentzelopoulos, whose foreignness was overlooked by virtue of his ownership of the hugely successful French supermarket chain of Felix Potin.

Since the Mentzelopoulos acquisition of Château Margaux, a combination of unparalleled investment and meticulous care and attention in the making of the wine has, in an incredibly short time, restored this Queen of the Médoc to her rightful throne. As soon after the purchase as the 1978 vintage, the wine is again superb, fulfilling the oft-quoted description of Charles Cocks 150 years ago, 'These wines are possessed of much finesse, a beautiful colour and a very sweet bou-quet; they are strong without being intoxicating; invigorate the stomach without affecting the head, and leave the breath pure and the mouth cool.' What more could anyone ask of a wine?

It is improvement and care, following the best traditions of winemaking, rather than change and technology, that mark the present regime of Margaux. In the vathouse one may note the capacious new doubled 'réception des vendanges' and the sophisticated electronic control panel, but the vats themselves are still of oak, albeit immaculately renewed and maintained. One of the most impressive sights in the Médoc is the vast, new cathedral-like underground second-year chai; it replaces the old Orangery chai on the other side of the château, which was adequate, but infinitely less workable. Margaux still has its own resident cooper, ensuring not only the quality of construction of the 1,000 new casks that are required each vintage, but also the proper ageing and provenance of the oak that is used.

The delicious, crisp white wine of château Margaux, Pavillon Blanc, is vinified and aged entirely separately at Château Abel-Laurent, a hundred yards up the road from the main buildings. One of the handful of three or four whites produced in the Médoc, Pavillon Blanc was first made in the 1930s. It is now vinified in the best 'new-wave' tradition of dry white wine production. There are 9 hectares planted with 100% Sauvignon grapes. The lightly-pressed must is put in to a stainless-steel tank for 24 hours to allow all the deposits to fall, and then racked into another tank. As soon as fermentation starts, the wine is drawn off into new oak casks and moved into a temperature-controlled chai where it stays for two weeks at about 19°C; it is then left on the lees for about 6 weeks to await clarification, racked back in to tanks for blending, and then back into cask. It is racked once more and filtered; the wine spends a total of some 6 to 7 months in cask before bottling.

Overall direction of Château Margaux is in the astonishingly capable hands of Mme. Corinne Mentzelopoulos-Petit, who has headed the Mentzelopoulos empire since her father André's death in 1980. She is supported by a talented team, which includes Philippe Barre, in charge of the vineyards, Paul Pontallier as general manager, a highly qualified and able oenologist, who spent his early career as a diplomatic attaché in Chile, advising on oenological matters, and, of course the redoubtable Jean Grangerou as maître de chai. The renaissance of Margaux also owes much to the counsel of the king of oenologists, Professor Peynaud.

TECHNICAL INFORMATION

General

Appellation:	Margaux
Area under vines:	*Red* 75 hectares
	White 10 hectares
Average production:	*Red* 25,000 cases
	White 3,750 cases
Distribution of vines:	In several parcels, but mainly grouped around the château
Owner:	Société Civile du Château Margaux
Director:	M. Paul Pontallier
Directeur d'Exploitation:	M. Philippe Barre
Maître de Chai:	M. Jean Grangerou
Consultant Oenologist:	Professor Emile Peynaud

Viticulture

Geology:	80% gravel, 20% clay/chalk
Grape varieties:	*Red* 75% Cabernet Sauvignon, 20% Merlot, 5% Cabernet Franc and Petit Verdot
	White 100% Sauvignon Blanc
Pruning:	Médocaine
Rootstock:	3309, 101-14
Vines per hectare:	Cabernet Sauvignon 10,000, Merlot 6,500
Replanting:	Regular

Vinification

Added yeasts:	No
Length of maceration:	Average 3 weeks
Temperature of fermentation:	28–30°C
Control of fermentation:	By circulation of cold water
Type of vat:	Oak
Age of casks:	100% new each vintage
Time in cask:	18–24 months
Fining:	Fresh egg-whites
Filtration:	None

Type of bottle:	Bordelaise lourde

Commercial

Vente Directe:	No
Sales:	Through the Bordeaux négociants, via the courtiers
Visits:	Yes, by appointment
	Telephone: 56 88 70 28
	Hours: 1000–1200, 1400–1700

THE TASTING AT CHATEAU MARGAUX,
28 November 1984
J.S., Wendy Seely, Paul Pontallier, Jean Grangerou

1983 Lovely deep blue-black. Nose still closed, but fruit, violets and new wood detectable. Beautiful, elegant, mouthfilling with tremendous length and finesse. A future star.

1982 Very dense, blackish red. Nose still quite closed, but lovely scent of sweet, dried fruits coming through. Big and round, yet has femininity and finesse; tannins excellent, no harsh aggression.

1980 Remarkable depth of colour. Bouquet attractive; elegant, soft fruit with flowery tones. Still very young with plenty of good tannin. Has elegance and charm, yet plenty of sinew behind it. Not ready. Certainly the best 1980 I have tasted in the Médoc.

1978 Colour good, with a hint of brown. Lovely cedary bouquet with hint of violets. Well made wine, with length, finesse and great complexity of flavours. Elegant.

N.B. Jean Grangerou says this vintage combines all that is most typical and best at Château Margaux!

Pavillon Rouge **1979** Good deep colour. Fragrant, soft bouquet, my idea of a Margaux nose. Has good fruit, finesse and some keeping qualities. A good second wine.

Pavillon Blanc **1981** Clear, very pale gold. Nose honeyed, but clean and fine. Excellent flavour of clean, ripe fruit, with a fine balance of maturity and freshness. A well-made white.

CHATEAU

Marquis D'Alesme-Becker

MARGAUX

Driving north on the D2 through the village of Margaux, you will find the wrought-iron gateway to Château Marquis d'Alesme-Becker on your right, opposite the Mairie.

One of the oldest vineyards in Margaux, Château Marquis d'Alesme was created by a nobleman of that name in 1585, and the name was registered in 1616. It was from this family, who were knights and cavalrymen by profession, that the horseshoe crest on the label originates. The d'Alesmes remained proprietors for two centuries, until they sold the estate to a Dutch négociant by the name of Becker in 1809, who added his name to that of Marquis d'Alesme, and it was under his ownership that the château was classified a Third Growth in 1855.

The owners of Marquis d'Alesme have been numerous and cosmopolitan. Starting with the Marquis himself, who was French, we then move to Becker who was Dutch; he sold to another Dutchman, who was followed by two Polish counts, another Frenchman, the English company of W.H. Chaplin, and finally Paul Zuger, whose son, Jean-Claude, the current owner, is Swiss.

By a long and convoluted series of property dealing and exchanges, it transpires that the present château of Marquis d'Alesme was originally the château of Desmirail, the name and vineyards of which belong to Lucien Lurton. The present Château Marquis d'Alesme, *née* Desmirail, is a large Victorian mansion, which owes its appearance to a former owner, Madame Sipière, who transformed it in 1870, while the original château of Marquis d'Alesme is now the offices of Château Lascombes.

Before Jean-Claude Zuger took over the management of the property in 1979, his father ran it in tandem with their other property, Château Malescot-St Exupéry, and there was a tendency to regard the wine of Marquis d'Alesme as a second wine of Malescot. It now has a totally separate and distinct identity, and Jean-Claude has made many improvements to the buildings and the wine. He has modernised the cuvier, installing stainless-steel vats, and built a new chai. He has also shortened the time spent in casks by the wine to 12 months, and the wines are somewhat softer and more readily appealing than in former years.

Jean-Claude has a total of 9 hectares under vines, but he also owns a further 7 hectares which are currently being farmed by his brother Roger, with a further 2 hectares that can be planted. These parcels will revert to him in 1995, so in 10 years the area of Château Marquis d'Alesme will be doubled.

TECHNICAL INFORMATION

General

Appellation:	Margaux
Area under vines:	9 hectares
Average production:	4,450 cases
Distribution of vines:	In 3 blocks
Owner:	M. Jean-Claude Zuger
Maître de Chai:	M. André Pelletan
Consultant Oenologist:	M. Boissenot

Viticulture

Geology:	Varied, typical of Margaux
Grape varieties:	40% Merlot, 30% Cabernet Sauvignon, 20% Cabernet Franc, 10% Petit Verdot
Pruning:	Guyot Double
Rootstock:	Riparia Gloire
Vines per hectare:	10,000
Average yield per hectare:	42 hectolitres
Replanting:	Yes, when necessary

Vinification

Added yeasts:	Yes
Length of maceration:	15–25 days
Temperature of fermentation:	Stabilised at 30°C
Control of fermentation:	By running water
Type of vat:	Stainless steel
Vin de presse:	Incorporated following tasting
Age of casks:	$\frac{1}{6}$ new each vintage
Time in cask:	12 months
Fining:	Egg whites
Filtration:	None
Type of bottle:	Bordelaise

Commercial

Vente Directe:	Yes, for private customers and France only
Direct ordering:	Yes
Agents:	Consult château for details
Visits:	Yes: Monday to Friday 0800–1200, 1400–1800 Telephone: 56 88 70 27

THE TASTING AT CHATEAU MARQUIS D'ALESME, 10 January 1985
J.S., Jean-Claude Zuger

1983 Very deep colour. Nose already showing well. Good rounded flavour, definite blackcurrant, with good tannins. Long in the mouth, and very supple for such a young wine.

1982 Incredibly dark red. Nose good, but not giving too much yet. Harder wine than 1983 with more pronounced tannin, will be excellent. To keep longer than its brother from the same vintage across the road at Malescot.

1981 Colour again very good and dark. Nose beginning to show typically Margaux. Fruit and tannin starting to harmonise, but still needs time. Will be lighter and more feminine than the two later vintages.

1980 Colour bright and much lighter. Pleasing, open bouquet. Lightish, already good to drink, but has some texture and will keep a while.

1979 Deep red. Assertive, fruity nose. Beginning to drink well, plenty of fruit and good length.

CHATEAU
Marquis de Terme
MARGAUX

Château Marquis de Terme is situated to the left of the village of Margaux, and can be seen to the right of Rausan-Ségla and Rauzan-Gassies as you drive between Issan and Margaux on the D2.

The vineyards of this, the only 4th Growth Margaux in the 1855 classification, used to form part of the estate of Pierre des Mesures de Rauzan in the first half of the 18th century. It passed in 1762 as a dowry for one of his nieces to her husband, a Gascon noble called the Seigneur de Peguilhan, who also enjoyed the title of Marquis de Thermes, an earlier spelling of the present name of the château. The vineyard was made up of various plots of land, bought from other properties whose names have long since disappeared from the Médoc scenario. The vines are still very fragmented, and are spread over the communes of Margaux, Cantenac, Soussans and Arsac.

The next proprietor, who really put Marquis de Terme on the map, was the rich merchant Oscar Solberg. He completely re-vamped the vineyard in the 1880s, and is known to have had considerable tussles with the local authorities over the wine that came from the lower, marshy 'palus' land. In fact, until the creation of the Appellations Controlées, there was always confusion between the 'graves' wine and the less good 'palus' wine of Marquis de Terme. Now the strict laws of the A.O.C. avoid any such uncertainty, and the palus wine is sold under the 'deuxième vin' label of Château (formerly Domaine) des Gondats.

After the Solbergs, Marquis de Terme changed hands several times, passing this century through the ownership of Frédéric Eschenauer and Armand Feuillerat, the last owner before Pierre Sénéclauze, a wine merchant from Marseilles, who bought it in 1936. It is Sénéclauze's three sons, Pierre-Louis, Philippe and Jean who are the proprietors today.

Until recent years, the wine of Marquis de Terme

has not been widely available on the world market, since the Sénéclauze family business tended to sell the major part of the crop on the domestic market. There is now a change of policy, and more of the wine is being made available through the Bordeaux négociants.

A great deal of building work has been carried out over the last three or four years here. The château has been restored and converted into apartments for the family, and a vast new chai has been constructed for ageing the wine in cask; this addition was completed in 1981, and, quite apart from its functional beauty, represents a considerable saving in time, transport and movement of personnel, since prior to its construction, the casks were stored in a chai on the other side of the village. At the end of the chai, separated from the casks by a plateglass wall, is a new reception-room where tastings and functions can be held, as well as, judging by the long dining-table, dinners and lunches.

Château Marquis de Terme is perhaps one of the most unyielding Margaux wines in its youth. The 1982, usually an open vintage full of fruit and ripe tannin, was still very unapproachable; certainly all the constituents of a fine claret were there, but one will have to wait longer for this one than for many of its neighbours. The 1980 also needed some time in bottle, whereas most wines of this light vintage are already being quaffed with enjoyment.

I much enjoyed the second wine of this property, Château des Gondats. The 1982 was excellent, fat and fruity with good, round tannins, already approachable, benefiting perhaps from the fact that the second wine does not age in wood.

TECHNICAL INFORMATION

General

Appellation:	Margaux
Area under vines:	40 hectares
Average production:	12,500 cases
Distribution of vines:	Spread over the communes of Margaux and Cantenac
Owner:	Société Civile du Château Marquis de Terme (The Sénéclauze brothers)
Régisseur:	M. Jean-Pierre Hugon
Maître de Chai:	M. Alain Gouinaud
Chef de Culture:	M. Pierre Salignan
Consultant Oenologist:	M. Couasnon, Laboratoire de Pauillac

Viticulture

Geology:	Gravel on subsoil of alios and clay

Grape varieties:	45% Cabernet Sauvignon, 35% Merlot, 15% Cabernet Franc, 5% Petit Verdot
Pruning:	Guyot Double Médocaine
Rootstock:	Riparia, 3309, 101-14
Vines per hectare:	10,000
Average yield per hectare:	35 hectolitres
Replanting:	As necessary to maintain average vine age of 35 years

Vinification

Added yeasts:	Yes, in difficult vintages
Length of maceration:	21–25 days
Temperature of fermentation:	30°C
Control of fermentation:	By heat-exchange pump
Type of vat:	Concrete
Vin de presse:	From 5% to 10% included, depending on vintage
Age of casks:	$\frac{1}{3}$ new each vintage
Time in cask:	18 months
Fining:	Egg-whites in cask
Filtration:	Sur plaque at bottling
Type of bottle:	Bordelaise

Commercial

Vente Directe:	Yes, for visitors
Sales:	Through the Bordeaux négociants and, in France, through the Sénéclauze business in Marseilles
Agents overseas:	Yes, contact château for information: Château Marquis de Terme 33460 Margaux
Visits:	Yes, all year, Monday to Friday Hours: 0900–1200, 1400–1700 Telephone: 56 88 30 01

THE TASTING AT CHATEAU MARQUIS DE TERME, 30 January 1985

J.S., Christian Seely, Jean-Pierre Hugon, Alain Gouinaud

1982 Very deep red. Nose good but still very closed. Big and hard, plenty of fruit, but tannins hard for 1982. Needs plenty of time to make a good bottle.

1980 Colour good, quite dark for 1980. Attractive fruit on nose. Pleasant to drink now, but still a bit astringent – I think this will soften up after a year in bottle.

1976 Very dark for the vintage, no brown. Ripe fruit bouquet. Becoming a little thin, with a dry finish. Pleasant enough to drink now, but no great future.

Château des Gondats

1982 Very dark, bluey red. Open nose with good powerful fruit. Big, generous wine, with ripe tannins. Already nice, but will get better.

CHATEAU

Martinens

MARGAUX

As you drive north up the D2, passing through the villages of Labarde, Cantenac and Issan, you arrive at the village of Margaux itself. Just after the signpost for Château Margaux on your right, there is a turning left, with a large wall-poster directing you to Château Lascombes, and underneath it a sign for Château Martinens. The simplest advice is to take this turning, and then follow the signs, which are very clear. Château Martinens is in fact about 2 km west of Cantenac.

The house is an elegant, classic maison bourgeoise of two storeys, beautiful in its 18th-century simplicity. One's first view of the house is framed by a wrought-iron gateway, over which hangs a black wooden sign, bearing the name of the château in gold Gothic script. Here everything is in proportion, the short avenue of trees, the pretty garden and the chai, the ageing-cellar and vineyard workers' cottages, which form the two enclosing walls of the garden.

In this neat and ordered setting, one can well imagine three – reputedly – pretty English sisters, who owned this corner of the Médoc in the middle of the 18th century. It is interesting to imagine the kind of life led by Elizabeth, Mary and Jane White at this time. It is for sure that it cannot have been a lonely one, as this was one of the more passionate periods of the long love affair between the English and the Bordeaux region.

In 1776, possibly due to rumblings of the upheaval to come in the following decade, the sisters sold the property to M. Pierre Changeur, a Bordeaux négociant, who considerably extended the vineyard. He sold shortly after this to Louis Mascou, who lived in Guadeloupe; he in turn sold the property to François-Auguste de Sautter, Comte de Beauregard, one-time chamberlain to the Emperor Napoleon, Consul-General of Tuscany, and owner of the Domaine de Beauregard in the Swiss canton of Vaud. Bernard Ginestet suggests in his excellent book on Margaux that the wines of Martinens must have made an agreeable counterpoint to the rather boring wines of his native canton!

The estate changed hands two or three times before Mme. Simone Dulos became the owner in 1945. The management of the property was taken

over by her son, Jean-Pierre Seynat-Dulos, in the difficult years of the mid-seventies. Until this time, his education and training had been entirely in the legal profession. One can only imagine the enormous scale of the task that lay before him – the market was very depressed, and the cellar was stacked to the roof with the last three or four vintages, all unsold, and there was nothing in the bank. Believing in and loving Martinens as he so patently does, he put his shoulder to the wheel without further ado. The first priority was to sell,

43

and Jean-Pierre tells of the joy he felt when the lorry arrived to collect the first order from Belgium, and how he literally wept with relief when the driver handed him a cheque. The first thing he did with this money was to start a renovation and modernisation programme for all the housing of his faithful staff.

Since that time, Martinens has gone from strength to strength under the increasingly capable direction of Jean-Pierre Seynat and his trusty band of helpers. His care and painstakingly acquired expertise are evident everywhere, in the chai, the cuvier and every corner of the meticulous and traditionally maintained vineyard, whilst his love for the property is equalled only by the warmth of the welcome he extends to his visitors.

I found the wines to be well-made, charming, if not great Margaux, though the later vintages, following the introduction of a significant proportion of new casks since 1979, have certainly a shade more backbone and finesse than the earlier years.

TECHNICAL INFORMATION

General

Appellation:	Margaux
Area under vines:	30 hectares
Production:	10,500 cases
Distribution of vines:	In one piece around the château
Owner:	Mme. Simone Dulos and M. Jean-Pierre Seynat-Dulos
Régisseur:	M. Delille
Oenological Consultant:	Laboratoire d'Oenologie de Pauillac, M. Quesnon

Viticulture

Geology:	Clay/gravel
Grape varieties:	40% Merlot, 30% Cabernet Sauvignon, 10% Cabernet Franc, 20% Petit Verdot
Pruning:	Guyot Double
Rootstock:	Riparia; 101-14
Vines per hectare:	6,500
Yield per hectare:	35–40 hectolitres

Vinification

Added yeasts:	Yes, if necessary
Length of maceration:	3 weeks
Temperature of fermentation:	28–30°C
Control of fermentation:	By heating and refrigeration
Type of vat:	Cement
Age of casks:	¼ new each vintage
Time in cask:	1 year
Fining:	Albumen of egg
Filtration:	Sur terre
Type of bottle:	Bordelaise

Commercial

Vente Directe:	Yes
Direct ordering:	Yes
Visits:	Yes, by appointment
	Telephone: 56 88 71 37
	Hours: 0800–1200, 1400–1800

THE TASTING AT CHATEAU
MARTINENS, MARGAUX, 16 November 1984
J.S., M. Seynat-Dulos

1983 (En barrique.) Deep, bluey red. Nose still very closed, slight vanilla from new wood. Strong taste of oak, fruit there, long in mouth.

1982 (Bottled May 1984.) Deep, ruby red. Soft Margaux nose beginning to come out. Good, well-balanced and mouthfilling. Will be a good bottle, profiting from proportion of Merlots, which were especially successful in '82.

1981 Beautiful, deep, bluey-red colour. Fine, elegant bouquet – classic Margaux, with blackcurrant. Well-balanced, supple and elegant. All elements combining well to give a good bottle in a couple of years.

1980 Shade lighter than later vintages, but excellent colour for 1980. Nose open, soft and elegant with good fruit. Attractive and easy enough to drink now, but enough fruit and tannin to keep for some time.

1979 Again a lovely deep red. Fine, elegant bouquet. Well-balanced, well-made wine with finesse and some backbone. First year to use new casks, and it shows. Will be a fine bottle.

1975 Lovely, brilliant mid-red. Very fine perfumed bouquet. Already very attractive, soft and elegant. Aromatic, with aroma of violets and blackcurrant. A 1975 which benefits from the Merlot, and perhaps from the lack of new casks, as it lacks the toughness of some of the '75s.

CHATEAU
Palmer
MARGAUX

Château Palmer is situated on the right-hand side of the D2 in the hamlet of Issan, as you drive northwards, between Cantenac and Margaux.

The present vineyard of Palmer was originally part of an estate called Château le Gascq, which belonged to a family of that name from the 16th century until 1814. The de Gascqs were leading Bordeaux parliamentarians, and their name crops up frequently in the history of the Bordeaux wine châteaux. It was the widow of a de Gascq, who, having just lost her second husband, Monsieur Brunet de Ferrière, sold the property to the legendary and rather tragic figure, General Charles Palmer, whose name the château now bears.

Palmer was an English general under Wellington, who arrived at the gates of Bordeaux with the conquering army in March 1814. He was the son of a brewer from Bath; originally destined for the church, Charles Palmer had other ideas. He quarrelled with his father over his choice of career, and was promptly put to work in a lowly capacity in the family brewery. Happily for the ambitious Palmer, his father died and left him a considerable fortune, which was further augmented by a belated payment of £100,000 from the government of the day for the first mail-coach system, invented and started by Palmer's father.

As part of his inheritance, young Charles was also owner of the Theatre Royal in Bath; by a none too subtle spot of graft, namely free theatre tickets for life for the Corporation of Bath, Palmer was elected Member of Parliament for that city. The now wealthy and respectable young man obtained a commission in the Prince of Wales' own regiment, and soon became an accepted member of the 'Carlton House set', the select entourage who frequented the salons of Carlton House and Prinny's oriental fantasy, the Brighton Pavilion.

This rich and socially adroit young soldier found himself, at the end of the Peninsula campaign, sharing a coach to Paris from Bordeaux with the attractive Marie Brunet de Ferrière. The journey took several days, and one can imagine the wiles employed by the merry widow, the purpose of whose journey to Paris was to sell her estate. Suffice it to say that by the time their destination was reached, Charles Palmer had agreed to buy Château de Gascq for 100,000 Francs, with a lifelong rent to the widow of 500 litres of wine. If the wine was stipulated to be the wine of the property, she had driven a hard bargain.

During the next 17 years, Palmer added to the domaine by progressive steps, until by 1831 he had spent the best part of half-a-million francs, giving him an estate of 162 hectares, 82 of which were under vines. Most of this land was bought from hard-pressed aristocrats and bourgeois absentee landlords living in Bordeaux, who could not be bothered with their Médoc properties.

General Palmer, with his court connections, divided his time between his Bordeaux estate and promotional visits to the English court. There is a story of a dinner at Carlton House to introduce the new and delicate wine of Château Palmer; Prinny, alas, favoured a meatier style of claret, heavily doctored with Rhône wine, and advised Palmer to go back to Bordeaux and see if he could not strengthen the character of his wine. Slavishly, Palmer went back to Issan, and set about a series of experiments, including the total replanting of his vineyard. These efforts cost him dear, and were the first steps down the road to Carey Street for the poor general. Times were difficult in the Médoc, what with punitive taxes and legislation on export, and the first ravages of oidium. All these troubles were compounded by Palmer's agent, one Mr Gray, a charming and personable gentleman, who robbed his employer systematically for twenty years. As if all this were not enough, the Reform Bill was passed in 1832, depriving Palmer of his parliamentary seat by the abolition of the rotten boroughs, of which Bath was one.

His fortune gone, Palmer started to sell off bits of his property, but nothing could save him. In 1834 his wife left him, and in 1843 the Caisse Hypothétique in Paris foreclosed his mortgage, repossessing the remaining, and best, parts of the vineyard, some 54 hectares, half of which was in Cantenac, and the other half, a vineyard called surprisingly, Boston, 4 km to the west near Virefougasse. Two years later, Charles Palmer, soldier, courtier and adventurer died penniless and alone.

Château Palmer now entered a happier phase. Around this time there were a number of financiers on the look-out for properties in the Médoc. Times were hard, and many owners were desperate, an ideal situation for the wise investor with the necessary capital. The Rothschilds were already well established at Mouton, Baron James was soon to become proprietor of Lafite, and Beychevelle was shortly to drop into the portfolio of the Paris bankers, Achille Fould. On to the stage at Château Palmer stepped the Pereire family, merchant bankers of Jewish-Portugese origin, with huge interests in railways and other burgeoning industries.

Isaac Pereire bought the vineyards and huge vinification, ageing and cooperage buildings of Château Palmer for 410,000 Francs from the Caisse Hypothétique in 1853. Since Palmer's death, the property had been in the hands of a Mme. Françoise Marie Bergerac, who, curiously enough, lived at the same address as M. Paul Estenave in the Allée de Tourny in Bordeaux; it was Estenave who was instrumental in arranging the sale of the property to General Palmer back in 1814. Could there have been dirty work at the crossroads?

The Pereires built the present château in classic Second Empire style, surely one of the most elegant of all Bordeaux châteaux. For all its beauty, Palmer has never really been home to anybody. I have been fortunate enough to enjoy Peter Sichel's kind hospitality at the château on two occasions, and it was wonderful to hear life, music and laughter and to enjoy good food and marvellous wine in such atmospheric surround

ings. Apart from such rare family dinners and parties, Palmer stands empty and rather forlorn.

It must have taken a while before the Pereires saw much return on their investment. In the latter days of Palmer's ownership and in the intervening years, the property had become sadly neglected. Morale on the estate cannot have been too high; records show that at the time Palmer's remaining land was seized by the bank, his régisseur, M. Lagunegrand was owed three months wages. The vineyard, or what was left of it, was in a sorry state, doubtless due to the poor general's ill-advised experiments, and had to be totally replanted in 1858. This possibly explains why Palmer was only placed among the Thirds in the 1855 classification, whereas it is generally recognised todays as coming somewhere between Second and First in terms of quality and price. The Pereires had two very essential ingredients for the successful running of a Grand Cru that Palmer, in his latter years, lacked – capital and business acumen.

In addition to the 54 hectares they acquired in 1853, the vineyard was gradually enlarged, until there was a total of 109 hectares under the vine by 1870. An extremely able viticulturist and winemaker, M. Lefort, was appointed régisseur and by rigorous selection and tireless effort, regardless of cost, the wine of Château Palmer continued to gain in quality and reputation, even through the desperate years of the late 19th century. At this time many vineyards suffered eclipses, due to the ravages of oidium, mildew and phylloxera, but the dedication and ceaseless investment of the Pereires took Palmer through it all with flying colours.

From the Pereire purchase down to the present day, Château Palmer has always owed much to the calibre of its régisseurs. M. Lefort was followed by the first of the Chardons, whose name is now synonymous with that of Palmer, and it is two Chardon brothers, Yves and Claude, maître de chai and chef de culture respectively, who carry on that tradition today. This continuity is assured; Yves's son Eric and Claude's son Philippe are both working at Palmer.

By the 1930s there were so many Pereire descendants owning shares in Château Palmer that agreeing on policy and taking decisions became practically impossible. The Médoc was entering into one of its dark and difficult phases, and the consensus of opinion among the Pereires was that enough was enough. Château Palmer was offered for sale, and in 1939 was bought for the cost of one year's outgoings.

For some years the Pereires had spent no money on the property, and the vineyard had shrunk

46

from 109 to 36 hectares. The difficult war years followed, and, in spite of a succession of good vintages in the late forties, it was not until 1953 that Palmer became profitable again.

Since 1939 the share-structure in the company that owns Palmer has shifted several times; the Sichel company now has the largest stake with 34%. The Mahler-Besse family holds 22%, and four participants 44%, one of whom, the Bouteiller family, in the person of Bertrand Bouteiller, is responsible for day-to-day management of the property.

The quality of Palmer is now unimpeachable, and it is one of the most sought-after wines by Bordeaux connoisseurs and, sadly, speculators the world over. This is directly reflected in the prices fetched for Palmer on the international fine wine market – always above the top Second Growths, and sometimes only just below the Firsts.

The wine of Château Palmer is always, first and foremost, well-bred, possessed of great charm, finesse and elegance, but at the same time having tremendous strength of character and backbone, taking it, even in the less good years, into a dignified old age. Palmer '61 is probably the best mature claret I have been lucky enough to drink, whilst I was most impressed with the 1979 when tasting the more recent vintages.

TECHNICAL INFORMATION

General

Appellation:	Margaux
Area under vines:	40 hectares
Average production:	15,000 cases
Distribution of vines:	Mainly around the château on both sides of the D2, plus three smaller blocks
Owner:	Société Civile Immobilière du Château Palmer (See text for more details)
Manager:	M. Bertrand Bouteiller
Maître de Chai:	M. Yves Chardon
Chef de Culture:	M. Claude Chardon
Consultant Oenologist:	M. Boissenot

Viticulture

Geology:	Deep gravel
Grape varieties:	40% Merlot, 55% Cabernet Sauvignon, 3% Cabernet Franc, 2% Petit Verdot
Pruning:	Guyot Double
Rootstock:	Riparia, 420A, 3309, 4453
Vines per hectare:	10,000
Replanting:	Between 1 and 2 hectares per year

Vinification

Added yeasts:	No
Length of maceration:	20–25 days
Temperature of fermentation:	28°C average
Control of fermentation:	By heat-exchange apparatus
Type of vat:	Oak
Age of casks:	⅓ new each vintage
Time in cask:	18–24 months, depending on vintage
Fining:	Egg-whites
Type of bottle:	Bordelaise lourde

Commercial

Sales:	By the two firms of négociants: Sté Sichel, 19 Quai de Bacalan, 33000 Bordeaux Sté Mahler-Besse, 49 rue Camille-Godard, 33000 Bordeaux
Visits:	Yes, telephone 56 88 72 72 Monday to Friday 0900–1200, 1300–1700

THE TASTING AT CHATEAU PALMER,
21 November 1984
J.S., Peter and Diana Sichel, Anthony Barton.

1983 Very deep, purplish colour. Powerful nose of fruit, violets and new oak. Enormously complex flavour, with a mass of fruit and soft tannins. Very long in mouth. One to wait for.

1982 (Bottled June 1984.) Colour as deep as '83. Nose very closed at the moment. Very big, round wine, with great concentration of flavour. Shut in at the moment.

1981 Deep, brilliant red. Nose good, with lovely, soft cassis overtones. Excellent balance, everything in harmony, great finesse and backbone. Will go on a long time, and become a lovely Palmer.

1980 Lovely bright medium red. Open fragrant bouquet. Beautiful 1980, open, fragrant mouthful of wine, delicious to drink now, but will keep.

1979 Very deep colour. Bouquet powerful, rounded and intense. A fat wine, with lots of power, fruit and tannin, but at the same time has plenty of finesse. Will last a long time, and be a winner.

1978 Colour has depth, but a shade lighter than the '79. Nose a little closed, more delicate than 1979. Flavoursome, aromatic and complex, long aftertaste. Peter Sichel says it has great potential.

1977 Colour quite tawny. Bouquet open with good fruit. A light vintage, good to drink now and for a few years.

CHATEAU

Pouget

MARGAUX

As you enter the village of Cantenac, driving north up the D2 towards Margaux, you will see a sharp left turn just before the church, signposted to Châteaux Boyd-Cantenac and Pouget. Take this road, pass under the railway bridge and follow the road for about 1 km and you will find Château Pouget on your right and the chais and cuvier of Boyd-Cantenac opposite.

In 1650 the Pouget vineyards belonged to Etienne Monteil, Canon of St Emilion; he left the property to his brother François-Antoine, whose granddaughter Thérèse Ducasse made one François-Antoine Pouget her residuary legatee on 9 April 1748. This worthy citizen, rejoicing in the titles of Bourgeois de Bordeaux, Conseiller du Roy and Receveur et Contrôleur des Consignations des Aides et Finances de Guyenne, gave his name to the property. His daughter Claire married in 1771 Pierre-François de Chavaille, Seigneur du Parc in the parish of Merignac, advocate and Secretary-General of the town of Bordeaux. These two families, the Pougets and the de Chavailles,

between them ran the vineyard for a century and a half.

The Pouget estates were confiscated at the time of the French Revolution, but were returned to the de Chavaille family in 1798 after a part of the vineyard had been nominated as a 'Bien National'. Presumably the de Chavaille grandson of François-Antoine Pouget, who had emigrated to England, was then allowed to return and take possession of the remaining portion of the property. The name of de Chavaille is clearly shown as proprietor in the 1855 classification, when Pouget was placed among the Fourth Great Growths.

Since 1906 the Elie-Guillemet family have been in charge of Pouget, and it is Pierre Guillemet, an able and traditionalist winemaker, who runs the property today. Winemaking clearly runs in the blood, for Pierre's son Lucien is the very able young régisseur at Château Giscours in neighbouring Labarde.

Pierre Guillemet lives in the attractive château of Pouget – in reality more an elegant farmhouse. He is also owner of Château Boyd-Cantenac, a Troisième Cru Classé, whose chais and cuvier are on the other side of the road. Until 1982 the two wines were vinified and aged at the same time in the same buildings, but Pierre Guillemet, feeling that a tendency had grown up for Pouget to be regarded as the second wine of Boyd-Cantenac, has built a new and completely separate chai and cuvier, and from the 1983 vintage onwards, Château Pouget will have its very own 'lieu de naissance'.

Château Pouget is marketed exclusively by the Bordeaux négociants, Dubos Frères, who have a strong traditional business; this Cru Classé is exported to Holland, England, Japan, and especially to Belgium.

TECHNICAL INFORMATION

General

Appellation:	Margaux
Area under vines:	11 hectares
Average production:	4,300 cases
Distribution of vines:	One block
Owner:	Guillemet Family – Groupement Foncier Agricole des Chx. Pouget et Boyd-Cantenac
Director/Régisseur:	Pierre Guillemet
Consultant Oenologist:	Professor Emile Peynaud

Viticulture

Geology:	Sand and gravel, on a clay/sand subsoil
Grape varieties:	66% Cabernet Sauvignon, 4% Cabernet Franc, 30% Merlot
Pruning:	Guyot Double
Rootstock:	101.14
Vines per hectare:	10,000 and 6,000
Yield per hectare:	35 hectolitres
Replanting:	As necessary

Vinification

Added yeasts:	No
Length of maceration:	15 days average
Temperature of fermentation:	25–30°C
Control of fermentation:	Cold-water circulation
Type of vat:	Cement
Vin de presse:	Incorporated according to vintage
Age of casks:	30% new each vintage, rest in casks of 1 vintage
Time in cask:	22–24 months
Fining:	Albumen of eggs
Filtration:	Sur plaque before bottling
Type of bottle:	Bordelaise lourde

Commercial

Vente Directe:	Yes
Sales:	Through Bordeaux firm of Dubos Frères
Visits:	Yes: telephone 56 88 30 58

THE TASTING AT CHATEAU POUGET,
14 November 1984
J.S., Pierre Guillemet

1982 Lovely, deep colour. Nose closed. Still very closed on palate, bags of fruit, good tannin and new oak.
1970 Full dark colour. Nose open, lots of ripe fruit. Quite open and evolved for this vintage; full, round flavour, but drying off at the finish.

CHATEAU

Prieuré-Lichine

MARGAUX

As you enter the village of Cantenac driving north towards Margaux on the D2, the entrance to Prieuré-Lichine is on your left just after the church, and there is a car-park opposite. The property is one of the easiest to find in the entire Médoc, as there are huge billboards all along the road directing you to the Prieuré.

It was with some trepidation that I first approached Alexis Lichine on the subject of this book, for he is the doyen of all wine-writers, one of the greatest living experts not only on Bordeaux but on the wines and spirits of the whole world; his *New Encyclopedia of Wines and Spirits* is now in its third edition, and his excellent *Guide to the Wines and Vineyards of France* has been reprinted and revised several times, and is now available in paperback. Not for nothing does he enjoy the sobriquet 'Le Pape des Vins'; he has probably done more, single-handed, for the sales and promotion of fine French wine in the United States than any other man. My fears were totally groundless – Alexis showed me great kindness and encouragement, as well as offering me the friendly and generous hospitality for which he and the Prieuré are justly renowned.

The history of Prieuré-Lichine, as the name suggests, has ecclesiastical origins. The Benedictine abbey of Vertheuil established a priory here in the Middle Ages; the monks, like many other orders, planted vineyards primarily to make wine for the altar and for their own consumption, and later to sell on a commercial basis to supplement their income. Records show that good wine was made here in the early 18th century, which sold at prices equal to the wines of d'Issan and the de Gascq vineyard that was later to become Château Palmer.

Like other church properties, Cantenac-Prieuré, as it was then called, was confiscated at the time of the Revolution, auctioned off and passed into private ownership. The 1855 classification, in which it was accorded the rank of Fourth Great Growth, shows the owner as the widow Pagès, possibly an ancestor of the present occupant of Château la Tour de By near Bégadan. The property changed hands several times in the second half of the last century, and in the 1920s belonged to

Monsieur Frédéric Bousset, who had inherited it in a good state from his father-in-law.

The bad vintages of the '30s, economic depression, the war of 1939–45 and the difficult post-war years combined to hit Le Prieuré even harder than most. When Alexis Lichine bought it in 1951, the price was low – and for good reason. The vineyard was reduced to a mere 11 hectares, the wine had lost its reputation and the château and buildings were in a sorry state. As we sat in the drawing-room after lunch, Lichine recalled that his chef used to sleep in this room, and that he could see the sky through the holes in the roof.

It has been a long haul bringing the Prieuré up to its present level of production and quality. The first task was to increase the area of productive vines, and over the years parcels have been added, exchanged and planted, many of them bought from illustrious neighbours like Palmer, Kirwan, d'Issan and Giscours. There are today 60 hectares of vineyard, fragmented in many small plots, although the main part straddles the railway line to the north of the château with a good depth of fine gravel.

As you enter the courtyard through the gateway from the road, the ivy-covered house is on your left, flanked by an office, which was being converted into a shop when I visited there in the winter of 1984; here the many thousands of visitors, who are welcomed 365 (yes, 365) days of the year, will be able to buy bottles of Prieuré-Lichine, as well as copies of the owner's many books. The wall from the gate to the château, which used to be a cloister, is, in fact, a range of cement fermentation vats, decorated with a collection of ancient firebacks. To your right is the entrance to the cuvier proper, which houses a range of fermenting-vats, and the right-hand side of courtyard is formed by the first- and second-year ageing chais. Behind this is situated a new building which is used for the bottling line and storage of wine in bottle.

The château is very much Alexis Lichine's home; he spends about half the year here, particularly when he is writing his books, and, of course, at vintage time. The atmosphere is warm and friendly, especially in the low, beamed kitchen

which serves as dining-room, with its huge open fire, massive oak table and winking ranks of copper pans that hang on the walls. On my visit, we ate a gargantuan and delicious lunch, and my standard vertical tasting of ten vintages was conducted by the two of us over the meal. We did not spit, and Alexis does not have a light hand when pouring; I seem to remember that the 1980 was a double magnum. I wisely decided to go swiftly through the vintages offered, before we started lunch, and made my notes before the 'tasting' became more horizontal.

Alexis changed the name of the Prieuré to Château Prieuré-Lichine, with the approval of the Syndicat des Grands Crus Classés du Médoc, starting with the 1952 vintage. He also produces an excellent deuxième vin under the name of Château de Clairefort. It should be emphasised that the Prieuré is Alexis Lichine's personal property, and is in no way connected with the négociant house of Alexis Lichine and Co. in Bordeaux, which he

sold to the English brewers, Bass Charrington, in 1967, nor with the American consortium, headed by Lichine, that owned and sold Château Lascombes to the same company in 1971. It is only in recent years that the wine of the Prieuré has been offered through the traditional marketplace of the Bordeaux négociants, and I confidently predict that it is a label that will be seen and appreciated on wider and wider markets as the years pass.

Lichine is an immensely attractive character, almost larger than life. Of Russian extraction, he has led a full, varied and fascinating life; during the war he served on the personal staff of both Churchill and Eisenhower. His contribution to Bordeaux and French wine in general is gigantic and worthy of greater recognition. Publicist and showman par excellence, Alexis is also a winemaker of great talent. Under his ownership the wine of the Prieuré has prospered and flourished; it has a style that is perhaps a shade more robust than many Margaux, and the quality is indispu-

51

table. His 1983 was one of the best wines of the commune that I tasted, and I am delighted to have bought some for my own cellar. By the turn of the century, I look forward to enjoying this fine vintage, which will bring back fond memories of the red-letter day of my 1984 audience with 'the Pope'.

TECHNICAL INFORMATION

General

Appellation:	Margaux
Area under vines:	60 hectares
Average production:	25,000 cases
Distribution of vines:	In many plots, scattered over the communes of Margaux
Owner:	M. Alexis Lichine
Director:	M. Philippe Lahondès
Régisseur:	M. A. Biraade
Maître de Chai:	M. A. Labarère
Consultant Oenologist:	Professor Emile Peynaud

Viticulture

Geology:	Varied, but mainly gravel
Grape varieties:	57% Cabernet Sauvignon, 33% Merlot, 6% Petit Verdot, 3% Cabernet Franc, 1% Malbec
Pruning:	Guyot Double
Rootstock:	3309, 101-14, SO4
Vines per hectare:	7,000
Average yield per hectare:	37.5 hectolitres
Replanting:	Average 8,000 vines per annum

Vinification

Added yeasts:	No
Length of maceration:	10–15 days for alcoholic fermentation, 10–15 days after the start of the malolactic
Temperature of fermentation:	28–30°C max.
Control of fermentation:	By heating/cooling apparatus
Type of vat:	Cement and stainless steel
Vin de presse:	Average 3% included in Grand Vin
Age of casks:	1–3 years
Time in cask:	19 months
Fining:	Fresh egg whites
Filtration:	Light filtration at bottling
Type of bottle:	Bordelaise lourde

Commercial

Vente Directe:	Yes
Direct ordering from château:	Yes
Exclusivities:	None
Trade Sales:	Through the Bordeaux négociants
Visits:	Yes, from 1000 to 1900 *365 days a year*

THE TASTING AT CHATEAU PRIEURE-LICHINE, 30 October 1984
J.S., Alexis Lichine

1983 Beautiful, clear, deep colour. Fine open bouquet, with fruit and oak. Big mouthful, with a huge amount of superb flavour and good tannins. Complete, structured – will be really splendid.

1982 Again a fine, deep colour. Nose very powerful. Only in bottle three months, but showing well – rounded with good fruit and soft tannins. Long aftertaste. Will be good fairly soon and keep well.

1981 Bright mid-red. Lovely, soft cassis-and-violets nose. Excellent balance, already showing classic Margaux elegance and poise. Will be lovely in three or four years.

1980 (Double magnum!) Good medium red, with a nice, soft, spicy bouquet. Pleasing, soft and easy to drink now. A little short.

1977 Colour good for year, hardly any brown. Curiously attractive, slightly animal bouquet. Round, with good fruit and some subtlety. An extremely good wine from a poor vintage, with lots of life in it.

1976 Deep, intense red. Bouquet attractive and soft, with good fruit. Pleasing, with good fruit, ready now and not a long future.

1974 Amazing colour for '74. Pleasing but muted bouquet. Flavour good, still has fruit and plentiful backbone, and will stay around for a while yet. A success.

1973 Lighter colour, showing quite brown. Nose ripe. A little past its best, but still perfectly good to drink, still some nice fruit.

1970 Very dense colour still, deep red with no brown. Lovely, powerful, aromatic bouquet. Intense concentration of flavour, still has lots of good fruit and tannin – and an indefinite life. Lovely wine.

CHATEAU
Rausan-Ségla
MARGAUX

As you drive north on the D2, pass through the village of Issan, with Château Palmer on your right, and you will see Château Rausan-Ségla across the vines on your left. The road to the property is clearly signposted.

The famous Pierre des Mesures de Rauzan was the creator of this vineyard in 1661; he was also owner of the vineyard in Pauillac which now comprises Pichon-Longueville-Baron and Pichon-Longueville-Comtesse de Lalande. De Rauzan was a successful merchant in Bordeaux, and good wine was one of the commodities from which he derived his revenue. It can be imagined how, in the course of visiting his suppliers in the Médoc, he became taken with the idea of becoming a proprietor himself. As proprietors, the de Rauzans became members of the haute bourgeoisie, marrying into the other aristocratic families of Bordeaux. By the 18th century the wine of Rauzan, which was still one property with the present Rauzan-Gassies, was of the highest quality. Thomas Jefferson, the great American connoisseur of Bordeaux wines and future American President, toured the vineyards of the Médoc in 1787, and listed 'Rozan' as the first of his selection of fine 'Seconds', and in 1790 bought ten dozen bottles, some of which may well have been destined for the presidential cellar of George Washington, for whom he bought much wine.

There is a story of an irascible member of the family, Jean de Rauzan, who was dissatisfied with the price currently being obtained for his wines. He set sail for England with a cargo of Rauzan in the mid-1700s, berthed in the Thames, and invited buyers to come and taste and make offers for the wine. So angry was he at the low prices offered that he started to throw the casks into the river. Not many casks had bobbed off downriver before the merchants began to make more satisfactory offers!

Around this time Rauzan was much bigger than it is today, comprising not only the vineyards of Rauzan-Gassies, but also Marquis de Terme and Desmirail. The latter two were split away from the main estate as dowries for two de Rauzan daughters when they married.

It was in 1792 that Rausan-Ségla and Rauzan-Gassies acquired their separate identities; two-thirds of the original vineyard became the property of the heirs of the Baroness de Ségla, and one-third went to a politician, the Seigneur de Gassies. The latter had married a Rauzan heiress, the former was herself a de Rauzan, who married the Baron de Ségla. The Baroness is commemorated by a rather touching plaque, set into the wall of the chai, which tells the passer-by that 'near this place, the Baroness de Ségla, 1761–1828, was pleased to cultivate hydrangeas.'

Rausan-Ségla passed from the Baron's widow to her son-in-law, the Comte de Castelpers, who was in turn succeeded by his son, the Baron d'Adeler. In 1866 his heirs sold to a 'minister of the reformed church', Eugène Durande-Dassier, for 730,000 Francs; his son-in-law, Frédéric Cruse, son of the founder of the great Cruse empire, succeeded him in 1903. During this period, Rausan-Ségla was in the ascendant; the wine improved and often realised prices nearer to those of First Growths than Seconds. Much of this improvement was doubtless due to the ability of the great Charles Skawinski, whom Frédéric Cruse appointed as régisseur. Skawinski was also régisseur of Pontet-Canet, another Cruse property. The present two-storey château was built by Frédéric Cruse, and Rausan-Ségla remained in the family until 1956. By this time ownership had become divided between several members of the Cruse family, and they sold it to a M. de Meslon, incidentally a descendant of the de Rauzans. The fortunes of Rausan-Ségla did not flourish under his ownership, as he appears to have been more interested in turning a quick profit on the property. After the terrible frost of 1956, de Meslon replanted a large part of the vineyard with Merlot grapes. The methods of vinification under de Meslon's direction were primitive to say the least; pressing was still done by treading, making this the last Cru Classé in the Médoc to employ this colourful but outmoded system.

In 1960 de Meslon reaped his profit, selling to an English firm, John Holt Limited of Liverpool, for three times his purchase price. The new owners also bought the old-established firm of négocians, Eschenauer, in Bordeaux, who now have the total

53

responsibility for the running and commercialisation of Rausan-Ségla, as well as Château Smith-Haut-Lafitte in the Graves.

Holts have invested prodigiously in the property; a large proportion of the Merlot vines planted by de Meslon have been replaced with Cabernet Sauvignon, and the old wooden vats were replaced with 12 epoxy-lined steel cuves in 1970. The vineyard now covers some 42 hectares, and by careful and painstaking purchases and exchanges the former 250 or so different plots of land have been reduced to four main blocks – a far more workable unit. Now that the increased area under vines is productive, the existing chais and cuvier have proved inadequate, and a huge new vinification and ageing unit is to be built during 1985 in the park to the rear of the château. The present cuvier is to be converted into a magnificent room for tastings and receptions. The château is not lived in permanently, but it is immaculately maintained and elegantly furnished with English antiques, and is used to received important visitors.

TECHNICAL INFORMATION

General

Appellation:	Margaux
Area under vines:	41 hectares
Production:	15,000 cases
Distribution of vines:	In four main blocks
Owner:	John Holt and Sons Ltd
Director:	M. René Baffert
Régisseur:	M. Michel Bruzaut
Oenologist:	Professor Emile Peynaud

Viticulture

Geology:	Deep gravel
Grape varieties:	51% Cabernet Sauvignon, 11% Cabernet Franc, 36% Merlot, 2% Petit Verdot
Pruning:	Guyot Double
Rootstock:	101.14, SO4, 420A
Vines per hectare:	8,200
Yield per hectare:	30–35 hectolitres
Replanting:	2 hectares per annum, approx.

Vinification

Added yeasts:	No
Length of maceration:	15–24 days
Temperature of fermentation:	25–28°C
Control of fermentation:	Water circulation
Type of vat:	Steel, epoxy-lined
Vin de presse:	Around 10% incorporated, depending on vintage
Age of casks:	50% new each vintage
Time in cask:	20 months
Fining:	Fresh egg-whites
Filtration:	None
Type of bottle:	Personalised up to 1977, now Bordelaise lourde

Commercial ·

Vente Directe:	Yes
Commercialisation:	Exclusively through Maison Eschenauer 42 Avenue Emile Counord 33300 Bordeaux
Visits:	Yes: telephone 56 81 58 90 (office)

TASTING AT CHATEAU RAUSAN-SEGLA, 4 December 1984
J.S., M. Baffert (Eschenauer), M. Bruzaut

1983 Deep, bluey red. Good nose, fruit and new oak. Very tannic, with great backbone, and a load of fruit. Will be very good, but needs a lot of patience.

1982 (Bottled September 1984.) Good, deep red. Nose a bit closed. Needs a rest from bottling-shock, but plenty of good, round, fruity flavour and ripe tannins present.

1981 (Probably first vintage to benefit from present encépagement.) Lovely, medium red. Nose good, very Margaux with fruit and violets. Elegant, with finesse, class and Margaux femininity. Good length – will be lovely in three or four years.

1979 Good medium red. Bouquet not giving much. A fairly easy wine with some power, but no complexity. Good now and for a few years.

1978 Beginning to brown a little. Ripe, soft bouquet beginning to evolve. Rich mouthfilling flavour, with fruit, tannin and backbone. A good 1978, but quite forward.

1977 Colour good for the vintage. Nose light, but pleasing. Good, light wine well made with fruit and tannins in harmony. Can be drunk with pleasure now, but will go on a while yet.

1961 Amazing depth of colour. Huge, concentrated bouquet of ripe fruit. Still surprisingly closed; great concentration of mouthfilling, complex flavour. Very long aftertaste – delicious wine that will go on for ever.

CHATEAU

Rauzan-Gassies

MARGAUX

As you leave the village of Issan, going north on the D2 towards Margaux, you will see a sign on your left pointing through the vineyard to Rauzan-Gassies, which lies next door to Rausan-Ségla.

I have covered the early history up to the time the estate was divided into the two properties Rausan-Ségla and Rauzan-Gassies in the chapter on Château Rausan-Ségla. We can therefore take up the story of Rauzan-Gassies in the mid-19th century, when it passed from the original Mademoiselle de Rauzan, who had married the Seigneur de Gassies, to one Chevalier de Puyboreau, who appears as the owner in the 1845 edition of Franck. At the time of the 1855 classification it had changed hands again, and the new proprietor is listed in the original document as Viguere or Vignère. At the time of the classification, Rauzan-Gassies, like the neighbouring Ségla vineyard, enjoyed a position and reputation only just behind Château Margaux itself, but over the ensuing century it has changed hands incessantly, which may in some measure have contributed to its decline in quality and recognition.

The present owner's father, Paul Quié, acquired Rauzan-Gassies just after the war from a Bordeaux lawyer named Puyo. He found the property in a very neglected state, with the area under vines sadly reduced, and the buildings in near ruins, a situation not uncommon in the Médoc after the ravages of the slump, the succession of poor vintages in the '30s and finally the war. Quié was already active in the area, having bought the Cru Bourgeois, Bel-Orme Tronquoy de Lalande, and more recently the Fifth Growth Croizet-Bages in Pauillac. He was an able and energetic proprietor, and in the twenty-odd years between the purchase of Rauzan-Gassies and his death in 1968, did much in the way of replanting and regrouping the vineyard; this work is being continued by his son Jean-Michel, who has also improved and modernised the chais and the cuvier. The combined efforts of father and son seem to be now paying off, as the quality of Rauzan-Gassies is steadily improving.

On the day in January 1985 when I visited Rauzan-Gassies, Bordeaux was enjoying, if such a word can be used, the coldest weather in living memory, with night-time temperaturs of −20°C and the vineyards covered in six inches of snow. Jean-Michel Quié and his régisseur, M. Espagnet, were delighted to show me their well-insulated chai and bottle store. They were also, quite rightly, pleased and proud that we were able to get a good bouquet off the sample of 1984 drawn off the vat – it was tasted outside in a temperature of −8°C, and the wine itself was only just above zero!

There is no château at Rauzan-Gassies, as the original house went to the Ségla portion at the time of the partition last century. The chais, cuvier and régisseur's house are grouped around an enclosed courtyard, immediately to the left of Rausan-Ségla.

The vineyard, like so many Margaux Grands Crus, is widely scattered around the parish, and the soil is correspondingly varied. I found the wine to be fairly typical Margaux, possessed of a fine, rounded softness, if a little more robust than some of its neighbours. The 1982 and 1981 were particularly successful, and I was also much impressed by the quality and potential of the 1978, a vintage which I have found generally is not living up to original expectations. The 1975 was still quite underdeveloped, but it is going to grow up into a very beautiful young lady indeed.

TECHNICAL INFORMATION

General

Appellation:	Margaux
Area under vines:	30 hectares, 25 in production
Average yield:	11,000 cases
Distribution of vines:	Very fragmented
Owner:	Société Civile du Château Rauzan-Gassies
Director:	Jean-Michel Quié
Maître de Chai:	M. Espagnet and his son
Consultant Oenologist:	M. Boissenot

Viticulture

Geology:	Varied, typical of Margaux
Grape varieties:	50% Cabernet Sauvignon, 25% Cabernet Franc, 25%

		Age of casks:	20% new each vintage
	Merlot with a little Petit Verdot	Time in cask:	17–20 months
Pruning:	Guyot Double	Fining:	Powdered egg-white in vat
Rootstock:	SO4, 420A, Riparia	Filtration:	Sur plaque before bottling
Replanting:	Around 3% per annum	Type of bottle:	Bordelaise lourde

Vinification

		Commercial	
Added yeasts:	No	Vente Directe:	Yes, to private customers
Length of maceration:	2–3 weeks	Sales in France:	Through own office in Paris; telephone: 1 368 08 41
Temperature of fermentation:	30°C	Export:	Through the Bordeaux négociants
Control of fermentation:	By heat-exchange pump		
Type of vat:	Cement and stainless steel	Visits:	Yes: telephone 56 88 71 88
Vin de presse:	Proportion included according to vintage		

THE TASTING AT CHATEAU RAUZAN-GASSIES, 16 January 1985
J.S., Jean-Michel Quié, M. Espagnet

1984 (Temperature of wine 1°C, ambient temperature −6°C.) Good deep purple. Amazingly, at this low temperature, the bouquet was strong and good! Taste was difficult, but there seemed to be plenty of fruit and tannins.

1982 Dark red, almost black. Nose open and generous. Rounded Margaux taste, well structured, lots of fruit and soft tannins, with long aftertaste.

1981 Medium to deep red. Bouquet fine, just beginning to open. Just entering aristocratic adolescence.

Elegant, fine and balanced, nothing too complex. Good future.

1979 Fine, deep colour. Bouquet good, with blackcurrant. Straightforward, good fruit and more backbone than 1981. Tannins quite dominant. Will reward patience.

1978 Lovely, brilliant scarlet. Very good, evolving nose. Typical Margaux with elegance and finesse, has good length.

1975 Good middle red. Bouquet quite closed. Very concentrated, complex flavour just beginning to come together; very long – a really good '75 with a future.

1971 Colour starting to show orange shade. Ripe smell, good fruit. Mature, right for drinking now – no great finesse, but very pleasing.

CHATEAU
Siran
MARGAUX

Take the D2 north from Blanquefort in the direction of Margaux. Pass through the small village of Labarde, and just at the end of the village you will see a milestone on your right with Siran written on it. Just after this you cross a level crossing, and turn immediately right – pass in front of the Rendez-vous des Chasseurs restaurant and turn right again. The gateway to Château Siran is 200 metres on your left.

Although the château as it exists today is in the Chartreuse style of the 18th century, the property is very much older, and is first mentioned in 1428, when Guilhem de Siran took the oath of fealty in the nearby Macau church of the priory of Ste Croix.

At the beginning of the 18th century, Siran belonged to the Baron de Bosq, whose descendants through the female line remained in possession until the middle of the 19th century. His daughter Anne-Marie, heiress of Siran, married the Comte de la Roque Bouillac, Mayor of Labarde. Their daughter in turn inherited Siran, and married Count Alphonse de Toulouse Lautrec-Monfa, whose great-grandson was to be the painter, Henri de Toulouse-Lautrec.

In 1848, the Toulouse-Lautrecs sold Siran to the ancestors of the present owners, the Miailhe family, who originally settled in Bordeaux as wine brokers in the 18th century.

I was fortunate enough to visit Siran for the first time in September, when a large part of the 15-acre park is carpeted with cyclamens. I was fortunate enough also to meet Alain Miailhe, sole owner since 1978, who spends only part of his time in Bordeaux. This energetic scholarly man has left the strong mark of his personality on the château, whose attractions include a collection of rare china, a gallery of Bacchanalian prints, and, unique to the property, a nuclear bunker solely for the protection of the château's collection of wine. (Building was commenced in the same year the French government decided to site one of the largest nuclear power stations in Europe on the opposite bank of the Gironde.) Here, great quantities of Château Siran from every vintage are stored, together with a selection of noble years from other properties in the Médoc. The decision to build the shelter was either an extremely expensive eccentricity, or an act of visionary inspiration. It is an interesting thought that should the worst ever come to the worst, and nuclear destruction fall on this part of Europe, it is possible that all that will remain of the life of the Médoc will be encapsulated in the bottles stored in this cellar.

Since 1980, the labels of Siran have been illustrated by distinguished contemporary artists: Decaris in 1980, Folon in 1981 and Joan Mirò in 1982. The 1983 label will have a painting by Cosco on the theme of computers; each year's artist is commissioned to base the design on something suited to the year – Decaris used Solidarnosc, Folon a space-shuttle and so on.

I did not have the opportunity of tasting the 1980 vintage, but evidently Alain Miailhe has considerable faith in both its quality and longevity, since he has presented a quantity of magnums of this vintage to the Station Oenologique et Agronomique de Bordeaux with which to celebrate their bicentenary, which will take place in the year 2080.

The Siran wine is of a consistently fine quality; it is always rounded and robust with lots of fruit, a fine deep colour which it holds well, and it is a wine which repays keeping, though it is perhaps less feminine in style than most Margaux. The power and depth of colour of Siran stems, perhaps, from the unusually high proportion (15%) of Petit Verdot planted. There is also – a Miailhe trademark – a fairly substantial quantity of Merlots in the vineyard.

A second wine is produced under the label Château Bellegarde, and there are also nine hectares of palus, which give a good wine with the Bordeaux Supérieur appellation under the brand of Château St Jacques.

Château Siran is supplied regularly to the Presidency of the European Parliament, and Château St Jacques has graced the tables of the Elysée Palace.

TECHNICAL INFORMATION

General

Appellation:	Margaux
Area under vines:	23 hectares
Average production:	12,000 cases
Owner:	M. W.-A. B. Miailhe
Régisseur/Maître de chai:	M. J. Daney
Consultant Oenologist:	Professor Emile Peynaud

Viticulture

Geology:	Sandy gravel plâteau
Grape varieties:	50% Cabernet Sauvignon, 25% Merlot, 10% Cabernet Franc, 15% Petit Verdot
Pruning:	Guyot Double
Rootstock:	SO4, Riparia Gloire, 101/14, 3309, 420A
Vines per hectare:	Circa 9,000
Yield per hectare:	40–45 hectolitres
Replanting:	When necessary to maintain high average age of vines – some parcels are 80 years old

Vinification

Added yeasts:	Very infrequently
Length of maceration:	15–25 days
Temperature of fermentation:	20–24°C
Control of fermentation:	Refrigeration
Type of vat:	Oak
Vin de presse:	$\frac{1}{10}$ of volume incorporated
Age of casks:	$\frac{1}{3}$ new each vintage
Time in cask:	24 months
Fining:	Albumen of egg
Filtration:	Kieselgur
Type of bottle:	Bordelaise, Grand Cru

Commercial

Vente Directe:	Yes
Direct Ordering at château:	Yes
Agents in foreign countries:	Yes, contact château for information
Visits:	Yes: telephone 56 81 35 01 (office), 56 88 34 04 (chais) Hours: 0900–1130, 1430–1730 Monday to Friday

THE TASTING AT CHATEAU SIRAN,
30 January 1985
J. S., Christian Seely, J. Daney

1982 Deep, bluey red. Open bouquet, with lots of blackcurrant fruit, in spite of only being bottled in September. Big, rounded mouthful, with good, ripe tannins. Will be a fine bottle.

1981 Same deep colour. Attractive, open nose. Well-structured, with fruit, tannins and backbone. An elegant wine.

1979 Same density of colour. Nose quite shut in, but plenty of fruit and power in background. More fleshy than 1981, long, but less finesse.

1978 Colour again deep red. Riper and rounder nose than the '79, quite forward for the year. Already filling out, and quite accessible.

1970 Dense, deep red, only just beginning to lighten a shade. Rich, ripe and concentrated, with slight dry finish. Long aftertaste, still showing quite young.

1961 Blackish colour, beginning to show brown at edges. Lovely bouquet of warm, ripe fruit. Delicious mouthful, reminiscent of ripe strawberries, tremendous concentration and length. Will last for many years. A great treat!

CHATEAU

Du Tertre

MARGAUX

From the village of Margaux, take the D105e to Arsac. Château du Tertre is on the left of this road, about 1 km before you reach Arsac itself. Two rather crumbling pillars mark the gateway and a track leads uphill through the vines to the château and chais.

At one time the vineyards of du Tertre belonged to the Marquis de Ségur, who also owned, among many other fine properties, Calon-Ségur, far away to the north in St Estèphe. There are many coincidences in the closely-woven tapestry of the Médoc's history, and one such occurred when Philippe Capbern-Gasqueton bought du Tertre in the early 1960s, for he also owns Château Calon-Ségur. The Gasquetons have lived at Château Capbern-Gasqueton in St Estèphe since the eighteenth century, and their ancestors must certainly have known the Prince des Vignes, since Calon was his favourite property and he spent much time there.

Du Tertre passed out of Ségur hands – in all probability slipping through the careless fingers of Nicolas Marie-Alexandre de Ségur, the spendthrift scion of the family who lost most of their considerable fortune. The property after two more changes of owner was acquired in the mid-19th century by M. Libéral, later to be immortalised in the name of Château Haut-Bages-Libéral, which he bought some years after. Château du Tertre changed hands several times over the next hundred years; during this century it has belonged to an Austrian family called Koenigswater and the Belgian de Wildes, one of whom now owns the successful La Mare aux Grenouilles restaurant at Lesparre. During the difficult years of the thirties and the ensuing war and post-war period, the property was sadly neglected, and when Philippe Gasqueton bought it, the place was practically derelict. There was not one productive vine in the vineyard, and the buildings and château were in ruins.

Gasqueton, an energetic, capable and traditional winemaker, set to and replanted the vineyard with a predominantly Cabernet Sauvignon encépagement. The chais and cuvier have been rebuilt, and a further extension to the buildings is currently planned. The château is still unoccupied, but the structure has received attention, and it is now wind- and weather-proof. Responsibility for du Tertre falls largely on the shoulders of Philippe Capbern-Gasqueton's daughter, who is a qualified oenologist, and her husband M. de Baritault, and they are doing a fine job.

Re-establishing a Grand Cru Classé that has fallen from grace poses many problems, quite apart from the sheer hard work and the capital investment. The first priority must be the quality of the wine, and this requires patience and a rigorous selection, rejecting all but the very best wine; even now, after twenty years, the yield per hectare is one of the lowest in the commune, but this is a sure sign of the pursuit of quality. Another prob-

60

lem, which requires much thought and planning, arises from the fact that the vineyard had to be totally replanted at the time of the purchase; this means that all the vines reach optimum maturity at about the same time, whereas an old-established vineyard is replanted on a rotation system, so that there is always a proportion of younger vines coming along to replace the oldest ones when they have passed their peak.

The 45-hectare vineyard is unusual for Margaux in that it is all in one piece, whereas most of the Crus Classés have their vines spread in small parcels all over the commune; it is surrounded by woods, and the soil varies from medium-sized to fine sandy gravel on a subsoil of ferruginous chalk. 'Tertre' is French for a small hill, and the property is aptly named, for the highest part of the estate, on which the château, buildings and the best part of the vineyard are sited, rises to 24 metres above sea-level − almost a mountain in the low-lying country of the Médoc. The vines neighbour those of Brane-Cantenac on one side and Monbrison and Angludet on the other.

The efforts of the Capbern-Gasqueton family are certainly meeting with success, judging by the only proper yardstick, the quality of the wine. The quality is consistent, and improving each year as the vines become established. In common with other family properties, du Tertre has the ability to produce excellent wines in the lesser vintages. The 1972 was a good example of this, as was the more recent 1980. The wine is one of the tougher Margaux, and requires patience; this stems partly from the large proportion of Cabernet-Sauvignon in the wine, and partly perhaps from the Gasquetons' traditional approach to winemaking, and the family's St Estèphe origins. The 1979 was a very big wine, with masses of fruit and plenty of good tannins, and needed a good three or four more years in bottle when I tasted it in December 1984. The 1983 and 1982 will also be lovely bottles in five or six years, though, of the two the '82 will certainly evolve more quickly.

TECHNICAL INFORMATION

General

Appellation:	Margaux
Area under vines:	45 hectares
Average production:	12,000 cases
Distribution of vines:	In one block
Owner:	M. Philippe Capbern-Gasqueton
Administrator:	M. de Baritault
Maître de Chai:	M. Michel Ellissalde
Consultant Oenologist:	M. Pascal Ribereau-Gayon

Viticulture

Geology:	Fine gravel and sand, chalky subsoil
Grape varieties:	80% Cabernet Sauvignon, 10% Cabernet Franc, 10% Merlot
Pruning:	Guyot Double Médocaine
Rootstock:	Riparia Gloire, 101-14
Vines per hectare:	5,600
Average yield per hectare:	30 hectolitres
Replanting:	Not yet necessary

Vinification

Added yeasts:	If necessary
Length of maceration:	21 days
Temperature of fermentation:	28–30°C
Control of fermentation:	Running water on exterior of vats
Type of vat:	Lined steel
Vin de presse:	Up to 10% included, according to vintage
Age of casks:	¼ new each vintage
Time in cask:	24 months
Fining:	Fresh egg whites
Filtration:	Light, sur plaque, at bottling
Type of bottle:	Bordelaise

Commercial

Vente Directe:	No
Sales:	Through Bordeaux négociants
Visits:	Yes, for appointment telephone: 56 59 30 08

THE TASTING AT CHATEAU DU TERTRE, 11 December 1984
J.S., M. de Baritault

1983 (From a 3-year cask.) Good dark colour. Fine, elegant nose, not giving much yet. Fine flavour, long and elegant with non-aggressive tannin.

1983 (From a new cask.) Same colour. Nose still elegant, but strong new oak smell. Flavour fine and long with loads of fruit, but dominated by much harsher tannin from the cask.

1982 Lovely deep red. Nose beginning to open up, with lots of soft fruit. Much rounder and more approachable than '83, with a lovely, long blackcurrant flavour, and lots of ripe tannin. Will develop more rapidly than the '83, but nonetheless a stayer.

1979 Very dense, dark red. Excellent, powerful bouquet of cassis. Still very young and tannic, but with a mass of good, aromatic fruit. Will be a lovely bottle in 3–4 years.

ST JULIEN

The smallest of the four great appellations of the Médoc, the vineyards entitled to the St Julien name cover only about 650 hectares. Between the northern limit of the Margaux appellation and the southern boundary of St Julien, the traveller passes through a stretch of low-lying, rather marshy land devoid of Crus Classés; there are, however, many fine properties of lesser status to either side of the D2 as you pass through Arcins, Lamarque, Vieux-Cussac, and Cussac-Fort-Médoc, the last being Château Lanessan on the higher ground to your left, just before you reach the sign bidding passers-by to bend the knee as they enter St Julien. As the D2 curves left-handed uphill just after this sign, you will see Château Beychevelle on your right, and the smaller, elegant Branaire-Ducru opposite. The vineyards covered by the St Julien appellation occupy an area about three-and-a-half kilometres square, the southern edge of which stretches from Beychevelle to Lagrange; the northern boundary divides the vineyards of Léoville-Las-Cases from those of Château Latour, and stretches westward to the edge of the vines of Larose-Trintaudon.

Saint Julien has no First or Fifth Growths, but boasts five of the best Seconds, two Thirds and four Fourths. There are two villages, Beychevelle and St Julien, both of which are on the D2 on the eastern side of the square. One of the best known and ugliest landmarks of the Médoc is the giant concrete St Julien bottle, situated among the vines of Château Beychevelle on the sharp right-hand bend of the D2, just before the minor road which takes you into the village of Beychevelle.

St Julien wines have a character that is somewhere between those of Margaux to the south, and the bigger, more unyielding style of Pauillac to the immediate north. They certainly have a tendency to show more of their charm in youth than the Pauillac wines, though this in no way lessens their ability to reach a graceful old age. Two of the St Julien properties, the Second-Growth Châteaux Ducru-Beaucaillou and Léoville-Las-Cases, have in recent years leapt ahead of most of the Deuxièmes Crus in terms of quality and price; these two, together with Pichon-Longueville-Lalande, a Pauillac property with a small part of its vineyard within the St Julien boundary, and Cos d'Estour-

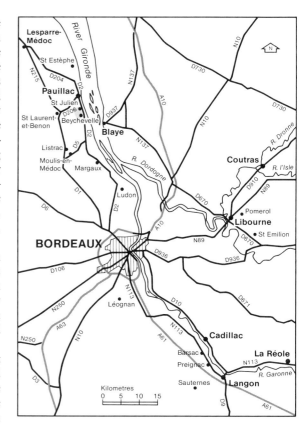

nel in St Estèphe, now consistently sell *en primeur* at prices somewhere between those of their peers and the Premiers Crus.

The commune boasts but one restaurant worth a visit, and that is in the sleepy village of St Julien. The Bar-Restaurant du Square, run by Henriette Moreau, is well patronised by local gastronomes, who drool over the best *escargots bordelais* in the area, and the *ris de veau* just like their grandmothers used to prepare. Henriette Moreau is one of the great characters of the Médoc, and, if she has the time and is in the mood, will regale her customers with anecdotes of the area from her encyclopedic memory. She is also a painter and a poet, but, as she both cooks and serves in the restaurant, it is a wonder that she has time for so many talents.

CHATEAU
Beychevelle
ST JULIEN

Château Beychevelle is the first property you encounter on the right-hand side of the D2 as you enter the appellation of St Julien from the south, just after the rather vulgar sign bidding travellers to bow low as they enter St Julien.

Early history attributes ownership of the lands of Beychevelle to one Archambaud de Grailly and to a Wagnerian-sounding Asshilde de Bordeaux; by 1446 it had passed into the hands of the powerful Foix de Candales, Seigneurs of Lamarque and lords over vast tracts of land throughout the region.

In 1587 the daughter of the last surviving Comte de Foix de Candale, by name Marguerite, married Jean-Louis Nogaret de la Valette, Duc d'Epernon, and the estate was part of her dowry. D'Epernon was an unsavoury character; a toady of Henri III, he was appointed Governor of Guyenne and by all accounts abused this position of trust to his own vast benefit and to the misery of the local inhabitants, whose property he seized and pillaged at will. Legend has it that he consorted with the Devil, and judging from the bulging black eyes and vulpine features of his portrait, nothing would surprise me. As a further mark of the King's favour, the Duke was made First Sea Lord of France, and the name of the château is purported to derive from the Gascon version of 'Baisse voile', the lowering of sails by passing ships in salute to the admiral; it is perhaps more likely that passing sailors had to heave-to and pay a tax, or simply they may have lowered the sails in order to keep a low profile in the hopes of escaping his rapacious attention.

His son Bernard, the last Duc d'Epernon, was a wastrel; on his death in 1666 the estate was sold to pay off the vast debts he had accumulated, and the lands that became Branaire and Ducru-Beaucaillou were split away from the property at this time. The portion that now forms the Beychevelle domaine was bought in 1674 by the Duc de Rendan, who took unto himself the title of Baron de Beychevelle. Less than twenty years later ownership passed to the d'Abbadie family, leading Bordeaux parliamentarians, who stayed there until the 1730s, when Beychevelle came into the hands of the Marquis de Brassier de Budot, Baron de Lamarque. It was he who built the present château and laid out the park and formal gardens much as we see them today in 1757. He pulled down the original fortified medieval manor to do this, and is said to have used most of the materials of the original building in the construction of the new one. The resulting château is one of the most imposing and elegant in the Médoc, having the rare architectural style that is a mixture of Louis XIV and XV; the grounds are worth a visit in their own right, though the name of Beychevelle picked out in bedding plants in front of the railings puts me in mind of municipal displays in English seaside resorts.

Brassier's son, François-Armand, ran the estate successfully until the Revolution. The family were huge landowners, and were forced to give up most of their property, and there is a record of the Marquis being hunted through the countryside 'like a wild beast' by the local populace. He appears to have survived this, however, only to get into hot water of a different kind, killing a man in a duel and going in to voluntary exile. The new people's government then tried to confiscate the property on the death of his widowed mother, but such attempts were successfully fought off by his sister, Madame de Saint-Heren, who promptly sold the estate to one Jacques Conte, a shipbuilder in Bordeaux.

Conte appears to have been too much taken up with his somewhat dubious shipbuilding activities to give proper attention to the Beychevelle vineyards; by the time he sold the estate to his nephew, Pierre-François Guestier, in 1825, the reputation of the wine was at a low ebb. Guestier, educated in England, son of Hugh Barton's trusted partner Daniel, brought new lustre to Beychevelle's name. It was due to the years of neglect under Conte's ownership that the vineyard was only rated as a Fourth in the 1855 classification. The quality and value of Beychevelle's wine has been in the ascendant ever since its acquisition by Guestier, and it was very soon fetching prices more suited to a Third or Second Growth, as it does today. Guestier was a keen racing man, which he may have picked up during his youth in England, or, more likely, from his family's close

association with the Irish Bartons. He founded a stud-farm at Beychevelle called the Ecurie Guestier, whose chief asset was a thoroughbred stallion appropriately named 'Young Governor'. Problems of succession soon caused financial headaches for Guestier – he had a large family of six daughters and only one son – and in 1866 another of his properties, Château Batailley, had to be sold, the same year that Beychevelle was awarded a gold medal by the Gironde Agricultural Society for the best-kept vineyard in the area. This sale presumably raised insufficient funds to provide dowries for his numerous daughters, for only eight years later in 1874 he sold Beychevelle to the Parisian banker, Armand Heine for 1,600,000 francs, an equitable profit on his original investment, bearing in mind the restoration of the property's tarnished image achieved under his aegis.

Heine's daughter, Marie-Louise, married a member of another powerful banking family, Charles Achille Fould, and Beychevelle thus passed in to the ownership of this rich and politically active family. Charles's grandfather, Aymar Marcus Fould, was Minister of Finance to Napoleon III, and succeeding members of the family have held government posts of similar importance. The present generation is represented by Aymar Achille Fould, who has held in turn the posts of Secretary of State for Defence, Transport and Post and Telecommunications. A new company has recently been formed, in which Aymar and his brother and sister retain a major holding; a large insurance company is also involved, together with a number of lesser shareholders.

Château Beychevelle, like other Médoc vineyards owned by banking families, has benefited and maintained its reputation not only due to the undoubted love and care of its owners, but also from the financial stability that has enabled them to weather the difficult periods that crop up with such monotonous regularity.

TECHNICAL INFORMATION

General

Appellation:	St Julien
Area under vines:	72 hectares
Average production:	30,000 cases
Distribution of vines:	One main block, two smaller parcels
Owner:	Société Civile du Château Beychevelle-Achille-Fould
Régisseur:	M. Maurice Ruelle
Maître de Chai:	M. Lucien Soussotte
Consultant Oenologist:	Professor Pascal Ribereau-Gayon

Viticulture

Geology:	Deep gravel
Grape varieties:	60% Cabernet Sauvignon, 8% Cabernet Franc, 28% Merlot, 4% Petit Verdot
Pruning:	Guyot Double Médocaine
Rootstock:	Principally 101-14, plus 420A and SO4
Vines per hectare:	10,000
Average yield per hectare:	46 hectolitres (10 years' figures)
Replanting:	2 to $2\frac{1}{2}$ hectares per annum

Vinification

Added yeasts:	No
Length of maceration:	20–25 days
Temperature of fermentation:	28–30°C max.
Control of fermentation:	By heat-exchange pump and water-cooling
Type of vat:	Stainless-steel, epoxy-lined steel and cement
Vin de presse:	Proportion included according to needs of vintage
Age of casks:	40% new each year, the rest casks of 1 and 2 vintages.
Time in cask:	20 months
Fining:	Fresh egg-whites in cask after a year
Filtration:	None
Type of bottle:	Bordelaise lourde

Commercial

Vente Directe:	A little to callers
Sales:	Through the négociants
Visits:	Yes, telephone: 56 59 23 00
	Hours: 0900–1130, 1400–1630

THE TASTING AT CHATEAU BEYCHEVELLE, 15 January 1985
J.S., Lucien Soussotte

1984 Formidable blackish colour. Nose very closed. Excellent fruit, great concentration and depth of flavour with a lot of tannin and tremendous length. This will be a good vintage, but with the reduced proportion of Merlot caused by the coulure, will take a long time.

1983 Deep, dark red. Nose good, exceptionally evolved for 1983. Long, full flavour with nice soft tannins. Will be a very fine bottle, but will need patience.

CHATEAU

Branaire-Ducru

ST JULIEN

Driving up the D2 from the south, you pass the sign welcoming you to St Julien on your right, with Château Beychevelle some 200 metres further on the same side. The entrance to Château Branaire-Ducru is 100 metres further on, round a left-hand curve, on your left.

Until his death in 1666, the lands of Branaire-Ducru were part of the estate of the notorious Duc d'Epernon, who owned not only Château Beychevelle opposite, but most of the commune of St Julien as well. The duke, powerful figure though he was, left a vast amount of debts, which had to be settled by the sale of the property. This part of the estate was separated and bought as 'Braneyre' by the du Luc family, who remained in possession for the best part of 200 years. The family must have been of some substance to have bought such an estate, but curiously little is recorded of them in either the political or commercial archives of Bordeaux. It is doubtless this 'low profile' that enabled them to hang on to their property so long, even through the desperate years of the French Revolution. So unaffected were they by the Terror, that they were even able to build the lovely Directoire château in 1794, a year when many aristocatic proprietors in the Médoc were looking their last into a basket, hightailing it to safer lands or, like the Baron de Pichon-Longueville, hiding in the bread oven.

The vineyard as we know it today was probably first established in the 1720s, and by the middle of the 18th century the wine of Branaire was enjoying a reputation on a par with those of Beychevelle, Talbot and Ducru-Beaucaillou, although none of these was yet known by its present name. It was Louis du Luc, or Duluc as it is sometimes written, who succeeded to the property in 1825, who is credited with having done most for Branaire; it was under his ownership that it was rated third of the Fourth Growths in the classification of 1855. In the original document the property is described simply as 'du Luc', and the owner as 'Du Luc Aîné'. Shortly after the classification Louis du Luc died, and was succeeded by his son Léo, who lost little time in cashing in his chips. He sold the estate to his cousin, Gustave Ducru, who had recently sold his share of Ducru-Beaucaillou to his sister, Marie-Louise Ravez.

Like Louis du Luc, Gustave Ducru was a conscientious owner and the estate prospered under his short régime. The names of these two are immortalised to this day on the label. Ducru died without a direct heir in 1879, and the property, now bearing its present name of Branaire-Ducru, passed to two of his nephews, Comte Ravez and the Marquis de Carbonnier de Marsac, who in turn passed it on to another noble pair, distant cousins by the name of the Vicomte du Périer de Larsan and Comte Jacques de la Tour. These last two are also remembered on the present label; it is their four coronets that embellish the corners of the design, as if, as Bernard Ginestet puts it, they had left them in the cloakroom.

At the end of World War I, Branaire-Ducru was bought by an industrialist, M. Mital, an iron-master from Lyons, with fingers in many other commercial pies. He was an absentee landlord, and while he did not actually neglect his property, there is no substitute for the physical presence of an owner. Inevitably the quality of the wine suffered, and things became worse as M. Mital became older and lost interest. Happily for Branaire-Ducru, a re-kindling spark appeared on the scene in the form of Jean Tapie, who bought the estate in 1952.

It is Jean's children, Jean-Michel Tapie and his sister, who is married to Nicolas Tari of Château Giscours, who are now co-proprietors of Branaire. The vineyard is in splendid condition, and the chais, cuvier and château have been carefully and harmoniously restored. The wine, too, has benefited enormously from the Tapie ownership, and is once more in world-wide demand.

TECHNICAL INFORMATION

General

Appellation:	St Julien
Area under vines:	48 hectares
Average production:	20,000 to 25,0000 cases
Distribution of vines:	In several parcels, scattered around Beychevelle.
Owner:	S.F.A. du Château Branaire-Ducru
President-Director General:	M. Nicolas Tari
Director General:	M. Jean-Michel Tapie
Maître de Chai:	M. Marcel Renon
Chef de Culture:	M. Berrouet
Consultant Oenologist:	Laboratoire de Pauillac

Viticulture

Geology:	Deep gravel, rich in quartz, on subsoil of alios
Grape varieties:	75% Cabernet Sauvignon, 20% Merlot, 5% Petit Verdot
Pruning:	Guyot Double
Rootstock:	Various
Vines per hectare:	6,600
Average yield per hectare:	35 hectolitres
Replanting:	½ hectare every 2 years

Vinification

Added yeasts:	No
Length of maceration:	18 days
Temperature of fermentation:	28°C
Control of fermentation:	By cold-water coil
Type of vats:	Epoxy-lined cement
Vin de presse:	Proportion of 1st pressing included according to vintage
Age of casks:	Between ⅓ and ½ new each vintage
Time in cask:	18 months
Fining:	Egg-whites
Filtration:	Very light sur plaque before bottling
Type of bottle:	Bordelaise lourde

Commercial

Vente Directe:	Yes, to visitors
Sales:	Through the Bordeaux négociants
Agents overseas:	Contact château for information
	S.F.A. du Château Branaire-Ducru, Saint Julien, 33250 Pauillac
Visits:	Yes, telephone 56 59 25 86 Hours 0800–1200, 1400–1700 Monday to Friday

---

THE TASTING AT CHATEAU BRANAIRE-DUCRU, 28 January 1985
J.S., Marcel Renon

1984 (Just in cask.) Dark bluey red. Good nose, Mouthfilling, already showing St Julien charm. Lots of tannin, more aggressive attack than the '83. Difficult to judge wine so young, but seems promising.

1983 Lovely colour, only a shade lighter than '84. Flowers, fruit and new oak on nose. Excellent long fruit flavour, already supple and feminine, with good rounded tannins.

1982 (Not yet bottled – from the cask.) Very dark red, almost black. Open nose with good ripe fruit. Rich, rounded and full with the right kind of tannins. Lovely, almost sweet, with a very long aftertaste. Will be a super bottle quite soon, but will last for years.

1978 (Half-bottle.) Brilliant medium red. Bouquet open and pleasing, with soft fruit and again the Branaire floweriness. Flavour quite closed still, with some complexity. Good fruits and tannins, very well structured. Will be a fine bottle in a year or two.

CHATEAU

Ducru-Beaucaillou

ST JULIEN

As you enter the village of Beychevelle from the south on the D2, pass Château Beychevelle itself on your right, and you come to the giant concrete St Julien bottle among the vines on a sharp right-hand bend. Château Ducru-Beaucaillou, instantly recognisable from the label, can now be seen across the vineyards to the right, and is reached by a clearly signposted road through the vines about 100 metres past the bend.

The vineyard was established in the late 18th century, when the property was known as Bergeron, though the actual vineyard was already called Beaucaillou, after the 'beautiful pebbles' – the deep gravel that gives that special quality to the wines of the Médoc.

Ducru was added to the name soon after the estate was purchased in 1795 by Bertrand Ducru. He was a good winemaker, and raised the quality of the wine from Third-Growth level to top of the

Seconds by 1840, when it sold on a par with Rauzan and Léoville. Ducru was married to the daughter of the chairman of Bordeaux's Chamber of Commerce, who is reputed to have so admired the wine from his son-in-law's estate that decanters of Ducru-Beaucaillou replaced the normal carafes of water at committee meetings. It is a nice idea, and, if true, must have enlivened many a dreary session.

The fine, vaulted cellars were already in existence when Ducru purchased the place, dating back to the beginning of the 17th century. Ducru built the elegant, long central part of the château in Directoire style on top of these cellars, making Ducru-Beaucaillou one of the very few properties in the Médoc with chais beneath the château. Such construction was usually not adopted because of the low-lying terrain of the area, and the consequent risk of flooding from the nearby Gironde estuary;

Ducru-Beaucaillou, however, is sufficiently elevated to be immune from this danger.

Bertrand Ducru had two children, Gustave, who married the widow of Jean-Baptiste Du Luc from Branaire, and Marie-Louise, wife of Antoine Ravez; these two inherited Ducru-Beaucaillou in 1829 on the death of their father. Shortly afterwards, Marie-Louise bought out her brother, who went to live at Branaire, which benefited greatly from his ownership.

Madame Ravez and her husband, later to be elevated to the rank of Comte by Charles X, remained in possession of Ducru-Beaucaillou for some thirty-five years, during which period they kept up the reputation and quality established by Bertrand Ducru; the property was classified ninth among the Second Growths in 1855. In 1866 Madame Ravez put Ducru-Beaucaillou up for sale, and it was bought by the wife of Nathaniel Johnston for the sum of 1,000,000 francs.

The Johnstons were of Scottish origin, having arrived in Bordeaux from Ireland some 150 years earlier. Unlike their fellow expatriates, the Bartons, they had taken out French citizenship and some became Roman Catholics. They were, and still are, a force to be reckoned with on the Bordeaux scene, firmly established as négociants, and already proprietors of another Cru Classé, Château Dauzac in Labarde.

This was a time of prosperity in the Médoc; there was a thriving trade with England, and prices of wines and properties rose to astronomic levels. The sun shone thus for some twenty years, to be followed by one of the bleakest chapters in the history of the vineyards of Bordeaux. The cause of the depression of the 1880s and 1890s was the appearance of the phylloxera beetle, run a close second by the ravages of mildew. The Johnstons were fortunately in a position of sufficient strength to survive these problems, and had the resources to combat these deadly enemies of the vine. Indeed, it was the joint régisseur of Ducru-Beaucaillou and Dauzac, M. David, who accidentally discovered the treatment for mildew at Château Dauzac, as I have described in detail in the chapter on that property. Thus Ducru survived this difficult period with its reputation and vineyard relatively unscathed, thanks to the now universally adopted 'Bouillie Bordelaise' treatment against mildew, and costly replanting with vines grafted on to the American phylloxera-resistant rootstock. So confident in fact were the Johnstons in their future, that they enlarged the château by the addition of the two square Victorian towers at either end of the existing structure.

In the early 1920s, however, the Johnston wine business was experiencing some difficulties. One of their strongest markets at that time was the United States, and the advent of prohibition dried up this source of revenue overnight. The world economic slump began to bite, and in 1928 Ducru-Beaucaillou was reluctantly sold to M. Desbarats de Burke, a partner in the négociant house of de Gernon Desbarats in Bordeaux. The late twenties were not a propitious moment for the acquisition of a Cru Classé, followed as they were by the horrendously bad vintages of the 1930s, and Desbarats de Burke sold the property, by then in a sorry state, to Francis Borie at the end of 1941.

Francis Borie, whose father, Eugène, had bought Château Caronne in 1889, set about the restoration and replanting of the property that was to take nearly twenty years to complete. Long before the programme was finished, the wine of Ducru-Beaucaillou was back on top. Francis Borie died in 1953, and was succeeded by his son, Jean-Eugène, the present owner, who lives at Ducru with his lovely wife Monique.

Ducru-Beaucaillou now enjoys a deserved reputation at the head of the Second Growths, together with Léoville-Las-Cases, Pichon-Longueville-Lalande and Cos d'Estournel. These four châteaux are almost in a classification of their own, realising prices in between the 1st Growths and the rest of the Seconds.

What is it that sets a wine like Ducru-Beaucaillou apart from the rest? As with every château, there is no single element that results in the whole end-product; it is, rather, a combination of many factors, and to produce a wine of exceptional quality, all these factors must be in unison. Firstly there are the God-given advantages, the soil and the weather, but even the soil needs a certain amount of attention; the weather, too, though it cannot be controlled, calls for the knowledge and experience of the owner when conditions are bad. It is here that the human factor comes into the picture; even given perfect geological and climatic conditions, great wine can only be made by that very special kind of man who pays meticulous attention to the tiniest detail, from vineyard to bottle, and is even prepared to sacrifice profit on the altar of excellence, should circumstances so demand. Jean-Eugène Borie is such a man, and will leave the stamp of his genius on Ducru-Beaucaillou. Words are superfluous, for bottled proof is abundant.

The château is a delight to visit; the exterior of the house, with its lovely gardens and trees, looking across green meadowland to the mighty Gironde, always puts me in mind of the carefree elegance of an Edwardian English country house and would make a perfect setting for the novels of L.P. Hartley or the plays of Oscar Wilde. Inside there are contrasts of style, from the warm comfort of Jean-Eugène's book-lined sitting-room and the light, airy salon that adjoins it, with its carefully restored murals depicting well-known proverbs, to the solid Victorian opulence of the sombre panelled dining-room, contrasting with the more often-used spacious, comfortable one beyond the study. In this setting, the Bories are the perfect host and hostess. Jean-Eugène is slight of build, dapper and unassuming, and has that rare gift of making comparative strangers feel totally at home. I well remember my first visit to Ducru-Beaucaillou, and a remark of Monsieur Borie's which illustrates his attitude to his wine. He had kindly given us two good vintages to taste, and my wife asked him which he liked best. 'You are a mother,' he said. 'Would you ask a father which of his two children he preferred?'

In 1970 Borie acquired 30 hectares of Château Lagrange's land and planted 18 hectares of vines; these vines produce the wine which is now vinified separately in a very modern winery, and sold as Château Lalande-Borie. Jean-Eugène and his son François-Xavier also make the wine at two other Crus Classés, Château Grand-Puy-Lacoste, which they own and where François-Xavier lives, and Château Haut-Batailley, which they manage for Jean-Eugène's sister, Madame des Brest-Borie.

TECHNICAL INFORMATION

General

Appellation:	St Julien
Area under vines:	50 hectares
Average production:	Between 12,000 and 20,000 cases
Distribution of vines:	2 large blocks, and several smaller parcels around the commune of St Julien-Beychevelle
Owner:	M. Jean-Eugène Borie
Régisseur:	M. André Faure
Maître de Chai:	M. René Lusseau
Consultant Oenologist:	Professor Emile Peynaud

Viticulture

Geology:	Gravel
Grape varieties:	65% Cabernet Sauvignon, 25% Merlot, 5% Cabernet Franc, 5% Petit Verdot
Pruning:	Médocaine (according to INAO regulations)
Rootstock:	Varied, to suit soils of different parts of the vineyard
Vines per hectare:	10,000

Average yield per hectare:	Between 30 and 45 hectolitres
Replanting:	By blocks of 1 hectare

Vinification

Added yeasts:	No
Length of maceration:	Varied according to vintage
Temperature of fermentation:	28–30°C max.
Control of fermentation:	By water-cooled coil
Type of vat:	Vitrified cement
Vin de presse:	Part incorporated depending on vintage
Age of casks:	50% new each vintage
Time in cask:	Average 20 months
Fining:	Egg-whites
Filtration:	None
Type of bottle:	Bordelaise

Commercial

Vente Directe:	No
Sales:	Through the négociants
Visits:	Yes, by appointment
	Telephone: 56 59 05 20

THE TASTING AT CHATEAU DUCRU-BEAUCAILLOU, 26/27 October 1984
J.S., Mme. Borie, Jean-Eugène Borie

1983 Incredibly dark, dense colour, almost black. Nose still closed, but lovely, concentrated fruit there and new wood. Big and mouthfilling, classically well structured with a load of blackcurrant fruit and good tannins. Superb, but will require a long bottle life before it realises its full potential.

1971 Deep red, just beginning to brown. Lovely ripe cassis bouquet. Full of St Julien charm, in harmony now, but still has lots of life. Long aftertaste. A lovely bottle.

1970 Dense, dark red with hints of brown. Superb, aromatic nose. Tremendous concentration of flavour and great complexity. Just about ready for drinking now, but will last and last. This is a superb wine that fully justifies the high price it now commands.

1961 Rich, dense and dark. Great depth of delicious ripe fruit on nose. Full, rich flavour, with great concentration of a much younger wine, even for such a marvellous vintage. Superb lingering aftertaste. A claret of nuclear proportions, certainly one of the best that has come my way. One of the world's great wines.

CHATEAU

Gruaud-Larose

ST JULIEN

As you come to the village of Beychevelle from the south along the D2, take the road straight through the village towards St Laurent, which is the D101. Gruaud-Larose is the first property on your left after you leave Beychevelle.

The vineyard of Château Gruaud-Larose as we know it today has its origins in the mid-18th century, when the Chevalier de Gruaud bought several parcels of land in the commune of St Julien and formed a large wine-poducing property. The estate was initially known as the Domaine de Fond Bedeau, the contemporary name of that part of the parish, though Gruaud soon gave it his own name. He must have been something of a martinet, for he had a tower constructed in the vineyard, from the top of which he would watch over his workers to see they all gave full measure.

In 1778 the vineyard, second in size only to the then undivided Léoville property, passed into the hands of Gruaud's son-in-law, Monsieur Larose, who lost no time in adding his name to that of his late father-in-law. Larose was, by all accounts, a remarkable man. He was a politician of note, President of the Presidial de Guyenne and Lieutenant-General of the province. Being a well-connected and much travelled man, mingling with the aristocracy and in court circles, Larose was able to introduce his wines in to the upper echelons of society; it was he who coined the motto '*Le roi des vins, Le vin des rois*', which has ever since adorned the labels of Gruaud-Larose.

Following Larose's death in 1795, there was a long and very expensive legal squabble between his heirs as to the ownership of the estate. By 1812 the costs of litigation had mounted to astronomic heights, and a solution had still not been found, so the property was put up for auction and bought by a consortium of three people, Baron Sarget, Pierre Balguerie and Monsieur Verdonnet. The latter died in 1836, and his share was bought by his partners. By 1867 many problems of inheritance had arisen, and the vineyard was split into two separate halves, one becoming known as Gruaud-Larose-Sarget, still owned by the Baron, and the other half taking the name of Gruaud-Larose-Bethmann, after Mme. de Bethmann, heiress to the Balguerie share. The latter half of the property

later became known as Gruaud-Larose-Fauré, after Mme. Adrien Fauré, daughter of Mme. de Bethmann.

In 1917 Désiré Cordier, grandfather of the present owner, Jean Cordier, bought Gruaud-Larose-Sarget from the Baron's widow, Mme. Adrienne Lavielle, Baronne Sarget de Lafontaine. Her husband the Baron had died many years before, his fortune greatly reduced by his love of pretty women and the card tables. Cordier, who had started a successful wine business in the province of Lorraine, moved his company to Bordeaux in 1914. The purchase of the Sarget portion of Gruaud-Larose was the first of many. Château Talbot was bought in 1918 by Désiré's son Georges, but it was not until 1935 that the Fauré half of Gruaud-Larose dropped into the Cordier portfolio of vineyards, thus re-uniting Château Gruaud-Larose as one property.

In 1934 Désiré Cordier gave a luncheon at Gruaud-Larose for everyone in the Médoc aged 100 or more, at which the French President Lebrun was guest of honour. Every centenarian present – history does not record their number! – was given a bottle of Château Gruaud-Larose 1834 to mark the occasion.

The château, a grandiose mansion built by Baron

Sarget in 1875, has a commanding view over the St Julien vineyards to the Gironde. It is not lived in, but there is accommodation for guests, and lunches, dinners and receptions are held in its elegantly furnished dining-room and salons. An interesting feature of the interior is the cunning design of the two fireplaces between the central dining-room and the two adjoining reception rooms; above the chimney-piece of each is an open space looking through to the next room, the flues being diverted to either side.

The wine of Gruaud-Larose has enjoyed the reputation of a top Second Growth since the very early days of its creation as a vineyard. The ancient house of Tastet-Lawton, Bordeaux négociants and courtiers since the 18th century, have a mention in their records of the sale of the wines of the Chevalier de Gruaud before 1750. The itinerant oenophile and future President of America, Thomas Jefferson, mentions the wine of 'La Rose' as being one of the top three Seconds in 1787, along with Rauzan and Léoville-Las-Cases. Again in the Lawton records, Gruaud-Larose is mentioned in 1815 as being 'the fullest, smoothest and at the same time sweetest of all the Grands Vins of St Julien'. Gruaud is, as it always has been, consistently worthy of its placement among the Second Growths; it is a full, rounded wine, with typical St Julien charm, and enough breeding and backbone to carry it, in good years, to sublime heights.

TECHNICAL INFORMATION

General

Appellation:	St Julien
Area under vines:	80 hectares
Average production:	35,000 cases
Distribution of vines:	Large parcels, one of 60 hectares, all around the château
Owner:	Société Civile du Château Gruaud-Larose
Director:	M. Georges Pauli
Régisseur:	M. Henri Puzos
Maître de Chai:	M. Lucien Moreau
Oenologist:	M. Georges Pauli

Viticulture

Geology:	Deep gravel on a base of deeply fissured chalky marl
Grape varieties:	65% Cabernet Sauvignon, 20% Merlot, 10% Cabernet Franc, 5% Petit Verdot
Pruning:	Guyot Double Médocaine
Rootstock:	Riparia 3309, 101–14
Vines per hectare:	7,500
Yield per hectare:	Average 42 hectolitres
Replanting:	1.5 hectares per annum

Vinification

Added yeasts:	No
Length of maceration:	18–20 days, depending on vintage
Temperature of fermentation:	30°C max.
Control of fermentation:	Water-cooled serpentine
Type of vat:	Glass-lined cement
Vin de presse:	6% to 8% included
Age of casks:	⅓ new each vintage
Time in cask:	20–22 months

Fining:	Fresh egg-whites
Filtration:	Light filtering sur plaque before bottling
Type of bottle:	Special Epoque-Cordier, but Bordelaise since 1979

Commercial

Vente Directe:	No
Exclusivity:	Yes, Ets Cordier, 7/13 Quai de Paludate, 33000 Bordeaux
Agents overseas:	Yes, enquiries to Ets. Cordier
Visits:	Yes, by appointment Telephone 56 92 70 00 0830–1200, 1400–1730 Monday to Friday

THE TASTING AT CHATEAU GRUAUD-LAROSE, 1 February 1985
J.S., Christian Seely, M. Daniel Vergely

1983 Fine, blue-black colour. Elegant bouquet, with fruit and finesse. Lovely mouthful of fruit and non-aggressive tannin, very long, with masses of backbone, but plenty of feminine charm. Will be very good.
1982 Dense, dark red. Nose open with lots of black-currant fruit. Rich and round, with masses of fruit and body. Tannins powerful, but not aggressive. Great!
1981 Lovely deep colour. Nose closed, but beginning to give of its charms. Very elegant, supple wine, typical St Julien charm and finesse. Long, lingering aftertaste – will be a beautiful wine.
1980 Good colour for 1980. Bouquet pretty and open. Charming, ready to drink, perhaps slightly less power-ful than brother Talbot, but delicious now and for a couple of years.
1979 Again very deep red. Nose good, but a little retiring. Excellent fruit with ripe tannins, long after-taste. Good, and not too complicated.
1978 Colour noticeably lighter than later years. Nose starting to show well. Loads of richness and fruit, but at same time has elegance and finesse. A fine 1978, but should be kept a while.
1964 (With lunch.) Colour still good, only a little brown. Nose ripe and beautiful. A lovely mouthfilling claret with charm and length. Perfect now, but will keep.
Author's note: This vintage is something of a rarity. In 1965 the chai was badly damaged by a great fire, and more than half the 1964 vintage was destroyed in cask, and much of the rest was affected by the heat. This bottle was a happy escapee!

Léoville-Barton and Langoa-Barton

ST JULIEN

The château of Langoa-Barton, which is also that of Léoville-Barton, is situated on the left-hand side of the D2, as you drive northwards between the villages of Beychevelle and St Julien.

The Barton family, originating from County Fermanagh in what is now Northern Ireland, arrived in Bordeaux in the early 18th century. The founder of the French family fortunes, Thomas Barton, known in the family as French Tom, arrived in Bordeaux in 1722 and by 1725 had established a wine business in the city. The firm still exists today as Barton and Guestier, the name it has borne since 1802, when Daniel Guestier was taken on as a full partner. It has been suggested that French Tom may have been drawn to Bordeaux by the lucrative two-way contraband traffic that existed between France and Ireland in wool and wine. Barton being of Irish birth and this type of trade being almost respectable, a little smuggling may well have contributed to the enormous fortune he amassed in commerce and property in France and Ireland, but there is, not surprisingly, a lack of documentary evidence on this subject.

Tom's only son, William, though he was officially a partner in the wine business, did not get on with his father, and spent a large part of his life on the family estates in Ireland. On his death in 1780, French Tom left the family properties in France and Ireland and the Bordeaux firm to William, and a bequest of £10,000 to each of William's six sons. The fourth of these sons, Hugh Barton, was made a partner in the wine business at the age of 20 in 1786. His five brothers were pursuing their own careers in Parliament and the army, and doubtless William was keen to involve a member of the family in a profitable business which did not interest him personally. Some time before his death, Tom Barton had formed a loose but trusting business arrangement with Daniel Guestier, who, though not officially a partner till 1802, virtually ran the business, and looked after the Barton interests with integrity and efficiency. How lucky were the family to have such a trustworthy friend, for at the time of the French Revolution Hugh Barton was arrested and interned; though he was released in 1794 and cleared of any suspicion of anti-republicanism, the French Republic was now at war with England, and Barton wisely kept a low profile, spending much time attending to his affairs in Ireland. His father William, already old and sick at the outbreak of the Revolution, was left in peace in his country house, and died there in October 1793.

Hugh was now in sole charge of the business, which, in spite of war and revolution, continued to prosper. In 1802, during a short peace, Hugh Barton visited Bordeaux, and ratified his faith in Guestier by entering into a formal partnership contract with him. (Ronald Barton is fond of the story that the 'contract' consisted of an exchange of letters saying, 'I put in 1 million francs, you put in the same and we divide profit and loss. Duration 25 years renewable.' This arrangement continued until 1925, when a limited company was formed.)

By 1820 Hugh Barton's fortune had doubled, and his thoughts turned towards owning a wine property. French Tom had been proprietor of Château le Boscq in St Estèphe, but this had by now passed out of the family. In 1821 he bought Château Langoa from Monsieur Pontet, who wanted to concentrate his efforts and capital on the huge estate of Château Pontet-Canet; a sum of 550,000 francs was paid. During the next two or three years he added and exchanged various parcels of land to round off the vineyard. He finally added to his property a quarter of the huge Léoville estate, which was to become Léoville-Barton. This vineyard was formerly the property of the Marquis de-Las-Cases-Beauvoice, and had become forfeit on the Marquis' emigration at the Revolution. There was no château on the property, since the house went with the portion now known as Léoville-Poyferré.

The two domaines were bought as private purchases by Hugh Barton, and were not then, nor are they now, any part of Barton and Guestier. It is perhaps a curious anomaly that a family of Anglo-Irish descent should have been continuously in possession of these two properties longer than any other family has held any Grand Cru in the Médoc. Indeed, apart from the Rothschilds at Mouton, the name of Barton is the only one appearing as proprietor on the 1855 classifica-

76

tion which still applies. Their purchase of Langoa preceded Baron Nathaniel's acquisition of Mouton by thirty-two years, so the Bartons may be justifiably regarded as the senior wine-producing family of the Médoc.

Ronald Barton, great-great-grandson of Hugh, and the present owner of Léoville and Langoa, is one of the great characters of the Médoc. Now virtually retired, this still twinkling octogenarian is a great debunker of the flowery pomposity with which the subject of wine is so often treated. He has been a strong traditionalist, and has consistently made his wines after the old style, firmly rejecting any tendency to vinify his wines in such a way as to mature more quickly for purely commercial reasons.

During the war he served first as an officer with the Royal Inniskillings, and later as a liaison officer with the Free French in the Middle East, in the Syrian campaign and finally in North Africa, and was decorated with the Légion d'Honneur, the Croix de Guerre and the Médaille Commemorative de la France Libre, as well as the British MBE (he is also CBE). It is said that the inhabitants of the Médoc had no fear of the RAF bombers, refusing to take shelter in the firm belief that Monsieur Barton was carefully directing all the raids from England.

Once more the Barton/Guestier relationship stood the Bartons in good stead; during his long absence from the Médoc in the war years it was another Daniel Guestier, great-great-grandson of French Tom's faithful friend and partner, who watched over not only the affairs of Barton and Guestier, but also those of Langoa and Léoville-Barton for Ronald.

On his return from the war, Ronald Barton found the vineyards, thanks to Daniel Guestier's vigilance, still in production. Much had to be done, however, since treatment of the vines and replanting had been virtually impossible during the occupation, due to lack of chemicals on one hand and manpower on the other. Many owners in the Médoc, finding their vineyards in the same state, adopted a policy of total replanting. Ronald, however, realising the importance of old vines in the constitution of fine claret, saved every old vine he could, only replanting where absolutely necessary. This is a much slower and more labour intensive way of doing things, but his efforts paid dividends, as he now has a well-balanced vineyard with the proper proportions of old, middle-aged and young vines.

Langoa and Léoville are a fascinating example of the current validity of the 1855 classification. The vineyards of the two properties, classified Third and Second Growths respectively, are virtually contiguous; their soil analysis is practically identical, grape varieties planted are the same, and vinification and ageing, though kept entirely separate, are done in the same way with the same equipment, in the same buildings and by the same people. In spite of all this Ronald Barton asserts that the wine of Léoville-Barton, the Second, is always slightly superior to that of the Third Growth Langoa.

Administration of the two properties is now carried out by Ronald's nephew, Anthony Barton, who also runs his own wine business. The old firm of Barton and Guestier has for some years now been part of the giant Seagram liquor conglomerate, who until quite recently had been the sole distributors of Châteaux Léoville and Langoa-Barton. Anthony Barton is now faced with the difficult task of re-establishing the wines at their proper price level on the world market through the traditional medium of the Bordeaux négociants. He is an able man, and the wine is as good as ever, so it is hardly surprising that his objectives are already being achieved.

TECHNICAL INFORMATION

General

Appellation:	St Julien
Area under vines:	54.5 hectares, with nearly 6 hectares planted with young vines
Average production:	27,000 cases
Distribution of vines:	Léoville – Principally in one block to the north-west of the château Langoa – Three parcels, 1 to the west of the château, 2 across the D2 from the château
Owner:	G.F.A. des Châteaux Léoville et Langoa-Barton (Barton family)
Regisseur and Maître de Chai:	M. Michel Raoult
Consultant Oenologist:	M. Jacques Boissenot

Viticulture

Geology:	Gravel on clay
Grape varieties:	75% Cabernet Sauvignon, 15% Merlot, 5% Cabernet Franc, 5% Petit Verdot
Pruning:	Guyot Double Médocaine

Rootstock:	Riparia Gloire 101.14, 3309
Vines per hectare:	9,000
Yield per hectare:	40–50 hectolitres
Replanting:	Replacement of vines as they become too old

Vinification

Length of maceration:	3 weeks
Temperature of fermentation:	28–30°C
Control of fermentation:	By cooling unit
Type of vat:	Oak
Vin de presse:	Incorporated, according to vintage, after assemblage
Age of casks:	⅓ new each vintage
Time in cask:	24 months
Fining:	Fresh egg-whites, in cask
Type of bottle:	Bordelaise lourde

Commercial

Sales:	By the Bordeaux négociants For information call Anthony Barton, telephone 56 59 06 05
Visits:	Yes, by appointment Telephone 56 59 06 05

THE TASTING AT CHATEAU LEOVILLE-BARTON, 25 September 1984

J.S., Christian Seely, Anthony Barton, in the cuvier
All the vintages tasted in the cuvier were Château Léoville-Barton

1983 Deep bluey red. Nose very closed. Tannic mouthful, quite aggressive, but loads of fruit and structure. A classic young Bordeaux that will take a long time to mature.

1982 (Bottled one month earlier.) Very dense, almost black appearance. Very fragrant bouquet. Suffering a little from the shock of bottling, but nonetheless a huge, generous mouthful with all the right ingredients.

1981 Very good, deep red. Nose closed, but beginning to evolve. Classic, well-structured wine. Balance good, with great elegance. Long aftertaste. Should make a lovely bottle.

1980 Lovely dark to mid-red. Bouquet soft and open. Pleasing and already quite open. Some oak. No hurry to drink this 1980.

1979 Deep ruby. Nose powerful, with lots of good fruit. Big and quite tannic, with sweetness and fruit beginning to show through.

1978 Very dense, dark red. Nose fine but a bit shut in. Well-made, accessible, balanced and harmonious. Complex and long in mouth. Will be good in 3–4 years.

1977 Slightly tawny colour. Nose open with a slight roasted smell. Some fruit there, a little thin and on the short side, but pleasant enough.

1976 Browning a little. Very ripe nose. Ripe and already good, but will go a while yet. A really good 1976.

1975 Bright medium colour, orangey tinges at edge. Muted, evolving nose, coming through stronger by the minute. Lovely, perfumed mouthful, long aftertaste. Plenty of fruit, but still tannic and a bit closed. Wait a while yet.

1971 Brilliant, almost russet, colour. Easy, soft fragrance. A good 1971, to drink now, tannins easing off a bit.

1970 Lovely colour, beginning to brown a little. Nose full and ripe, quite complex. Lovely mouthful, with lots of concentrated flavour. Supple wine with great finesse, and staying power.

At lunch

Château Langoa-Barton **1967**. Good deep colour, with only a trace of brown. Ripe bouquet. Well-made '67, with good fruit. A little short. Perfect to drink now.

Château Léoville-Barton **1964**. Colour still very deep and dense. Rich, concentrated nose. Big and ripe, with great concentrated fruit flavours. Long aftertaste. Will stay well.

Château Léoville-Barton **1950**. Deep browny colour. Nose overripe, vegetal. 1950 was not a good year, but this still had good fruit and was quite long in the mouth. To be drunk up quickly.

CHATEAU
Léoville-Las-Cases
ST JULIEN

The offices, chais and vathouses of Château Léo-ville-Las-Cases are on your right as you enter the village of St Julien on the D2 from the south, and the vineyard is mainly situated behind the long wall that runs along the right-hand side of the D2 from St Julien right up to the gates of Château Latour; in this wall is set the famous gateway which adorns the label.

The huge vineyard that was to become the Léo-ville estate, encompassing the two other present-day Léovilles, Poyferré and Barton, was first created in 1638 by Jean de Moytié, a powerful Bordeaux merchant, whose son became Président des Trésoriers de la France. In the early 1700s the estate passed into another important Bordeaux family, through the marriage of a Moytié heiress to Blaise Antoine Alexandre de Gasq-Léoville. He was President of the Bordeaux parliament, and the de Gasqs were also large landowners in Margaux; the vineyards that were to become Château Palmer, as well as those of Château d'Issan, were among their properties.

De-Gasq-Léoville died in 1769 without issue, and the estate passed to four of his nephews and nieces, the senior of whom was the Marquis de Las-Cases Beauvois. At the time of the Revolution the Marquis emigrated in fear of his life, and the estate was promptly sequestrated. His brother and two sisters embarked on a protracted petition to have the property restored to them, since they had stayed put. The dispute was eventually settled, and three-quarters of the estate was given back to them, while the Marquis's share was sold as a 'Bien National'; this was the portion that was acquired by Hugh Barton in the 1820s, and is now Château Léoville-Barton.

The new Marquis, Field-Marshal Pierre-Jean, was a trusted friend of Napoleon, and joined him in his exile on St Helena, where he wrote Bonaparte's biography. He retained the major share of the property, the rest belonging to his sister Jeanne who was married to Bertrand d'Abbadie de St Germain, Baron de Nocarelles, a Bordeaux family of an importance matching its name.

Jeanne gifted her third share of Léoville to her daughter, Madame de Bonneval, who caused the third splintering of the great estate by selling her share in 1860 to her sister, the Baronesse de Poyferré.

The remaining part, now known as Léoville-Las-Cases, passed from Pierre-Jean, through his son Adolphe, to his three grandchildren, Gaston, Marquis de Las-Cases, Gabriel and Clothilde in 1880. The Marquis sold his share to his brother Gabriel soon afterwards, and in 1900 Gabriel too decided to cash in his chips. At this point a company was formed to administer the property, and Clothilde, now Madame d'Alauzier, retained the largest number of shares, eight of a total of twenty. The other shares were acquired by an assortment of négociants, and one by the estate manager, Théophile Skawinski, whose son-in-law was André Delon, grandfather of the present Administrator, Michel Delon.

The Delons have gradually acquired 13 of the present 21 shares, and the rest belong to the heirs of Madame d'Alauzier, thus keeping a substantial portion of the property in the de Las-Cases family. Since the splitting away of the Poyferré section of the vineyard, the château, chais, vathouses and other buildings have been intermingled in a most confusing way. Basically Las-Cases has its cuverie, first-year chai and offices on the left-hand side of the courtyard as you drive through the gates, while the Poyferré vathouse and one chai are on the right. The main portion of the château itself belongs to Las-Cases, though it is not lived in, and has never been used for the label. Across the road is a large stockroom for the storage of wines in bottle and some casks, together with the bottling line and labelling and packaging unit. With all these buildings there is still need for more space at Las-Cases, and a large new extension to the stocking area is planned, with a loading bay and apron for lorries.

The vines of Château Léoville-Las-Cases enjoy one of the most enviable sites in the Médoc, the majority being in the section known as Grand Clos: this is a perfectly aspected slope, running from the D2 down towards the Gironde, with a thick layer of large gravel. This vineyard, almost entirely enclosed within a wall, runs in one continuous block of 50 hectares from the village of St Julien to the Jalle de Juillac, a small stream that divides the communes of St Julien and Pauillac,

and the grapes of Léoville-Las-Cases and Château Latour. It is the situation of this vineyard, perhaps, that contributes most of the style of this, the biggest and sturdiest of the St Julien wines. It has been called 'the Latour of St Julien', and this is hardly surprising, as the vines of the two properties run hand-in-hand together down the slope towards the river.

There is, of course, much more than geography and geology in the making of a great Grand Cru;

81

given the right site and the right microclimate, the next most important element is the human contribution. Here Léoville-Las-Cases is truly blessed with the talents of Michel Delon; capably assisted by Jacques Depoizier, his Directeur d'Exploitation, Delon moves quietly about his business with the calm assurance of knowledge born of generations of experience. A softly-spoken man, he has no need to raise his voice, for his confidence and assurance impart themselves to everyone he deals with and brook no argument. His ability as a winemaker and a businessman is beyond question, and the proof is there for all to see. As well as making one of the top-flight Deuxième Cru wines at Léoville-Las-Cases, which often justifiably commands a price nearer to that of a First Growth than a Second, Michel Delon also runs the highly successful A.C. Médoc, Château Potensac, the property of his parents; Château Pichon-Lalande, another of the 'First Seconds', also owes some of its present status to Delon, who ran the property for the Miailhe family for some years before Madame de Lencquesaing took personal charge in 1978. I learnt more in a couple of afternoons from Michel Delon about the making of fine Bordeaux than could be gathered in months of reading, and I shall remember him for that.

Every aspect of the winemaking process at Léoville-Las-Cases receives the same degree of meticulous attention. The vineyards, the chais, and the vathouse with its array of oak vats, as well as the stock warehouse and bottling line are all spotlessly clean, always a clear indicator of care and pursuit of excellence. It is perhaps the all-important assemblage, the moment of selection and blending of the various vats before the wine goes into cask, that is the pivot on which the quality of Léoville-Las-Cases rests. Dozens of samples are tasted time and again over a period of weeks by Delon, his colleagues and the celebrated Professor Peynaud. It is only after this rigorous selection that the component parts of the Grand Vin de Léoville are chosen, while the remainder, only marginally less perfect, goes into the casks destined for the excellent 'deuxième vin', Clos du Marquis, a label that has been in use since the 1902 vintage, and which represents, thanks to the strictness of the selection at Las-Cases, exceptional value for money.

TECHNICAL INFORMATION

General

Appellation:	St Julien
Area under vines:	86 hectares
Average production:	Château Léoville-Las-Cases 20,000 to 25,000 cases Clos du Marquis 10,000 to 15,000 cases
Distribution of vines:	2 main blocks
Owner:	Société Civile du Château Léoville-Las-Cases
Administrator:	M. Michel Delon
Directeur d'Exploitation:	M. Jacques Depoizier
Maître de Chai:	M. Michel Rolland
Consultant Oenologist:	Professor Emile Peynaud

Viticulture

Geology:	Slopes of deep gravel, with large pebbles
Grape varieties:	65% Cabernet Sauvignon, 12% Cabernet Franc, 20% Merlot, 3% Petit Verdot
Pruning:	Guyot Double
Rootstock:	Riparia Gloire, 101-14 with a few 420A
Vines per hectare:	8,000
Yield per hectare:	40–45 hectolitres
Replanting:	As necessary, maintaining average vine age of 30 years

Vinification

Length of maceration:	15–20 days, depending on vintage
Temperature of fermentation:	26–29°C, depending on vintage
Control of fermentation:	By water-cooled coil system
Vin de presse:	From 10% to 15% incorporated depending on vintage
Age of casks:	35% to 50% new, according to requirements of vintage
Time in cask:	18 months
Fining:	Fresh egg-whites in cask
Filtration:	Sur plaque before bottling
Type of bottle:	Bordelaise lourde

Commercial

Sales:	Through the négociants
Exclusivities:	None
Agents overseas:	World-wide distribution by the négociants
Visits:	Yes, appointment advised Telephone: 56 59 25 26 Weekdays only 0900–1200 1430–1700 (1600 Fridays)

THE TASTING, AT CHATEAU LEOVILLE-
LAS-CASES, 30 January 1985
J.S., Christian Seely, Michel Delon, Jacques Depoizier,
Michel Rolland

Château Léoville-Las-Cases
1983 Amazing deep blue/black. Excellent nose, with powerful fruit. A lot of wine, filling the mouth with fruit and non-aggressive tannin. Very long in the mouth. A wine for 2000 and beyond!
1981 Colour almost as deep as '83. Nose attractively open with loads of good fruit. A big wine for 1981, with a lot of flesh on a great frame. Also has elegance and charm. A winner.
1980 Superb colour for 1980, quite purple. Bouquet quite shut-in. Lots of fruit, with good tannin and some backbone. Very backward for this 'petite année', a really well made 1980 that will repay keeping.
1979 Deep red, with blue shades. Powerful fruit bouquet. Quite tough for '79 with good fruit and quite hard tannin. Lacks the 'supple' character of the later vintages.
1978 Fine, dense, medium-dark red. Nose only just beginning to open. Complex and still evolving; all the elements, fruit, body, backbone, tannin and finesse are there to make this into a really great bottle, but one needs to wait a few years.

Clos du Marquis
1983 Deep, almost black colour. Nose fine, surprisingly evolved. Big, powerful wine, lots of fruit and good tannin, very long; will be exceptional for a deuxième vin.
1981 Dense, bluey red. Nose aromatic, good fruit. Big for 1981 with fruit and tannins a-plenty. Wait 3 years for a good-value bottle.
1980 Medium dark red, good for '80. Attractive open bouquet of good fruit. Well-made 1980, with plenty of fruit and ripe tannin – excellent to drink now, but will keep.
1979 Good red, still some blue. Slightly 'roasted' on nose. Fruit and tannin here, but has quite a dry finish. Nice, but not for laying down.
1978 Bright, medium-red. Good open nose, quite complex. Flavour good, concentrated and ripe with some good tannin. Will keep.

FURTHER TASTING AT CHATEAU
LEOVILLE-LAS-CASES, 10 May 1985
J.S., Wendy Seely, Michel Tesseron, Michel Delon,
Jacques Depoizier

Château Léoville-Las-Cases
1984 Colour almost black. Nose very closed, a huge wine, big, hard and tough. Fruit there in plenty and quite aggressive tannins – it will take a long time to achieve potential.
1982 Amazingly deep colour, almost black. Bouquet very good, but more closed than Clos du Marquis. A nuclear explosion of fruit; tannin excellent and not at all aggressive. Tremendous length and ageing potential – possibly the best 1982 I have tasted.
1977 Really good colour for 1977. Good open bouquet with excellent fruit. Tasting blind, there is no way I would judge this as a 1977; just beginning to open with plenty of fruit and enough backbone to last a long while.
1976 Lovely bright scarlet with a good, open bouquet. Plenty of good ripe fruit and a certain nutty taste. Plenty of length, now approaching readiness.
1975 Colour still very dense and dark without a trace of brown. Powerful, concentrated nose. Flavour also very concentrated. Enormous complexity and potential with excellent fruit and beautiful ripe tannin.
1974 Palish red. First of the Léoville-Las-Cases wines to show any brown. Bouquet very open. Some fruit, but tannin almost gone. Quite pleasant but finished very dry and is ready for drinking now.
1973 Pale garnet colour. Soft attractive nose. Flavour still quite lovely. Elegant and perfect for current drinking. This wine is now on a plateau and will continue for some years.
1972 Medium good colour. Bouquet excellent for 1972. A little thin, but still has good fruit. Not the best year for Léoville-Las-Cases.
1971 Excellent deep colour, only just beginning to shade towards brown. Ripe bouquet with lovely fruit, a classic ripe St Julien, full of finesse and charm with a beautiful long aftertaste. Ready now, but will last for several years.
1970 Amazing depth of colour for a 15-year-old wine. Nose still quite closed in. The wine is still shy and shut in. Flavours and aromas very complex, just beginning to unfold. Tremendous concentration. This will be one of the all-time great clarets.

Clos du Marquis
1984 Dense, blue-black colour. Very good nose, strong cassis. Excellent fruit and tannins. Very big for a second wine. To keep for several years.
1982 Dense, blackish red. Bouquet well evolved, beautiful with lots of fruit. A very big, mouthfilling wine, tannins more aggressive than usual for 1982. Lots of good fruit with an excellent long aftertaste. For a second wine, this is a blockbuster.

CHATEAU
Léoville-Poyferré
ST JULIEN

As you enter the village of St Julien on the D2 from the south, the offices and part of the chais are on your left, while the cuvier and another chai are through a gateway opposite, shared with Château Léoville-Las-Cases. Poyferré's buildings are on the right of the courtyard, and the cuvier, chais and offices of Las-Cases are on your left.

The story of Léoville-Poyferré really begins in 1860, when Jeanne d'Abbadie sold her share of the great Léoville estate to her sister, the Baronesse de Poyferré-Céres, whose husband's name originated from his property in the commune of Céres in the Landes, some 10 km north of Mont de Marsan. After the death of the Baron, his son, Jean-Marie, made some speculative investments in Russian railway shares on the advice of his bankers in Bordeaux, and as a result was virtually ruined. Château Léoville-Poyferré went under the hammer, and was bought in 1866 by the Bordeaux négociant, Armand Lalande, who was already proprietor of Cantenac-Brown in Margaux.

His daughter was married to Edouard Lawton of the powerful négociant firm of Tastet-Lawton, into whose hands the property passed on the death of Armand Lalande in 1894. Lawton's grandsons, Daniel and Hugues, are still négociants in Bordeaux today, the former carrying on the old family business of courtier and négociant, the latter running his own merchant firm of Hugues Lawton S.A. on the Quai de Bacalan in Bordeaux. They are a delightful pair, and have a fund of knowledge and anecdotes about the Bordeaux wine business that has proved of immeasurable amusement and fascination to me during my researches. They were brought up in the best Anglo-French tradition; Hugues recalls that only English was spoken in the nursery, and remembers the days when Savile Row tailors came in ships to Bordeaux, and the Chartronnais establishment used to visit them on board to be measured and fitted for their suits.

Their ownership of Léoville-Poyferré was relatively short, however, although the Lawton family crest remains on the label to this day. The château was purchased in 1920 by a company called the Société Civile des Domaines de St Julien, formed by the Cuvelier family, who had been established

as négociants in Lille since the beginning of the 19th century. They already owned Château le Crock in St Estèphe, which still belongs to them, and also owned Château de Camensac until 1964, when it was sold to the Forners. Léoville-Poyferré had been managed by one of the fascinating Skawinski family under Lawton ownership, and their descendants, the Delons, ran it for the Cuveliers until 1979, when Didier Cuvelier took over responsibility for the administration of both Léoville-

84

Poyferré and Le Crock. The Skawinskis were a family of Polish émigrés, who arrived in Bordeaux in the mid-19th century, and left their mark on many a property in the Médoc. The unmistakable design of Skawinski cuviers can be seen at several Crus Classés, notably properties that belonged to the Cruse family, for whom the Skawinskis worked, such as Giscours and Pontet-Canet.

The Delons, like their Skawinski forebears, are inspired winemakers, but for some reason, possibly lack of investment during the difficult thirties and postwar years, Léoville-Poyferré, with a few notable exceptions like 1961 and 1970, has not been producing particularly exciting wines in the last few decades. It is generally recognised that until the advent of Didier Cuvelier, the last really great wine made here was the fabled Léoville-Poyferré 1929, a claret of tremendous distinction that it has been my great good fortune to drink on two occasions.

Didier Cuvelier, whose father, Max, established a négociant office in Bordeaux just after the war, is a qualified oenologist, and is setting about the renaissance of Léoville-Poyferré in a serious way. A massive investment programme is under way; already the old cuvier has been totally re-equipped with large metal fermentation vats, a new and up-to-date reception des vendanges and an Amos crusher, and a large new building is under construction on the western side of the road for stocks of wine in bottle. Further improvements include a modern bottling-line, the increased use of new oak casks, and, most important of all perhaps, a far more strict process of selection than has been adopted in past years; the counsel of the eminent Professor Peynaud has also been sought. The Cuveliers also own the vineyards of the Cru Bourgeois Château Moulin Riche, and the produce of the young vines and those cuves not considered suitable for the Grand Vin are sold under this label. Château Moulin Riche is effectively the second wine of Léoville-Poyferré, and is distributed exclusively in France by the family wine business.

The results of all these improvements are already apparent in the vintages since 1979, and continuity of quality is assured by the watchful eye of Didier Cuvelier, who is ably assisted by the bright young maître de chai, Francis Dourthe, who has recently joined the team. The last three vintages which I tasted at the château showed tremendous promise for the future, and I predict that in years to come the competition between the three Léovilles will become again the close contest that it was in years past.

TECHNICAL INFORMATION

General

Appellation:	St Julien
Area under vines:	61.3 hectares, with a further 19 hectares potential
Average production:	22,000 cases
Distribution of vines:	In four main blocks, the largest being to the west and north-west of the buildings, opposite the Grand Clos of Léoville-Las-Cases
Owner:	Société Civile des Domaines de St Julien (Props: Cuvelier family)
Director:	M. Didier Cuvelier
Maître de Chai:	M. Francis Dourthe
Chef de Culture:	M. Jean-Pierre Fatin
Consultant Oenologist:	Prof. Emile Peynaud

Viticulture

Geology:	Deep gravel
Grape varieties:	65% Cabernet Sauvignon, 10% Cabernet Franc, 25% Merlot
Pruning:	Guyot Double
Rootstock:	Varied to suit soil and drainage
Vines per hectare:	9,200
Average yield per hectare:	40 hectolitres
Replanting:	Replacement of oldest vines to maintain average age of 25 years

Vinification

Added yeasts:	Sometimes used in first vat in difficult years
Length of maceration:	15–21 days
Temperature of fermentation:	30°C
Control of fermentation:	Water-cooling
Vin de presse:	Very little incorporated, depending on vintage
Age of casks:	⅓ new each vintage (50% for 1984)
Time in cask:	18 months
Fining:	Fresh egg-whites in cask
Type of bottle:	Bordelaise lourde

Commercial

Vente Directe:	Yes, to callers
General Sales:	Through Ets Cuvelier et Fils, 72 Rue Regnier, 33000 Bordeaux as well as the other négociants Château Moulin-Riche: French distribution only through Ets Cuvelier et Fils
Visits:	Yes: telephone 56 49 08 30 (Château) 56 40 03 92 (Office) Closed August Hours: 0800–1200, 1400–1800

THE TASTING AT CHATEAU LEOVILLE-POYFERRE, 21 January 1985
J.S., Didier Cuvelier, Francis Dourthe

1983 Fine, deep, bluey red. Nose still closed, but perfectly correct, with blackcurrant and new oak. A big, powerful mouthful of wine, with quite aggressive tannins but a huge amount of fruit and body to offset. Very long; a classic St Julien vin de garde.

1982 Colour beautiful, even denser and darker than 1983. Lovely, open nose of sweet, ripe fruit. A huge, fat wine with plenty of good fruit and soft tannins; already most approachable, but has the backbone to take it into a graceful old age.

1981 Deep, intense ruby. Good bouquet with cassis and a little oakiness. Well structured, feminine and elegant, already showing great charm. Everything in its right place; will be a classic.

CHATEAU
St Pierre

ST JULIEN

As you enter the village of Beychevelle-St Julien, Château St Pierre is on your left on the sharp right-hand bend of the D2, opposite the huge St Julien bottle.

The story of Château St Pierre is one of ups and downs culminating in a happy ending. From the 16th to the end of the 18th century, the property was known as Château Serançan, and belonged to a family called Chaveny. They sold it to a M. de St Pierre, who gave the estate his name. In the 1830s, there were two daughters of the St Pierre family who inherited the estate. One of them married a M. Bontemps-Dubarry, and the other married a Swede called Luetkens. It was at this time that the property was divided in two; Mme. Luetkens decided to sell her share, which she did to a M. Sevaistre, and thus were born Châteaux St Pierre-Sevaistre and St Pierre-Bontemps.

In the late 1800s, Château St Pierre-Bontemps, which had now passed into the hands of a M. Kappelhoff, began gradually to disappear, as small parcels of vines were sold off. The Bontemps half of the property included the château and the chai, and it was for the use of the latter that Henri Martin's father, who was a cooper by trade, took the buildings and a few vines on a tenancy from M. Kappelhoff. By 1920 there were practically no vines left, and Kappelhoff decided to sell what remained, keeping just the château for himself. The remnants of the property were first offered to M. Martin, who said 'no thank you' to the vineyard, but bought the chais for his cooperage business. The name of Château St Pierre Bontemps and the few vines that were left were bought by an entrepreneur, who very soon sold them to M. Sevaistre, thus reuniting the two properties, albeit diminished to some 25 hectares from the original 40.

M. Sevaistre sold the property to a family of Belgian négociants called Van Den Bussche, in whose hands it stayed until 1982, and it was from Mme. Castelein, *née* Van Den Bussche, that Henri Martin bought the vineyard and marque of Château St Pierre. Henri Martin was already proprietor of Château Gloria next door, which he had bought with 1 hectare of vines in 1940; in the ensuing 30 years he built it up by clever buying

and exchanging of parcels of vines from his friends and neighbours, to its present size of 44 hectares, where he makes an extremely correct wine. It is interesting that amongst his purchases were 10 hectares that originally formed part of St Pierre-Bontemps, which he has kept as part of Château Gloria.

In 1981, Martin bought the château and park of Château St Pierre from a daughter of M. Kappelhoff and plans to construct a new chai and offices in the grounds; the chai and buildings of Gloria, originally part of St Pierre, are now too small for the modern scale of vinification, ageing and stocking.

It has been a lifetime ambition of M. Martin to own a Cru Classé, and this is the satisfactory end of St Pierre's story. There is, however, much to be done. Through the Van Den Bussche connection, the wine has had a good following in Belgium, Luxembourg and Holland, but its name and reputation have lost much ground in France, the United Kingdom and other important markets. The first aim and objective of Martin's son-in-law, M. Triaud, is to re-establish the wine of St Pierre to its proper level as a top 4th Growth; this he is achieving by concentrating on quality above all else; an astonishingly rigorous selection at the assemblage of the abundant 1982 vintage resulted in a very low yield – only 20 hectolitres per hectare – but the quality of the wine is there, and the price demanded has been justified. St Pierre is definitely on its way back to where it should be, first of the 4th Growths in the 1855 classification.

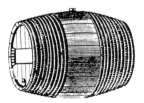

TECHNICAL INFORMATION

General

Appellation:	St Julien
Area under vines:	20 hectares
Average production:	9000 cases
Distribution of vines:	Grouped around centre of Beychevelle
Owner:	Domaines Henri Martin
Director:	M. Triaud
Régisseur:	M. Audron
Maître de Chai:	M. Galley-Bardier

Viticulture

Geology:	Gravel, subsoil of sandy clay
Grape varieties:	70% Cabernet Sauvignon, 25% Merlot, 5% Cabernet Franc
Pruning:	Guyot Double
Rootstock:	Riparia, 101-14
Vines per hectare:	10,000
Yield per hectare:	40 hectolitres
Replanting:	73 ares in 1982

Vinification

Length of maceration:	1 month
Temperature of fermentation:	29°C, finishing at 32°C
Control of temperature:	Automatic water-cooling
Type of vat:	Enamelled steel
Vin de presse:	Incorporated according to vintage to a maximum of 4%
Age of casks:	New for 50% of the crop, the rest in wooden vats
Time in cask:	18–20 months, according to vintage
Fining:	Fresh egg-whites
Filtration:	Very light filtration before bottling

Commercial

Vente Directe:	Yes, to private customers
General Sales:	Through the Bordeaux négociants.
Visits:	Yes; for appointment, telephone: 56 59 08 18 Hours: Monday to Friday 0800–1200, 1400–1800

TASTING AT CHATEAU ST PIERRE,
14 January 1985
J.S., M. Triaud

(The temperature outside was −15°C, and the wines were almost too cold to taste properly.)

1983 Deep, intense red. Nose already good, in spite of youth and cold! Elegant, rounded. Has the elements of a classic Bordeaux vin de garde.

1982 Colour even denser and darker than 1983. Nose not giving very much, but some fruit coming through. Excellent fruit and well-balanced. Seemed less open and fat than many 1982s, but this could be due to the very low temperature, which tends to emphasise the tannins in a wine.

(M. Triaud, in a letter of March 1985, confirms that the cold was responsible, and that the '82 stands comparison with any of its contemporaries.)

CHATEAU
Talbot
ST JULIEN

As you enter the village of St Julien on the D2 from the south, turn left towards St Laurent, opposite the buildings of Château Léoville-Las-Cases, on the D101e. Soon after leaving the village, you will see a road through the vines pointing to Château Talbot, on your right.

The estate is named after the English General Talbot, who commanded the army in the fateful battle of Castillon in 1453, when England finally relinquished her rule of Aquitaine. Whether or not Talbot ever actually owned the property is open to question, but for English claret-lovers it is nice to think so. There is a popular and also probably apocryphal story that Talbot buried a vast treasure on the estate before leaving for battle. Despite several excavations permitted by the present owner, Jean Cordier, nothing has been found so far, except a collapsed secret passage. The idea is a romantic one, not unlike the story of King John's baggage lost in the Wash, and it will doubtless die hard.

The high repute of Talbot dates from the early

19th century, when it came in to the ownership of the Marquis d'Aux de Lescaut, from the Armagnac area, who is known to have been a devoted and successful winemaker. Tastet-Lawton have a note in their journals of 1815, testifying to the finesse and cleanliness of the wines of Talbot. The d'Aux family owned the property until 1899, when it was sold to a M. and Mme. Claverie; they, in turn, sold to the present owner's father, Georges Cordier, in 1918.

Jean Cordier lives at Château Talbot, like his father before him. He is the owner of nine wine properties in the Bordeaux region, as well as vineyards in other parts of France. He is assisted, especially in the field of public relations, by his daughter Nancy.

There is a white wine, Caillou Blanc, made at Talbot, one of only four white wines produced in the Médoc. It owes its birth to Georges Cordier, who planted a small area of Sauvignon grapes in the 1930s to make a white wine for his private consumption. After the war it was decided to increase the production of this clean, crisp Sauvignon, and commercialise it. It has been most successful, and now demand exceeds supply; there are now six hectares under 100% Sauvignon grapes, producing some 32,000 bottles of Caillou Blanc each year.

The Grand Vin of Château Talbot, classified as a Fourth Growth, and, in my opinion, frequently surpassing that level, comes from one of the largest vineyards of the Médoc. Vinification takes place in glass-lined vats in the hospital-clean cuvier – this cleanliness is a feature of all Cordier-run properties – and ageing is traditionally in oak casks, of which one third are new each vintage. The wine of Talbot is always thoroughly good, and, again my own judgment, sometimes, as with the 1980, better than big brother Gruaud-Larose across the vineyard! There is certainly an atmosphere of friendly rivalry between the two properties, which only serves to keep both on their toes.

TECHNICAL INFORMATION

General

Appellation:	St Julien
Area under vines:	Red 87 hectares
	white 6 hectares
Average production:	40,000 cases
Distribution of vines:	All in one piece around the château
Owner:	M. Jean Cordier
Director:	M. Georges Pauli
Régisseur:	M. Jean-Marie Bouin
Maître de Chai:	M. Serge Potier
Oenologist:	M. Georges Pauli

Viticulture

Geology:	Large plateau of quaternian silico-gravel, sloping gently to the west.
Grape varieties:	*Red* 70% Cabernet Sauvignon, 5% Cabernet Franc, 20% Merlot, 5% Petit Verdot
	White 100% Sauvignon
Pruning:	Guyot Double Médocaine
Rootstock:	Riparia 3309, SO4, 5BB, 101.14
Vines per hectare:	10,000
Yield per hectare:	Average 45 hectolitres
Replanting:	2 hectares per annum

Vinification

Added yeasts:	No
Length of maceration:	18–20 days average
Temperature of fermentation:	30°C max.
Control of fermentation:	By serpentine cooler
Type of vat:	Glass-lined steel
Vin de presse:	8–10% incorporated
Age of casks:	⅓ new each year
Time in cask:	18–20 months
Fining:	Fresh egg-whites
Filtration:	Light, sur plaque, before bottling
Type of bottle:	Bordelaise lourde, before 1979 special Epoque-Cordier bottle

Commercial

Vente Directe:	No
Exclusivity:	Yes, Ets Cordier, 7/13 Quai de Paludate, 33000 Bordeaux
Agents overseas:	Yes, for information, contact Ets. Cordier
Visits:	Yes, by appointment Telephone: 56 92 70 00

THE TASTING AT CHATEAU TALBOT,
1 February 1985
J.S., Christian Seely, Serge Potier, Daniel Vergely.

1983 Good, deep blackish colour. Nose good and open, strong cassis. Powerful and mouthfilling, soft tannins, has charm and suppleness of St Julien.

1982 Very dark, blue-black. Lovely nose of blackcurrant. Very ripe, round and full of flavour and softish tannins; has elegance and finesse, with lots of hidden power.

1981 Good colour, shades lighter than 1982. Nose more delicate than 1982, but lovely. Surprisingly approachable already, has great femininity and breeding. Will be lovely.

1980 Excellent deep red for this light vintage. Beautiful bouquet, open and lots of good cassis. Very good – one of the best 1980s I have tasted, with fruit and backbone and length. Will stay quite a while.

1979 Good medium dark colour. Nose has some delicacy and character. Rounded and elegant, with some skeleton and not a little flesh, quite voluptuous in fact. I was seduced.

1978 Lighter colour than 1979. Bouquet complex, and delightful, evolving beautifully. Powerful wine, with attractive, complex flavour, still has some way to go, and will be excellent.

PAUILLAC

Pauillac is the commune in which lie three of the most renowned wine properties in the world, Lafite-Rothschild, Latour and Mouton-Rothschild. Some 1,000 hectares may carry the magic Pauillac appellation, from Château Latour in the south to Château Lafite-Rothschild on the northern border. Between these two crowned heads, clustered around the harbour town of Pauillac and its satellite villages, to the east and west of the D2, lie the sixteen other members of the royal family of Pauillac. Their grouping within the classification of 1855 is the most uneven of the four great communes of the Médoc, with three Premiers Crus, two Seconds, not a single Third, only one Fourth and no less than a dozen Fifths. It is perhaps in Pauillac that the need for an updating of the classification is most evident; within the twelve Fifth Growths there are several properties that consistently produce wines of a quality and price more on a par with the Fourth, Third and even Second Growths of neighbouring communes. Only in Pauillac has there been an official change in the old order, when Château Mouton-Rothschild, after a long campaign waged by Baron Philippe de Rothschild, was rightly elevated in 1973 from Second to First Growth status.

In the past the little township of Pauillac enjoyed considerable prosperity as a port, but now that the huge traffic in wine goes through the international port of Bordeaux itself, the only ships that call are the tankers discharging at the huge Shell refinery and the countless pleasure-craft that use the new marina. It is hard to imagine how the hideous and foul-smelling refinery was ever allowed to be sited in this most precious piece of wine land, and it is only due to ceaseless campaigning at the highest levels by Philippe de Rothschild that the complex is not even larger than it is today.

The wines of Pauillac are bigger and more full-bodied than those of Margaux and St Julien, and slightly less robust then the 'blackstrapping' wines of St Estèphe to the north. There is great variation in style within the appellation, ranging from the towering, masculine strength of Latour to the aristocratic femininity and finesse of Lafite; for my personal taste it is the wine of Pauillac that epitomises all that is best in red Bordeaux, combining suppleness, elegance, backbone and an

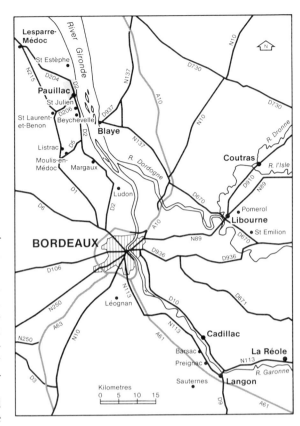

astonishing longevity.

Nowhere in the Médoc is the absence of good restaurants more sharply accentuated than here in Pauillac; surrounded by the world's greatest vineyards, the town does not even rate an entry in the *Guide Michelin*. I have often commented on this curious anomaly to the Bordelais, and their answer is usually that all the entertaining is done in the châteaux themselves. This may well be the case, but for six or seven months of the year the Médoc is the Mecca for hundreds of thousands of vinous pilgrims, who do not have the good fortune to be invited to the tables of the proprietors. When will some enterprising restaurateur heed the gastric rumblings from the Médoc and open an establishment worthy of the area? Such an undertaking would surely be to the mutual benefit of *patron* and diner alike.

92

CHATEAU

Batailley

PAUILLAC

Take the main Pauillac – St Laurent road, the D1e, and you will find Château Batailley and its buildings on your left-hand side, 1½ km out of Pauillac, just across the level-crossing.

Batailley, as one might imagine, probably owes its name to a battle, alleged to have been fought here when du Guesclin was busy mopping up the fleeing remnants of the English, defeated at Castillon in 1453.

Records exist from the late 18th century, when it was owned by three people named Saint Martin, two sisters and a brother; it appears that their vocation was spiritual rather than vinous, since one of the sisters was a nun and the brother was a priest. Such holiness, however, did not stand in the way of the two sisters, who sold their portion to a Bordeaux wine-merchant named Pécholier in 1791 for a tidy lump sum, linked with an annuity for the nun!

Batailley came into the capable and powerful hands of the négociant Daniel Guestier in 1819, who bought it from Admiral Bedout, son-in-law of Pécholier and veteran of Chesapeake Bay. Guestier introduced modern methods to Batailley, improving production and quality, and did much to promote the name on the world wine market through his négociant firm, Barton and Guestier. On his death in 1847, Batailley was left to his three children; Pierre François received a half-share, while the other half passed to his two married sisters, Mesdames Phélan and Lawton. In 1866, the distaff holding having been further watered down by passing to married daughters of the married daughters, the family decided to sell, and the purchaser was a Parisian banker named Halphen.

The Médoc tapestry is liberally sprinkled with bankers – Rothschilds at Mouton, Lafite and their subsidiary properties, the Achille Foulds at Beychevelle and, in the past, the Perreires at Palmer – and they all appeared at around this time. Problems both fiscal and viticultural besieged owners in the Médoc in the mid-1800s, and who was in a better position to benefit from this depression than the beleaguered clients' bankers? Although one's natural instinctive sympathies tend towards the troubled *ancien régime* proprietors, there is no doubt that this influx of new capital saved many a good vineyard from virtual annihilation.

The Halphen family owned Batailley for nearly 70 years until they sold the property to the Borie family in 1929. At the death of M. Marcel Borie, Batailley passed in to the ownership of Madame Casteja, *née* Borie. Her husband, Emile Casteja, head of the négociant house of Borie-Manoux, now runs Batailley, as well as Château Lynch-Moussas, another 5th Growth Pauillac, which he inherited from his father, and the wine of Batailley is commercialised exclusively by Borie-Manoux.

Batailley is one of the loveliest châteaux of the Médoc; built around the beginning of last century, the mellow sandstone house stands in a 6-hectare park, in which fine specimen trees have been planted by various owners. In late September the park is a carpet of cyclamens, the little pink and white flowers that locals call the vendangeurs, because they always appear at harvest time. The Castejas have a fine collection of furniture and porcelain, and yet the atmosphere is very much that of a loved and lived-in house.

The wine of Batailley leans towards the sterner style of Pauillac, and only mellows with the passage of time. A mature Batailley, such as the delicious 1964 I drank recently, is well worth the wait, while the 1961, also tasted last year, is still wonderfully concentrated and long, and could be kept for many years.

TECHNICAL INFORMATION

General

Appellation:	Pauillac
Area under vines:	50 hectares
Average production:	Variable, according to vintage
Distribution of vines:	In 2 parcels
Owner:	M. Emile Casteja
Maître de Chai:	M. H. Valade
Chef de Culture:	M. L. Servant
Consultant Oenologist:	M. Pascal Ribereau-Gayon

Viticulture

Geology:	Gravel
Grape varieties:	80% Cabernet Sauvignon, with a few Cabernet Franc, 20% Merlot
Pruning:	Médocaine
Rootstock:	101-14, 3309
Vines per hectare:	9,000 and 8,000
Yield per hectare:	Varies from vintage to vintage
Replanting:	Vines renewed as necessary

Vinification

Added yeasts:	No
Length of maceration:	15–20 days
Temperature of fermentation:	28–30°C
Control of fermentation:	Regulated by cooling system
Type of vat:	Steel and oak
Vin de presse:	Proportion of first pressing incorporated according to vintage
Age of casks:	⅓ new each vintage
Time in cask:	16–18 months
Fining:	Egg-white
Filtration:	None
Type of bottle:	Bordelaise

Commercial

Vente Directe:	Yes
Direct ordering from château:	Yes
Exclusivity:	Distribution by Borie-Manoux in Bordeaux
Visits:	Yes, for appointment telephone 56 59 01 13 Hours: 0800–1200, 1400–1800

THE TASTING AT CHATEAU BATAILLEY, 8 January 1985
J.S., Emile Casteja

1984 Good deep purple. Fine bouquet of blackcurrant and new wood. Fruit and new oak also plentiful on taste, should be very fair.

1983 Good depth of colour. Nose closed, but what's there is good. Very good blackcurrant fruit, but lots of tannin and oakiness. This will take a long time, but will be very well worth the wait.

1982 Superb, blackish colour. Bouquet very promising, but shy. Rounded and powerful, with a mass of fruit and good tannins; already quite approachable.

1981 Same lovely depth of colour. Good bouquet, but quite closed in. More elegance and femininity than the '82. Should make a lovely bottle in two or three years.

1980 A shade lighter than the '81. Nose open and easy. Very drinkable now, fruit and tannins in harmony. It will last a while.

1979 Very deep bluey red. Soft bouquet with lots of fruit. Big, rounded and powerful, with good keeping qualities.

1978 Good deep red. Nose of cassis quite well developed. Quite an open 1978, with good fruit but not particularly structured for a long evolution.

1977 Fine medium red for '77. Bouquet not very pronounced, but some fruit there. A lightish wine, very pleasing to drink now.

1976 Deep, brilliant red. Ripe but not overripe nose. A ripe, full wine with lots of fruit and staying power for some years yet. A good '76.

1975 Colour similar to '76. Bouquet quite complex, good but still shut in. Concentrated complexity of fruit and good tannins; has charm, fruit and length. Just beginning to come together.

1974 Fairly light colour, but not much brown. Good bouquet. Surprisingly good mouthful of wine, harmonious and ripe. Ready and should be drunk now. A success for a poor year.

94

CHATEAU
Clerc-Milon
PAUILLAC

The vineyards of Château Clerc-Milon are grouped around the small village of Mousset, on the right of the D2, more or less opposite Château Lafite.

The name of Château Clerc-Milon derives from Monsieur Clerc, who was the owner in the middle of last century, and Milon, a small hamlet on the banks of the Jalle de Breuil to the north of the property. In Cocks and Feret's first *Bordeaux et Ses Vins* it is listed simply as Château Clerc, but in the 1855 classification, when it was placed among the 5th Growths, the name appears in full. There was one more change of name when the owner at the beginning of this century, a notary named Mondon, added his name to that of Clerc-Milon;

though I have never seen a bottle labelled Château-Clerc-Milon-Mondon, I am told they still exist.

In 1970 Baron Philippe de Rothschild, recognising the fine quality of the soil and aspect of the vineyard, bought the property from M. Mondon's granddaughters, Mlle. Vialard and Mme. Louis Hedon. His instincts were certainly right, but he was presented with a formidable exercise when it came to reconstituting the vineyard. Over the years, Clerc-Milon had become dismembered, and the Baron's first objective was to bring it back into one; some plots were as small as a couple of rows of vines, and it can be imagined how the owners held out for high prices, especially bearing

95

in mind the identity of the new owner!

The vineyard has almost identical soil with that of Mouton-Rothschild, and is most favourably situated with the traditionally vital 'view of the river', and is very rarely affected by the dangerous spring frosts. Vinification and ageing is very similar to that of Mouton-Rothschild, save that only 20% new casks are used, and fermentation is in vats of lined steel.

The wine of Clerc-Milon has a dignity and reserved power that is typical of fine Pauillac, and I was pleased to have this impression confirmed by no less a pundit than the great Raoul Blondin of Mouton-Rothschild, who adjudges Latour, Clerc-Milon and Lynch-Bages to be the archetypal wines of the commune. Of the recent vintages of Clerc-Milon tasted at Mouton-Rothschild, the 1983 was perhaps the finest, with a lovely dense colour and enormous concentration of flavour and excellent tannin, perfectly structured to carry the wine through a long journey to maturity – in short a classic Médoc vin de garde.

TECHNICAL INFORMATION

General

Appellation:	Pauillac
Area under vines:	30 hectares
Average production:	8,000 cases
Distribution of vines:	In several parcels
Owner:	Baron Philippe de Rothschild G.F.A.
Maître de Chai:	M. Dupuy
Oenologist:	Company's own team

Viticulture

Geology:	Deep gravel, with clay/marl subsoil
Grape varieties:	85% Cabernet Sauvignon, 7% Cabernet Franc, 8% Merlot
Pruning:	Guyot Double
Rootstock:	Varied to suit soil
Vines per hectare:	8,000 to 10,000
Average yield per hectare:	35 hectolitres
Replanting:	By complantation

Vinification

Added yeasts:	No
Length of maceration:	3 weeks

Temperature of fermentation:	28–30°C
Control of fermentation:	Electronic, manual control
Type of vat:	Metal
Vin de presse:	Part incorporated, according to vintage
Age of casks:	20% new each vintage, rest in used Mouton casks
Time in cask:	22–24 months
Fining:	Fresh egg-whites
Filtration:	None
Type of bottle:	Bordelaise lourde

Commercial

Vente Directe:	No
Sales:	Through the Bordeaux négociants, as well as La Baronnie
Agents overseas:	Contact La Baronnie, B.P. 32, 33250 Pauillac for information
Visits:	Contact La Baronnie for appointment as above Telephone 56 59 20 20 Closed week-ends and August

THE TASTING AT CHATEAU MOUTON-ROTHSCHILD, 31 January 1985
J.S., Christian Seely, Raoul Blondin, M. Houben

1983 Excellent deep, dense red. Nose fine and quite closed up. Concentration of fruit flavours, tannins good, not harsh, has balance and structure to keep for a long time. A classic Pauillac for laying-down.

1981 Deep ruby colour. Elegant nose with good cassis. Again a beautifully structured wine with great charm and finesse, and a certain richness. Very long in the mouth, has enough backbone to make it last.

1979 Medium-dark colour. Good nose with plenty of ripe fruit. Has lots of 'puissance' with perhaps a shade less finesse and complexity than 1981 and 1982. Still needs a year or two. Will be good.

CHATEAU
Croizet-Bages
PAUILLAC

As you approach Pauillac from the south on the D2, Château Croizet-Bages is clearly signposted to the left halfway between the village of Saint-Lambert and the outskirts of Pauillac. It lies behind the little village of Bages.

The name derives from the Bages plateau on which the vineyard is happily sited, and two brothers called Croizet, who created the vineyard in the 18th century. They sold it in the early 1800s to a Monsieur le Puytarac, who in turn sold it on to Julien Calvé in 1853. Two years later it was classified among the ranks of the Fifth Great Growths of the Médoc.

In 1875 Julien Calvé had a house built, not at the property, but a kilometre distant, on the quay in Pauillac. It was this house that used to appear on the Croizet-Bages label, but it was sold away from the property many years ago, and in fact now serves as a youth centre. For this reason the label is now basically a typographical design, showing the medals that have been awarded to the wine; the silver and gold ones that were won at the Exposition Universelle de Paris in 1878 and 1889 respectively show us that Croizet-Bages did well under the Calvé family ownership.

The Calvés owned the property until 1930, when they sold it to a M. Monod, of American extraction, who brought the Klaxon company to France. He lasted until 1945, when the vineyard passed into the hands of Paul Quié, whose widow Lucienne and son Jean-Michel now own it, following Paul Quié's death in 1968. They are also owners of the 2nd Growth Rauzan-Gassies in Margaux, and Bel-Orme, Tronquoy de Lalande, a good Cru Bourgeois Haut-Médoc near Saint Seurin de Cadourne.

Although Château Croizet-Bages shares some of the best gravelly terroir of Pauillac, the Bages

97

plateau, with neighbours like Lynch-Bages, it has never, to my way of thinking, produced a typically Pauillac style of wine. This may be due to the encépagement, which is, for Pauillac, relatively low in Cabernet Sauvignon – only 40% – while there is a correspondingly high proportion of 25% Cabernet Franc and 35% Merlot. The wine during the '60s and '70s has certainly been more ready to give of its charms in its youth than most Pauillacs, and this is probably also due to the absence of new casks in the ageing process.

Severe losses due to the 1977 frosts have caused problems, and the 1978, especially, lacked the body and finesse that one normally associates with this vintage. However, I was much impressed by

the energy and dedication of Monsieur Quié, and he seems to be well in control of the situation. He is gradually increasing the amount of Cabernet Sauvignon as he replants, and the 1981 and, even more so, the 1982 are looking extremely good prospects.

Jean-Michel Quié is a friendly and likeable man, and we spent a most enjoyable and instructive afternoon tasting the wines of Croizet-Bages and Rauzan-Gassies at the latter property. He told me that the French commercialisation of all the Quié wines is handled from his Paris office through a network of 25 agents covering the country. He believes firmly in a healthy domestic market being the key to export, and the wines are sold overseas by the Bordeaux wine trade.

TECHNICAL INFORMATION

General

Appellation:	Pauillac
Area under vines:	Total 22 hectares; in production, 18 hectares
Average production:	8,000 cases
Distribution of vines:	One block
Owner:	Héritiers de Paul Quié
Director:	M. Jean-Michel Quié
Maître de Chai:	M. Ribeaux
Consultant Oenologist:	M. Boissenot

Viticulture

Geology:	Gravel plateau
Grape varieties:	40% Cabernet Sauvignon, 25% Cabernet Franc, 35% Merlot
Pruning:	Guyot Double
Rootstock:	S04, 420A, Riparia
Vines per hectare:	6,500/7,000
Replanting:	1.5 hectares per annum

Vinification

Added yeasts:	No

Length of maceration:	2–3 weeks
Temperature of fermentation:	30°C
Control of fermentation:	By heat-exchange pump
Type of vat:	Concrete
Vin de presse:	Part incorporated, according to requirements of each vintage
Age of casks:	2 years
Time in cask:	About 18 months
Fining:	Powdered egg white, in vat
Filtration:	Sur plaque before bottling
Type of bottle:	Bordelaise lourde

Commercial

Vente Directe:	Yes, to private customers
Commercialisation in France:	Handled by own office in Paris: telephone 1 368 08 41
Export sales:	Through Bordeaux négociants
Visits:	Yes, for appointment, telephone 56 59 01 62

THE TASTING AT CHATEAU RAUZAN-GASSIES, 16 January 1985
J.S., Jean-Michel Quié, M. Espagnet

1982 (Bottled Sept. '84.) Dense, dark colour. Powerful bouquet. A very big wine with lots of fruit and good tannins. Will be a fine Pauillac, and will need a long time in bottle.

1981 Dark bluey colour. This bottle had just a hint of corkiness about it, which was a pity, because overall the wine was well-structured with good balance, and this vintage will be a success for Croizet-Bages.

1979 Good, deep red. Good nose of blackcurrant. Big,

generous wine, honest with no great complexity.

1978 Lightish, clear scarlet. Nose very open and evolved for 1978. Sweet and rounded, lacking a bit in body and finesse. Shortish, but good now.

1976 Dense, deep red. Quite closed bouquet, atypical of '76, but, with aeration, coming out well. Taste good, full and ripe with plenty of life.

1973 Light colour, with an open, ripe bouquet. Light, clean and correct, with taste of strawberries. Not at all tired, as many '73s are. Delicate wine, perfect now.

1971 Palish colour. Good evolved nose. No great complication here, straightforward, ripe wine, ready for drinking, with good fruit and medium length.

Duhart-Milon-Rothschild

The vineyard of Duhart-Milon is to the west of those of Châteaux Mouton-Baronne-Philippe, Mouton-Rothschild and Lafite-Rothschild, but the chais and cuvier are located in the centre of the town of Pauillac itself.

At the end of the 18th century, Duhart-Milon belonged to a gentleman by the name of Manda-vid, and it is interesting to speculate on the possible connection between this family and the hugely successful Robert Mondavi of California. For over a hundred years the Castejas owned this, the only Fourth Growth in Pauillac; it is their name which appears as proprietors in the 1855 classification, and it was from them that the Rothschilds acquired it in 1962. Prior to 1855, the wine of Duhart-Milon enjoyed similar price and status, as is borne out by the records of the firm of Tastet-Lawton as early as 1815.

There is not now, nor ever has been, an actual château on the property, although the Casteja family used to own a house on the quays in Pauillac, which was sold just after the Second World War. The elegant building shown on the Lafite-style label therefore owes its provenance more to the artist's imagination than to reality.

On their acquisition of the property in 1962, the new owners had much to do before they were happy to add the magic Rothschild name to that of Duhart-Milon. There were only 16 hectares in production, and an extensive drainage programme necessitated an almost total replanting of the vineyard. The chais and cuvier were in a very sorry state, and it was not until 1974 that the present immaculate new buildings were brought in to use.

The wine of Château Duhart-Milon-Rothschild is one more illustration of how different the produce of two neighbouring vineyards can be with

virtually the same encépagement and the same vinification, under the same management. It is probably the minuscule differences in soil, subsoil and microclimate that make the wines of Duhart-Milon harder, more tannic and less refined than those of Lafite. A combination of severe pruning and even severer selection at the time of assemblage produces a wine that is classically Médocain in style, deep-coloured and closed in infancy, in spite of the comparative youth of the vineyard, developing slowly with finesse and supple elegance as it approaches maturity. In recent years the proportion of Merlot has been increased to tone down the toughness of the wine in some measure.

TECHNICAL INFORMATION

General

Appellation:	Pauillac
Area under vines:	45 hectares
Average production:	2,000 to 2,500 cases
Distribution of vines:	In 1 block, on the Carruades plateau
Owner:	Société de Gestion des Domaines Barons de Rothschild
Régisseur:	M. Gilbert Rokvam
Maître de Chai:	M. Francis Huguet
Consultant Oenologist:	Professor Emile Peynaud

Viticulture

Geology:	Deep gravel, some clay skimmings
Grape varieties:	70% Cabernet Sauvignon, 10% Cabernet Franc, 20% Merlot
Pruning:	Guyot Double
Rootstock:	Riparia
Vines per hectare:	8,500
Average yield per hectare:	30–50 hectolitres
Replanting:	Average vine age of 40 years, sometimes longer if the condition of the vine allows it

Vinification

Added yeasts:	No
Length of maceration:	Varied according to vintage, 12–21 days
Temperature of fermentation:	26–30°C
Control of fermentation:	Tubular exchange apparatus
Type of vat:	Stainless steel
Vin de presse:	Incorporated according to vintage
Age of casks:	⅓ new each vintage, ⅔ one or two vintages
Time in cask:	18–24 months
Fining:	Yes
Filtration:	No
Type of bottle:	Bordelaise

Commercial

Vente Directe:	No
Sales:	Through the Bordeaux négociants

THE TASTING AT THE CHAIS OF CHATEAU DUHART-MILON-ROTHSCHILD, 22 January 1985
J.S., Christian Seely, M. Guy Schÿler, M. Gilbert Rokvam, M. Francis Huguet

1983 Deep, almost black colour. Nose good, with fruit and new wood. Big and powerful, with lots of fruit and hard tannin. A wine to wait a long time for.

1982 Same dark colour. Nose quite closed, but elegant. More rounded and fruity than the '83, with less dominant tannin and more finesse.

1981 Lovely, bright medium-red. Again elegant, but shy on the nose. Structured wine, well balanced, with good fruit and classic Pauillac breeding. Will be a good bottle in 2–3 years.

1980 Deep colour for the vintage. Bouquet open and attractive. Perfumed and aromatic in the mouth, though shortish with a dry finish.

1979 Very dark red. Powerful blackcurrant bouquet. Big, mouthfilling wine with good balance, lots of fruit and good tannin; wait a year or two and this will be a very nice bottle.

1978 Colour very similar to '79. Nose fuller and softer. Supple and ripe, with good complexity of flavours, and quite a long aftertaste.

1977 Bright scarlet. Bouquet attractive with nice fruit. Good fruit on the palate, with more body than many '77s, but finishes a bit thin and dry.

1975 Medium garnet colour. Good open nose. Well-made, harmonious and long, quite approachable for 1975.

CHATEAU
Grand-Puy-Ducasse
PAUILLAC

The château of Grand-Puy-Ducasse is in the heart of the town of Pauillac, halfway along the quay facing the Gironde river.

The early origins of Château Grand-Puy-Ducasse are somewhat obscure. It certainly formed part of a much larger estate, the Domaine de Grand Puy, which was split in two in the 17th century by the then owner, Monsieur Déjean; he had a son, Bertrand Déjean, and a daughter who married a gentleman called de Cormière, the former inheriting what is now Grand-Puy-Lacoste, the latter Grand-Puy-Ducasse. The de Cormières sold their portion to a M. Ducasse; his name, however, was not to be attached to that of the property for a long time, since it was designated in the 1855 classification as Château Artigues-Arnaud. Part of the present vineyard is near the village of Artigues, and the name of Château Artigues-Arnaud is still used for the second wine of Grand-Puy-Ducasse.

From Ducasse, the estate passed by inheritance in to the Duroy family, owners of the noble Château Suduiraut in Sauternes, who were listed as owners in 1855 when it was classified a 5th Growth.

Coincidentally the Duroy family later became owners of Château Grand-Puy-Lacoste with the Lacoste family, thus for a period reuniting the two properties.

Prior to the purchase in 1971 of Grand-Puy-Ducasse by the Bordeaux company of Mestrezat-Preller, the wine of this 5th Growth had passed through a period of relative obscurity. Since 1971, however, the area under vines has been enlarged, and a magnificent array of stainless-steel vats and other modern vinification equipment have been installed; a significant proportion of new oak casks is purchased for each vintage and Grand-Puy-Ducasse is now back on the map.

The owning company is also sole proprietor of Château Rayne-Vigneau in Sauternes, four other growths in the Médoc, and Château Tourteau-Chollet in the Graves, which produces both red and white wine. The seven properties boast a total of 335 hectares under vines. The Président-Directeur Général of Mestrezat SA is Jean-Pierre Angli-viel de La Beaumelle, a direct descendant of the Mestrezat from Switzerland, who formed the

company in 1814. He is responsible for the administration of all the wine properties whose entire production is sold exclusively by his company with the exception of Rayne-Vigneau and Grand-Puy-Ducasse, of which a proportion is offered on the Bordeaux marketplace.

Until quite recently the actual château of Grand-Puy-Ducasse served as the Maison du Vin in Pauillac, and also as the headquarters of the Commanderie du Bontemps des Graves et du Médoc. The pretty 18th-century house, with its courtyard flanked by staff houses and winemaking buildings, has now come back into the hands of the present owners, and they have great plans for its restoration and refurbishment. Behind the château there is a large area where further building work and landscaping is to take place.

The vineyard of Grand-Puy-Ducasse is spread widely over the Pauillac appellation. Basically it is split into three parcels; the most northerly is right nextdoor to Château Pontet-Canet, the central and smallest parcel is between Château Lynch-Bages and Grand-Puy-Lacoste, while the third and most southerly part borders on Château Batailley and Lynch-Moussas. It is interesting to note once again the validity of the 1855 classification; all the neighbouring vineyards of these three plots also belong in the ranks of the 5th Growths. The wine of Grand-Puy-Ducasse is typically Pauillac; slow to give off its charms when young, with a power and degree of finesse which evolve slowly to produce an elegant and well-structured wine in due course.

TECHNICAL INFORMATION

General

Appellation:	Pauillac
Area under vines:	35 hectares
Owner:	Société Civile de Grand-Puy-Ducasse (Parent Co: Mestrezat SA)
Average production:	17,500 cases
Distribution of vines:	3 parcels (see text)
Director:	M. J.-P. Angliviel de La Beaumelle
Régisseur:	M. Patrice Bandiera
Maître de Chai:	M. Michel Fontagnères
Consultant Oenologist:	M. Bernard Monteau

Viticulture

Geology:	70% gravel, 30% sandy gravel
Grape varieties:	70% Cabernet Sauvignon, 30% Merlot, and a very little Petit Verdot
Pruning:	Guyot Double
Rootstock:	Riparia Gloire, 101.14, 3309
Vines per hectare:	10,000
Yield per hectare:	About 45 hectolitres
Replanting:	As necessary. Average age of vines: $\frac{2}{3}$ 30 years, $\frac{1}{3}$ 10 years

Vinification

Added yeasts:	No
Length of maceration:	21 days average
Temperature of fermentation:	30–32°C
Control of fermentation:	Cold water circulation, and thermostatic control of cuvier
Type of vat:	Stainless steel
Vin de presse:	Incorporated totally or partly, after 12 months in cask
Age of casks:	One to three years
Time in cask:	15–18 months
Fining:	Albumen of egg in cuve
Filtration:	Sur plaque before bottling
Type of bottle:	Bordelaise lourde

Commercial

Vente Directe:	Yes
Sales:	Through Mestrezat-Preller, 17 Cours dela Martinique, B.P. 90, 33027 Bordeaux Cedex, and on the Bordeaux market
Visits:	By appointment: telephone 56 52 11 46

THE TASTING AT CHATEAU GRAND-PUY-DUCASSE, 21 January 1985
J.S., Jean-Pierre Angliviel de La Beaumelle

1983 Deep blackish colour. Nose good, but closed. Big, tannic, lots of fruit. A wine to wait a long time for.

1982 (Not yet bottled.) Dark, dense colour. Nose rich and full of fruit. Rounder and fatter than '83, with masses of fruit and tannin. More aggressive than many 1982s.

CHATEAU

Grand-Puy-Lacoste

PAUILLAC

Take the main D1e road from Pauillac in the direction of Saint Laurent, and Château Grand-Puy-Lacoste is the first château you come to on your right: it is clearly marked.

The first recorded owner of the Grand Puy estate was a Monsieur de Guiraud, who was the lord of the manor at the end of the 15th century. His is the first of two Sauternais names to be associated with Grand Puy, the other being Duroy de Suduiraut, the family who owned the Ducasse part of the property in the late 19th and early 20th century. De Guiraud's daughter married a M. de Jehan, whose son Bertrand de Jehan had two daughters; it was on his death that Grand Puy was split into

the two parts that are now known as Grand-Puy-Lacoste and Grand-Puy-Ducasse.

Another peculiarity of the history of Grand-Puy in general, and the Lacoste part in particular, is the extraordinary number of times it has passed through the female line. Lacoste passed from de Jehan's oldest daughter, who married a M. d'Issac, to her daughter whose husband's name was Saint-Guirons (which still appears on today's label) to her youngest daughter who married the M. Lacoste whose name the property now bears. François Lacoste was one of the few owners who managed to leave a son, Frédéric, in charge, but he again had only a daughter, Madame la Comtesse

103

de Saint-Léger. The property then passed into the ownership of two men, MM. Hériveau and Néel, who sold Grand-Puy-Lacoste in 1932 to Raymond Dupin.

Dupin was, by all accounts, a splendid and slightly eccentric character. He was a great gourmet, and very rich, owning large areas of forest in the Landes. He never lived in the château, preferring cosier quarters in Bordeaux. Though comfortably placed, while never allowing the quality of the Grand-Puy-Lacoste wine to fall off, yet he was reluctant to spend money on the property. Many of his friends, who all speak of him with great affection, have told me of gargantuan and delicious meals shared with him in crumbling, sparsely-furnished surroundings. The pennies may have been pinched on decor and maintenance, but apparently never on food or wine. Jacques Marly of Malartic-Lagravière and Jean-Eugène Borie both have fond memories of his unbelievable collection of old and rare vintages of all the best châteaux, which he would open at the drop of a hat. The only trouble was that he had the greatest difficulty laying his hand on any particular bottle; it seems that open cases and old bottles,

some from the last century, just lay about all over the place in wild profusion. To dine with Raymond Dupin was an experience to remember, especially if one was lucky enough to be served with 'Agneau de Pauillac'; Dupin was the only man in Pauillac to own a flock of sheep, and exceedingly proud of the fact.

In 1978 Raymond Dupin did a deal with Jean-Eugène Borie, who bought 50% of the shares in Grand-Puy-Lacoste and took over the management of the property; the balance of the shares were bought by Borie before Raymond Dupin's death in 1980. The château is now under the very able direction of François-Xavier Borie, who, with his attractive wife Marie-Hélène, lives in the skilfully converted cooperage at the back of the old château. Grand-Puy-Lacoste is a typical imposing Médoc château, built by Frédéric Lacoste around the time of the 1855 classification. It is empty, and somewhat derelict, but no doubt the Bories will in due course restore it to its original splendour. Their first priority has been the wine, and the vineyard has received much attention since 1975; so also has the vathouse, the original wooden vats having been replaced with an impressive array of dark red enamelled-steel cuves.

As I have already said, the wine of Château Grand-Puy-Lacoste did not suffer in terms of quality under Dupin's ownership, but the actual area under vines sank as low as 25 hectares in the mid-1960s. There are now 45 hectares in production and François-Xavier Borie strives constantly and successfully in pursuit of excellence; the quality of the wine goes from peak to peak, and it is now one of the hottest properties on the international claret market, commanding prices equal to some Second Growths. It is always full and well-structured, developing a smooth, elegant texture as it ripens and matures. The fine, typically Pauillac style of Grand-Puy-Lacoste comes from the usual combination of natural and human factors – the deep gravel and favourable aspect of the Bages plateau on the one hand, and, on the other, the care and attention of the owners and their team. The young cellar-master, Philippe Gouze, learnt his skills under Raoul Blondin of Mouton-Rothschild; Monsieur Blondin speaks well of him, and there can be no higher recommendation than this.

As a result of the continuing search for quality, the selection at Grand-Puy-Lacoste is especially rigorous; this is a happy circumstance for wine lovers, since all wine that is less than perfect is marketed as a 2ème vin under the label of Lacoste-Borie. It is always of outstanding quality, and sells at a reasonable price.

TECHNICAL INFORMATION

General

Appellation:	Pauillac
Area under vines:	45 hectares
Average production:	8,000–16,000 cases
Distribution of vines:	In one piece around the château
Owner:	Société du Château Grand-Puy-Lacoste
Director:	M. F-Xavier Borie
Régisseur:	M. Roland Seriat
Maître de Chai:	M. Philippe Gouze
Consultant Oenologist:	Professor Emile Peynaud

Viticulture

Geology:	Deep gravel
Grape varieties:	75% Cabernet Sauvignon, 25% Merlot
Pruning:	Médocaine
Rootstock:	Varied according to soil type
Vines per hectare:	7,500–10,000
Average yield per hectare:	35–45 hectolitres
Replanting:	¾ hectare per annum

Vinification

Added yeasts:	No
Length of maceration:	Varied according to vintage, generally long
Temperature of fermentation:	30°C
Control of fermentation:	Running water on exterior of vats
Type of vat:	Enamelled steel
Vin de presse:	Part incorporated according to vintage
Age of casks:	⅓ new each vintage
Time in cask:	18–20 months
Fining:	Egg whites
Filtration:	None
Type of bottle:	Bordelaise lourde

Commercial

Vente Directe:	No
Sales:	Through the Bordeaux négociants
Visits:	Yes, by appointment Telephone 56 59 05 20

THE TASTING AT CHATEAU GRAND-PUY-LACOSTE, 30 January 1985
J.S., Christian Seely, M. François-Xavier Borie, M. Philippe Gouze

1983 Very good blackish colour. Nose good, with cassis fruit. Big, tannic wine with lots of 'puissance' and skeleton. One to put away for a long time.

1982 Colour almost black. Nose good, but not giving off much at the moment. At first a bit closed in the mouth, but huge, concentrated flavour begins to develop; enormous wine with a mass of good fruit and muted tannins. Aftertaste beautiful and very long. I wish I had some in my cellar.

1981 Colour again very dark. Lovely, fine bouquet. Superb and stylish, with complex, elegant flavour, finesse and power. Will be a lovely bottle.

1980 Good, medium-dark colour. Attractive, soft nose with some blackcurrant. A very well structured 1980, with fruit and backbone to keep it going for some time.

1979 Deep plummy red. Ripe, lovely scent. Good, powerful wine, evolving well, with lots of aromatic flavour. Very long, with good tannins and some keeping quality. One of the nicest 1979s I have tasted.

At lunch at Grand-Puy-Lacoste, where we were joined by François-Xavier's wife Marie-Hélène, and his father, Jean-Eugène, from Ducru-Beaucaillou.

1978 Fine medium-dark red. Nose ripe and rounded. Well balanced wine with some complexity and lots of finesse. Needs a couple more years, and will be excellent.

1970 Good, dense colour, just beginning to brown. Full, mature bouquet. Aromatic, still concentrated flavour, with good length. Ready now, but will stay a while.

1955 Colour still amazingly good and deep, browning a bit. Nose round, ripe and flowery. Good concentration of summery fruitiness, tannins still present, only just starting to fade. A lovely mature claret.

105

CHATEAU
Haut-Bages-Libéral
PAUILLAC

As you drive on the D2 from St Julien to Pauillac, pass between the two Pichons, Longueville-Baron and Longueville-Lalande, past the goods entrance to Château Latour, and the driveway to Château Haut-Bages-Libéral is shortly after this on your right. From the road you can see the name in faded black lettering on the side of the buildings.

At the time of the 1855 classification this property belonged to M. Libéral, whose family had been 'courtiers' in the area since 1736. Over the years they had acquired some of the best Pauillac land in and around St Lambert, which was the site of Pauillac's oldest church, dating back to the 11th century. The derivation of the name Haut-Bages is slightly curious, since less than half of the vineyard is on the Bages plateau, the greater part being around the house and cellars, between the D2 and the river; this part of the vineyard is mainly bordered by the vineyard of Château Latour, though it is on a slightly lower 'croupe' of considerably poorer gravel.

During the first part of this century, Haut-Bages-Libéral has suffered a period of relative obscurity, but a large resurrection programme was instigated when the Cruse family acquired it under a company name in 1960. They started replanting the vineyard, and installed a very modern cuvier of ten 150-hectolitre stainless-steel vats, and three smaller ones, all with thermostatic temperature controls. There are also two vast tanks for the assemblage, which are used at bottling time as well. The work on the vathouse was carried out in 1973, the year that Château Pontet-Canet passed out of the Cruse ownership, and until that time the wine was vinified at Pontet-Canet.

In November 1983 the property was acquired by a consortium, which includes the Parisbas bank, and the successful Bernard Taillan group, whose brand leader is the table wine Chantovent. The Taillan company is headed by Jacques Merlaut, who took over the Ginestet wine business in the

106

late seventies; it is his very able daughter, Mme. Bernadette Villars, who runs the affairs of the château, together with the excellent Château Chasse-Spleen, in which the family also has a major holding, as well as Château La Gurgue, a Margaux Cru Bourgeois.

I have always found the wine of Haut-Bages-Libéral to be almost uncompromisingly hard, even after several years bottle age, and this was borne out by the tasting of the last five vintages I was given at Chasse-Spleen. Changes are afoot, however, and there is certainly a very able team running the properties. I detected a definite change in style in the 1983 vintage, already showing signs of dropping its guard and becoming quite soft and approachable.

TECHNICAL INFORMATION

General

Appellation:	Pauillac
Area under vines:	23 hectares
Average production:	9,000–10,000 cases
Distribution of vines:	12 hectares on gravel 'croupe' around château, 11 hectares across D2 on Bages plateau
Owner:	Société Fermière du Château Haut-Bages-Libéral
Director:	Mme. Bernadette Villars
Régisseur and Technical Director:	Mr. Michael Conroy
Maître de Chai and Chef d'Exploitation:	M. Jean Lafforgue
Consultant Oenologist:	Laboratoire de Pauillac

Viticulture

Geology:	60% gravel on clay/chalk, with some loamy clay by the river
Grape varieties:	80% Cabernet Sauvignon, 15% Merlot, 5% Petit Verdot
Pruning:	Guyot Double
Rootstock:	101.14, 3309, S04
Vines per hectare:	9,000–10,000
Yield per hectare:	40 hectolitres average
Replanting:	As necessary to maintain average vine age of 35 years – roughly 3–5% per year

Vinification

Added yeasts:	No
Length of maceration:	21–24 days
Temperature of fermentation:	28–30°C
Control of fermentation:	Running water on exterior of vats
Type of vat:	Stainless steel, 10 of 150 hectolitres, and 3 of 75 hectolitres capacity
Vin de presse:	From 5% to 8% of first pressing included, according to vintage
Age of casks:	Under new management from 30% to 45% are new each vintage
Time in cask:	18–20 months
Fining:	Egg albumen
Filtration:	Light sur plaque before bottling
Type of bottle:	Bordelaise lourde

Commercial

Vente Directe:	Yes
General Sales:	Wide distribution through the Bordeaux négociants
Visits:	Yes, by appointment Telephone: 56 58 17 54

THE TASTING AT CHATEAU CHASSE-SPLEEN, 31 January 1985
J.S., Christian Seely, Michael Conroy

1983 Blue-black colour. Nose hard, quite peppery. Good fruit and soft tannins, surprisingly accessible. Long aftertaste. Will develop fairly quickly.

1982 (Bottled July 1984.) Very dark, almost black. Nose closed, but lots of fat fruit beginning to come through. Huge, blackstrapping mouthful of fruit and tannin, lots of backbone. Will be a really fine bottle, but needs time.

1981 Deep bluey red. Nose quite closed, but some good fruit there. Fairly rounded, but still has a lot of tannin. Tough, but has finesse and structure at back. Will be OK.

1980 Colour lighter, but deep for this vintage. Nose quite open with honest fruit aroma. More approachable than all the other vintages, but still tough, with a metallic edge to it. Could soften out in a year or so.

1979 Deep, dense blue-black colour. Powerful bouquet of blackcurrant. Big, with lots of fruit, but hard and tannic. Not ready to drink yet.

CHATEAU
Haut-Batailley
PAUILLAC

There is no château at Haut-Batailley, but the vineyard is to be found on the left of the D1e from Pauillac to St Laurent, about 2 km out of Pauillac. It is situated on both sides of the railway line.

Before 1942 Batailley and Haut-Batailley were one property, and, since I have dealt with the history of Batailley in an earlier chapter, I will confine my treatment of Haut-Batailley to the last forty-odd years.

In 1942 part of the vineyard of Batailley as well as Château la Couronne and the curiously-named Château la Tour l'Aspic were left to Marcel Borie's older brother, Francis, and Château Haut-Batailley came into existence. Francis Borie died in 1953, leaving Ducru-Beaucaillou to his

son, Jean-Eugène, and Haut-Batailley to his daughter, Madame de Brest-Borie. The property is run by Jean-Eugène on his sister's behalf, but day-to-day running is the responsibility of Jean-Eugène's son, François-Xavier of Château Grand-Puy-Lacoste.

As a result of the 1942 partition, the chai and the château stayed with Marcel Borie's portion.

Until 1974, vinification of Haut-Batailley's wines was carried out at Ducru-Beaucaillou, which must have involved much expensive and time-consuming transport at vintage time. Since 1974, the curious Swiss-chalet style building of La Couronne has served as chai and cuvier. The cuvier, based on the specifications of the Bordeaux

108

University of Oenology, is one of the most efficient and spectacular of the Médoc, allowing for perfect cleanness and temperature control during the fermentation process. At the same time, the chai has been enlarged to facilitate ageing in wood. Continuing his efforts, in 1985 Borie will be building a bottling plant and storage cellar next to the existing building.

Both the Bories and Emile Casteja, whose wife owns Château Batailley, are skilled winemakers, and it is inevitable that a spirit of competition should exist between the two Fifth Growths that used to be one property. It is a contest which neither side wins, for both make excellent wine, but the styles are completely different. Either due to soil difference, or more likely due to an unconscious tendency of Jean-Eugène Borie's family to strive after the St Julien style, Haut-Batailley seems to have the softer, more approachable character of the two, while Batailley leans more towards the Pauillac tradition of severity and slow maturation. This is not to say that the wine of Haut-Batailley is not long-lived; I have tasted many an older vintage from this property which has given enormous pleasure, not least of which was the fabulous 1961.

TECHNICAL INFORMATION

General

Appellation:	Pauillac
Area under vines:	20 hectares
Average production:	Between 6,000 and 9,500 cases
Distribution of vines:	Divided in 2 main parcels, one behind Château Batailley, the other on the Bages plateau
Owner:	Mme. des Brest-Borie
Directors:	MM. Jean-Eugène and François-Xavier Borie
Régisseur:	M. André Faure
Maître de Chai:	M. René Lusseau
Consultant Oenologist:	Professor Emile Peynaud

Viticulture

Geology:	Gravel
Grape varieties:	65% Cabernet Sauvignon, 10% Cabernet Franc, 25% Merlot
Pruning:	Médocaine
Rootstock:	Varied according to soil in different parts of vineyard
Vines per hectare:	10,000
Yield per hectare:	30–40 hectolitres

Replanting:	$\frac{1}{2}$ hectare per annum

Vinification

Added yeasts:	No
Length of maceration:	Variable according to vintage, but usually long
Temperature of fermentation:	28–30°C
Control of fermentation:	Cooling by running water on exterior of vats
Type of vat:	Enamelled steel
Vin de presse:	Part incorporated according to vintage
Age of casks:	$\frac{1}{3}$ new each vintage
Time in cask:	Average 20 months
Fining:	Egg-whites
Filtration:	None
Type of bottle:	Bordelaise lourde

Commercial

Vente Directe:	No
Sales:	Through Bordeaux négociants
Visits:	Yes, by appointment Telephone 56 59 05 20

THE TASTING AT CHATEAU HAUT-BATAILLEY, 30 January 1985
J.S., Christian Seely, François-Xavier Borie, René Lusseau

1983 Excellent clear deep red. Nose good, but closed (just fined). Fruit, structure and balance very good. Long aftertaste.

1982 Deep blackish red. Ripe, roasted, slightly farmyard nose. Very big, rounded with lots of fruit and non-aggressive tannins. Already quite accessible, but will be a great stayer.

1981 Good depth of colour. Nose just beginning to come out. Medium body, and good structure, with finesse and backbone. Will develop into a lovely wine.

1980 Bright garnet red. Light, flowery and attractive bouquet. Open and easy to drink now; long for 1980, a well-made wine with some life.

1979 Colour darker than '80. Good nose, quite complex. More complicated and has more finesse than a lot of '79s I have tasted. Very good.

1978 Good middle red. A bit shy on the nose. Is at a stage between youth and adolescence. Good, fairly complex flavour with a long aftertaste. Will be a very good '78.

1976 (Tasted at lunch at Ducru-Beaucaillou 27 October 1984.) Dense, blackish colour. Good ripe nose. Ripe but not overripe flavour, with plenty of good fruit and tannins to keep it going. Long aftertaste.

CHATEAU

Lafite-Rothschild

PAUILLAC

Travelling north on the road from Pauillac to Lesparre, Lafite appears on the left, set well back from the road and marked only by a small sign at the entrance to the drive.

In 1670 the property passed into the Ségur family when Jacques de Ségur, owner of Calon Ségur, married the widow of Saubat de Pommiers, owner of Lafite and member of the Bordeaux parliament. Their son, Alexandre de Ségur, made an equally fortunate alliance by marrying Marie-Thérèse Clausel, heiress of Château Latour, in 1695. Ownership of Lafite, Latour and Calon Ségur thus passed into the hands of one man, their son Nicholas Alexandre de Ségur, born in 1697, later to become known as the 'Prince des Vignes', with good reason.

In 1755, the year of his death, Lafite was introduced to the court of Louis XV by Maréchal de Richelieu, where it became enormously popular both with king and courtiers. Despite this, Nicholas Alexandre's heir, his grandson the Comte Marie-Nicholas Alexandre de Ségur, got into desperate financial straits and was forced to sell the property in 1784.

At the time of the Revolution in 1789, Lafite was owned by Nicholas Pierre de Pichard, who although a Baron, remained in France. A great many owners of châteaux in Bordeaux at the time chose not to flee from the Revolution, and were generally rewarded by being allowed to keep their property. Unfortunately, the Baron de Pichard had a daughter, Anne-Marguerite-Marie-Adelaide de Puységur, who fled the country with her husband. They were proscribed as émigrés, and her parents were arraigned as accomplices, tried and guillotined. As an émigrée, the daughter forfeited her right to inherit, and so Lafite became the property of the Republic.

On 15 July 1797, the château was put up for auction, and bought by a Dutch consortium headed by a Mr de Witt. In 1803 the syndicate sold out to Ignace-Joseph Vanlerberghe, a Frenchman despite his name, who among other things was Napoleon's head of General Supplies. Although he was at this time able to pay FF 1,200,000 for Lafite, he was later to run into serious financial troubles through a speculative partnership with a

man named Gabriel Julien Ouvrard. The pair declared bankruptcy in 1808, and in 1818, with proceedings still dragging on, Vanlerberghe sold Lafite to his wife for 1,000,000 francs in order to keep the château out of his creditors' hands. She in turn 'sold' Lafite on to her son for the same sum of money in 1821, covering the transaction by using the services of a London banker, Sir Samuel Scott, in whose name the château was held and administered, until the death of the younger Vanlerberghe in 1866 when Sir Samuel's bank revealed that they had held Lafite on his behalf. In 1868 the property was put up for auction for the benefit of Vanlerberghe's heirs, and was purchased by Baron James Rothschild. The total purchase price was 4,400,000 francs. Bearing in mind that the rate of wages for vendangeurs was one franc per day in 1899, almost 30 years later, this was an astonishing price.

James Rothschild was an old man at the time of the purchase; he died the same year, and never saw Lafite. The property has belonged to his heirs in succession ever since.

During the Revolution the iron railings that enclosed the garden in front of the château were removed by the rebellious populace to be used as makeshift weapons. Perhaps to ensure against a recurrence of such an act of lèse majesté, they were never replaced when the château passed back into private ownership. To this day the terrace in front of the château is enclosed by railings made of wooden spikes, cunningly disguised to resemble cast iron. It is reassuring to the nervous visitor to observe that the 'iron' gates of Lafite have noticeably been chewed at the bottom by the resident Alsatian.

This blend of apparent grandeur and actual informality is one of the characteristics of Lafite. Seen from the immaculate gardens which extend from the road to the terrace of the house, the imposing wall of the raised terrace, topped by its balustrade, gives the property an air of inaccessibility to ordinary mortals. In fact, if one takes the trouble to make an appointment by telephone to the Rothschild offices in Paris, a visit to the chais where Lafite is made can be arranged. On closer inspection, it will be seen that the château itself is

really quite modest in size, and the atmosphere is as generally friendly as it is bound to be on an estate where successive generations of employees have lived and worked on the property in harmony with generations of the same family of proprietors.

The château itself is less grandiose in appearance than many of the Médoc houses. It is basically a 16th-century manor house, while the majority of 'châteaux' of the region owe their outward grandeur to the social and political aspirations of much later times. Inside there are but four modestly-proportioned reception rooms. The 'salon rouge', with its rather heavy dark-red damask-covered furniture, is preserved, like a fly in amber, as it was at the time of the Rothschild purchase. Here is the famous desk on which the terms of the Franco-Prussian treaty were drafted in 1871, complete with the ink stain said to have been caused by Bismarck; the story goes that he banged the desk – so violently that the ink-well overturned – on learning that the Rothschild bank had put up the vast indemnity imposed on the French nation with the intention of crippling her economy for generations. Leading from this room is the lighter 'summer' drawing-room, that opens onto the terrace.

The dining-room is painted in white and pale green, and contains some fine pieces of Bordeaux porcelain commissioned by the Rothschilds from the Johnston factory. Leading off the dining-room is the comfortable library, with its dark-green furnishings and wall-coverings. In all the rooms, generations of Rothschilds gaze down from their gilt-framed portraits, but the pictures in the library are all of children. On the wall to the right of the door there is a framed requisition or 'shopping list' from Napoleon in exile, in which he rather modestly requests 4 bottles of Château Lafite.

Beneath the château is a treasure-house of red gold. This is the private cellar, started by the famous régisseur of the property in the early 19th century, Monsieur Goudal. The youngest bottle dates from the 1920s, and the oldest vintage is 1797.

There is no special secret, no single ingredient that makes Château Lafite the 'Premier des Premiers', the most sought-after and expensive wine in the world that has graced the tables of 'amateurs' of Bordeaux wine both rich and royal for two hundred years. It is, rather, a combination of many factors – special soil, microclimate and the human element of unflagging care and labour at every stage of viticulture and vinification.

To try to describe the wine of Lafite in all its wonderful complexity has taxed the minds and imaginations of generations of writers more qualified than me. In the aristocracy of Bordeaux it has always been, in my mind, the Queen; its style, finesse and subtle perfume combine to give an impression of femininity, when compared, for example, with the assertive masculinity of Château Latour. In lesser vintages, perhaps due to its very delicacy, Lafite can sometimes be a little disappointing: in the good and great years, however, it is sublime – beyond comparison, almost beyond description.

TECHNICAL INFORMATION

General

Appellation:	Pauillac
Area under vines:	90 hectares
Average production:	3,000 to 3,500 cases
Distribution of vines:	Mainly around the château, 2 small parcels near Pontet-Canet, and one to the north in St Estèphe
Owner:	Direct heirs of Baron James de Rothschild
Maître de Chai:	M. Robert Revelle
Régisseur:	M. Gilbert Rokvam
Consultant Oenologist:	Professor Emile Peynaud

Viticulture

Geology:	Deep gravel, some clay skimmings
Grape varieties:	70% Cabernet Sauvignon, 10% Cabernet Franc, 20% Merlot
Pruning:	Guyot Double
Rootstock:	Riparia
Vines per hectare:	8,500
Yield per hectare:	30–40 hectolitres
Replanting:	As necessary to maintain average vine age of 40 years, sometimes more if the condition of the vine allows it

Vinification

Added yeasts:	No
Length of maceration:	Varies according to vintage, 12–21 days
Temperature of fermentation:	26–30°C
Control of fermentation:	Tubular exchange apparatus
Type of vat:	Oak
Vin de presse:	Incorporated
Age of casks:	Entirely new each vintage; oak casks constructed on the property
Time in cask:	18–24 months
Fining:	Fresh egg-white
Filtration:	None
Type of bottle:	Bordelaise

Commercial

Vente Directe:	No
Sales:	Through Bordeaux négociants
Visits:	Yes, by appointment Telephone 1 256 33 50 (Paris) Hours: 0900–1100, 1500–1700 Monday to Friday Closed from 15.9 to 15.11

THE TASTING AT CHATEAU LAFITE-ROTHSCHILD, 22 January 1985
J.S., Christian Seely, M. Guy Schÿler, M. Gilbert Rokvam

1983 Deep bluey red. Bouquet very perfumed, scent of violets. Huge concentration of flavour. Very long, will become an all-time great Château Lafite.

1982 (Bottled September '84.) Denser colour, almost black. Nose very open and rounded with cassis and lots of power. Rich and rounded flavour, full of fruit and fairly typical of the vintage. Will be a great bottle, but relatively soon.

1981 Colour considerably lighter than later vintages. Nose beautiful and flowery with good fruit. A complex, elegant and feminine Lafite with good backbone. Will be a classic.

1980 Colour very pale. Nose light and elegant, slightly disappointing on palate, shortish but very pleasant to drink now.

1979 Deep ruby colour. Bouquet beginning to evolve. Rich with suggestion of Christmas pudding. Concentrated flavour, long with unusual degree of finesse for 1979. Hard tannins predominate but has a lot of elegance and breeding. One begins to see Château Lafite in this wine.

1978 Medium red colour. Nose quite open and evolved. Fruit and tannin almost in harmony. An elegant and delicate wine, quite long, but for me lacks the power and possibility of '79.

1977 Bright medium red. Light and pleasant bouquet, not excessively fine. Quite light but has some finesse and lacks the unpleasant acidity associated with this vintage.

At lunch

1976 Very dense colour, almost black. Rich aromatic nose. Good fruit. Well balanced and approaching the plateau of maturity.

1975 Very dark dense red. Bouquet a little shy, but promise of greatness coming through. Enormous concentration of flavour. This is a 1975 that will surely get where it is going and, having arrived, will stay there a very long time indeed.

CHATEAU
Latour
PAUILLAC

Driving from St Julien to Pauillac on the D2, you pass the walled vineyard of Léoville-Las-Cases with its famous gate, and the entrance to Château Latour is next on your right, immediately before Château Pichon-Longueville-Lalande.

The name of the château goes back to the 14th century when 'La Tor à St-Maubert en Médoc' was constructed as a fortress. In 1378 this was held by a troop of Breton soldiers, loyal to the French King, against a besieging force of Anglo-Gascons. Nothing remains today of the original fortress, which stood on the site of the present chai, though the famous tower is said to have been built of stones from its ruins.

The estate, which had produced some wine since the 14th century, belonged at one time to Jean-

Denis D'Auléde de Lestonnac who also owned the Margaux estate; in 1670 he sold the Latour domaine to a François Chanevas, a parvenu who had made a fortune in the service of the King. Chanevas left the property to his niece, whose daughter, Marie-Thérèse de Clauzel, heiress to the property, married Alexandre de Ségur in 1695. It was their son, Nicholas Alexandre de Ségur who was to become the 'Prince des Vignes', acquiring and inheriting among other properties Châteaux Latour, Lafite, Mouton and Calon-Ségur. Of all these fine estates, it was in Latour that the de Ségur interest was to remain for the longest period, for the numerous shareholders in the Société Civile du Château Latour who sold to the English in

113

1963 were all descendants of the Prince of the Vines. Nicolas-Alexandre de Ségur died in 1755, leaving a fortune of two million livres, which included Château Latour valued at 500,000 livres and Lafite at 700,000. This inheritance was divided chiefly among his four daughters, one of whom, Marie-Thérèse, the eldest, married a cousin, Alexandre de Ségur, thus keeping the Ségur name as proprietors. Of the other three sisters to whom Ségur assigned Latour in 1760, one married the Comte de Coëtlogon and died childless, the second, Angélique-Louise, had a son, the Comte de Ségur-Cabanac, and the third, Marie-Antoinette-Victoire, had two daughters who married well – one to the Comte de la Pallu, and the other to the Marquis de Beaumont.

At the Revolution, Ségur-Cabanac fled the terror, and his share of the property became a 'Bien National' and was put up for sale. For some unknown reason, the other members of the family failed to buy it, and the 'trade' moved in and it was sold to Jeanne Courregeottes-Teulon and M. Monbalon. In 1833 and 1840 Barton and Guestier and Nathaniel Johnston acquired Ségur-Cabanac's 27·06% share of the property. The presence of these middlemen as part owners of Latour was an irritation to the family shareholders, and in 1841 they put the property up for auction and bought it back in its entirety for a sum of 1,511,000 francs, giving Barton and Guestier as part of the deal the exclusivity for the production from 1844 to 1853. The shareholders then formed the Société Civile du Vignoble de Latour which still exists today.

At this time there was no château as such on the property, only a simple farmhouse, where the régisseur lived, and in which an apartment was kept for visiting shareholders. Following the successful vintages of 1857 and 1858, which produced an income of over half a million francs, the family, wishing to follow the contemporary fashion and visit their rural property more often, started to discuss the possibility of building a suitable château. The 1861 crop was another outstanding success, and building work began. By 1864 the present château was completed, together with the new improved chais and cuvier.

For the next hundred years Latour continued and prospered under the ownership and administration of the de Ségur descendants, chief among whom were the Courtivron and de Beaumont families.

By 1963 there were no less than 68 owners of the 155 shares in the company, when the English Pearson Group – the family company of Lord Cowdray – and the wine merchants, Harveys of Bristol, acquired a controlling interest in Latour;

Pearson's bought 51% and Harveys 25% for a reputed price of $2.7 million – about £900,000 at the rate of exchange in 1963. I myself was present at one of the critical moments in Latour's history. Staying with Tommy Brand, chairman of Lazards, the merchant banking arm of the Pearson Group, I remember a telephone call coming through from Reggie Maudling, then Chancellor of the Exchequer, telling the banker that Treasury permission for the purchase had been given.

Since the English purchase an extensive investment programme has been pursued. One of the first innovations was the replacement of the old oak fermentation vats with stainless steel. This is a normal enough sight in the cuviers of the Grands Crus today, but in 1964 the gleaming array of 14 stainless-steel vats with their automatic cooling apparatus caused raised eyebrows in the wine world. Any fears were groundless – the quality and character of Latour's wine are as wonderful as ever.

Plots of land, such as the part known as Petit-Batailley, that had lain fallow for years, were replanted, other parcels of land, such as the vineyard called Les Forts de Latour, which had previously been part of the property, were purchased, and a further 5 stainless vats were installed in the petit cuvier.

The second wine of Latour, sold since 1966 under the label Les Forts de Latour, is made principally from wines grown in the Petit-Batailley vineyard, and another small plot known as Comtesse de Lalande, but also includes the produce of vines of less than ten years age from the main part of the vignoble. It is always of a very high quality, and represents exceptional value for money.

The wine of Château Latour is perhaps the most regal and masculine of all the Grands Crus of the Bordeaux region, possessed of amazing body, finesse and almost legendary longevity. It is a wine that in good years should be laid down by the unselfish and dynastically-minded for their children and grandchildren, while in lesser vintages it never disappoints. This ability to produce excellent wine in the 'petites années' is one of Latour's great strengths. Only in one year, 1915, has the château failed to produce any of the Grand Vin.

Latour is today administered by an extremely able team; the Board of Directors is headed by Alan Hare, late of the English *Financial Times*. Harry Waugh, grand old man of the English wine trade and man of letters, is an active consultant, and day-to-day running is carried out by the capable Jean-Louis Mandrau, under the watchful eyes of Jean-Paul Gardère and Henri Martin.

TECHNICAL INFORMATION

General

Appellation:	Pauillac
Area under vines:	60 hectares, 47 hectares Château Latour, 13 hectares Les Forts de Latour
Average production:	Grand Vin and Les Forts – 28,000 cases
Distribution of vines:	One main block around the château, with two smaller parcels near Château Haut-Batailley
Owner:	Société Civile du Vignoble de Château Latour (See text)
President:	A. Hare
Director:	Jean-Louis Mandrau
Maître de Chai:	Jean-Noël Malbec
Chef de Culture:	Guy Faure

Viticulture

Geology:	Gunzian gravel
Grape varieties:	80% Cabernet Sauvignon, 10% Cabernet Franc, 10% Merlot
Pruning:	Guyot Double
Rootstock:	Riparia, 3309C
Vines per hectare:	10,000
Yield per hectare:	40–45 hectolitres
Replanting:	By complantation

Vinification

Added yeasts:	Occasionally
Length of maceration:	3 weeks
Temperature of fermentation:	30°C
Control of fermentation:	By running water on exterior of vats
Type of vat:	Stainless steel
Vin de presse:	Added following careful tastings
Age of casks:	100% new each vintage
Time in cask:	20–24 months
Fining:	Egg whites
Filtration:	None
Type of bottle:	Bordelaise lourde

Commercial

Vente Directe:	No
Exclusivities:	None
Agents overseas:	None
Sales:	Through the Bordeaux market
Visits:	Yes, by appointment Telephone: 56 59 00 51 Hours: 0900–1130, 1400–1700 Monday to Friday

THE TASTING AT CHATEAU LATOUR,
18 January 1985
J.S., Jean-Louis Mandrau

1983 The blackest, densest colour I have yet seen in this vintage. Bouquet completely closed. Tremendous richness, with huge tannin. Enormous fruit, and very, very long legs. One for the grandchildren!

1979 Again very deep, blacky red. Nose beginning to evolve, with great power and rich cassis. Very pronounced blackcurrant in mouth, long with tannin still very dominant. Less complex than one might expect from Latour, but time is needed.

1976 Colour very dense, but shading to brown. Powerful, ripe bouquet of rich fruit. Quite evolved for such a 'young' Latour, rich in fruit flavours, but finishes quite dry.

1973 Colour only a shade lighter than 1976. Nose quite open, and giving off lovely ripe fruit scents. Ripe and rounded in the mouth, still has lots of life. Staggering for 1973, but then this *is* Latour.

The 6 following vintages were tasted in England in March 1985, through the kind generosity of Harveys of Bristol.

1981 Lovely deep blue/red. Nose very powerful, absolutely typical of Latour, full of blackcurrants, with lots of reserve. Fine and powerful, with a mass of fruit and plenty of good tannin. Has elegance and backbone, and a fine, lingering aftertaste. Will be superb.

1980 Good deep colour. Nose good, with cassis fruit. Not at all 1980 in style. Quite tannic with good fruit and structure enough to keep it going quite a while.

1978 Beautiful deep and dense colour. Latour nose again, great wafts of sun-warmed fruit, especially cassis. Fat and tannic, with slight roasted flavour. Balance superb – a 1978 to wait another 10 or 15 years for.

1977 Dense rusty red. Nose quite evolved, with some cassis. A middleweight for Latour, but amazing for 1977. Fruit very good and still has tannin and backbone to keep it going a while.

1975 Colour brilliant, deep garnet. Nose very fragrant, summer fruits. Wealth of complex flavours, still almost too concentrated to identify. Certainly there is a suggestion of ripe strawberries, but so much more besides. Still very tannic, with stupendous aftertaste.

1972 Medium colour, browning at edges. Nose very open and ripe. Easy to drink, still has some weight and good fruit, but not a lot of tannin left. An everyday Latour, if there can be such a thing.

CHATEAU
Lynch-Bages
PAUILLAC

Château Lynch-Bages is some two hundred yards to the left of the D2, as you approach Pauillac from the south, in the small village of Bages.

Although the estate has existed more or less in its present form since the 16th century, the first official deeds relate to the sale of the property in 1728 by Bernard Dejean to 'Chevalier Président' Pierre Drouillard, who was General Treasurer for the province of Guyenne; the purchase price was paid in 'a simple cash payment, all in gold or silver'. On Drouillard's death in 1749, the 'Domaine de Batges', as it is described in his will in the Bordeaux archives, passed to his sister Elisabeth, who had married Thomas Lynch in 1740, thus beginning 75 years ownership by the Lynch family, who gave their name to the property.

Lynch was the son of an Irish immigrant from Galway, John Lynch, who fled to France, along with many of his compatriots, after the defeat of James II at the battle of the Boyne in 1690. He set himself up as a merchant in Bordeaux, dealing in wool and leather, and soon became a successful and respected member of the community, marrying a beautiful local girl, Guillemette Constant, who gave him two sons, Thomas and Jean-Arthur.

In 1749 Thomas and Elisabeth made over the estate to their elder son, Jean-Baptiste, on the occasion of his marriage. Jean-Baptiste was an ambitious and political animal, cast in the mould of the famous Vicar of Bray, a contemporary Irish cleric who changed his religion according to the reigning monarch, so that, as the song records, 'Whatsoever King shall reign, I'll still be the Vicar of Bray, Sir'. Lynch's shifting affiliations were of a political rather than a religious nature, but they kept him in power and possession of his extensive properties through the most turbulent times of France's turbulent history. He was created Comte Lynch, and elected to the Chambre des Pairs under Louis XVIII. He was Mayor of Bordeaux from 1809 to 1814, remaining in this office for a further year after his elevation to the Chambre des Pairs, following a petition from the people of Bordeaux to the King. Jean-Baptiste's political manœuverings kept him absent from Pauillac for long stretches, and the management of the estate

was entrusted to his brother, Sir Michael Lynch, until it was sold in 1824.

The new owner of Lynch-Bages was Sébastien Jurine, a successful Swiss wine-merchant, whose business was based in Bordeaux. The Jurine family, who bult the present château, sold it to another Bordeaux wine-merchant, Jérome Cayrou, in whose family it remained until it came under the management of the present owning family in 1934.

Jean-Charles Cazes, father of André and grandfather to Jean-Michel, was already the owner of Château les Ormes de Pez in St Estèphe when he took on Lynch-Bages as a tenant in 1934; he did not become the official owner until 1937. He was a winemaker of great repute, and a well-known and respected figure in the Médoc; he died in 1972 at the ripe age of 95. His son André, mayor of Pauillac since 1947, has run Château Lynch-Bages since 1966, energetically assisted by his son Jean-Michel, who lives at the château. The family also has a thriving insurance business based in Pauillac, and are said to look after the insurance of almost all the wine properties in the Médoc.

The vineyard of Château Lynch-Bages is situated on croupes of gravel to the south and south-west of the town of Pauillac, commanding a fine view of the Gironde estuary. The combination of large round gravel on a subsoil of light clay and sand, shading to a lower stratum of chalk or heavy clay, sand and pebbles, is too poor for the cultivation of anything but the vine, to which it is ideally suited. The 75 hectares are planted with a classical mixture of predominantly Cabernet Sauvignon vines, with some 10% Cabernet Franc and 15% Merlot. A great deal of rebuilding and modernisation is currently under way at Lynch-Bages, although the vast Skawinski-designed cuvier has been carefully preserved, with its array of oak vats, and the upper floor, where the grapes arrived and were trodden in former times; vinification now takes place in a battery of 25 steel vats of 200 or 250 hectolitre capacity of which 7 are stainless steel. Ageing, however, is still completely traditional in oak casks, of which half are renewed each vintage, and fining, with six fresh egg whites, is done in cask during the second winter.

Château Lynch-Bages is said to be the Englishman's idea of what claret should be, though a high accolade was given to this wine by a very French Frenchman, Raoul Blondin of Mouton-Rothschild; he told me that the wine of Pauillac was for him most typified by three châteaux – Latour, Lynch-Bages and Clerc-Milon. The English love of Lynch-Bages may owe something to the ease of pronunciation – it is often merrily referred to as 'Lunch-Bags' among the young English members of the wine trade – but it is certainly among my personal favourites. The colour is always of a lovely depth, intensifying as the wine matures, and the bouquet is soft and aromatic with a distinctive suggestion of cedarwood which often

helps me to identify Lynch-Bages in blind tastings; it is a wine which ages well, and is often surprisingly good in generally disappointing vintages, two characteristics well illustrated by the delicious 1957. In good years it develops a creamy texture, but always has lots of underlying character and backbone. Lynch-Bages merits a higher rating than 5th Growth, as is consistently borne out by the prices it achieves.

Selection is careful when the final assemblage of the wine is made, and an excellent second wine is sold as Château Haut-Bages Averous. Jean-Michel Cazes also makes a delightful, crisp, dry white wine, but this is not commercialised.

117

TECHNICAL INFORMATION

General

Appellation:	Pauillac
Area under vines:	75 hectares
Average production:	Château Lynch-Bages 25,000 cases
	Château Haut-Bages-Averous 6,000 cases
Distribution of vines:	Mainly grouped together, south of the town of Pauillac
Owner:	Société Civile de Lynch-Bages (André and Jean-Michel Cazes)
Director:	M. Daniel Llose
Maître de Chai:	M. Guy Bergey
Consultant Oenologist:	Laboratoire d'Oenologie de Pauillac

Viticulture

Geology:	Deep gravel on subsoil of marl and clay/sand gravel (alios)
Grape varieties:	75% Cabernet Sauvignon, 10% Cabernet Franc, 15% Merlot
Pruning:	Guyot Double
Rootstock:	Riparia 101-14, 420A, 4453
Vines per hectare:	8,500
Average yield per hectare:	36 hectolitres
Replanting:	Complantation, with occasional replanting of parcels in a bad state
	Average vine age is 35 years

Vinification

Added yeasts:	No
Length of maceration:	Average 2 weeks
Temperature of fermentation:	30°C
Control of fermentation:	Running water on exterior of vats
Type of vat:	18 lined steel of 200 hectolitres, 7 stainless steel of 250 hectolitres
Vin de presse:	From 0–10% incorporated, according to the vintage
Age of casks:	50% new each vintage
Time in cask:	Average 15 months
Fining:	Fresh egg-whites
Filtration:	Sur plaque before bottling
Type of bottle:	Bordelaise lourde

Commercial

Vente Directe:	No
Sales:	Through the Bordeaux négociants
Visits:	Yes, by appointment Telephone 56 59 19 19 Hours: 0900–1200, 1400–1700

THE TASTING AT CHATEAU LYNCH-BAGES, 11 October 1984
J.S., Jean-Michel Cazes, Miklos Dora

Château Lynch-Bages

1983 Deep colour, almost black. Beautiful bouquet beginning, with mass of cassis and new oak. Tannins present in plenty, but not dominating the fruit. Very Lynch-Bages, with subtlety, fruit, backbone and lots of promise.

1982 Blue-black colour. Generous, powerful nose of cassis and cigar-boxes. Big and mouthfilling, rounded with lovely quality of tannin, this will be a superb claret.

1981 Again a lovely, dense blackish colour. Fine, rich nose developing. Well-made wine, with everything there to make a classy, elegant claret. Very fine in 3–4 years.

1980 Colour still very dark, amazing for such a light vintage. Open cassis nose, elegant. Well-made, easy on the palate already, with fruit and ripe tannins, but could wait a year or two yet.

1979 Medium/dark red. Bouquet a bit shy but typical cedarwood coming through. A good '79 with some way to travel, with plenty of fruit and good tannin. Long aftertaste.

Château Haut-Bages Averous

1983 Same depth of colour as the Grand Vin. Bouquet closed. Harmonious and balanced, with good blackcurrant flavour and non-aggressive tannin. A very good deuxième vin from a fine vintage.

1982 Blackish red. Open, luscious fruity bouquet. Big, rounded wine, still very tannic. Well-structured, and already showing very well.

118

CHATEAU
Lynch-Moussas
PAUILLAC

Drive on the D1e from Pauillac towards Saint Laurent; about 1½ km outside Pauillac you cross a railway line, and pass Château Batailley on your left. Turn right at the next crossroads, and Château Lynch-Moussas is less than a kilometre along on your right.

Formerly a property of the famous Comte Jean-Baptiste Lynch of Irish extraction, Lynch-Moussas belonged at the time of the 1855 classification to a Spanish-sounding gentleman named Vasquez. Evidently he was a serious enough winemaker, since the estate was classified as a Fifth Growth; in the following half-century or so, however, his descendants must have either lost interest or become financially embarrassed, since, when Emile Casteja's father, Jean, bought it in 1919, production had virtually ceased.

The difficult years of the world economic slump followed Casteja's purchase, then the bad vintages of the 1930s, and then the war, hardly a propitious epoch for heavy investment. Jean Casteja died in 1955. Little was, in fact, done until Emile Casteja took over in 1969. Since then the vineyard has been totally replanted, so that there are now some 40 hectares under vines, with the possibility of some further expansion. When a vineyard is re-created from virtually nothing, planting must be done in stages in order to achieve an eventual correct balance of young and old vines. This means that a period of as much as twenty years must elapse before the wine can begin to reach its full potential. Already, in the early 1980s, one can see the steady evolution of quality at Lynch-Moussas; by 1987, with the combination of good terroir and the Casteja expertise, the wine at Lynch-Moussas will undoubtedly have returned to its proper place in the hierarchy of the Médoc Crus Classés.

The soil of Lynch-Moussas's vineyards is virtually the same as that of Château Batailley and the neighbouring Grand Puy, the two parcels sandwiching and touching Batailley, to the north and the south. Vinification is also almost identical, and is carried out by the same team as at Batailley, under Emile Casteja's watchful eye. It therefore follows that the style and quality of the wines of the two properties will eventually bear marked similarities, which must be good news for the commercial future of this long-neglected property.

119

TECHNICAL INFORMATION

General

Appellation:	Pauillac
Area under vines:	40 hectares
Average production:	Varied according to vintage
Distribution of vines:	Mainly in one block near the château, with another parcel near Batailley
Owner:	M. Emile Casteja
Chef de Culture:	M. L. Servant
Maître de Chai:	M. H. Valade
Consultant Oenologist:	M. Pascal Ribereau-Gayon

Viticulture

Geology:	Gravel
Grape varieties:	70% Cabernet, 30% Merlot
Pruning:	Médocaine
Rootstock:	101-14, 3309
Vines per hectare:	6,000
Yield per hectare:	Variable according to vintage
Replanting:	Vineyard in process of recreation since 1969

Vinification

Added yeasts:	In difficult years
Length of maceration:	15–20 days
Temperature of fermentation:	28–30°C
Control of fermentation:	Cooling by running water on exterior of vats
Type of vat:	Lined steel
Vin de presse:	Proportion incorporated according to year
Age of casks:	¼ new each vintage
Time in cask:	18–20 months
Fining:	Egg white
Filtration:	None
Type of bottle:	Bordelaise

Commercial

Vente Directe:	Yes
Sales:	Through the Bordeaux négociants
Visits:	Yes, telephone 56 59 57 14 Hours: 0800–1200, 1400–1800

THE TASTING AT CHATEAU
BATAILLEY, 8 January 1985
J.S., Emile Casteja

1984 Medium to light colour. Nose all right, still has carbonic acid gas from malolactic fermentation. Difficult to taste at this stage, but fruit and tannins seem OK.

1983 Good deep colour. Attractive bouquet with blackcurrant fruit. Balanced and well made, with the right structure of tannins and fruit flavours to make a good bottle. Long aftertaste.

1982 Deep blackish red. Nose open, again with good cassis smell. Already rounded and fat, with good fruit and soft tannins.

1981 Colour a bit lighter than later vintages. Fine attractive nose. Elegant, well-balanced and supple wine. Quite forward.

1980 Bright medium red. Open, honest nose with good fruit. Easy and lightish with no faults. Good for current drinking.

1979 Good medium dark colour. Nose not giving much. Good fruit, but not particularly exciting. Ready, and will not get very much better.

1978 Slightly darker red than 1979. Pleasing and not very powerful bouquet. Quite a complex flavour, well-made wine with some backbone and a good future.

1977 Colour quite light and brownish. Nose tired. Tastes a bit over the hill and not very pleasant.

1976 Medium colour tending to brown. Bouquet a little overripe. Tastes better than it smells, a bit short, but quite good to drink now.

1975 Quite a light colour for 1975. Soft, nice fruit on nose. Good wine with some finesse, but a bit disappointing for this fine vintage, finishing dry.

CHATEAU
Mouton-Baronne-Philippe
PAUILLAC

As you drive on the D2 between Pauillac and le Pouyalet, you will come to a small turning on the left by a roadside Calvary; about 1 km along this road you come to the entrance to Château Mouton-Rothschild on your right, opposite the distinctive gilded Star of David. The entrance to Mouton-Baronne-Philippe is a little further on the same side of the road.

The vineyard of Mouton-Baronne-Philippe was created in the early 18th century, by Dominique d'Armailhac; he put together several pieces of land, and the property became known as Château d'Armailhac.

In the early part of the 19th century, the Bordeaux wine market was in a serious depression, due to a combination of wars, export restrictions, taxes and diseased vines; in 1840 the d'Armailhacs tried to sell the property, together with the half-finished château, which they had started to build in expectation of plenty. The obvious purchaser was Monsieur Thuret, who had recently bought the neighbouring Brane-Mouton; Thuret, however, wanted none of it – he had problems of his own, and in fact sold Mouton in 1853 to Nathaniel Rothschild for less than he had paid twenty years before.

It appears that the d'Armailhacs' financial worries were solved by raising a mortgage on the property for 400,000 francs, which was redeemed only three years later by Madame d'Armailhac, whose husband had meanwhile left her. The running of the estate was taken over by her son, Armand d'Armailhac. This gentleman appears to have been something of an oenologist, for in 1855 he published a book *La Culture des Vignes, la Vinification et les Vins dans le Médoc*. He is also reputed along with his erstwhile neighbour Baron Hector 'Napoléon des Vignes' Branne, to have been responsible for the introduction of the Cabernet Sauvignon to the Médoc. This, if it be true, makes him a key figure in the history of Bordeaux wine. Presumably Armand d'Armailhac had no children, as the property passed through his sister to the de Ferrande family at the end of the last century.

1933 finds the ageing Comte de Ferrande living in genteel poverty in the demi-château. He sold the estate, together with his Pauillac-based wine business, the Société Vinicole de Pauillac, to the Baron Philippe de Rothschild, his neighbour at Château Mouton-Rothschild. The property, now named for Baron Philippe's later wife Château Mouton-Baronne-Philippe, was previously called in turn Mouton d'Armailhac, Mouton-Baron-Philippe, and, for a short period, Mouton-Baronne-Pauline. The current label bears a touching tribute to the Baron's late wife; where it used to carry a picture of a pair of sphinxes, there is now but one. The

wine business, through which the Baron sells part of the produce of Mouton-Rothschild, and Clerc-Milon, all of Mouton-Baronne-Philippe, the hugely successful brand Mouton-Cadet and many other wines, is now known as La Baronnie, and is based in Pauillac in a small street opposite the church.

After the purchase in 1933, an extensive programme of replanting, rebuilding and restoration was entered upon, but the war years came along before the new vineyard was in proper production. After the war, Baron Philippe was able to realise his long-cherished ambition of making an attractive park out of Mouton d'Armailhac's gardens, which now makes for a better approach to Mouton itself. The first vintage to be made on the property was the unfortunate year of 1956, and the chais and cuvier were not rebuilt until the late 1960s. The Daliesque half-château remains. The 50 hectares of Mouton-Baronne-Philippe give a wine that is perceptibly related to Mouton-Rothschild, but is softer and more supple in youth, lacking the stature of its nobler neighbour. It is an attractive wine that gives generously of its charms while relatively young; this accessibility is probably due to the relatively high proportion of Merlot grapes planted (20%), and to the use of fewer new casks. Cement tanks are used for fermentation, and ageing takes place in casks of which only 20% are new, the rest being casks of one vintage from Mouton. In high-yield vintages, the wine spends some of its ageing period in large wooden 'foudres' or barrels, holding 100 hectolitres. Vinification is overseen by Monsieur Bueno, the young maître de chai, who learnt his job from the master nextdoor, Raoul Blondin.

TECHNICAL INFORMATION

General

Appellation:	Pauillac
Area under vines:	50 hectares
Average production:	15,000 cases
Distribution of vines:	One block
Owner:	G.F.A. du Baron Philippe de Rothschild
Maître de Chai:	M. Bueno
Oenologist:	Company's own team

Viticulture

Geology:	Gravel on clay/marl subsoil
Grape varieties:	65% Cabernet Sauvignon, 15% Cabernet Franc, 20% Merlot
Pruning:	Guyot Double Médocaine
Rootstock:	Varied to suit soil
Yield per hectare:	35 hectolitres
Vines per hectare:	8,000 to 10,000
Replanting:	By complantation

Vinification

Added yeasts:	No
Length of maceration:	3 weeks
Temperature of fermentation:	28–30°C

Control of fermentation:	Electronic, manually controlled
Type of vat:	Cement
Vin de presse:	Incorporated according to vintage
Age of casks:	20% new, rest of one vintage from Mouton
Time in cask:	22–24 months
Fining:	Egg-whites, less used than at Mouton because of colour loss
Filtration:	None
Type of bottle:	Bordelaise lourde

Commercial

Vente Directe:	No
Sales:	Entire commercialisation by La Baronnie, B.P. 32, 33250 Pauillac Telephone 56 59 20 20
Visits:	By appointment Telephone La Baronnie – see above Closed weekends and August

THE TASTING AT CHATEAU MOUTON-ROTHSCHILD, 31 January 1985
J.S., Christian Seely, Raoul Blondin, M. Houben

1983 Deep purple colour. Nose soft, very forthcoming. Large, rounded, tastes of good ripe fruit. Already quite approachable.

1981 Good medium red. Nose open, with round, attractive fruit. Easy on the palate, soft and rounded, with some length and good tannin. Approaching readiness.
1979 Bright scarlet. Opening charming bouquet, good fruit. Balanced wine, with elegant charm, very feminine. Perfect for drinking now and for a year or two.

CHATEAU

Mouton-Rothschild

PAUILLAC

Driving north on the D2 between Pauillac and Pauillac-le-Pouyalet, you turn left at a wayside Calvary, from where Château Mouton-Rothschild is signposted. The entrance is about 1 km along this road on your right, unmistakably marked by a large, gilded, three-dimensional Star of David, set on top of a stone column that faces the gateway.

The vineyard at Mouton was established, more or less in its present form, in the 1730s by the Baron Joseph de Branne. Brane-Mouton, as it was then called, remained in that family for the best part of a century. It was in 1830 that Baron Hector de Branne, whose sobriquet was the 'Napoléon des Vignes', sold Mouton to a Monsieur Thuret for 1,200,000 francs, ostensibly in order to concentrate his efforts and resources on Brane-Cantenac, purchased ten years earlier. One is tempted to wonder whether perhaps the sale owed more to the Baron's known penchant for gambling and

pretty women, which eventually led to his financial ruin.

During the next couple of decades, Mouton suffered a partial eclipse, due to a combination of neglect and the ravages of oidium, a fungoid malady affecting the vines, also known as 'powdery mildew', which first made its appearance in the Médoc at this time; it still occurs, but in the mid-19th century there was no known treatment. It was at this stage that Baron Nathaniel de Rothschild, great-grandfather of the present owner, stepped on to the Médoc stage and snapped up Mouton for considerably less than the embarrassed Thuret had paid 23 years earlier.

The Rothschild purchase was in 1853, only two years before the classification, and the timing, from this point of view, could not have been worse. First of the Seconds was, by any standard, a fair enough rating, especially when one bears in mind the difficult times affecting the vineyard

during the preceding twenty years, but subsequent generations of Rothschilds did much to revitalise Mouton, and it took the present owner, Baron Philippe, over fifty years of vigorous and incessant campaigning at the highest levels before the injustice of 1855 was finally rectified.

Though Mouton-Rothschild, as it had now become, prospered and flourished under the successive aegis of his great-grandfather, grandfather and father, it is undoubtedly Philippe de Rothschild who is totally responsible for its elevation to Premier Cru status. Evacuated to Mouton from Paris during the First World War, he has been in love with the place ever since. When he first saw Mouton, it was nothing more than a farmhouse, which his father, a Parisian whose life was devoted to the theatre, had never even visited. In 1922 when Philippe persuaded his father to put the future of Mouton in his hands, the small house, now known as Petit Mouton and used for housing guests, was virtually derelict, and Grand Mouton, where the Baron now lives, was a delapidated stable-block.

The life and times – and loves – of Philippe de Rothschild have been fully and ably chronicled by other pens. His extraordinary persistence and ability as a campaigner have benefited not only Mouton, but the entire Bordeaux region and its devotees as well. He was the first proprietor to instigate total château-bottling of his wines in 1924, now adopted by all Crus Classés. It is also thanks to this remarkable man's intervention, at presidential level, that the further insane development of the Shell oil-refinery complex in Pauillac was halted.

Château Mouton-Rothschild is now a showplace of the Médoc, of interest as much to wine lovers as to connoisseurs of the arts. Philippe de Rothschild, aided by his lovely American-born second wife, the late Baronne Pauline, has amassed a wonderful collection of glass, silver, tapestries, paintings and other objets d'art, all associated with the making, drinking and love of good wine. The converted stable-block which houses the Museum is an Aladdin's cave; the exhibits are displayed and lit with taste and care, and range from pottery pre-dating history to modern pictures by Picasso and Giacometti. There is almost an *embarras de richesses* here, but my own favourites include the magnificent intricately carved ivory drinking cup, which must have taken years of agonising work, the English biscuit figure of the drunkard from the Bow porcelain works and the pair of box-wood and silver-gilt owl drinking cups, a present from her lover to Catherine the Great of Russia.

Another tradition linking Mouton with the arts was established, appropriately enough, in 1945, the fabled 'année de la Victoire', a great vintage for Mouton-Rothschild as well as civilisation in general. It was in this year that the Baron first commissioned a well-known painter to decorate the Mouton label, and his first choice was Philippe Jullian, who has been followed by a dazzling succession of names, including Dali, Jean Cocteau, Braque, Henry Moore, Chagall and Picasso. It is the Picasso design that surmounted the label of 1973, the most significant year in Mouton's history, the year in which Baron Philippe finally won the right to sell Mouton as a Premier Cru. The latest label design, that of the 1982 vintage, is by way of a departure from tradition. It is a charming, symbolic water-colour, combining a happy sheep, blue skies, sunshine and grapes; what is unusual is that its painter, John Huston, is better known as a film director and actor than as an artist; he has been a personal friend of Baron Philippe for many years, and has touchingly written beneath his design, 'In celebration of my beloved friend Baron Philippe's 60th harvest at Mouton.' The artists have always been paid in wine for their work – five cases of mature Mouton-Rothschild, and five cases of the vintage which their design adorns – a handsome remuneration, and possibly tax-free, since many countries' tax officials look upon wine as a 'wasting asset'.

The Mouton vineyard has a soil of large, deep gravel, with a subsoil of clay and marl on a limestone base. The proportion of Cabernet Sauvignon grown is one of the highest in the Médoc, accounting for the breeding, finesse and longevity of its wine.

Vinification is traditional, fermentation and maceration taking place in oak vats; the wine is aged in 100% new oak casks for an average of two years, and is racked every three months and fined with beaten fresh whites of egg. Every stage of the winemaking process is minutely observed by the venerable cellar master, Raoul Blondin, one of the great characters of the Médoc. His knowledge of the district, and of Mouton in particular, is encyclopedic. Blondin was at Mouton when Baron Philippe arrived, and between the two there is an almost tangible bond composed of mutual love and respect. This curious blend of feudality and affection is evident in all who work at Mouton, Mouton-Baron-Philippe, Clerc-Milon and the offices at La Baronnie in Pauillac, and imparts itself to the visitor in a feeling of family pride and solidarity.

TECHNICAL INFORMATION

General

Appellation:	Pauillac
Area under vines:	73 hectares
Average production:	20,000 cases
Distribution of vines:	Basically one block
Owner:	Groupement Foncier Agricole du Baron Philippe de Rothschild
Technical Director:	M. L. Siolleau
Maître de Chai:	M. Raoul Blondin
Oenologist:	Company's own team

Viticulture

Geology:	Gravel, on subsoil of marl and clay
Grape varieties:	85% Cabernet Sauvignon, 7% Cabernet Franc, 8% Merlot
Pruning:	Guyot Double Médocaine
Rootstock:	Various, as suited to soils
Vines per hectare:	8,000 to 10,000
Average yield per hectare:	35 hectolitres
Replanting:	By complantation

Vinification

Added yeasts:	No
Length of maceration:	3 weeks

Temperature of fermentation:	28–30°C
Control of fermentation:	Electronic, but manually operated
Type of vat:	Oak
Vin de presse:	Portion of 1st pressing sometimes included in lighter vintages
Age of casks:	100% new each vintage
Time in cask:	22–24 months
Fining:	Fresh egg-whites
Filtration:	No
Type of bottle:	Bordelaise lourde

Commercial

Vente Directe:	No
Sales:	Through the Bordeaux négociants, and La Baronnie, Pauillac
Agents overseas:	Contact La Baronnie, 33250 Pauillac, for information
Visits:	Yes, by appointment only
	Telephone: 56 59 20 20 (office)
	56 59 22 22 (château)
	Closed weekends and August

THE TASTING AT CHATEAU MOUTON-ROTHSCHILD, 31 January 1985
J.S., Christian Seely, Raoul Blondin, M. Houben

1984 Deep dense red. Nose powerful with plenty of fruit. Amazingly rounded, excellent concentration of fruit with good tannins. (Interestingly, Monsieur Blondin said it compared well with the 1981.)

1983 Clear, dark almost black colour. Nose good, but very closed. Massive weight, excellent structure, with fruit and good tannins in tandem. Tannins not at all harsh; will be a classic Mouton.

1981 Very deep colour. Lovely ripe cassis bouquet. Balance superb. Has charm, finesse and roundness. A young Mouton, with splendid promise of development.

1979 Lovely, deep plummy colour. Nose beautifully perfumed with good cassis, just beginning to open. Lovely, well structured wine with lots of elegance and backbone. Raoul Blondin comments that this is typical Mouton, and at present shows better than the '78. (See also my notes on Lafite and Petrus.)

It is worth recording one of Raoul Blondin's observations. He does not regard Mouton Rothschild as typical Pauillac, a description, he says, that best fits three wines – Latour, Lynch-Bages and their own Clerc-Milon.

CHATEAU
Pédésclaux
PAUILLAC

As you leave Pauillac on the D2 in the direction of St Estèphe, pass the small road to your left which leads to Château Mouton-Rothschild, and you will see a squat concrete building in the middle of part of Pédésclaux's vineyard bearing the château's name. Some 100 metres further on you will see a sign to Château Pédésclaux to your right.

The vineyard of Château Pédésclaux is one of the more recently created of the Crus Classés; it dates from 1825, when Monsieur Urbain Pédésclaux, a courtier, put together some plots of land, part of which neighbour Château Grand-Puy-Lascoste, and the rest butt on to the vines of Château Mouton-Baronne-Philippe. M. Pédésclaux is given as the proprietor in the 1855 classification, when the property was placed among the 5th growths.

Pédésclaux's widow sold the château and its vineyard to the Comte de Gastebois in 1891. Lucien Jugla, the present owner's father, bought Pédésclaux in 1950, although he had been renting it from de Gastebois' heirs since 1933. The Jugla family have a solid Médocain winemaking background; Bernard's grandfather was for 30 years régisseur in charge of Château Duhart-Milon when it belonged to the Casteja family. They also own other properties in Pauillac, including Château Grand-Duroc-Milon and Château Haut Padarnac; a second wine is sometimes produced at Pédésclaux under the label of Château Belle Rose.

Bernard Jugla, a helpful and friendly man, obviously in love with his work, has run the property since his father's death in 1965; he is assisted by his brother Jean, who lives in an apartment on the first floor of the small but elegant 19th-century château. The ground floor is simply and tastefully furnished, and is used for tastings and receptions.

I was agreeably surprised by the firm, Pauillac quality of this Fifth Growth. The surprise was due not so much to any adverse reputation, but more to the fact that the wine is not particularly well known in England. This is, I think, mainly due to an exclusive arrangement, by which most of the 75% of the crop that is exported each year goes across the Atlantic.

126

TECHNICAL INFORMATION

General

Appellation:	Pauillac
Area under vines:	18 hectares
Average production:	8,000 cases
Distribution of vines:	In three parcels: 7 hectares around château, 5 hectares near Mouton and Pontet-Canet, 6 hectares west of Pauillac
Owner:	Société Civile du Château Pédésclaux
Director:	M. Bernard Jugla
Maître de Chai:	M. Jean Jugla
Consultant Oenologist:	M. Couasnon

Viticulture

Geology:	Gravel and clay/chalk in the home and Mouton-neighbouring vineyard, gravel and silica in the part west of Pauillac
Grape varieties:	70% Cabernet Sauvignon, 10% Cabernet Franc, 20% Merlot
Pruning:	Guyot Double Médocaine
Rootstock:	Riparia Gloire, 3309, 420A
Vines per hectare:	8,000
Replanting:	½ hectare per annum, giving average vine age of 39 years

Vinification

Added yeasts:	Yes, when necessary
Length of maceration:	18–22 days
Temperature of fermentation:	28°C max.
Control of fermentation:	By refrigeration and heat-exchange pump
Type of vat:	Steel, epoxy-resin lined
Vin de presse:	Incorporated according to vintage
Age of casks:	At least 50% new each vintage
Time in cask:	20–22 months
Fining:	Fresh egg-whites in cask
Filtration:	Sometimes sur terre before wine goes in cask
Type of bottle:	Bordelaise lourde

Commercial

Vente Directe:	No
Exclusivity:	Yes, since 1983 with C.V.G.B. Parempuyre
Agents abroad:	USA, Bacardi
Visits:	Yes, by appointment Telephone: 56 59 22 59 Hours: 0900–1200

THE TASTING AT CHATEAU PEDESCLAUX, 14 January 1985
J.S. and Bernard Jugla

1982 Deep, dark red. Nose closed, but very promising. Rich, round and powerful with a degree of sweetness and plenty of ripe tannins.

1981 Excellent colour, shade lighter than 1982. Nose good, peppery with some vanilla. Long in mouth, has finesse and elegance, just beginning to come together.

1978 Colour deep, but has just a shade of orange. Bouquet rich and slightly burnt. Very long, with lots of power, fruit and good tannins. Will go on a long while.

1973 Colour still very good for '73. Light, pleasant and perfumed nose. Quite light, with elegance and good flavours. Good aftertaste. A very good 1973.

Pichon-Longueville-Baron

As you approach Pauillac from the south along the D2, passing the vineyards of Léoville-Las-Cases and Latour on your right, you come to the two Pichons. Pichon-Longueville Comtesse de Lalande is on your right, and Pichon-Baron is on the left.

As I have dealt in some detail with the earlier history of the Pichon-Longueville estate in the chapter on the sister-château of Pichon-Longueville Comtesse de Lalande, we may take up the story of Pichon-Baron in 1933, when the Bouteiller family acquired the property.

The Bouteillers have wide interests in the Médoc, which started in 1907 when Etienne Bouteiller

married Marie-Louise Delbos, who inherited Château Lanessan and the neighbouring Château Lachesnaye. Until 1971, when it was acquired by Mestrezat-Preller, the Bouteillers were major shareholders and made the wine at Château Grand-Puy-Ducasse. The family also have a holding in Château Palmer, where Bertrand Bouteiller is responsible for administration. It is Château Pichon-Longueville-Baron, however, which is undoubtedly the jewel in the Bouteiller crown.

There is something rather sad about the appearance of the château of Pichon-Baron. Built on the site of a former 'maison noble' in 1851 by Baron Raoul de Pichon-Longueville, this Victorian fairy-tale castle, with its conical turrets and elegant balustraded double stairway to the front door, has the dejected air of an abandoned film-set. It has, in fact, been empty for over fifty years, apart from a brief period during the war, when evacuees from the bombing in Pauillac took shelter here. The basement is now used for storing the bottled wine, and one of the spacious ground-floor salons is used by the local Rotary club for meetings. It seems a sorry fate for so fine a building, but the structure has suffered from years of neglect, and a vast fortune would be needed to render the château habitable once more. Could this be yet another possibility for the 'Grand Hôtel du Médoc' which I feel is so sorely lacking?

Château Pichon-Longueville-Baron is relatively small in terms of production and vineyard; 30 hectares are under vines, and an average of thirty thousand cases are produced. Of the two Pichons, the Baron, as one might expect by the name, is certainly the more masculine of the two. The wine has a severity of style which takes many years to soften and mature, while the wine from the Comtesse is ampler and more rounded in the right places, probably due to the high proportion of Merlot grapes grown there. Though the wine of the Baron has not for some years enjoyed the same level of reputation or price as its sister-château there are definite signs of improvement and softening of style in the wine since the 1979 vintage. A slightly lower fermentation temperature – around 26°C – may be partly contributory to this change, since this means that less colour and tannins are extracted from the must.

TECHNICAL INFORMATION

General

Appellation:	Pauillac
Area under vines:	30 hectares
Average production:	35,000 cases
Distribution of vines:	In two parcels, mainly to the south of the château, with a smaller piece to the west near Château Haut-Batailley.
Owner:	Société Civile du Château Pichon Longueville
General manager:	M. Bertrand Bouteiller
Maître de Chai:	M. Coucharrière
Consultant Oenologist:	M. Boissenot

Viticulture

Geology:	Quaternian gravel
Grape varieties:	75% Cabernet Sauvignon, 25% Merlot
Pruning:	Guyot Double
Rootstock:	Riparia, 420A, 3309, 44-53
Vines per hectare:	10,000
Yield per hectare:	35–40 hectolitres
Replanting:	About 1 hectare per year

Vinification

Added yeasts:	No
Length of maceration:	Minimum 21 days
Control of temperature:	Heat-exchange apparatus
Type of vat:	Lined cement
Age of casks:	⅓ new each vintage
Time in cask:	24 months
Fining:	Egg-white
Filtration:	None
Type of bottle:	Bordelaise lourde

Commercial

Vente Directe:	Yes
Direct ordering from château:	Yes
Exclusivity:	Yes
Agents overseas:	Yes, for information contact M. Bertrand Bouteiller Château Lanessan Cussac-Fort-Médoc 33460 Margaux
Visits:	Yes, telephone 56 58 94 80 Hours: Monday to Friday 0900–1200, 1400–1700 Closed 15–30 August and 25 December–2 January

THE TASTING AT THE LION D'OR RESTAURANT, ARCINS, 13 November 1984
J.S., Bertrand Bouteiller

1983 (Cask sample.) Deep, purple colour. Nose strong cassis and new oak. Big, tannic wine with lots of fruit and power and a very long aftertaste.
1982 Dense, blackish red. Nose good but quite closed. Much more classic Médoc and less forward than most 1982s. Fruit, good tannin and spine in plenty. Will be very good, but will take time.
1975 Colour bright medium scarlet. Complex, fine bouquet just beginning to open, with hints of violets. A typical Pichon-Baron, according to Bertrand Bouteiller. Very long, concentrated flavour, with good aftertaste. Still has lots of fruit and tannins and a long life ahead.

CHATEAU

Pichon-Longueville-Comtesse de Lalande

PAUILLAC

As you approach Pauillac-St Laurent from the south on the D2, pass the walled vineyard of Château Léoville-Las-Cases and the entrance to Château Latour on your right. Château Pichon-Longueville-Comtesse de Lalande is the next property on the same side of the road; the château is almost hidden by trees, but the entrance to the chais and cuvier is a little further along the road, clearly marked.

Before the 17th century this estate was known variously under the names la Baderre, la Batisse and la Bastide. The land on the side of the road opposite the present property belonged in the 16th century to a family called Brun de Boysset, who owed allegiance to the Seigneurs of Latour, and were forced to pay a toll every time they used any of the roads bordering the Latour lands; this must have made work on the estate both tiresome and expensive, though at this time it was mostly woodland.

The first Pichon who really relates to the history of the vineyard was Bernard de Pichon, born at the dawn of the 17th century. He married in 1646 the only daughter of the Baron de Longueville, and the title appears to have passed to his family as part of her dowry. Their second son, Jacques de Pichon, also made a favourable marriage, to Thérèse des Mesures de Rauzan in 1694. Her father, Pierre des Mesures de Rauzan, nicknamed 'le Sorcier des Vignes', was owner of the important Rauzan estate in Margaux. He had also acquired land in Saint Lambert, where he had begun to plant vines, and it was this vineyard that passed into the Pichon-Longueville family as Thérèse's dowry. Under the magic influence, perhaps, of its origin, the vineyard prospered, and by the middle of the 18th century the wine enjoyed a reputation and price on a par with that of Mouton, Ducru-Beaucaillou, Gruaud and Beychevelle.

The next Baron Pichon-Longueville to concern us is the legendary Joseph, born in 1755. This remarkable man was immortalised by that flowery versifier of the Médoc, the poet Biarnez, both for the ripeness of his years and the quality of his

wine. He died in 1850, aged 95, having survived la Terreur of 1793 by hiding in the bread oven of the château for eight days. He had five children, Raoul, the eldest, who only survived his father by a few years, Louis, who died unmarried, and three daughters, Sophie de Pichon-Longueville, the Vicomtesse de Lavaur and Marie-Laure, who became the Comtesse de Lalande, having married the Comte Henri in 1820.

A sagacious man, the Baron Joseph decided to split the state between his children in the 1830s, thus avoiding any possible problems or family wranglings over inheritance, so common under the new Napoleonic Code. Two-fifths went to Raoul, which included his late brother Louis' share, and the remainder was divided among the three sisters. The property was, however, still run as one vineyard, and there was but one château, on the site of Pichon-Longueville-Baron.

The Comtesse de Lalande, Marie-Laure, had the present château of Pichon-Lalande built in the 1840s for herself and her two sisters to live in. She was by this time a widow and her lover, the Comte de Beaumont, owner of Château Latour, gave her the land on which the château stands. The architect was Duphot, later to be responsible for the design of Château Latour. As there was no château at Latour when Pichon-Lalande was built, it must have been a most convenient place for Beaumont to stay on his frequent trips to the Médoc.

Visiting Pichon-Lalande today, I find it easy to enter a time-warp and imagine life there in the 19th century. Most of the original furnishings are still there, together with books and paintings of the period. Sophie de Pichon-Longueville studied under the painter Gérard in Paris, and there is a lovely portrait by her of her brother-in-law, Henri de Lalande. There are also two pictures by her of scenes in the Pyrenees on the Spanish border; in one of them there are two figures picnicking, said to be her and her lover, and the other, later on, shows the girl alone. There could possibly be a sad love story behind these two pictures, which might

explain why Sophie de Pichon-Longueville took the veil and became a nun. The huge collection of archives, recently discovered in an attic, also gives a rich insight in to the life and economies of a great wine property in the last century. Madame de Lencquesaing has kindly said that I may return and study these at length and I am greatly looking forward to this exercise.

Across the road, Raoul de Pichon-Longueville built the present Gothic fairy-tale château in 1851, but it was not until his death in 1864 that the two portions of the estate were physically separated, and two separate wines were made. The 'female' portion of the vineyard lay, as it does today, to the west of Pichon-Baron, with 4·5 hectares on the château side of the road, bordering the vineyard of

Château Latour; the Baron vines were and are grouped immediately around its own château and chais.

None of Joseph de Pichon-Longueville's children had issue. Pichon-Longueville-Baron passed from Raoul to a nephew, also named Raoul, who took over the title as well as the property, while Pichon-Lalande was left by Marie-Laure, Comtesse de Lalande, to a niece, Elisabeth de Narbonne-Pelet, who almost incestuously married another Lalande, Comte Charles, son of the Marquis de Lalande. They had two daughters, Henriette, who never married, and Sophie de la Croix, who died in 1916 leaving five children. These five children and their aunt Henriette sold Pichon-Lalande in 1925 to the brothers Edouard and Louis Miailhe. It is Edouard Miailhe's daughter and her husband, Général Hervé de Lencquesaing, who own and run the property today.

The Miailhe family have a long history in Bordeaux and the Médoc. Originating from Portets in the Graves, the family have been involved in the wine business for the best part of 200 years, but it was Madame de Lencquesaing's grandfather Frédéric, and her father and uncle, Edouard and Louis, who first began to buy wine properties in the 1920s. Château Coufran and Verdignan were acquired by Louis, while Château Siran in Labarde was inherited by Edouard. In partnership they became owners of Pichon-Lalande, Citran, shareholders in Palmer and in 1966 added Dauzac in Labarde to their bag of tricks. The latter had to be sold due to inheritance problems in 1978, and the share in Palmer has also been disposed of. Madame de Lencquesaing inherited a part of Pichon-Lalande on her father's death in 1959, but it was not until 1978, on the General's retirement from a long and distinguished military career, that they took over the full-time running of the château. From 1975 to 1978, Pichon-Lalande was managed by their neighbour Michel Delon of Léoville-Las-Cases, and he did a great deal to improve the quality and reputation of the wine. It is now grouped among the 'first four' of the Second Growths, with Ducru-Beaucaillou, Cos d'Estournel and Léoville-Las Cases; in terms of price this bunch of four have opened a wide gap in the field, and are currently way out in front, commanding nearly double the opening price of some of their peers of the 1855 classification.

In the half-dozen years since Madame de Lencquesaing took over, there has been much building and renovation work at Pichon-Lalande. A vastly enlarged second-year chai has been added, as have a new building for bottling and storage-in-bottle and a magnificent reception room with commanding views across the vineyards of Latour to the estuary and beyond. The houses of the vineyard and cellar workers, which are grouped like a small village around the chais and cuvier, have also been extensively modernised, and the cuvier itself is equipped with stainless-steel fermentation tanks.

The wine of Pichon-Lalande fully merits its high reputation. It is perhaps more rounded and supple than most Pauillacs, and this stems partly from the unusually (for Pauillac) high proportion of Merlot grapes used, a preference shared by other Miailhe-owned properties, and partly from its proximity to the St Julien vineyards. At one time, indeed, the wine that came from the St Julien part of the vineyard had to be separately labelled as Appellation Saint Julien. The 1949 is one such bottle. The last five vintages have been outstanding successes; the 1979 is one of the best wines from this year I have tasted, and even the 1980 is outstandingly well structured for such a generally light year. As they mature, the wines of Pichon-Lalande retain their lovely, intense depth of colour and have a distinctly feminine element of finesse, charm and breeding. Strict selection at the assemblage gives us a really excellent Deuxieme Vin, sold as 'Réserve de la Comtesse'.

TECHNICAL INFORMATION

General

Appellation:	Pauillac
Area under vines:	60 hectares
Average production:	Between 20,000 and 30,000 cases
Distribution of vines:	Basically in one block
Owner:	M. le Général and Madame de Lencquesaing
Director:	Madame de Lencquesaing
Régisseur:	M. J.J. Godin
Maître de Chai:	M. F. Lopez
Consultant Oenologist:	Professor Emile Peynaud

Viticulture

Geology:	Gunzian gravel on clay subsoil
Grape varieties:	50% Cabernet Sauvignon, 35% Merlot, 7% Cabernet Franc, 8% Petit Verdot
Pruning:	Guyot Double
Rootstock:	SO4, Riparia 101-14
Vines per hectare:	9,500
Average yield per hectare:	40–50 hectolitres
Replanting:	3–4% replanted each year

Vinification

Added yeasts:	No
Length of maceration:	20 days
Temperature of fermentation:	26–28°C
Control of fermentation:	By cooling plant
Type of vat:	$\frac{1}{3}$ stainless steel, $\frac{2}{3}$ epoxy-resin lined cement
Vin de presse:	Proportion of first pressing included according to necessity
Age of casks:	50% new each vintage, 50% 2-year-old casks
Time in cask:	18–20 months
Fining:	Fresh egg-whites
Filtration:	None
Type of bottle:	Frontignan

Commercial

Vente Directe:	Yes, for visitors
Sales:	Through the Bordeaux négociants
Visits:	Yes, telephone 56 59 19 40 for appointment Hours: 0900–1130, 1430–1700 Monday to Friday

THE TASTING AT CHATEAU PICHON-LONGUEVILLE, COMTESSE DE LALANDE, 24 January 1985

J.S., Christian Seely, Mme. and Général de Lencquesaing, M. J.J. Godin, M. Lestapis, Prince Henri-Melchior de Polignac

1983 Deep, intense red. Good round fruit and new wood on nose. Rounded, rich mouthful of fruit; tannins less aggressive than most 1983 Médocs, probably due to Merlot influence.

1982 Same lovely, velvety, dark colour. Nose showing strongly, with big, powerful fruit. Big, generous flavour, with excellent tannins. 1982 was a great year, especially for the Merlot, and Pichon-Lalande of this vintage will be one of the great ones.

1981 Colour almost as dark as '82 and '83. Lovely bouquet developing, with some cassis. Elegant, fine and feminine, a classic Pichon-Lalande with superb length and structure, confirming my first impression when tasted in 1982.

1980 Amazingly good, deep red for 1980. Open, attractive bouquet with good, blackcurrant fruit. Very full and rounded, with flesh and backbone. Tasted blind, I would have suspected this to be an '81.

1979 Dark colour, almost black. Generous, rounded nose. Big, mouthfilling, with powerful fruit and ripe tannins. A really good 1979, with great keeping qualities.

1978 Colour even darker than '79. More complex bouquet. Still quite closed, but beginning to show its form. Great complexity and concentration of fruits and tannins, very long – will be a fine bottle.

1977 Fine, medium-dark ruby. Light, charming nose. Some fruit and flesh, lacks acidity of most '77s. Finishes a bit short, but a very nice luncheon wine.

1976 Colour browning a little, but dark. Lovely ripe nose of a hot-weather vintage. Ripe and rounded, with good fruit and respectable length. To drink now.

1975 Still black. Nose just beginning to open, complex and delicious. Concentrated, slightly roasted flavour, still full of youth and vigour. The orchestra is just warming up, and soon everything will be in harmony, but the crescendo is still a long way off!

1971 Palish, tawny colour. Very ripe, evolved nose. Pleasing, open flavour, slight suggestion of boiled sweets. 'A point'.

At lunch

1970 Intense, dark red. Bouquet quite closed in, but promising much. Great concentration of rich flavours, very long in the mouth. Will improve and stay a long while.

1966 Deep colour, tending to brown. Rich, spicy nose. Good, fruity taste, with some sweetness; generous and rounded with excellent long aftertaste.

1964 Colour quite orangey. Bouquet pleasing, open and ripe. Soft, agreeable wine with good fruit and some length, but no great finesse.

CHATEAU

Pontet-Canet

PAUILLAC

Driving north on the D2 between Pauillac and Pauillac-le-Pouyalet, look for a turning on your left marked by a large wooden crucifix; Château Pontet-Canet is signposted from here, and is situated about 1 km along this road on the left-hand side.

Pontet-Canet owes its name to Jean-François Pontet, who started the vineyard in 1725, gradually piecing together parcels of land until there were some 20 hectares under vines by 1740. Pontet was an influential lawyer, who rose to great power in local and national politics; he served as private secretary to Louis XV, and was appointed Major-General of the area in his later years. Over the next eighty years the property grew in size and importance, until in 1821, the year that Bernard de Pontet sold his St Julien property to Hugh Barton, Pontet-Canet was producing up to 200 tonneaux of wine, which sold at Fourth-Growth prices.

It would appear that during the next forty-odd years the standard of the wine suffered a minor eclipse. By the time the last de Pontet, an old lady, sold it to Hermann Cruse in 1865 for 700,000 francs, Pontet-Canet had only been classified as a Fifth Growth in 1855, and he found the vineyard somewhat neglected. The power and resources of the mighty Cruse family, whose star was by now very much in its ascendant, combined over the ensuing century to put the wine of Pontet-Canet on a level that was always at the top of the Fifths and often among the Fourths, Thirds and sometimes as high as the Seconds in terms of quality and price. Among the many properties to have benefited from Cruse ownership one can list Rausan-Ségla, Giscours, Haut-Bages-Libéral and d'Issan, the only property to remain in the family's hands after their firm's demise in 1974, as well as a host of good Crus Bourgeois.

Though the Cruses always produced a wine of persistent high quality at Pontet-Canet, they were the last Cru Classé in the Médoc to adopt the now universal practice of château-bottling. Until the early 1970s all Pontet-Canet was either bottled at the Cruse cellars on the Quai des Chartrons in Bordeaux, or it was sold in cask for bottling by the importing customer. This leads to many variations between one bottle and another of the same vintage prior to this time.

The range of buildings for the making and ageing of the wine at Pontet-Canet is impressive in its sheer size. The vast cuvier with its huge array of oak vats is an archetypal Skawinski design; the upper floor, where the grapes arrive at vintage time, is used for dinners and receptions during the rest of the year, and can comfortably house 600 seated diners. The chais for ageing the wine in cask were constructed by Hermann Cruse in the late 1860s, and are of a size appropriate to house even the most abundant vintage from the 65-hectare vineyard. The upkeep of the roofs alone, of which there are some three hectares, is a daunting thought. Unusually for the Médoc, Château Pontet-Canet also boasts a large underground cellar, where some casks, but mainly bottled wines are kept.

Pontet-Canet was bought in 1975 by Guy Tesseron, already owner of Lafon-Rochet in St Estèphe. The Tesseron business was originally that of Cognac merchants; indeed they still have a thriving business there, although they are now very much part of the Bordeaux establishment. Guy's son Alfred lives at Pontet-Canet, and is in charge of the three wine properties, which include Lafon-Rochet and Château Malescasse near Lamarque.

Since the Tesseron acquisition, all Château Pontet-Canet has been bottled at the château, and some exceptionally fine wine has been made. The good vintages are classic Pauillacs with lots of sinew and refinement that will repay long keeping – the 1983, 1982 and 1981 are all fine examples of these vintages, while the 1978 and 1975 will be really outstanding bottles in a few years. Lesser years, like 1980 and 1977, are well-made and correct, both very good to drink now, while one waits for the babies to grow. An excellent Deuxième Vin is made and sells under the label 'Chateau les Hauts de Pontet'.

The château itself is basically a small early 18th-century house, with two wings and a third floor added in the prosperous mid-19th century to make it a more grandiose and fit dwelling-place for the large Cruse family; the furnishings and decor

are contemporary with these alterations. There is a particularly fine panelled dining-room, a billiard-room and an elegant drawing-room, all of which are situated on the first floor. There are fine panoramic views of the Médoc to the south over the formal garden, and the approach to the west-facing front of the house is through a wooded park which contains several splendid cedars of Lebanon.

135

TECHNICAL INFORMATION

General

Appellation:	Pauillac
Area under vines:	70 hectares (soon to be increased to 75)
Average production:	33,000 cases
Distribution of vines:	Mainly in one pacel to the south and south-east of the château, with 20 hectares across the D2 near Château Pédésclaux
Owner:	Société Civile du Château Pontet-Canet
Administrator:	M. Alfred Tesseron
Régisseur:	M. Pierre Geffier
Maître de Chai:	M. Alain Coculet
Consultant Oenologist:	C.E.I. OE. Pauillac

Viticulture

Geology:	Garonne gravel, clay/silica subsoil on ironstone base
Grape varieties:	70% Cabernet Sauvignon, 20% Cabernet Franc, 10% Merlot
Pruning:	Guyot Double
Rootstock:	Riparia, 3309, 101-14, 16149
Vines per hectare:	8,300
Average yield per hectare:	45 hectolitres
Replanting:	About 1½ hectares per annum

Vinification

Added yeasts:	Yes, if necessary
Length of maceration:	4–6 weeks
Temperature of fermentation:	30°C average
Control of fermentation:	Cooling by water-cooled jackets, water heating by jackets with Alfa-Laval system
Type of vat:	Oak and epoxy-resin lined cement
Vin de presse:	Incorporated according to necessity
Age of casks:	⅓ new each vintage
Time in cask:	18–24 months
Fining:	Egg-white
Filtration:	Sur plaque before bottling
Type of bottle:	Bordelaise lourde

Commercial

Vente Directe:	Yes, to visitors only
Direct ordering from château:	Yes
Sales:	Through Bordeaux négociants
Visits:	Yes, by appointment Telephone: 56 59 04 04 or 56 52 15 71 (office) Hours: 0900–1200, 1400–1730 Monday to Friday

---

THE TASTING AT CHATEAU PONTET-CANET, 29 October 1984
J.S., Alfred Tesseron, Alain Coculet

1983 Good deep red. Open nose with fruit and new oak. Long in the mouth with very good fruit and tannins. Will be very good, but will take some years.

1982 Dark, dense colour. Full and rounded bouquet with rich fruit. Big and tannic, less rounded at this stage than lots of '82 Médocs, with dominant tannins; will take time.

1981 Fine bluey-red colour. Attractive, slightly curious, peppery bouquet. Balanced, structured wine with finesse and backbone. Will be a very classic bottle.

1980 Good medium garnet colour. Pleasing, open fruit on the nose, suggestion of cedarwood. A good, light claret, well made, a little on the short side, but very good to drink now and for a year or two.

1979 Dense, purplish colour. Good fruit on nose, but still quite closed. A firm, well-made wine with quite a lot of flesh, fruit and good tannin. Good in 2–3 years.

1978 Brilliant, scarlet colour. A lovely, blackcurrant bouquet opening up. This is what 1978s ought to be like, though they often disappoint. A fine, structured wine with good fruit flavours, but still quite tannic. Long aftertaste, needs a year or two yet.

1977 Good colour for '77, not much browning. Nose agreeable, with a touch of caramel. Good fruit on palate, slight roasted flavour. All right to drink now.

1976 Deep red, quite dense. Ripe on nose, typical enough of this very hot year. Pleasing but slightly overripe fruit on palate, finishing a bit short. Good to drink now, but don't keep it around too long.

1975 Very nice medium red colour, with depth. Nose complex, and still shy. Just beginning to open up, complex, tannic and long. Should like to taste again in three or four years.

ST ESTEPHE

This most northerly of the four great wine communes of the Médoc peninsula has the fewest classified growths, two Seconds and one each in the Third, Fourth and Fifth sectors; there are also a few excellent Bourgeois growths, and among these Château de Pez would almost certainly merit a placing in a revised classification. St Estèphe has the largest area of the 'big four' entitled to the communal appellation, and produces a total of some six million bottles in an average year, though the proportion of top-quality wine is lower than in its three sister communes.

All the Crus Classés and the better Crus Bourgeois, from the majestic oriental fantasy of Cos d'Estournel to the rather sombre Calon-Ségur, enjoy a fine view of the Gironde estuary; this is said to be an essential for the production of great wine in the Médoc. St Estèphe boasts one château which has risen head and shoulders above its classification; like Châteaux Léoville-Las-Cases, Ducru-Beaucaillou and Pichon-Longueville-Lalande, Château Cos d'Estournel has outstripped its fellow Second Growths in terms of price by a considerable margin; in any re-classification based on price, these four would form a distinct group between the Premiers Crus and the rest of the Deuxièmes.

St Estèphe wines are the biggest and toughest members of the Médoc family; they have a huge bouquet, and in youth are characterised by enormous fruit and very pronounced tannin. The wine of this commune has been likened to that of St Emilion, but for me it has more of the backbone of the Médoc, and in old age it has a breeding and finesse rarely found on the other side of the Dordogne. The wines of Châteaux Montrose and de Pez are certainly among the author's personal favourite clarets.

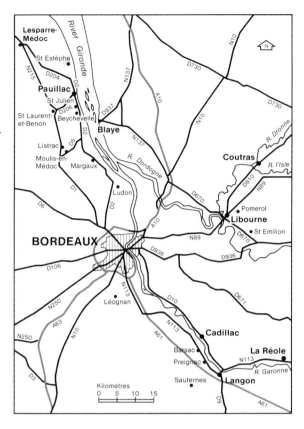

Although I have been lucky enough to enjoy the best food and the most memorable bottles of my life at the tables of Robert Dousson and Jean-Louis Charmolüe, again the hungry traveller will be hard put to it to find sustenance in this commune; surely another opportunity for an enterprising restaurateur?

CHATEAU
Calon-Ségur
ST ESTEPHE

The château and vineyard of Calon-Ségur lie to the north of the small road that leads out of the village of St Estèphe, back to the D2 between Pez and St Corbian. The main part of the vineyard is surrounded by an old stone wall, which runs along the right-hand side of this road.

There has been an important estate or Maison Noble here since Gallo-Roman times. There are several versions of the origin of the name Calon, but the consensus of opinion tends towards the Latin word *calonis*, a barge-type craft which was used for ferrying timber on the Gironde estuary and through the inland waterways of the Médoc. The name of the commune was for centuries de Calones, and right up to the 18th century it was called Saint-Estèphe-de-Calon.

The lands of Calon were certainly among the earliest in the area to be planted with the vine; taxes on wine produced here were levied as early as the 13th century, at which time Calon was the principal fief of the Seigneurs of Lesparre, passing in 1362 to a junior branch of the family called the Gombauds. After the conquest of Guyenne, the vineyard became the property of the powerful d'Albrets, who owned vast tracts of the Médoc including 'la noble Mothe de Margaux'.

By the 18th century, when individual wine-producing estates had begun to assume their present-day significance, Calon had passed by marriage into the hands of 'the Prince of Vines', the Mar-

quis Nicolas-Alexandre de Ségur, owner of Latour and Lafite. Evidently Ségur preferred Calon to all his other properties, and is reputed to have declared, 'I make wine at Lafite and Latour, but my heart is at Calon'; hence the heart that adorns the label to this day.

On the death of de Ségur in 1755, Calon was assigned to his cousin, Alexandre de Ségur-Calon, who built the château as it is today. His son, Nicholas-Marie-Alexandre, inherited the estate on his father's death, but was something of a black sheep; he got into serious financial difficulties, and Calon had to be sold in 1798, when it was bought by Etienne-Théodore Dumoulin. His son, also called Etienne, concentrated his considerable energies and talents on the creation of the vineyard that was to become Montrose, and sold the major part of the Calon estate, including the present vineyard, to the Lestapis family in 1824 for over half a million francs.

The Lestapis, originating from Paris, were substantial vineyard owners in the Médoc, though Calon-Ségur was their only property of great importance. Under their ownership it was rated a Third Growth in 1855, though it had enjoyed a higher placing in Ségur's days. It would appear that the Lestapis lost interest in the estate in the latter part of the 19th century, and Calon-Ségur was put up for sale in a rather run-down state in 1894.

139

The new proprietors of this 'Premier Cru de St Estèphe', as it was then known, were Georges Gasqueton from Château Capbern in St Estèphe, and his uncle Charles Hanappier of the old-established négociant family. The Hanappier share has passed through the female side of the family to Bertrand Peyrelongue, and the Gasquetons are represented by Philippe, grandson of Georges, who now lives at and runs Château Calon-Ségur. The house is one of the most imposing in the Médoc, and the tapestries and antiques collected by the Capbern-Gasqueton family are worth a special visit.

Philippe Capbern-Gasqueton is very much a traditionalist, and the wine of Calon-Ségur reflects his philosophy. From a mixture of principally Cabernet grapes, grown on the relatively low-lying, gravelly 60 hectares of vineyard, the wine is fermented in lined-steel vats and aged for a minimum of two years in casks, one-third of which are new each vintage. Calon-Ségur is typical St Estèphe, tannic and unapproachable in its youth, but emerging with bottle-age into a claret of great finesse, while retaining some of its youthful reserve. The 1982 which I tasted at the château was one of the most tannic and well-structured wines from this generally round and approachable vintage that I have encountered; it will be a very fine bottle, but will require patience on the part of the consumer. I was surprised recently by a bottle of the 1961 vintage, which, though superb, ripe and concentrated, showed more of the softer charms of the southerly parts of the Médoc; I suspect this may be due to the higher proportion of Merlot which was used then.

TECHNICAL INFORMATION

General

Appellation:	St Estèphe
Area under vines:	60 hectares
Average production:	20,000 cases
Distribution of vines:	In two main blocks, north-east and north-west of the village of St Estèphe
Owner:	Héritiers Capbern-Gasqueton and Peyrelongue
Director/Régisseur:	M. Philippe Capbern-Gasqueton
Maître de Chai:	M. Michel Ellisalde
Consultant Oenologist:	Professor Pascal Ribereau-Gayon

Viticulture

Geology:	Gravel
Grape varieties:	65% Cabernet Sauvignon, 15% Cabernet Franc, 20% Merlot
Pruning:	Guyot Simple
Rootstock:	Riparia
Vines per hectare:	6,000
Average yield per hectare:	35 hectolitres
Replanting:	1 hectare per annum

Vinification

Added yeasts:	None
Length of maceration:	3 weeks
Temperature of fermentation:	30°C
Type of vat:	Lined steel
Vin de presse:	Not incorporated in grand vin
Age of casks:	⅓ new each vintage
Time in cask:	24 months
Fining:	Egg-whites
Filtration:	None
Type of bottle:	Bordelaise antique

Commercial

Vente Directe:	No
Exclusivities:	None
Sales:	Through the négociants
Visits:	Yes, by appointment Telephone: 56 59 30 08 or 56 59 30 27 Hours: 0730–1230, 1400–1800 except weekends

THE TASTING AT CHATEAU CALON-SEGUR, 7 December 1984
J.S., Philippe Capbern-Gasqueton, M. Ellisalde

1983 Good deep red. Nose open, with fruit and new wood. Surprisingly light, with a lot of wood, but fruit and tannins good.

1982 (Still in cask.) Amazingly dark and dense. Very closed on nose. Very complex, concentrated, mouthful. Enormous fruit and tannin, the most 'skeletal' 1982 I have tasted. A great keeping wine – will be superb. Philippe Gasqueton preferred it to the '83, and I agree.

1980 Nice, medium dark red. Nose a bit more open, with some good fruit. Very well structured for 1980, with tannin and spine as well as fresh fruitiness. May be drunk now, but will keep and improve.

CHATEAU
Capbern-Gasqueton
ST ESTEPHE

Drive up the D2 until you come to the right-handed fork in the road, pointing to St Estèphe. Château Capbern-Gasqueton is in the centre of St Estèphe, right next to the church.

The only remarkable thing about the history of Château Capbern-Gasqueton is that it has remained in the same family since the middle of the 18th century. Philippe Capbern-Gasqueton, the present representative of the family, owns and runs the property along the same strict, traditional lines as his other vineyards at Calon-Ségur nearby, and du Tertre in Margaux. He and his two children are the ninth and tenth generations of Capbern-Gasquetons, and continuity is assured; his daughter is a qualified oenologist, and she and her husband are currently responsible for the resurgent Château du Tertre.

The vineyard is in two main parcels, one near Calon-Ségur and the other bordering the vines of Château Meyney. The grape varieties grown are 40% Cabernet Sauvignon, 20% Cabernet Franc and 40% Merlot. The high proportion of Merlot is very necessary, since the wine of Capbern-Gasqueton is typically St Estèphe in its sternness and slow maturation; even with this quantity of the softer, suppler Merlot vine, a minimum of five years is necessary before the wine begins to open up and lose its sharp edges.

Vinification is carried out in the cuvier opposite the château, where the wine is fermented in lined-steel vats. For ageing, no new casks are used, as these would only add to the wine's tough intractability; instead casks of one or two vintages are bought in from other Crus Classés. The casks are stored partly in the chai attached to the vathouse, and partly in the cellar, which runs under the whole length of the rather sombre-looking château. The maître de chai, a portly Dickensian figure with a fine pair of whiskers, is Monsieur Michel Ellisalde, who also attends to vinification at Château Calon-Ségur.

The wine of Château Capbern-Gasqueton is also marketed under the label 'Le Grand Village Capbern'.

TECHNICAL INFORMATION

General

Appellation:	St Estèphe
Area under vines:	30 hectares
Average production:	9,000 cases
Distribution of vines:	In two main blocks
Owner:	M. Philippe Capbern-Gasqueton
Director:	M. Philippe Capbern-Gasqueton
Maître de Chai:	M. Michel Ellisalde
Consultant Oenologist:	M. Pascal Ribereau-Gayon

Viticulture

Geology:	Gravel
Grape varieties:	40% Cabernet Sauvignon, 20% Cabernet Franc, 40% Merlot
Pruning:	Guyot Simple
Rootstock:	Riparia
Vines per hectare:	6,000
Average yield per hectare:	30 hectolitres
Replanting:	As necessary

Vinification

Added yeasts:	No
Length of maceration:	3 weeks
Temperature of fermentation:	30°C
Control of fermentation:	By cold-water circulation
Type of vat:	Lined steel
Vin de presse:	Not used
Age of casks:	Casks of one or two vintages
Time in cask:	24 months
Fining:	Egg-white
Filtration:	None
Type of bottle:	Bordelaise

Commercial

Vente Directe:	No
Sales:	Through the négociants
Visits:	Yes, for appointment telephone: 56 59 30 27 Hours: 0730–1200, 1400–1800 Monday to Friday

THE TASTING AT CHATEAU CAPBERN-GASQUETON, 10 May 1985
J.S., M. Philippe Gasqueton

1984 Good, deep red. Bouquet quite open with some blackcurrant. Good structure with fruit and tannins in balance; will take some time, but will be a good bottle. (No Merlots in the assemblage.)

1981 Deep red with blue tinges. Nose good but quite closed. An elegant wine with lots of charm and backbone; will drink very well in two or three years.

1979 Good deep colour. Nose still quite closed. Fairly hard and tannic, but has plenty of fruit and should be good in a couple of years.

1978 Good, bright medium colour. Bouquet much more open than the '79. Flavour already nicely evolved and beginning to drink well.

1975 Good depth of colour with no browning. Fine nose with plenty of blackcurrant fruit. Still quite tannic and closed but all the elements there for a really great bottle.

CHATEAU
Cos D'Estournel

ST ESTEPHE

Take the D2 towards St Estèphe, through Pauillac and Pauillac-le-Pouyalet, pass Château Lafite-Rothschild on your left, and you will see the oriental gateway and façade of Cos d'Estournel at the top of a rise on the right-hand side.

The name of Cos d'Estournel derives from the word *caux*, a small hill of *cailloux*, or gravelly pebbles, and the family name of Estournel, the first recorded owners of the property, wealthy landowners in the southern part of the commune of St Estèphe.

In the early 19th century, the property was inherited by the last of the Estournels, Louis Gaspard, a noted eccentric. His chief love at that time, and his main business, was the importation of Arab horses into France. As his ships were frequently outward-bound without cargo, he decided to send out some of the wine made on his estate to test the Middle-eastern market. His contacts, being strict abstaining Muslims, were, not surprisingly, unenthusiastic and the wine returned on board the same ships to Bordeaux. This story may well be apocryphal, but the conclusion is that the journey across the bounding main under hot eastern skies so improved the quality of the wine that M. d'Estournel was able to sell it at a high price in Bordeaux, and the price and popularity of his wines never looked back.

In 1811, Louis Gaspard d'Estournel sold Cos, and the buyer was a civil servant from Paris named Lapeyrière. There was a clause in the contract, giving d'Estournel the right to re-purchase within 5 years; this option was not taken up, but Lapeyrière did, in fact, sell the property back to d'Estournel in 1821. From the re-purchase until 1853, Louis Gaspard devoted his life and a great deal of money to building Cos into a much larger, more reputable and indeed a model vineyard. The area under vines increased from a mere 14 hectares in 1821 to its present size of 65 hectares. He also bought several other vineyard properties including Château Cos Labory, next door.

From the 1830s the great work of building the ornate 'Chinoiserie' chais and cellars commenced. The principal style of architecture was doubtless inspired by M. d'Estournel's eastern travels, whereas the triumphal archway giving onto the very minor road from Pauillac to St Estèphe, bearing his coat of arms and motto, possibly owes more to Louis Gaspard's sense of his own importance. The effect is nonetheless imposing, albeit a surprise for the unready traveller. The odd thing is that all this oriental flight of fancy was expended on the chais and cellars and no living accommodation was included in the scheme, nor has any been built to this day; for this reason, the property is sometimes known simply as 'Cos d'Estournel', there being no actual Château. The imposing carved oak doors to the main entrance, with its clove-head motive, are not part of d'Estournel's original dream. They used to belong to the Sultan of Zanzibar's palace, and Bruno Prats bought them at auction.

In 1852 Louis Gaspard, having exhausted his funds in his quest for perfection, was forced to sell his properties once more, and died a year later. The purchaser was a wealthy and somewhat mysterious Englishman named Martyn, who paid a staggering FF 1,125,600. Martyn was an absentee landlord, but continued with d'Estournel's work of investment and care for the property. Cos was awarded the Deuxième classification in 1855, and in 1866 was awarded the 'prix d'ensemble' by the Agricultural Society of the Gironde for cleanliness and modern methods employed on the property, combined with humanitarian treatment of the workers. Apart from capital investment, the cleverest move by Martyn was his appointment of one M. Gerome Chiapella as administrator of the property. Chiapella was a Bordeaux négociant, as well as being proprietor of Château La Mission Haut-Brion; possessed of formidable skills, both vinous and commercial, he did much to improve the fortunes of the property.

Martyn sold the property to a M. d'Errazu in 1869, who held Cos d'Estournel for 20 years, a period during which the château was mainly noted for an extravagantly high style of living. In 1889 – d'Errazu's money having run out – the property was acquired by the Brothers Hostein, and in 1894 devolved upon one of the Charmolüe family of Château Montrose, which they still own, by virtue of his marriage to a Hostein daughter.

In 1917 Fernand Ginestet, founder in 1899 of the

143

famous Bordeaux shipping firm of that name and grandfather of the present owner, bought Cos d'Estournel as his first venture into vineyard ownership; many other properties followed, including, during the 1930s, Château Margaux. Cos passed to Fernand's son Pierre, his sister Mme. Jean Prats in 1971, and subsequently to her son Bruno, who now runs the property in a dynamic and efficient way in partnership with his two brothers, Yves and Jean-Marie.

The estate marches with Château Lafite-Rothschild, which it overlooks, and the two properties are divided by the Jalle du Breuil, a stream running through a marshy tract to which Professeur Henri Enjalbert attaches great geological significance; he says that it 'played the role of a tectonic "throw"', which isolated the peculiar 'graves' of Cos, throwing them up into a high ridge with perfect drainage. This ridge is definitely noticeable as you approach the château from the direction of Lafite.

The vineyards, some 65 hectares of a total estate of about 80 hectares, stretch behind the chais as far as the railway line; in front of the impressive buildings, with their copper-roofed bell-towers and triumphal arch, the vines slope down to the marshy land around the Jalle du Breuil. The Cabernet vines, both Sauvignon and Franc, are planted on the higher ground to gain maximum benefit from the outcrops of gravelly soil, whilst the Merlot are planted lower down on the more chalky soil. The proportions of the encépagement, 60% Cabernet and 40% Merlot, are about average for St Estèphe.

The wines of St Estèphe in general tend to be on the hard and aggressive side; indeed, they can sometimes be so tough that, by the time some of this fibre and backbone has toned down, the fruit has also diminished, leaving an unsatisfactory and thinnish wine. Cos, however, having a higher percentage of gravelly soil than most of St Estèphe, tends to have more elegance and finesse, and has had remarkable success with some of the lighter, quicker-maturing vintages as a result. 1958, 1960 and more recently 1974 and 1977 are good examples of this.

The vinification is overseen by the régisseur, M. Jacques Pelissié, but oenological help is at hand both from M. Hallay of the Prats' shipping company and in the person of Professor Pascal Ribereau-Gayon of the Bordeaux Institute of Oenology. Fermentation takes place in either enamelled metal or stainless-steel vats, firstly at a temperature of 28°C or lower to catch the maximum of aromatic elements, and then the fermenting must is heated up to 35°C so as to extract the tannin and colour until alcoholic fermentation is complete. The period of ageing en barrique varies according to vintage, and two types of filtration are employed, sur terre before the wines go into cask, and sur plaque before bottling – to give maximum cleanliness and brilliance. In short, all that is best and most up-to-date, consistent with tradition and high quality, is used at Cos d'Estournel.

In the past a 'non-vintage' Cos d'Estournel has been marketed, without much success, by Ginestet. The first was a blend of 1960, some 1964 and 1965, but it did not sell well, as purchasers had no idea what the wine was, or when they should drink it. It was a clever idea for selling off-vintages, and, if properly thought out and marketed could well have a useful application throughout Bordeaux. The second wine of Cos, such as the production from young vines, carries the label of the neighbouring Château de Marbuzet, also the property of the Prats family, where all the entertaining takes place.

TECHNICAL INFORMATION

General

Appellation:	St Estèphe
Area under vines:	60 hectares
Average production:	200 tonneaux per annum
Owner:	G.F.A. des Domaines Prats
Director:	M. Bruno Prats
Régisseur:	M. Jacques Pelissié
Maître de Chai:	M. Jean-Baptiste Irigaray
Consultant Oenologist:	Professor Pascal Ribereau-Gayon

Viticulture

Geology:	Gunz gravel on a base of St Estèphe chalk
Grape varieties:	60% Cabernet Sauvignon, 40% Merlot
Pruning:	Guyot Double Médocaine
Rootstock:	Riparia Gloire, 101.14
Vines per hectare:	10,000
Average yield per hectare:	35 hectolitres
Replanting:	Programme giving average age of 40 years

Vinification

Added yeasts:	If necessary, depending on vintage
Length of maceration:	20–28 days, according to vintage
Temperature of fermentation:	Varied to the optimum extraction of tannins
Control of fermentation:	Cuves equipped with thermostatic circulatory pump
Type of vat:	Cement, enamelled steel and stainless-steel
Vin de presse:	Not added to the Grand Vin
Age of casks:	100% new in big years, 70% in average years and casks of one vintage for light years
Time in cask:	Between 20 and 24 months according to vintage
Fining:	Egg-whites
Filtration:	Sur terre before putting in cask, sur plaque before bottling
Type of bottle:	Special Grand Cru

Commercial

Vente Directe:	Yes, to callers in France only
Sales:	Through the Bordeaux négociants
Visits:	Yes, by appointment Telephone: 56 44 11 37 Hours of opening: 0900–1200, 1430–1730

THE TASTING AT CHATEAU COS D'ESTOURNEL, 28 September 1984
J.S., Monsieur Hallay

1983 Deep, blackish red. Excellent and powerful Cabernet nose. Huge and full of 'puissance'; a typical young St Estèphe of outstanding potential. Concentration of multiple flavours and good tannins, very long aftertaste. Will be a great wine.

1982 Slightly less dark, but still very dense. Aromatic and spicy bouquet, with lots of fruit. Big and rounded, with tannins not at all dominant. Very soft for such a young St Estèphe, but will last a very long time.

1981 Deep, purplish red. Ripe bouquet, with a touch of gaminess. Starting to open a little. Similar in style to 1983, but more finesse and less power. Will be a lovely and elegant Cos.

1979 Very deep, bluey red. Powerful nose, with lots of fruit and some elegance. Well structured, with fruit and tannins together. Already very good, but with lots of future. '79 at Cos, as with many Médocs, is much better than was originally thought.

1971 (Tasted at lunch at the 'Chapon Fin' in Bordeaux, with M. Jacques Marly of Château Malartic-Lagravière.) Lovely deep colour, very dense, hardly a trace of brown. Beautiful, open cassis nose. Long, elegant and classic. Approaching maturity, but still has lots of life. A really good bottle.

CHATEAU
Cos Labory
ST ESTEPHE

As you drive northwards towards St Estèphe from Pauillac, leaving Château Lafite on your left, you climb a small hill and arrive at the elaborate fantasy of Château Cos d'Estournel. Immediately after the buildings of Cos d'Estournel there is a turning on your right, and the gateway to Cos Labory is on the northern side of this junction.

Not a great deal is known of the early history of Cos Labory, mainly, I suspect, because it was until late in the 19th century part of the domaine of Cos d'Estournel next door. It is for sure that Mr Martyn, the English owner of Cos d'Estournel from 1853 to 1869, was also owner of Cos Labory, and the property no doubt derived much benefit from the very capable administration of Martyn's manager, M. Gerome Chiapella.

In 1922 Cos was bought by an Argentine family by the name of Weber, who were distant cousins of Madame Audoy, the present owner, who acquired Cos Labory in 1959. She and her hus-band, François, completely restored the elegant little château during the 1970s, and later built a large warehouse to the rear of the house which gives ample room for stock and also houses the bottling line, with two large stainless-steel vats.

François Audoy sadly died in 1984, and it is his son Bernard who now runs Cos Labory. He studied oenology at Talence, and started working with his father in 1978.

The wine produced at Cos Labory tends to be somewhat less austere and to mature a little earlier than most St Estèphe wines, mainly due to the fairly high proportion of Merlot vines planted. Since 1981 they have used one-third new casks for each vintage, and I certainly noticed an increased backbone in the last three vintages as a result.

The vast majority of Cos Labory's production goes for export, finding its best market in the United States and Great Britain, as well as Belgium, Holland and Switzerland.

146

TECHNICAL INFORMATION

General

Appellation:	St Estèphe
Area under vines:	15 hectares
Production:	6,000 cases
Distribution of vines:	In three parcels, one behind the château, and two across the road at the foot of the hill
Proprietor:	Mme. Cecile Audoy
Director and winemaker:	M. Bernard Audoy
Consultant Oenologist:	M. Bernard Audoy and Laboratoire Oenologique de Pauillac

Viticulture

Geology:	Gravel
Grape varieties planted:	30% Merlot, 40% Cabernet Sauvignon, 25% Cabernet Franc, 5% Petit Verdot
Pruning:	Guyot Double
Rootstock:	Riparia 420A, 3309, etc.
Density of planting:	9,600 vines per hectare
Yield per hectare:	45.5 hectolitres
Replanting:	0.5 hectare per annum

Vinification

Added yeasts:	No
Length of maceration:	20–25 days
Temperature of fermentation:	28–30°C
Control of fermentation:	Water circulation in stainless steel; water-cooled 'serpentine' for concrete vats
Type of vat:	Stainless steel and lined concrete
Vin de presse:	Incorporated in Grand Vin
Age of casks:	One-third new each year, one-third one vintage old, one-third two vintages old
Time in cask:	15–18 months
Fining:	Egg-whites
Filtration:	Sur terre end of first winter, sur plaque before bottling
Type of bottle:	Bordelaise

Commercial

Vente Directe:	Yes
Direct ordering from château:	Yes
Agents in foreign countries:	Thorman Hunt Limited, 42 Monmouth Street, London WC2
Visits:	Yes, by appointment Telephone 56 59 30 22 Normal office hours, not weekends

THE TASTING AT CHATEAU COS LABORY, 25 October 1984
J. S. Bernard Audoy

1983 (En barrique, 1 year cask.) Clear medium red. Good nose, with fruit and oak. Quite light, but with backbone. Long aftertaste.

1982 Dense, blackish red. Good, open bouquet – blackcurrants. Rounded, mouthfilling, already approachable with a mass of fruit and muted tannins.

1981 Attractive medium red. Nose excellent with plenty of fruit. Well-made wine with good structure and balance. Already pleasant, but in two or three years will make a good bottle.

1980 Good colour for 1980. Nice straightforward fruity bouquet. Light, rounded, and already good to drink, but no need to rush!

1979 Good medium colour. Pleasant fruit on nose. Round, with good fruit. Long, with slightly dry finish.

1978 Colour similar to '79. Nice bouquet – fruity and slightly truffly. Ripe and harmonious, a little short with dry finish.

1977 Lightish colour. Faint mushroomy smell. Good, but beginning to dry off. Short, to be drunk now.

1976 Beginning to go brown. Very ripe, hot-weather nose. Very ripe taste, dry finish. Beginning to go over.

1975 Good medium red. Nose a bit closed. Beginning to open up but still a bit tough. Lovely strawberry fruit taste. Will be good bottle.

CHATEAU
Lafon-Rochet
ST ESTEPHE

Château Lafon-Rochet is situated on the left-hand side of the D2, just after you pass through the hamlet of Cos on your way north to St Estèphe.

The property owes its name to the Lafon family, who were the owners from the 17th century until 1888. The first M. Lafon was a counsellor to the Bordeaux parliament in the late sixteen hundreds, and it is a widow Lafon-Camarsac who appears as proprietor in the 1855 classification, when Rochet, as it was then known, was graded among the Fourth Growths.

Little remains of historic interest for the eye to see, except for an old chapel in the garden behind the château, built by one of the Lafon family as a resting-place for weary pilgrims. It has been at some time converted for use as a water-tower, but Madame Tesseron has plans to restore it to some of its former beauty. When her husband, Guy Tesseron, bought Lafon-Rochet in 1959, it was, as they say, for the second time of asking; he had already made an offer for the property five years earlier, which had been turned down.

This highly successful Cognac merchant had long cherished an ambition to own a property in Pauillac, not to be fulfilled until 1974, when he bought Pontet-Canet. Lafon-Rochet, however, was close; its vines neighbour those of Duhart-Milon to the south of the property. I have the distinct impression that a Pauillac style of wine is aimed at and, moreover, frequently achieved. As a first step in this direction, Tesseron had a large number of Merlot vines replaced with Cabernet Sauvignon, which did not noticeably affect the character of the wine until the mid-sixties, when the new vines started to mature. The Cabernet Sauvignon influence is more noticeable with each succeeding vintage, and I find the wines of the late seventies and early eighties are showing a marked increase of finesse and breeding. In an incredibly difficult blind tasting of sixteen 1981 St Estèphes, I had no hesitation in picking out Lafon-Rochet as one of the five Crus Classés of the commune.

Following a very proper policy, subsequently adopted at the family's other properties, Château Pontet-Canet and Château Malescasse, Tesseron made his first priority the extension and replanting of the vineyard, coupled with the restoration and improvement of the chais and the cuvier; only after this work was well in hand did he turn his attention to the château itself, or rather the place

where the château should have been. According to Guy's son, Alfred, who runs the three properties, there was nothing here but a concrete blockhouse. Guy Tesseron gave his architect an open-ended commission to design a house that would blend properly into the Médoc landscape, and the long, single-storey house with its squat central tower certainly fits the bill. It nestles comfortably amid the vines, backed by some fine trees in the park beyond, for all the world as if it had been there for two hundred years. Inside there is a certain *Mary Celeste* atmosphere about the place; it is spotless and immaculately furnished with a subtle combination of antique and modern pieces, the beds are made up and there are almost pans simmering on the kitchen stove, but nobody lives here! It was Tesseron's idea, when he built the place, that he would retire here to live in rural tranquillity at Lafon-Rochet, but he thrives on the busy world of commerce, and pipe and slippers are not yet for him.

TECHNICAL INFORMATION

General

Appellation:	St Estèphe
Area under vines:	42 hectares
Average production:	21,000 cases
Distribution of vines:	In one block
Owner:	Société Civile du Château Lafon-Rochet
Director:	M. Alfred Tesseron
Maître de Chai:	M. Paul Bussier
Consultant Oenologist:	M. Gérard Gendrot

Viticulture

Geology:	Garonne gravel
Grape varieties:	70% Cabernet Sauvignon, 8% Cabernet Franc, 20% Merlot, 2% Malbec
Pruning:	Guyot Double
Rootstock:	420A, Riparia, 3309
Vines per hectare:	8,300
Average yield per hectare:	45 hectolitres
Replanting:	$1\frac{1}{2}$ hectares per annum

Vinification

Added yeasts:	Yes, in difficult years
Length of maceration:	4–6 weeks
Temperature of fermentation:	30°C
Control of fermentation:	Cooling by damp jackets, warming by electric system
Type of vat:	Oak and cement
Vin de presse:	Proportion incorporated according to vintage
Age of casks:	$\frac{1}{3}$ new each vintage
Time in cask:	18–24 months
Fining:	Egg-white
Filtration:	Sur plaque at bottling
Type of bottle:	Bordelaise lourde

Commercial

Vente Directe:	Yes, to visitors only
Sales:	Through the Bordeaux négociants
Visits:	Yes, for appointment telephone: 56 52 15 71 Hours: 0900–1200, 1400–1730 Monday to Friday

THE TASTING AT CHATEAU MALESCASSE, 30 January 1985
J.S., Christian Seely, Michel Tesseron

1982 Deep, blacky red. Powerful bouquet. Big, strapping wine with a lot of tannin and rich in fruit. Will be very good.

1981 Deep, dense red. Excellent bouquet, with definite Cabernet cassis. This will be a fine bottle, already showing a good balance of fruit and tannins with length and finesse. Should wait three or four years.

1980 Brilliant, medium dark colour. Open, fresh nose. Straightforward, correct wine, with good fruit and some backbone. Nice, clean aftertaste. Good for 1980.

1979 Good bluey red. Strong fruit on nose, suggests blackberries. Nice fruit flavour, still quite hard and tannic; not a huge wine, but well-made and worth waiting a couple of years for.

1978 Excellent medium red colour. Lovely open nose of ripe fruit. Good and complex flavour, with some length; although already attractive and approachable, still has a long way to go.

1977 Medium bright red, shading to orange. Bouquet light, but pleasant – crushed strawberries. Lightish, with same strawberry flavour promised on the nose, some acidity and a bit short.

1976 Pale colour, going brown. Very ripe on bouquet. Good ripe taste of summer fruits; no great length, but ready and good to drink now.

CHATEAU
Montrose
ST ESTEPHE

Driving north along the D2 from Pauillac towards St Estèphe, turn right between the Chinese fantasy of Château Cos d'Estournel and Château Cos Labory. Follow this road, the D2e, past Château Marbuzet, and you will come to a turning on your right, signposted to Château Montrose.

Château Montrose is perhaps one of the youngest Crus Classés of the Médoc. Towards the end of the 18th century it was a piece of rough moorland, known as the 'Lande de l'Escargeon', covered with heather and scrub, and formed part of the great estate of Calon-Ségur. In 1778 there was a legal action, presumably for debt, brought against Nicolas-Marie-Alexandre de Ségur, son of the great 'Prince des Vignes', Alexandre de Ségur. As a result, one M. Etienne Théodore Dumoulin became the owner of this piece of land for around FF 300,000; he died in 1808, and the property passed to his son, also Etienne Théodore, who was not slow to realise the potential of this scrubland for the cultivation of the vine, and for the production of quality wine.

Dumoulin started cleaning and planting the ground around 1815, at the same time putting up the basic buildings for winemaking. He also built the château, which is really more aptly described as a substantial country house, for occupation only during the summer and the vintage. There is an element of *trompe l'oeil* in the architecture of Château Montrose, giving it an illusion of greater than actual size when viewed from the river. The ground floor is wider than the first, which consists of only two large bedrooms and a large landing, while above this is a second floor which is in reality only a 'dormer' tower-room. It was almost certain that M. Dumoulin christened the property Montrose, as it appears on the first official survey map of St Estèphe in 1825 under this name, showing only 6 hectares of vines and a few buildings. The origin of the name is not recorded, but it is a pleasant and poetic notion to ascribe it to the colour of the heather in flower before the vineyard existed.

Dumoulin continued to enlarge and improve the property at a great rate; by 1832 there were 31 hectares under vine, and extensive new buildings for vinification, stables and housing for the workers. His efforts were rewarded by the classification of Montrose in 1855 among the 2nd Growths. The latter half of the 19th century was 'easy street' for the Grands Crus, until the phylloxera struck. Records show vintages such as 1858, 1862, 1864 and 1865 selling in totality, en primeur, for prices ranging from 2,100 to 4,000 francs a tonneau. In 1866 the valuable cellar of T.B.G. Scott, British Consul in Bordeaux from 1832 to 1866, a great connoisseur of Bordeaux wines, was sold and it included some Château Montrose 1848 which fetched FF 15.50 a bottle.

During these prosperous years, Dumoulin enlarged Montrose still further by the purchase and exchange of numerous plots, cleverly managing to keep the entire estate within one boundary. By 1866 the property had increased in size to some 100 hectares, nearly two and a half times bigger in only 34 years! By this time Dumoulin had died, and the property had passed to his heirs, who were all his adopted children. They sold Montrose in June 1866 to Mathieu Dollfus, an Alsatian, for FF 1,050,000.

Dollfus appears to have been a model proprietor, investing enormous sums in improved vinification – the last oak vats that he built were only replaced 15 years ago – new housing for the vignerons, stabling of amazingly advanced design for the horses and oxen, with automatic measured feeding for each animal, construction of underground cellars to avoid sacrificing precious vines and further additions and refurbishments to the château itself. This paragon also introduced many benefits for the workers, including free medical care, payments to pregnant mothers from the time they stopped work till the children were weaned, and payment of 10% of the profits divided among the workers each New Year's Day. This last, progressive move was doomed to a short life, however, with the arrival of the dreaded phylloxera beetle. Dollfus pumped money into the battle against this plague like a man possessed. He sank a 735-foot well, and saturated the vineyards through a network of galvanised iron piping which must have cost a fortune, resulting in yields that hardly diminished from normal. The investment may have been too onerous, however, for

150

the Société Anonyme, which he founded in the year of his death, sold Montrose in May 1889 to two brothers, Jean-Justin and Jean-Jules Hostein for 1,500,000 francs. Jean-Jules soon took control of Montrose, but sold it to Louis Victor Charmolüe, husband of his niece and heiress, Marie-Thérèse Hostein, in 1896 for 800,000 francs.

Louis Victor Charmolüe, already a substantial vineyard owner, with Cos d'Estournel, Pomys, where he lived, and domaines at Troussas and Condissas near Bégadan as well as Château Romefort near Lesparre in his portfolio, added Montrose to his bag by this opportune marriage. The happy couple were joined in wedlock at the church in St Estèphe by Cardinal Lecot, Archbishop of Bordeaux, connoisseur of fine wines and a familiar figure at Montrose, where a special chapel and suite of rooms were built for his use. Difficult years followed, in which grafting to new phylloxera-resistant rootstocks was undertaken, followed by the First World War; then followed one of the Médoc's sunnier decades, with the great vintages of the '20s, 1926, 1928 and 1929, but it was in the midst of this period of prosperity that Louis Victor died in 1925.

It is curious how periods of light and shade seem to follow one another in the Bordeaux wine picture. The '30s must have been one of the most difficult, with a succession of bad vintages and a world slump, terminating with the Second World War. Albe Charmolüe, son of Louis Victor, steered Montrose through these troubled waters with skill and perseverance, reducing the area under vines and keeping expenditure to the bare minimum, and Montrose survived with its reputation intact; as if all these problems were not enough, a devastating fire in 1933 deprived the property of the entire 1932 vintage and much of its buildings.

In wartime, the French army sited an anti-aircraft battery at the château, which was taken over by the Germans after the fall of France. Although the invaders did not occupy the château, the A-A battery became an important target for the RAF bombers; luckily the château and buildings survived, though a number of bombs fell among the vines.

In January 1944, Albe Charmolüe died unexpectedly, leaving his widow, Mme. Yvonne, with two small children and the burden of a war- and depression-ravaged Montrose to cope with. How she shouldered this load and brought the name of Montrose through these years must serve as a monument to a remarkable lady.

Jean-Louis Charmolüe took over the running of the property in 1960, and has since maintained the traditions of improvement and investment that mark the history of this estate. The magnificent oak cuvier, entirely reconstituted between 1960 and 1970, with its tiled floor, improved and modernised housing for the estate workers and the impressive reception room made out of the old billiard-room are among the visible signs of Jean-Louis's work here. He has also added a vast new building for storage in bottle, and a new ageing chai.

The quality, elegance and longevity of the wine of Château Montrose continue undiminished and the warmth of the reception that visitors receive from the Charmolüe family is in the very best traditions of the Médoc.

151

TECHNICAL INFORMATION

General

Appellation:	St Estèphe
Area under vines:	67 hectares
Average production:	24,000 cases
Distribution of vines:	In one block
Owner:	Jean Louis Charmolüe
Maître de Chai:	Jean Louis Papot
Régisseur:	Roger Bareille
Oenological Consultant:	M. Pascal Ribereau-Gayon and M. Couasnon (Laboratoire de Pauillac)

Viticulture

Geology:	Gravel to a depth of 3–4 metres, on subsoil of clay and marl
Grape varieties:	65% Cabernet Sauvignon, 10% Cabernet Franc, 25% Merlot
Pruning:	Guyot Double
Rootstock:	44.53, SO4 and 101.14
Vines per hectare:	9,000
Yield per hectare:	32 hectolitres
Replanting:	As necessary to maintain average age of vines of 40 years

Vinification

Added yeasts:	Not normally, but yes if need arises
Length of maceration:	20–25 days
Temperature of fermentation:	Temperature taken at least 3 times daily during fermentation, and cooling if necessary
Type of vat:	Oak
Vin de presse:	Part added or not, according to quality
Age of casks:	$\frac{1}{4}$ to $\frac{1}{3}$ new per annum, to maximum 6 years old
Time in cask:	2 years
Fining:	Always 6 fresh egg-whites per cask
Filtration:	None
Type of bottle:	Bordeaux, Grand Cru

Commercial

Vente Directe:	Yes, to passing tourists
Direct ordering from château:	Yes
Exclusivities:	None
Visits:	Yes, for appointment telephone: 56 59 30 12 Hours: 0730–1230, 1400–1800 weekdays only

THE TASTING AT CHATEAU MONTROSE, 29 November 1984
J. S. M. Jean-Louis and Mme. Charmolüe, Mlle. Charmolüe, Wendy Seely

1983 Deep, almost black red. Nose quite approachable, soft. Surprisingly soft and rounded, new oak and tannins not overpowering. Long flavour, but not typical of this vintage.

1982 Very deep purple. Nose good, but very closed. (Only just bottled.) Big, hard and tannic. Lots of firm fruit, but a wine with less instant fatness than many 1982s and considerable elegance and style. Will be a very great bottle.

1981 Good medium to dark red. Bouquet just beginning to show fruit and style. Fine, elegant and supple wine with more femininity than 2 later vintages, but plenty of sinew to keep it going a long time.

1978 Colour beginning to lighten a shade. Perfumed nose starting to come out of its shell. Complex, developing well, elegant, good in 3–4 years and then some.

1976 Very good red for 1976, no orange. Good powerful ripe nose, with none of the hot, cooked smell sometimes found in this vintage. Flavour excellent, rich and long – still needs a year or so. Among best of 1976 I have tasted.

1975 Deep, dense red. Very closed on nose. This is a 1975 which will definitely be worth waiting 5, 10, even 20 years for. Still very tannic, but has also huge concentration of richness, fruit and complexity of flavours. Very long in mouth.

At lunch

1970 Still very dense, blackish colour. Nose powerful and ripe. Flavour very concentrated, with a mass of fruit and tannin. Will go on and on.

1964 Deep, clear red. Luscious ripe bouquet. Just coming to perfect readiness, though has enough concentration to last for a long time. A fine example of what could be done in this vintage if the grapes were picked before the rain.

1961 Colour still dense and dark. Nose powerful and very aromatic. An amazing wine, considering its 23 years. Concentrated, still not entirely open, with great, complex elegance and finesse. A St Estèphe from a great vintage and a great château that will probably outlive us all.

CHATEAU

Les Ormes de Pez

ST ESTEPHE

Follow the D2 north from Pauillac through Leyssac and continue until you reach the village of Pez. In the centre of the village there is a very sharp right-hand bend, and the gateway to Château les Ormes de Pez faces you as you enter the bend. Proceed with extreme caution, watching for traffic from your right.

At one time the vineyards of les Ormes de Pez formed part of the estate of de Pez itself, but became separated during the 18th century. The nicely proportioned château and extensive range of winemaking and farm buildings were constructed in 1792. There is nobody living at the château presently, but Jean-Michel Cazes tells me that a relation of his may move in there shortly. Certainly there is enormous potential here; the house has an elegant, terraced façade on the side away from the road, and looks out over an extensive, though sadly neglected park. A feature of the property is the fine array of mature trees in the park and gardens, though the magnificent elms, or 'ormes', from which the château derives its name, have been decimated by the ubiquitous Dutch elm disease.

The estate has been the property of the Cazes family since the 1930s, when they also bought Lynch-Bages. It is run today by André Cazes and his son, Jean-Michel, assisted by the Lynch-Bages team of Daniel Llose, Technical Director, and Guy Bergey as Maître de Chai.

The cuvier has been recently equipped with 12 stainless-steel vats of 190 hectolitres capacity, each fitted with thermostatic temperature control, which allow for a carefully regulated fermentation of even the largest vintage and in difficult conditions. Ageing is conducted in the usual oak casks over a relatively short period of up to 15 months, and the casks are of one or two vintages from either Lynch-Bages or other Crus Classés.

The vineyard lies on both sides of the village of Pez, and covers 29 hectares of sandy clay and gravel, on a subsoil of chalky marl. This soil composition and the fairly typical St Estèphe encépagement of 55% Cabernet Sauvignon, 10% Cabernet Franc and 35% Merlot gives a wine of some body and backbone which, like most of the wines of this commune, requires some years in bottle to be properly appreciated.

153

TECHNICAL INFORMATION

General

Appellation:	St Estèphe
Area under vines:	29 hectares
Average production:	14,000 cases
Distribution of vines:	In two principal parcels, on either side of the village of Pez
Owner:	G.F.A. les Ormes de Pez (the Cazes family)
Technical Director:	M. Daniel Llose
Maître de Chai:	M. Guy Bergey
Consultant Oenologist:	Laboratoire d'Oenologie de Pauillac

Viticulture

Geology:	Gravel and sandy clay on subsoil of chalky marl
Grape varieties:	55% Cabernet Sauvignon, 10% Cabernet Franc, 35% Merlot
Pruning:	Guyot Double
Rootstock:	Riparia 101-14, 420A, 4453
Vines per hectare:	9,000
Average yield per hectare:	40 hectolitres
Replanting:	By complantation, maintaining average vine age of 40 years

Vinification

Added yeasts:	None
Length of maceration:	Average 2 weeks
Temperature of fermentation:	30°C
Control of fermentation:	Running water on exterior of vats
Type of vat:	Stainless steel, 12 × 190 hectolitres
Vin de presse:	5% to 10% incorporated, according to vintage
Age of casks:	2–3 years
Time in cask:	12–15 months
Fining:	Egg-whites
Filtration:	Light, before bottling
Type of bottle:	Bordelaise

Commercial

Vente Directe:	No
Sales:	Through the Bordeaux négociants
Visits:	Yes, by appointment Telephone: 56 59 19 19

THE TASTING AT CHATEAU LYNCH-BAGES, 11 October 1984
J.S., Jean-Michel Cazes, Miklos Dora

1983 Dark, dense red. Good, open bouquet with cassis. Lots of fruit with some sweetness, surprisingly approachable with softish tannins; will be a lovely bottle, but quite soon.

1982 Dark, bluey red. Open, generous nose. Typical of this fat vintage, well-made and rounded, already giving generous fruit flavours. Long in the mouth, with muted tannins.

1981 Dense blue/black colour. Nose closed, but fine. Plenty of fruit, but tannins harsher and quite some backbone. Much more typical St Estèphe than the two later vintages. Will be an elegant claret in three years or so.

154

CHATEAU

De Pez

ST ESTEPHE

As you drive north up the 'Route des Châteaux' from Pauillac towards Le Verdon, you will pass through the village of Pez; in the middle of the village there is a sharp and dangerous right-hand bend, and the gateway to Château de Pez is on the left hand elbow of the corner.

I will always have the happiest memories of Château de Pez, as it was the first property I ever visited in the Médoc, more years ago than I care to remember. I went there with my good friend the late Martin Bamford from Château Loudenne. Martin told me at the time, and his words hold good today, that if I wanted to learn about the making of good Bordeaux, or the problems – and their solution – in any particular vintage, I could do no better than talk to Robert Dousson.

The whole ambiance of de Pez is typically and traditionally Médocain in the very best sense, with its oak fermentation vats, cool and well-ordered ageing cellar and the dark, earth-floored cellar where the older bottles lie in tempting dust-covered ranks; the very smell of the place embodies Bordeaux.

Pez is historically one of the original noble houses of St Estèphe, together with Château Calon-Ségur, although the vineyard as it is today was not created until 1680, under the ownership of the Pontac family, owners of Haut-Brion and Margaux. The wine of de Pez was used for topping-up the casks at Château Haut-Brion until 1749, so Pez found its way, albeit in a very diluted form, in to the City of London Pontac tavern at the same time as Haut-Brion!

Before the de Pontac ownership, de Pez had two earlier recorded seigneurs, Jean de Briscos in 1452 and the 'Noble Homme' Ducos in 1526. Jean de Pontac took possession in 1585, and his family owned it for 170 years until it passed to the Marquis d'Aulede in 1744. Eleven years later de Pez became the property of the Comte de Fumel, Governor of Château Trompette and Commandant of the province of Aquitaine. At the revolution the estate became a 'Bien National', and was bought by M. Tarteiron, whose widow sold to Jean Charles Balguerie in 1820; 47 years later this fine vineyard passed in to the famous Irish/Bordeaux Lawton family. After one more change of ownership in 1902, de Pez was acquired by Robert Dousson's maternal grandfather, Jean Bernard, in 1920.

Robert Dousson was born at de Pez in 1929. Although he claims in a carefully prepared 'Product Fact' sheet to have 'no distinctions', I would hotly contest such typical modesty. Since taking over the running of de Pez, Robert has consistently produced wine of the highest quality, even in difficult years. I am not alone in my opinion that, should there be a re-classification, de Pez would undoubtedly rank among the 4th or 3rd Growths.

I think perhaps personal supervision and constant attention to detail at every stage of the winemaking process are the major keys to the continued success and reliability of de Pez. On almost every occasion that I have visited or telephoned the château, Robert Dousson has been in the chais, the cuvier or the vineyard, which I find significant.

The vineyard, which is all in one piece around the château, covers just over 23 hectares of good gravelly soil, with a chalk subsoil. The ground forms an east-west 'croupe' or bank, which makes for perfect natural drainage, and is planted with 70% Cabernet Sauvignon, 15% Cabernet Franc and 15% Merlot.

Vinification is traditional: a magnificent range of oak vats has been completely remade over the last 10 years, and ageing is in oak casks over 20 months, during which time racking takes place every 3 months. An average of 25% of the casks are new every vintage. Fining takes place, using fresh egg-whites, at the end of the first year's ageing in cask. As a result of his care of the wine during its long cask ageing, Robert Dousson never finds it necessary to filter his wine before bottling.

The vin de presse is never included in the Grand Vin, but is declassified and is used for the wine given to the staff. Another example of the rigorous care exercised at Château de Pez is the existence of a 'deuxième vin' label, Château la Salle de Pez, for wine not considered worthy of the grand vin, and the fact that Robert Dousson has only found it necessary to use it once, in 1974.

Since 1968 the wine of Château de Pez has been exclusively marketed by Gilbey de Loudenne,

which has proved of mutual benefit to both parties. This was due to the high regard in which the late Martin Bamford held the wines of Château de Pez; the link also formed a close personal friendship between the Doussons and this remarkable young Englishman, so sadly missed throughout the Bordeaux region since his untimely death in 1982. Robert and Edith shared with Martin a passionate love and an encyclopedic knowledge of fine wine and the gastronomic arts, and talk fondly of memorable bottles shared and restaurants visited in every corner of France.

Mme. Dousson is a formidable cook herself, as all who have been lucky enough, including the author, to have had their feet under the Dousson table, will readily bear witness! I salute this happy pair for their knowledge and their willingness to impart it to others, and I thank them for their kindness and the warmth of their welcome.

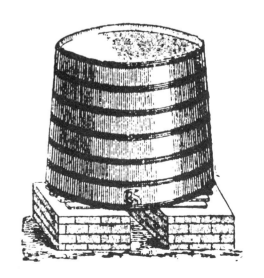

TECHNICAL INFORMATION

General

Appellation:	St Estèphe
Area under vines:	23.23 hectares
Distribution of vines:	In one piece around the château
Owner:	Société Civile du Château de Pez
Director:	M. Robert Dousson
Maître de Chai:	M. Pierre Faugère
Consultant Oenologist:	M. Quertinier

Viticulture

Geology:	'Gunzienne' gravel on a chalky subsoil, distributed on an east-west 'croupe' or bank rising to 18 metres above sea-level, with excellent natural drainage to the roadside ditches surrounding the property
Grape varieties:	70% Cabernet Sauvignon, 15% Cabernet Franc, 15% Merlot
Pruning:	Guyot Double
Rootstock:	Exclusively Riparia Gloire de Montpelier
Vines per hectare:	6,750
Replanting:	Complantation as necessary – average 5,500 vines per annum

Vinification

Length of maceration:	3 weeks average
Temperature of fermentation:	28–29°C maintained day and night until end of alcoholic fermentation
Control of fermentation:	By water-cooled serpentine pipes
Type of vat:	Oak
Vin de presse:	Not used in grand vin
Age of casks:	Average $\frac{1}{4}$ new in each vintage
Time in cask:	20–22 months
Fining:	Fresh egg-whites
Filtration:	Never
Type of bottle:	Bordelaise

Commercial

Commercialisation:	Solely and exclusively through I.D.V. France, Gilbey de Loudenne, Château Loudenne, St Yzans-de-Médoc, 33340 Lesparre. Telephone: 56 41 50 23
Visits:	By appointment only Weekdays: 0800–1200, 1430–1800, Saturdays: 0800–1200 Telephone: 56 59 30 07 or Château Loudenne

THE TASTING AT CHATEAU DE PEZ,
26 November 1984
J.S., M. Robert Dousson and, at lunch, Mme. Edith Dousson

1983 Good, deep colour. Bouquet already good, oaky. Hard and tannic, but plenty of fruit and length. Will be very good, but needs plenty of time.

1982 (Not yet bottled at time of tasting.) Similar density of colour. Nose attractive, slight tang of iodine. Rounded, complete, easy in the mouth, but very big and classic. Will go a long way.

1981 Deep bluey red. Nose quite closed. Well structured and balanced, with plenty of backbone. Classic Médoc to keep 3 or 4 years, and then some.

1980 Colour good and bright, only a little lighter than later years. Attractive and mouthfilling with fruit, and good long aftertaste. Plenty of backbone for a 1980.

1979 Colour deep, clear ruby. Nose open and attractive. Well-made wine, already easy in the mouth with some length and elegance.

1978 Good, deep colour again. Nose beginning to develop well, cassis. All the elements are in harmony here, but still quite shy. A big, complex and classic wine that will make superb drinking in a few years.

1977 Excellent colour for 1977, no browning. Nose open and attractive with lots of fruit. Simple and easy to drink now. Typical Château de Pez expertise in a difficult year.

1975 Colour again very good, starbright red. Nose just beginning to come out, but still closed. Fruit there, but wine still very closed and tannic. When this comes together, it will be a great de Pez.

1973 Lighter red, no trace of brown. Nose ripe and open, with hint of strawberries. Pleasant, aromatic and quite long for the vintage, strawberries in mouth too. Balance good – just right now.

At lunch

1967 Good depth of colour. Nose powerful and ripe. Complex, no hint of tiredness, good now but will last. A very good 1967.

1961 Excellent deep, dense red. Powerful nose. Complete, concentration of flavour extraordinary. A beautiful claret, well up to expectations of this marvellous year. Aftertaste goes on and on. Classic.

HAUT-MEDOC, MEDOC, MOULIS, AND LISTRAC

These four appellations cover a vast area, from the very south of the Médoc to the far north, and include five Crus Classés and countless excellent properties of lesser status producing fine red Bordeaux.

The five Crus Classés are all in the Haut-Médoc; Château la Lagune near Ludon is the nearest classified Médoc property to the city of Bordeaux, with Château Cantemerle only a kilometre or so further north on the opposite side of the D2. The other three, de Camensac, La Tour Carnet and Belgrave, are all in the sub-commune of Saint-Laurent to the west of St Julien.

Moulis, which includes Château Maucaillou and the excellent Château Poujeaux, lies to the west of the D2 on a level with the village of Arcins; slightly to the north-west of Moulis is the area entitled to the appellation of Listrac, centred around the village of that name on the main D1 from Bordeaux to Le Verdon. It is in Listrac that Baron Edmond de Rothschild has staked his chips in the huge vineyards of the re-born Château Clarke.

The vineyards entitled to the appellation of plain 'Médoc' are all to the north of the village of St Seurin de Cadourne, and include such fine properties as Loudenne, which makes one of only four white wines produced in the Médoc, and Châteaux Greysac and la Tour de By to the north of St Christoly, both of which are good Crus Bourgeois, and can be relied upon to produce wines of consistent quality and value.

The very size of the appellations covered in this section obviously precludes any uniformity of character or style, and each wine is best studied in its own right, and on its own particular merits.

As to the restaurants within the far broader limitations of these appellations, I ate both well and often in Arcins at the Lion d'Or, a small, unpretentious Bar/Restaurant owned by its highly volatile and talented chef Aimé Barbier. He will, I know forgive me if I describe our first meeting; I was taken there to be introduced to le patron at about 10 o'clock one Sunday morning, to find Aimé in his underpants in the kitchen; he had just returned from la chasse, and was changing out of his wet clothes, yelling at a howling dog next door, stirring a savoury pan of civet de lièvre, having a row with his wife and welcoming me and my companion all at the same time. From nowhere appeared a bottle of Sauternes, glasses,

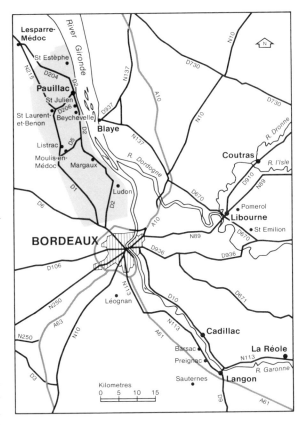

knife and fork, bread, plate and a huge dollop of steaming and delicious civet from the bubbling pot. I don't know if you've ever eaten jugged hare, accompanied by copious drafts of sweet white wine, at 10 o'clock on a Sunday morning, just after a large breakfast of bacon, sausages, eggs and black pudding, but I can tell you that it is a gastronomic feat of heroic proportions, not easily forgotten. For the promotion of the Entente Cordiale I should be given at least the Légion d'Honneur.

Another Lion d'Or, this time in St Laurent, the 'mid-west', of the Médoc, also serves good food and has a respectable wine list. I have also eaten very well at La Mare aux Grenouilles just to the north of Lesparre, where the à la carte menu is impressive in its sheer size, and the wine list is in proportion. The owner, Monsieur de Wilde, is a member of a Belgian family with long associations in the Bordeaux wine trade.

160

CHATEAU
Beaumont
HAUT-MEDOC

Château Beaumont is clearly signposted on the left of the D2 as you drive northwards, just before you enter the village of Cussac.

Early history of Château Beaumont is difficult to trace, since all the archives were lost at the time of the French Revolution. Cussac has certainly been a wine-producing area since the 10th century, though the Beaumont estate is not identified as such until the early 19th century. The name of the property possibly derives from one Louis de Beaumont who was one of eight commissars responsible for condemning to death a certain Pierre de Montferrand in the 15th century. De Montferrand was the Seigneur of Cussac during the Hundred Years War and had sided with the English. It is not unlikely that the traitor's lands would have been seized by one of his judges.

The huge and imposing château, with its turret and four pointed towers, was built by a Monsieur Bonin, who had amassed a vast fortune from his plumbing business. He installed himself at Beaumont, with a pretty young wife, all set to be part of the Médoc aristocracy. His fellow proprietors, many of them fairly 'new rich' themselves, and consequently sensitive to the subtle nuances of social climbing, found the plumber unacceptable, and Bonin sadly decided to make the best of a bad job and sold up. The sad M. Bonin was followed by the eminently acceptable Comte de Gennes, an artist and draughtsman of some talent.

Around the beginning of this century, the owner was M. Jean Germain, and under his aegis Château Beaumont prospered and flourished. At this time there were 100 hectares under the vine, and some 250 to 300 tonneaux of wine were produced each year. *Les Grands Vins de la Gironde Illustrés*, produced by Henry Guillier of Libourne, states that the cuvier was the most modern in the area, where all vinification work was done mechanically, and which had a capacity of 3,600 hectolitres. He also states, that, among others, the négociants Calvet, Cruse, Eschenauer and de Luze were regular buyers of Beaumont's wine, and that no less than ten gold medals had been awarded to

161

the château between 1882 and 1907.

Germain was followed by a succession of proprietors, including a Venezuelan, Señor Ignacio Andrade. In 1966 another Venezuelan, Monsieur de Bolivar, an architect from Caracas and a soi-disant descendant of Simon Bolivar, El Liberador, bought the property. He gave it to his third wife, some 30 years his junior, and shortly afterwards he left her and returned to Venezuela. Mme. de Bolivar did her best; the vineyard was, through a succession of owners and hard times, reduced by now to only 10 hectares, which she managed to increase to 38, but it proved too much of a burden for her, and in 1979 she sold Château Beaumont to the present owner, Bernard Soulas.

Monsieur Soulas is a grain-merchant and farmer, and has completely revitalised Beaumont in the five short years since he bought it. There are now 88 hectares planted, of which 79 are currently in production. Planting has been carried out in stages, so as to give a correct balance of young and old vines, and the work will continue until 1990, by which time there will be a total of 120 hectares under vines. He has also restored and re-equipped the vathouse with stainless-steel cuves. On the advice of his oenologist, M. Boissenot, Soulas ages the crop in oak casks, one-third of which are renewed every year. I was most impressed by the quality and finesse of the vintages made under the new ownership, and the standard is certainly improving with each succeeding vintage. They are charming, elegant and well balanced, with a distinctly spicy bouquet and a lovely and consistent deep colour.

TECHNICAL INFORMATION

General

Appellation:	Haut-Médoc
Area under vines:	88 hectares, 79 in production
Average production:	31,000 cases
Distribution of vines:	Principally in one block
Owner:	M. Bernard Soulas
Director:	M. Paradivin
Régisseur:	M. E. Grangerou
Maître de Chai:	M. F. Panozzo
Consultant Oenologist:	M. Boissenot

Viticulture

Geology:	Deep bank of Garonne gravel
Grape varieties:	58% Cabernet Sauvignon, 7% Cabernet Franc, 34% Merlot, 1% Petit Verdot
Pruning:	Guyot Médocaine
Rootstock:	SO4 or 101.14 depending on subsoil
Vines per hectare:	6,600
Average yield per hectare:	35/40 hectolitres
Replanting:	Continuing programme

Vinification

Length of maceration:	20 days
Temperature of fermentation:	28°C
Control of fermentation:	Running water on exterior of cuves
Type of vat:	Stainless steel
Vin de presse:	Vinified and aged separately
Age of casks:	⅓ renewed every year
Time in cask:	18 months
Fining:	Egg-white
Filtration:	Sur plaque before bottling
Type of bottle:	Bordelaise lourde

Commercial

Vente Directe:	Yes
Direct ordering from château:	Yes
Agents overseas:	None
Visits:	Yes: telephone 56 28 15 53 Hours: 0800–1200, 1400–1800 Monday to Friday

THE TASTING AT M. BERNARD SOULAS' HOUSE IN EYSINES, 14 January 1985
J.S., Bernard Soulas

1982 Good deep blackish red. Nose closed. Taste also rather dumb, but tannin and fruit in plenty there, with backbone and length.

1981 Same good depth of colour. Good smell of blackcurrant starting to develop. Well made and balanced, with elegance, charm and length. Will be a very nice bottle.

1980 Excellent limpid, medium dark red. Nose open and attractive. Extremely well made wine with good fruit and surprising backbone for this vintage.

1979 Good medium red. Spicy, open bouquet. Easy on the palate, but lacks the finesse of the later vintages. Good now.

Also tasted: 1983 Moulin d'Arvigny, entirely made from young vines, and currently enjoying a 'vogue' in some restaurants.

Nose fresh and fruity. Fruity and round, very little tannin, a good fresh red with some bite.

CHATEAU
Belgrave
HAUT-MEDOC

As you enter the village of St Julien, from the south on the D2, take the left turning, signposted to St Laurent, opposite the buildings of Château Léoville-Poyferré. Follow this road in the direction of St Laurent for about 2 km, and Château Belgrave is on your left-hand side, just after the gateway to Château Lagrange.

Château Belgrave has been through a bad patch. This is not an exaggeration; the few bottles that have come my way of vintages prior to the takeover of the present owners, have been, to say the least, disappointing. If you see the photo-graphs taken of the property in 1979, this will hardly surprise you. The chai and cuvier were virtual ruins, with daylight showing through all the roofs, and the vineyard was in no better state. No less than ten tons of wire were needed to replace the rusted vine supports, and practically every one of the stakes had to be renewed. When the cost of the new chai, cuvier and equipment, and the massive replanting programme are added, the capital investment can only be guessed at. The new owners are a 'Groupement Foncier Agricole', which is an owning and managing syndicate of

163

numerous shareholders, headed by the firm of Dourthe Frères at Parempuyre.

Patrick Atteret, son-in-law of Jean-Paul Jouffret, a director of Dourthe Frères, lives at Belgrave and runs the property. He has been there now some five years, and 1980 was his first vintage on the estate. Apart from all the rebuilding work and the care, attention and rigorous selection he gives to the winemaking, probably the two most important factors that will contribute to the reinstatement of Château Belgrave to its proper level will be the increased use of new casks, and the gradual change of grape-varieties planted. This latter change was counselled by Professor Peynaud; when the G.F.A de Château Belgrave arrived, the vineyard had a very high proportion of Merlot – some 70% – and his first advice was to reduce this to 35% and increase the Cabernet. This has now been achieved, but it will obviously be some years before the full benefits will be felt, as the vines mature and reach optimum production level.

The first proprietor of whom I have been able to find trace was one M. Bruno-Devez, who was the owner at the time of the 1855 classification, at which time the property was called Coutenceau; five years earlier, in Charles Cocks' first 'tourist guide' to the Médoc, M. Devez is shown as being the owner of a vineyard called Darroutty, producing some 75 tonneaux of St Laurent wine, and one presumes that this is again the same property under an even earlier name. In 1906 the owner was a M. Alibert, who was followed by Jules Canaferina, a Frenchman of North African origin, who did much for the property, and built new cellars in 1934.

The next owners were the Guges family, who occupied the château, but were not concerned with the winemaking side of the estate, and it was under their ownership that Belgrave went into eclipse. The renaissance of this 5th Growth is hopefully assured with the expertise and huge investment of the new owners, and results are already evident from the recent vintages I tasted.

TECHNICAL INFORMATION

General

Appellation:	Haut-Médoc
Area under vines:	55 hectares
Average production:	21,000 cases
Distribution of vines:	In one block
Owner:	Groupement Foncier Agricole du Château Belgrave
Director:	M. Patrick Atteret
Régisseur:	M. Pierre Desmorets
Consultant Oenologist:	Professor Emile Peynaud

Viticulture

Geology:	Gravel
Grape varieties:	60% Cabernet Sauvignon and Cabernet Franc, 35% Merlot, 5% Petit Verdot
Pruning:	Guyot Double
Rootstock:	101.14
Vines per hectare:	40 hectares @ 10,000, 15 hectares @ 6,500
Yield per hectare:	40 hectolitres
Replanting:	Annual complantation

Vinification

Added yeasts:	'Pied de cuve' – yeast starter employed
Length of maceration:	Average 15 days
Temperature of fermentation:	28°C
Control of fermentation:	By cold water circulation, and heating apparatus
Type of vat:	Stainless steel and cement
Vin de presse:	Incorporated according to vintage
Age of casks:	New
Time in cask:	Up to 2 years
Filtration:	Yes, before bottling
Type of bottle:	Bordelaise lourde

Commercial

Vente Directe:	Yes
Direct Ordering:	Yes
Exclusivity:	Yes, with C.V.G.B., Parempuyre
Visits:	Yes; telephone 56 59 40 20 Hours: 0830–1230, 1400–1700

THE TASTING AT CHATEAU BELGRAVE,
11 January 1985
J.S., M. Patrick Atteret

AND AT THE 'LION D'OR, ARCHINS
J.S., Christian Seely, M. Michel Tesseron

1983 Good deep red. Powerful bouquet of fruit and new wood. Tannic, but not aggresively so; well made with a degree of finesse, good fruit and some backbone. Will be a good bottle.

1981 Nice medium red. Nose pleasing, not very pronounced. A 'middle-weight' wine, with fruit and tannin quite nicely balanced now.

1980 Light to medium red. Bouquet quite attractive. An honest, straightforward 1980, pleasant enough for current drinking, with no pretensions to nobility.

CHATEAU
De Camensac
HAUT-MEDOC

As you approach Beychevelle-St Julien on the D2 from the South, you will see the enormous concrete St Julien bottle on your right among the vines. Do not follow the main road round the corner, but carry straight on into the village, and keep on this road towards Saint Laurent. Pass Gruaud-Larose and Lagrange on your left, and de Camensac is the next property, well signposted, on the left.

I have not been able to trace much of the history of Château de Camensac, except that it belonged for quite a time to a family by the curious name of Popp. They were certainly the owners in 1868, according to the Cocks of that date, and were also there 13 years earlier at the 1855 classification when de Camensac was designated a 5th Growth. The inexhaustible poet-laureate of the Médoc, Biarnez says of the property, 'Camensac d'un cinquième a déjà tout le lustre, et doit peut-être encore devenir plus illustre.' Does this mean that the poet thought it was not doing its best? The estate then passed through the hands of a family called de Tournardre, until it was acquired by M.H. Cuvelier et Fils, who were négociants in the north of France. They owned it until 1965, by which time it had become sadly neglected.

The brothers Elisée and Henrique Forner, of Spanish origin, bought de Camensac in 1965, and set about the huge and expensive task of restoring it to its proper place as one of the best classified growths of St Laurent. The Forners, also owners of a fine Rioja property, Marqués de Caceres, had been large vineyard proprietors in Narbonne, producing table wine for the mass market. Facing a decline in consumption of cheaper wine, and being by inclination more interested in the making of high-quality wine, they left Corbières, and bought first de Camensac, and shortly afterwards the huge abandoned vineyards of Château la Rose Trintaudon, a bare kilometre to the north.

It is Elisée who has been primarily concerned with the Médoc properties, while his brother Henrique runs the Rioja enterprise. The effort and investment that have been put into the restoration of these two vineyards have been both prodigious and successful. At de Camensac, Professor Peynaud's help was immediately enlisted, and on his

advice, over three-quarters of the vineyard was completely replanted, and for the first few vintages 100% new casks were used every year, and a rigorous selection process employed. Now that the vineyard has become properly established, only 40% new casks need to be bought each year. The wine has improved beyond all recognition, especially in recent years, having a good consistent colour, supple and fleshy in character, with good length and traditional Médocain keeping qualities.

Renovation and new building work on the chais, cuvier and other buildings at de Camensac was going on apace when I visited there at the beginning of 1985, and the pretty and elegant Chartreuse château will be completely restored when the present work is finished. The end result will be a compact, symmetrical, and, above all, beautiful working château. Cuvier and chais will be housed in three long contiguous buildings to the left of the house, with the château in the middle, and on the other side of the courtyard, three matching buildings will house the bottling line, packaging and stockrooms.

165

TECHNICAL INFORMATION

General

Appellation:	Haut-Médoc
Area under vines:	60 hectares
Production:	26,000 cases
Distribution of vines:	2 blocks, (48 hectares round the château, with 12 hectares nearby)
Owners:	Société Civile du Château de Camensac
Director:	M. Elisée Forner
Maître de Chai:	M. Bras
Chef de Culture:	M. Fescaux
Consultant Oenologist:	Professor Peynaud

Viticulture

Geology:	Deep gravel on various sub-soils, chiefly clay
Grape varieties:	60% Cabernet Sauvignon, 20% Cabernet Franc, 20% Merlot
Pruning:	Guyot Double
Rootstock:	Various
Vines per hectare:	10,000
Yield per hectare:	38 hectolitres
Replanting:	As necessary

Vinification

Added yeasts:	No
Length of maceration:	15–21 days
Temperature of fermentation:	30°C
Control of fermentation:	Heat exchange, and circulation of cold water from own well
Type of vat:	Some concrete, but mainly stainless steel
Vin de presse:	1st pressing incorporated, according to vintage
Age of casks:	40% new each vintage
Time in cask:	14–18 months
Fining:	Egg albumen in vat
Filtration:	Sur terre, before going in cask, sur plaque before bottling
Bottle:	Bordelaise lourde

Commercial

Vente Directe:	Yes
Sales:	On Bordeaux market
Visits:	Yes, by appointment Telephone: (56) 59.41.72 Hours: 0900–1200, 1400–1800 except at weekends

THE TASTING AT CHATEAU LAROSE TRINTAUDON, 21 January 1985
J.S., M. Elisée Forner

1983 Deep colour. Nose already very good. Rounded and fleshy, with ripe tannins; a big, classic 'vin de garde'.

1982 (Bottled September 1984.) Colour bright mid-red. Nose a bit closed. Touch of bottle sickness, but everything is there.

1981 A good medium dark red. Nose a bit closed, touch of cork. Corkiness there in mouth again, but not badly so; balance good, with charm and finesse, will be a good bottle.

1980 Lightish scarlet. Bouquet open and soft. Very pleasant, balanced wine. Very agreeable to drink now, but will go on a while yet.

1979 Good medium red. Bouquet pleasant, slightly peppery. Quite open and advanced for 1979, a bit lighter than some. Good now.

1978 Bright mid red. Nose good, with fruit and promise. A well structured 1978, with sinew and backbone. Already good, but will continue and improve.

1975 A shade darker than the '78. Nose very good, and quite open. Concentrated flavour, ripe fruit. Long in mouth. Will improve, but quite a forward 1975.

1970 (Elisée Forner said that the vines were still too young to make a great '70.) Colour quite orange. Nose slightly overripe. Flavour excellent now, quite short. Not far away from the end.

CHATEAU
Cantemerle
HAUT-MEDOC

Driving north up the D2 from Blanquefort, the gateway to Château Cantemerle is on your left just before you come to the village of Macau-en-Médoc.

Jean de Villeneuve purchased 'the noble house of Cantemerle' in 1579 for 12,500 livres; de Villeneuve was the second President of the Parliament of Bordeaux, and his family remained in possession here for over three hundred years. Wine was produced at Cantemerle even before the first de Villeneuve; there is a record in the archives stating that three tonneaux of wine were made in 1575.

The style of the château is asymmetrical and of varying periods, but the whole effect is utterly charming. This haphazard appearance reflects the continuous ownership of one family, who have obviously added bits here and changed bits there as and when the need arose, or fashion and fancy dictated; this has been done with a happy disre-

gard for tradition, in a way that more timid, new-rich proprietors would not have dared to emulate. The property passed in 1892 into the hands of the Dubos family, Bordeaux négociants of old-established reputation. In their hands, Cantemerle prospered and flourished until the late 1960s, but during the 70s the wine suffered a partial eclipse, possibly due to lack of investment. In 1980 Château Cantemerle was acquired by a French company, Goulet-Turpin, with extensive interests in property, foodstuffs and restaurants. Jean Cordier is also a shareholder in the new set-up, and the property has been administered by the Cordier company since 1980. Since then the wine has certainly improved enormously; the vineyard has been considerably extended, a new and typically Cordier spotless cuvier installed, and an immense programme of restoration work is in progress on the château and its impressive range of chais and other buildings.

Rumour has it that Château Cantemerle may be turned into an hotel. It is an unsubstantiated rumour, but it would make an ideal and picturesque base from which to tour the Médoc and, indeed, the whole Bordeaux region. It is beautifully situated, screened from the road by mature trees, at the end of a long drive, and the atmosphere is one of rural peace, yet it is, after Château la Lagune, the nearest Médoc Cru Classé to the heart of Bordeaux.

Apart from a beautiful 1966 which I drank at a dinner in Bordeaux this year, the only vintages I tasted were the first four made under Cordier management, and I was most impressed by the style and soft elegance of the wine that is now coming from Cantemerle. It has been suggested that its placing at the bottom of the list of 5th Growths in the 1855 classification was a clerical error, as it appears on the original handwritten document to have been squeezed in at the end in much smaller writing, and could easily have been originally meant to occupy a more elevated situation. This, of course, is mere speculation, but there is little doubt that, should there ever be a revised classification, Cantemerle would merit a higher rating on present form.

TECHNICAL INFORMATION

General

Appellation:	Haut-Médoc
Area under vines:	34 hectares in production, with the possibility of expansion to 53
Average production:	15,000 cases
Distribution of vines:	In parcels grouped around the château
Owner:	Société Civile du Château Cantemerle
Director:	M. Georges Pauli
Régisseur:	M. Jean Constantin
Maître de Chai:	M. Jean Fraysse
Oenologist:	M. Georges Pauli

Viticulture

Geology:	Spread of silico-gravel on a subsoil of Aquitaine chalk
Grape varieties:	40% Cabernet Sauvignon, 40% Merlot, 15% Cabernet Franc, 5% Petit Verdot
Pruning:	Guyot Double Médocaine
Rootstock:	Riparia Gloire 3309, 101.14
Vines per hectare:	10,000
Replanting:	1 hectare per annum

Vinification

Added yeasts:	No
Length of maceration:	18–20 days
Temperature of fermentation:	Around 30°C
Control of fermentation:	By serpentine water-cooling apparatus
Type of vat:	Stainless steel and oak
Vin de presse:	10% to 12% included, according to vintage
Age of casks:	$\frac{1}{3}$ new each vintage
Time in cask:	18–20 months
Fining:	Egg-whites
Filtration:	Light filtration 'sur plaque' before bottling
Type of bottle:	Bordelaise

Commercial

Vente Directe:	No
Exclusivity:	Yes: Ets. Cordier, 7/13 Quai de Paludate, 33000 Bordeaux
Visits:	Yes, by appointment Telephone: 56 92 70 00 Hours: 0830–1200, 1400–1730 Monday to Friday

---

THE TASTING AT CHATEAU
CANTEMERLE, 1 February 1985
J.S., Christian Seely, Daniel Vergely, M.J. Fraysse

1983 Blackish red. Powerful cassis bouquet. Perfect balance, at the same time powerful, yet soft and rounded, possibly due to high Merlot content.
1982 Good deep colour. Lovely nose of ripe fruit. Big and rounded with finesse. Large proportion of Merlot evident in a tip-top year for this variety. Will be a very good bottle.
1981 Bright rich red. Bouquet a bit closed. Lots of fruit, tasting a bit hard at the moment, but has elegance and backbone to be very good.
1980 Lovely bright garnet red. Nose open and soft. Quite a good bottle to drink now, a little more astringent than most wines of this vintage. Cordier's first wine at Cantemerle.

CHATEAU
Citran
HAUT-MEDOC

Driving north on the D2 from Margaux towards Pauillac, pass through Soussans and you come to the village of Tayac; there is a turning on your left, signposted to Château Citran. Go along this road, past Château Paveil de Luze on your left, and Citran will be found after about 2 km on your right.

This property, like many others in the area, had a difficult time during the '30s, the war years, and immediately after the war. So bad, in fact that when the Société Miailhe Frères took over in 1947, the buildings were nearly in ruins, there were sheep in the château, and there was not one productive vine on the huge estate!

There has been a château on this site since the 15th century, but this was demolished towards the end of the 17th century, and the present house was built on the original foundations by a family called Donissan, who stayed there for about a hundred years. In Charles Cock's *Bordeaux et ses Vins* of 1850, Citran is shown as belonging to M. Boyrie,

and producing some 230 tonneaux of wine. The Clauzel family were the owners until they sold to the Miailhe family company in 1947. The Miailhes, in particular Louis Miailhe, sole owner since 1950, put their collective shoulders to the wheel, and over the past quarter of a century re-established the quality and reputation of this Cru Bourgeois to its proper level.

In 1980, Jean Cesselin and his wife Françoise, daughter of Louis Miailhe, became sole owners of Citran. They have continued the work begun by Louis Miailhe, and have completely rebuilt the cask chai, the vats (4,500 hectolitres in stainless steel) and the bottling line. With the assistance of their manager, a qualified oenological graduate of the University of Talence, M. Jean-Marc Pons, they continue in pursuit of quality. The pretty château has also been restored, and the Cesselin family are frequently in residence to receive friends and customers both from France and overseas.

169

TECHNICAL INFORMATION

General

Appellation:	Haut-Médoc
Area under vines:	90 hectares
Distribution of vines:	One block
Owner:	M. Jean Cesselin
Director/Régisseur:	M. Jean-Marc Pons
Maître de Chai:	M. Manuel Fernandez
Consultant Oenologist:	Professor Emile Peynaud

Viticulture

Geology:	Gravel
Grape varieties:	60% Merlot, 40% Cabernet Sauvignon
Pruning:	Guyot Double
Rootstock:	101/14, 3309, 420A
Vines per hectare:	6,666 (sic!)
Yield per hectare:	40 hectolitres
Replanting:	3 hectares per year

Vinification

Length of maceration:	3 weeks
Temperature of fermentation:	28°C
Control of fermentation:	Water-cooled jackets on vats
Type of vat:	Stainless steel
Vin de presse:	Incorporated up to 7%
Age of casks:	$\frac{1}{4}$ new each vintage
Time in cask:	18 months
Fining:	Gelatine of eggs
Filtration:	Sur terre
Type of bottle:	Bordelaise

Commercial

Vente Directe:	Yes
Direct Ordering:	Yes
General Sales:	Through the Bordeaux négociants
Visits:	Yes
	Appointment for parties of 10 or more is advised
	Telephone 56 58 21 01
	Hours: 0800–1200, 1400–1800 weekdays
	0900–1200 Saturday

THE TASTING AT CHATEAU CITRAN,
12 January 1985
J.S., Christian Seely, M. Jean-Marc Pons

1982 (Bottled June 1984.) Medium dark red. Nose very powerful, ripe fruit. Good attack, rounded but with a mass of non-aggressive tannin. All possibilities there to make a very good bottle. Typical predominantly Merlot wine in a really good year for this variety.

1981 Pretty, medium dark red. Bouquet open, elegant and attractive, with ripe fruit. More finesse and less punch than 1982, well balanced and well made.

1979 Deep, blackish colour. Good rounded nose, with some cassis. Well structured, with lots of ripe fruit. Still quite hard, should improve.

1978 (In magnum.) Mid scarlet colour. Nose much more open and riper than younger vintages. Sound, well-made wine, with some backbone.

CHATEAU

Clarke

LISTRAC

Château Clarke lies between Listrac and Moulis, and is well signposted. It may be approached either from the D1 Bordeaux–Le Verdon road, from which you turn right in Listrac, or from the D2 from which Clarke is signposted to the left at the Lamarque/Moulis crossroads.

The history of Château Clarke, such as it is, does not bear much relevance to the new property, since the vineyard was virtually created in 1973, when Baron Edmond de Rothschild bought the long-abandoned property. The previous owner was a Monsieur Bidon, who demolished the château in the early 1950s. Feret, in the 1929 edition of *Bordeaux et Ses Vins*, likens the contemporary red wine of the property to that of St Emilion, even going so far as to describe it as a 'Vin de Bourgogne de la Gironde'; there is also mention of a white wine called Merle Blanc, produced from 10 hectares of 'terrain Sauternais', and described as 'ni doux, ni sec'.

Briefly, the origin of the Clarke name is from an Irish family who emigrated to France in 1692, having taken the side of James II against William of Orange. The Lord of Blanquefort sold the property, then known as Granges, to the Clarkes in 1750. It was a member of the family, one Luc-Tobie Clarke, a judge in the criminal court of Bordeaux, who built a château on the estate in 1810 and gave it his name.

A second and even bigger property was added to the Clarke domaine, when Château de Peyrelebade, also abandoned and château-less, was bought in 1979, making the total area of the estate a huge 177 hectares. At present 105 hectares are under vines, and a further 35 will be planted by 1990. The post-impressionist painter Odillon Redon lived at Peyrelebade in his early years, and is said to have been much influenced by the countryside of the area.

The creation of Château Clarke by Baron Edmond de Rothschild, great-great-grandson of Mayer Amschel Rothschild of Frankfurt, founder of the Rothschild dynasty, is the translation of a dream into reality. Although he is already the largest shareholder in Château Lafite-Rothschild, here he is sole owner, and more important, creator. The vast and futuristic winemaking instal-

lations, the huge underground stock-cellar, over one hundred hectares of vineyard totally replanted, to say nothing of the purchase of the entire estate, represents an investment of a magnitude that would terrify anyone but a Rothschild. All this has been done out of the Baron's personal fortune, and when one considers the somewhat indifferent wine-growing terrain of Listrac, one can begin to realise the tremendous faith behind this venture.

In addition to the competent team at Château Clarke, headed by Gérard Colin and counselled by the great Professor Peynaud and his successor M. Boissenot, there is an impressive public-relations machine at work. The Cercle Oenologique de Clarke, housed in the village of Moulis-en-Médoc, 150 yards from the church, offers a whole range of services to all who would learn more about the new Rothschild property. Here one can taste the wines, buy them by the bottle or case and have them delivered in France or exported, and there is even a restaurant offering a delicious lunch with which one may savour the wines of the property – always the best way to judge a bottle. Lectures, combined with a tasting, can be organised for parties of 10 to 30 people, introduced by the general manager and oenologist of Château Clarke, Gérard Colin, and given notice, this can be followed by a dinner. Charges for food are modest.

Great care has been taken over the planting of the vineyard, and nearly 100 separate analyses of soil were taken from different sections. It was only after careful consideration of these analyses that decisions were taken as to what grape varieties were to be planted, in what proportions and in which parts of the vineyard. 150 separate plots have been carefully identified, and the grapes from each plot are individually monitored for maturity, and are vinified separately to ensure complete control and to identify any problem areas.

Fermentation takes place in stainless-steel vats, and, following the malolactic fermentation, the new wine is drawn off into an impressive range of 150-hectolitre oak 'foudres' or barrels. Before the wine is transferred to traditional oak casks for

171

ageing, the wine is given its first racking. The wine spends only twelve months in cask, and is fined with albumen of egg. Only a light filtration through cellulose is performed just before bottling. The wine is then stored in the cavernous 1,000,000-bottle-capacity underground cellar to await shipment.

When all is said and done, Edmond de Rothschild has placed his vinous chips on the green baize of the Médoc, and Listrac is a long-odds sector of the table. The presentation, the public relations and the magic of the Rothschild name are almost a guarantee of success in themselves; the wine is very well made, but only time will show whether this newcomer to the ancient hierarchy of the Médoc will find acceptance among the connoisseurs of Bordeaux wine. I, for one, love a gambler, and wish every success to this brave essay.

172

TECHNICAL INFORMATION

General

Appellation:	Listrac
Area under vines:	105 hectares, to expand to 140 by 1990
Average production:	30,000 cases due to very strict selection
Distribution of vines:	One vineyard
Owner:	Cie Vinicole des Barons Edmond et Benjamin de Rothschild
Director and Oenologist:	M. Gérard Colin
Director-General	M. J. C. Boniface
Maître de Chai:	M. Philippe Bonnin
Chef de Culture:	M. Bazingette
Consultant Oenologists:	Professor Emile Peynaud and M. Boissenot

Viticulture

Geology:	Chalky clay and a little sandy gravel
Grape varieties:	46% Cabernet Sauvignon, 45% Merlot, 9% Petit Verdot and Cabernet Franc
Pruning:	Guyot Double
Rootstock:	Riparia Gloire, SO4, 101-14
Vines per hectare:	6,500
Yield per hectare:	45 hectolitres
Replanting:	None at present

Vinification

Length of maceration:	10–15 days, dependent on vintage
Temperature of fermentation:	30°–33°C
Control of fermentation:	By running water
Type of vat:	Stainless steel
Vin de presse:	Proportion incorporated, according to vintage, decided at final assemblage
Age of casks:	25% to 30% new each vintage
Time in cask:	12 months
Fining:	Albumen of egg
Filtration:	Sometimes sur terre before going in cask, and light sur plaque before bottling
Type of bottle:	Bordelaise lourde

Commercial

Vente Directe:	Yes, through Cercle Oenologique de Clarke
General Sales:	Enquiries to: Château Clarke Listrac 33480 Castelnau de Médoc Telephone: 56 88 88 00
Agents:	Yes: enquiries to château
Visits:	Yes: telephone 56 88 88 00 for details of Cercle Oenologique de Clarke

THE TASTING AT CHATEAU CLARKE,
15 January 1985
J.S., M. Gérard Colin

1983 Good depth of colour. Nose good and woody. Quality of Clarke now really beginning to come through. Really well-structured, with fruit, good tannins, finesse and backbone. This is a Rothschild baby.

1982 Good intense blackish colour. Powerful bouquet with some oak. Has power and roundness of 1982s, but harder tannins than many. This will be good, but needs plenty of time.

1981 Beautiful colour, with blue tinges. Nose quite shy, but has charm and again some oakiness. Well made, beginning to come together nicely. Has elegance and will be a nice bottle.

1980 Good red, lightest of all vintages tasted – except the rosé! Straightforward, pleasing nose. Easy, fresh and ready to drink now.

1979 Clear, bright, deep red. Nose not giving much, but good fruit coming through. Good fruit, quite long with a touch of acidity. Quite drinkable, but should get better.

1978 Ruby colour. Nose evolving well. Quite complex, supple wine with faint bitterness on aftertaste, indicating good tannins. Overriding impression of blackcurrant. Nice bottle, which should improve.

Also tasted

1977 Château Malmaison. This was the first wine made and bottled here, but it was not commercialised. Colour was light and quite brown, and the bouquet suggested a degree of overripeness. It tasted pleasant enough with some fruit there, but no length. Bearing in mind the youth of the vines and the difficulty of the vintage, not a bad first try.

1983 Rosé. The colour is medium pale pink. Nose distinctly reminiscent of pear-drops. Fruity and soft, very refreshing. This rosé is made by drawing off the juice of the red wine after only twelve hours skin contact. It helps to concentrate the colour and tannins of the red. It is a favourite summer wine of the Baron.

CHATEAU
Coufran
HAUT MEDOC

Château Coufran lies to the left of the D2, just after the village of Cadourne, as you drive northwards towards St Yzans-de-Médoc.

Coufran belonged in the mid-19th century to the Comte de Verthamon, under whose aegis production increased from 65 tonneaux in 1850 to 150 tonneaux in 1868. At this moment de Verthamon sold the property to the Celerier family, in whose hands it remained until it was bought by Louis Miailhe in 1924.

The Miailhes are a remarkable family; they have been brokers in Bordeaux since 1818, which makes them one of the oldest firms in the city. It was not until 1891 that Frédéric Miailhe, grandfather of Jean, purchased the first vineyard in a chain that was to make them today's largest owners in the Médoc. That first château was Siran, still in Miailhe ownership, though the current proprietor, Alain Miailhe, is a cousin of

Jean, and there is no business connection. Jean Miailhe recalled his grandfather telling of the amazing vintage of 1893, his second at Siran; harvesting began on 15 August, a record yet unbroken, and the crop was so abundant that casks became at such a premium that coopers were able to demand one full cask for every two empty ones supplied.

Coufran was the next acquisition, followed by Château Pichon-Longueville-Lalande, where Jean's cousin Madame de Lencquesaing still presides; in 1938 Jean's father Louis Miailhe and his uncle Edouard acquired a quarter share in Château Palmer, which to the family's great regret they later sold. After the war the abandoned Château Citran was taken in hand, and now belongs to Jean's sister, Madame Cesselin and her husband, Jean. In 1972 Jean bought Château Verdignan, and the final piece of the jigsaw was fitted in when

Jean's son Eric bought and re-created the vineyard of Château Soudars, an Haut-Médoc vineyard not far from Coufran, which had been derelict for 50 years.

Louis Miailhe planted Coufran with 100% Merlot grapes, a revolutionary step in the predominantly Cabernet Sauvignon-planted Médoc. It is a trademark of all Miailhe properties to have a high proportion of this variety, and even today Coufran still has 85% Merlot. Jean Miailhe took over the running of Château Coufran in 1950, and succession is assured by his son Eric, large and friendly, rather like the wine of Coufran. Eric has been responsible for winemaking since 1973 on all his father's properties.

On my visit to Coufran, Jean Miailhe told me, with a roar of laughter, that he had now retired. He is one of the least retired and retiring of men; he is extremely active in the sales and promotion of the Miailhe wines, as well as being the President of the Syndicat des Crus Bourgeois du Médoc, travelling the world and cementing the ties the family have built up with their overseas importers. Miailhe is one of the few owners in the area who handle the total commercialisation of their wines.

Jean's father, Louis Miailhe, died in June 1982 at the ripe old age of 92, and since then the château has not been lived in. The house is now somewhat neglected, but this is certainly the only part of any of the properties about which this could be said. In 1973 Jean Miailhe went to California as a consultant, and on his return he constructed a new cuvier at Coufran, followed by another at Verdignan. The layout and general appearance of these vathouses, with their gleaming ranks of stainless-steel vats, put one very much in mind of a Napa Valley winery. The old oak cuves at Coufran are no longer used, but they have been kept for appearance, and the later cement vats are now only used for storage and assemblage.

The wine of Coufran is consistent and reliable, even in the lesser vintages. It is always rounded and charming, not particularly complicated and with a great and constant depth of colour.

TECHNICAL INFORMATION

General

Appellation:	Haut-Médoc
Area under vines:	64 hectares
Average production:	30,000 cases
Distribution of vines:	In one block
Director, Régisseur and Maître de Chai:	M. Eric Miailhe
Chef de Culture:	M. Christian Surget (born at Coufran)
Consultant Oenologist:	M. Boissenot

Viticulture

Geology:	80% pure gravel to a depth of 10 metres, 10% sandy gravel, 10% clay
Grape varieties:	85% Merlot, 15% Cabernet Sauvignon
Pruning:	Guyot Double Médocaine
Rootstock:	Teleki, 5BB, 420A, some SO4
Vines per hectare:	80% 8,200, 20% 7,000
Average yield per hectare:	48–50 hectolitres
Replanting:	Currently 2–3 hectares per annum

Vinification

Added yeasts:	Yes, systematically
Length of maceration:	16–21 days
Temperature of fermentation:	First $\frac{2}{3}$ of fermentation at 26°C, rest at 30°C
Control of fermentation:	Water circulation
Type of vat:	Stainless steel
Vin de presse:	1st pressing practically always incorporated, some 2nd pressing occasionally used after malolactic fermentation
Age of casks:	From 1981 vintage, $\frac{1}{4}$ new each vintage
Time in cask:	13–18 months according to vintage
Fining:	Egg albumen in vat
Filtration:	Sur terre before going in cask and again after fining
Type of bottle:	Bordelaise lourde

Commercial

Vente Directe:	Yes, for French customers and tourists at wine shop at the château
Sales:	Contact M. Jean Miailhe, Château Coufran, St Seurin de Cadourne, 33250 Pauillac
Agents overseas:	Yes, for information apply as above
Visits:	Yes, by appointment Telephone 56 59 31 02 or 56 44 90 84 Office hours

THE TASTING AT CHATEAU COUFRAN,
25 January 1985
J.S., Christian Seely, M. Jean Miailhe, M. Eric Miailhe, M. Boissenot

1984 Tasted 5 different cuves for assemblage. General impression: excellent depth of colour. Nose soft with good fruit. Quite tannic, with plenty of fruit and a degree of acidity.

1983 Very dark colour. Nose powerful and rounded. Big, fat mouthful with plenty of easy tannins. Will make a very good bottle with keeping qualities.

1982 Dark almost black red. Nose quite closed. Big, velvety wine, a mouthful of rich Merlot fruitiness. Good length, opens up after a while in the glass.

1981 Slightly lighter colour. Nose beginning to open up and show promise. Has elegance and finesse, beginning to come together – excellent in a year or two.

1980 Colour only a shade lighter than younger vintages. Nose good and open with some blackcurrant. Ready and pleasing, with lots of fruit and some tannin to enable keeping a little while.

1979 Good depth of colour. Showing well on nose with lots of good fruit. Powerful mouthful of fruit and ripeness, still quite tannic; could be a few years before this is at its best. Very good '79.

1978 Dense red. Bouquet good with suggestion of sappy wood. Good balance, harmonious. A good, structured wine with length and backbone.

1977 Excellent colour for '77, shade darker than '80. Nose not very pronounced, but quite pleasant. Good fruit and lacks acidity of some '77s, shortish but very good for the year.

1976 Beginning to go brown. Nose good and ripe, but not overly so. Ripe and easy on the palate, with a slightly roasted flavour. Lovely to drink now, but no hurry.

At lunch at Château Verdignan

1976 (In magnum.) Even better and less developed than the bottle sample.

1974 Very good deep colour for this scorned vintage. Nice ripe nose. Full wine, with good fruit. A very nice claret for drinking now, and outstanding for the vintage.

1973 Lightish red. Nose faint, but pleasing. Light, easy and a bit short. Needs drinking now.

1970 Going quite brown. Nose very ripe and evolved. Ready to drink now, good ripe Bordeaux of no great pretension, lacking the concentration of most 1970s, perhaps due to high proportion of Merlot.

176

CHATEAU
Fourcas-Dupré
LISTRAC

Drive north from Bordeaux towards Le Verdon on the main D1. The gateway to Château Fourcas-Dupré is clearly marked on the right-hand side of the road in the village of Listrac.

Together with Châteaux Clarke and Fourcas-Hosten, Fourcas-Dupré stands head and shoulders above most of the Listrac vineyards. There have been vines at Fourcas since the 18th century, witnessed by the map of Belleyme, geographer-royal to Louis XV. Maître Dupré, whose name is joined to that of Fourcas, was a Bordeaux solicitor of some note, and owned the property in the middle of last century. In 1875 the château and vineyard were acquired by another legal gentleman, a notary by the name of Cathala, and his descendants ran the property until it came into the hands of the present Société Civile in the late 1960s. Evidently Cathala was a most capable winemaker; from 1895 to 1905 the wine of Four-

cas-Dupré won ten consecutive Gold Medals, a tradition followed by Guy Pagès since he took over the administration of the property in 1970.

Guy Pagès, whose family had large agricultural holdings in Tunisia, and whose brother, Marc, runs Château la Tour de By near Bégadan, died unexpectedly in March 1985, and is succeeded by his able son Patrice who has for some years been régisseur at Château Fourcas-Hosten nearby. A gentle, humorous man, Guy Pagès was also a gifted and innovative winemaker, and made many improvements to the vineyard, buildings, and wine of Château Fourcas-Dupré; he is sadly missed, not only by his family, but also by his numerous friends. It is a fitting tribute to the man that the property was admitted in May 1985 to the ranks of the Union des Grands Crus de Bordeaux.

The style of Fourcas-Dupré's wine is not entirely typical of Listrac; it has more finesse than many of the properties in the commune, which is probably due to the relatively high proportion of gravel in the soil of the vineyard. During the period of his administration, Guy Pagès built a new cuvier, and vinification is carried out in vats of stainless-steel as well as epoxy-resin-lined cement. The wine is aged in casks, of which between 15% and 25% are new each vintage, and spends from 12 to 18

months in wood before bottling. It is an excellent Cru Bourgeois, always very sound in quality even in the lesser vintages, and can be relied upon to give excellent value for money.

Visitors are welcome at Fourcas-Dupré; it is an attractive and well-run property, and I am sure will continue as such under the administration of Patrice Pagès.

TECHNICAL INFORMATION

General

Appellation:	Listrac
Classification:	Cru Bourgeois
Area under vines:	40 hectares
Average production:	20,000 cases
Distribution of vines:	In one piece
Owner:	Société Civile du Château Fourcas-Dupré
Director/Régisseur:	M. Patrice Pagès
Maître de Chai:	M. Alain Bouscarrut
Consultant Oenologist:	M. Jacques Boissenot (formerly Prof. Emile Peynaud)

Viticulture

Geology:	Pyrennean gravel and chalky clay, with subsoil of alios
Grape varieties:	50% Cabernet Sauvignon, 10% Cabernet Franc, 38% Merlot, 2% Petit Verdot
Pruning:	Guyot Double
Rootstock:	Riparia Gloire, SO4
Vines per hectare:	7,000 to 10,000
Average yield per hectare:	45 hectolitres
Replanting:	By complantation, new parcels of 1 to 2 hectares being planted each year to a maximum eventual area of 50 hectares

Vinification

Added yeasts:	Yes, when necessary
Length of maceration:	From 15 to 21 days, according to vintage
Temperature of fermentation:	30°C
Control of fermentation:	Water-cooled coil for cement vats, running water on vats for stainless steel
Vin de presse:	Percentage added according to vintage
Age of casks:	15% to 25% new each vintage
Time in cask:	12–18 months
Fining:	Gelatine, in vat
Filtration:	Sur terre
Type of bottle:	Standard

Commercial

Vente Directe:	Yes, to private callers, during working hours, including Saturdays
General Sales:	Mostly direct, but also through a few négociants
Agents overseas:	Yes, but no exclusivities
Visits:	Yes: 0900–1200, 1400–1800 including Saturdays

THE TASTING AT CHATEAU FOURCAS-DUPRE, 10 May 1985
J.S., Patrice Pagès

1983 Deep, bluey red. Nose attractive with plenty of good fruit and some wood. Rounded, with almost sweet fruit taste. Good, soft tannins; will make a fine bottle.

1982 Same deep colour as '83. Soft, elegant bouquet. Round, full and velvety, but with good backbone. Excellent long aftertaste.

1981 Good medium red. Nice blackcurrant on nose. Supple mouthful, with finesse, backbone and charm. Approaching readiness; has a good future.

1980 Brilliant medium red. Open, pleasing and uncomplicated nose. Easy and drinkable with good fruit; no great complexity – an honest wine with enough tannin to keep it going for a while yet.

1978 Medium dark colour. Nice soft fruit on the nose. A well-made wine, quite forward but has plenty of future. A success.

CHATEAU

Fourcas-Hosten

LISTRAC

Château Fourcas-Hosten is situated behind the ancient church in the village of Listrac, to the right of the D1 Bordeaux–Le Verdon road.

Hosten is quite a common family name in the Médoc, and Hostens were proprietors here in the 18th century. In 1810 the Baron de Saint-Affrique bought the property and built the elegant château, which is now unoccupied; he also had the lovely 3-hectare park laid out by an English landscape gardener in 1840. There are many fine and rare trees, including a huge tulip tree and a Siberian elm, happily immune to the ravages of Dutch elm disease.

The de Saint-Affriques owned Fourcas-Hosten for five generations, until it was acquired in 1971 by an American syndicate of 30 shareholders, headed by Philip Powers. The last de Saint-Affrique had allowed the property to deteriorate somewhat,

and the new owners injected some much-needed capital, re-equipping the cuvier with a range of steel fermentation vats and embarking on a re-planting programme in the vineyard. As a result of this major investment, and thanks to the skill and care of Bertrand de Rivoyre, the wine of Fourcas-Hosten has improved greatly over the past ten years, and is now certainly one of the best Listracs.

In recent years the majority of the shares in the owning company were acquired by the late Guy Pagès of Château Fourcas-Dupré, Jean-Henri Schÿler, M. de Rivoyre and some Danish investors. Following the untimely death of Guy Pagès in March 1985, his son Patrice, régisseur at Fourcas-Hosten for the past three years, will be concentrating his energies on Fourcas-Dupré, and a new manager, Bernard Coucharrière has replaced him

179

at Fourcas-Hosten. The original American consortium still have their shares, and it is therefore hardly surprising that the wine enjoys a healthy export trade with the United States. Château Fourcas-Hosten is now commercialised exclusively by the négociant houses of Schröder and Schÿler and de Rivoyre et Diprovin, achieving a wide diffusion of sales on the export and domestic markets.

The quality and finesse of Fourcas-Hosten is due largely to the gravelly soil of the Fourcas plateau on which two-thirds of the vineyard is situated, and which is planted mainly with the noble Cabernet Sauvignon grape. This high quality is further augmented by careful selection at the assemblage, and by a gradual increase in the use of new casks for ageing.

TECHNICAL INFORMATION

General

Appellation:	Listrac
Classification:	Cru Bourgeois
Area under vines:	38 hectares, with the possibility of planting up to 46 hectares
Average production:	18,000 cases
Distribution of vines:	⅔ on the Fourcas plateau, ⅓ on lower-lying clay/chalk land
Owner:	Société Civile du Château Fourcas-Hosten
Director:	M. de Rivoyre and M. Patrice Pagès
Régisseur:	M. Bernard Coucharrière
Maître de Chai:	M. Claude Bibeyran
Consultant Oenologist:	M. Claude Barthe (formerly Prof. E. Peynaud)

Viticulture

Geology:	Fourcas plateau: Pyrennean gravel. Lower ground: Clay and chalk
Grape varieties:	50% Cabernet Sauvignon, 10% Cabernet Franc, 40% Merlot
Pruning:	Guyot Double
Rootstock:	Riparia Gloire, SO4
Vines per hectare:	8,000 to 10,000
Average yield per hectare:	45 hectolitres
Replanting:	Complantation, and 2 hectares of new ground annually

Vinification

Added yeasts:	Yes, when necessary
Length of maceration:	15 to 21 days
Temperature of fermentation:	30°C
Control of fermentation:	Water cooling
Type of vat:	Stainless-steel, lined steel and cement
Vin de presse:	Part incorporated, according to vintage
Age of casks:	Currently 10% to 15% new each vintage, increasing to 25%
Time in cask:	12–18 months
Fining:	With gelatine in vat
Filtration:	Sur terre
Type of bottle:	Bordelaise lourde

Commercial

Vente Directe:	Yes, to passing customers
General Sales:	Through the négociants houses of: Schröder and Schÿler & Cie, 97 Quai des Chartrons 33300 Bordeaux, and De Rivoyre et Diprovin 33440 St Loubès
Agents overseas:	Contact either of the above for information
Visits:	Yes, during working hours

THE TASTING AT KELVEDON, 15 May 1985
J.S.

1984 Dark, bluey red. Good nose with oak and powerful blackcurrant. A tough, tannic mouthful, but good fruit and backbone. Will be a good bottle, but will need patience.

1983 Deep, intense red. Nose rich and powerful, good Cabernet smell. Well-structured, fruit, tannin and backbone will combine to make an excellent wine – long aftertaste.

1982 Same intense dark colour. Nose less assertive than '83 and '84 – lovely soft fruit. Big, rounded and mouthfilling, already nearly drinkable, but with enough good tannin to keep it going for a long time.

1981 Again a lovely deep red, shade lighter than '82. Nose a bit closed, but fine. Well made wine with nice balance and plenty of finesse. Will drink well in a year or two.

1980 Amazingly, deeper colour than the 1981. Nose good. A really good 1980, drinkable now but with plenty of fruit, and tannin enough to give it years of life.

1979 Deep red, bluey tinges. Strong blackcurrant bouquet. Big, rounded mouthful, with lots of power, fruit and good tannin; already very good to drink, but has a long life ahead.

1978 Good bright scarlet. Fruit evident and quite evolved on nose. Ripe, quite complex; good aftertaste. Already attractive, but will develop further.

CHATEAU
Greysac
MEDOC

Château Greysac, along with Château la Tour de By, is the most northerly of the properties in this book. Follow the D2 to St Christoly-de-Médoc, and continue north with the Gironde on your right. After about 1½ km, you will come to a left turn, signposted to Lesparre. Château Greysac is about half a kilometre along this road on your left. Château Greysac emerged from virtual obscurity when it was purchased by the Baron François de Gunzburg in 1973. De Gunzburg, a Parisian of Russian ancestry, had a long and colourful career, much of it associated with the wine of Bordeaux; for eight years he headed the old-established firm of Barton and Guestier. He left them in 1972 and formed a consortium, largely Italian-owned, and purchased three properties in Bordeaux, of which Château Greysac was the most important. Sadly de Gunzburg died in 1984, but his widow, the Baronne Mercedes de Gunzburg, is still actively interested in the property and stays frequently in the very pretty, elegantly furnished Chartreuse château.

In the ten years prior to his death, the Baron expanded the vineyard from 14 to 53 hectares, now producing an average 300 tonneaux of wine each year. He also installed a modern vathouse with stainless-steel cuves. Knowing the market as well as he did, he set out to produce a sound Cru Bourgeois that would sell at a reasonable price, and that would mature relatively quickly. This has been achieved by judicious mixture of grape varieties, and by ageing the wine for a comparatively short time in casks, one-third of which are replaced annually with casks of one vintage from Premier Cru châteaux.

Largely due to his Seagram American connections, the wine of Greysac has a regular following in the United States, whither some 30% of the production is currently exported, but a programme of sales expansion is being actively pursued both in France and other overseas markets.

I found the wines to be of thoroughly sound and likeable quality; though never especially exciting, they are always rounded and balanced, and even with some bottle age, the lighter years such as 1977 and 1974 are still lively with a beautiful depth of colour. In short, Château Greysac produces a wine that is perfectly adapted to current market trends, when the wine lover is looking for château-bottled claret of some finesse and reliability at a price more suited to everyday consumption than the more exalted Crus Classés.

The property is currently managed by Monsieur Philippe Dambrine, who operates from the owning company's office in Bordeaux, while day-to-day running is in the hands of the young Chef d'Exploitation, Philippe Coudoin.

TECHNICAL INFORMATION

General

Appellation:	Médoc
Area under vines:	53 hectares
Average production:	30,000 cases
Owner:	Domaines Codem S.A.
Director:	M. Philippe Dambrine
Chef d'Exploitation:	M. Philippe Coudoin
Consultant Oenologist:	M. Boissenot

Viticulture

Geology:	Mixture of silico-gravel, with some parcels of chalky clay
Grape varieties:	50% Cabernet Sauvignon, 10% Cabernet Franc, 38% Merlot, 2% Petit Verdot
Pruning:	Guyot Double
Rootstock:	Riparia, SO4
Vines per hectare:	From 4,500 to 10,000
Yield per hectare:	40–45 hectolitres
Replanting:	As necessary, maintaining average vine age of 35 years

Vinification

Added yeasts:	Sometimes, depending on condition
Length of maceration:	15–18 days
Temperature of fermentation:	26–28°C
Control of fermentation:	Water-cooling, governed by thermostat
Type of vat:	Stainless steel
Vin de presse:	Proportion incorporated according to necessity
Age of casks:	⅓ of casks replaced each vintage with casks of one vintage bought from Premiers Crus châteaux
Time in cask:	18 months
Fining:	Egg albumen in vat
Filtration:	Lightly, sur plaque before bottling
Type of bottle:	Bordelaise

Commercial

Vente Directe:	Yes
Direct ordering from château:	Yes
Exclusive contracts:	Yes, for information, contact M.P. Dambrine, Domaines Codem S.A., 26 Quai de Bacalan, 33075 Bordeaux Cedex
Visits:	Yes, by appointment Telephone 56 41 50 29 Hours: 0800–1200, 1400–1800 Monday to Friday (Closed in August)

THE TASTING AT CHATEAU GREYSAC,
19 November 1984
J.S., M. Philippe Dambrine, M. Philippe Coudoin, M. Daniel Vergely (Cordier)

1983 Deep, bluey red. Nose just beginning with fruit and touch of oak. Well balanced, with fruit, supple roundness, perhaps stemming from Merlot.

1982 Dark, plummy colour. Nose open and quite complex. Still fairly closed, but plenty of power and fruit behind. Very attractive.

1981 Medium to dark red. Nose already elegant and open. Long in mouth, balanced and well structured. To keep for up to five years.

1980 Lovely garnet red. Lovely generous bouquet of good fruit. Good, balanced wine with lots of fruit and fragrance, if a little short on finish.

1979 Again good deep colour. Nose evolved and soft. Good balance and structure. Good long aftertaste.

1978 Medium deep red. A bit closed on nose. Some power; length and backbone here, will repay waiting a year.

1977 Colour very good for 1977. Soft, pleasing nose. Good easy fruit on palate, a bit short on finish, but good for drinking now.

1976 Colour hardly showing brown. Nose good and quite ripe. A good example from a vintage that in some châteaux is beginning to fade a bit. This one has some fruit and strength, and will last a while yet.

1975 Still good colour. Bouquet a bit shy, but starting to come out. Fruit and tannins together, and will keep it going for some years.

1974 Colour good for this vintage, only just beginning to brown. Nice, open bouquet. Lightish wine, finishing dry, but still very pleasant.

1973 Still has a very good colour. Nose still pretty light, but with some fruit, if a little short. To drink now.

CHATEAU
La Lagune
HAUT-MEDOC

Château la Lagune is the most southerly of all the Crus Classés of the Médoc, and is to be found 14 km north of Bordeaux between the D2 and the village of Ludon. It is clearly signposted on the right-hand side of the road.

The château belonged to the family of Seguineau de Lognac in the early 18th century, who had the elegant Chartreuse style house built, designed by the great architect Victor Louis.

In 1819 Château Grand la Lagune, as it was then known, was acquired by M. Jouffrey Piston, who originated from Périgord. It was under his owner-ship that the wine of la Lagune started to gain its reputation, and by the classification of 1855, when his widow is shown as the owner, it was deemed worthy of inclusion among the ranks of the Third Growths. The lady was succeeded by her son, and by the end of the century there were 50 hectares in production, with an average yield of some 80 tonneaux of wine. In 1886 the estate was sold to Monsieur Louis Sèze.

Sèze was obviously a successful winemaker, as witness the numerous medals won by the property during his ownership.

On the death of Sèze's son-in-law, M. A. Galy, who had succeeded him in 1911, la Lagune went in to a sad decline, plunging finally after the end of the last war to such an extent that only a few hectares of vines remained. The château and build-ings were allowed to fall into ruins. So desperate was the state of the property that even Alexis Lichine, the great bargain-hunter of the post-war years, turned it down as being beyond recall.

Fortunately for la Lagune, a fairy godfather appeared on the scene in the form of one Monsieur Georges Brunet, an idealist with the means to bring substance to his dreams. In 1958 he bought the estate and set to with a will and a large bank balance, restoring château and buildings and totally replanting the vineyard. By 1961 Brunet had either run out of capital, or simply decided, like many idealists, that the grass was greener elsewhere. The latter seems the more likely, since he is now making one of the best red wines in Provence, Château Vignelaure, made with 100% Cabernet Sauvignon.

Brunet was followed by another owner dedicated to the reinstatement of la Lagune to its rightful place. Brunet's work was carried on by the next proprietor, M. René Chayoux of the Champagne house of Ayala. He and his régisseur, Monsieur Boyrie, continued the work of restoration and modernisation, installing an incredibly advanced cuverie with a unique system of transferring the wine direct from vats to casks by a network of pipes; the wine is impelled by gravity and com-pressed air, and the system is controlled from a central panel. The wine is not fatigued by high-pressure pumping, and an enormous saving of labour and cost is effected at racking time. The idea seems to the inexperienced eye so compara-tively simple and logical that I am surprised it has not been widely adopted. Under the Ayala owner-ship, parcels of vineyard that previously belonged to la Lagune have been bought back, and the restoration of the château and buildings has been

183

completed to the very highest standard.

Since his death some years ago, the administration and day-to-day running of the property have been in the hands of Monsieur Boyrie's widow. Anyone with chauvinistic views on the ability of women to make great wine has only to meet the tough and likeable Madame Boyrie and taste the wine, and their conversion will be assured. The house of Ayala is now represented by M. Jean-Michel Ducellier, who visits and stays at the château at least twice a year.

The soil of Château la Lagune is quite different from the rest of the Médoc, being composed of deep but very light, almost sandy gravel. The wine, probably as a result of this particular soil, also has its own character. Pierre Casteja of Châ-

teau Doisy-Vedrines, a great connoisseur of fine wine, told me that he finds the young wines of Domaine de Chevalier and la Lagune almost indistinguishable. It is not altogether surprising, when one considers that the suburb of Eysines, only a few kilometres to the south of la Lagune, has the Graves appellation. Be that as it may, it is certain that la Lagune, now restored to its proper level, is making classic Bordeaux of Grand Cru quality; the wines are firm and have perhaps more flesh and backbone than one associates with the southerly vineyards of the Médoc. It is certainly highly sought after on the world claret market, and all thanks are due to the combined efforts of Ayala and Madame Boyrie.

TECHNICAL INFORMATION

General

Appellation:	Haut-Médoc
Area under vines:	55 hectares
Average production:	25,000 cases
Distribution of vines:	One single vineyard
Owner:	Société Civile du Château la Lagune, M. Jean-Michel Ducellier
Régisseur and Maître de Chai:	Madame Jeanne Boyrie
Consultant Oenologist:	Professor Emile Peynaud

Viticulture

Geology:	Light, sandy gravel
Grape varieties:	55% Cabernet Sauvignon, 20% Cabernet Franc, 20% Merlot, 5% Petit Verdot
Pruning:	Guyot Simple
Rootstock:	Various, principally Riparia 6,600
Vines per hectare:	
Average yield per hectare:	30–35 hectolitres
Replanting:	Total replanting in 1958/1959, will therefore start renewal programme in two to three years as necessary

Vinification

Added yeasts:	Sometimes in very difficult years
Length of maceration:	Average 18 days
Temperature of fermentation:	28–30°C max.
Type of vat:	Metal, epoxy-resin lined
Control of fermentation:	Heat-exchange apparatus
Vin de presse:	1st pressing included occasionally, according to vintage
Age of casks:	100% new every vintage
Time in cask:	Normally 20 months, varying according to vintage
Fining:	Fresh egg-whites
Filtration:	Sometimes very light filtration before bottling
Type of bottle:	Bordelaise lourde

Commercial

Vente Directe:	No
Sales:	Through Bordeaux négociants
Visits:	Yes, by appointment Telephone 56 30 44 07 Monday to Thursday: 0900–1200, 1400–1800, Friday: 0900–1200, 1400–1700, except August

---

THE TASTING AT CHATEAU LA LAGUNE AND AT KELVEDON November, December 1984 J.S., Mme. Boyrie

1984 Very deep colour, almost black. Powerful nose, lots of new oak and good blackcurrant fruit. Tannins pronounced, a typical young Médoc of high quality, promising a great future for a decried vintage.
1978 Fine, brilliant garnet colour. Beautiful bouquet, with lots of fine fruit just beginning to open out. A wine of some complexity and class, just beginning to show indications of a really good development. Fruit, good tannin, finesse and backbone are all present. A very good 1978.
1970 Colour fine scarlet, hardly any browning. Perfect open bouquet of cassis. Just ready for drinking, but with plenty of life. In balance with good, concentrated flavour, and a long aftertaste. Surprisingly, when decanted this wine had virtually no sediment.

CHATEAU
De Lamarque
HAUT-MEDOC

Going north on the D2, pass through Arcins, and take the second turning signposted to Lamarque. Halfway down the main street of Lamarque there is a square on your left, with the gates to Château Lamarque on the far side.

One of only three real castles in the Médoc, the original Château de Lamarque was built at the end of the 11th century for defence against invasions from the Gironde by the Vikings and other marauders. During the Hundred Years War it was one of three principal fortresses used by the English in their struggle to hold possession of Guyenne; the others were châteaux at Blanquefort and Lesparre. After the English were defeated in 1453 at the battle of Castillon, the castle fell back into French hands.

Over the centuries Château de Lamarque has been as renowned for its historical connections as for its wines, since the Roman occupation until the present owners took possession in 1841. Roger Gromand, husband of the present owner, who is one of the powerful and aristocratic d'Evry family, took over the running of the estate in 1963, and has battled tirelessly to raise the quality of the wine of Château de Lamarque. Gromand is a widely-travelled and well-connected intellectual, politician and homme d'affaires. He is President of Mercedes France, and has published many articles on important global issues such as European defence and the Cyprus question in the monthly *Revue des Deux Mondes*. Talking of the status of his wine, he told me with a twinkle that his wife's great-grandparents were ardent loyalists, and for this reason samples of the wine of Château de Lamarque were not submitted for consideration at the 1855 classification, instigated by the radical republican Prince Napoléon! Be this as it may, the wine today is certainly well made, but tends more to top Cru Bourgeois level than that of a Cru Classé.

Since Roger Gromand took over 22 years ago, the vineyard has been totally replanted, and the cuvier has been modernised; I find the *trompe l'oeil* facing of oak over the cement vats curious – but *chacun à son goût* – and the vats *are* in the style of the château. Every stage of vinification and ageing is carefully supervised by Madame Coulary, one of the very few lady régisseurs in the Médoc. The

wine is noticeably smooth and rounded, and tends towards early maturity. If tasted blind, I might be inclined to place its provenance on the other side of the river, perhaps in Pomerol or St Emilion. Although the dominant grape is the Cabernet, with 70% of the vineyard planted with Cabernet Sauvignon and Cabernet Franc, I got more of an impression of Merlot style from the vintages I tasted.

The château, redolent with history, is a fascinating place to visit. The library where Monsieur Gromand received me is hung with family portraits and escutcheons of the d'Evrys, and their predecessors the de Fumels. There is a chapel dating from the 12th century, and a 14th-century guard-room which has been converted into a private cellar. The overall impression of the château, park, gardens, courtyard and winemaking buildings is one of an important and historic property, yet lived in, loved and well cared for.

TECHNICAL INFORMATION

General

Appellation:	Haut-Médoc Bourgeois Supérieur and Grand Bourgeois
Area under vines:	50 hectares, of which 47 are currently in production
Average production:	26,000 cases
Director:	M. Roger Gromand d'Evry
Owner:	S.C. Gromand d'Evry
Régisseur:	Mme. Coulary
Maître de Chai:	M. Guionnet
Consultant Oenologist:	Professor Emile Peynaud

Viticulture

Geology:	Good gravel on alios
Grape varieties:	50% Cabernet Sauvignon, 20% Cabernet Franc, 25% Merlot, 5% Petit Verdot
Pruning:	Guyot Double Médocaine
Rootstock:	SO4, Riparia, 44-53, 3309, 420A, 101-14 5DB
Vines per hectare:	6,400
Average yield per hectare:	43 hectolitres
Replanting:	Continuous

Vinification

Added yeasts:	Sometimes, in cold vintages
Length of maceration:	Average 20 days
Temperature of fermentation:	19°C to maximum 30°C
Control of fermentation:	Thermostatic
Type of vat:	Cement faced with oak, also stainless steel
Vin de presse:	1st pressing used, following tasting
Age of casks:	20% new each year, the rest are 3 and 4 years old
Time in cask:	20 months
Fining:	Egg-white
Filtration:	Before bottling
Type of bottle:	Bordelaise

Commercial

Vente Directe:	Yes
Direct ordering:	Yes
Exclusivities:	Yes, in certain countries
Agents overseas:	Yes, in U.S.A., Belgium, Denmark and Holland
General Sales:	Contact Château de Lamarque, Lamarque, 33460 Margaux
Visits:	Yes: telephone 56 58 90 03 Hours: 0800–1200, 1400–1800 Monday to Friday

THE TASTING AT CHATEAU DE LAMARQUE, 1 December 1984
J.S., Wendy Seely, M. Roger Gromand d'Evry, Mme. Coulary

1983   Good deep colour. Nose quite open. Quite full and round, with some finesse, but more accessible than many Médocs of this vintage.
1982   Very dark colour. Bouquet soft and rich. Big and mouthfilling with plenty of power and long aftertaste. Already very approachable.
1981   Good colour, bright and clear. Elegant, feminine bouquet. Supple and easy on the palate, not complex and quite drinkable for a wine so young.
1981   Reserve des Marquis d'Evry. A special blend, only sold in France. Very similar to the usual château wine, but has more length and finesse.
1980   Bright medium red. Open attractive nose. Well-made 1980, easy, supple and perfectly ready to drink. Very agreeable wine with no great pretensions.

CHATEAU
Lanessan
HAUT-MEDOC

Château Lanessan lies well back from the D2 on the left as you approach Château Beychevelle from the village of Cussac-Fort-Médoc. The drive to the château and museum of horse-drawn carriages is well marked.

Thanks to some carefully conserved parchments, we can trace the sale of the estate in 1310 by the widow of Henry de Lanessan to the Sieur de Blaignan. It remained in the same family, passed down through the distaff side, until 1793, when it was bought by Jean Delbos, négociant and ship-builder of Bordeaux. His son, Louis, was a man of some pride, and since he had no difficulty in selling his wines at satisfactory prices, considered the 1855 classification to be an unnecessary bureaucratic exercise and refused to submit samples to the Chamber of Commerce. In 1832 Jullien placed the wine of Lanessan at a level corresponding to a 4th Great Growth on today's scale, and this quality has been more or less consistently maintained for over 150 years. Though Louis Delbos' draconian contempt for the classification may have cost his descendants dear in terms of prices achieved, it has benefited claret-lovers, who

can acquire wine of Cru Classé quality at Cru Bourgeois prices.

The Château was built in distinctly Scottish Baronial style in 1878, and the architect was Abel Duphot. In 1907 André Delbos's daughter married Etienne Bouteiller, grandfather of Hubert and Bertrand, and Lanessan has remained in Bouteiller ownership since then. The Bouteiller family can trace their connection back to an ancestor who was 'bouteiller', or cellarmaster to Louis the Fourteenth. Hubert, who lives at nearby Château Lachesnaye, is currently responsible for running Lanessan and Lachesnaye, while his brother Bertrand administers Château Pichon-Longueville-Baron, also a family property, and Château Palmer in which the Bouteillers have a substantial shareholding.

Château Lanessan has always been something of a showplace; in the mid-19th century André Delbos, who did much to improve and enlarge the property, had a second great passion, his love of horses. He had the most beautiful range of stables built, with marble mangers and automatic feeding devices. The names of the horses can still be seen

187

on plaques in each horse-box; Whisky, Darling, Major and Tommy owed their names to the coachmen and stable-lads of the day, who were always, following the dictates of fashion, imported from England. The family, also acquired over the years an impressive collection of carriages, traps, phaetons and brakes, and these have all been carefully preserved to form, with stables and tack-room, an interesting 'Musée du Cheval'. All the vehicles, except a London mail-coach and a yellow carriage presented to the Bouteillers in 1961 by the Exshaws, were in daily use by the Delbos and Bouteiller families, and are painted in the 'house colours' of black and dark red. The museum is open to the public, and well worth a visit.

The wine of Lanessan is a classic Médoc, made from a traditionally Cabernet-dominated encépagement, which is grown on a good depth of Garonne gravel. It is a wine which, like all good Médocs, requires time to develop its finesse and complex flavours, and handsomely rewards the patient connoisseur. A second wine is made from the produce of young vines and those cuves that are not considered suitable for inclusion in the Grand Vin; it is sold under the label Domaine de Ste Gemme, not to be confused with the nearby Château Caronne Ste Gemme.

TECHNICAL INFORMATION

General

Appellation:	Haut Médoc
Area under vines:	40 hectares
Average production:	20,000 cases
Distribution of vines:	One block
Owner:	G.F.A. des Domaines Bouteiller
Director and Maître de Chai:	M. Hubert Bouteiller
Consultant Oenologist:	Centre d'Information Oenologique de Pauillac

Viticulture

Geology:	Garonne gravel
Grape varieties:	75% Cabernet Sauvignon, 20% Merlot, 5% Petit Verdot and Cabernet Franc
Pruning:	Médocaine
Rootstock:	101.14, 420A, Riparia Gloire, 3309
Vines per hectare:	10,000
Yield per hectare:	30–35 hectolitres, depending on vintage
Replanting:	As necessary, maintaining average vine age of 40 years

Vinification

Length of maceration:	Average 3 weeks
Temperature of fermentation:	28–30°C
Control of fermentation:	By tubular circulation with cold water
Type of vat:	Cement, epoxy-resin lined
Age of casks:	3–5 years
Time in cask:	18–24 months
Fining:	Egg-whites, sometimes egg albumen
Filtration:	Yes, before bottling
Type of bottle:	Bordelaise lourde

Commercial

Vente Directe:	Yes
Direct ordering:	Yes
Exclusivities:	None
Agents overseas:	Switzerland – Machler
Visits:	Yes; telephone 56 58 94 80 Hours: 0900–1200, 1400–1800 Monday to Friday
For general information write:	M. Hubert Bouteiller Château Lanessan Cussac-Fort-Médoc 33460 Margaux

THE TASTING AT CHATEAU LANESSAN AND AT THE LION D'OR, ARCINS,
13 November 1984
J.S., M. Bertrand Bouteiller

1978 Good, deep, garnet colour. Nose good, typical Médoc, lovely cassis fruit. Well balanced wine with fruit and tannins in harmony. Already good, but has plenty of distance to travel.

1976 Very good red for the vintage. Good, ripe fruit bouquet, with none of the overripeness associated with this year. Flavour ripe and pleasing, ready now, but has enough to keep it going for quite a while. A successful 1976.

THE TASTING AT KELVEDON,
23 December 1984
J.S., Christian Seely

1982 Fine, clear, dark red. Powerful, rounded nose, lots of lovely blackcurrant fruit. A big, rounded mouthful, with soft tannins, and a good degree of finesse. Already very accessible, but has breed and skeleton to age well.

1981 Brilliant garnet. Fine bouquet with good fruit. Elegant flavour, good fruit/tannin balance, more feminine than '82. Will make a lovely bottle in a couple of years.

1980 Fine garnet red. Nose open and very attractive. Easy on the palate, with no great pretensions to grandeur; good now.

CHATEAU
Loudenne
MEDOC

Loudenne is situated between the villages of St Seurin-de-Cadourne and St Yzans. After leaving St Seurin on your way north towards St Yzans on the D2, you come to the lodge and driveway of Château Loudenne on the elbow of a sharp left-hand bend after about half a kilometre.

The lands of Loudenne formed part of the great domaines of the Comtes de Castillon until the 17th century. By the end of the 18th century it had emerged as a property in its own right, and was bought by a M. Verthamond d'Ambloy. It was one of his female descendants, the sonorously named Marie-Angélique Joséphine Eudoxie de Verthamond, dowager Vicomtesse de Marcellus, who sold the estate to the adventurous Gilbey brothers, Walter and Alfred, in 1875.

The Gilbeys were a remarkably dynamic pair. Returning from the Crimea, where they served as civilian clerks, they had found their father, owner of a coaching business, financially ruined by the advent of the railway. They started their own wine business, importing wines from South Africa, which they sold by mail order. In 1860, after only three years in business, they had become the third largest wine importers in England, shipping in over a million bottles a year. In 1861 the Gilbeys' expansion really took off due to a piece of legislation called 'The Single Bottle Act'. This permitted retailers to sell by the bottle for the first time, and the brothers set about appointing thousands of exclusive agents up and down the country. All over the British Isles the emerging middle-class wine consumer was able to purchase the wines and spirits imported by the Gilbeys from grocers, chemists and small shops everywhere. The fascinating success story of the Gilbey enterprise is readably chronicled in Nicholas Faith's book, *Victorian Vineyard, Château Loudenne and the Gilbeys*, and there is no need for further elaboration on this theme.

Suffice it to say that by the 1870s the firm felt the need for a base in the Bordeaux area, where stocks of Bordeaux and other French wines, notably a sparkling Saumur which was selling like the proverbial hot cakes, could be assembled, stocked and prepared for shipment. It was with this objective that the two brothers bought Loudenne in 1875,

rather than for the modest production of medium-quality red wine that the estate then produced.

Without delay, the Gilbeys embarked upon a prodigious programme of building and replanting that was to cost them in a very short time more than twice the initial purchase price of £28,000. Bearing in mind their prime reason for buying Loudenne, the first project was the construction of a vast chai for storage of wines. Advice was taken from the famous Skawinski of Château Laujac, and Ernest Miniveille was appointed as architect. Incredibly, the vast building was completed in less than a year, as was a small port on the Gironde and

189

a railway line from chai to jetty. Miniveille, incidentally, was the architect of the great Gothic pile of Château Cantenac-Brown, a style very much to the taste of English Victorian tycoons, and it was doubtless the sight of Cantenac-Brown that inspired the brothers in their choice of architect. Ships could now put in at Loudenne, load up with Gilbey wines and return to London, avoiding both the merchants and the port of Bordeaux, an entirely new concept for the era.

In every way the Gilbeys were natural innovators. Although there was already some white wine being produced on the property, it was of a rough and ready quality and destined for consumption by the estate workers. In 1899 a significant portion of the vineyard was planted with Semillon grapes to give a white wine of quality for the export market. Today Château Loudenne is still one of the only three or four properties in the Médoc producing white wine, though the style has changed and improved greatly since those early days. Walter Gilbey, no mean judge of horseflesh, was the first man to use horses for vineyard work. He imported Shire horses from England, which did twice the work of the traditional oxen, and twice as quickly. Horses remained in service at Loudenne until the advent of the tractor in the 1930s. In 1923 Loudenne was one of the first châteaux to install glass-lined fermentation vats, which allowed for easier control of excessive temperatures during the fermentation process.

As far as the château itself and the winemaking side of Loudenne was concerned, one gets the distinct impression that the Gilbey family uncharacteristically let their hearts rule their normally hard heads. The diaries and the visitors' books of the last half of the century bear witness to the pleasure and frequency of the regular visits to Loudenne, that became a regular twice-yearly habit for many members of the family. The records also show how money was more or less continuously invested and lost in the vineyard, especially during the difficult years when mildew and the phylloxera beetle wrought such havoc in the Médoc. It must have been the peculiar magic and charm of Château Loudenne, that invested the place then as it does today, that seduced this aggressive and cost-conscious family. Their unflagging efforts were recognised in 1887 by the award of a Gold Medal for the best-kept vineyard in the Médoc.

Apart from the obvious benefits of summer holidays in such an idyllic spot, the Gilbeys, always ahead of their times in matters of advertising and promotion, were not slow to realise the value of a property like Loudenne as the flagship of a huge organisation such as the company had now become, and the château featured prominently in advertisements and promotional literature. In the 1920s and 1930s, however, times became difficult, and if it had not been for the efforts of Gordon Gilbey, Loudenne's chief advocate of that era, the family would have sold the property.

Château Loudenne suffered badly from the German occupation, and the consequent lack of investment. These difficulties were to continue for fifteen years after the war, due to post-war shortages and problems of exchange control.

In 1963 the English wine, beer and spirits giant International Distillers and Vintners was formed, and the old company of W. and A. Gilbey became part of this group. Geoffrey Hallowes, a director of I.D.V., whose own family wine business had also been merged in to the group, was responsible for Château Loudenne, and it was his inspired casting that put a remarkable young man, Martin Bamford, at the helm of Loudenne.

Although Martin went on to wider fields, becoming finally Président Directeur Général of I.D.V. France before his untimely death during the 1982 vintage, his heart was always at Loudenne. Apart from the myriad improvements and innovations he introduced at Loudenne, the impressive wine museum established in the chais, his love and care for the fabric and decor of the château, the installation of the beautiful vintage kitchen, the conception of the Wine School, and much, much more besides, Martin Bamford has left a wider, deeper, if less visible mark on the Médoc as a whole. He was universally liked and respected by all who knew him; the countless visitors who enjoyed the special Loudenne magic and the warmth of his hospitality, the people who worked with him, and his peers, the many owners throughout the entire Bordeaux region, all hold his memory dear. He is buried in the simple country graveyard at St Yzans, fittingly surrounded by vines.

Life goes on, and so does the work of Loudenne. The long, single-storey pink-washed château still extends its special welcome to visitors from all over the world; the museum of vineyard and winemaking equipment is well worth a visit, and regular art exhibitions are held in the chais. The five-day Wine School seminars continue under the direction of Master of Wine Charles Eve; they include lectures, tastings, visits to other properties in the Médoc, Pomerol and St Emilion and accommodation and all meals and wine. The course is most instructive and extremely enjoyable, and enquiries should be addressed to Miss Pamela Prior at Château Loudenne.

The activities of Gilbey de Loudenne as négociants dealing with all the wines of the Bordeaux region as well as the wines of Loudenne, Giscours and de Pez, which they represent exclusively, are based at the château. The company has also developed one of the leading Bordeaux branded wines, La Cour Pavillon red and white.

Château Loudenne Bordeaux Blanc is a delicate, crisp, dry white wine, one of only four whites made in the Médoc. It is made from 60% Sauvignon and 40% Semillon grapes, fermented at a low temperature of 18°C, and during the vinification and six-month period in vat before bottling, the wine is kept under inert gas. The wine is delicious when young, but keeps its clarity and freshness for several years.

The red wine of Loudenne is a Cru Bourgeois of excellent and reliable quality, with elegance, finesse and good ageing properties. Vinification of the red and white wines of the château is carried out under the watchful eye of the able cellar-master and oenologist, Jean-Louis Camp.

TECHNICAL INFORMATION

General

Appellation:	*Red* Médoc
	White Bordeaux Blanc
Area under vines:	*Red* 43 hectares
	White 12 hectares
Average production:	*Red* 17,000 cases
	White 6,500 cases
Distribution of vines:	All one block around the château
Owner:	W. & A. Gilbey
General Manager:	M. Francis Fouquet
Régisseur:	M. Alain Bouilleau
Maître de Chai:	M. Jean-Louis Camp
Oenologist:	M. Jean-Louis Camp

Viticulture

Geology:	*Red* Clay/gravel on chalk bed
	White Clay soil, with tertiary sediments
Grape varieties:	*Red* 48% Cabernet Sauvignon, 41% Merlot, 8% Cabernet Franc, 3% Malbec and Petit Verdot
	White 60% Sauvignon, 40% Semillon
Pruning:	Guyot Double
Rootstock:	Basically Riparia, with different varieties according to soil type
Vines per hectare:	5,000
Yield per hectare:	*Red* 43 hectolitres (10-year average)
	White 48 hectolitres (10-year average)
Replanting:	*Red* (1984) 7.10 ha
	White (1984) 5.73 ha

Vinification

Added yeasts:	Yes

Length of maceration:	*Red* 3 weeks	Type of bottle:	Bordelaise with embossed logo
	White 10 days		
Temperature of fermentation:	*Red* 26–30°C	*Commercial*	
	White 18°C	Vente Directe:	Yes, to private customers calling at the château
Control of fermentation:	*Red* Heat exchange	Direct Ordering for export:	Possible for the trade
	White Thermostatically controlled water-cooling	Exclusivity:	Yes, Gilbey de Loudenne S.A.
Type of vat:	*Red* Epoxy-resin lined cement	Agents overseas:	Yes, in all major importing countries of the world. For information contact the château
	White Stainless steel		
Vin de presse:	*Red* Incorporated		
	White Kept separate from Grand Vin	Visits:	By appointment. Telephone 56 41 15 03
Age of casks:	*Red* ¼ new each vintage		1 May–30 September
	White No casks used		Hours: 0930–1200, 1400–1630
Time in cask:	15–18 months for red wine		
Fining:	*Red* Powdered egg-white		
	White Bentonite		
Filtration:	*Red* Sur terre before going in cask, sur plaque before bottling	Address for all information:	Gilbey de Loudenne S.A., Château Loudenne, St. Yzans de Médoc, 33340 Lesparre, France
	White Sur plaque before bottling		Telephone 56 41 15 03

THE TASTING AT CHATEAU
LOUDENNE, 17 October 1984
J.S., Jean-Loup Taupin, Jean-Louis Camp

Château Loudenne, Médoc – Red

1983 Good, bluey red. Bouquet good fruit and new wood. Plenty of fruit, with good, ripe tannins.

1982 (Not yet bottled.) Dense, blackish red. Powerful, fragrant cassis on nose. Big, mouthfilling wine, with lots of fruit and tannin, everything there for an outstanding bottle.

1981 Deep purplish red. Very fragrant with lots of fruit. Well balanced, structured wine, with fruit and backbone. Already approachable, but worth waiting a year or two yet.

1980 Fairly light red. Ripe, open nose. Pleasing and ready to drink, good fruit, a little short.

1979 Brilliant medium to dark red. Nose open and appealing. Fruit there, but flavour still developing. Well made and balanced, good now, but will keep and improve.

1978 Surprisingly light colour. Bouquet a touch over-ripe. Ripe and easy on the palate. Perhaps a little short. To drink now.

1977 Pale red, browning. Not much nose, but quite nice. Light, fruity and ready. Good luncheon wine.

1976 Beginning to brown. Ripe, pleasant nose, a bit roasted. Balance right to drink now, with good fruit. Long aftertaste of ripe strawberries.

1975 Good medium red. Bouquet good, but quite shy. Well structured, forward for 1975. Some complexity, with fruit and tannin not yet perfectly in harmony. Will keep.

1974 Pale, amber colour. Bouquet very ripe, and still good. Shortish, but very pleasing. Fruit still there, not much tannin left.

Château Loudenne, Bordeaux Blanc

1984 (From the vat.) Sample of Sauvignon, fermentation finished, SO2 added. Wine still very hazy. Very pronounced Sauvignon grapey nose. Lovely, balanced, with lots of fruit. Will be excellent.

1983 Very pale straw. Fresh, fruity bouquet. Undeveloped, with acidity dominating fresh, fruity taste.

1982 Bright and clear, with brilliant gold edges. Nose slightly heavier, with honeyed tones. Balanced and harmonious, fresh and clean with long aftertaste.

1981 Pale, clear, bright gold. Open, fresh bouquet. Crisp and clean, with lots of grapey fruit. Lovely *fruits de mer* partner.

1980 Colour similar to 1981. Nose quite luscious. Ripe and clean, with relatively low acidity. Lovely to drink now.

1979 Very pale, clear straw, like the 1983 in colour. Nose a bit closed, with hint of vanilla. Surprisingly muted on the palate, lacking a little in fruit and acidity.

1978 Medium light gold. Nose elegant, with fresh fruit. A touch oxidised, but still very charming.

1977 Darkest colour of all whites tasted. Very ripe on nose. Good, ripe wine, fruit and acidity together. Semillon grape dominant.

1974 Still good medium gold colour. Nose quite shy, but developing after 15 minutes in glass. Quite ripe flavour, still fresh, long in mouth, with surprisingly good aftertaste.

192

CHATEAU
Malescasse
HAUT-MEDOC

As you drive north up the D2 towards Pauillac, pass through the village of Arcins, and you will shortly see a large sign in the fields pointing to Malescasse. The turning to Château Malescasse is on your right, just before a petrol station.

Château Malescasse is situated in the heart of the Médoc, and also has a very special place in the heart of the author. Michel Tesseron, who lives there, is the son of Guy Tesseron, the owner, and Michel's brother, Alfred, is responsible for the running of Malescasse, as well as the Tesserons' other two properties, Château Pontet-Canet and Château Lafon-Rochet. I am pleased to count Michel as one of my few real friends, and thanks to his generous hospitality I lived at Château Malescasse during the many months of work on this book. In addition to lodging me, he gave me unstinting help, and received little in return, save an introduction to English breakfasts, hot curry and vintage port. I shall always remember my

time at Malescasse as one of the happiest of my life, and only hope that no great Médocain palates have suffered permanent damage from over-indulgence in Oriental spices! Special thanks are also due to the régisseur and his wife, Monsieur and Madame Dufau, who kept me well-supplied with firewood during the bitter freeze of January 1985, and were always on hand to give willing help and advice; on one occasion they quite literally had to bale me out, when the pipes burst during the night and the ceiling of my bedroom, mixed with a great deal of cold water, descended on my sleeping form!

Guy Tesseron, a successful Cognac merchant, bought the elegant 19th-century Malescasse in 1978; it was formerly the property of an American consortium, headed by Mr John Train, who bought it from the widow of a Parisian stock-broker, Mme. Philippe, in 1970. The good Dufaus have been régisseurs at Malescasse since the days of the Philippe ownership. The Tesserons have replanted much of the vineyard, and the classic chais and cuvier on either side of the courtyard have been restored and re-equipped. I have not had the occasion to taste any pre-Tesseron Château Malescasse, with the exception of an outstanding bottle of 1959 presented to me by the Dufaus; however, I was much impressed with the clearly visible improvement in the wine over the 6 vintages that have been made there since the Tesseron family came into power. The 1983 vintage is superb, and Monsieur Dufau is justifiably proud of it, as, of course, are his employers.

The soil is exceptionally good for this part of the Médoc, with a good depth of gravel and well drained; the encépagement is right for making classic Médoc wine, and the people and the will are also there. I have every reason to believe that Malescasse will continue to improve, and will take its place among the top Crus Bourgeois of the Médoc.

TECHNICAL INFORMATION

General

Appellation:	Haut-Médoc
Classification:	Cru Bourgeois
Area under vines:	30 hectares, with a possibility of planting up to 40
Distribution of vines:	In several parcels around the château
Owner:	Société Civile du Château Malescasse
Director:	M. Alfred Tesseron
Maître de Chai:	M. Roland Dufau
Consultant Oenologist:	M. Dubois-Arnaux Gendrot

Viticulture

Geology:	Deep gravel
Grape varieties:	70% Cabernet Sauvignon, 20% Merlot, 10% Cabernet Franc
Pruning:	Guyot Double
Rootstock:	R99, 3309, 420A, Riparia
Vines per hectare:	5,800
Average yield per hectare:	45 hectolitres
Replanting:	½ hectare per annum

Vinification

Added yeasts:	Yes, in difficult years
Length of maceration:	3–6 weeks
Temperature of fermentation:	30°C
Control of fermentation:	Cooling by damp jackets, warming by electric system
Type of vat:	Enamelled steel
Vin de presse:	Proportion incorporated according to vintage
Age of casks:	Used casks from Château Pontet-Canet
Time in cask:	14–16 months
Fining:	Egg-whites
Filtration:	Sur plaque at bottling
Type of bottle:	Bordelaise lourde

Commercial

Vente Directe:	Yes, to visitors
General Sales:	Through the Bordeaux négociants
Visits:	Yes, telephone 56 58 90 09 Hours: 0800–1200, 1400–1700 Monday to Friday

THE TASTING AT CHATEAU MALESCASSE AND AT KELVEDON, December 1984 and February 1985 J.S., Christian Seely, M. Michel Tesseron

1984 Good, deep blackish colour. Powerful nose, strong blackcurrant smell. Quite tough and tannic, but with really good mouthfilling fruit. A really well-made 1984, promising a very good development.

1983 Fine, deep red. Good bouquet, with fruit and some finesse. Has the right balance of fruit, tannin and backbone to promise character for the future.

1982 Deep red. Good open nose. Fat and rounded, with fruit and some good ripe tannins. Will be a good bottle soon, but will keep well.

1981 Lighter colour than 1982. Nose more reserved, but good. A lighter, more feminine style than '82 as one would expect from this vintage. I like it.

1980 Bright, medium red. Clean, straightforward and pleasing nose. An honest, well-made 1980, with good fruit and some backbone. Drinks well now, but may be kept.

1979 Good depth of colour. Nose quite open and attractive, with hints of blackcurrant. Balance good, with some finesse and backbone. Long and pleasing aftertaste.

CHATEAU

Maucaillou

MOULIS

Going north up the D2, pass through the village of Arcins, and after about 1 km you will come to a crossroads with a garage on the right. Turn left here, and Château Maucaillou is clearly signposted. You will soon see the large sprawl of Maucaillou's buildings, with the name in large white letters on the side of the chai.

Before Maucaillou was purchased by the Dourthe family in 1929, the vineyard was very much smaller, and was owned by the Petit-Laporte family. Before buying Maucaillou, Georges Dourthe, grandfather of Philippe, used to own Château du Moulin à Vent, an appropriately rustic name, since it was only comparatively recently that anything but corn was grown in the parish of Moulis. The name of Maucaillou doubtless dates from the time it was discovered that the bad pebbles or 'mauvais cailloux' were by no means bad for the cultivation of the noble vines.

It was the remarkable Roger Dourthe who took over in 1961 and built Château Maucaillou into what it is today. He extended the vineyard from 20 to the present 55 hectares, which are spread over the parishes of Moulis, Listrac and Lamarque, and the chais and cuvier have been enlarged and modernised to accommodate the present level of production. He was a skilled and traditional winemaker – the grapes were trodden by foot as late as 1954 – and it was under his direction that the wine of Maucaillou attained its current level of quality. Roger Dourthe died in 1984 at the age of 84, and I am sad not to have met him; he was an amazingly fit man, even up to the year of his death, making a 7-km walking tour of his vineyard every morning, which took him exactly one hour, followed by a vigorous session on his rowing machine. At the age of 72 he completed a two-way crossing of the Atlantic, in a ketch built by Illingworth, with the present owner, Philippe Dourthe, who recalls that it was a particularly arduous voyage due to the failure of the Trade Winds.

The négociant business of Dourthe Frères, now part of CVGB based at Parempuyre, was run from here for many years. Philippe now runs his own company, Dourthe Père et Fils, on the same premises, as well as two other businesses. One of these is a marketing and distribution organisation, the SICA des Châteaux du Bordelais, which looks after the commercialisation of a handful of wine properties in the Bordeaux region; the other is the Centre d'Embouteillage Girondin S.A., which, as the name implies, bottles the wines of other

châteaux. This work is carried out either on the premises at Moulis, or at the châteaux who avail themselves of this service, in one of the enormous mobile bottling units which the company owns. These juggernaut trailers are crammed with a mass of high-tech equipment, represent a vast capital investment and require constant and immaculate maintenance, but they show a good return; the company is the biggest of its kind, and is currently responsible for bottling over fifteen million bottles.

Philippe Dourthe looks what he is, a forceful man of action, successfully making fine wine and carrying on the family tradition of trading in wine that was established in the early part of last century.

TECHNICAL INFORMATION

General

Appellation:	Moulis		
Area under vines:	55 hectares		
Average production:	30,000 to 32,000 cases		
Distribution of vines:	55% in Moulis around château, 30% in Listrac, 15% in Lamarque		
Owner:	Société Civile Agricole des Domaines Dourthe Frères		
Director:	M. Philippe Dourthe, Oenologist and Ampelologist		
Régisseur:	M. Francis Goulary		
Maître de Chai:	M. Jean- Marc Gobineau		

Viticulture

Grape varieties:	58% Cabernet, Sauvignon and Franc, 35% Merlot, 7% Petit Verdot
Pruning:	Guyot Double
Rootstock:	101-14, SO4, Riparia
Vines per hectare:	5,855
Average yield per hectare:	50 hectolitres

Replanting:	Replacement of vines by complantation, $\frac{1}{5}$ hectare per annum

Vinification

Added yeasts:	None
Length of maceration:	3 weeks
Temperature of fermentation:	25–26°C
Control of fermentation:	By heat-exchange apparatus
Type of vat:	Stainless steel
Age of casks:	$\frac{2}{3}$ renewed each vintage, $\frac{1}{6}$ casks of 2 vintages, $\frac{1}{6}$ casks of 3 vintages
Time in cask:	18 months
Fining:	Egg-white
Type of bottle:	Bordelaise, Grand Cru

Commercial

Vente Directe and ex-château sales:	Yes, accounts for 20% of production
Visits:	Yes, for appointment telephone 56 58 17 92

THE TASTING AT CHATEAU MAUCAILLOU, 10 December 1984
J.S., M. Gérard Colin of Château Clarke, M. Philippe Dourthe

1984 Just finished malolactic fermentation. Medium bluey red, still opaque. Nose very young and closed up. Fruit and tannin good. Should be all right.

1983 Excellent deep colour. Bouquet fine, but still closed. Well structured wine with fruit and backbone and some finesse. Will be a good bottle.

1982 Blacky red. Nose very powerful and evolved with huge fruit. This is a big wine, with a mass of good fruit and tannins. Will drink fairly young, but will last.

1981 Good, dark red. Nose pleasant, but not giving much yet. Balance good, with finesse and charm. Classic claret, going through slight adolescence at the moment, but will be civilised when it grows up.

1980 Good, bright medium red. Bouquet open, with very nice fruit. Absolutely drinkable now, but has some tannins and keeping qualities.

1979 Same constant dark colour, with assertive and open bouquet. Not complicated, strong blackcurrant fruit, long in mouth with slight woody taste. Will keep.

1977 Bright medium red. Nose good. Very full for 1977, with lovely lingering cassis aftertaste.

1976 Orangey colour. Nose very ripe, but not too much so. Has taste of hot vintage. To drink now. Again distinct cassis aftertaste.

1975 (Interesting wine, because hail killed all Cabernets at Maucaillou, wine made from 95% Merlot.) Colour quite tawny. Nose elegant and quite open. Good now, softer and rounder than most 1975s. Mouthfilling, but has some finesse.

1974 Colour going quite brown. Nose soft and beginning to fade a little. Again this has the very distinct blackcurrant flavour. Finishes a little short and dry, but a good success for such a year, and holding up well.

196

CHATEAU

Poujeaux

MOULIS

Driving north up the D2 towards Pauillac, pass through the village of Arcins. After about 1 km, you will come to a crossroad, with a petrol station on your right. Turn left, signposted Castelnau; 500 metres along this road, follow the left-hand fork, still signposted to Castelnau. Soon you enter the village of Grand Poujeaux; the offices of Château Poujeaux are on your right immediately after you enter the village, and the chai and cuvier are opposite.

In the middle of the 16th century, Château Poujeaux, known then as La Salle de Poujeaux, was the property of Gaston de l'Isle, as witnessed by a title deed dated 1544, referring to him as the 'Noble et puissant Seigneur Gaston de l'Isle, Seigneur de la terre de la Salle de Poujeaux...' Later, in the 18th century, the property belonged to one Mme. de Montmorin Saint-Heren, sister of the Marquis de Brassier who owned Château Beychevelle; she sold it in 1806 to M. André Castaing, in whose family it remained until 1920, when it was acquired by M. F. Theil on the death of M. Philippe Castaing.

The Theils were one of the many families who made the break from the impoverished Corrèzes Département in the second half of last century. They came west to work in the wine trade; these 'wioneers' must have been determined hard workers. Many of them, like the Moueix family, stopped when they reached Libourne, and sought work there; others crossed the second river and travelled on to Bordeaux, taking jobs as sales representatives to the Northern parts of France and Belgium. One can imagine the hard life they lived, travelling in discomfort by train or boat, laden with samples, and, in those days, certainly no expenses. Many of them, like the Bories and the Manous, prospered and set up their own businesses, and some, like M. Theil, managed to buy their own vineyards. They bought Poujeaux when it was only one-third of the size it had been in 1880, when it was divided into three separate properties. By dint of hard work and perseverance, the family have re-united the three parts, and Poujeaux is now restored to its original boundaries.

Jean Theil, eldest son of the original purchaser,

died in March 1981, leaving seven children. Two of his sons, François and Philippe, now run the property with undiminished zeal and love. All too often in Bordeaux, a property becomes the subject of succession wrangles in such circumstances, but all the children were determined that their inheritance should remain intact. A Société Anonyme was in the process of being formed at the time of my visit, to make continuity possible.

François Theil is deeply concerned with the responsibility of his heritage; he believes that his wine has a soul, an 'esprit' that must be carefully nurtured and preserved. Whilst he is in no way impervious to the technological improvements and advances in oenology that are available to today's winemaker, he will make no changes unless he is totally convinced that they will improve the quality of Château Poujeaux without in any way changing the character of the wine.

The quality, finesse and elegance of Poujeaux are undeniable. At a blind tasting of the 1953 vintage of Poujeaux, Lafite, Mouton-Rothschild, Latour and Margaux, at which were present Jean-Paul Gardère, now a director of Château Latour, Henri Martin, owner of Châteaux St Pierre and Gloria, and M. Jean Theil, Poujeaux and Lafite were placed first and second by each taster. There is also a famous story of a dinner at the Elysée palace, where Poujeaux was served. Baron Elie de Rothschild was one of the guests, and on tasting the Poujeaux, which was obviously served from a decanter, voiced his pleasure at being served with his own wine! On being told of its provenance, he

197

refused to believe it, and demanded to be shown the bottle. The sommelier was then shooed away with some embarrassment.

This similarity with the wine of Lafite undoubtedly springs from the soil-type and exposure of the vineyard, which René Pijassou has compared almost precisely with that of the great Premier Cru. The Theils are proud of the fact that M. Pijassou, one of the most erudite writers on the Médoc, is among their most regular private customers, buying a hogshead for his personal cellar in most vintages.

Poujeaux is not commercialised through the Bordeaux market: the Theils handle all their own sales both abroad and on the domestic market, where they have an amazing mailing list of no less than 12,000 customers who buy their wine direct from the property.

The wine has an extraordinary depth of colour, which is constantly evident even in lighter vintages. François Theil believes that this evenness of quality is partly due to the broad choice of grape varieties grown, and in particular the unusually high proportion of Petit Verdot used.

TECHNICAL INFORMATION

General

Appellation:	Moulis		
Area under vines:	45 hectares		
Owner:	Indivision Theil – Company under formation	Control of fermentation:	Heat-exchange pump
		Type of vat:	Concrete and stainless steel
Viticulture		Age of casks:	20–30% new each vintage, balance from one- to four-year casks
Geology:	Sand/gravel, with good drainage		
		Time in cask:	18 months
Grape varieties:	40% Cabernet Sauvignon, 36% Merlot, 12% Cabernet Franc, 12% Petit Verdot	Fining:	Egg-whites
		Filtration:	Never
		Type of bottle:	Bordelaise or Grand Cru, according to vintage
Pruning:	Guyot Double		
Rootstock:	101.14, 420A, 3309		
Replanting:	Complantation, as necessary to maintain average vine age of 50 years	*Commercial*	
		Vente Directe:	Yes
		Direct ordering	
		at château:	Yes
Vinification		Exclusivities:	Yes, in some countries
Added yeasts:	When necessary	Visits:	Yes, by appointment
Length of maceration:	4 to 6 weeks		Tel. 56 58 23 69 or 58 22 70
Temperature of fermentation:	28–30°C max.		Hours: 0900–1200 1400–1800

THE TASTING AT CHATEAU
POUJEAUX, 3 December 1984
J.S., François Theil

1983 Colour good, clear and deep. Nose new wood with good fruit. Lots of tannin and rich fruit. Well structured, long. Will be good.

1982 (Bottled July, as every year.) Deep, blackish colour. Nose very powerful and rounded, cassis. Big with lots of fruit and good tannin. Has more complexity than many wines of this vintage.

1981 Same excellent deep red. Bouquet still closed, but elegance and fruit beginning to show. Balanced, well made, with more femininity and elegance than the

two later vintages. Tannins muted; will age well.

1980 Beautiful deep red, only a shade lighter than the 1981. Nose open and fragrant, distinct blackcurrant. Perfumed, elegant, aromatic and long in the mouth. Excellent structure for a 1980.

1979 Lovely deep red again, shade darker than 1980. Nose aggressive and open. Cassis flavour, easy, rounded. (François describes it as a *vin d'hiver*, which I found accurate and evocative.)

1928 What an amazing treat! François Theil and his lovely wife gave me a bottle of this staggering vintage one evening. It was still remarkably alive, and even after an hour in the glass, I was still placing it as '61 or later.

CHATEAU

La Tour de By

MEDOC

Follow the D2 into the far north of the Médoc, through St Yzans-de-Médoc, through St Christoly-de-Médoc and on along the edge of the river. After about 2 km you will come to the gates of Château la Tour de By on your left. Visitors should turn left immediately before the entrance to the château, and a gateway after 100 yards on your right takes you to the courtyard, with the office and winemaking buildings around it.

'By' is an old Norse word for port or harbour, and indicates that this corner of the Médoc may have attracted the attention of those pillaging and looting Vikings on their raids up the Gironde estuary ten centuries ago. It is hard to imagine what drew the horn-helmeted Scandinavians to this quiet stretch of the river bank; today there is little to be seen in the way of loot and even less of ravishable maidens.

The origin of the name is probably more prosaic; de By is a Dutch family name; and it was under Louis XV that a vast programme of drainage and reclamation of the Médoc marshlands was carried out by Dutch experts. Most likely, then, a de By settled here and left his name behind him.

The property was known until 1876 as Château la Roque de By, and there is still a smaller château of that name on the property which was built in 1730. 1876 is the date the present château was built by one M. Rubichon who evidently overreached himself financially – the pillars supporting the balcony along the whole façade of the château are unfinished! In 1910 la Tour de By was bought by the wine merchant Monsieur Damoy; he loved the place, and spent his last years living here. Damoy had two daughters, one of whom married a doctor from Paris, and the other married the régisseur's son. After the war they sold La Tour de By to M. Kaskoref, of Russian extraction, who was more interested in the estate as a property speculation than as a serious winemaking exercise. It was acquired in 1965 by a trio of Tunisian Frenchmen, Messrs Pagès, Cailloux and Lapalu; Marc Pagès, whose family owned a huge farming business in Tunisia, which they lost when independence came to that country, now runs and lives at Château la Tour de By. A happy, philosophical gentleman farmer, Marc loves the land and

the whole ethos of winemaking, though he still speaks nostalgically of his 'orange-blossom' days in North Africa.

I know this property well, as Marc has been kind enough to appoint me as his agent in Great Britain. It is a joy to represent la Tour de By, as Pagès is a skilled vigneron and is incapable of producing bad wine, even in the less good years. When we put on a tasting at Trinity College, Cambridge, of all the vintages made during his ownership the assembled dons and wine-buyers, experts to a man, were deeply impressed by the consistent quality and breeding of this fine Cru Bourgeois.

199

When the three partners were on the lookout for a wine property in the Médoc, they considered several châteaux closer to the heartland of the area, but Pagès was most taken with the potential of the terroir of la Tour de By. The main 40-hectare section of the vineyard has two prime ingredients for making fine claret – an excellent 'croupe' of deep Garonne gravel, and a fine view of the estuary. From the top of the actual Tour de By, originally a windmill and later a lighthouse, one has a commanding view of the property, the surrounding countryside and the estuary; in certain weather conditions le Verdon and the Point de Graves, some twenty miles away at the mouth of the Gironde, appear startlingly close.

In 1971 an additional 29-hectare section near St Christoly was added, making a total vineyard area of 69 hectares. The selection of grape varieties grown is classically Médocain – 70% Cabernet Sauvignon, 4% Cabernet Franc and 26% Merlot, and the wine has a fine deep colour, almost black in youth, and in a good vintage needs eight to ten years to reach its full potential. The 1970 has still some way to go, with great intensity of colour and a huge concentration of flavour and tannin. 1982 and 1983 were outstandingly successful, particularly the latter; the *Revue du Vin de France* singled out la Tour de By 1983 with only five other properties in the Médoc, three of which were 1st Growths, as being of special merit in this exceptional vintage. Such recognition is the norm for Marc Pagès; he has won dozens of Gold Medals for his wine, and it is always well placed in blind tastings. La Tour de By is to be found on the wine list of some seventy Paris restaurants, including many of the three-star rated establishments; this surely is the ultimate accolade for any winemaker. Visitors are welcomed at la Tour de By, and if you are lucky enough to be shown round by the owner, you can learn a great deal about how good wine is made. The château has a fine display of old vineyard equipment and cooperage tools collected by Marc Pagès, some of them rare and valuable, and on the wall of the ageing-chai there is a beautiful wooden statue of the Madonna and Child, which the owner rescued from the disused chapel and has painstakingly cleaned and restored. It is perhaps the vathouse, half of which houses traditional and immaculately maintained oak cuves, while the other half boasts a range of gleaming stainless-steel vats, which best illustrates the blend of tradition and technology employed to produce a very fine Cru Bourgeois.

The wine is also sold under the label Château la Roque de By, and the produce of the young vines and the cuves that are not selected for the château label are sold as an excellent Vin de Table under the name of Les Tourterelles. For the future, watch out for a wine called Château Noaillac; this is a vineyard of 30 hectares, purchased in 1981 by Marc Pagès and run by his son Xavier. It is a few kilometres away in the parish of Dignac, and has been totally replanted. With the Pagès know-how and eye for good terroir, one may justifiably hope for good things.

TECHNICAL INFORMATION

General

Appellation:	Médoc
Area under vines:	69 hectares
Average production:	37,500 to 41,500 cases
Distribution of vines:	40 hectares west of the Château, 29 hectares near St Christoly
Owners:	MM. Pagès, Cailloux and Lapalu
Director:	M. Marc Pagès
Maître de Chai:	M. Raymond Ziga
Chef de Culture:	M. Bernard Mehaye
Consultant Oenologist:	M. Jacques Boissenot (formerly, for 16 years, Professor Emile Peynaud, who chose M. Boissenot to take over from him)

Viticulture

Geology:	Mainly Garonne gravel, with 7 hectares of clay/chalk
Grape varieties:	70% Cabernet Sauvignon, 4% Cabernet Franc, 26% Merlot
Pruning:	Guyot Double
Rootstock:	SO4, 420 A, R 140, 3309, 101.14, Riparia Gloire
Vines per hectare:	6,000/7,000
Yield per hectare:	40–55 hectolitres
Replanting:	Regular annual programme

Vinification

Added yeasts:	Yes
Length of maceration:	From 20 to 40 days depending on vintage and state of grapes
Temperature of fermentation:	28–30°C
Control of fermentation:	Tubular cooling system, and running water on exterior walls of vats
Type of vat:	Stainless-steel and oak
Vin de presse:	Incorporated in Grand Vin, depending on year and tannin content
Age of casks:	20% new each vintage, oldest 5 vintages old
Time in cask:	10–15 months
Fining:	Egg-white
Filtration:	Sur terre before going in cask, sur plaque before bottling
Type of bottle:	Ceti standard (lighter than Bordelaise lourde)

Commercial

Vente Directe:	Yes
Direct ordering from château:	Yes
Exclusivities:	Yes, consult château for details
Visits:	Yes: telephone 56 41 50 03 Hours: 0800–1200, 1400–1800

THE TASTING AT CHATEAU LA TOUR DE BY, 6 December 1984
J.S., Christian Seely, M. Marc Pagès, Mr and Mrs David Nutting

1984 Deep blue-black. Very good nose, lots of fruit. Very big and tannic – 95% Cabernet – excellent fruit flavour, will take quite a few years.
1983 Fine dark red. Lovely complex bouquet. Round, supple with lots of backbone and good length. Will be very good in three or four years.
1982 Amazing depth of colour. Powerful rich nose, with a mass of ripe fruit. Big and mouthfilling, complete with good ripe tannins and plenty of skeleton. Will drink soon and last long.
1981 Lovely, medium-dark colour. Nose opening up, good with some blackcurrant fruit. Just beginning to come together nicely, has elegance and finesse, well-balanced with good aftertaste. Classic.
1980 Pretty garnet red. Open, attractive and fruity bouquet. Easy wine, no great complexity, but honest and well made. Good now and for a year or two.
1979 Colour still very deep. Good rich fruit on nose. A very good la Tour de By, elegant, rounded with plenty of length and fruit. Will keep well and get better.
1977 Colour on the light side, going a bit brown. Nose has slight vegetal undertones, but not bad. Light, but still has fruit, and a slightly roasted flavour. To drink now.
1976 Good, dense red. Open nose of ripe fruit. Not at all overripe like some '76s, well-made, balance right for drinking now, but will go on a while yet.
1973 Lightish red, only a little brown. Pretty and ripe bouquet. Good, well-structured wine from this light vintage. Still has some running, with a very attractive fruity flavour and good aftertaste.
1970 (90% Merlot.) Very dark and dense. Powerful, concentrated bouquet. Big concentration of fruit, with plenty of good tannin and lots of mileage left.

CHATEAU

La Tour Carnet

HAUT MEDOC

As you drive north up the D2 in the direction of Pauillac, you come to the village of Beychevelle, with the giant St Julien bottle on your right. Do not follow the main road here, but carry straight on through Beychevelle in the direction of St Laurent. Pass Gruaud-Larose, Lagrange, Camensac and Belgrave, and the drive to Château la Tour Carnet is on your left, about 2 km out of Beychevelle.

Château la Tour Carnet is one of three wine estates in the Médoc to boast a real castle, along with Château de Lamarque and Château d'Issan. The oldest part of the château, dating from the 13th century, is the gatehouse tower that faces you as you drive up the tree-lined avenue to the property. The original castle was known as the Château de St Laurent, but took its present name from the seigneur of the manor of Carnet, who lived here in the 15th century; this noble gentleman fought on the side of the English in the Hundred Years War. The estate was even then producing wine of great quality, for documents exist proving that the wine of la Tour Carnet was being sold as early as 1407 at nearly double the price of red wine from the Graves.

In the early 18th century, la Tour Carnet was bought by a M. de Luetkens, a gentleman of Swedish origin, King's counsellor and military adviser; at the time of the great classification of 1855, in which it was placed among the 4th great growths, it was still in the same family – the owner was a M. O. de Luetkens, whose wife was also owner of the half of Château St Pierre later to be known as St Pierre-Sevaistre.

In 1962 the property was in a very sad state; the vineyard had run wild, and the château was practically a ruin. It was in this year that Louis Lipschitz, a shipping executive of Polish extraction, bought la Tour Carnet. There were so few productive vines when M. Lipschitz bought the property, that the first two years – 1963 and 1964 – only yielded 20 tonneaux, against today's rendement of around 130 tonneaux. The vineyard was almost entirely replanted by Lipschitz in his first two years of ownership, giving today's vines an almost uniform age of 22 years. There are now 31 hectares under vines, with the possibility of adding a further 14.

Château la Tour Carnet now belongs to M. Lipschitz's daughter, Marie-Claire Pelegrin, who runs the property with her husband, Guy-François, who has quit the world of publishing and assumed the mantle of winemaker with great enthusiasm. At the time of writing, a great deal of work was in hand; a new cuvier was being built, and a garden in the formal French style of the 18th century was being laid out between the ornamental blue-painted gateway and railings and the moated castle. On the moat, which completely surrounds the château, float stately swans, white ones, imported in some strange way from England, and a pair of rare black swans.

There is a well-known story of some English visitors to la Tour Carnet, who were amazed to discover that there was no ghost to haunt such a venerable property. On their return to England, they placed an advertisement in the personal column of *The Times* – 'Ghost required for 13th-century castle in Bordeaux'! Only in England could this advertisement have elicited such a volume of replies – so many, in fact, that a second announcement had to be made, saying that the vacancy had been filled. I have seen some of the replies, which range from two New Zealand spirits, able to drive a hearse and willing to supply two hauntings for the price of one, food and wine included, to a young, attractive, female phantom, tired of Irish castles, who seemed to have misunderstood her spiritual duties altogether!

The recent vintages of la Tour Carnet which I had the pleasure of tasting showed the results of the care and work that two generations of the Lipschitz family have lavished on the property. They are perhaps a shade less demanding and complex than some Crus Classés, but are well structured, with a degree of finesse, and a tendency to mature relatively quickly. Visitors are welcome, by appointment, and the Pelegrins are more than ready to impart their enthusiasm and love of this fine property to all and sundry.

TECHNICAL INFORMATION

General

Appellation:	Haut-Médoc
Area under vines:	31 hectares, with a further 14 hectares planned
Production:	12,000 to 14,000 cases
Distribution of vines:	In one block
Owner:	G.F.A. du Château la Tour Carnet
Director:	Mme. Marie-Claire Pelegrin
Maître de Chai:	M. Bertrand Pascal

Viticulture

Geology:	⅓ of vineyard – la Butte de la Tour Carnet – an outcrop of chalk with clay slopes; ⅔, sloping south-south-west, consists of strongly chalky clay, covered by a thick layer of mixed gravel from the Garonne and the Pyrenees
Grape varieties:	53% Cabernet Sauvignon, 33% Merlot, 10% Cabernet Franc, 4% Petit Verdot
Vines per hectare:	8,400
Average yield per hectare:	From 36 to 45 hectolitres depending on year
Replanting:	As necessary to maintain age of vineyard – 22 years

Vinification

Added yeasts:	If necessary, in difficult years
Length of maceration:	15–21 days
Temperature of fermentation:	30°C
Control of fermentation:	By cooled coil, and thermostatically controlled cuvier
Type of vat:	Oak, concrete and lined steel
Vin de presse:	1st pressing included, according to vintage
Age of casks:	¼ to ⅓ renewed per vintage
Time in cask:	17–20 months
Fining:	Egg-whites, in vat
Filtration:	Light sur terre before mise en barrique, sur plaque before bottling
Type of bottle:	Bordelaise lourde

Commercial

Vente Directe:	Yes, to private customers and tourists
Sales:	Through the traditional Bordeaux market
Agents for foreign countries:	Yes – contact M. Pelegrin at Château la Tour Carnet for details
Visits:	Yes: by appointment only Telephone 56 59 40 13 Hours: 0900–1200, 1400–1800 Monday to Friday

THE TASTING AT CHATEAU LA TOUR CARNET, 19 January 1985
J.S., M. and Mme. Guy-François Pelegrin

1984 Medium deep red, blue at edges. Nose good, some blackcurrant. Medium weight, good fruit, tannin pronounced.
1983 (In cask.) Good depth of dense colour. Good bouquet, new oak. Fruit and ripe tannin present. Has some finesse, and quite a lot of charm. Long aftertaste.

Should be excellent bottle in 3–4 years.
1982 Good dark red. Nose surprisingly 'giving' and open. Wine going through 'unhappy phase' due to bottling, but all the right elements seem to be there. Would benefit from tasting again in 6 months.
1981 Beautiful, mid-dark colour. Bouquet elegant, and already very fragrant. Well-made, balanced wine, with finesse and backbone. Good, long aftertaste. Will be good to drink quite soon, but will also keep.

GRAVES

The properties enjoying the right to the Graves appellation are divided into two distinct geographical groups. The northern Graves include Château Haut-Brion, La Mission Haut-Brion and its satellites La Tour Haut-Brion and the white wine section of its vineyard Laville-Haut-Brion, Pape-Clément and the tiny Château les Carmes Haut-Brion; only these few have resisted the urban sprawl of Bordeaux. In former times there were many more vineyards in this area to the southwest of Bordeaux, but they are now covered by the bricks, concrete and tarmac of Pessac, Talence and Mérignac. The larger, southern area is situated around the town of Léognan to the west of the A61 Bordeaux-Toulouse autoroute and the Garonne river.

Probably due to their proximity to Bordeaux, the wines of the Graves were recognised a long while before those of the Médoc, and Haut-Brion's name was known in Pepys' London when most of the Médoc was still a marsh. The quality of Château Haut-Brion was recognised in the great classification of 1855, when geography was ignored so that this great red wine could take its place among the Premiers Crus of the Médoc.

The wines of the Graves were only classified as recently as 1953, and the listing was revised in 1959. The main difference between the Graves and the other great appellations of the Bordeaux region is that the production of most of the Grands Crus properties is of both red and white wine; of the thirteen red wine châteaux in the 1959 classification, all but two make a white wine, and there is only one property among the Grands Crus, Château Couhins, which produces only white wine.

Red Graves varies in style with the differing soil types and encépagements of its widespread area; it is possibly more Médocain in style than anything else, especially in the case of the northern, gravelly vineyards of Talence and Pessac; the grapes employed are certainly those of the Médoc, and the Cabernet Sauvignon is the dominant variety throughout the Grands Crus vineyards.

White Graves, to the uninitiated, equates with indifferent quality, medium-dry wine produced in large quantities, and sold under the generic 'Graves' name. The superb, delicate dry white with its marvellous ageing qualities that is made at the Grand Cru properties, both northern and southern, is quite a different ball-game. Haut-

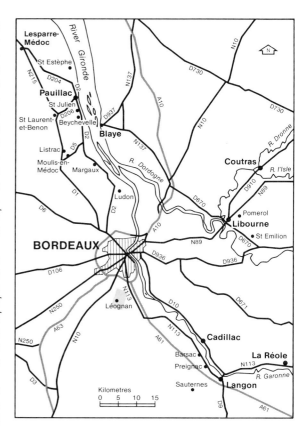

Brion Blanc is superb, but sadly made in such tiny quantities that only a lucky few ever get to try it; Laville-Haut-Brion, the white of La Mission, has an amazing depth of golden colour, increasing as it ages, and develops the most luscious Sauternes bouquet for a dry wine. Of the southern Graves perhaps Domaine de Chevalier Blanc is my favourite white wine in the whole world; Malartic-Lagravière also makes an exceedingly fine white, from, unusually, 100% Sauvignon grapes. The varieties normally employed are Sauvignon and Sémillon, with the former dominant, plus a very little Muscadelle in some vineyards.

The northern Graves is well-served by the superb restaurant and comfortable rooms of La Réserve in Pessac, very close to Château Haut-Brion. The southern Graves is not so well-blessed, though there are several adequate bistros. I have often fared well at the simple restaurant in the centre of Labrède.

CHATEAU
Bouscaut
GRAVES

Take the RN113 south from Bordeaux towards Langon. Château Bouscaut is about 4 km out of Bordeaux on the right-hand side of the road, and the entrance is down a long, tree-lined drive just after the D111 turn-off to Léognan.

Château Bouscaut is a property with a great deal to offer, both in terms of charm and winemaking potential. The château, originally an 18th-century house, with 19th-century additions and embellishments, was virtually rebuilt following a major fire in 1962. The restoration was done with care and taste, and the house sits, solid and settled as if nothing had disturbed it in two hundred years, looking over its ornamental pond across the vines, with not a care for the ever-encroaching urban sprawl that surrounds it.

In 1969 a group of Americans, headed by one Charles Wohlstetter, bought Bouscaut for a million dollars. They proceeded to invest prodigious sums, replanting the vineyard and spending a small fortune on the buildings and the château. The most important step they took, and the wisest, was in appointing Jean-Bernard Delmas of Château Haut-Brion to oversee the re-equipping of chais and cuvier, and the restoration of the vineyard. His wife, Annie, was put in charge of furnishing and decorating the château for the reception of guests and shareholders, a task which she performed with taste and enjoyment.

Possibly the return on capital proved insufficiently attractive for the consortium, for in 1980 Château Bouscaut was acquired by the 20th-century 'Princes des Vignes', Lucien Lurton, owner of Château Brane-Cantenac, as well as enough lesser châteaux to go round each of his ten children. His portfolio also includes Durfort-Vivens, Desmirail, Villegeorge and the Barsac Premier Cru, Château Climens.

Lurton makes a good, reliable red and a typical dry white with excellent ageing potential here at Bouscaut. He is greatly assisted by the groundwork done by his predecessors, as well as by his numerous children; one of his daughters, the attractive Brigitte, is in charge of public relations for all the Lurton properties, and another daughter is a fully qualified oenologist. One may, perhaps, be forgiven for not remembering the names of all

Lucien's offspring, for at Brane-Cantenac, where I have been nobly entertained on more than one occasion, they buzz in and out like so many bees in a hive.

TECHNICAL INFORMATION

General

Appellation:	Graves
Area under vines:	*Red* 45 hectares
	White 10 hectares
Average production:	*Red* 15,000 cases
	White 3,000 cases
Distribution of vines:	One block
Owner:	Société Anonyme du Château Bouscaut
Director:	Lucien Lurton
Régisseur	M. Eynemard
Maître de Chai:	Patrice Grandjean
Consultant Oenologist:	Professor Emile Peynaud

Viticulture

Geology:	Pyrenean gravel
Grape varieties:	*Red* 60% Merlot, 35% Cabernet Sauvignon, 5% Cabernet Franc
	White 70% Semillon, 30% Sauvignon
Pruning:	Guyot Simple and Double
Rootstock:	Riparia-Gloire, 420A
Vines per hectare:	7,000
Average yield per hectare:	*Red* 30 hectolitres
	White 40 hectolitres

Replanting:	5% per annum

Vinification

Added yeasts:	No
Length of maceration:	20 days
Temperature of fermentation:	*Red* 28–30°C
	White Maximum 20°C
Type of vat:	Lined steel and stainless steel
Vin de presse:	Approx. 7% incorporated for red wine
Age of casks:	25% new each year
Time in cask:	*Red* 18 months
	White 6 months
Fining:	Egg-white
Filtration:	Sur plaques before bottling
Type of bottle:	Bordelaise lourde

Commercial

Vente Directe:	No
Direct ordering from château:	Yes
Exclusivities:	None
Agents overseas:	Château and Estate Wines Co., New York, U.S.A.
Visits:	Yes, by appointment only Telephone 56 30 72 40

THE TASTING AT CHATEAU BOUSCAUT, 28 January 1985
J.S., Christian Seely, Brigitte Lurton

White

1983 Very pale yellow colour. Bouquet strong and grapey. Light and clean, with no great weight or length, good now.

1982 Slightly darker gold than '83. Nose more assertive and quite honeyed. Good fruit and acidity, with some length; will improve with time in bottle.

1981 Very similar colour to '82. Good fruit on nose. A little short, enough fruit at the moment, but not enough spine to improve much.

1980 Quite a deep gold. Nose very Sauternes – pourriture. Quite a different style of wine, fermented in cask. Has more classic Graves ageing possibilities. I prefer it to the later style.

Red

1983 Deep, blue-red. Nose very strong with open blackcurrant smell. Lots of good ripe fruit and non-aggressive tannins that will make a fine bottle in 5 to 10 years.

1982 Very deep red. Forthcoming bouquet – again blackcurrant. Big and mouth-filling, almost sweet fruit taste; very long in the mouth, will be a good bottle quite quickly.

1981 Again a good, deep colour. Good classic bouquet. Well-made '81 with backbone; already drinkable, but will be better in 2 to 3 years.

1980 Quite light scarlet colour. Honest bouquet, open but not very exciting. Good, straightforward wine, pleasant to drink now with good fruit, but will last a year or two.

CHATEAU
Carbonnieux
GRAVES

Chateau Carbonnieux lies between le Bouscaut and Léognan, on the small DIII. Leave Bordeaux by the NII3 and turn right in Le Bouscaut, and you will reach Carbonnieux after about two kilometres on your right.

Carbonnieux is one of the oldest and largest vineyards of the Graves; it has been consistently planted with vines since the early part of the 13th century, when it was owned by a nobleman named Ramon Carbonnieu, from whom the name derives. In 1519 the property was bought by the de Ferrons, one of the leading families of Bordeaux, prominent in the Jurade or Parliament of the city. They remained proprietors through difficult periods of civil and religious insurrection until 1740, when they sold Carbonnieux to the powerful Benedictine foundation of Sainte Croix, owners of many vineyards throughout the Bordeaux region. They would appear to have been fortunate in numbering among their brothers a

bon-vivant called Dom Galeas, who was by all accounts something of a 'Mr Fix-it' to the sophisticated high society of that time, being very well connected with the local aristocracy. It follows that he was well-placed to dispose of the wines of Carbonnieux, as is shown by invoices to the local gentry for quantities of up to 200 bottles at a time. The wine would have been mainly white and sweet at that time. There is a story that while the monks were at Carbonnieux, they used to export their white wine to a French favourite of the Ottoman Emperor for whom it was labelled 'Eau Minerale de Carbonnieux' so as not to offend her lord and protector's religious scruples; it is said that the gentleman tasted the wine on one of his seigneurial visits, and asked the lady why the French made such a fuss about wine, when they had such excellent water available!

By the time of the Revolution, the monks had built a great reputation for the wines of Carbonnieux, and the estate totalled some 200 hectares. The monks were kicked out by the revolutionary government and Carbonnieux was designated a 'Bien National', and sold to a M. Elie Bouchereau, who just happened to be the administrator of government finances for south-west France. The Bouchereaus ran the property on sound and scientific lines until 1887, when it was sold to a M. Allendy, whose family owned it until 1894, when it was sold to a triumvirate, Dr Martin and Messrs Mure and Ballet. Martin was a dedicated and professional vigneron, who took Carbonnieux to new heights of quality and reputation. In 1920, being childless, and his partners having died, Dr Martin sold Carbonnieux to the Bordeaux shipping company Doutreloux et Cie, who in turn sold it during the difficult years of the thirties to the wealthy Chabrat family.

After the war, M. J.J. Chabrat, shoe manufacturer and successful political figure, perhaps found that he did not have enough time to devote to Carbonnieux, and in 1956 he sold it to M. Marc Perrin, father of the present owner, Antony Perrin. The Perrins come from Algeria, where they were substantial vineyard owners since 1850. In 1962, along with many others, they lost all their Algerian property and the family still bless the foresight of Marc Perrin in acquiring this beautiful property in the Graves.

From the moment he left school Tony Perrin worked with his father, whom I had the pleasure of meeting just before his death in 1982. He has certainly inherited his father's love of the prop-

erty, and that love has demonstrably been of great benefit to Carbonnieux. The house, basically unchanged in format for centuries, is built around a great courtyard, with the cuvier, chai and 'reception de la vendange' on either side of the gateway. There are bright flowers everywhere, and white tumbler pigeons clatter lazily from rooftops to courtyard. Carbonnieux is a jewel among the Graves.

Situated on one of the highest points in the parish of Léognan, the 70 hectares of vines are planted with half red and half white grape varieties. The gravelly soil has a clay subsoil, and the vineyard has a slight north-west facing slope, with perfect drainage in to a stream called L'Eau Blanche.

The white grape harvest is usually one of the earliest in the Bordeaux area, and the low-temperature fermentation is of 3 to 4 weeks duration. The wine is then kept in new oak barrels for up to 2 months. The vinification process for the red wine is more traditional; ageing is for between 18 months and 2 years in oak casks, a quarter of which are new each year. The most remarkable characteristic of the wines of Carbonnieux, both red and white, is the consistency of their colour, quality and dependability. The whites are crisp, dry and agreeable, maintaining their youthful colour and quality for a surprising number of years, while the reds are sound, reliable Graves with excellent ageing qualities. The 1966 red which Tony Perrin kindly gave me for lunch was vigorous, full of fruit and with enough backbone to keep it going for a long time yet.

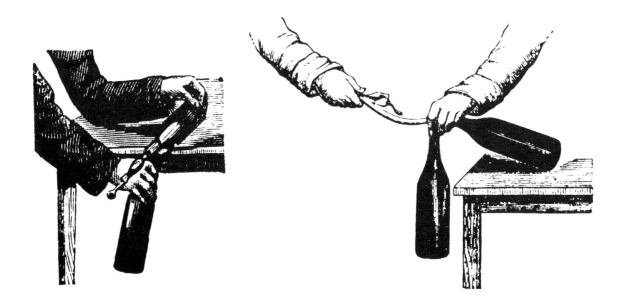

210

TECHNICAL INFORMATION

General

Appellation:	Graves, Grand Cru Classé
Area under vines:	*White* 35 hectares
	Red 35 hectares
Production:	*White* 15,000 cases
	Red 15,000 cases
Distribution of vines:	In one piece
Proprietor:	Société des Grandes Graves
Director:	M. Antony Perrin
Maître de Chai:	M. Jean Henriquet
Régisseur:	M. René Besse
Oenological Consultant:	M. André Vaset

Viticulture

Geology:	Deep gravel on clay subsoil
Grape varieties:	*White* 65% Sauvignon, 34% Semillon, 1% Muscadelle *Red* 55% Cabernet Sauvignon, 30% Merlot, 10% Cabernet Franc, 5% Petit Verdot & Malbec
Pruning:	Guyot Simple
Rootstock:	101–14, Riparia Gloire 3309
Vines per hectare:	7,100
Average yield per hectare:	40 hectolitres per hectare
Replanting:	$\frac{1}{50}$ per annum

Vinification

Added yeasts:	*Red* Yes *White* Yes
Length of maceration:	1 month
Temperature of fermentation:	*Red* 30°C *White* 18°C
Control of fermentation:	Water cooling
Type of vat:	*Red* Cement & stainless steel (200 hectos), *White* stainless steel (140 hectos)
Vin de presse:	*Red* 5%–10%
Age of casks:	*Red* 25% new *White* new
Time in cask:	*Red* 18–24 months *White* 1–2 months
Fining:	*Red* Yes
Filtration:	*Red* Yes
Type of bottle:	Bordelaise

Commercial

Vente Directe:	Yes, to visitors
Direct ordering from Château:	No
Exclusivities:	No
Agents in other countries:	Château and Estates in USA
Visits:	Yes, by appointment Telephone: 56 87 08 28 Hours: 0800–1200, 1400–1800

THE TASTING AT CHATEAU CARBONNIEUX, 19 September 1984
J.S., Tony Perrin

White

The most remarkable facet of the range of vintages was the amazing consistency and lightness of colour. Tony Perrin puts this down to light pressing, and a short stay in barrel.

1983 Pale, greeny yellow. Clean, sharp fruit on nose. Good balance, slight limey fruit taste.

1982 Pale straw, with greeny tinge. Soft muted fragrance with fruit. Delicious mouthful, with refreshing acidity. Again slight lime juice flavour.

1981 Very bright yellow gold, less green. Ripe honeyed fragrance. Well structured, riper than the '82. Semillon flavour developing.

1980 Palest greeny gold. Soft bouquet, good fruit. A little short, but enough fruit there.

1979 Pale straw. Fresh grapey–Sauvignon?–bouquet. Good balance, well made, crisp attractive wine.

1978 Colour a shade darker. Ripe nose, but a bit muted. Ready; soft, but with good fruit.

1977 Pale greeny gold. Perfumed, slightly spicy nose. A little short on fruit, but still harmonious and pleasant.

Red

1982 Good ruby colour. Powerful nose, new wood. Big wine, tannins not aggressive, will develop quite quickly.

1981 Brilliant red with bluey edges. Fragrant, round bouquet, not woody. Well structured, a good keeping wine, to drink after the 1982.

1980 Lighter red, but no browning. Good, open, ripe bouquet. Light, agreeable luncheon claret.

1979 Good red. Nose beginning to develop well. Quite tannic still, but promises well for drinking in a year or two.

1978 Dense red. Nose still closed and complex. Flavour also complex, but fruit and tannin in abundance. Will be a very good bottle in 2 or 3 years.

1977 Good garnet red. Nose very open and attractively fruity. Excellent for 1977, not acid, with plenty of fruit still.

1976 Lighter colour. Open ripe nose, a 'hot year' smell. A ripe mouthful, ready now. Good aftertaste.

1975 Dense deep red. Beautiful bouquet, opening out. Great complexity of flavour, with everything there if you wait.

1974 Colour good for year, only a little brown. Not a lot of bouquet, but what there is is good. Becoming a little tired, but still has some fruit.

1973 Colour browning a bit. Ripeness going over a bit on nose. Still has fruit but wants drinking now.

CHATEAU
Chantegrive
GRAVES

Driving south on the RN113 from Castres, take the first turning to the right after entering the village of Podensac, which is the D115E, signposted to St Michel de Rieufret. Château Chantegrive is about 1 km along this road on the right-hand side.

Chantegrive is to all intents and purposes a new vineyard, started by the present owner, Henri Lévêque.

M. Lévêque can trace his family's involvement with wine back to 1753, when they owned vineyards in Bergerac; in the course of time they left these properties, but Henri's grandfather owned a vineyard at Parsac in the commune of Puisseguin, St Emilion. This was sold during the war due to labour problems, but the family had a 'courtier' business, which Henri inherited from his father and which he still runs with his brother.

Henri Lévêque, clearly a man of foresight and great energy, wanted to get back into wine production; in the early sixties his eyes lit upon this piece of land, which he judged to have just the right combination of soil, exposure and microclimate for the making of fine wine. At that time the land was owned by a multitude of separate people, and much of it was woodland – even those parts that were under vines were not being properly utilised. Nothing daunted, he set about acquiring the present area of 60 hectares. It took several years and a great deal of patience and determination; the whole purchase involved no less than

67 separate legal conveyances, and the ensuing labour of clearing, soil preparation, planting and the building of a modern and sophisticated cuvier and chai can only be guessed at. Finally, he built the 'château', an elegant and well-designed modern villa, and a suite of offices in the garden.

Henri and his wife are the sole proprietors of Château Chantegrive, while his brother helps in the 'courtier' business. He decided to keep the existing name of Chantegrive, appropriate by reason of the large quantity of migrating thrushes that rest in the area on their southerly migration around vintage time. The thrush is his trademark, and appears on the labels.

The Lévêques are clearly an able family. There is yet another brother, who on Peter Sichel's recommendation, went to work as a commis waiter at Durrants Hotel in London to perfect his English; he stayed, and is now the general manager of that fine establishment. Henri himself, as well as demonstrating extraordinary drive and ability by creating a vineyard from scratch and elevating it in just a few years to Grand Cru status, is also President of the Syndicat des Courtiers de Bordeaux.

The production at Chantegrive is divided equally between red and white wine, planted with 50% Cabernet Sauvignon, 40% Merlot and 10% Cabernet Franc for the red, and 60% Semillon, 30% Sauvignon and 10% Muscadelle for the white.

212

Fermentation takes place in stainless-steel cuves, and the very latest in temperature-control equipment is used. The ageing-chai is air-conditioned and humidified. New barriques are used each year, and the wine spends just one year in cask before bottling.

The white wine is of a pale, greeny-gold colour, full, dry and fruity with a predominant Semillon flavour. The red is classic red Graves, big and generous, with undoubted ageing potential. Henri believes his red wines are not ready to be judged until they are five years old at least.

TECHNICAL INFORMATION

General

Appellation:	Graves
Area under vines:	*Red* 30 hectares
	White 30 hectares
Production:	*Red* 15,500 cases
	White 16,500 cases
Proprietor;	H. & F. Lévêque
Maître de Chai:	·M. Christian Elia
Oenological Consultant:	M. Pascal Ribereau-Gayon

Viticulture

Geology:	Alluvial gravel on chalk/clay subsoil
Grape varieties:	*Red* 50% Cabernet Sauvignon, 40% Merlot, 10% Cabernet Franc
	White 60% Semillon, 30% Sauvignon, 10% Muscadelle
Pruning:	Guyot Simple
Rootstock:	Various – 101.14, R99
Density of planting:	6,300 vines per hectare
Yield per hectare:	40/60 hectolitres

Vinification

Added yeasts:	Yes
Length of fermentation:	*Red* 15 days
Temperature of fermentation:	*Red* 30°C
	White 20°C
Control of fermentation:	Water-cooling system
Type of vat:	Stainless steel
Age of casks:	New each year
Time in cask:	1 year
Fining:	*Red*; Egg-whites
Filtering:	Yes – sur-terre
Type of bottle:	Bordelaise

Commercial

Vente Directe:	Yes, to private customers
Direct ordering:	Yes
Exclusive contracts:	Yes, in USA
Agents in Foreign Countries:	Yes
Visits:	Yes – for appointment, telephone 56 27 17 38
	Hours for visits: 08.00–1200, 1400–1800 (except Saturday mornings and Sundays)

THE TASTING AT CLOS ST JEAN, LATRESNE, 17 July 1984
J.S., Christian Seely

White

1983 Pale, greeny gold. Nice fresh bouquet. Clean, crisp and well balanced wine, good to drink now, but will improve. Definite Semillon character.

Red

1982 Good, deep red. Attractive and open nose. Rounded, with lots of fruit and a nice earthy robustness. Already very easy to drink, but will keep and improve.

1981 Slightly lighter colour than '82. Nose good. Pleasing, medium-bodied red Graves, with some finesse and elegance; should keep and make a nice bottle.

1980 Brilliant, medium red. Nice open bouquet, quite soft with good fruit. Straightforward, not too much sublety, very nice to drink now.

1979 Deep, clear garnet. Earthy, fruity, Graves bouquet. A good winter wine, with lots of fruit, body, tannin and not too much complexity.

Domaine de Chevalier

GRAVES

Take the D109E from Léognan in the direction of Cestas; after half a kilometre turn left along a small country lane, and 500 metres further on, a small sign on your right indicates the private road through the vineyard to Domaine de Chevalier.

As soon as you enter the vineyard, you will see the entire vignoble, neatly embraced on three sides by pinewoods, the house white and unassuming, with its chai and outbuildings nestling in the centre of the far boundary against a background of tall trees.

It is generally assumed that the name Chevalier is a corruption of Chibaley, the first recorded owner of the domaine and probably the creator of the vignoble. It is the name of Chibaley that appears on Belleyme's map of the area dated 1763, of which a fine print hangs in the house. In the 17th and 18th centuries some of the finest vineyards in the Bordeaux region were here in the Graves, and the wines of the area were known outside France, while most of the Médoc was still marshland.

In the 1820s the name had been changed to Chevalier, but around this time the vineyard was uprooted and the land returned to the pine trees. In 1865 it was purchased by Jean Ricard, great-grandfather of the present occupant, Claude Ricard. Jean's father owned Haut-Bailly, and he himself already owned Fieuzal and La Gravière (now known as Malartic-Lagravière). The Ricard family name appears as a strong thread throughout the vinous tapestry of the Graves, and Jean was an energetic and capable vigneron; he cut down the pines and re-instated the vineyard, rapidly restoring it to its former glory. It was he who built the large Cave in Léognan, next to the Mairie, which bears the names of Malartic-Lagravière and Fieuzal, and is now used by the present owners of both these properties.

At the turn of the century, Domaine de Chevalier passed to Jean's son-in-law, Gabriel Beaumartin, a Bordeaux timber merchant. Gabriel fell totally in love with the vineyard, calling it his *danseuse*; apart from his love and care, he brought two other benefits to the property – a plentiful supply of oak for new barrels, at a time when the Bordeaux wine trade was just beginning to realise the beneficial effect of new wood in the ageing process, as well as a ready and willing work force from his sawmills to pick the grapes quickly at the optimum moment.

On the death of the redoubtable Beaumartin in 1942, Domaine de Chevalier came into the hands of Jean Ricard, grandson of the original Jean, who, with the help of an agricultural engineer from Leognan named Marcel Doutreloux, brought the vineyard and its wines to an even higher standard of excellence. In 1948 the property passed into the hands of Jean's son Claude, perfectionist and man of extraordinary ability, totally devoted to the excellence of his wines.

In 1983 Domaine de Chevalier was sold to the Bernards, a family of distillers. Claude Ricard, however, remains at Chevalier in a consultant capacity until 1988, which will be his fortieth vintage; during this period he will pass on his skills, perfectionism and, above all, his love and enthusiasm for Chevalier, to Olivier Bernard, who will doubtless run the property with the same care and attention to detail that have made Domaine de Chevalier what it is today.

Although the new owners are now the Bernard family, it seems appropriate to write of Claude Ricard, since he still lives in the house and will continue to run the property until 1988. On his retirement, Claude tells me that he will live nearby and looks forward to having time for his beloved piano, but will always be available for help and advice when called upon. I get the distinct feeling that, in spirit at least, Claude will never leave Domaine de Chevalier: like Gabriel Beaumartin before him, the vineyard has been a lifelong love affair, and such devotion does not die with the signing of deeds.

Courtly is perhaps an old-fashioned word, but it seems to fit Claude Ricard well. Athlete and aesthete, he plays real tennis with the best and at one time was a concert pianist of note. He has an acute wit, and a dry, very French, but never cruel, sense of humour. A kind and welcoming man, he immediately imparts even to casual visitors his great love and enthusiasm for the remarkable wines of Domaine de Chevalier.

There are those aficionados who rate Domaine de Chevalier Blanc as the finest dry white wine in the

world; Claude's comment summed up the wine and the man quite neatly. 'If one can compare wine to women, I like to think of the great classic white Burgundies as Sophia Loren; my wine is to me more like Audrey Hepburn!'

Although it is only a small part of the total production of Chevalier – three hectares as opposed to fifteen of red – I am sure that it is the white wine that Claude loves best. It is in the production of this superb wine perhaps that one can best see his almost fanatic perfectionism.

The picking of the white grapes always begins ten days to a fortnight before the red. After a first, very selective 'tri', or passage through the vines, in which only perfectly ripe grapes are picked, Claude analyses the total acidity; on the result of this analysis, he decides how the picking will

proceed. For instance, if the total acidity is too high, the vendangeurs have to go through the vines as many as five times, selecting only the ripest grapes. After the last tri, any unripe grapes are left on the vines for the birds; all overripe and rotten grapes are carefully picked out and thrown away.

Fermentation takes place in cask, as Claude finds control easier in small volume; the process takes about three to four weeks at a low temperature. He uses only a maximum of 25% new wood for the white wine. Domaine de Chevalier is perhaps the last property to keep its white wine in wood for so long. Bottling takes place at the end of the second winter after the vintage. Finally, to ensure that his white wine is never drunk too early, even after bottling, and even though much has already

215

been sold, the wine is locked away in a special building for another two years before it is allowed to leave the property.

The same rigorous process applies to the red as to the white grapes at the vintage; Claude himself, or his régisseur, Monsieur Grassin, inspects every bunch that goes into the cuves, and a smart ticking-off is administered to any picker whose standards slip! Claude, though slightly manic in his perfectionism, is well loved and all is taken in good part. I somehow feel that as long as Claude is around, Chevalier will be the last vineyard to be picked by machine!

Fermentation takes place in specially constructed steel cuves in parallelepiped form, with large trap doors in the top, which allows for 'bombage', the process of breaking up the 'chapeau' or cap of grape skins that forms over the surface of the must. Another peculiarity of Claude's vinification at Chevalier is that he believes in a much higher temperature for the fermentation than any of his colleagues. The cuves are heated up to 32°C. On one occasion Claude went out for an evening's bridge, telling his régisseur that he would check the temperature of a certain cuve on his return and switch off the heater before going to bed. For once Homer nodded, and he forgot. In the morning he was awoken by a call from his régisseur, telling him that the temperature was over 34°! Later,

Professor Peynaud, oenological consultant to Chevalier, came to taste the various cuves for tannin, and pronounced that particular one to be the best!

The wine is aged in barriques for two years, half of which are new, and half are those used for the vintage two years before. After their second use, the barrels are disposed of. During the ageing, the wine is racked alternately from new to old casks to ensure uniformity and balance.

This combination of meticulous selection of grapes, rigorous and immaculate treatment of the wine during vinification and ageing, and strict attention to detail at all stages of development, is the secret of Claude's ability to produce wines of such consistent quality and longevity, even in the lesser vintages.

The proof of the pudding may be demonstrated by the result of a fascinating tasting experiment conducted in the presence of a group of top wine journalists and oenological experts. Claude presented three groups of three vintages of Chevalier red which were as follows: 1962, 1963 and 1964 – 1965, 1966 and 1967 and 1968, 1969 and 1970. He then set the tasters the problem of finding the 'bad' vintage in each group. In the first two groups only Claude Ricard and his oenological adviser got it right, and in the third, only Claude himself was successful! Quite a tribute.

TECHNICAL INFORMATION

General

Appellation:	Graves
Area under vines:	*Red* 15 hectares
	White 3 hectares
Production:	*Red* 5,000 cases
	White 800 cases
Distribution of vines:	In one piece
Proprietor:	Société Civile du Domaine de Chevalier
Régisseur and Maître de chai:	Loïs Grassin
Directeurs:	Claude Ricard and Olivier Bernard
Oenological Consultant:	Professor Peynaud

Viticulture

Geology:	Siliceous gravel on an iron-clay subsoil
Grape varieties planted:	*Red* 65% Cabernet Sauvignon, 5% Cabernet Franc, 30% Merlot
	White 70% Sauvignon, 30% Semillon
Pruning:	Guyot Double
Rootstock:	3309 (95%)
Vines per hectare:	10,000

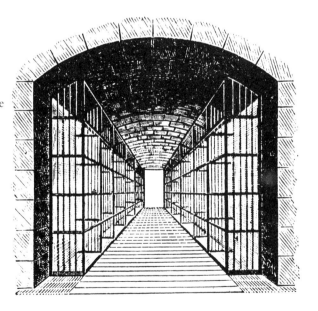

216

Average yield per hectare:	35 hectolitres	Time in cask:	*Red* Nearly two years
			White 18 months
Replanting:	Annual replacement of failing vines, replanting every 50 years	Fining:	*Red* Whites of 6/7 fresh eggs
			White Bentonite
		Filtration:	*Red* Light at bottling
			White None
Vinification		Type of bottle:	*Red* Grand Cru
Added yeasts:	No		*White* Bordelaise
Length of fermentation:	*Red* 20–25 days		
	White 21–28 days	*Commercial*	
Temperature of fermentation:	*Red* 32°C–33°C	Vente Directe:	No
	White Low	Direct ordering:	No
Regulation of fermentation:	*Red* By remontage and 'bombage'	Exclusive contracts:	None
		Agents in foreign countries:	None
	White None	Visits:	Yes; for appointment, telephone: 56 21 75 27
Type of vat:	*Red* Epoxy-resin lined steel tanks, 100 hectolitres		Hours for visits: 0900–1200, 1400–1700
	White Barriques		
Vin de presse:	*Red* Partial inclusion, depending on tannin level		
Age of barriques:	*Red* half new each year, half two years old		
	White 20–25% new each year		

THE TASTING AT CHEVALIER,
27 September 1984
J.S., Christian Seely, Claude Ricard, Olivier Bernard, E. Penning-Rowsell, Mrs Penning-Rowsell

Red

1983 Lovely depth of colour. Some fruit and new wood on nose, but quite closed. Big wine with finesse, elegance and backbone. Tannins supple and not aggressive. A Domaine de Chevalier to wait for.

1982 Not a good sample. Mise finished only 15 days ago. Not fair to judge.

1981 Deep, dense colour. Round, ripe fruit on nose. Good balance, tannins to the fore, plenty of fruit. Will be an excellent bottle.

1980 Lighter, brilliant colour. More open, fragrant bouquet, typical Graves nose. Well-made 1980, elegant, mouthfilling and well-structured. Good now, but will stay well for the vintage.

1979 Very deep red, with bluey edges. Good, if muted bouquet. A fat wine with fruit and tannin in abundance, and a good long aftertaste. A Chevalier to keep.

1978 Deeper colour than the '79. Ample, rich fragrance. Powerful, ripe fruit, with good tannin at back, but not aggressive. More forward than 1979, but also a stayer.

White

1983 Pale, gin-clear, light gold. Good Semillon nose. Full of fruit, slight new wood. Needs plenty of time; very complex and elegant, like all white Chevaliers, and will be a classic.

1982 Slightly darker colour, with hint of green. Distinctive, powerful nose. A bit fuller than the '83 – fruit more evident. Again this needs time.

1981 Colour very like '82. Perfumed nose, honeyed. Fruit and acidity a bit unbalanced, but will even out and become a winner.

1980 Star bright, pale gold. Honeyed, fragrant bouquet. Easier taste with lots of fruit. Lovely now, but not especially typical.

1979 Slightly darker colour. Beautiful nose, just beginning to show elegance of Chevalier. Ripe, mouthfilling and complex. A young daughter of the house, beginning to blossom into lovely womanhood.

Wines served at dinner at le Rouzic in the Cours du Chapeau Rouge

1976 Fine deep red. Open, attractive and heady fragrance. Approaching readiness. Round, supple wine, with long, pleasant aftertaste. Will stay well.

1975 Brilliant, deep colour. Attractive nose, just beginning to open up. Very complex flavour, fruits and tannins in harmony. An aristocrat, but still an adolescent. Will be a really fine bottle, but needs another five to ten years, and then will last many more.

1970 Beautiful dark red. Nose full, but refined and elegant. A wine to keep for some years yet, mouthfilling, with a superb structure, fleshed out with fruits and supple tannins.

1964 Still has deep intense red of Chevalier wine. Lovely ripe bouquet of fruit and flowers. Perfectly balanced, a good Chevalier and a good 1964, the harvest having been, as usual, picked at exactly the right moment, before the rains of that year. A point now.

White

1976 Lovely medium gold. More rich and ripe. A white Chevalier in perfect condition for drinking, elegant, supple with delicious fruit and correct degree of acidity. Very long aftertaste.

1975 Bright gold, a shade lighter than 1976. Bouquet beautiful, more reserved than the '76. Slightly more finesse and delicacy than the '76, with quite a lot in reserve. White Domaine de Chevalier at its superb best.

217

CHATEAU

Ferrande

GRAVES

Château Ferrande is to be found on the right-hand side of the N113 just after you leave the village of Castres, driving south towards Barsac and Langon.

Henri Delnaud bought Ferrande in 1954, making it one more in the chain of wine properties in the Bordeaux area to benefit from *pied noir* ownership. Delnaud was a landowner in Algeria until Independence, but had the foresight to buy Château Ferrande some time before. The property used to be the estate of the family of Seguineau de Lognac, and later belonged to M. Jean Descacq. Delnaud died in 1970 and it is his daughters who now own Château Ferrande, though the property is run for them by the firm of Castel Frères, under the general managership of M. Delbois; day-to-day running is in the capable hands of Monsieur Bortoletto, who has been régisseur at Ferrande since 1969.

The part of the vineyard nearest to the main road is the oldest section, and formed part of the original Domaine de Ferrande, and slopes upwards, away from the road, to a plateau of some 15 hectares, bordered by pine woods. The most remarkable feature of the vineyard is the size, volume and colour of the gravel. In places, particularly on the slopes, the pebbles are the size of a man's fist and they have a curious yellowy colour, deriving from the coating of clay and sand.

The old vathouse, which I remember well from my first visit to Ferrande, consisted of a series of concrete cuves built two high, and seemingly crammed higgledy-piggledy into every available corner of the building. This made for difficult working conditions, and moreover the capacity was inadequate for big-volume vintages. A new cuvier has now been built, some 500 metres from the château and chais, on the plateau section of the vineyard. It is equipped with steel and stainless-steel vats of sufficient volume to cope with the largest imaginable crop; it also contains the latest temperature-control equipment, and is well-insulated against extreme external conditions.

The estate produces both red and white wine in a proportion of 75% to 25% respectively. The red is a typical southern Graves, with a good depth of colour and a certain vigour of style; it also has some finesse, and ages well. The white wine is vinified according to the latest techniques at very low temperatures; after an 8–10 day period of maceration, the assemblage is made, the wine is fined and filtered and then goes back into vat for a period of from 3 to 5 months before bottling. The end product is a crisp, dry, fruity wine with a lovely fresh bouquet; it is probably at its best when a couple of years old.

The attractive, if modest, chartreuse château sits back from the road, protected by a small park containing old cedars and walnut trees. It is not permanently lived in, but M. Delnaud's daughters and their families use the house during the summer.

TECHNICAL INFORMATION

General

Appellation:	Graves
Area under vines:	44 hectares – 43 in production, 9 hectares white, 34 hectares red
Average production:	*White* 4,500 cases
	Red 17,000 cases
Distribution of vines:	In one block
Owner:	Société Civile du Château Ferrande (Héritiers Delnaud)
Régisseur:	M. Bortoletto
Consultant Oenologist:	M. Laffort

Viticulture

Geology:	Gravel on sandy clay
Grape varieties:	*Red* 33⅓% Merlot, 33⅓% Cabernet Franc, 33⅓% Cabernet Sauvignon
	White 35% Sauvignon, 65% Semillon
Pruning:	Guyot Simple
Rootstock:	Mainly 420 A
Vines per hectare:	4,500
Average yield per hectare:	45 hectolitres
Replanting:	As necessary

Vinification

Added yeasts:	Used in difficult years

Length of maceration:	*Red* 8–15 days
	White 8–10 days
Temperature of fermentation:	*Red* 30–33°C
	White 19–20°C
Control of fermentation:	By running water on exterior of vats
Type of vat:	Stainless steel and epoxy-resin-lined steel
Vin de presse:	1st pressing used according to vintage, 2nd pressing very rarely
Age of casks (for red only):	10% renewed each vintage
Time in cask (red only):	15 to 18 months
Fining:	Egg albumen in vat
Filtration:	Sur terre before going in cask, sur plaque before bottling
Type of bottle:	Bordelaise

Commercial

Vente Directe:	Yes, to private callers
Sales:	Through the Bordeaux market, and some commercialisation direct by the château
Visits:	Yes: telephone 56 50 90 20 for appointment

THE TASTING AT CHATEAU FERRANDE,
1 February 1985
J.S., M. Bortoletto

White

1983 Light, greeny gold. Clean, fresh and fruity bouquet. Delicious, crisp, dry flavour, with good aftertaste. Balance excellent. (Gold Medal, Concours Agricole, Paris.)

Red

1982 Bright, medium red. Nose a little closed (bottled September 1984) Already pleasing to drink, rounded and well-balanced, with a good, slightly earthy taste.

1980 Fairly light colour. Bouquet quite nice, but not very strong. Light and easy to drink now, a little short, but all right for a year or so.

1979 Good medium red. Good nose with some blackcurrant. Firm, straightforward wine with no great finesse. Good to drink now.

1978 Colour similar to 1979, with a touch more ripeness on the nose. Good fruit with body and some finesse; more backbone than the '79. Will stay a while.

1966 Bright scarlet. Lovely nose of summer fruits – raspberries. No great length, but perfect to drink now, with lovely fruit taste promised on the bouquet.

CHATEAU
De Fieuzal
GRAVES

The chai and cuvier of Château de Fieuzal are to be found on the right-hand side of the D651, about 1 km out of Léognan as you head for Saucats.

There is no château here, the totally dilapidated house having been demolished some 5 years ago to make way for more vines. Administration and sales are handled by the able director of the owning company, Gérard Gribelin, from the old office-cum-cuvier complex in Léognan next to the Mairie. This was originally built by the Ricard family when they owned de Fieuzal, Domaine de Chevalier, Malartic-Lagravière and Haut-Gardère at the turn of the century.

During the monarchy, Château de Fieuzal belonged to the noble family de la Rochefoucauld; the writer of the family is quoted as believing that 'sobriety is a form of impotence'.

Abel Ricard bought de Fieuzal from one Alfred de Griffon in 1893, and it was in this year that the wines of the property were sold to the Vatican for the table of Pope Leo XIII.

The vineyard certainly prospered and flourished under Ricard ownership; I have a price list of 1900 of the Maison J. Ricard, and it is interesting to note that, across the board, the prices asked for de Fieuzal and Malartic-Lagravière were about equal, and always a little higher than Domaine de Chevalier.

Just after the First World War, Abel Ricard's daughter, Odette, married a Swede, Erik Bocke, who came to France as an American volunteer soldier during the war. His civilian metier was the theatre, and he managed the Alhambra in Bordeaux during the inter-war years. At the outbreak of the Second World War, he and Odette left France for Morocco, where they stayed for the duration. On their return in 1945, Odette's father

had died, the vineyard was in a desperate state and there was no stock to sell. Bocke abandoned the theatre, and put his hand to the vigneron's plough. His achievement at de Fieuzal can be measured both by the quality of the wines of the 60s, and by the price of FF8,000,000, at which, at the age of 80, he sold the property to the present company.

Gérard Gribelin, dynamic director and general manager of the Société Anonyme du Château de Fieuzal, runs a thriving négociant business, as well as an attractive retail shop in the fine old Ricard building in Léognan, as adjuncts to the company's winemaking activities. Some 5 years ago, Gribelin bought a very old run-down property called Château Ferbos. The house was a virtual ruin, and the vineyard had been grubbed up in the 1930s; now all is revitalised – the vines replanted, the house restored and beautifully furnished, and it is here that Gérard Gribelin lives, with his pretty blonde wife and their four children.

Vinification of both the red and white wine produced at Château de Fieuzal takes place in the cuvier and ageing cellar where the old château once stood. Gérard Gribelin had lined steel cuves installed here in 1977, with electronic temperature-control for each one. The red wine process is traditional – a three-week maceration period with the alcoholic fermentation at around 30°C, followed by transfer into wooden barrels, of which 60% are new each vintage, in which the wine will age for between 18 and 20 months depending on the vintage. The white wine, of which there is only a small production – some 850 barrels – is fermented in new casks, and bottled after around 5 to 6 months.

The red de Fieuzal, especially from 1979 onwards, is a very well-made wine, with excellent and

220

constant depth of colour, firm body and fruit and considerable backbone. Even the 1980 would repay keeping for two or three years. The white is elegant and well balanced, with, in the case of the young 1984, a luscious and extraordinary bouquet of ripe white peaches; like all correctly made white Graves, it has excellent ageing potential. At the turn of the century, the white wine was commercialised under the name Sable-d'Or, as I have seen from a Ricard family menu from the early 1900s, and also from an old label.

Sadly this book was a year too soon to include details and photographs of the impressive array of new buildings that is planned on the site of the old château. These will include a large stock warehouse, offices, a reception area, guest suite and tasting-room. I look forward to my next visit, when M. Gribelin and I have a date with a bottle of vintage port!

221

TECHNICAL INFORMATION

General

Appellation:	Graves
Area under vines:	*Red* 21 hectares
	White 2 hectares
Production:	Red 8,500 casks
	White 850 casks
Owner:	Société Anonyme du Château de Fieuzal
Director:	M. Gérard Gribelin
Régisseur:	M. Guy Chaussat
Maître de Chai:	M. Arnaud Andres
Oenological Consultant:	Laboratoire Oenotechnique de Portets

Viticulture

Geology:	Deep white gravel
Grape varieties:	*Red* 60% Cabernet Sauvignon, 30% Merlot, 5% Cabernet Franc, 5% Petit Verdot
	White 60% Sauvignon, 40% Semillon
Pruning:	Guyot Double
Rootstock:	Riparia Gloire, 101.14, 420A, 3309
Vines per hectare:	9,000
Average yield per hectare:	35–40 hectolitres

Vinification

Added yeasts:	Yes, own strains
Length of maceration:	21 days
Temperature of fermentation:	30–32°C
Control of fermentation:	Electronically controlled for each cuve by cold-water sprinkling
Type of vat:	Lined steel
Vin de presse:	All or part used in the Grand Vin, depending on vintage
Age of casks:	60% new annually
Time in cask:	18–20 months
Fining:	White of eggs
Filtration:	Sur terre, and sur plaque before bottling
Type of bottle:	Bordelaise

Commercial

Vente Directe:	Yes
Direct Ordering:	Yes
Exclusivity:	None
Agents abroad:	Yes
Visits:	Yes, by appointment only Telephone: 56 21 77 86

THE TASTING AT THE CUVIER,
23 November 1984
J. S., M. Gérard Gribelin

White

1984 Clear, pale, greeny gold. Astounding and delicious nose of ripe white peaches. Excellent, clean and crisp, but plenty of fruit and new wood indicating longevity.

Red

1984 Colour deep, luscious purple. Nose closed, slight malolactic fermentation still going on. Seems to have an excellent balance of fruit and non-aggressive tannins. A tough one, but should be really good.

1983 Deep, dense red. Bouquet open, with some blackcurrant and new wood. Tannic and quite aggressive in the mouth, but has fruit and backbone with good long aftertaste.

1982 Colour almost as deep as 1983. Nose a bit closed (bottled in June) but very correct. Good, mouthfilling and long, tannin agreeable. Will be drinkable much quicker than '83.

1981 Again deep, bluey red. Bouquet beginning to give off good fruit. Quite hard and tannic, not dissimilar to 1983 in style, but less powerful. Should make a good bottle.

1980 Surprisingly – again the same depth of colour. Nose good, but still closed. Amazingly well structured for 1980, with tannin and fruit and backbone. Needs 2/3 years.

1979 Good. Cassis nose beginning to evolve. Another well made wine with structure, backbone and fruit. Plenty of life here.

1978 Same deep red colour. Nose attractive, but quite closed. Very complex flavour, but shut down. (Gérard Gribelin says it has just gone into this phase, and will stay like it for a few years before opening up again into a really good wine.)

1977 Colour a bit lighter. Nose of overripe fruit. Not bad for the vintage, but lacks flesh and character of other years tasted. Not a lot of future.

1976 Beginning to brown a little. Ripeness on bouquet, but very pleasant. Good for 1976, not powerful but agreeable to drink now, with good fruit and some aftertaste.

1975 Good medium red, no browning. Nose good, but not giving much. Very tannic, but luscious fruit – strawberries. Needs another 3–5 years.

At lunch at Château Ferbos

1971 Colour good, beginning to go orangey. Ripe on nose, Good ripe mouthful, beginning to dry off at the end.

1970 Dense red. Lovely ripe nose. Together and harmonious, with everything in balance, still plenty of fruit and life. Very good.

CHATEAU

De France

GRAVES

From the village of Léognan, take the D651 in the direction of Saucats. Château de France is about 1 km out of Léognan, and is clearly signposted on your right.

I have not been able to find out much about the early history of this property, which probably stems from the fact that it has changed hands countless times in the past 50 years, and all early records have been lost. It would seem that at one time it formed part of the Domaine of Château Olivier.

The present owner, Bernard Thomassin, bought de France in 1971, at which time there were only a few hectares under badly neglected vines. M. Thomassin is a distiller of industrial alcohol, has a large factory near Paris, and has applied a great deal of his technical expertise to the equipping of an impressive new vathouse and bottling line. He tells me that this task was simplified for him by the almost total absence of any such buildings when he arrived, enabling him to suit the construction to the plant, rather than the other way round.

Since 1971 the vineyard has been totally replanted, and there are now 27 hectares under red vines; a further 4 hectares, on lower ground, have just been planted with a mixture of Sauvignon, Semillon and Muscadelle for the production of a white wine, whose first vintage will be in 1987. Modern technology is also at work among the vines; behind the château, the vineyard slopes down to a stream, and is very susceptible to damage by frost. M. Thomassin has laid out a system of water-pipes above the vines; spraying the vines has proved an effective remedy in other parts of France, and although the system had not been used when I visited the property, M. Thomassin felt that it was a necessary and comforting piece of insurance.

The cuvier, completed in 1978, contains stainless-steel tanks for the alcoholic fermentation, and a further 20 metal vats which are used for the malolactic fermentation, assemblage and bottling; all are thermostatically and individually controlled from a central panel. Although the first stages of vinification are conducted with every modern technological aid, ageing is in traditional oak casks, of which some 30% are new each vintage. The wine spends from 12 to 18 months in cask, and is bottled in the château's own bottling plant. Until 1976 the bottling was done by a contractor with a mobile unit, but this was found to be less than satisfactory, and the new bottling-line ensures perfect, clean work and an exactly controlled level of wine in each bottle. Thomassin's aim is to produce classic red Graves with good ageing

qualities, and immaculate bottling is a prerequisite for a long life.

The owner visits the château at least once a fortnight, and in his absence Château de France is ably cared for by the young régisseur, Guy Beyris. The house is extremely pretty, but not currently lived in, although restoration work has started, now that the vineyard, chais and cuvier are in order. In front of the château stands an ancient Cognac still, a reminder, perhaps, of M. Thomassin's other activities.

In the early years of his ownership, the produce of the then young vines was sold under the appellation Bordeaux Supérieur, and was labelled Château Coquilles, and the Château de France name was not used until the vines became more mature.

TECHNICAL INFORMATION

General

Appellation:	Graves
Area under vines:	*Red* 27 hectares
	White 4 hectares (not yet in production)
Average production:	12,000 cases
Distribution of vines:	One parcel
Owner:	Bernard Thomassin
Régisseur:	Guy Beyris
Consultant Oenologist:	M. Latapie

Viticulture

Geology:	Gravel and sandy clay
Grape varieties:	*Red* 50% Merlot, 50% Cabernet
	White 50% Sauvignon, 30% Semillon, 20% Muscadelle
Pruning:	Guyot Simple
Rootstock:	3309, SO4
Vines per hectare:	5,000
Average yield per hectare:	40 hectolitres
Replanting:	As necessary

Vinification

Added yeasts:	Yes
Length of maceration:	20 days
Temperature of fermentation:	30°C max. (generally between 26 and 28°C)
Control of fermentation:	Running water on exterior of vats and by thermostatic control
Type of vat:	Stainless steel for alcoholic fermentation, lined steel for malolactic
Vin de presse:	Proportion of 1st pressing added to Grand Vin
Age of casks:	⅓ new each vintage, rest casks of 1 and 2 vintages
Time in cask:	12 months
Fining:	Albumen
Filtration:	Kieselguhr, and sur plaque before bottling

Commercial

Vente Directe:	Yes
Exclusivities:	None
Agents overseas:	Yes, contact château for information
Visits:	Yes: telephone 56 21 75 39 Hours: 0900–1200, 1400–1700

THE TASTING AT CHATEAU DE FRANCE, June 1984
J.S., Guy Beyris

1982 Good deep red, without purple of 1981. Powerful, fruity nose with some oak. Attractive, rounded and mouthfilling, success of Merlot in '82 evident; a supple, generous wine with soft tannins – will be ready quite quickly.

1981 Colour dark with purple tones. Bouquet soft and quite evolved. Good fruit, but still quite tough with plenty of tannin and backbone. More Médoc than Graves in style, will repay keeping for two or three years.

1979 Good scarlet colour. Attractive, soft nose with some cassis. Light and very pleasing to drink now, but will keep some time.

1975 Colour good, beginning to brown. Slight gamey smell. Ready to drink, but still has enough tannin and backbone to keep it going for some years.

CHATEAU
Haut-Bailly
GRAVES

Take the Saucats road out of Léognan, and turn left on the sharp right-hand bend just before you leave the village. Château Haut-Bailly is the second property on the left of this road after about 1½ km, between Châteaux Larrivet Haut Brion and La Louvière.

Haut-Bailly is one of the most recent creations of the vineyards of the Graves, first established around 1840, at which time it belonged to a member of the Ricard family, owners then of de Fieuzal, Domaine de Chevalier and Malartic-Lagravière.

In 1872 Pierre Ricard sold Haut-Bailly to an eccentric and zealous new proprietor, M. Bellot de Minières, for 115,000 francs; this was not a great sum, but the vineyard was relatively small and there was no house on the property. Bellot de Minières was an individualist with fixed ideas and the determination to put them into practice. He was violently opposed to the universally adopted practice of grafting the traditional French vines on the phylloxera-resistant American rootstocks, maintaining that wine produced from such 'bastard' vines must be degenerate and not worthy of the great Bordeaux traditions, and he used a treatment of his own invention which must have cost him dear; he is also reputed to have employed a somewhat dubious practice of cleaning out his vats with old cognac, which he conveniently forgot to remove before the must of the new vintage began its fermentation.

Unorthodox though his approach to winemaking may have been, the wine of Haut-Bailly prospered under his ownership and achieved recognition as the First of the Léognan Growths, realising prices on a par with the Deuxièmes Crus of the Médoc; he himself was known as the 'Roi des Vignerons', surely a mark of high praise among the conservative winemakers of the region.

Bellot de Minières died at Haut-Bailly in 1906, and the property was sold by his heirs after the First World War to another innovator, Frantz Malvesin, author of a recognised history of the wines of Aquitaine. He introduced the shocking practice of pasteurising the wine of Haut-Bailly, and continued the policy of growing ungrafted French vines. His reign was short, since he died in

1923, and happily pasteurisation was abandoned forthwith.

The new châtelain of Haut-Bailly was Paul Beaumartin, kinsman of the great Gabriel, owner of Domaine de Chevalier. Beaumartin was initially in partnership with the Comte Lahens, a Parisian financier, also grandfather of the present owner of the jewel-like Château de Malle in Preignac, Comte Pierre de Bournazel. Beaumartin bought his partner's share in 1937, but was forced to sell the entire property in the early years of the war; he was by now an old man, and the difficult years of the depression and the bad vintages of the '30s had taken their toll of both Haut-Bailly and the man himself.

The next ten years were dark ones for the property, and little was done by the proprietors, two industrialists from the north of France, who appear to have had no interest in the making of wine. The resurgence of Château Haut-Bailly began in 1955, when it was bought by a Bordeaux wine merchant of Belgian origin, Daniel Sanders. He had spent a period of convalescence in Bordeaux after being wounded in the First World War, fell in love with a wine merchant's daughter and with the wine business; he married the lady and started his own firm. The wine of Haut-Bailly first attracted his attention when he bought some of the 1945 vintage, and although he knew the property to be in a parlous state, was impressed by its potential. He finally bought Haut-Bailly, unloved and unwanted by anybody else, for a modest price in 1955. He was already proprietor of Château du Mayne in Barsac, where he lived, and where his widow lives to this day.

Since Daniel Sanders' death a few years ago, Haut-Bailly has been run by his son Jean, who lives on his own property, Château Courbon near Toulenne, where he makes a very pleasant white Graves. The Sanders family have done great things for Château Haut-Bailly; the wine is of excellent quality, full and rounded, showing great charm from its earliest stages and ageing superbly. This quality stems partly from the vineyard itself, situated on some of the best gravel in the Léognan district, partly from the very great age of many of the vines, but largely from the care and conscien-

tious attention of Jean Sanders. Selection is particularly rigorous, and a very large proportion, often as much as 30% of the crop, goes into the second wine, 'La Parde de Haut-Bailly'. My first experience of this fine Graves was at a fortieth birthday dinner-party given for me by the late Martin Bamford at the Restaurant Jacques-Cagna in Paris, when we drank the delicious 1964; it was a revelation, and I have enjoyed other vintages of Haut-Bailly on many occasions since.

My visit with Jean Sanders was one of the most enjoyable days I spent whilst working on this

book. We met him at Château du Mayne, where his mother received us, and we enjoyed two delicious vintages of the excellent Barsac they make there. We then drove to Jean's house, where we had an *al fresco* lunch in the company of a coach-load of Belgians, whom Madame Sanders fed regally, in spite of having received notice of their arrival only two hours before. After lunch we drove to Haut-Bailly, and I had the greatest difficulty in keeping up with Monsieur Sanders, whose daughter told me that he worries the life out of his family with his rate of travel. He

226

showed us the gleaming new chai that had just been completed, filled with rank on rank of casks of the 1983 vintage. The square, stone-built château is in the course of restoration, and will soon be once more an elegant house, having stood empty since the war. Jean Sanders' English is excellent, and I was therefore most surprised when he showed us the open fireplace in the old kitchen where, he said, they used to roast a donkey every Christmas! Amid much hilarity, I explained that *dinde* was more accurately translated as turkey, and all were agreed that the meat would make a more fitting accompaniment to the wine of Haut-Bailly.

TECHNICAL INFORMATION

General

Appellation:	Graves
Area under vines:	25 hectares
Average production:	12,500 cases in total
Distribution of vines:	In one block
Owner:	S.C.I.A. Sanders
Administrator:	M. Jean Sanders
Chef de Culture:	M. Serge Charritte
Consultant Oenologist:	Professor Emile Peynaud

Viticulture

Geology:	Uniformly deep gravel
Grape varieties:	60% Cabernet Sauvignon, 10% Cabernet Franc, 30% Merlot
Pruning:	Guyot Simple
Rootstock:	420A
Vines per hectare:	10,000
Average yield per hectare:	45 hectolitres
Replanting:	In parcels of 2 hectares

Vinification

Added yeasts:	No
Length of maceration:	Varied according to year, average 16 days
Temperature of fermentation:	32°C

Control of fermentation:	By passing through a system of 55 metres of copper pipe, cooled by cold water.
Type of vat:	50% cement, resin-lined, 50% steel, resin-lined
Vin de presse:	Incorporated in grand vin, according to needs of vintage
Age of casks:	From 40% to 55% new each vintage
Time in cask:	Average 20 months
Fining:	Powdered egg-white in vat
Filtration:	None
Type of bottle:	Grand Cru

Commercial

Vente Directe:	Yes
Direct ordering from château:	Yes
Exclusivities:	None
Agents overseas:	Yes, in Great Britain and the USA, but not exclusive
Visits:	Yes, by appointment Telephone 56 21 75 11 (Château) 56 27 16 07 (Barsac) Normal office hours

THE TASTING AT CHATEAU HAUT-BAILLY, 9 May 1985
J.S., M. Serge Charritte

1984 Good, deep colour, plenty of fruit and some new oak on the nose. Flavour good, with nice tannins and some taste of oak.

1983 Again, good deep colour. Nice bouquet with plenty of ripe fruit. A supple, well made wine with good tannins, plenty of finesse and a long aftertaste.

1982 Slightly darker colour. Bouquet rounded and more open than 1983. A big, supple mouthful, already quite approachable, but has good tannins and plenty of length. Will be a super bottle.

1981 Same fine depth of colour. Lots of fruit and elegance on the nose; a fine delicate wine with lots of supple elegance, but also has enough backbone to give it a long life.

1980 Very good colour for this vintage; open, straightforward nose, good fruit, well made wine, excellent to drink now, but has the potential to stay for several years. A very good 1980.

1979 Same consistent deep red. Bouquet good and quite spicy. A big and well rounded wine with masses of fruit, body and backbone.

1978 Good, medium dark red. Ripe, open nose, quite a forward 1978 with good fruit and ripe tannin.

1977 The lightest colour of all the vintages tasted, starting to brown a little. Lively bouquet with nice ripe fruit. In balance now and good for current drinking. None of the unpleasant acidity associated with 1977. (Almost 100% Cabernet Sauvignon.)

1976 Fairly light red. Bouquet open and ripe. A nice, open, hot-weather vintage, pleasing to drink now, but not a great way to go.

1975 Good, medium colour. Bouquet nice, but not over-assertive; complex and concentrated flavour of ripe fruit. Very evolved for this vintage. To drink – and enjoy greatly – now. The wine may be going through a phase, but I found it surprisingly ready.

CHATEAU

Haut-Brion

GRAVES

Leave Bordeaux on the Route Nationale 250 in the direction of Arcachon; about 5 km south-west of the centre of Bordeaux, Château Haut-Brion is on the right-hand side of the road in the suburb of Pessac, just before you reach the centre of the town. Turn in at the main gate, and arrows will direct you to your left down through the vines to the offices and the château.

The origins of Haut-Brion as a vineyard date back to 1525, when Jean de Pontac married Jeanne de Bellon, daughter of the mayor of Libourne, whose dowry included lands in the area known as Haut-Brion. In 1533 Pontac bought the 'Maison Noble de Haut-Brion' from a Basque named Jean Duhalde, and added it to his wife's property. He also built the château in 1549, part of which still exists. Jean de Pontac married three times, had many children and died reputedly the richest, and possibly the oldest, man in Bordeaux at the age of 101.

The de Pontacs were wealthy merchants of great power in Bordeaux, and bore the hereditary title of First President of the Bordeaux Parliament. It was a grandson of Jean de Pontac, Arnaud, who did much to improve the quality of the wine; he was fascinated by the art of winemaking, and is said to have been one of the prime innovators of ageing the red wine in bottles. It was his son, François-Auguste, who was despatched to London to promote the sales of the Haut-Brion wine, and in 1666 opened the Pontac's Head tavern. This fashionable eating-house was to remain open for over a hundred years, and the wine of Haut-Brion, selling at the relatively high price of seven shillings a bottle at the table, became a firm favourite with the cosmopolitan elite of London; it was also the first Bordeaux wine to be sold in England under its own name. Some three years before the Pontac's Head opened its doors, the diarist Samuel Pepys records that he drank 'a sort of French wine called Ho Bryan' in the Royal Oak Tavern in Lombard Street. Certainly the de Pontacs were largely responsible for opening up the trade with England in fine claret, and for many years the price realised for Haut-Brion far outstripped all other Bordeaux wines. In 1714 the Bordeaux merchant Wischfold records that the

'wine of Pontac' fetched 550 livres a tonneau, as against 450 for Latour and only 410 for Lafite.

François-Auguste died childless in the last years of the 17th century, and the estate was shared between the families of his two married sisters. Two-thirds went to Joseph de Fumel, heir to Châteaux Margaux and de Pez in the Médoc, who had married Thérèse de Pontac, while the remaining third passed to the other sister, Marie-Anne's husband, Jean-Baptiste, Comte de La Tresne.

Joseph de Fumel was a soldier and had a brilliant military career, finishing up as a Lieutenant-General, and was appointed Governor of Guyenne with the Grand Cross of St Louis in 1781. A man of such obvious leadership did not find sharing the command of Haut-Brion to his liking, and came to a speedy arrangement with his brother-in-law, whereby a portion of the vineyard known as Chai Neuf was annexed as the separate property of La Tresne; Fumel thus became the sole proprietor of Château Haut-Brion. He made vast improvements to the estate, laying out the park and gardens, and enlarging the château to the proportions now known to wine-lovers and label collectors the world over. He also built the large orangery, and the various offices, outbuildings and porter's lodge which surround the courtyard.

At the time of the Revolution, Fumel set about buying a little insurance for himself and his property. He donated the Château Trompette, of which he had been made Governor in 1773, to the city of Bordeaux, as well as digging deep into his private purse to alleviate the sufferings of the poor and needy citizens; Bordeaux duly showed its gratitude by electing him Mayor in 1790. Only four years later, however, all these efforts were to avail him naught; the Terror came to Bordeaux, and a Revolutionary Committee, under the presidency of one M. Lacombe, tried Fumel, sequestrated all his property and executed him on 27 July 1794. Too late, alas, for poor Fumel, only four days after his execution the self-same Lacombe was himself arrested and he and his committee went to the guillotine.

Fumel's nephews managed to regain most of their uncle's property, including Haut-Brion, but understandably decided to emigrate. They sold

Haut-Brion to no less a personage than Charles-Maurice de Talleyrand, Minister for Foreign Affairs under Napoleon I. Talleyrand was too busy with his ministerial duties to spend much time at his newly acquired property, but it is certain that the wine of Haut-Brion frequently complemented the cuisine of his peerless chef, Carême.

Thus did Haut-Brion survive the French Revolution and the turbulent years of the early 19th century, until it passed, like so many Bordeaux properties, in to the hands of a Parisian banking family; Talleyrand sold the estate in 1836 to Eugène Larrieu, in whose family it remained until 1922. Eugène's son, Amédée Larrieu, bought back the portion known as Chai Neuf in 1840, thus reuniting the property. He also did much to improve and modernise the vinification process, including the installation of a new cuvier. His efforts were rewarded in 1855, when Haut-Brion was counted one of the First Great Growths, the only wine in the entire classification outside the Médoc. Amédée was also a public figure of some importance, twice elected a deputy in the National Assembly and finally appointed Prefect of the Gironde Department; there is to this day a square in Bordeaux that bears his name.

On his death in 1873, Amédée was succeeded by his son Eugène, who only survived him by 23 years; on his death in 1886 the property passed into the hands of several nephews and their families. This joint ownership forced Haut-Brion onto the market in 1922, one of Eugène's nephews having been foreclosed upon by his bankers, the Compagnie Algérienne. They sold the property to a company called the Société des Glacières de Paris, and one of their directors, a Monsieur André Gibert, took Haut-Brion as a sort of golden

handshake on his retirement in 1924; he appears to have been something of an opportunist, since he wasted little time in selling off parts of the château's fine park for building land, and entered into lengthy and principally unsuccessful lawsuits with various properties who were incorporating the words 'Haut-Brion' in their names. The difficulties that beset the wine business in the late twenties and early thirties caused Gibert to put Haut-Brion up for sale, and in 1935 the powerful American financier Clarence Dillon came to the rescue.

There is a story, somewhat contested, that Dillon originally wanted to purchase Château Cheval Blanc, but the day was so cold and foggy, and the journey by unheated motor-car took so long, and Dillon became so uncomfortable that, disgruntled, he decided to plump for something nearer to civilisation. Part of this is certainly true, as Hugues Lawton, son of the courtier Daniel Lawton who was in the car with the financier on his safari to St Emilion, has pointed out to me the actual shop where they stopped to buy a rug to wrap up the frozen Dillon.

Whatever the truth may be, it is certain that both Dillon and his heirs on the one hand, and the name and fame of Haut-Brion on the other, have benefited mutually from the purchase. The estate has enjoyed continuity of investment, even in difficult times, and from a purely real-estate point of view, the value of the property must have multiplied at a far greater rate than anything on the eastern bank of the Dordogne.

Clarence Dillon's son, Douglas, was appointed United States Ambassador in Paris in 1953, and, on his return to America, rose to the heights of Treasury Secretary in the Kennedy administration. His daughter, like all the Dillons, was a

229

Francophile, and stayed in France at the end of her father's mission in Paris. In 1967 she married Prince Charles of Luxembourg, a direct descendant of Henry IV, and they became responsible for Haut-Brion; the Princess took over from her cousin, Henri Seymour Weller, as President of the company in 1975.

After the death of Prince Charles of Luxembourg, Princess Joan remarried in 1978; her new husband was the Duc de Mouchy, who also has great historical connections with this corner of France. One of his ancestors, Maréchal de Mouchy, was Governor of Guyenne in the 18th century, when the de Pontacs and Joseph de Fumel were establishing the name of Haut-Brion. The Duc and Duchesse de Mouchy are now Director and President of the company that owns and runs Haut-Brion.

The continued level of quality of the wines of Château Haut-Brion owes as much to the Delmas family as to the interest and direction of the Dillons. Georges Delmas came to Haut-Brion in 1921, and his son, Jean-Bernard, born at Haut-Brion, succeeded his father as régisseur and is now Directeur Vinicole. There may yet follow a third generation of Delmas; as Jean-Bernard told me with a characteristic twinkle, 'I have a son who is certainly showing great interest in wine.'

Delmas is probably one of the most knowledgeable winemakers in the whole Bordeaux region. He studied oenology at the University at Talence, and took over his father's job as régisseur in 1960. Profound as his expertise may be, he is striving constantly by slow and painstaking experiment to improve every aspect of viticulture and vinification. Perhaps the most important work in progress at Haut-Brion, not only for the property but for the wine world in general, is that of research into vine-cloning, started in 1972. The purpose of this exhaustive study is to determine not only which grape varieties, grafted to which rootstocks, suit which particular soil and subsoil, but to find the best individual vines within each variety. To this end, a nursery of 'mother-vines' is kept in part of the vineyard, and the offspring are planted throughout the main body of the vineyard and are carefully tagged and computerised, giving the exact provenance of every vine planted since 1972. Literally hundreds of individual macerations and vinifications are made each year, tasted, analysed and annotated at every stage of development and the results are fed into the computer. Delmas is encouraged and assisted in this programme by the National Institute of Agricultural Research as well as the Department of Oenology at Talence, and its importance cannot be overestimated.

Clonal selection is just one of the many innovations instigated at Haut-Brion. Stainless-steel vats were installed in 1961, the first in a Grand Cru property, after much careful experimentation, and with the help of the distinguished oenologist, Professor Emile Peynaud.

Exclusion of all but the most perfectly mature grapes is another of Delmas's keys to the making of great wine; every load of grapes that arrives at the cuverie is sorted by hand on large stainless-steel tables, and all leaves, unripe, split or rotten grapes are eliminated. This is characteristic of the minute attention to detail at every stage of vinification that keeps Château Haut-Brion in the exalted position that it has held in the Bordeaux hierarchy for four hundred years.

The red wine of Château Haut-Brion is perhaps the closest in style to the Grands Crus of the Médoc that is not made on that famous peninsula, and this similarity almost certainly derives from the outcrop of deep Garonne gravel on which the vineyard is sited. The late Henri Enjalbert, professor of geology, compared the soil here with that of the Latour vineyard. The wine has perhaps more friendly approachability in youth than its Médocain counterparts, and in old age it has a warmth and soft charm that are beyond compare. A non-vintage wine called Bahans-Haut-Brion results from the rigorous selection of the vats at the assemblage. It is the only non-vintage wine currently produced by a Bordeaux Grand Cru; it is only sold when it is ready for drinking, and is marketed exclusively by the négociant house of Nathaniel Johnston in Bordeaux.

A tiny quantity of exceptionally fine dry white wine is also produced at Haut-Brion from about 2·5 hectares planted with Sauvignon and Semillon grapes. The production is indeed so minuscule that one hardly ever sees the wine offered for sale, and the only bottles I have been lucky enough to taste have been offered at the château. The 1966, drunk at lunch there in October 1984 with Jean-Bernard Delmas, his wife Annie and Pascal Ribereau-Gayon, was still amazingly fresh and youthful, with a beautiful light golden colour, a fine grapey bouquet and a lovely, long, complex flavour.

Jean-Bernard has been described by one of my fellow wine-writers as looking like 'a successful night-club proprietor'. I am not sure I would go along with this, but he is certainly a kind and attentive host, and I shall always remember and be grateful to him and his wife Annie for the kindness and willing help that they gave me in the preparation of the chapters on Haut-Brion and La Mission.

TECHNICAL INFORMATION

General

Appellation:	Graves
Area under vines:	*Red* 40 hectares
	White 3 hectares
Production:	*Red* 13,000 cases
	White 1,000 cases
Proprietor:	Domaine Clarence Dillon S.A. (Pt Duchesse de Mouchy)
Director-General:	Duc de Mouchy
Director:	M. J.B. Delmas
Maître de chai:	M. Jean Portal

Viticulture

Geology:	Gunzian gravel, clay/sand subsoil
Grape varieties planted:	*Red* 50% Cabernet Sauvignon, 25% Cabernet Franc, 25% Merlot
	White 50% Semillon, 50% Sauvignon
Pruning:	Guyot double
Rootstock:	Riparia Gloire, 3309–420A
Vines per hectare:	8,000
Average yield per hectare:	*Red* 35 hectolitres
Replanting:	Every 40–50 years

Vinification

Added yeasts:	No
Length of maceration:	15 days
Temperature of fermentation:	30°C
Regulation of temperature:	Running water
Type of vat:	Stainless-steel cylinders
Age of casks:	New casks for each harvest
Time in cask:	2 years
Fining:	Egg-whites
Filtration:	At bottling
Type of bottle:	Special Haut-Brion

Commercial

Vente Directe:	No
Direct ordering:	No
Exclusivities:	No
Agents in foreign Countries:	None
Visits:	Yes, exclusively on recommendation and by appointment: telephone 56 98 28 17 Hours 0830–1130, 1400–1700, closed at weekends and public holidays, and from 15 July to 31 August.

THE TASTING AT CHATEAU HAUT-BRION, 24 October 1984

J.S., Jean-Bernard Delmas, Professor Pascal Ribereau-Gayon

1983 Deep, blue-tinged red. Rounded, powerful nose with distinct cassis. Big and complex, with excellent fruit and non-aggressive tannins, and a superb structure.

1982 (Not yet in bottle.) Dense, dark bluey colour. Lovely rounded bouquet. Generous, fat mouthful of wine, already very approachable, with enormous fruit and ripe tannin. Will be a great wine, relatively soon, but will stay for ever.

1981 Beautiful deep ruby. Generous, soft bouquet with classic Haut-Brion blackcurrant. Balanced and harmonious, full of finesse and elegance, with good backbone. Will be a classic Haut-Brion.

1980 Brilliant medium dark colour. Bouquet open and attractive. Supple and easy on the palate, already very drinkable but with enough body and tannin to keep for some years.

1979 Good depth of colour. Refined Cabernet Sauvignon smell. Well-structured wine, evolving well, with good fruit and supple characteristics which Jean-Bernard Delmas says typify Haut-Brion.

1978 Fine, bright medium red. Classic cassis bouquet. Excellent and complex flavour, with great length. (This was a late vintage of small quantity; Pascal Ribereau-Gayon comments that '78 is the only vintage of its sort to produce a great wine.)

1976 Good red, with no browning. Bouquet nicely evolved, truffly and slightly roasted. Delicious already, balanced, with fruit and tannins together, approaching plateau of maturity.

1975 Very dense, dark colour. Nose quite closed still, but with powerful fruit beginning to show. Still quite undeveloped taste, with big concentration of flavours and tannins starting to evolve. Very long in mouth, will be a great bottle.

At lunch

1966 Château Haut-Brion Blanc. Colour still very young – lovely medium golden. Nose fresh and grapey, very concentrated. Clean and fresh, with crispness and good body – perfect with the delicious turbot.

1959 (Red.) Dense colour, with brownish tones. Lovely rich bouquet of ripe fruit. Fills the mouth with fat concentrated and complex flavours, and leaves a lingering and superb aftertaste. A superb vintage at the peak of maturity, but one that will last for decades.

CHATEAU
Larrivet-Haut-Brion
GRAVES

Drive out of Léognan towards Saucats. Take the left turning on the sharp right-hand bend after passing the Mairie; this is signposted as the Route Touristique des Crus Classés de Graves, and leads to Larrivet-Haut-Brion, Haut-Bailly, La Louvière and Carbonnieux. The chais and cuvier of Larrivet-Haut-Brion are the last buildings on your right as you leave Léognan, and the house is opposite.

At the time of the French Revolution the property formed part of a large estate, belonging to the Marquis de Canolle, and was then known as Château de Canolle. The lands were confiscated and sold off, and over the next century-and-a-half changed owners many times.

After the de Canolle family lost the estate, the name was changed to Haut-Brion-Larrivet; 'Brion' was a local dialect word for gravel, and the Larrivet is a small brook that runs through the property. The name stuck until 1940, when a lawsuit, brought by the owners of Château Haut-Brion, enforced the change to Larrivet-Haut-Brion, though what difference this made to either party is hard to see.

The vineyard has a good depth of gravel, and produces a firm, sturdy red wine that needs a good five years in bottle to be best appreciated. There is also a small quantity of white made, which I have only tasted when it was very young; a year after bottling it was clean and fresh and very enjoyable, but would have kept and possibly improved for a year or two.

Madame Guillemaud is gradually changing over her fermenting vats to stainless steel, although a proportion of them are still of cement with a plastic lining. She is ably assisted in the vinification of her wines by her régisseur, M. Airoldi, and also calls on the services of Professor Peynaud for oenological advice.

TECHNICAL INFORMATION

General

Appellation:	Graves		
Area under vines:	*Red* 15.5 hectares		
	White 0.5 hectare		
Average production:	*Red* 8,000 cases		
	White 500 cases		
Distribution of vines:	One block		
Owner:	Madame Guillemaud		
Maître de Chai:	M. Airoldi		
Consultant Oenologist:	Professor Emile Peynaud		

Viticulture

Geology:	Typical Léognan gravel/sand mixture
Grape varieties:	*Red* 60% Cabernet Sauvignon, 40% Merlot; *White* 40% Semillon, 60% Sauvignon
Pruning:	Guyot Simple
Rootstock:	Various
Replanting:	As necessary

Vinification

Added yeasts:	No
Length of maceration:	Average 15 days
Temperature of fermentation:	28°C
Control of fermentation:	Water circulation
Type of vat:	25% new each vintage (No casks for white)
Time in cask:	18 months
Fining:	Gelatine
Filtration:	Sur terre before going in cask, sur plaque before bottling
Type of bottle:	Grand Cru

Commercial

Vente Directe:	Yes
Sales:	Through Bordeaux négociants
Visits:	Yes, by appointment Telephone 56 21 75 51

THE TASTING AT CHATEAU LARRIVET-HAUT-BRION, 12 November 1984
J.S., Madame Guillemaud, M. Airoldi

1983 Nice medium deep red. Fruit and new wood on nose. Well-constituted wine with fruit and tannins to make an elegant bottle in three years or so.

1982 Colour a shade darker than '83. Nose very good and fragrant with distinct whiff of blackberry. Rounded and approachable, has a lot of fruit and very muted tannin. Not typical of Larrivet-Haut-Brion, as Merlot seems to be showing through the Cabernet. Will keep, however, and be very good for a long while.

CHATEAU
La Louvière
GRAVES

Leave Léognan on the small DIII, Route Touristique des Crus Classés de Graves, in the direction of Cadaujac. After passing Châteaux Larrivet-Haut-Brion and Haut-Bailly, you will come to the driveway to Château la Louvière on your left after about 200 metres.

The name of this property suggests a connection with the time when wolves roamed the forests that covered the land around Léognan. La Louve certainly means she-wolf, and although I have not found the word in any dictionary, La Louvière surely indicates a den-full of cubs!

The property was bought in 1791 by M. J.B.

Mareilhac, Mayor of Bordeaux, and a financier and businessman of no little weight, for a sum of 228,000 livres. Mareilhac built the château, for me one of the loveliest buildings in the whole of the Bordeaux region. It is said to have been designed by Louis, the architect of the Grand Théatre in Bordeaux, but André Lurton thinks it more likely to have been one of his associates or pupils. The château has not been lived in for a long time, and much of the original decoration can be seen inside, including a magnificent painted ceiling in the great hall by the Flemish painter Lonsing; the central figure is Mareilhac's wife, depicted as a flying and naked angel. Whether overcome by the beauty of his subject, or an excessive intake of the château's produce, it is said that the unfortunate artist died while finishing the painting.

The Mareilhac family owned La Louvière until 1911, when they sold it to a Monsieur Bertrand-Tacquet, who was Mayor of Léognan.

The property was acquired in 1965 by André Lurton, one of a dynamic family of winemakers who collect and restore châteaux at an amazing rate. André's own properties include La Louvière, de Rochemorin, de Cruzeau, Couhins-Lurton and Bonnet, a total of over 350 hectares. André employs some 70 people full-time, 15 of whom are working the whole time on building and machinery maintenance.

When I visited him at La Louvière, André took me to see the work in progress on the extension of another vineyard, Château de Rochemorin, on the road between Labrède and Léognan. Watching the huge amount of plant at work, removing trees, clearing debris, ploughing, draining and preparing for planting, one begins to appreciate the energy and vision of this man. In passing, it is interesting to note that de Rochemorin used to be part of the estate of Montesquieu in Labrède, though it was not planted with vines in his day. Had he known the quality of the soil beneath his forests, he might well have rivalled the de Pontac family at Haut Brion in the quality of his wine. The wine from Château de Rochemorin is vinified at La Louvière, together with that of Couhins-Lurton.

André is, characteristically, restoring the château

at La Louvière, though he has no plans to live there. 'I was born at Bonnet, and I have been happy there for sixty years. Why move?'
55 hectares are planted with vines. The vineyard, bounded on one side by Château Haut-Bailly and on the other by Château Carbonnieux, has a mixture of soils, gravel, chalk and silicate. The white varieties are 15% Semillon and 85% Sauvignon, whilst the red are 80% Cabernet Sauvignon and 20 % Merlot.

Vinification is by traditional methods, but using the best in modern equipment. The red is aged in oak casks, one third of which are new.
The white wine is dry, sinewy and fruity, with a delicate pale gold colour with a hint of green, typical of the elegant dry whites of the Léognan district. The red has firmness, body and power, which with the added qualities of elegance and charm, make for a wine which ages well.

TECHNICAL INFORMATION

General

Appellation:	Graves Léognan	Temperature of fermentation:	*Red* 28–30°C *White* 16–18°C
Area under vines:	55 hectares	Control of fermentation:	Cooling by compressor and water cooling
Distribution of vines:	André Lurton	Type of vat:	*Red* stainless steel or coated cement
Owner:	M. Jean Yves Arnaud		
Maître de Chai:	M. Joseph Pessotto		*White* stainless steel or glazed steel
		Age of casks:	*Red* $\frac{1}{3}$ new each vintage
Viticulture			*White* in new casks
Geology:	Deep gravel, varied topsoil: gravelly, silicate, light chalk in a small area	Time in cask:	*Red* 12 months
			White a few months
		Fining:	Egg-whites
Grape varieties:	*Red* 70% Cabernet Sauvignon, 20% Merlot, 10% Cabernet Franc	Type of bottle:	Bordelaise
	White 85% Sauvignon, 15% Semillon	*Commercial*	
Pruning:	Guyot Double	Vente Directe:	Yes
Rootstock:	101.14, SO4, Riparia Gloire, etc.	Sales:	By mail order for private customers in France, export through the Bordeaux négociants
Vines per hectare:	6,500		
		Visits:	Only by appointment Telephone 57 84 52 07
Vinification			
Added yeasts:	Sometimes, when necessary		

THE TASTING AT KELVEDON, 22 December 1984
J.S., Christian Seely

White

1983 Pale, greeny, gold. Pleasing, clean and grapey on the nose. Nice, crisp and clean on the palate, showing signs of ageing potential.
1982 Slightly darker colour. Good ripe Sauvignon nose. A shade fuller and more luscious than '83, but also lovely, clean and crisp.
1981 Pale straw colour, with a hint of green. Boquet typically Sauvignon and grapey. Perfect now, lovely balance of fruit and acidity – very good with oysters!

Red

1982 Deep, plummy red. Nose open and nicely rounded. A fat mouthful of wine, with lots of fruit and soft, muted tannins; already very good, but will get better.
1981 Shade lighter than '82. Nice elegant bouquet with good fruit, still a bit reserved. Well-balanced, with good tannins and some finesse. Will be a nice bottle.
1979 Good deep colour. Rounded bouquet with some power. Biggish mouthful and has some finesse and staying power.
1978 Medium red, bright and clear. Nice open nose with a touch of new-mown grass. Light, easy, feminine wine with some good fruit, but tannins almost gone. A little short, but lovely to drink now.

CHATEAU
Malartic-Lagravière
GRAVES

Take the D651 from Léognan towards Saucats, and Château Malartic-Lagravière is half a kilometre out of the village on the left.

The château itself is an elegant, if modest building, dating from the late 18th or early 19th century.

The story of the property is really summarised in the history of four families.

de Malartic A famous Gascon family, whose name crops up all over South-Western France. Comte Hippolyte de Maurès de Malartic, born at Monttauban in 1730, was Governor of Mauritius, then Ile de France, in 1792. A mausoleum stands in the Champs de Mars in the capital, Port Louis, containing his remains, and bears the inscription 'To the saviour of the Colony'. The Comte de Maurès de Malartic had soldiered in Nouvelle France with Montcalm, and it was in his honour that the town of Malartic, Quebec, was named. A nephew of his, Pierre de Malartic, acquired the Domaine de La Graviere in 1803, and added his own name.

Ricard: In 1850 Mme. Arnaud Ricard became the owner of Malartic-Lagravière, and proceeded to reconstitute the original vignoble, which had become divided. Ten years later, in 1860, Mme. Ricard and her son, Jean, purchased Domaine de Chevalier; Jean became sole proprietor of Château de Fieuzal in 1892.

In point of fact Malartic-Lagravière has remained consistently in Ricard family ownership, under the name Ridoret-Marly.

Ridoret: The Ridorets were a seafaring family, originally from Cambes in the Premières Côtes de Bordeaux, where they also owned vineyards. They were 'long cours' or deep-sea captains, who sailed three-masted barques, such as the *Arnaud* and the *Marie Elisabeth*, of which a fine oil painting hangs in the château. The custom appears to have been for the men to sail away, leaving the vineyard management to their wives.

The son of one of these doughty sailors, Lucien Ridoret, married Angèle Ricard in 1876, and took on the running of Malartic-Lagravière; Angèle was the granddaughter of Mme. Arnaud Ricard, and it was her own granddaughter, Simone, who in 1927 married Jacques Marly, the present owner, to whom she bore ten children.

Marly: Established in Bordeaux in 1835, the Marly industrial mirror business was one of the largest in France.

Henri Marly, Jacques' grandfather, owned a fine vineyard in Merignac called Château Marbotin. The château, a fine Chartreuse building, still stands, but the vineyard has disappeared beneath the suburbs of Merignac, though Jacques clearly remembers taking part in the vendange there in 1915. It was Jacques who put in the final piece of the jigsaw which completed the reconstitution of Malartic-Lagravière started by Mme. Arnaud Ricard over a hundred years ago, by the acquisition of a very important piece of the vineyard, which had hitherto eluded all would-be purchasers.

Jacques Marly, the present owner, a kind, courteous and knowledgeable man, has given me much of his time and hospitality, and, more important still, a wealth of information on not only his own property, but on the history of the Graves and Bordeaux in general.

Jacques is very much a family man; his wife Simone, née Ridoret, gave him ten children, neatly alternating their sexes with each birth, and they in turn have made him a grandfather twenty-six times. A widower now, he lives alone at the château, but his numerous family visit him often, and most weekends are filled with children, grandchildren, tennis, bridge, billiards and the enjoyment of food, wine and family life. Between times he has for company a 15-year old, totally deaf spaniel and a parrot; since I first met Jacques, the original parrot has departed, having succumbed to cirrhosis of the liver – Jacques maintains he would still be with us if he had stuck to the wines of Malartic-Lagravière, but, hélàs!, in his latter years he took to whisky – this remarkable bird also used to answer the telephone, though how was not precisely explained.

Jacques came to the property in 1947, and undertook the renovation and refurbishment of the vineyard and château – a Herculean task after the hard times of the thirties, followed by four years of occupation by the German army; the drawing-room was used as a garage for motor-cycles!

Jacques is a man of strong views, and is not afraid to air them, though he often finds he is a lone

voice crying in the wilderness. One of his hobby-horses is the law that sets a limit on production. If God is good, and sends ideal weather conditions and an abundant harvest, can it be right, he asks, provided that he sticks to all the regulations regarding viticulture, soil treatment, etc., that he should be obliged to send away for distillation a large portion of the grapes or must, which would produce an identical wine to the portion which is permitted? Surely this is bureaucracy gone mad?

Jacques is most conscious of not only the quality of his wines, but also of their public image. He designed a new label for the 1964 vintage, which carried a mirror-image of the name of the château, reversed above the existing lettering in silver ink.

The powers that be did not like it, as they said it looked like Russian, and he was forced to withdraw it. He is now working on a very elegant label, which has as background the three-masted barque *Marie-Elisabeth* in silhouette. He intends to add a back label, explaining the seafaring connection, which should avoid any problems with officialdom.

Continuation of the Marly name and tradition at Malartic-Lagravière is assured by the co-direction of his youngest son, Bruno, who will run the property on Jacques' retirement.

In the production of white Malartic-Lagravière, Jacques Marly again shows his independent spirit. Against the opinion of all the pundits, he grows

237

only Sauvignon grapes. The proof of the wine is definitely in the drinking; a bottle of the 1970, 13 years old when he opened it for us, still had a light greeny-gold colour, the bouquet was honeyed, almost Sauternais, and the flavour was still young and lively, with a complexity I have never encountered in a wine made solely from the Sauvignon grape.

It seems a not unreasonable conclusion that it is probably the soil and the micro-climate of the Graves, rather than the grape variety used, which gives the fine dry white Graves their amazing ageing qualities.

Fermentation of the white wine takes place at a controlled 18°C maximum in stainless-steel cuves in the simple, but highly efficient cuvier 100 metres from the house. The wine then spends 7–8 months in new casks before bottling in May or June.

The red wines of Malartic-Lagravière have tended in the past to be on the tough and austere side; however, a somewhat softer, more elegant style has been achieved in recent years, following certain changes in vinification and encépagement recommended by Professor Peynaud, consultant to the property. The resultant wines are firm, classic, red Graves with excellent keeping qualities. After fermentation at 30°C (32°C max.) the wine remains in cask for one year at the château, and the casks are then moved to the ageing chai in Léognan, to await bottling some 20 months after the vendange.

TECHNICAL INFORMATION

General

Appellation:	Graves
Area under wines:	*Red* 12.84 hectares
	White 1.65 hectares
Production:	*Red* 6000, to 8000 cases
	White 800 to 1000 cases
Distribution of vines:	In one piece
Proprietor:	Héritiers de Madame Jacques Marly-Ridoret
Director:	Jacques Marly
Co-Director:	Bruno Marly
Oenological Consultant:	Professor Emile Peynaud

Viticulture

Geology:	Mixture of gravel, chalk and clay
Grape varieties:	*Red* 41% Cabernet Sauvignon, 34% Cabernet Franc, 25% Merlot
	White 100% Sauvignon
Pruning:	Guyot Simple
Rootstock:	420A
Vines per hectare:	10,000
Yield per hectare:	60–70 hectolitres
Replanting:	Every 30 years by rotation

Vinification

Added yeasts:	No
Length of maceration:	Varied, according to necessity
Temperature of fermentation:	*Red* 30°C maximum
	White 18°C
Regulation of fermentation:	Water cooling system
Type of vat:	Stainless steel
Vin de presse:	Not used
Age of barriques:	One-third new barriques each year
Time in cask:	*Red* 20–22 months
	White 7–8 months
Fining:	Egg-whites
Filtration:	Yes
Type of bottle:	Bordelaise

Commercial

Vente Directe:	No
Direct ordering:	No
Exclusive contracts:	Yes, with 10 regional partners
Agents in foreign countries:	None
Visits:	Yes
	Telephone for appointment: 56 21 75 08

THE TASTING AT CHATEAU MALARTIC-
LAGRAVIERE, 4 November 1984
J.S., M. Jacques Marly, M. Bruno Marly.
(This was the day that 'Hurricane Hortense' hit south-
western France. A 200-year-old cedar was blown down
while we were tasting).

White

1984 Alcoholic fermentation only just complete.
Almost all sugar gone; aromas and flavours beginning
to develop. (The sugar-level had descended in a correct
manner over a thirteen-day period from 1080 to 997.
Monsieur Marly was well pleased with the potential.)

1983 Bright golden colour. Good fruit and some oak
on nose. Good Sauvignon flavour, still very closed and
woody, will be good.

1982 Colour lighter than '83. Bouquet good and open.
Balance of fruit and acidity correct; this is a wine with
good ageing potential, but one can already see its fine
character.

1981 Bright gold, similar to '83. Bouquet evolving
well, with Sauvignon character. Less weight than '82 or
'83, but has charm and finesse. Already very pleasing to
drink.

1980 Bright, medium to light golden. Ripe fruit on
nose. Balanced and well-made, good to drink now.

1979 Golden straw colour. Nice, delicate bouquet of
ripe fruit, just beginning to develop. Still quite reserved,
but classic Malartic, with good ageing possibilities.

1978 Pale, greeny gold. Rich, honeyed fruit on nose.
Well-structured, balance perfect. Slight Sauternes overtones, though completely dry.

1976 Pale straw. Elegant nose, with a suggestion of
warm hay. Slightly flat on palate, could be due to very
hot weather at vintage time.

1975 The darkest colour of all the vintages tasted, but
still quite light after ten years. Rich, honeyed bouquet.
Lovely flavour, ripe and complex, with long aftertaste.

1974 Colour still amazingly light. Open bouquet,
with plenty of ripe grapiness. Acidity very low, but nice
fruit. Good as apéritif.

1972 Colour a shade darker than '74. Bouquet elegant
and complex. Mouthfilling, with loads of good fruit
and long aftertaste. Excellent.

1971 Good, bright gold, very similar to '72. Rich,
honeyed fragrance. Lots of fruit with a touch of sweetness. Balanced, well-made wine, ageing very well.

Red

1983 Lovely deep red, bluey edges. Good nose with
new oak. Complex wine with good tannins. All the
elements there for long keeping.

1982 Again deep red, less blue. Nose still closed, but
good, if slightly gamey, fruit coming through. A lot of
wine, although still quite closed; less accessible than
many wines of this vintage.

1981 Bright, deep colour, almost as dark as '82.
Typical Graves nose beginning to come out. Well-
made, with charm and finesse, will make an elegant
bottle.

1980 Light, brilliant red. Nice, straightforward and
open nose. Quite evolved and easy on the palate. Has
enough to keep it going a year or two.

1979 Colour similar to '81, with bluish tinges. Powerful, fragrant bouquet. Quite a tough mouthful, with
summer fruit taste, but still very tannic; will repay
keeping.

1978 Deep red, beginning to go brown. Bouquet ripe
and open. Already quite approachable, with fruit and
tannins harmonious. Will stay.

1977 Excellent colour for the vintage, similar to '78.
Pleasing, fruity nose. A very good '77, with more than
average weight and some quite good tannin.

1976 Deep colour, with no brown. Aromatic and
flowery bouquet. Good to drink now, with fruit,
elegance and some finesse.

1975 Very deep, intense red. Nose just beginning to
give off lovely powerful fruit aromas. Still very closed,
big and tannic, with a wealth of delicious fruit flavours,
like raspberries and redcurrants, just waiting to explode.
Vin Nucléaire!

1974 Good colour, a bit light. Very ripe nose. Still
alive with some fruit there; finishes dry and a little
short.

1971 Still very deep red. Bouquet fragrant, evolved
and ripe. Perfect wine to drink now, everything in
harmony, lightish, but good fruit and lovely aftertaste.

1947 Deep, dark plummy colour, with only hints of
brown. Powerful aromatic bouquet, with a suggestion
of freshly-picked mushrooms. Vinified in Malartic's old
style, this has developed after nearly forty years into a
lovely, harmonious wine, with great length and a
delicious flavour of wild strawberries. Wonderful!

CHATEAU

La Mission Haut-Brion

GRAVES

Drive out of Bordeaux in the direction of Arca-chon, on the RN250. Just before you get to the centre of the suburb of Pessac, some 5 km from the centre of Bordeaux, Château La Mission Haut-Brion is on your left, opposite Haut-Brion's main gate.

Haut-Brion is a place name, and earliest references to it date from the 14th century. La Mission once formed part of the Château Haut-Brion estate, but when, why or how it became a separate vineyard is not known.

The first recorded owner of the land on which La Mission stands appears to be a lady by the name of Dame Olive de Lestonnac, presumably a relation of Pierre de Lestonnac, creator of the vineyard of Château Margaux at the end of the 16th century. On her death she willed the land to Jean de Fonteneil, who was Director-General of the Bordeaux clergy.

In 1682 the property was transferred to one R.P. Simon, who was the Superior of an order called the Prêcheurs, or preachers, de la Mission. This order of monks, also known as Lazaristes, was founded in 1625 by Saint Vincent de Paul and established in the college of St Lazare in Paris. Their principal activity was the founding of missions to help poor country people; they cleared some woodland on the Haut-Brion land and built a chapel to Notre Dame de la Mission, hence the name La Mission Haut-Brion. Like many of their calling, they lost no time in planting a vineyard, and the wine that they made was good, for by the middle of the next century it was fetching prices on a par with the First Growths of the Médoc.

At the Revolution, La Mission, in common with other church properties, was confiscated and designated a 'Bien National', and was bought by Martial-Victor Vaillant for 302,000 livres; this was a high price, and one can imagine the quality of the wine from the yield – little over 20 hectolitres per hectare, low enough to indicate careful selection even in those days of far smaller crops.

In 1821 Célestin Chiapella was in charge at La Mission; he and his son Jérôme were négociants in Bordeaux, but they also managed several other properties for absentee landlords, such as the Englishman, Martyn, of Château Cos d'Estournel

in St Estèphe. The Chiapellas were dedicated and gifted winemakers, and did much to enhance the quality and reputation of the properties that they owned or managed.

In spite of the Chiapella administration, the wine of La Mission appears to have suffered a minor downgrading over the next 50 years. The 1845 edition of Franck lists it as a Fifth Growth; it was not included in the 1855 classification, and the 1868 edition of Cocks et Feret grades it below Pape-Clément. From 1870 onwards, however, things looked up, and La Mission Haut-Brion was achieving the same prices as the Second Growths of the Médoc. In 1880 the property was acquired by a Paris company, Etablissements Duval, who sold it in 1895 to the négociant firm of Schroeder and de Constans, who in turn sold to M. Victor Coustau in 1903. Prior to these last two transactions, a Russian émigré, M. Frédéric Woltner, had joined Schroeder and de Constans, opened their Paris office, and was made a partner. He became a friend of M. Coustau, and made an agreement with him that if he ever decided to sell La Mission, he would be given first refusal. This occurred in 1919 when Coustau retired, and Woltner became the owner. The Woltner régime took La Mission to new heights of excellence, and it was possibly Frédéric's son, Henri, who did most for the wine. He was a pioneer of controlled fermentation, and first installed two glass-lined steel fermentation tanks in 1926, a move at that time as revolutionary as turning up on a grouse moor with a machine-gun. The prototype vats came, of all places, from a brewery, but Woltner experimented carefully and slowly, conducting the alcoholic fermentation below 30°C by cooling the outside of vats with running water. It was not until 1950 that the cuvier was completely re-equipped with the squat, rectangular white-painted vats, after Henri Woltner was totally satisfied with the results.

After a long illness, Henri Woltner died in 1974, followed shortly after by his brother Fernand, whose daughter, Françoise Dewavrin inherited La Mission-Haut-Brion and took over responsibility for its running with her husband Francis.

It was perhaps during the 1960s that the red wine of La Mission hit its peak; 1964 and 1966 were

outstanding successes as, of course, was the fabulous 1961. Prices paid in the auction houses for good vintages of La Mission are often near and sometimes even equal to those realised by Haut-Brion itself.

When Château La Mission Haut-Brion was put on the market in 1983, it was, perhaps logical that the best offer should have come from none other than Domaine Clarence Dillon S.A., the company owning Château Haut-Brion, across the road. The future of the property, once under threat of total extinction from urban development, now seems quite safe, as does that of the wine in the more than capable hands of Jean-Bernard Delmas of Haut-Brion, aided by Professor Peynaud, who has agreed to continue as Consultant Oenologist.

La Mission is totally different in character from Haut-Brion, being fuller, more tannic and slower to yield its charms, and the new owners intend to retain its very separate identity. The white wine, made from 60% Semillon and 40% Sauvignon grapes, and sold as Château Laville Haut-Brion, is best drunk after a minimum of five years, and gets better and better with age. When mature it has a beautiful, deep golden colour and a rich almost Sauternes bouquet; it is luscious and complex on the palate, with a long and lingering aftertaste.

TECHNICAL INFORMATION

General

Appellation:	Graves
Area under vines:	*Red* 20 hectares
	White 5 hectares (Château Laville Haut-Brion)
Average production:	*Red* 7,000 cases
	White 1,500 cases
Director-General:	Duc de Mouchy
Director:	J.B. Delmas
Maître de Chai:	M. Jean Portal
Consultant Oenologist:	Professor Emile Peynaud

Viticulture

Geology:	Gunzian gravel, clay/sand subsoil
Grape varieties:	60% Cabernet Sauvignon, 20% Cabernet Franc, 20% Merlot
	White 60% Semillon, 40% Sauvignon
Pruning:	Guyot Double
Rootstock:	Riparia Gloire, 3309–430A
Vines per hectare:	10,000
Average yield per hectare:	37 hectolitres
Replanting:	Every 40–50 years

Vinification

Added yeasts:	No
Length of maceration:	15 days
Temperature of fermentation:	30°C
Control of fermentation:	Refrigeration, according to need
Type of vat:	Parallelipiped, in coated steel
Vin de presse:	Proportion incorporated in Grand Vin according to necessity
Age of casks:	New casks for each harvest
Time in cask:	2 years
Fining:	Egg-whites
Filtration:	At bottling
Type of bottle:	Bordelaise

Commercial

Vente Directe:	No
Direct ordering:	No
Exclusivities:	No
Agents in foreign countries:	None
Visits:	Yes, exclusively on recommendation and by appointment: telephone 56 98 28 17 Hours 0830–1130, 1400–1700, closed at weekends and public holidays, and from 15 July to 31 August

THE TASTING AT CHATEAU LA MISSION HAUT-BRION, 27 November 1984

J.S., Wendy Seely, Professor Emile Peynaud, Jean-Bernard Delmas

Chateau La Mission Haut-Brion

1983 Very deep red. Nose very rich and open, with lots of new oak. Very concentrated flavour, with a mass of fruit and good tannin. Will take a very long time, but will be a really superb bottle.

1982 Deep, blue/black colour. Bouquet still very closed. Big, fat and mouth-filling, with lots of good tannins. More rounded and approachable than 1983, but still needs plenty of time.

1981 Same lovely deep colour. Bouquet open and evolved, with good fruit. Excellent flavour, supple and elegant, with less 'puissance' than 1982 or 1983, very delicate; will be a classic La Mission.

1980 Colour good, lighter than later vintages. Pleasing, spicy bouquet. Lightish, with good fruit and enough backbone to keep it going for a year or two; already very pleasant to drink.

1979 Fine, deep red. Bouquet well-developed, with good fruit. Well-balanced with good fruit, and long aftertaste; will keep well.

1978 Excellent medium dark red. Fine open bouquet, some cassis. Complex and long on palate, with balanced fruit and tannin. A typical 'vin de garde' of La Mission; will be a really good bottle.

Château Laville Haut-Brion, White

1983 Pale gold. Fresh bouquet, Sauvignon to the fore at this stage. Wine still in cask and not yet fined, but fruit/acid balance good.

1982 Colour a shade darker than '83. Bouquet already quite assertive. Big and fat, with good acidity level and great potential.

1981 Colour still very light gold. Nose slightly strange – I thought it a little oxidised, but Professor Peynaud said that it was just showing too much new oak. This will disappear, and the wine will age well.

At Lunch

1971 Château Laville Haut-Brion – Deep golden colour. Rich, Sauternais bouquet. Still has lots of fruit and body and lovely, ripe complex flavour, with a good, lingering aftertaste.

1970 Château Laville Haut-Brion – Colour even deeper gold than '71. Nose very ripe and 'liquoreux', almost overcooked. Less finesse than '71, shade flatter, but still rich in ripe fruit.

1976 Château La Mission Haut-Brion – Deep, dense red, no brown. Excellent open bouquet of ripe fruit. This is La Mission in good condition for current drinking, though not a great vintage.

1966 Château La Mission Haut-Brion – Colour very deep, with just a shade of brown. Big, powerful bouquet of spices and fruit. Rounded and ripe, with fruit and tannins harmonising; ready now, but on a plateau that will extend for years.

CHATEAU

Olivier

GRAVES

Take the Autoroute A61 out of Bordeaux in the direction of Langon, and turn off at the interchange signposted to Cadaujac. On leaving the motorway, follow the signs to Léognan. About halfway between the built-up areas of Cadaujac and Léognan, the drive to Château Olivier is on the apex of a sharp right-hand bend, through a thick wood.

The Seigneurie, or manor, of Olivier has been in existence since the 12th century, and documents survive showing feudal dues paid to the King as early as 1273. In 1350 Rostang d'Olivey – Olivier – married Elisabeth de la Lande, heiress to Arnaud de la Brède, who was the owner and lord of the great Château de la Brède, probably not the first, and certainly not the last judicious marriage of vineyards.

The Black Prince, who lived in Bordeaux for about ten years in the 1360s, used to visit Château Olivier accompanied by all the gallant knights of England and Aquitaine for the excellent hunting in the forests that covered the area. Their quarry was mainly deer and wild boar, but wolves roamed the woods then as well, as is witnessed by the names of some properties in the neighbourhood such as La Louvière and Lagueloup.

In 1409 the Jurats, or councillors, of Bordeaux became owners of the County of Ornon, and laid claim to the seigneurial rights of all the manors in the parish of Léognan, of which Château Olivier was one. The Seigneur of Olivier contested the claim, and a legal wrangle ensued that lasted nearly 300 years and finally ended in favour of the Seigneurs of Olivier.

In 1521 Arthur d'Olivier was lord of Léognan, Cabenac and other places too numerous to mention. After him came Jehan d'Olivier, who was probably his son, and is mentioned as having entered holy orders around 1540. He had a sister, named in official documents as the 'Souveraine d'Olivier', and she left one son who became co-seigneur with his uncle, and this is the last recorded member of the Olivier family to have been at the property.

The next recorded Seigneur of Olivier was the nobleman Jacques de Lasserre, whose only daughter, Marie de Lasserre, married in April 1663 Pierre Penel, Baron de la Brède; she brought to her marriage the château and estate of Olivier, the second connection by marriage between the two properties.

Pierre Penel had inherited his title and the château de la Brède from his grandfather, Gaston de l'Isle, whose other properties included Château Poujeaux near Moulis in the Médoc. Penel and Marie Lasserre had an only daughter who married Messire Jacques de Secondat, Baron de Montesquieu – it was their son who became the famous writer. They sold Olivier in 1687 to Messire Bernard Joseph de Mulet, Seigneur of Queyssac and first Jurat of Bordeaux.

In the next 150 years the château and its lands changed hands no less than six times. In 1886 the estate passed into the hands of Monsieur and Madame Alexandre Wachter, who held a mortgage on the property. It is likely that the previous owners, the Comte and Comtesse d'Etchegoyen, overextended themselves with the extensive, and ugly, restorations that they had made to the castle; they had sold it in the meantime to a buyer who failed to fulfil the terms of his contract. Perhaps hoping to destroy some of the evidence of his obligations, this gentleman saw fit to burn all the documents and archives relating to the property. Happily for posterity, a good deal of documentation on the early history survived in the archives of Château de la Brède from the time when the Montesquieus owned Olivier.

One of Madame Wachter's heirs, Mlle. Agatha Wachter, married Jacques de Bethmann, a member of the old Frankfurt banking family who had a branch of their business established in Bordeaux for several generations. In 1945 the de Bethmanns became sole proprietors of Château Olivier.

The château is certainly 'worth a detour', as Michelin has it. In spite of the efforts of an early 18th-century owner, one Messire Fossier de Lestard, to turn Olivier into a house of the Grande Siècle, and the later Victorian contributions of the Comtesse d'Etchegoyen, Olivier can still without doubt be termed a real, fortified castle. The moat which completely surrounds it, the drawbridge and the walls, some three metres thick, are clearly there to keep out uninvited guests. It is not, however, a forbidding place; de Lestage's work on the north façade of the castle, his creation of an open inner courtyard, the construction of the winemaking buildings and vignerons' houses built at a cunning angle combine to give a feeling of space and grace. Lestage also put in larger windows, and put a flying bridge over the moat on the south façade, giving on to a formal French garden, which boasts an elegant stone fountain.

Inside, there is a beautiful tiny chapel, consecrated in 1500. Jean-Jacques de Bethmann's family are protestants, and he tells me that he used to listen to services in the chapel with his family on the radio. Above the old kitchen is the bedroom, and indeed the very bed, in which the Black Prince is reputed to have slept; the walls are of such thickness here that it has been possible to build a bathroom between the outer and inner surface.

Great care is taken to preserve Olivier as a proper balanced estate, with meadow land and mature forests of pine and oak. The vineyard, which is one block of 33 hectares, is situated to the north-east of the château. Production is divided almost equally between red and white wine, which have been of a steady and reliable quality for many years. The Bordeaux firm of Eschenauer held a lease on the property from the beginning of this century, but the de Bethmanns took over the running of the vineyard in 1982, and from the autumn of 1984 they will also commercialise their own wine. Many improvements in vinification have already been made, and there are also plans to enlarge the vineyard.

TECHNICAL INFORMATION

General

Appellation:	Graves, Grand Cru Classé
Area under vines:	*Red* 19 hectares
	White 16 hectares
Average production:	*Red* 9,000 cases
	White 9,000 cases
Distribution:	In one block
Owner:	The de Bethmann family
Director:	M. Jean-Jacques de Bethmann
Maître de Chai:	M. Dubile
Oenological Consultant:	M. Gimberteau

Viticulture

Geology:	Gravel on higher ground, where most of the red wine grapes are planted, and clay/sand and alios on the lower
Grape varieties:	*Red* 79% Cabernet Sauvignon, 21% Merlot *White* 60% Semillon, 35% Sauvignon, 5% Muscadelle
Pruning:	Guyot Simple and Double
Rootstock:	Various
Vines per hectare:	Between 6,000 and 10,000
Yield per hectare:	45 hectolitres
Replanting:	As necessary to maintain average age of vines

Vinification

Added yeasts:	Yes for white, and sometimes for red
Length of maceration:	Depending on vintage
Temperature of fermentation:	*Red* 25–32°C *White* Maximum 19°C
Control of fermentation:	Warming by heat exchange, cooling by a circulation of estate's own well water, which is always 12°C
Type of vat:	Glass-lined steel
Vin de presse:	Included in red grand vin according to vintage
Age of casks:	*Red* 1–4 years old *White* All new, part fermented in cask
Time in cask:	*Red* 18 months *White* From 1 to 3 months according to vintage; wine is tasted twice weekly in cask, and racked accordingly
Fining:	Egg-whites
Filtration:	Sur plaque before bottling
Type of bottle:	Bordelaise

Commercial

Vente Directe:	Yes
Direct ordering:	Yes
Exclusivities:	None
Visits:	Yes, by appointment only Telephone: 56 21 73 31

THE TASTING AT CHATEAU MALESCASSE, 1 February 1985
J.S., Christian Seely, Michel Tesseron.

White

1983 Pale, clear, greeny gold. Not yet giving much on nose, but very pleasing. Clean, crisp and correct, an unexceptionable white Graves.

1982 Shade darker than '83. Boquet a little flat – more Semillon than Sauvignon. A little 'fatter' than '83 or '82, but still a very pleasant wine.

1981 Lovely, brilliant greeny-gold. Nice Sauvignon bouquet. Beautiful crisp and delicate; dry, white Graves at its best – perfect with any sea food.

Red

1982 Good depth of colour. Nice, rounded, open bouquet with good fruit. Easy and mouthfilling, with good tannins – not aggressive; already nice to drink, but will keep.

1981 Shade lighter than '82. Nose still quite reserved. More finesse and less round than '82; good balance, nearly ready and will be good.

1979 Full, dark red. Good powerful fruit on nose. A good mouthful of Graves, some body and nice fruit, not too complicated – nice now, but still has plenty of life.

CHATEAU

Pape-Clément

GRAVES

Château Pape-Clément is in the sprawling Bordeaux suburb of Pessac, and is situated on the right of the RN250 from Bordeaux to Arcachon. Coming out of Bordeaux on this road, pass Château Haut-Brion on your right, go through the centre of Pessac, and you will find Pape-Clément on your right after another 2 km.

In spite of its depressingly suburban situation, Château Pape-Clément has what is probably the longest history of any wine-producing estate in the Bordeaux area, a history, moreover, as the name of the property suggests, that is closely linked with the church.

In 1300 the Archbishop of Bordeaux, Bertrand de Goth, bought himself a country estate within easy reach of the city by horse, and thereon planted a vineyard. This 'local boy made good' (he was born at Villandraut, near Langon) ascended to the papacy in 1306 and became Clement V. Relations between the Vatican and the French King were somewhat strained at that time, so with a degree of prudence the new pope decided to establish the papal court in France, which he did at Avignon. Clément must have had an eye for good wine-producing soil, for the new palace became none other than – Châteauneuf du Pape!

When he became pope, de Goth bequeathed his estate to his successor and to all the succeeding Archbishops of Bordeaux. The property remained in the hands of the church right up to the Revolu-

tion, and the wine, of excellent quality, was used entirely for the enjoyment of the Archbishops' court, and was known as Vigne du Pape Clément. The estate, along with other ecclesiastically owned properties, was confiscated by the revolutionary administration and sold.

Pape-Clément then passed through several hands, one of the most important owners being a Monsieur J.B. Clerc, who did much to improve the property and establish the high quality of the wine between 1858 and his death in the late 1870s; he won the Gironde Agricultural Society's gold medal in 1861, and a further award in 1864.

The next owner was a gentleman named Cinto, who built the château in its present Gothic form. After his death, Pape-Clément was acquired by the English Maxwell family, and the vineyard then began a serious decline, partly due to the prevailing economic problems, but culminating in a catastrophic hailstorm which decimated the vines in 1937. It was at this time that Pape-Clément nearly disappeared altogether, to be sold for urban development; plans can be seen from this period showing new roads and housing projects, where happily the noble vineyard still exists. The saviour of Château Pape-Clément was the poet Paul Montagne, who wrote under the name of Pol des Causses; he bought the estate in 1939 and set about the restoration of the château and the replanting of the sadly dilapidated vineyard. The war delayed the completion of his work until 1950, and it was not until the 1953 vintage that the wine returned to its former glory. Montagne lived to the age of 94, dying only a few years ago. It is his heirs who now own the property, through the Société Montagne & Cie. Administration is carried out by M. Pujol, and responsibility for winemaking rests, as it has for nearly 30 years, in the very able hands of the régisseur, M. Michel Musyt. The château is currently undergoing renovation following a serious fire in 1983. When complete, it will be used as a conference centre, though the régisseur will retain an office on the ground floor.

The wine of Pape-Clément tends to be rather more austere than many Graves, requiring a full ten years for a good vintage to develop to its best potential. There is a small production of elegant, dry white wine made – between 3 and 5 casks a year – and very little of this small quantity is available on the open market; this is a pity, for it is a wine that ages well, and can hold up its head in company with the top white wines of the Graves.

TECHNICAL INFORMATION

General

Appellation:	Graves, Grand Cru Classé
Area under vines:	*Red* 27 hectares
	White 0.3 hectares
Production:	*Red* 13,500 cases
	White 150 cases
Distribution of vines:	One large block, and several smaller parcels north of the château
Proprietor:	Société Montagne & Cie
Régisseur:	M. Michel Musyt
Maître de Chai:	M. René Raymond
Oenological Consultant:	Prof. Emile Peynaud

Viticulture

Geology:	$\frac{1}{3}$ gravel, $\frac{1}{3}$ sand, $\frac{1}{3}$ chalky clay
Grape varieties:	*Red* 60% Cabernet Sauvignon, 40% Merlot *White* 33% Semillon, 33% Muscadelle, 33% Sauvignon
Pruning:	Guyot Double
Rootstock:	420A
Vines per hectare:	7,500
Average yield per hectare:	50 hectolitres
Replanting:	By sections of 0.5 hectare

Vinification

Added yeasts:	Rarely
Length of maceration:	8–15 days
Temperature of fermentation:	26–28°C
Control of fermentation:	Heat-exchange pump
Type of vat:	Wood and cement
Vin de presse:	Part of first pressing mixed with Grand Vin
Age of casks:	$\frac{1}{3}$ new each vintage
Time in cask:	2 years
Fining:	Fresh egg-whites
Filtration:	None
Type of bottle:	Monogrammed Bordelaise

Commercial

Vente Directe:	Yes
Direct Ordering:	Yes
Exclusivities:	None
Agents abroad:	None
Visits:	Yes, by appointment Telephone: 56 07 04 77 Hours: 0800–1200, 1400–1700

THE TASTING IN THE CHAI AT PAPE-CLEMENT, 25 October 1984
J.S., M. Pujol, M. Michel Musyt

Red

1983 (In cask.) Deep red, almost black. Vanilla and fruit on nose. A big wine, well-structured with fruit, tannin and backbone in the right quantities to make a really good Graves to drink in the years ahead.

1982 Again deep, blackish red. Open bouquet, blackcurranty fruit. Large, fat and mouthfilling, with muted tannin. Long and rounded. Ready long before the 1983.

1981 Shade lighter than first two, but still very dark. Nose has some fruit, but a bit closed. Well-made wine, approachable, not very exciting.

1979 Deep bluey red. Nose soft with good fruit fragrance. Concentrated flavour, in balance. Could be drunk fairly soon.

1976 Colour lighter, but good for year, hardly any brown showing. Bouquet ripe. Flavour ripe and in balance. A good 1976, ready now and will keep a while.

1967 Slightly bricky red. Powerful, ripe nose. A good example from this generally disappointing vintage, with plenty of fruit left. Long aftertaste, drying a little at the end.

White

1983 A rare treat! Only 4 or 5 casks are made each year. Pale gold with slight greeny tinges. Aromatic, fruit and vanilla on nose. Dry and clean with excellent fruit/acidity balance. Very pleasant now, but will improve in bottle.

247

CHATEAU
Picque-Caillou
GRAVES

Leave Bordeaux by the RN250 Arcachon road; as you enter the suburb of Pessac, you will pass Château Haut-Brion on your right, and then the hotel La Reserve. At the next traffic light, turn right; follow this road for about 2½km, and you will eventually find a sign for Château Picque-Caillou on your right.

Picque-Caillou was something of a revelation to me, in that I had not realised that there was still a wine-producing property left in the essentially suburban area of Mérignac. Before the French Revolution there were many fine vineyards here and in neighbouring Pessac and Talence, but all but a few such as Haut-Brion, Pape-Clément, La Mission and Les Carmes-Haut-Brion have now been swallowed up by the concrete and tarmac sprawl of Bordeaux. Both here and at Château Chêne-Vert across the road, also the property of M. Alphonse Denis, you can stand in the vineyard and imagine that you are in the heart of the country – only the persistent hum of traffic reminds you that you are in fact surrounded by suburban Bordeaux.

Both châteaux are lovely; Picque-Caillou was rebuilt on the original Louis XIV foundations, having been burnt to the ground at the time of the Revolution, while Chêne-Vert is a jewel of a château, built by one Etienne Laclotte in the middle of the 18th century. Alphonse Denis, a courteous French gentleman of the old school, has an old-established family company in Paris, trading in the Far East, though he visits the property frequently; he has done much to improve the vineyard and the wine of both properties. The château of Picque-Caillou is currently let, but he is in the process of restoring Chêne-Vert. At the moment the vineyard of Chêne-Vert extends over 4 hectares, and that of Picque-Caillou is 14 hectares, though new parcels are being planted annually, which will give an eventual total area of 20

248

hectares. The dominant grape variety is Merlot, with 50% of the encépagement, but new plantings are almost totally Cabernet Sauvignon. There is a good depth of gravel on a subsoil of clay, and the resulting wine has elegance, finesse and good ageing qualities. The 1984 was most impressive, and will, I think, be relatively quick to yield up its undoubted charm, while the 1981 had great quality, excellent fruit and enough backbone to carry it into old age.

The vineyard is now coming into full maturity following almost total replanting by M. Denis between 1960 and 1964, and it is definitely a wine to watch. Commercialisation is handled by the négociants Johnston and Coste, and the former has done much to enhance its reputation in the United States through the firm of Châteaux and Estates, who market Picque-Caillou's wine across the Atlantic.

TECHNICAL INFORMATION

General

Appellation:	Graves de Pessac
Area under vines:	14 hectares Picque-Caillou, 4 hectares Chêne-Vert
Average production:	7,000 cases
Distribution of vines:	In one piece, Château Chêne-Vert also across the road
Owner:	Société Civile et Immobilière du Château Picque-Caillou (Alphonse Denis)
Régisseur:	M. Jean Renaud
Chef de Culture:	M. Drillaud
Consultant Oenologist:	Frères Rolland

Viticulture

Geology:	Deep gravel on clay subsoil
Grape varieties:	50% Merlot, 40% Cabernet Sauvignon, 10% Cabernet Franc
Pruning:	Guyot Simple
Rootstock:	Various
Vines per hectare:	10,000
Average yield per hectare:	40 hectolitres
Replanting:	By rotation, and new plantings to an eventual size of 20 hectares

Vinification

Added yeasts:	No
Length of maceration:	15–18 days
Temperature of fermentation:	30°C
Control of fermentation:	By water circulation
Type of vat:	Steel, lined with epoxy-resin
Vin de presse:	Proportion incorporated, depending on vintage
Age of casks:	$\frac{1}{3}$ new each vintage
Time in cask:	12 months
Fining:	Gelatine, in vat
Filtration:	Light, sur plaque at bottling
Type of bottle:	Standard, changing to Bordelaise lourde

Commercial

Vente Directe:	A little, mainly on Saturday mornings
General Sales:	Commercialised through Nathaniel Johnston and Maison Coste
Visits:	Yes, Saturday mornings only at present, by appointment Telephone: 56 47 37 98

THE TASTING AT CHATEAU PICQUE-CAILLOU, 11 May 1985
J.S., Michel Tesseron, Alphonse Denis

1984 Medium-dark red, bright. Good nose of ripe fruit. Has charm and roundness, with some finesse, and will drink quite soon. Tannins not too pronounced, excellent ripe fruit and long aftertaste.

1983 Pale, tawny red. Bouquet a bit flat. Curious taste, quite good fruit and some tannins. This may have been an unfortunate bottle, but it was not quite up to the standard of the other vintages tasted.

1982 Colour quite dark, but still on the light side for 1982. Good nose of ripe fruit. Elegant and rounded, quite forward, with nice aftertaste.

1981 Much deeper red, with bluish edges. Soft, elegant nose. Good fruit taste, with a suggestion of boiled sweets. Has finesse and some backbone and should stay well.

1980 Lightish red. Pleasing, light bouquet. Some fruit, with the same boiled-sweet characteristics. Light and easy to drink now, with no great future.

CHATEAU
Rahoul
GRAVES

Driving south-west from Bordeaux towards Langon on the RN113, you will come to a traffic light just as you enter the village of Portets; turn right at these lights, and the gates of Château Rahoul are about 250 metres along on your right.

The first recorded owner was Le Chevalier Guillaume de Rahoul in 1646, and there is a stone – possibly his gravestone – let in to the south facade of the château bearing proof of this. In 1814 it was acquired by a family called de Balguerie, the de Rahouls having lost both the prperty and their heads in the Revolution. The estate then passed to the Comte de Camiran in 1862. The next proprietor I have been able to trace was a notaire called Landais, who was imprisoned for fraud.

In 1972 an Englishman called David Robson bought Rahoul, and completely restored the château. For family reasons, Robson sold the property in 1978 to two Australians, the famous antipodean vinocrat, Len Evans, and an entrepreneur with fingers in many pies called Peter Fox. The latter was tragically killed in a car accident, and Rahoul was sold in 1982 to a Danish wine-merchant from Copenhagen, Lothardt Dahl, who is the present owner.

The estate has been administered by the very capable Peter Vinding-Diers, also a Dane, since 1977. He and his English wife, Suzanne, live at the château. Peter also ran a property in Barsac, Château Padouen, until it was sold recently, where he made a very good, correct wine. He also has a property of his own, Domaine la Grave, which produces an excellent red Graves, which is vinified at Rahoul. When he arrived at Rahoul, Peter found the vineyard in good heart, but the cellar needed change. He set about cleaning it up, installed new machinery, including stainless steel vats, an Amos crusher and lately, his pride and joy and the first of its kind in the area, a large pneumatic tank press.

Although the production at Château Rahoul is predominantly red wine, it is the white which has brought it fame. Peter Vinding and his wife went to Australia to see the vintage in February and March 1979, and there three of the top winemakers, Gerry Sissingh at Rothbury, Murray Tyrell of Tyrrells and Brian Croser in Adelaide, all took tremendous trouble to explain and discuss why and when one had to do what. It is no mere accident that has placed Australia in the forefront of white winemaking, and these three persons, have, more than any others, paved the way.

The result was an adaptation of their methods to suit the climate and wines of the Graves, in order to develop the true varietal tastes in this part of the world. Peter Vinding was the first to apply the method of harvesting white grapes at optimum maturity, and to experiment with skin-contact in order to maximise the fruit flavours. It caused a stir when the first of his white wines came out, and some professionals even thought he had used aromatics in order to obtain the very fine flavours. These were accentuated by the R2 yeast, one of five base yeasts found in the wild state on the estate. This innovation came to the Graves at a time when several people were already working in the same direction. Controlled temperatures, optimum ripeness and skin-contact were all recognized in time.

In 1981 several other properties followed Rahoul, and today the method has been generally accepted. However, the notion that the yeasts should have such a big influence on taste struck many traditionalists as being a bit far-fetched. Only now are a few beginning to realise the enormous influence yeasts have on quality white wines.

Peter Vinding is also a strong believer in the important influence of new oak in the making of quality white wine; following much experimentation, the wine now spends some time in casks, which are made only from oak from Nevers and Alliers. On my visit we made a fascinating comparison between three samples of Château Padouen 1980, all of which had remained in cask for three years; one cask was of Nevers oak, one of Costa Rican and the third of Limousin. There was little to choose between the Nevers and Costa Rican casks, though my choice was the former, while the sample from the Limousin oak was definitely inferior, showing signs of oxidation which probably results from the larger pores in the oak from that region.

The white wine of Rahoul is of excellent quality, with an attractive, fruity clarity of style, and demand exceeds supply; the larger share goes to the United States, followed by the United Kingdom, Denmark, Belgium and France. The red is a typical southern Graves with firmness, style and good ageing qualities, which continues to improve as the proportion of Cabernet Sauvignon is gradually increased.

TECHNICAL INFORMATION

General

Appellation:	Graves
Area under vines:	*Red* 15 hectares
	White 2.5 hectares
Production:	*Red* 6,000 cases
	White 1,000 cases
Distribution of vines:	In one piece
Owner:	Société Civile du Château Rahoul de Balguerie (Mr. L. Dahl)
Director and Wine Maker:	Peter Vinding-Diers
Maître de Chai:	M. H. Broussy

Viticulture

Geology:	Deep gravel and clay
Grape varieties:	*Red* 70% Merlot, 30% Cabernet Sauvignon
	White 100% Semillon
Pruning:	Guyot Simple
Rootstock:	R100; SO4
Vines per hectare:	5,500
Yield per hectare:	36 hectolitres (red)
	40 hectolitres (white)
Replanting:	Replacement of vines as necessary – 'complantation'

Vinification

Added yeasts:	Own strains used, R2 only for the white and five strains for the red.
Length of maceration:	2–3 weeks
Temperature of fermentation:	*Red* 30°C maximum
	White 14°C
Control of fermentation:	Refrigeration
Type of vat:	Cement and stainless steel
Vin de presse:	Developed and incorporated
Age of casks:	$\frac{1}{3}$ new per annum
Time in cask:	*Red* 18 months
	White 3–4 months
Fining:	Egg-whites
Filtration:	Yes
Type of bottle:	Bordelaise Lourde or Grand Cru

Commercial

Vente Directe:	Yes
Agents in foreign countries:	Denmark: Molt Wengels Vinimport
	USA: Barry Bassin Inc. New York
	UK: Bordeaux Direct for white
Visits:	Yes, by appointment Telephone 56 67 01 12 Office hours.

THE TASTING AT CHATEAU RAHOUL,
15 October 1984
J.S., Mr and Mrs Peter Vinding-Diers

White

1983 Good clear pale gold. Open fruity bouquet. Well made, harmonious wine with lots of fruit. Will be excellent.

1982 Deeper colour than 1983. Fresh fruity nose. Balanced flavour, slight botrytis, lots of fruit – a good bottle.

1981 Bright, light gold. Bouquet quite closed. Coming together, fruit and acidity in balance. Beautiful.

1979 Lovely clear colour, slightly darker than later vintages. Rich, ripe fruit on nose. Well structured harmonious wine with firm flesh.

Red

1983 Deep, bluey red. Good nose with fruit and some new wood. Good, with backbone, fruit and non-aggressive tannins.

1982 Good deep red. Open, soft fruit on bouquet. Already very approachable with lots of fruit and muted tannins.

1981 Again lovely deep colour. Nose open with lots of good fruit. Well made, balanced with some finesse. Will be excellent in two years.

1980 Excellent depth of colour for 1980. Attractive, rich fruit on nose. Pleasant easy wine, fragrant mouthful, surprisingly long for 1980.

1979 Good medium red. Good fruit on nose. Well made wine, with some oakiness. Needs a little time.

1978 Good depth of colour. Slightly overripe nose. Complex, and a little disappointing for the vintage.

1973 (With lunch.) A good colour, with very little browning; nose still good with ripe fruit. A big wine for such a 'little' vintage, probably due to higher proportion of Cabernet Sauvignon still in vineyard at that time.

CHATEAU
Smith-Haut-Lafitte
GRAVES

Drive south from Bordeaux on the RN113 in the direction of Toulouse. When you reach the village of Bouscaut, turn right just before Château Bouscaut on the D111. After about 200 metres, you will come to a small turning to your left, at which Smith-Haut-Lafitte is signposted, along with several Graves châteaux. The château and vineyards are about 2 km along this road on your right, and are reached by a small road, also on the right.

As early as the 12th century, the property was part of an estate belonging to the noble house of Du Boscq, but the first record of an important vineyard on this plateau of Garonne gravel dates from 1549, when it belonged to a family called Verrier. In 1720 the vineyard was bought by an Englishman named George Smith, and it was then that it became Smith-Haut-Lafitte; Lafitte derives from old French, and means 'a small hill'.

In 1856 the powerful M. Sadi Duffour-Dubergier, Mayor of Bordeaux and President of the Chamber of Commerce, bought the estate; he was a fine figure of a man, as can be seen from his Romanesque bust in the underground chai. He was also an able and dedicated winemaker, and Smith-Haut-Lafitte enjoyed a period of prosperity and expansion under his ownership; in 1876 the vineyard was awarded the 'Grande Médaille d'Or' by the Société d'Agriculture for the best-kept estate in the Département; at the end of the 19th century, before it passed out of his family's hands, the total area of the estate was 273 hectares, with 68 hectares of red vines and 5 of white.

During the first half of this century, Smith-Haut-Lafitte became the property of a succession of different owners, most of whom were more interested in property speculation than serious wine-making, and the size of the vineyard and the reputation of the wine went in to a decline. As early as 1902, the name of Eschenauer first became associated with the property, when Frédéric Eschenauer first signed a contract for the exclusive distribution rights of Smith-Haut-Lafitte. The estate belonged from the early 1900s to a German company, the Handels Gesellschaft, until it was sequestrated at the outbreak of war in 1914, when Frédéric's son, Louis Eschenauer, became the tenant. It was during the twenties that the speculators moved in, and the property suffered greatly from lack of investment.

It was not until 1958 that the Société Eschenauer managed to acquire the property, and there followed the Phoenix-like resurgence of the vineyard and its wines. By this time there were only 10 hectares under productive vines, and Eschenauer set about a massive programme of replanting and building. The reconstitution of the vineyard to its former 19th-century dimensions lasted well in to the 1960s, and it was not until the 1975 vintage that the results of all this work really began to take effect.

The elegant 18th-century château did not form part of the Eschenauer purchase, but the building and restoration of the chais, cuvier, régisseur's house, reception room and other buildings have been tastefully executed, and the property has a uniform and cared-for appearance. The crowning glory of all these works was the completion in 1974 of the vast underground cask-cellar, capable of holding over 2,000 hogsheads, humidified at a constant 85% and air-conditioned at a perfect 17°C.

There are now about 46 hectares planted with red grapes, which are predominantly Cabernet Sauvignon, giving a sound, fairly typical red Graves of good colour with a pleasing Cabernet nose; the structure and potential keeping quality is noticeably improving in the later vintages, as the re-planted vines become better established. The white wine is fresh and crisp, best appreciated in its youth, and comes from 6 hectares of Sauvignon vines. Eschenauers, finding that demand exceeds supply for white Smith-Haut-Lafitte, also market a white wine which is bought in from other Graves growers, and sold under the label of Les Arcades de Smith – it is not the same wine, and is not quite so good. The white wine is not a Cru Classé, and is simply sold under the appellation Graves Sec. A second label exists for the red wine, Les Hauts de Smith-Haut-Lafitte, which is used for the cuves not thought good enough for inclusion in the Grand Vin, and for the produce of the younger vines.

The property is administered by René Baffert of Eschenauer, who also manages Château Rauzan-Ségla in Margaux, while the running of day-to-day matters has been for nearly twenty years in the hands of the régisseur, Claude Guérin, who is aided by his son, Jean-Jacques, as maître de chai.

TECHNICAL INFORMATION

General

Appellation:	Graves
Area under vines:	*Red* 45.4 hectares
	White 5.6 hectares
Average production:	*Red* 22,500 cases
	White 3,000 cases
Distribution of vines:	One block
Owner:	S.C.A. d'Exploitation des Vignobles Eschenauer
Director:	M. René Baffert
Régisseur:	M. Claude Guérin
Maître de Chai:	M. Jean-Jacques Guérin
Consultant Oenologist:	Professor Emile Peynaud

Viticulture

Geology:	Garonne gravel
Grape varieties:	*Red* 73% Cabernet Sauvignon, 11% Cabernet Franc, 16% Merlot
	White 100% Sauvignon
Pruning:	Guyot Simple
Vines per hectare:	6,300
Average yield per hectare:	45 hectolitres
Replanting:	As necessary

Vinification

Added yeasts:	In very difficult years
Length of maceration:	21 days
Temperature of fermentation:	*Red* 28–31°C
	White 17°C
Control of fermentation:	By running water, but new system being installed of exchange pumps
Type of vat:	Lined steel
Vin de presse:	Red only – proportion included, according to vintage
Age of casks:	50% new
Time in cask:	15 months
Fining:	Egg-whites
Filtration:	Sur terre before going in cask, sur plaque before bottling
Type of bottle:	Bordelaise lourde (prior to 1981 special bottle was used)

Commercial

Vente Directe:	Yes, to private customers
Sales:	Exclusively by Sté. Eschenauer, 42, Ave Emile Counord, 33300 Bordeaux
Visits:	Yes: Monday to Friday By appointment on Saturdays Telephone: 56 30 72 30 (château) 56 81 58 90 (office)

THE TASTING, Part at Château Smith-Haut-Lafitte, July 1984, but mainly at Château Rausan-Ségla, January 1985
J.S., M. René Baffert, M. Bruzaut, and M. Guérin at Smith-Haut-Lafitte

White

1983 Clear, light-greeny gold. Assertive Sauvignon grapiness on nose. Clean and crisp fruit, typical Sauvignon taste. Quite high acidity but will be lovely after a few months in bottle.

Red

1983 Deep purple colour. Lovely strong blackcurrant bouquet. Quite complex flavour with good tannins, some backbone and keeping qualities.

1982 Deep red, less blue than '83. Softer on the nose, with some oakiness. Rounded and supple, well-made. Big mouthful, with lovely long aftertaste.

1979 Medium-light red. Open, attractive bouquet. Straightforward wine, with good fruit and tannins; will improve.

1978 Colour good, shade darker than '79. Powerful nose, typical Graves. Quite tannic, but plenty of fruit and weight to make a good bottle in 2 or 3 years.

1977 Good light red, very little browning. Bouquet light and fruity. Flavour good and honest, a little short, but very pleasing light claret for lunch-time drinking.

1961 Very dense, dark colour, only tinges of brown. Nose excellent, but not particularly strong. Great concentration of ripe fruit, finishes a little dry, but has a superb aftertaste.

CHATEAU
La Tour Martillac
GRAVES

Château la Tour Martillac is reached by the small road that heads off to the right of the La Brède – Léogan road, the D109, clearly signposted to Martillac. The property is on a small road just behind the church in Martillac.

The Domaine de Martillac once formed part of the estates of the powerful Montesquieu family of Château de la Brède, whose ancestors built the tower that stands in the courtyard, and to which the property owes its name. This tower is extremely old, probably dating back to the 12th century, and the vineyard was known simply as La Tour, until the name of the village was added quite recently in order to avoid confusion with the First Growth Château Latour in the Médoc. It is a quiet, rural backwater of the Graves, and one can well understand the Montesquieu who preferred its quiet seclusion to the splendour of his great château at La Brède; he was an important parliamentarian, however, and had to stay in the grandeur of his castle as it was more suited to his elevated station.

The vineyard as we know it today was planted in the mid-1880s, and has some of the oldest vines in the area. Alfred Kressmann bought the property in 1930, and it is his son Jean who runs it now, assisted by his son Loïc. The Kressmanns are a large family of German origin, and are widely disseminated throughout the Bordeaux wine trade. The founder of this dynastic line was Edouard Kressmann, who arrived as an apprentice in Bordeaux in 1858. His arrival and subsequent life and times are described in an evocative biography, *Le Défi d'Edouard*, written by his scholarly grandson Jean, the present owner.

Jean Kressmann's knowledge of the history of Bordeaux, indeed of European history generally, is nothing short of encyclopedic. I spent an enthralling afternoon with him, and three of his carefully reasoned, if slightly unusual, historical theories have stuck in my mind; firstly he doubts that Joan of Arc was ever burned at the stake, secondly that the English invented Champagne, and lastly that the French Revolution was caused entirely by an increase of nine sous on the tax on a litre of wine.

Both red and white wine are made at Château la Tour Martillac. The red is one of the more refined of the Léognan Graves, and comes from a Caber-

net Sauvignon–dominated encépagement; this variety was planted in great profusion by Alfred Kressmann, Jean's father, when he arrived here in 1930, and is still favoured by Jean. The white wine, an excellent, crisp, dry Graves, has represented until recently only a small proportion of the total production, though this is now being considerably increased to meet a healthy demand. It is interesting to note that when the Kressmanns first purchased la Tour Martillac the accent was very definitely on white wine production; of the 12 hectares then under vines, 8 were planted with white varieties, some of which dated back nearly fifty years, and it was these ancient vines which gave, albeit in small quantity, a wine of remarkable quality and with great ageing potential. Jean Kressmann has always been fiercely proud of his white wine, and I am pleased that it is currently meeting with such success.

The white wine is now vinified according to the best modern oenological techniques. Small stain-

254

less-steel vats are used for fermentation, and the temperature is kept below 20°C by water cooling the exterior of the vats. Half the crop finishes its fermentation in casks, where it remains until the blending prior to bottling. The wine is usually bottled in the June following the vintage. The principal grape variety used is Semillon with 30% Sauvignon and a small percentage of the very old vines of unknown origin, which contribute much to the individuality of the wine.

Vinification and ageing of the red is more traditional; the wine is fermented at 33°C, with a maceration period of up to four weeks, and is then aged in cask for 15 to 18 months, depending on the vintage.

All La Tour Martillac is now bottled at the château, following present-day custom. Bottling was always done at the Kressmann négociant firm's cellars in Bordeaux in the past; the now universal château-bottling, and the consequent necessity for storing as many as three vintages at the property at any one time have created a considerable space problem; this is being solved by the construction of a vast new chai and storage area alongside the original buildings, which will be completed in 1985.

TECHNICAL INFORMATION

General

Appellation:	Graves de Léognan
Area under vines:	*Red* 19 hectares, increasing to 23 *White* 4 hectares, increasing to 4·5
Average production:	*Red* 8,500 cases *White* 1,500 cases
Distribution of vines:	One block
Owner:	M. Jean Kressmann
Régisseur:	M. Loïc Kressmann
Maître de Chai:	M. Jean Kressmann
Consultant Oenologist:	M. Castaing

Viticulture

Geology:	Gravel of Pyrenean origin
Grape varieties:	*Red* 60% Cabernet Sauvignon, 25% Merlot, 6% Cabernet Franc, 5% Malbec, 4% Petit Verdot *White* 55% Semillon, 30% Sauvignon, 15% Old vines
Pruning:	Mixture of Guyot Double and Simple
Rootstock:	420A, 3309, 1103 Paulsen, 5. BB
Vines per hectare:	7,200
Average yield per hectare:	*Red* 40 hectolitres *White* 30 hectolitres
Replanting:	As necessary to maintain high average age of vines

Vinification

Added yeasts:	No
Length of maceration:	*Red* 6–15 days
Temperature of fermentation:	*Red* 32–33°C *White* Max. 20°C
Control of fermentation:	By water-cooled coil, and water-cooling on stainless-steel vats
Type of vat:	Metal and stainless steel
Vin de presse:	1st pressing included in red, sometimes second
Age of casks:	*Red* only, ⅓ new each vintage
Time in cask:	*Red* only, 5–18 months
Fining:	egg-whites, powdered
Filtration:	*Red* sur plaque at bottling
Type of bottle:	Bordelaise

Commercial

Vente Directe:	Yes
Direct ordering:	Yes
Exclusivities:	Yes, wine sold through négociant house of Kressmann
Visits:	Yes, telephone 56 21 71 21 or 56 23 78 40

THE TASTING AT CHATEAU LA TOUR MARTILLAC, 9 May 1985
J.S., M. Jean Kressmann

White

1984 Very pale greeny colour, almost gin-clear. Nose very grapey, Sauvignon to the fore at this stage. Lovely concentration of fresh fruit; a touch of sweetness, but very dry finish and good aftertaste.

1983 Beautiful pale greeny colour; nose less assertive. Rich and smooth with lots of good Semillon flavour. Excellent.

Red

1984 Deep purplish red. Nose oaky, but plenty of good fruit also. Quite hard and tannic, but plenty of good fruit there; a wine to keep.

1983 Good depth of colour; good open bouquet. Lovely flavour of summer fruits with good tannins and some finesse. Will be a really fine bottle.

1982 Very deep almost black colour. Bouquet good, but as yet undeveloped. A fat, round wine with a touch less finesse than the '83 – a bit dumb at the moment.

1975 Fine bright scarlet, beginning to brown a little. Bouquet very ripe – has lovely taste of summer fruits, but still has good tannin and ageing potential.

SAUTERNES

The miracle fungus growth, *botrytis cinerea*, which results in the noble rot and gives the luscious, honeyed dessert wines of Sauternes, occurs only here between the villages of Barsac and Sauternes, in certain vineyards along the Rhine and Moselle and in the Tokay properties of Hungary. Given this tiny area, and adding the enormous cost of harvesting the minute quantity of shrivelled grapes and the all too frequent non-occurrence of the *botrytis*, it is a wonder that anyone bothers to make Sauternes at all, and moreover, that it can be bought at such a relatively modest price.

There are five communes entitled to the Sauternes appellation: Sauternes itself, Bommes, Preignac, Fargues and Barsac. Barsac is entitled to use the name of its own commune as well as that of Sauternes, and its wines are in fact of a distinctly different character to those of the other four communes; the vineyards are on lower, flatter ground, and the soil is less stony, yielding a wine that is usually lighter and less luscious than the communes of the slopes.

The difficulties that beset the owners of properties in the Sauternais are Herculean, and are described in some detail, along with the viticultural and vinification methods for the production of Sauternes, in the chapter on Château d'Yquem. Many proprietors offset the vicissitudes of their precarious existence by producing dry white wine as well, and some even make a little red, though neither of these are entitled to the magic Sauternes name.

The vineyards and châteaux of the Sauternes are among the prettiest in Bordeaux, and it has been sad to see the hardships and problems endured by their owners in recent years. The winds of change are gently ruffling the vine-clad slopes, however, and I sense a renaissance in these fabulous wines. One of the most encouraging signs in recent years has been the acquisition by the Rothschilds of the Premier Cru Château Rieussec, a gesture of faith in the future of Sauternes if ever there was one.

Of the restaurants in the area, I have had most pleasure from two, and those for entirely different reasons. The Auberge des Vignes in the village of Sauternes has tremendous atmosphere; the service

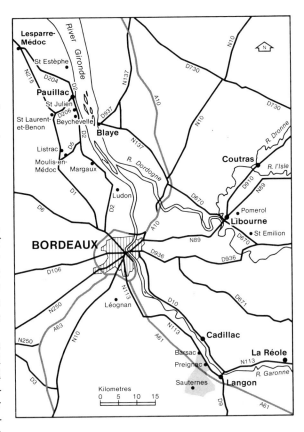

is friendly, the wine list adequate and the food simple, but delicious – entrecôtes cooked on an open fire of *sarments de vigne* are a speciality. It was here that I was first introduced to the joyous marriage of blue cheese and Sauternes – a delicious glass of Rieussec 1970 with a generous tranche of Roquefort was a sublime combination. The second restaurant is not truly in the commune, but at Claude Darroze in the nearby town of Langon you can eat some of the very best food in the Bordeaux area, accompanied by wines chosen from a superbly balanced wine list. It is a watering-hole well worth a detour, but if you choose to stay the night, ask for a room at the back of the hotel away from the noisy traffic of the main road.

258

CHATEAU
Broustet
BARSAC

Take the small road north from the village of Barsac; just outside the village you will cross the railway line, and after another 250 metres you will see Château Broustet on your right-hand side. Beware the spreading roots of the two enormous plane trees on either side of the gateway – low-slung cars can suffer!

The vignoble was originally part of one estate called 'Broustet-Nairac' and was so classified in 1855.

There is not much to tell before the end of last century, when Eric Fournier's great-grandfather bought the land to build a large cooperage. Records in the Bordeaux Chamber of Commerce show that a model of the official 'Barrique Bordelaise' was supplied by the factory to serve as a pattern for all coopers.

The Fournier family have been winemakers since the early part of this century, and also own Château Canon, a Premier Grand Cru of St Emilion.

There is no château as such at Broustet, only a small attractive house occasionally occupied by Daniel Fournier, together with the maître de chai's cottage and a range of buildings – chai, ageing cellar, cuvier and stock rooms – surrounding a pretty courtyard with an old well and a line of shady plane trees.

The vineyard extends to some 16 hectares with a soil that is half large alluvial gravel and half red clay with a high iron content, which gives Barsac wines their special character. The situation of the vineyard, near to the Garonne, gives rise to those special conditions in sunny autumns, when the morning mists followed by hot days favour the development of the all-important 'noble rot'.

The vines are planted in the average proportion of 63% Semillon, 25% Sauvignon and 12% Muscadelle to give, in a favourable vintage, the typical luscious but refined dessert wine of the Haut-Barsac. The vines are severely pruned, and this, combined with the concentrating action of the noble rot, gives a low average yield of some 12 hectolitres to the hectare, perhaps only one or two glasses of wine per vine.

Vinification is traditional, though in 1984 a range of small stainless-steel vats was installed, each just large enough to contain the harvest of one day. This will enable the owners to conduct a controlled fermentation of each day's picking before the wine is transferred into oak casks, where it will age for at least one year. There is also a small quantity of excellent dry white wine made at Broustet, which is sold under the label 'Vin Sec de Château Broustet'.

259

TECHNICAL INFORMATION

General

Appellation:	Barsac-Sauternes, Grand Cru Classé
Area under vines:	16 hectares
Production:	Average 2,000 cases
Distribution of vines:	In one block
Owner:	Fournier family
Chef de Culture:	M. Faugère
Director:	Eric Fournier
Oenological consultant:	M. Sudraud

Viticulture

Geology:	Red clay and gravel on chalk sub-soil
Grape Varieties planted:	63% Semillon, 25% Sauvignon, 12% Muscadelle
Pruning:	Courte: à cot
Rootstock:	3309, 101–14
Vines per hectare:	5,400
Average yield per hectare:	12 hectolitres
Replanting:	When necessary, and maintaining an average vine age of around 40 years

Vinification

Added yeasts:	No
Temperature of fermentation:	24°C maximum
Control of fermentation:	By refrigeration
Type of vat:	Stainless steel
Age of casks:	10% new annually
Time in cask:	12 months
Fining:	Yes
Filtration:	Yes
Type of bottle:	Bordelaise, clear

Commercial

Vente Directe:	Yes, for retail customers
Direct ordering:	Yes, for retail customers
Exclusivities:	No
Visits:	Yes, by appointment Telephone 56 27 16 27 or 57 24 70 79 Normal office hours

THE TASTING AT CHATEAU BROUSTET, 2 October 1984
J.S., M. Eric Fournier, sundry Belgian buyers

1983 Very pale, clear gold. Already very perfumed, honeyed nose with some oak. Great concentration of fruits and sugar. Very mouthfilling, with lovely long aftertaste and backbone. Will be a superb Barsac.

1982 Fractionally darker than the '83. Muted but fragrant perfume, very grapey. Flavour strongly Muscadelle, not so charpenté as '83, nor as long, but very good.

1981 Pale gold with greeny tinge. Bouquet quite closed, but lots of fragrance there. Not so big as '82 and '83, more acidity and less concentrated.

1980 Very pale, brilliant gold. Nose coming out, fruity and honeyed. Well-balanced, with good complex flavours. Delicious already.

1979 Richer and darker gold. Strong, aggressive pourriture bouquet. Big and powerful, with ripe concentrated flavour. Good now.

1978 Lighter, greeny gold. Elegant perfumed bouquet, less aggressive than '79. Lighter than later years, well structured with fruit and acidity in harmony. Sings well already.

1975 Lovely deep gold. Nose rich, like a Madeira. Very ripe, tastes like an older wine, delicious now but not for keeping.

1972 Clean bright gold. Bouquet attractive, less honeyed than '75, but elegant. Perfumed and light, long aftertaste. Good, in balance, but not special.

1971 Colour deeper than '72, bright and clear. Delicate, perfumed and fragrant. Good now.

1970 Deep, golden, syrup colour. Concentration of fruit on nose. Luscious flavour with backbone and lots of fruit. Best of '72, '71 and '70.

CHATEAU
Climens
BARSAC

Drive south-east on the N113 from Bordeaux towards Langon; just after the village of Barsac there is a turning to your right with a large poster-map of the major vineyards of Barsac and Sauternes, clearly marked. Turn right here and follow the signs, past Château Doisy-Vedrines and turn right in the small village of La Pinesse. Climens is about 1 km out of La Pinesse on a small cross-roads.

In the middle years of the 19th century, Château Climens belonged to the Lacoste family, in whose ownership it was accorded the rank of Premier Cru in the great classification of 1855, and it has been consistently producing one of the best wines of Barsac ever since.

In 1855 the property was bought by the Gounouilhou family, whose main business was printing, and it remained in their hands until 1971, when it was bought by the latter-day Napoléon des Vignes, Lucien Lurton. Day-to-day running at Climens was then, as it is now and has been for three generations, in the hands of the Janin family, who have been régisseurs at Climens for the best part of a hundred years.

The Gounouilhou family never lived at Climens, and the front of the low single-storey house with its flanking square towers still has a blind, shut-tered appearance. The back of the château has an attractive, tree-shaded courtyard with the chais and other buildings on either side. Brigitte, Lucien Lurton's daughter, prefers this to all of her father's properties, and she and her husband may well come to live here before very long.

The situation of Climens is Himalayan by Barsac standards; at 20 metres above sea-level it is the highest vineyard in the commune, and it may be that this elevation has contributed to its consis-tently maintained reputation, for it has never been affected by the periodic floodings of the Garonne, which have from time to time inundated more low-lying vines. The soil is a mixture of fine gravel and reddish sand on a limestone base, and enjoys exceptionally good drainage. Vinification and viticulture are carried out on traditional lines. In the vineyard, severe pruning and harvesting in series of three or more 'tris' result in a low yield of around 12 hectolitres per hectare of precious botrytis-affected must; the fermentation takes

261

place in oak casks, around a third of which are new each vintage, and the wine then spends at least two years in cask before bottling, at which time it is lightly filtered.

The wine is a typical Barsac in the best tradition, being luscious, rich and complex, but always light and perhaps more feminine than the slightly hea-vier wines of the communes of Sauternes. The 1964 was a fine example of what can be done here, when neighbouring vineyards experienced more difficulty. The wine is still excellent, though the colour is going quite dark; in this vintage not one drop of wine was bottled at Château d'Yquem.

TECHNICAL INFORMATION

General

Appellation:	Barsac
Area under vines:	32 hectares
Average production:	6,000 cases
Distribution of vines:	In one block
Owner:	M. Lucien Lurton
Director:	M. Maurice Garros
Régisseur:	Mme. Janin
Maître de Chai:	M. Christian Broustaut
Consultant Oenologist:	Prof. Emile Peynaud

Viticulture

Geology:	Fine gravel and red sand on a subsoil of fissured limestone
Grape varieties:	100% Semillon
Pruning:	A cot
Rootstock:	Riparia Gloire, 101.14
Vines per hectare:	6,600
Average yield per hectare:	12 hectolitres
Replanting:	3–4% per annum

Vinification

Fermentation:	In cask
Temperature of fermentation:	20°C
Age of casks:	$\frac{1}{4}$ to $\frac{1}{3}$ new each vintage
Time in cask:	2 years
Fining:	Egg whites
Filtration:	Sur plaque at bottling
Type of bottle:	Bordelaise blanche

Commercial

Vente Directe:	No
Ordering from château:	Yes
Exclusivities:	None
Agents overseas:	No
Visits:	Yes, by appointment Telephone 56 88 70 20

THE TASTING AT CHATEAU CLIMENS,
28 January 1985
J.S., Christian Seely, Brigitte Lurton

1982 Colour very pale, greeny-gold. Nose open and attractive, beginning to show a slightly roasted richness. Rich, very good, honeyed fruit – at the same time tastes both roasted and of 'pourriture'. Will be a superb Barsac.

1981 Shade deeper than 1982. Rich, ripe and honeyed bouquet. Perfectly balanced, a classic, correct Barsac with the most marked finesse and elegance of all the vintages tasted. Fat and silky, with a long, subtle, rich aftertaste. Lovely.

1980 Medium to light gold. Nose quite shy, but some botrytis there. Quite rich and fat, but at the same time has finesse of Barsac and the proper taste of 'noble rot'. Quite long. Good.

1978 Light gold with greenish tinge. Flowery nose of ripe grapes, more 'roti' than 'pourriture'. Clean, with plenty of concentrated fruit and sweetness and good length, but has slightly less finesse than the three later vintages.

262

CHATEAU
Doisy-Vedrines
BARSAC

Château Doisy-Vedrines is situated on the D114 between Barsac and Pujols, about 1½ km south-west of Barsac just before the hamlet of La Pinesse. The Vedrines family were landowners in Barsac in the 17th and 18th centuries, and it is from them that the château derives its name, although there was a house here as early as the 16th century. The history of the Vedrines has been exhaustively investigated and documented in a book written in 1981 by Jacqueline Olivier Vidrines, whose ancestor, Jean-Baptiste Vedrines, emigrated to the New World in the mid-1700s, founding a branch of the family in Louisiana. Jean-Baptiste, a marine officer, is reputed to have fled his native France following a duel over a lady, in which he killed his rival, though this has not been clearly proved.

The property remained in the hands of the Vedrines until the early 19th century, but by the 1855 classification in which it was ranked a Deuxième Cru, it belonged to M. Daëne of the neighbouring château. In the early 1900s Doisy-Vedrines passed into the ownership of a family called Boireau-Teyssonneau, one of whom, the present owner, married M. Pierre Casteja, who lives at and runs the property today. Casteja is a member of an old-established Bordeaux wine family who owned Château Duhart-Milon in Pauillac for over a century, and his cousin Emile makes wine at two Crus Classés, Châteaux Batailley and Lynch-Moussas, in the Médoc. It is worth noting that Casteja, by virtue of their presence at Duhart-Milon in 1855, is one of only four names listed as owners in the great classification who still own Crus Classés today; the other three are Rothschild, Barton, and de Lur-Saluces. Pierre Casteja is head of the successful négociant firm of Roger Joanne in Bordeaux, and at Château Doisy-Vedrines makes a very correct Barsac along traditional lines, capably assisted by his son Eric. There is also some red wine made here, which is sold as Château la Tour

Vedrines, and in the early seventies Casteja started to produce a dry white wine on the property which was christened Chevalier de Vedrines. This latter experiment, started as a boost to the economy of the property, was so successful that demand soon far outstripped supply. Chevalier de Vedrines, of which there is also a red version, is now a branded wine, skilfully blended from wine purchased from other properties, and marketed by Roger Joanne; very little of the blend is now produced at Château Doisy-Vedrines.

The 'vin liquoreux' of Doisy-Vedrines comes from a mixture of 80% Semillon and 20% Sauvignon grapes, the latter variety giving the wine a delightful freshness. The vineyard has a typically Barsac soil, a mixture of reddish sandy clay and fine gravel, and is well situated on a gentle, south-west-facing slope.

Fermentation takes place in casks, in which the wine ages for about 18 months before bottling. The resulting wine is a delicate Barsac of great quality with a very full flavour, developing many hidden nuances and deepening to a lovely dark golden colour as it matures in bottle.

The atmosphere at Château Doisy-Vedrines is very much that of a family home, and the old house is furnished with love and taste. Pierre Casteja is a great connoisseur of the wines of Bordeaux, and is recognised as having an extremely good palate. He showed me tasting notes from the series of blind tastings which he and a group of friends hold regularly, and they included some truly memorable wines from all the classic Bordeaux vintages; I would give my eye-teeth to have been a fly on the rim of the glass at any of these occasions! He is a fund of anecdotes about the Bordeaux wine scene, most of which are unrepeatable. He also told me two things which stuck in my mind; for the wines of Sauternes and Barsac, a truly great vintage can only happen if the whole harvest can be picked wearing sandals, and, secondly, any vintage that starts on 13 September, whether for the white or red wines of Bordeaux, is destined to be a great year. There is much truth in both these adages; 1962 and 1983 were 'sandal' vintages, and picking started on 13 September in 1947 and in 1982.

TECHNICAL INFORMATION

General

Appellation:	Barsac
Area under vines:	20 hectares
Average production:	2,500 cases
Distribution of vines:	In one block
Owner:	Société Civile du Château Doisy-Vedrines
Administrator:	M. Pierre Casteja
Régisseur:	M. Eric Casteja
Consultant Oenologist:	M. Llorca

Viticulture

Geology:	Red clay and fine gravel on limestone subsoil
Grape varieties:	80% Semillon, 20% Sauvignon
Pruning:	A cot for Semillon, Guyot Simple for Sauvignon
Rootstock:	420A, Riparia Gloire, 3309, 101–14
Vines per hectare:	6,600
Average yield per hectare:	14–15 hectolitres
Replanting:	As necessary to maintain average vine age of 25 years

Vinification

Temperature of fermentation:	18°C average
Age of casks:	⅓ new each vintage
Time in cask:	18 months
Fining:	Bentonite at fermentation
Filtration:	Light, sur plaque, at bottling
Type of bottle:	Bordelaise blanche

Commercial

Vente Directe:	No
Sales:	Through Roger Joanne and other négociants
Agents oveseas:	Yes, for information contact: Roger Joanne, B.P.9, Fargues St. Hilaire, 33370 Tresses
Visits:	Yes, by appointment Telephone: 56 21 20 15

THE TASTING AT CHATEAU DOISY-VEDRINES, 2 February 1985
J.S., Monsieur and Madame Pierre Casteja, Eric Casteja

1983 Pale straw. Slight whiff of sulphur due to recent racking, but still has good 'rot' bouquet. Very nice and concentrated, honeyed flavour, distinctly pourriture-affected grapes. Lovely long aftertaste – will be a really good Barsac in time.

1982 Pale, bright gold. Bouquet excellent and concentrated, full of ripe fruit a little more closed than the '83. Lovely complexity of honeyed sweetness and sun-warmed grapes. Very good, but a shade less elegance than '83.

1976 Lovely, dark gold. Nose rich and full of flowers and ripe grapes. Silky luscious flavour, has the proper taste of 'noble rot'. Very good Barsac, coming into full bloom.

CHATEAU
Guiraud
SAUTERNES

Château Guiraud, one of the largest estates in the Sauternes district, is situated on the right-hand side of the D8 as you drive from Barsac towards La Saubotte. It is well signposted, and a long, rather bumpy drive takes you to the front of the château.

The house is beautiful, and basically very old. There has been a dwelling here since the 16th century, and probably earlier, when it was called Château Bayle, the name under which it was classified as a Premier Cru in the 1855 classification. As it stands now, the format of the château is mainly 19th century, when it was considerably extended, and the top floor added.

Shortly after the 1855 classification the name of the château was changed to Guiraud, which was almost certainly the name of the owning family. In 1862 Guiraud was bought by the Bernard family, under whose direction wines of great quality were made, winning 1st prize at the

Exposition Universelle in Paris in 1900, and being placed Hors Concours at Antwerp in 1904. Guiraud changed hands once more in 1935, when it was purchased by M. Rival for FF1,000,000. The house was not lived in by M. Rival, but it was occupied by the German army in the last war, witnessed by the SS and swastika emblems still to be seen in an unmodernised room on the first floor. Guiraud remained unoccupied until its purchase in 1981 by the Canadian Narby family, industrial magnates whose wealth derives principally from shipping.

Hamilton Narby, a man of only 30, but possessed of bull-like determination and passionate love for his property, found himself at the age of only 25 in the enviable position of having the means to do exactly what he wanted with his life.

Educated in France, having attended the University of Grenoble, Hamilton decided that France was the best country in the world to live in, and

265

that agriculture, and in particular viticulture, was to be his métier. The family had always been lovers of Bordeaux wines, so it was to this magical south-western corner of France that he took himself. Armed with an introduction to the charming Bordeaux savant, Hugues Lawton, he started on his quest. Having looked at many properties, including Crus Classés in the Médoc, he eventually plumped for Guiraud, a choice that may have in part been influenced by his father's penchant for fish, and the potential for dry white wine production at the property!

Fascinated and attracted by the history of the Sauternes area, Hamilton Narby told me the legend of the birth of Sauternes, the vin liquoreux that we know today. Apparently during the 1840s, the owners of a local château, who were absentee landlords living in Paris, decided to pay their annual visit, as was then the custom, with a party of friends for a holiday of pastoral delights during the vintage. The journey by carriage was long and fraught with hazards, and the party was delayed by some three weeks. The staff at the château, mindful of their station, and not wishing to spoil the rural idyll of their lords and masters, touched not a grape, though the harvest, for traditional dry white wine, was perfectly ready. The house-party finally arrived, and the vintage took place, though the grapes were shrivelled raisins, and clearly fit for nothing; but, they thought, 'noblesse oblige'. The resulting wine was put to one side as being of academic interest only, until a visit was paid by one of the Russian Grand Dukes, a brother to the Tsar, Constantin by name; he tasted this sweet wine, pronounced it delicious and bought the entire vintage for the Russian Imperial court. The taste caught on, and the Russian nobility, always eager for anything modish and French, developed an insatiable appetite for 'vin liquoreux' from Sauternes, and from there the demand spread and grew.

It is noteworthy that at the great classification of 1855 there were no less than 14 Premiers Crus in the area and one Premier Cru Exceptionnel, d'Yquem, whilst the red wines of the Médoc could muster only three, with Haut-Brion from Pessac as the fourth.

Hamilton believes very strongly that, with the application of funds and minute attention to quality, the wines of Guiraud, and Sauternes in general, can regain their former glory. It is for him a supreme exercise in mental and cultural stimulation, and I, for one, believe that he will succeed.

Of the total estate of 118 hectares, 55 are currently under white vines, and 16 devoted to the production of a red wine, sold as 'Le Dauphin' under the appellation Bordeaux Supérieur; red wine has been made at Guiraud since 1947, and sold as Pavillon Rouge until the Narby family bought the property in 1981 and changed the name, partly to

avoid confusion with other marques with similar names, and partly because a dolphin figures on the Narby coat of arms. Another Narby innovation was to start the production of an excellent dry white wine, sold as Château Guiraud 'G', of which an average of 3,000 cases are made each year.

The major capital investment in the property is evident wherever you look. For the vinification of the sweet white wine, an impressive computerised cuvier has been installed; a range of stainless-steel vats of varying capacity can be temperature-controlled down to −4°C from a central control panel, which allows the juice of each day's harvest to be fermented in perfect condition before transfer to barrels for ageing. This completely does away with the need for sulphur for fermentation control, and apart from Château d'Yquem, Guiraud is the only property to boast such a facility. A separate new fermentation unit for the dry white wine has been installed in the old stables, where there were still 14 horses when Hamilton Narby arrived in 1981! There is also a further separate unit for the vinification of the red wine, and a large stock warehouse. All this re-building and re-equipment has been done within the old buildings, retaining the original style and appearance of the property.

TECHNICAL INFORMATION

General

Appellation:	Sauternes, Premier Cru Classé	Density of planting:	4,000 vines per hectare
		Yield per hectare:	*White* Sauternes 18 hectolitres
	Bordeaux Blanc ('G')		Sec 50 hectolitres
	Bordeaux Supérieur (Le Dauphin, Red)		*Red* 45 hectolitres
		Replanting:	Permanent rotation 5 hectares per annum
Area under vines:	*White* 55 hectares		
	Red 16 hectares	*Vinification*	
Production:	Château Guiraud, Sauternes:8,000 cases	Added yeasts:	None
		Length of maceration:	Red and 'G' traditional
	Château Guiraud, 'G': 3,000 cases	Temperature control:	Computerised thermo-refrigeration
	Le Dauphin, rouge; 10,000 cases	Type of vat:	Stainless steel of multiple capacities
Distribution of vines:	In one block	Age of casks:	50% new, 50% casks of one vintage
Owner:	Société Civile Agricole de Château Guiraud	Time in cask:	2½ years (Sauternes)
Director:	Hamilton Narby	Type of bottle:	Grand Cru Bordelaise
Maître de Chai:	Roland Dubile		
Régisseur:	Xavier Planty	*Commercial*	
Oenological Consultant:	Professor Sudraut	Vente Directe:	Yes
		Direct Ordering:	Yes
Viticulture		Exclusivity:	None
Geology:	Sand, gravel and clay	Agents abroad:	Yes
Grape varieties:	*White* 47% Sauvignon, 51% Semillon, 2% Muscadelle	Visits:	Telephone 56 63 61 01
	Red 50% Merlot, 50% Cabernet Sauvignon		Hours 0900 to Midday, 1400 to 1800
Pruning:	Bas – 2 buds		

THE TASTING AT CHATEAU GUIRAUD,
1 October 1984
J.S., Hamilton Narby

1983 Very pale, star-bright, young colour. Muted bouquet of fruit and new wood, no great subtlety as yet, but beginning to show. Tremendous weight and depth of flavour. Voluptuous taste that stays long and beautifully in the mouth. Will be a great Sauternes from a great year.
1981 Pale, clear gold, beginning to darken a shade.

Lovely, rich fragrance, honeyed and complex. Delicious and perfumed in the mouth, long, with the right balance of acidity, fruit and pourriture concentration. A wine to wait for. (Won a Gold Medal at Macon. First vintage harvested by H. Narby.)
1979 Perceptibly darker. Powerful, aromatic nose, with more attack than the 1981. Big, open, with great richness. A typical Sauternes of Grand Cru quality, but lacking the finesse and elegance of 1981. (Won Gold Medal at the Comice Agricole. Although not harvested by H. Narby, was assembled and bottled by him.)

CHATEAU

Nairac

BARSAC

As you drive south on the NI13 from Bordeaux to Langon, Château Nairac is the first property on your right as you enter the village of Barsac. Turn right immediately before you reach the château, and the gateway is on your left.

Château Nairac is one of the loveliest houses in the Sauternes area, which is hardly surprising, since the great Victor Louis was the architect. We know this for sure, as his original drawings were found in one of his portfolios when an exhibition was mounted in 1980 to celebrate his bicentenary.

The Nairac family, who gave their name to the property, were powerful négociants and ship-builders in Bordeaux during the 18th century, and had a fine town house, the Hôtel Nairac in the Cours de Verdun, also Louis-designed. The family dispersed at the time of the French Revolution; there are still Nairacs living in Holland, whither one branch of the family fled; a Charles-Auguste Nairac was Burgermeister of the town of Barneveld from 1841–1883, one Diane Nairac is a translator, living in Paris and there are Nairacs also living in Mauritius. Tom Heeter tells me that on several occasions he has received unannounced visits from members of the Nairac family, and he is always pleased to welcome them 'home'.

At the beginning of the 19th century, Château Nairac came into the possession of a family named Burnet-Capdeville, who also owned Château Broustet nearby, and appear as the owners in the 1855 classification when Broustet-Nairac was nominated a Deuxième Cru. Evidently the Burnet-Capdevilles made excellent wine, for in 1867 at the Exposition Universelle in Paris, Nairac won a Silver Medal in competition with all the sweet white wines of France and Germany. Tom wishes that more such international competitions for great 'vins liquoreux' were held today. The vineyard suffered terribly with the phylloxera beetle, and Capdeville even tried his hand at making red wine.

Just before the First World War, Nairac was bought by a family named Mas-Perpezat, who ran it successfully for many years. The next proprietor, a land speculator, was not interested in making wine, and when Tom and Nicole Heeter came here in 1971, both house and vineyard were in poor shape.

Tom, a wine buff from Dayton, Ohio, originally came to Bordeaux to work as a 'stagiaire' at Château Giscours, where he met and married the daughter of the house Nicole Tari. To say that Tom was passionate about his wine would be grossly understating the case. He is, at times, almost manic. Château Nairac was lucky in Tom and Nicole, for they both did much to restore both ambience and reputation. He took the hard and correct line for the production of fine Barsac – severe pruning, conscientious and expensive picking of the botrytis-affected grapes in series of from three to as many as ten 'tris', fermentation in new oak casks and above all, rigorous selection. The result of this policy can be heart-breaking in 'off' years, for it can mean, as in 1977 and 1978, that no wine at all is bottled under the château's label; the other side of the coin, however, is that in good years Nairac produces beautiful, elegant and luscious wine in the very best tradition of the area. Nicole, on the other hand, was and is a promoter par excellence; she is also an admirable home-maker, cook and gourmet of considerable expertise. A public-relations 'natural', she has done great things for Nairac and the wine of the Sauternais in general, editing, with the aid of the great chefs of the South-West, a collection of recipes to match the great 'vins liquoreux' of the region under the title *La Grande Cuisine au Barsac-Sauternes*. The aim was to encourage people to drink these superb wines on a wider variety of occasions and with a far broader selection of complementary dishes. Her crusade was absolutely justified; over the past fifty years, the wines of Barsac and Sauternes have tended to be relegated to the end of the meal and served with – and overpowered by – over-sweet and cloying desserts. They are, in fact, delicious on their own as apéritifs, with fish and shellfish, foie-gras – divine marriage – and are superb with tangy blue cheese like Roquefort, English Stilton or Dolcelatte.

Sadly Tom and Nicole are now divorced, but Tom staunchly carries on the campaign at Nairac with continuing success. On the morning that I visited him in early October of 1984 he was putting out a promotional mailing-sheet to all his customers, licking and stuffing envelopes between puffs at the inevitable Havana that is almost a permanent part of his face, talking to me with authority and knowledge about his property, its wine and history, worrying about the weather prospects for the '84 vintage, and finally, before I left, conducting a bus-load of American tourists on a tour of the chais and vineyard, followed by an instructive talk and tasting. Château Nairac makes fine Barsac, and deserves to succeed.

A letter from Tom in April 1985 tells me that he is quite happy about the 1984 vintage.

TECHNICAL INFORMATION

General

Appellation:	Barsac
Area under vines:	15.26 hectares
Average production:	Very variable, but around 2,000 cases
Distribution of vines:	13 hectares around the château, the rest mainly touching Climens
Owner:	M. and Mme. Thomas Heeter-Tari
Régisseur, maître de chai:	M. Tom Heeter
Consultant Oenologist:	M. Sudraut

Viticulture

Geology:	Gravel
Grape varieties:	90% Semillon, 6% Sauvignon, 4% Muscadelle
Pruning:	A cot
Rootstock:	Riparia Gloire
Vines per hectare:	6,600
Average yield per hectare:	Variable, but around 15 hectolitres before 'selection'
Replanting:	As necessary

Vinification

Added yeasts:	Yes, since 1977

Length of fermentation:	5 to 6 weeks in cask
Temperature of fermentation:	15–17°C
Control of fermentation:	By watering down the floor of the chai, or by heating the chai if too cool
Age of casks:	50% to 60% new each vintage
Time in cask:	From 2 to 3 years
Fining:	Bentonite
Type of bottle:	Bordelaise blanche

Commercial

Vente Directe:	Yes
Direct ordering at château:	Yes
Agents overseas:	Yes, contact M. Tom Heeter, Château Nairac, Barsac, 33720 Podensac for information
Visits:	Yes, for appointment telephone: 56 27 16 16

THE TASTING AT CHATEAU NAIRAC,
2 October 1984
J.S., Tom Heeter, sundry tourists

1980 Fine, medium-light golden. Nose delicate, with good botrytis fruit. Rich and elegant, silky, with subtle nuances of raisins and honey, with a lovely lingering aftertaste. Will be a great vintage that will keep and improve for many years.

1975 Quite a deep gold, but still has a slight greeny tinge. Luscious fruit on nose, honeyed. Beautiful, rich and honeyed, but in no way cloying. Has all the finesse and elegance of a fine Barsac, and can be kept a long while. Super.

CHATEAU
De Rayne-Vigneau
SAUTERNES

Rayne-Vigneau lies to the left of the small D125e, that leads down the hill from the village of Sauternes towards Preignac.

In the 17th century the land on which the present vineyard is situated was the property of a Monsieur La Vigneau, who gave his name to the estate. The first part of the name derives from the château's 19th-century owner, the Baron de Rayne, whose widow, a member of the great Pontac family, was recorded as the owner when the vineyard was designated a Premier Cru in the 1855 classification.

The wine made here in the second half of the 19th century certainly seems to have been of superb quality, surpassing even the wine of d'Yquem itself on some occasions. In 1867 there was a gigantic blind tasting, a sort of competition between the wines of France and Germany to determine the best sweet wine in the world, and Rayne-Vigneau took the prize with its 1861 vintage.

The de Rayne family retained ownership of the vineyard until 1961, when they sold the vines and winemaking buildings away from the château to a négociant by the name of Raoux. It was a member of the de Rayne family, the Vicomte de Roton, a well-known local writer and journalist, who used the *nom de plume* Notor, who made a particular study of the rather remarkable geology of the Rayne-Vigneau 'butte' or outcrop. It appears that the glacial shift of Pyrenean soil that formed this land mass contained a substantial quantity of precious and semi-precious stones, of which he amassed an important collection. It contained white sapphires, jasper, various types of agate, onyx, cornelian, chalcedony and quartz, and is now in the hands of museums and private collectors. De Roton lived to be 98, and his mother before him reached 101 – a tribute, perhaps, to the life-giving quality of the wines of Sauternes.

In 1971 the property changed hands again, and passed in a very sad state in to the hands of the

270

present owners, the Bordeaux firm of Mestrezat S.A. The château itself is still entirely separate from the wine side of the property, which has benefited from the injection of much capital investment. The area under vines has been greatly increased, and the chai and cuvier are equipped with the latest in vinous techology. The wine ferments in huge stainless-steel vats of double thickness, and the temperature is controlled down to between 19 and 20°C by an automatic system of circulating coolant.

It would, I think be fair to say that the commercially-minded owners have opted for the production of a high-yield – for Sauternes – good-quality wine that will appeal to the newly emerging generation of Sauternes drinker, rather than the ultra-expensive, traditionally made 'vin liquoreux' that is made, for example at Château d'Yquem or Château Rieussec. Survival is the name of the game in the troubled Sauternes region, and Mestrezat have found one way of overcoming the almost insoluble problems. They also produce a crisp, dry white wine that sells under the label 'Le Sec de Rayne-Vigneau'.

I found both the sweet and the dry wine to be of more than acceptable quality, though the former lacks the complexity and ageing potential of more traditionally vinified Sauternes. A second wine of the vin liquoreux is sold as Clos l'Abeilley.

TECHNICAL INFORMATION

General

Appellation:	Sauternes (Vin liquoreux)
	Bordeaux (Rayne Sec)
Area under vines:	65 hectares
Average production:	14,500 cases (total)
Distribution of vines:	In one block
Owner:	Société Civile du Château de Rayne-Vigneau
Administrator:	M. J.-P. d'A. de la Beaumelle
Maître de Chai:	M. Cyrille Rey
Oenologist:	M. Bernard Monteau
Consultant Oenologist:	M. Sudraut

Viticulture

Geology:	Gravel
Grape varieties:	60% Semillon,
	40% Sauvignon
Pruning:	A cot and Guyot Simple
Rootstock:	196.17, 101–14, SO4
Vines per hectare:	7,700, 6,600 and 5,000

Average yield per hectare:	20 hectolitres

Vinification

Added yeasts:	Selected strains
Temperature of fermentation:	19–20°C
Control of fermentation:	By circulation of coolant in double-walled vats
Type of vat:	Stainless steel
Age of casks:	18–24 months
Fining:	Silica gel and gelatine
Type of bottle:	Bordelaise lourde

Commercial

Vente Directe:	No
Sales:	Through Mestrezat SA and other négociants
Visits:	Yes, by appointment
	Telephone: 56 52 11 46

THE TASTING AT CHATEAU DE RAYNE-VIGNEAU, 16 January 1985
J.S., M. Olivier Merceron, M. Cyrille Rey

Rayne Sec

1984 (In vat.) Very light pale colour, greeny tinge. Wine was so cold that nothing was detectable on the nose. Very light, crisp, dry – typical young Sauvignon.

1983 Medium-light gold. Not much on nose, but clean, slightly Sauterney. Much more evolved than '84, fruit showing ripe, refreshing acidity. Nice balance, good to drink young.

Chateau de Rayne-Vigneau, Sauternes

1984 (In vat.) Light yellow colour. Fruity, aromatic bouquet, with no rot. Lots of aromatic fruit in mouth, but no hint of pourriture.

1983 Medium golden colour. Light but luscious fruit on nose. Full and rich without being cloying. Well-made wine, the style of Sauternes at which the owners are aiming.

1982 Good medium golden, a shade darker than '83. Nose OK, but less aromatic and fruity than '83. Less acidity, more sugary and concentrated than '83 – not such a good wine.

CHATEAU
Rieussec
SAUTERNES

Château Rieussec is to be found on the right-hand side of the small D8 road as you drive from Langon towards the village of Haut-Bommes. It is about 4 km out of Langon, just before the cross-roads where the D8 becomes the D116e.

Before the French Revolution, Rieussec belonged to a religious order based in Langon, but their properties were confiscated and sold off as a 'Bien National'. The vineyard has known many owners since then, but at the time of the classification of 1855, when it was accorded the rank of Premier Cru, it belonged to a M. Mayne, presumably the owner also at Château du Mayne in Barsac. The last owner before Albert Vuillier bought Rieussec in 1971 was M. Balaresque, who had acquired the property twenty years earlier from an American named Berry who had run it in partnership with his French half-brother, the Vicomte du Bouzet. The estate had formerly been in the hands of the Gasqueton family, owners of Châteaux Calon-Ségur and Capbern-Gasqueton in St Estèphe.

In spite of its numerous changes of ownership, and the fact that Château Rieussec has been almost permanently under the direction of absentee land-lords, the wine has maintained a surprisingly high standard of quality and reputation. Since 1971 Albert Vuillier and his wife have lived in the comfortable but modest accommodation, and the wine has benefited greatly from the personal care and attention of this retiring, courteous but extre-mely able winemaker. Albert and Chantal Vuillier are fervent and active supporters of the traditional 'vins liquoreux' of Sauternes and have laboured

valiantly and successfully against all the problems and adversities that beset the Sauternais for thir-teen years. In 1984 an offer was made by the Domaines des Barons Rothschild, owners of Lafite and Duhart-Milon in Pauillac, which the Vuilliers found acceptable, though Albert will remain here for a time in a consultant capacity. It is encouraging to see important investors like the Rothschilds buying into Sauternes vineyards, and goes some way towards supporting my theory that this hard-pressed area is about to enjoy a long-deserved renaissance. I shall be fascinated to watch the progress of Château Rieussec over the coming years, since I firmly believe that the only path for the Sauternais to follow is to make the wine that only they in the whole world can make; the methods of producing such wine are expensive, and the only way to arrive at a correct end product is to follow these precepts, sacrificing quantity for quality, and to charge accordingly for the wine. In order to reach the level of excellence at which one can demand an economic price for a really fine Sauternes, a situation currently enjoyed by neigh-bouring Yquem, three ingredients are required – technical knowledge, patience and capital. Vuillier has the knowledge, and the Rothschilds can sup-ply the capital that allows the luxury of patience. Only time will show the end result.

Apart from the fermentation, which is now con-ducted in vats of stainless steel, the vinification of Château Rieussec is conducted along traditional lines, the wine spending anywhere between 18 and 30 months in wood, depending on the characteristics of each vintage. About 35% of the casks used are renewed each vintage. Selection is very strict, and a large proportion of the crop is sold under a second label, Clos Labère, also entitled to the Sauternes appellation. There is an excellent dry white wine produced at Château Rieussec, made from the first grapes harvested, unaffected by the pourriture that is so essential for the Grand Vin; it is pale in colour, clean, crisp and refreshing, and is called simply 'R'. About 2,000 cases are made each year, and must form a welcome and stable source of revenue in the always uncertain balance sheet of a Sauternes property.

Château Rieussec will always be rather special for me, firstly because of the warmth of the Vuilliers' hospitality and secondly because my first introduction to the marvellous combination of Sauternes and Roquefort was by way of a complimentary glass of Château Rieussec 1970 in the Auberge des Vignes in the village of Sauternes. On my first visit to the château in the summer of 1982, the Vuilliers gave me a most memorable evening, starting with a bottle of the 1971 drunk as an apéritif in the ivy-clad tower that commands a wonderful view of the vine-covered slopes, followed by the most delicious dinner, accompanied by numerous vintages of this fine Premier Cru Sauternes.

TECHNICAL INFORMATION

General

Appellation:	Sauternes		
Area under vines:	60 hectares		
Average production:	4,500 cases		
Distribution of vines:	In one block	Temperature of	
Owner:	Château Rieussec S.A.	fermentation:	18–20°C
President-Director-		Type of vat:	Stainless steel
General:	M. Albert Vuillier	Age of casks:	35% new each vintage
Régisseur/Maître de		Time in cask:	18–30 months
Chai:	M. Louis Gouze	Fining:	Varied according to the year
Consultant Oenologist:	M. Albert Bouyx	Filtration:	Sur terre
		Type of bottle:	Bordelaise blanche

conditions, such as external temperature, degree of alcohol, etc.

Viticulture

Geology:	Fine gravel on clay/limestone	*Commercial*	
Grape varieties:	80% Semillon, 19%	Vente Directe:	Yes
	Sauvignon, 1% Muscadelle	Direct ordering from	
Pruning:	Guyot Simple (6 to 7 buds)	chateau:	Yes
Rootstock:	SO4, 420A, Riparia Gloire	Sales:	Through the négociants
Vines per hectare:	7,000	Agents overseas:	Contact château for
Average yield per			information
hectare:	13 hectolitres		Château Rieussec,
Replanting:	By a planned 50-year rotation		Fargues de Langon,
			33210 Langon
Vinification		Visits:	Yes, by appointment
Length of maceration:	15 days to 2 months,		Telephone; 56 63 31 02
	according to various		Hours: 0900–1700 (except
			weekends and holidays)

THE TASTING AT CHATEAU RIEUSSEC,
18 January 1985
J.S., Albert Vuillier

'R' de Château Rieussec

1983 Clear, pale gold. Honeyed, Sauternais nose. Round and rich, with a good length; has suggestion of sweetness although essentially dry with lovely clean fruit.
1982 Similar colour to 1983. Nose not giving as much, but has honeyed undertones. Drier than the '83, has

suggestion of new wood, more complex and backward than the younger wine. Excellent.

Château Rieussec, Sauternes

1983 Quite deep gold. Extraordinarily honeyed pourriture bouquet. Remarkable concentration of rich fruit and taste of noble rot. A beautiful classic Sauternes of great length. Will keep and improve.
1982 Star-bright, medium gold. Lovely nose of fruit and flowers, some pourriture, but light and fresh. Luscious, but quite light. Already very attractive and drinkable.

CHATEAU

Suduiraut

SAUTERNES

Take the Route Nationale 113 from Bordeaux in
the direction of Langon. Some 40 km south of
Bordeaux, you wll come to the village of Preignac. In the village, take the second turning right,
the D8 E4, signposted to Villandraut; go over a
level crossing, over the Autoroute, and you will
shortly come to the gateway to Château Suduiraut, well-marked, on your right.

The label of Suduiraut bears the legend 'Ancien
Cru de Roy'. There are two schools of thought as
to the origin of these words, and perhaps the truth
lies in a mixture of the two. It is possible that a M.
Duroy who married one of the lady owners in the
distant past may have added the motto, or the
words could refer to the special subsidy that was
paid to Château Suduiraut by Louis XIV in recognition of the quality of its wines. What a pity that
such subsidies are not awarded to the hard-pressed
Sauternais today!

The present château was largely constructed in the
mid-17th century, on the site of an earlier fortress
that had been razed to the ground on the orders of
the notorious Duc d'Epernon, Governor of Aquitaine under Louis XIII, in the course of a wrangle
with the Bordeaux Parliament. This same gentleman owned and lived at Château Beychevelle in
the Médoc. The rebuilt château is at the same time
imposing and attractive; the approach is by a long
drive, with a small lake to the left, and the façade
of the house, turreted at either end, looks onto a
courtyard formed by two wings which are joined
by wrought-iron railings. The right-hand of these
two wings is the only part of the original fortress
left standing.

The other façade of Suduiraut looks over a fine
park, laid out by the great landscape gardener, Le
Nôtre, creator of the gardens at Versailles. In the
centre there is a fine triangular pediment bearing
the crests of the Suduiraut and Duroy families,
and over the front door, a lovely wrought-iron
balcony that came from the Hôtel de Richelieu in
Paris.

Château Suduiraut is currently back in its rightful
position, making one of the very best, correct
wines of the Premier Cru Sauternes. One of the
less glorious periods of its winemaking history
preceded the Second World War, but much was

done by M. Fonquernie, a wealthy cloth manufacturer, who bought Suduiraut in 1940. The property now belongs to his five daughters; Mme.
Olivier is Director, Mme. Frouin handles the sales
side of the estate from her Paris ofice. They are
most ably assisted by their régisseur, M. Pierre
Pascaud, a passionate believer in the wines of
Sauternes, and himself an owner of a small property in Barsac, Château Pernaud near Doisy-
Vedrines. Pascaud maintains that Sauternes is all

274

about high-quality 'vin liquoreux', made in the traditional way in this, the only corner of the world where microclimatic and soil conditions combine to make it possible; he is proud to say that at Suduiraut there is no dry white wine and no red wine made.

Great emphasis is placed on the importance of new wood in the making of fine Sauternes. One-third of the casks are new each vintage – the wine spends its first year in cuve, and it is then aged for 18 months to 2 years in wood. Pruning is among the severest I have seen, even in Sauternes – usually only one bud is left. This has the double benefit of a tremendous concentration of sugar and flavour in the grapes, and a harvest that is usually about 8 days in advance of most of the neighbouring properties.

1978 was Pierre Pascaud's first vintage at Suduiraut, and the quality was certainly well above average for that year in Sauternes. In good years Château Suduiraut has a lovely depth of colour, a fragrant honey bouquet, and a delicious complex and honeyed flavour typical of good Sauternes at its best. M. Pascaud's favourite dishes to accompany Sauternes are duck's liver, cooked in Sauternes, and any fish with a beurre blanc sauce.

TECHNICAL INFORMATION

General

Appellation:	Sauternes
Area under vines:	72 hectares (a further 10 hectares are being planted)
Average production:	7,700 to 10,000 cases
Distribution of vines:	In one block
Owner:	S.A.R.L. Héritiers de Léopold Fonquernie
Director:	Mme. Olivier
Sales Manager:	Mme. Frouin
Régisseur:	Pierre Pascaud
Maître de Chai:	Claude Laporte
Consultant Oenologist:	M. Llorca, Laboratoire Oenologique, Chambre d'Agriculture de la Gironde

Viticulture

Geology:	Gravel, clay
Grape varieties:	85% Semillon, 15% Sauvignon
Pruning:	A cot, very severe
Rootstock:	SO4, 420A, Riparia 3309
Vines per hectare:	6,850

Replanting:	2–3 hectares per year

Vinification

Length of fermentation:	15 days
Vats:	Stainless steel, 50 hectolitres
Age of casks:	⅓ new for each vintage, wine spends 1st year in vat
Filtration:	Sur terre before going in cask Sur plaque before bottling
Fining:	Bentonite at fermentation time
Bottle:	Bordelaise

Commercial

Vente Directe:	Yes
Direct ordering:	Yes
Agents in Foreign Countries:	Yes, contact office for details
Visits:	Yes: telephone 56 63 27 29 Monday to Friday Hours: 0900 to Midday, 1400 to 1800

THE TASTING AT CHATEAU SUDUIRAUT, 18 January 1985
J.S., M. Pascaud

1983 (In vat.) Light gold, with greeny tones. Bouquet still closed. Lightish, with delicate fruity sweetness and concentrated pourriture flavours. Complex, long, a great Sauternes for the future.

1982 (In cask.) Noticeably darker colour. Rich, honeyed bouquet beginning to emerge. Same concentrated, rich flavours, very long, but perhaps lacking some of the finesse of the '83.

1982 Crème de Tete – A special selection of 20 casks of the finest vats. Superb, rich and complex. Will be a tremendous wine.

CHATEAU
D'Yquem
SAUTERNES

Take the D8e from Preignac in the direction of Villandraut; cross the railway line by a level crossing, go over the Autoroute and Château d'Yquem is about 2 km out in the country on your right, at the top of a steep hill.

The situation of Château d'Yquem is in keeping with its origins as an early fortified castle, commanding extensive views of the surrounding countryside which must have made surprise attacks a virtual impossibility. The house as it stands today was started in the 16th century and completed in the 17th, when the estate belonged to a family called Sauvage d'Yquem. Just before the Revolution in 1785, Joséphine d'Yquem married the Comte Louis Amédée de Lur Saluces, whose family had been Seigneurs de Fargues since 1472,

when a de Lur Saluces married Isabel de Montferrand; Château de Fargues is still owned by the family. Château d'Yquem was Joséphine d'Yquem's dowry, and has remained in the de Lur Saluces family in an unbroken line ever since.

Only two years after this dynastic marriage, the ubiquitous Thomas Jefferson, later to become President of the United States of America, visited the region. He is on record as having said, 'The white wines of Sauternes are the best in France after Champagne and Hermitage Blanc, and M. de Lur Saluces makes the best of these.' In the 18th century the general taste was for sweet white wines, and the Sauternes area was already mainly devoted to the production of this sort of wine; the benefit of late picking was already well known,

276

and there is evidence that the practice of harvesting the grapes by passing through the vines more than once, only picking the ripest grapes each time, was also adopted at this time. It is generally agreed, however, that the vital ingredient of good dessert wine, the mushroom growth known as *botrytis cinerea*, or pourriture noble, was not fully understood until some time in the 19th century.

In the 1830s a man named Focke, who originated from the winelands of the Rhine, was proprietor of Château La Tour Blanche. German winemakers were well aware of the significance of the noble rot, or *Edelfaule* as it is called in German, and were already producing the fabulous honeyed wines of Beerenauslese and Trockenbeerenauslese quality. Focke was not slow to appreciate the natural microclimatic conditions of Barsac and the Sauternais – the morning mists and sunny autumn days – that encourage the spores of *botrytis cinerea* to attack the skins of the ripe grapes – and is credited with being the first proprietor in the area to do so.

There is also a story – somewhat more romantic – concerning the first discovery of the beneficial effects of the 'rot'. It seems that the 1847 vintage was picked far later than was then the custom, due to the then de Lur Saluces being detained by social obligations, which made him late for his annual visit to the château at vintage time – to start picking before the proprietor arrived would have been a dreadful act of lèse majesté! The grapes, shrivelled and concentrated by the fungus growth, produced a wine so totally different to the normal style of d'Yquem that the wine was put aside and forgotten. A decade later, Grand Duke Constantine, brother of the Tsar of all the Russias, visited the property and tasted the 1847; so overwhelmed was he by the extraordinary bouquet, richness and subtlety of the wine that he paid 20,000 gold francs for a tonneau, about four times the usual price of the day for d'Yquem. The taste of the Russian court at that time was for everything French; d'Yquem's fame rapidly spread throughout Europe's aristocracy, and from 1859 the château concentrated its efforts on producing 'botrytis' wine, rapidly followed by the other vineyards in this lucky corner. I say lucky because in the whole world only the Sauternes area, parts of the Rhine and Moselle, and the Tokay vineyards of Hungary enjoy the special microclimate that favours the correct development of the noble rot.

The importance of the Sauternes area in the mid-1800s can be judged by the great classification of 1855. Above all the rest, d'Yquem was awarded the classification of Grand Premier Cru Classé, but there were also no less than nine graded as Premier Cru, while only four red wines achieved this level of distinction; there are now eleven Premiers Crus, following two divisions of properties – Sigalas-Rabaud and Rabaud-Promis, and Lafaurie-Peyraguey and Haut-Peyraguey. Sadly, drinking habits and fashion change, and these changes have worked to the detriment of the Sauternais over the last half-century, though there are encouraging signs of a re-awakening of interest in these fabulous 'vins liquoreux'.

Of all the great Crus Classés of the Sauternes communes, Château d'Yquem has perhaps suffered least from the vicissitudes of popular taste. Doubtless this is due in part to the great wealth of the de Lur Saluces family and their consequent ability to ride out the storm; it is perhaps this same stability that has enabled them to keep up the immaculate standard of their wine, a standard that can only be maintained at enormous cost, resisting every temptation to cut corners, and sacrificing everything on the altar of excellence. The price asked by de Lur Saluces and his forebears for their liquid gold has always been high, but there has never been a shortage of devotees to pay it. A policy of releasing only 5,000 cases of the wine each year, spread among selected Bordeaux négociants, results in Alexandre de Lur Saluces receiving begging letters and telephone calls from all over the world, beseeching him to part with a few more cases, but he is adamant.

Why is d'Yquem so special, and what makes it so expensive? To answer the last question will provide the answers to the first. Primarily, as Alexandre de Lur Saluces points out, correctly made Sauternes is ruinously expensive to produce; he does not sell his wine expensively, it is rather the case that the other proprietors sell too cheap, thus creating a chicken-and-egg situation, since, if the income of the estate is insufficient, they cannot afford to make good Sauternes, but if they are not making good wine, they cannot ask higher prices. It is therefore hardly surprising that so many Sauternais are in such dire straits, and that so many châteaux change hands so often. Initially, vast capital resources are required, and it will be most interesting to see what will happen to neighbouring Château Rieussec, now that it has been acquired by the Domaines des Barons Rothschild of Lafite.

Let us attempt to analyse some of the costs of producing the precious liquid of Château d'Yquem. Firstly the soil – only the very best parts of the 102 hectares of vineyard entitled to the appellation are suitable, and at any one time only about 80 are in production, and these 80 hectares of special gravelly slopes have to be maintained and drained so as to give of their best. Only

organic fertiliser is used, and the 60 miles of drainage pipe installed by Alexandre's great-grandfather have to be regularly checked and kept in good repair. Some parts of the vineyard are so steep and difficult to work that horses were used right up till 1984, when technology produced suitable machinery to replace them. All this requires immense labour, as do the later stages of viticulture and vinification, and there is a permanent work-force of over forty people employed at Château d'Yquem. Here, as at other great wine properties, quality is only obtained at the expense of quantity; the vines are pruned with swingeing severity, and this, combined with the incredibly concentrating effect of the pourriture noble on the juices of the grapes, results in a yield equivalent, in a good year, of one glass of wine per vine.

Now to the harvest; a team of between 100 and 150 specially trained pickers, over and above the permanent employees, is brought in when the first grapes are at exactly the right state of rot. They will go through the vines on an average six times, picking only the grapes – yes, the individual grapes – that have reached the precise stage of maturity required; picking stops if there is rain or if it is too hot or too cold, and the army marches on its stomach! In 1964 as many as 13 'tris' were made, and in the end none of the wine was good enough to bear the d'Yquem label. This process can be extremely lengthy, and on several occasions the harvest has continued well into December.

In the 'réception des vendages' one's first reaction is surprise at the small scale of the vinification equipment. There are three small, vertical hydraulic presses, but these are more than adequate to cope with the minute quantities of grapes brought in on any one day. There are three pressings; the 'must' of each successive pressing decreases in volume as it increases in concentration of sugar. The juice is transferred rapidly into new oak casks, where the fermentation takes place over a period of between two weeks and a month, and stops naturally when the alcohol content reaches around 14°.

The wine then spends three years or more in cask, and there are three separate cask chais, the wine of each succeeding vintage being moved each year. During its long stay in oak, the wine is racked every three months, and vital 'ouillage', or topping-up, is carried out twice weekly, to eliminate contact with the air and consequent damages of oxidation. These operations result in the loss of over twenty per cent of each crop by evaporation.

We are not finished yet. The ultimate moment of arbitration is the 'sélection'. In spite of all the care and work involved, the standard at Château d'Yquem is so high that in some years no wine is allowed to carry the famous yellow label. This was the case in 1930, 1951, 1952, 1964, 1972 and 1974.

Perhaps this goes some way towards explaining the reasons for Yquem's price, and why it is one of the most highly prized and sought-after wines in the world.

Alexandre, Comte de Lur Saluces, and his family do not live at the château, but he is an active and conscientious proprietor, visiting the property regularly, and actively interested in every aspect of vinification, viticulture and the marketing of his wine. A small quantity of dry white is made, selling under the label Ygrec; it is a very good quality medium-dry wine, with good ageing potential, and contains a higher proportion of Sauvignon than the 'vin liquoreux' of Château d'Yquem. Because of the cost of production and tiny quantity made – around 2,500 cases – and, possibly, because it comes from Château d'Yquem, it is always expensive.

De Lur Saluces kindly opened a bottle of the 1980, which we drank in the rather chilly salon of the château while he talked to me about d'Yquem and what goes on there. I find the wine of Yquem

278

defeats my powers of description utterly; it has so many complex and subtle nuances of flavour – fruit, honey, flowers and blossoms, and no two vintages are ever alike. The 1980 was no exception, and the owner opined that it has great ageing potential. This was no surprise, as this is characteristic of almost every vintage of Yquem, though some have it to a more pronounced degree. I have especial memories of three astounding examples, all of which I shared with the late Martin Bamford, the first two at Château Loudenne, and the last at the table of Robert Carrier, when he lived at Hintlesham Hall in Suffolk. These were the 1949, 1959 and 1967 vintages. Any one of these constituted a tasting experience to spoil a man's palate for any other dessert wine for life.

TECHNICAL INFORMATION

General

Appellation:	Sauternes
Area under vines:	102 hectares, 80 in production
Average production:	5,500 cases
Distribution of vines:	One block
Owner:	M. le Comte Alexandre de Lur Saluces
Régisseur:	M. Pierre Meslier
Maître de Chai:	M. Guy Latrille
Oenologist:	M. Meslier, M. P. Ribereau Gayon, M. P. Sudraut, Chauvet

Viticulture

Geology:	Diverse
Grape varieties:	20% Sauvignon, 80% Semillon
Pruning:	À Cot
Rootstock:	Riparia Gloire, 420A

Vines per hectare:	6,500
Average yield per hectare:	From 9 to 11 hectolitres
Replanting:	3 hectares per annum

Vinification

Added yeasts:	No
Age of casks:	100% new each vintage
Time in cask:	3½ years
Fining:	Before bottling, albumen and bentonite
Filtration:	None
Type of bottle:	Frontignan

Commercial

Vente Directe:	No
Sales:	Through selected négociants
Visits:	Yes, professionals only
	Times: 1430, 1530 and 1630
	Monday to Friday

THE TASTING AT CHATEAU D'YQUEM,
11 January 1985
J.S., M. le Comte Alexandre de Lur Saluces

1980 Beautiful mid-golden colour. Delicious bouquet, redolent of flowers, honey and apricots. The flavour was incredibly rich and ripe without for an instant cloying the palate; we sat and drank the bottle over a period of an hour or so, and the flavour continually unfurled like the petals of a flower, revealing new delights with every mouthful. Superb – this is what Sauternes is all about.

Author's note
Alexandre de Lur Saluces wrote to me after my visit, promising to invite me to the next specialist trade tasting of Chateau d'Yquem. I look forward to this with immense pleasure, and shall certainly include notes of the occasion in the next edition of *Great Bordeaux Wines*.

ST EMILION

The medieval town of St Emilion lies on a hilltop some 40 km to the east of Bordeaux across the Dordogne river. Even were it not for the numerous fine vineyards and the delicious macaroons, which are a local speciality, St Emilion merits a detour in its own right. The steep, cobbled streets – hazardous in the rain – the lovely old limestone houses, the wine shops, and the church hewn out of the solid rock, attract tourists by the thousand in the summer. The square, where one may sit and enjoy a drink or a meal, resounds to a babel of many languages and the clicking of countless camera-shutters. I wrote many of the chapters of this book sitting here in the sun, though the uneven cobbles on which the tables of the little bar and crêperie stand gave rise to a few curious red stains on my pages!

The majority of the best vineyards of St Emilion are on the 'côtes' or slopes around the town itself; Château Cheval Blanc and Château Figeac lie some five kilometres to the west of the town, and enjoy a different soil, containing a goodly proportion of gravel, while the côtes vineyards are mostly on a mixture of clay and limestone. There are seven small communes surrounding the town which are entitled to the St Emilion appellation, St Christophe-des-Bardes, St Laurent-des-Combes, St Hippolyte, St Etienne-de-Lisse, St Pey d'Amens, Vignonet and St Sulpice-de-Faleyrens; there are also four communes north of the town, St Georges, Puisseguin, Montagne and Lussac, which are allowed to attach the name of St Emilion to that of their commune. None of the twelve Premiers Grands Crus are in these lesser communes, though they produce some very fine wines.

St Emilion wines were classified in 1955. They are divided into Premiers Grands Crus, of which there are twelve, two of which, Cheval Blanc and Ausone, head the list with the suffix 'A', and Grands Crus, which number more than seventy. There is also a further category of principal growths, numbering well over five hundred, as well as the properties of the lesser communes of which there are in excess of two hundred. The St Emilion appellation alone produces an average of over two million cases of wine a year, and the properties of St-Georges, Puisseguin, Montagne and Lussac St Emilion another million.

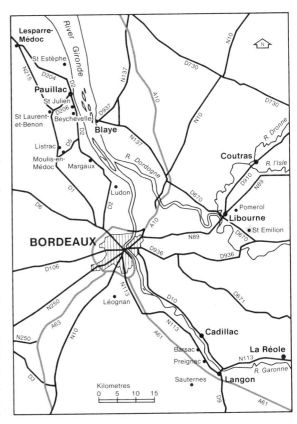

The wines of St Emilion are open, rounded and friendly, and tend to earlier maturity than their Médocain cousins; the dominant grape variety is the Merlot, followed by the Cabernet Franc, or Bouchet as it is known locally. The Premiers Grands Crus and many of the Grands Crus are capable of great finesse and elegance, and the two 'gravel' properties, Cheval-Blanc and Figeac, as well as Château Ausone, can rank with the best of Bordeaux red wines in terms of breed and ageing potential.

The St Emilionais, like their wines, are the most Burgundian, if they will forgive the word, of the Bordeaux wine-growers; this is certainly reflected in the restaurants of St Emilion, and one may eat very well at Chez Germaine, the Hostellerie Plaisance, the Logis de la Cadène and the Auberge de la Commanderie; the wine lists are, not surprisingly, very long on St Emilions.

CHATEAU
L'Angelus
ST EMILION

Leave St Emilion by the small country road which passes Château Canon and runs along the middle of the famous south-facing Côtes. After one kilometre, you will pass the château on your left; turn immediately left after the château into the yard in front of the graceful new sandstone buildings.

The de Bouard family have owned the property since the middle of last century, though their connection with the area and their interest in the wine business go back much further than that. In 1564 Georges du Bouard, a Counsel in the Bordeaux parliament, was Jurat de St Emilion.

The name of the property was originally Château Mazerat: in 1924 Hubert de Bouard's grandfather bought a small vineyard of three hectares called L'Angelus, but it was not until 1945 that Hubert's father and uncle regrouped the vineyards, then 21½ hectares, and changed the name to Château L'Angelus.

From 1963 to 1968 there was a period of expansion and modernisation, culminating in the purchase of three hectares from the neighbouring vineyard of Beausejor. Since 1979, when Hubert finished his oenological studies and started to manage the property, there has been further modernisation, including the building of the huge warehouse where the production of each vintage is kept between the bottling and collection for delivery and shipment, reorganisation of the *reception de vendange*, and the installation of eight gleaming stainless-steel cuves, each of 125 hl capacity.

Beneath the new buildings there is an extensive cellar holding some 30,000 bottles of older vintages; an average of 10% of each crop is set aside, so that there is always a quantity of mature L'Angelus available for the Bordeaux négociants to satisfy the demands of their restaurant and wine-merchant customers. This is an admirable practice and its wider adoption would, I am sure, benefit everyone from the proprietors to the consumer, who is all too often faced with a restaurant list containing only wines that are too young to be appreciated.

Château L'Angelus is owned by a family company. Hubert de Bouard de la Forest is responsible for day-to-day management, assisted by various cousins in the office. Fresh-faced, keen and passion-

ate about his wine, Hubert studied oenology under the famous Pascal Ribereau-Gayon. He is married with two young daughters; they do not live in the château at the moment, since it is not in good repair, but he hopes to rectify this situation in the next two or three years.

From some 24½ hectares of some of the best land in St Emilion, from a mixture of 50% Cabernet Franc, 45% Merlot and 5% Cabernet Sauvignon, Château L'Angelus produces a wine of quality and finesse; it is, justifiably, one of the most expensive Grands Crus Classés of St Emilion.

Until 1979, there were no wooden casks used at L'Angelus; the maturation took place for a period of 18 months to two years in concrete vats. Since 1979, however, possibly under the influence of

Ribereau-Gayon, an increasing proportion of each vintage is aged for a year to 16 months in new casks. In 1979 it was only 10%, but by 1983 it was over 65%. This wine is blended with the vat-aged wine before bottling, and I, for one, certainly noticed a definite change in style for the better, and an increased finesse in the wines of 1979 onwards.

TECHNICAL INFORMATION

General

Appellation:	Grand Cru Classé, St Emilion
Area under vines:	28 hectares
Production:	1,500 cases
Proprietor:	Hubert de Bouard de Laforest
Distribution of vines:	In one piece

Viticulture

Geology:	Chalky clay on the high ground, sandy clay on the 'côtes', with some alluvial clay
Grape varieties planted:	50% Cabernet Franc, 5% Cabernet Sauvignon, 45% Merlot
Pruning:	Guyot Simple
Rootstock:	Riparia, 3309, 101.14, 420A, 41B
Vines per hectare:	6,600
Yield per hectare:	30–45 hectolitres
Replanting:	By slow rotation

Vinification

Length of maceration:	3 weeks
Temperature of fermentation:	Circa 30°C
Regulation of fermentation:	Running water and refrigeration
Type of vat:	Stainless steel and concrete
Age of casks:	All new
Time in cask:	12 months
Fining:	Egg-whites

Commercial

Vente Directe:	No Sales exclusively through Bordeaux négociants
Agents in foreign countries:	Yes: contact château for addresses
Visits:	Yes, by appointment Telephone: 57 24 71 39 Hours for visits: 0830–1200, 1400–1800

THE TASTING AT CHATEAU L'ANGELUS, 4 September 1984
J.S., M. Hubert de Bouard de la Forest

1983 Very dense, deep red. Superb bouquet, full of power, fruit and tannins. A big wine of great potential, a quantity of fruit and plenty of tannin, but not aggressive. Will be a superb bottle in 5/6 years.

1982 Good, brilliant red. Bouquet a bit closed, but probably resulting from recent bottling. A generous, mouthfilling flavour; tannin more evident that the '83 – long aftertaste. (N.B. The 1982 had only been in bottle two or three weeks, so allowances should be made.)

1981 Lighter in colour than '82 or '83. Beautiful smell of cherries, ascribed by Monsieur Bouard to a vineyard that is wholly situated on the 'côtes'. Much tannin evident but fruit also; a wine to keep.

1980 Light colour, but good for 1980. Soft agreeable nose. A lightish wine, but excellent to drink now and for a few years; a really good 1980.

1979 Colour showing brownish tinges. Pleasant, slight mushroomy smell. Round, well balanced wine; good to drink in twelve months.

1978 Quite a light colour. Soft, fruity, and slightly roasted nose. Well balanced, with fruit and acidity in harmony. Can be drunk now and for several years.

1977 Light browny-red. Not much on the bouquet. A little lacking in fruit, but pleasant enough for this vintage. To drink now.

1976 Slight brownish tinge. Not very pronounced bouquet. Absolutely ready and good for current drinking.

1975 Surprisingly brown colour for a 1975. Soft and fruity bouquet, redolent of summer flowers. Tannin still predominant, but fruit sufficient to offset. A fine bottle to keep.

1974 Very light browny red. Delicate bouquet of spring flowers. Light and thinnish. To be drunk now.

CHATEAU
Ausone
ST EMILION

From the car-park outside the Maison du Vin in St Emilion, turn left down the grandiosely named Avenue 18th Mai 1945; after about 200 metres you will come to a fork in the road, with Berliquet and Canon to your right, and Ausone and Belair to your left. Follow the road to your left, and Ausone is clearly signposted after about 500 metres.

Château Ausone was so named in 1781, after the Latin poet Ausonius, who was born in Burdigala, the Roman name for Bordeaux, in AD 320. His early career was an academic one, teaching rhetoric in the Roman equivalent of a university in Bordeaux. One of his pupils, happily for Ausonius, later became the Emperor Gratianus, and in recognition of his services, appointed his former dominie as governor and later Consul of Gaul. The poet-politician loved the country around Bordeaux, and praises its beauty and its wine in his poems. He records that his large estate had some 40 hectares of vines, but a passing reference to the colours of these vines reflecting in the waters of the Garonne gives the lie to the long-held belief

that St Emilion was his home. He may, of course, have had another property in this part of the Gironde, and it is beyond doubt that the Romans planted vines at St Emilion, or Lucaniacum as they called it. There is clear evidence of this both at Ausone itself, and in the vineyards of Château Fonplegade; in both places one can see trenches cut into the limestone rock of the plateau, the method used by the Romans for planting their vines. The mosaic floors of a large Roman villa have been uncovered in the vineyards of Château la Gaffelière at the foot of Ausone's slopes, and the central motif in the main room is a vine in full fruit; there are also Roman ruins in an abandoned part of the vineyard behind the château at Ausone. Ausonius certainly praised the St Emilion wines, so although there is no direct evidence, the legend could easily be founded in fact.

As with most of St Emilion, the importance of Ausone as a quality vineyard does not truly begin until the 19th century, with the building of the bridges over the Garonne and the Dordogne and the coming of the railway, establishing easier

contact with the commercial centre of Bordeaux. Up to this time, the vineyards were mostly part of a more generalised agriculture, for the most part in the hands of peasant farmers; the wine they made was for home use and for sale in the locality. In 1808 the Ausone vineyards were gifted by one Jean Cantenat to his son Pierre. The property is first referred to as an autonomous vineyard in the 1868 edition of Cocks et Feret, when it had passed into the hands of a Monsieur Lafargue, a nephew of the Cantenats. It was listed as the fourth of the named 'Côtes' growths of St Emilion, after Belair, Troplong-Mondot and Canon, and was at that time producing only around 10 tonneaux of wine. Lafargue's widow appointed her nephew, Edouard Dubois-Challon to run the property, and under his aegis Ausone prospered and flourished. In the 1893 Cocks it had climbed to second place, and by the 1920s the wine enjoyed a reputation second to none on this side of the Dordogne river. I myself have been lucky enough to taste the '29 recently, and it was still remarkably alive and a fine example of that great year; and that was only a half-bottle.

Edouard Dubois-Challon bought the neighbouring Château Belair in 1916, and the properties have been run in tandem ever since, though the wines have always been kept totally apart, vinification and ageing being carried out in separate cuviers and cellars. Dubois-Challon had two children, a son named Jean, who became a senior and well respected figure in the St Emilion hierarchy, and a daughter, Cécile, who married Marcel Vauthier. Ausone now belongs 50% to Madame Dubois-Challon, the widow of Jean, who died in 1974, and 50% to the Vauthier family. The château, a Gothic mish-mash resulting from periodic additions and extensions, but nonetheless charm-

ing, is divided into two parts; one is occupied by Madame Dubois-Challon, and the other by the Vauthiers.

I think it is fair to say that for a period of about 25 years, from the early 50s to 1976, Ausone suffered a minor eclipse, and for no clear reason. I use the word 'minor' advisedly, since the level to which this wine had risen was so high, and it is a level to which it has happily now returned. At many châteaux this marginal but definite lowering of standards could be laid at the door of the disastrous spring frosts of 1956; this was certainly not the case with Ausone, since the main part of the vineyard that lies on the steep slope down from the château to the D122 was luckily unaffected. Whatever the cause, or combination of causes, may have been, 1975 saw the arrival of a remarkable young régisseur and oenologist, Pascal Delbeck, and since the excellent 1976 the wine of Château Ausone is once more firmly in the ascendant.

The comparatively tiny vineyard is situated mainly on the very sharply inclined slope that borders the left-hand side of the road as you approach the town of St Emilion from the main Libourne–Bergerac road, with small parcels both on the lower ground near La Gaffelière, and behind the house and buildings on the plateau. Some parts of the vineyard are so steep that they have had to be terraced to prevent erosion by rainfall, and still have to be worked by horses due to their inaccessibility by tractor. Vinification, too, is quintessentially traditional, fermentation and maceration still take place in immaculately maintained oak vats, while the newly installed stainless steel tanks are used principally for the malolactic fermentation and the assemblage. These new tanks are housed in a section of the

286

cuvier that is hermetically sealed so that the wine can be kept at an ideal 20–22°C for the malolactic fermentation.

Ageing is in traditional oak casks, 100% new each vintage, which lie in the cavernous underground chai, where the temperature varies by less than 2° throughout the year. This cellar is yet another quarry from which stone was hewn in past centuries for the building of the houses of St Emilion and the surrounding area; at one point there is a chimney, or light-well, glazed at the top, cut through some twenty feet of solid rock. In the small portion of the vineyard that lies directly above this underground cellar, there is a small 13th-century chapel, the floor of which is carpeted with human bones, unearthed when the vines were planted.

Madame Dubois-Challon is a charming lady, full of joie de vivre, with a lively sense of humour. She entertained me for an hour or so in her rather sombre Victorian drawing-room, in front of a cosy log fire, and was most apologetic that her wine was so scarce, and that she could not offer me more than a limited selection of vintages to taste. I was more than content to sample the last three vintages, as well as the elegant 1975, and I am happy to report that the reputation and price of the 'reborn' Château Ausone are well justified, fully meriting its classification of Premier Grand Cru Classé 'A', a rating only accorded to one other St Emilion, Château Cheval-Blanc.

TECHNICAL INFORMATION

General

Appellation:	St Emilion, Premier Grand Cru Classé 'A'
Area under vines:	7 hectares
Average production:	2,000 cases
Distribution of vines:	One block
Owner:	Madame Dubois-Challon and the Héritiers C. Vauthier
Régisseur/Wine maker:	M. Pascal Delbeck
Maître de Chai:	M. Lanau
Consultant Oenologist:	C.B.C.

Viticulture

Geology:	Clay/limestone
Grape varieties:	50% Merlot, 50% Cabernet Franc
Pruning:	Guyot Poussard
Rootstock:	41.B, 333.EM, 120A
Vines per hectare:	6,000
Average yield per hectare:	25 to 30 hectolitres
Replanting:	½ hectare every 4 years

Vinification

Added yeasts:	Own culture, 'pied de cuve'

Length of maceration:	3–4 weeks, depending on tasting
Temperature of fermentation:	28° to 31°
Type of vat:	Oak for alcoholic fermentation (50 hectolitres) Stainless steel for malolactic (30 hectolitres)
Vin de presse:	Part incorporated according to vintage, following tasting
Age of casks:	100% new each vintage
Time in cask:	16–22 months
Fining:	Egg-whites, in cask
Filtration:	None
Type of bottle:	Bordelaise lourde

Commercial

Sales:	Very limited, due to tiny production, through the négociants
Visits:	Yes, telephone: 57 24 70 94 or 57 24 70 26 Hours: 0900–1200, 1500–1700

THE TASTING AT CHATEAU BELAIR,
22 November 1984
J.S., Pascal Delbeck

1983 (In cask.) Deep ruby red. Nose good with rich fruit and vanilla smell of new oak. Rich, full flavour, good tannins. Very long in mouth. A real 'vin de garde', very complex with great potential.
1982 (Bottled September '84.) Deep, rich red. Fine, elegant bouquet, quite closed up. A little fatigued from bottling, and therefore somewhat muted; nonetheless has plenty of puissance, a wealth of fruit and the right sort of tannin – bags of backbone. Will be a great wine.
1981 Same lovely, dark red. Nose beginning to open up, with lots of fruit and some oakiness. Structure and style beginning to show; excellent balance, long; will be a classic – lovely.
1975 Still very dark colour. Nose a bit shy, suggestion of tobacco or dried grass. Very good complex flavour, slightly meaty; tannic still, with a dry finish, but enough there to be worth waiting for.

CHATEAU

Balestard La Tonnelle

ST EMILION

Emerging from the main street of St Emilion, you come to the main crossroads on the northern edge of the town. Take the right turning, the D243, signposted to St Christophe-des-Bardes. After only 500 metres you will see the 'tonnelle', or tower, standing among the vines on your right. 250 metres further, and you come to a driveway, clearly marked, to the château itself.

Wine was certainly made here in the 15th century, witnessed by a prayer to the blessed Virgin, written in the form of a poem by François Villon who died in 1485. He begs to be taken to paradise, among the elect who savour the divine nectar which bears the name of Balestard. The canon of St Emilion, Balestard, after whom the property is named, presumably kept his finest vintages for the 'gens fortunés' amongst whom the poor poet was not numbered.

The tower, la Tonnelle, stands proud among the vines to the west of the château; it was once an observation post on the old road from Ville Maure to St Emilion. In the early part of this century the property belonged to a Parisian by the name of Bertants-Couture, who, though an absentee land-lord, still managed to win medals in London, Paris and America with the wine of Balestard. He sold the property to M. Berthon, father-in-law of Roger Capdemourlin, who managed the vineyard for some thirty years. Roger's capable son, Jacques, has been in charge now for more than ten years.

Jacques Capdemourlin is a member of one of the oldest families in St Emilion; Capdemourlins have certainly been in this locale for five hundred years, and the name crops up again and again in the vinous history not only of St Emilion, but of the whole region as well.

Other properties under the care of Jacques are Château Cap de Mourlin itself and Château Roudier, which is a Montagne St Emilion wine, and where Jacques has his office. Jacques lives in the château with his attractive blonde wife, who is a teacher in Libourne, and their two sons. When he came to the property in the early 1970s, the house had stood empty for some 30 years, but he has done a wonderful job of restoration. As with the château, so with the rest of the property: little by little, year by year, the same love, care and

attention to detail have been expended on the chai, the cuvier, the vineyard and the tower. It is a delightful place to visit, and reflects in every way the artistry and feeling for the *qualité de la vie* that are the guiding principles of the owner.

The vines, which are all in one piece, are on the summit of a clay–limestone plateau, with bedrock never too far below the surface. From the tower, as from the garden of the château, there is a superb view, with the imposing Château Soutard in the foreground, over the vineyards of Montagne St Emilion, with Puisseguin St Emilion to the right.'

In all there are 10.6 hectares under vine, planted with 65% Merlot, 20% Cabernet Franc, 10% Cabernet Sauvignon and 5% Malbec. Fermentation is in traditional cement cuves, and maturation is one-third in new casks, one-third in two-year-old casks, and one-third in stainless-steel cuves.

The wine has power and finesse, and is one of the more *charpenté* of the St Emilion wines. Jacques ascribes this quality to the proximity of the rock. A very dense dark colour is characteristic.

Jacques is keen to control the marketing of Balestard la Tonnelle himself, and sales are done through all avenues – the négociants in Bordeaux, direct to foreign agents, direct to private customers and direct to the Paris restaurateurs, with whom Jacques established good contacts very early on in his career. He sells to, and visits personally, merchants right across the United States, where his wine has a good following.

TECHNICAL INFORMATION

General

Appellation:	St Emilion, Grand Cru Classé
Area under vines:	10.6 hectares
Production:	5,000 cases
Distribution of vines:	In one piece
Proprietor:	G.F.A. Capdemourlin
Director:	Jacques Capdemourlin

Viticulture

Geology:	Limestone and clay
Grape varieties planted:	65% Merlot, 20% Cabernet Franc, 10% Cabernet Sauvignon, 5% Malbec
Pruning:	Guyot Simple
Rootstock:	41B
Density of vines per hectare:	5,300

Vinification

Length of maceration:	Average 15 days
Type of vat:	Concrete
Age of casks:	$\frac{1}{3}$ new
Time in cask:	Up to two years
Type of bottle:	Dark Bordelaise

Commercial

Direct ordering from Château:	Yes
Agents in foreign countries:	Yes
Visits:	Yes, telephone for appointment 57 84 02 06 or 57 24 74 35 Hours: 0800–1200, 1400–1700 Closed weekends and holidays

THE TASTING AT CHATEAU BALESTARD, 7 September 1984
J.S., Jacques Capdemourlin

1983 Very dense, deep colour, almost black. Rich nose, full of fruit – blackcurrants. Huge wine, enormous fruit and tannins, taste of the rock. Will be great wine.

1982 Lovely depth of colour. More soft and rounded bouquet, a little dumb, but probably caused by recent 'mise'. Plenty of both fruit and tannin there, and more accessible than '83.

1981 Good red, but noticeably lighter. Bouquet quite developed. Well balanced, nearing readiness – perhaps in eighteen months.

1980 Slight browny tinges, but lovely clear colour for 1980. Good grapey nose. Acidity surprisingly pronounced, but plenty of fruit. Not typical of 1980, needs a bit of time, but will come round.

1979 Good, brilliant red. Generous fruity nose. Well made, nearing readiness.

1978 Brilliant scarlet colour. Nose still a bit closed. Complex flavour, mouthfilling, plenty of fruit and tannin. Will make a good bottle.

1977 Light browny red. Open bouquet with plenty of fruit. As you would expect from this vintage, but quite pleasant to drink now.

1976 Good, clear, intense red. Rounded, open bouquet. Still tannins present, but fruit to balance. Approaching its best.

1975 Splendidly young and lively colour. Nose full of fruit and promise. Big wine with plenty of backbone. To keep.

1974 Light, brownish tinges. Slight toffee nose. Pleasant, slight caramel flavour. Good for the vintage.

289

CHATEAU
Belair
ST EMILION

Leave the car-park outside the Maison du Vin in St Emilion, and take the small road to your left, the Avenue 18th Mai 1945. After about 200 metres you will come to a fork in the road, with Châteaux Ausone and Belair signposted to your left. Follow the signs for about half a kilometre, and you will come to the entrance, which serves both châteaux, on your right.

The early history of Belair is English. During the Hundred Years War there was a fortress on these rocky heights, and it belonged to the Governor of Guyenne, General Robert Knolles. This worthy soldier married a French lady and Gallicised his name to de Canolles.

His family stayed in possession until after the French Revolution, by which time it had passed through the distaff side into the de Marignan family. There is a story of touching loyalty and faith that occurred during The Terror. Apparently the current de Marignan, fearing for his neck, emigrated, and the property, like so many others, was duly confiscated and put up for sale as a 'Bien National'. The purchaser was the family's faithful régisseur, who must have appeared to be acting in the most exemplary and revolutionary fashion, taking his master's place. This was not the case; as soon as the black shadow of La Terreur was past, the owner returned, and the steward gladly sold Belair back to his master for the same price he had paid.

The property was bought in 1916 by Monsieur Edouard Dubois-Challon, who already owned the neighbouring Château Ausone, where he had done great things since taking over the running from his aunt, Madame Lafargue. He was followed by his son, Jean Dubois-Challon, a well-respected figure in the area and Premier Jurat of St Emilion. Jean died in 1974, and his widow is the sole owner today; she lives in part of Château Ausone, in which she has a half share with the Vauthiers, who are also grandchildren of Edouard Dubois-Challon on the female side.

Like Ausone, Belair is currently enjoying a little renaissance; from the early 1950s to the mid-1970s the wine was definitely in a decline. In 1975, however, a very remarkable young régisseur was appointed, a qualified oenologist called Pascal

Delbeck. He is an interesting and dedicated man, with a huge bushy beard, and his eyes gleam with evangelical fervour when discussing his three pet subjects, Belair, Ausone, where he is also régisseur, and the cooking and eating of good food. He is well-known for his Epicurean skills, and I look forward to taking up his open invitation to take a meal with him in the very near future.

The vines of Château Belair are half on the slopes to the west of Ausone, and half on the plateau, and the encépagement has a higher proportion of Merlot than that of Ausone. The wines of Belair and Ausone have been made under the same direction since Edouard Dubois-Challon bought Belair seventy years ago, but vinification has

290

always been kept strictly separate; anyone having the good fortune to taste the two side by side, as I did, can immediately see that the two have totally different styles. Belair has more richness and the immediate charm of St Emilion, while Ausone is a reserved lady, perhaps more of a Médocaine aristocrat, slow to lower her defences, but when she does, you have a friend for life. The variation in character is probably mainly due to the soil, and partly to the higher proportion of Merlot used at Belair. The other factor that contributes to Belair's somewhat lighter, less tannic style lies in the cuvier; here Pascal Delbeck has had stainless-steel vats installed in the one-time quarry, while the alcoholic fermentation at Ausone still takes place in traditional oak cuves.

Every now and then in the history of Bordeaux wine-making there emerge régisseurs of exceptional talent, whose names are remembered for the contribution they have made, names like Chiapella, Skawinski, the Chardons of Palmer, the Grangerous of Margaux and Raoul Blondin at Mouton. It is my opinion that Pascal Delbeck may well form part of this scroll of honour in years to come.

TECHNICAL INFORMATION

General
Appellation:	St Emilion
Area under vines:	13 hectares
Average production:	5,000 cases
Distribution of vines:	One block, half on slopes, half on plateau
Owner:	Mme. Dubois-Challon
Régisseur/Wine-maker:	M. Pascal Delbeck
Maître de Chai:	M. Lanau
Consultant Oenologist:	C.B.C.

Viticulture
Geology:	Clay/limestone
Grape varieties:	60% Merlot, 35% Cabernet Franc, 5% Cabernet Sauvignon
Pruning:	Guyot Poussard
Rootstock:	41B, 333EM
Vines per hectare:	6,000
Average yield per hectare:	35–40 hectolitres
Replanting:	1 hectare every 4 years

Vinification
Added yeasts:	Own strain, *pied de cuve*
Length of maceration:	3–4 weeks, following tasting
Temperature of fermentation:	28°–31°C
Control of fermentation:	By heat-exchange apparatus
Type of vat:	Stainless steel of 70–80 hectolitres
Vin de presse:	Not incorporated
Age of casks:	35% new, rest casks of Ausone
Time in cask:	16–20 months
Fining:	Fresh egg-whites, in cask
Filtration:	None
Type of bottle:	Bordelaise lourde

Commercial
Vente Directe:	Yes
Sales:	Exclusively through one négociant
Visits:	Yes, by appointment Telephone: 57 24 70 95/94 Hours: 0800–1200, 1400–1800

THE TASTING AT CHATEAU BELAIR,
22 November 1984
J.S., Pascal Delbeck

1983 (This was a sample taken from two casks, one new and one from an Ausone '82 cask.) Great depth of colour, Bouquet very concentrated, and still very closed up. Very rich, almost voluptuous fruit in the mouth, good, non-aggressive tannins, great aftertaste.

1982 Fine mid-red colour. Nose starting to evolve with good ripe fruit. Generous, rounded mouthful of wine, with loads of fruit and soft tannin. Will be drinkable quite soon, but also has a great future.

1981 Brilliant scarlet, almost orange. Nose very ripe, a little cooked. Aromatic in the mouth, very ripe, roasty flavour. Good, to drink quite soon.

CHATEAU
Canon
ST EMILION

Leaving St Emilion from the car-park outside the church and the Maison du Vin, turn left along the Avenue 18 Mai 1945; after some 200 metres, you arrive at a fork in the road. The walled section of Château Canon's vineyard is immediately in front of you: take the right fork, signposted Berliquet and Château Canon, and after about 500 metres you will find the gateway to the château on your right.

It may be assumed that M. Kanon, a naval officer on the King's frigate, and owner of this estate until 1770, had already dedicated this property to the production of Grands Vins, using the new processes of the 'révolution viticole': these included the culture of selected grape varieties, long fermentation, separate vinification of red and white varieties, and keeping and ageing in wooden vats or barriques. This assumption derives from the comparatively high price of 49,000 livres paid for the property to Kanon by Raymond Fontemoing, a rich négociant from Libourne, in 1770.

Evidence of the continued production of quality wine in the Fontemoings' ownership is provided by records of the price at which the wine of Saint-Martin, as they called it, sold in 1790 – 420 livres per tonneau, as against 200 livres for the vin ordinaire of the district.

Although records show that the chai was 'modernised' by Kanon, it was Raymond Fontemoing who built the very attractive château between 1770 and 1780; it was to stand him in good stead, since it was here that he fled, already an old man, to escape Madame la Guillotine in 1793, and here that he passed his remaining years until his death in 1800 aged 97.

Before the Fontemoing purchase, the property almost certainly bore the name of its owner, M. Kanon or Canon, as this was the current practice. However, in 1777 Raymond Fontemoing bought an important vineyard at Canon-Fronsac, at that time an equal of Haut-St Emilion in the production of quality wine. It was to avoid confusion between his two fine properties that Fontemoing adopted the parish name of Saint-Martin for the Canon vineyard.

It was not until 1853 that Virginie Hovyne de Tranchère, granddaughter of Raymond Fontemo-

ing, having no direct connection with the Canon-Fronsac property, changed the name back to Château Canon.

In 1858 the estate passed to her son Jules Hovyne de Tranchère, who was a brilliant scholar, poet and dilettante; he led an expensive life, and was hugely in debt, so, without delay, sold Canon to a Comte de Bonneval.

This fine estate was to survive the difficult years of oidium and phylloxera intact, passing through the hands of two more owners, until it was bought by Mme. André Fournier's father in 1919, and it is her grandsons, Daniel, Christian and Eric Fournier, who own Canon today.

Eric Fournier, the younger brother of the family, runs Canon along very traditional lines. He lives in Bordeaux, and comes daily to his office at the château, from where he administers not only Canon, but also their other fine property in Barsac, Château Broustet, which he visits regularly.

The château is not lived in full-time, but the family stay there for holidays and at vintage time.

The 18-hectare vineyard, some two-thirds of which is in front of the château enclosed by an ancient wall – the remainder lies to either side – is planted with 55% Merlot, 40% Cabernet Franc, 3% Cabernet Sauvignon and 2% Malbec.

The vineyard is situated both on the plateau and the south-west slope of St Emilion, and the soil, some of the best for vines in the area, is predominantly limestone/clay on a subsoil of chalk and stone.

Continually in pursuit of quality, the viticulture at Canon is conducted along traditional lines. Replanting is undertaken only when necessary, in order to maintain the optimum age of the vines,

292

which is on average 35 years. Horses were in daily use here until as recently as 1979.

Again, in the vinification process, Eric sticks resolutely to the use of oak fermentation cuves. This, he insists, is not for reasons of economy – a new oak cuve now costs more to instal than one of stainless steel – but because contact with the lining wood is beneficial to the wine, whereas stainless steel is completely neutral.

The resulting wines have good deep colour, an attractive fragrance, and a good concentration of flavour. In the tasting, I must admit to being more impressed by the produce of the last five years than by the earlier ones; this is by no means a damning criticism, since the earlier years, with the exception of 1975, which was good anyway, tended to be light vintages for everybody.

TECHNICAL INFORMATION

General

Appellation:	St Emilion, Premier Grand Cru Classé
Area under vines:	18 hectares
Production:	8,000 cases
Distribution of vines:	In one piece
Owner:	Fournier family
Directeur:	Eric Fournier
Maître de Chai:	Paul Cazenove
Chef de Culture:	Gérard Gerémie
Consultant Oenologist:	Laboratoire Legendre

Viticulture

Geology:	Limestone-clay on a subsoil of chalk and stone
Grape varieties:	55% Merlot, 40% Cabernet Franc, 3% Cabernet Sauvignon, 2% Malbec
Pruning:	Guyot Simple
Rootstock:	41B
Density of vines per hectare:	5,400
Average yield per hectare:	38 hectolitres
Replanting:	As necessary, to maintain average age of 35 years

Vinification

Length of maceration:	Three weeks
Temperature of fermentation:	30°C maximum
Control of fermentation:	Refrigeration
Type of vat:	Oak
Vin de presse:	Sometimes, depending on vintage
Age of casks:	50% new in normal years
Time in cask:	20 months
Fining:	Fresh egg-whites
Filtration:	No
Type of bottle:	Bordelaise lourde

Commercial

Vente Directe:	Yes, for retail orders
Direct ordering:	Yes, for retail orders
Exclusivities:	None
Agents in foreign countries:	No
Visits:	Yes, for appointment telephone: 57 24 70 79 Normal office hours – not weekends

THE TASTING AT CHATEAU CANON,
13 September 1984
J.S., M. Eric Fournier

1983 Intense dark purple, almost black. Powerful fragrance of oak and fruit. Mouthfilling, full of fruit and tannin, with long aftertaste. One to wait for, and it will repay the waiting.

1982 Also a very deep colour. Nose closed, but blackcurrant comes through. Rounded and approachable, with excellent fruit and body, and good non-aggresive tannins. Will be a really fine bottle.

1981 Colour a shade lighter, but brilliant. Open fruity and aromatic bouquet. Good mouthful, well balanced, well-made wine, good to drink in two years.

1980 Light, clear red, but good colour for 1980. Pleasant, slight caramelly nose. Good wine to drink now, but no great hurry.

1979 Deep red. Good open fruit on nose, black-currant. A well-structured wine with long aftertaste. Plenty of fruit and tannin, to keep a while.

1978 Brilliant, garnet red. Soft pleasant bouquet. Balance good, nearly ready.

1977 Pale but bright red, browning a little at edges. Slight dank vegetation smell. Light and lacking fruit a little.

1976 Clear almost rusty red. Soft, perfumed and fragrant. *A point*, a ripe wine, smooth and rounded, good to drink now.

1975 Good scarlet and bright. Nose still closed. Still hard and astringent, but will be interesting in two or three years.

1974 Very light brown. Caramelly and not very pleasing on nose. Very light wine, not much remaining here.

1973 Pale russet. Muted bouquet, but still some fruit there. Delicate, a bit short, but a good wine to drink now, perhaps with chicken or some cold meat.

CHATEAU
Canon La Gaffelière
ST EMILION

The château and buildings of Canon la Gaffelière are just before the level crossing as you approach St Emilion from the Libourne Bergerac road, having turned left just after the village of Les Bigaroux.

At the end of the 18th century, this estate belonged to a M. Boitard de la Poterie, and was then known as Canon-Boitard. In 1953 the property was bought by M. Pierre Meyrat, who undertook to re-establish the vineyard, which had been neglected for many years. M. Meyrat, who did a fine job with Canon la Gaffelière, was mayor of St Emilion, and died in 1969.

In 1971 a German, Count von Neipperg, who had wine estates in Germany, purchased the property, and his three sons are the owners today: the administration of the vineyard is in the hands of Michel Boutet of Château Peyreau, who also runs Château la Tour Figeac and two other properties in which he is a shareholder, Peyreau and Clos de L'Oratoire.

The vineyard of Canon la Gaffelière, although officially one of the 'Côtes' vineyards of St Emilion, is mainly on flat land which has a limestone/chalk soil, with some sand on the foot of the slopes.

The wines are agreeable, attractive St Emilion, and are vinified to mature and be enjoyed comparatively young. One-third of the casks are renewed annually, but Michel Boutet conducts the ageing on a rotation system, with the wine alternating between 3-month periods in cask and 3 months in the impressive battery of stainless-steel cuves, installed in 1974.

294

TECHNICAL INFORMATION

General

Appellation:	St Emilion
Area under vines:	19 hectares
Average production:	10,000 cases
Distribution of vines:	In one piece
Owners:	Les Comtes Neipperg
Administrator:	M. Michel Boutet
Maître de Chai:	M. Eresue
Consultant Oenologist:	M. Cassignart

Viticulture

Geology:	Clay/chalk and ancient sand
Grape varieties:	65% Merlot, 30% Cabernet Franc, 5% Cabernet Sauvignon
Pruning:	Guyot Simple
Rootstock:	Varied to suit soil
Vines per hectare:	6,500
Average yield per hectare:	50 hectolitres
Replanting:	Average 5% per year

Vinification

Added yeasts:	Yes, in difficult years
Length of maceration:	15–21 days
Temperature of fermentation:	28–32°C
Control of fermentation:	Running water on exterior of vats
Type of vat:	Stainless steel
Vin de Presse:	Proportion incorporated according to needs of vintage
Age of casks:	$\frac{1}{3}$ new each vintage
Time in cask:	18 months
Fining:	Egg albumen in vat
Filtration:	Light, sur plaques, before bottling
Type of bottle:	Bordelaise lourde

Commercial

Vente Directe:	Yes to callers
General sales:	Through the Bordeaux négociants
Visits:	Yes, for appointment telephone 57 24 71 33 Normal office hours

THE TASTING IN THE AGEING CELLAR AT CHATEAU CANON LA GAFFELIERE, 28 September 1984

1983 Bright scarlet colour. Slight sulphur on nose and taste due to recent racking. Very light tannin, agreeable fruit.

1982 Same scarlet colour as 1983. Open fruity bouquet. Round, pleasant wine. Open and forward. Tannin very mute, to drink fairly soon.

1981 Bright medium red. Nose not so open as 1982. Good balance, slightly more tannin and keeping qualities than 1982.

1980 Lighter colour, browny tinges. Not much nose, but quite pretty. Open and easy to drink with enough fruit, but lacking tannin and backbone.

1979 Same bright scarlet as later vintages. More asser-tive grapey nose. Well made, with more skeleton. Has good aftertaste. Good now, but will stay a while.

1978 Browning a little. Good fruity fragrance. Quite open and ready, with good fruit and pleasant aftertaste.

1977 Pale red, quite brown. Ripe bouquet. Pleasant enough, but on the thin side with nothing much to come.

1976 Pale bright garnet. Good open nose with ripe fruit. Quite long, ideal for current drinking, with fruit and some elegance.

1975 Pale red. Nose not giving much but quite agreeable. Surprisingly thin. Tannin certainly there, but is there enough fruit to balance out and keep it going?

1974 Pale rather watery red, browning. Quite distinct, overripe nose. Not disagreeable, though very light, with a faintly roasted taste.

CHATEAU
Cap De Mourlin
ST EMILION

Take the D122 north from the town of St Emilion, and the gateway to Château Cap de Mourlin is about 1 km on your left, between large, neatly-clipped box hedges.

The Capdemourlin family, whose name the château bears, have been settled here for nearly 500 years. There is a record of a sale of wine in the property's archives dating back to 1647.

Recent history is somewhat complex. Since 1936, when the vineyard was divided between two Cap de Mourlin brothers, Jean and Roger, there have been two separate wines made at the château; the labels were the same, except for the names of the proprietors, Jean, and Jacques, son of Roger. The wine of Jean was from the vines around the château, where his widow still lives, and the wine of Jacques came from vineyards behind the property, where there is no house, but which has a separate cuvier. From 1983 Mme. Jean Capdemourlin turned over the management of the Jean vineyard to her nephew Jacques, so the property is now re-united, and the

continuity of the Cap de Mourlin name is possible through Jacques' two sons.

On my visit I was welcomed by Mme. Jean Capdemourlin, a neat, compact and hospitable lady, who still takes an active interest in the property, which she ran from her husband's death in 1976 till 1983. She is justly proud of her husband, who was a tireless worker and champion of the wines of St Emilion; he was largely responsible for the official classification of the wines of the region in 1954, maintaining that classement should be earned by quality, and that same quality should be monitored regularly.

An indication of Jean Capdemourlin's dedication to quality was the introduction of the Château la Rose Faurie label. This was for the wine from the young vines replanted after the ravaging frosts of 1956. He continued to use the label until 1974 when he was happy for the wine to go out as Jean Cap de Mourlin.

During the years that the Jean and Jacques wines

296

have been made separately, the Jean Cap de Mourlin has been a consistent and typical St Emilion; soft, undemanding and relatively quick to give of its best, the wine was usually ready to drink in three to four years.

The 1983, under Jacques management, will show whether there is to be a change in style. When I tasted the cask sample in September 1984, it certainly had a fine deep colour and strongly pronounced tannins, but it was still very young and it is difficult to judge a wine's eventual genre at such an early stage.

TECHNICAL INFORMATION

General

Appellation:	Grand Cru Classé, St Emilion
Area under vines:	13.81 hectares
Production:	6,000 cases
Owner:	Jacques Capdemourlin
Oenological Consultant:	M. Rolland

Viticulture

Geology:	Part limestone/clay, part sand, on an iron-pan base
Grape varieties:	60% Merlot, 25% Cabernet Franc, 12% Cabernet Sauvignon, 3% Malbec
Pruning:	Guyot Simple
Density of vines per hectare:	5,300

Vinification

Length of maceration:	12–15 days
Type of vat:	Cement
Age of casks:	⅓ new each year
Time in cask:	Nearly two years
Type of bottle:	Bordelaise

Commercial

Vente Directe:	At the château
Direct ordering:	Yes, from the château
Visits:	Yes, weekdays only and by appointment
	Telephone: Jacques Capdemourlin 57 84 02 06 or Mme. Capdemourlin 57 24 70 83

THE TASTING AT CHATEAU CAP DE MOURLIN, 3 September 1984
J.S. Mme. Jean Capdemourlin

(N.B. All the wines up to 1983 were Jean Cap de Mourlin.)

1983 Good deep bluey red. Powerful, rounded Merlot bouquet. Well-made wine, with massive fruit and pronounced tannins. Long aftertaste. Will be excellent.

1982 Garnet red. Slightly peppery nose. Good, fat, generous, mouthfilling wine – ready to drink quite soon.

1981 Lightish red. Soft elegant nose. Good fruit, acidity softening. Lighter than the '82 – almost ready.

1980 Light garnet red, not showing brown. Slightly burnt nose. Well-balanced; quite light, but pleasant to drink now.

1979 Pale red. Light, very perfumed nose. Tannins predominate, but there is enough fruit to balance.

1978 Deep colour. Nose still quite closed. Big mouthful; well made wine, balanced, rounded – nearing readiness, but should keep.

1977 Light colour, with brownish edges. Good nose. A light wine, excellent for its year. Good to drink now and for two or three years.

1976 Lightish red. Attractively fruity bouquet. Balance right, but no depth. To drink now.

1975 Fine, deep colour still. Nose still shut in, but beginning to open. Big wine with lots of fruit and tannin and a prolonged aftertaste. Will go on for years.

1974 Brownish colour. Bouquet a bit maderised. A bit unfair to taste after the 1975, being a poor vintage; light and lacking fruit, but good enough to drink now.

CHATEAU
Cheval-Blanc
ST EMILION

Château Cheval-Blanc is to be found on the route D21 from Libourne to Pomerol and Montagne St Emilion. About 5 km east of Libourne take the right turning, sign-posted to St Emilion, and the entrance to Cheval-Blanc is 400 metres on your left.

To all intents, Château Cheval-Blanc is one of a very small number of properties in the Bordeaux region that has stayed in the ownership of the same family for its entire history. In 1852 Jean Laussac Fourcaud married a Mlle. Henriette Ducasse, also from a vineyard-owning family – they were then, and still are, the proprietors of Château L'Evangile across the road in Pomerol. Mlle. Ducasse brought, as her dowry to this marriage, a property of 15 hectares called Cheval-Blanc; it was at this time producing some 25 tonneaux of wine of no great importance.

Jean Laussac Fourcaud wasted no time in adding to the vineyard by buying suitable parcels of adjacent land. By 1870 the size was 42 hectares – the same as it is today – producing some 60 tonneaux, about half the present production. Other writers suggest that Cheval-Blanc's wines only started to gain distinction in the last years of the 19th century – 1893, 1899 and 1900 being particular examples. Medals were however won as early as 1862 in London and 1878 in Paris, as can clearly be seen on the labels.

On his death in 1893, Jean was succeeded at Cheval-Blanc by Albert, one of his eight children; Albert promptly bought out the rest of his family, and changed his name to Fourcaud-Laussac. It was he who created the present Société Civile du Château Cheval-Blanc, to be owned by his five children, one of whom, Jacques, ran the property till his death as recently as 1972.

The Société is now owned by an assortment of heirs of the Fourcaud family, and is run by Jacques Hébrard, an impressive figure of a man who came to Cheval-Blanc in 1970; he is married to one of Albert's granddaughters. Jacques' background is both vinous and naval; his grandfather was a broker in Libourne, and his father a distinguished sailor in the Fleet Air Arm, finishing his career as an admiral – he was also president of the French airline Air Inter. Jacques himself wanted to follow his father's career and joined the Navy; he was, however, badly wounded in action during the war, and spent many years in Indo-China and later in Central Africa, where he gained a wealth of agricultural experience.

Jacques Hébrard lives in the small, elegant but comfortable château. Two-storeyed and painted white, the house has on one side a small chapel and an orangery, and is flanked on the other by the impressive chai, built in 1974.

TECHNICAL INFORMATION

General

Appellation:	St Emilion, Premier Grand Cru Classé A
Area under vines:	36 hectares
Average production:	12,500 cases
Distribution of vines:	In one block
Owner:	Société Civile du Château Cheval-Blanc
Director:	M. Jacques Hébrard
Chef de Culture:	M. Pierre Perdigal
Maître de Chai:	M. Gaston Vaissière
Consultant Oenologists:	MM. Legendre and Pauquet

Viticulture

Geology:	Mixture of gravel, sand, clay and alios
Grape varieties:	66% Cabernet Franc, 33% Merlot, 1% Malbec
Pruning:	Guyot Simple
Rootstock:	Riparia
Vines per hectare:	5,800
Average yield per hectare:	34 hectolitres
Replanting:	As necessary

Vinification

Length of maceration:	Average 3 weeks
Temperature of fermentation:	29°C
Control of fermentation:	By cooling apparatus
Type of vat:	Cement
Vin de presse:	1st pressing generally used
Age of casks:	100% new every vintage
Time in cask:	Average 20 months
Fining:	Fresh egg-white, in cask
Filtration:	None
Type of bottle:	Bordelaise lourde

Commercial

Vente Directe:	No
Sales:	Through 7 négociants in Bordeaux and Libourne
Visits:	Yes, by appointment Telephone: 57 24 70 70 Hours: 0900–1130, 1430–1730 except Saturday, Sunday and Feast Days

THE TASTING AT CHATEAU CHEVAL-BLANC, 29 January 1985 (My birthday, and what a way to celebrate it!)
J.S., Christian Seely, Jacques Hébrard, Daniel Lawton, Max Lestapie

1983 Dense, blackish colour. Bouquet powerful with cassis and new wood. Huge wine, with great concentration of flavour and good, dominant tannins. A long-distance runner.

1982 (Bottled July 1984.) Same incredible deep colour as '83. Nose 'fermé'. Not typical of vintage, as it was very tannic and closed; very big, with loads of fruit and good tannin. Very long in the mouth.

1980 Colour astonishing for this 'petite année'. Nose good and quite open, with lovely blackcurrant fragrance. Quite evolved flavour, but lots of bottle-life. Along with Château Margaux, probably the best 1980 tasted.

1978 Dense, medium-to-dark red. Magnificent nose, full of fruit and power. Still very closed, with tannins dominating. Complex, concentrated flavour, with a combination of finesse, richness and backbone to develop into a fine bottle. Very long aftertaste.

1976 Medium red, shading to orange. Bouquet quite open. Just starting to harmonise, with a rich, slightly roasted flavour. Will be perfect in a couple of years.

1975 Very dark, dense red, just beginning to go a little tawny. Full, aromatic nose starting to evolve. A huge and concentrated mouthful with great complexity of good flavours and ripe tannins. Classic Cheval-Blanc that will stay and stay.

1973 Fine scarlet colour. Nose open and ripe. Not a big wine, but an elegant, charming claret. On a plateau, and will stay there for a while yet.

1971 Deep red, beginning to brown. Delicate and ripe on the nose, with some blackcurrant. In balance, everything together; fruit and tannin harmonious, this wine has just arrived, but will stay and improve.

Clos Fourtet

ST EMILION

Clos Fourtet is the closest vineyard to the heart of St Emilion itself. It lies opposite the collegiate church of St Emilion, alongside which is the Maison du Vin and a small car-park.

Fourtet is an old French word for a small fort; there was a military garrison billeted here in the 19th century, and the property was known until the middle of the 19th century as Campfourtet.

Clos Fourtet was acquired just after the first war by Fernand Ginestet, who also bought Château Petit-Village in Pomerol in the same year. The reputation and quality of the wine had declined a little in the years prior to the Ginestet purchase, but the new owners were skilful and successful winemakers, and by the late twenties Clos Fourtet was back among the top St Emilions.

The Ginestet regime lasted until 1947, when they exchanged Clos Fourtet for the Recapet/Lurton 40% holding in Château Margaux. It is François Lurton's four children, Lucien, André, Dominique and their sister Monique who now own Clos

Fourtet, and Dominique's son Pierre Lurton now runs the property on the family's behalf. He now lives in the régisseur's house at the right-hand end of the château; the main part of the château has stood empty for many years, but there are plans for its restoration and eventual occupation by Pierre and his wife Odile.

The Clos Fourtet vineyard has all of its wines on the limestone plateau of St Emilion. 13 of the total 17 hectares are within the 'Clos' or walled section around the château, the remainder being to the north of the St Emilion-Pomerol road. The fermentations, alcoholic and malolactic, take place in a mixture of stainless and enamelled-steel vats, and ageing is in casks of oak, up to half of which are new each vintage, and which are housed in the cavernous disused limestone quarry which runs beneath the vines and the château. It is from these endless rock-chambers, and others like them, that stonemasons have for centuries hacked the soft limestone blocks with which the fine houses of the

300

area are built.

In past years the wine of Clos Fourtet (the word Château is seldom attached to the name) was a classic 'vin de garde', and required a minimum ten and an optimum twenty years in bottle to give of its best. In recent years the wine has definitely softened in style, without losing any of its fine quality. Pierre Lurton impressed me enormously with his love of the job, and with his keen, professional approach. I am most grateful for the time he gave me, and the many things he taught me about the art and the science of modern winemaking, to say nothing of the vertical tasting of a dozen vintages which he talked me through with the benefit of first-hand experience.

TECHNICAL INFORMATION

General

Appellation:	St Emilion
Area under vines:	17 hectares
Average production:	5,500 cases
Distribution of vines:	In two main blocks
Owner:	Lurton Frères
Director/Régisseur:	Pierre Lurton
Consultant Oenologist:	Professor Emile Peynaud

Viticulture

Geology:	Light soil on limestone base
Grape varieties:	70% Merlot, 15% Cabernet Franc, 15% Cabernet Sauvignon
Pruning:	Guyot Simple
Vines per hectare:	5,000
Average yield per hectare:	30 hectolitres
Replanting:	3% per annum

Vinification

Added yeasts:	None
Length of maceration:	20–25 days
Temperature of fermentation:	27°–30°C
Control of fermentation:	Water cooling
Type of vats:	Stainless steel and enamelled steel
Age of casks:	⅓ new each vintage
Time in cask:	12–18 months
Fining:	Sur terre before going in cask, sur plaque before bottling
Type of bottle:	Bordelaise lourde

Commercial

Vente Directe:	Yes
Sales:	Through the Bordeaux négociants
Visits:	Yes, for appointment telephone: 576 24 70 90

THE TASTING AT CLOS FOURTET,
21 September 1984
J.S., Pierre Lurton

1983 (In cask, racking just completed.) Fine deep colour. Nose has good fruit, and vanilla of new oak. Fine depth of flavour, good backbone, needs some time to develop.

1982 Dark, bluey red. Bouquet very forward, ripe and open. Very big, rounded and open mouthful of wine, already very drinkable, but has a mass of generous fruit and ripe tannins to keep it going for many years. Excellent.

1981 Dense colour. Vanilla very strong, redolent of new wood. A complex wine of some finesse with a touch of sweetness. Forward for '81, but has enough tannin and backbone to age well.

1980 A good medium red. Bouquet open and appealing, with plenty of fruit. More structure and tannin than some 1980 St Emilions; though atractive now, will stay for a year or two.

1979 Excellent deep red, with blue tinge. Powerful blackcurrant bouquet. Appealing, generous and mouth-filling, with enough structure and tannin to keep it going.

1978 Very deep red. Rounded, cassis nose of great power. Beautiful, aromatic and complex flavour. good tannins and long in the mouth; a stayer.

1977 Good, lightish red, no brown. Nice fruit on nose. A very pleasing mouthful of fruit with little of the acidity encountered in so many wines of this vintage. one of the best 1977 St Emilion tasted.

1976 Bright scarlet. Nose pleasing and open with ripe fruit. in balance, and very good to drink now.

1975 Brilliant medium red. Open fruity bouquet. Lightish for '75, with good fruit and a touch of astringency. No great future, but lovely to drink now and for a few years.

1974 Very pale red. Not much on nose. A little thin, but some fruit there, quite a pleasing luncheon wine.

1973 Bright, pale red. Ripe and mature bouquet. An honest, straightforward wine, very agreeable to drink now, with not a lot of life left.

CHATEAU

Dassault

ST EMILION

Take the D122 north from St Emilion in the direction of Montagne; after about 1½ km take the right turning at the crossroads. Follow this small country road across one crossroads, and Château Dassault is on your left after about 500 metres.

Unfortunately not much of the early history of this very pretty property is known, since such documents as there were disappeared with the previous owner, and the archives in St Emilion relating to the property were destroyed in a fire. In 1864 Victor Fourcaud, an elder brother of Laussac Fourcaud at Cheval-Blanc, built the château in the middle of a 25-hectare vineyard. The property appears, as Château Couperie, in the 1881 edition of Cocks et Feret.

The château was purchased in 1955 by M. Marcel Dassault, a tycoon who manufactures aircraft and owns newspapers, among many other business activities. He changed the name of the property from Château Couperie to Château Dassault. With the financial backing of the Dassault industrial empire, it has been possible to turn the château into a model property.

M. Vergriette, who now manages the property for the owning company, Château Dassault SARL, has been there since 1972. He attended the University at Talence to study oenology at the age of fifty, and both he and Château Dassault have clearly profited thereby.

The château is a compact, elegant house, built in 1864, standing in its own small park, with a wealth of old trees. As you approach the château, you will pass the chai/cuvier, which has been extensively re-equipped under M. Vergriette's supervision. The whole building has been lined with brick, insulating it completely against all extremes of temperature. There is a modern cuvier with stainless-steel vats, a new bottling line, an ageing-chai for wines in cask, and a cellar for storage of wines in bottle. This is currently being enlarged, as M. Vergriette is adopting a laudable policy of keeping a proportion of each crop in bottle to sell when it is mature.

The vineyard, which surrounds the château, comprises 23 hectares of AC Grand Cru, St Emilion vines. A further 3–4 hectares are, by rotation, permanently under replanting, and the wine from

these young vines is marketed under a lesser appellation. The encépagement is 55% Merlot, 35% Cabernet Franc and 10% Cabernet Sauvignon, growing on a mixed soil of old sand and siliceous clay.

The resultant wine is a generous, fairly full-bodied St Emilion which ripens early, but also has good ageing properties.

302

TECHNICAL INFORMATION

General

Appellation:	St Emilion, Grand Cru, Classé
Area under vines:	23 hectares
Production:	Average 9,150 cases
Distribution of vines:	In one piece
Proprietor:	Château Dassault SARL
Manager:	M. André Vergriette
Maître de Chai:	M. J.-C. Barge
Oeonological Consultant:	M. Roland

Viticulture

Geology:	Ancient siliceous sand and siliceous clay
Grape varieties planted:	55% Merlot, 35% Cabernet Franc, 10% Cabernet Sauvignon
Pruning:	Guyot Simple
Rootstock:	SO4, 1104, 41B, 3309, 420A
Density of vines per hectare;	5,000 to 5,500
Yield per hectare:	About 39 hectolitres
Replanting:	By rotation

Vinification

Added yeasts:	Very rarely, if fermentation is difficult
Length of maceration:	About 28 days
Temperature of fermentation:	27–30°C
Control of fermentation:	By water circulation
Type of vat:	Stainless steel
Vin de presse:	Kept in cask for use if necessary
Age of casks:	$\frac{1}{3}$ new, $\frac{1}{3}$ one year old, $\frac{1}{3}$ in vat
Time in cask:	About 12 months
Fining:	Freeze-dried egg-white in vat
Type of bottle:	Dark bordelaise

Commercial

Vente Directe:	A little
Direct ordering;	Yes
Agents abroad:	Château and Estate Wine Co., New York, U.S.A. S.E.V.E.S., Brussels for Belgium, Holland, Denmark, Great Britain, Luxembourg and West Germany
Agent in France:	Michel Querre, négociant in Libourne
Visits:	Yes, by appointment Telephone: 57 24 71 30 Weekdays only

THE TASTING AT CHATEAU DASSAULT,
8 October 1984
J.S., M. Andre Vergrielle

1983 Colour already very clear, good bluey red. Bouquet fine and plenty of fruit and tannins. Complex, excellent flavours, surprisingly approachable. Will be very good.

1981 Very dense red, purply colour. Closed nose, but great fatness developing – cassis. Very well balanced wine with elegance, and backbone. Long aftertaste.

1980 Very good, bluey red for 1980. Delicious, fairly closed nose for '80, wine very cold – 15°C which did not help, but bouquet evolving. Lots of fruit, but still very young. Plenty of tannin. Still has some way to go. A very good '80.

1978 Good brilliant colour, slightly orangey. Good nose, pleasant, slight vanilla and slight whiff of milky caramel. On plateau; good, well-balanced, all right to drink now, but will keep for a long time. Good, long aftertaste.

1977 Again an excellent colour for a light year. Open pleasant fruit, slight cassis on nose. Very good bouquet. Quite light, good fruit. Ready and no need to hurry. A good 1977.

1975 Very deep dense colour. Slightly woody nose, fruit good, still quite closed. First of new style – new barriques – new vinification. Still very closed, but very complex and mouthfilling. Finesse, elegance and fruit. Will be an excellent bottle.

1973 Colour bright orange tinge. Nose soft, but still agreeable. Not a lot of weight, but still has tannin and fruit, though not much length.

CHATEAU

Figeac

ST EMILION

Château Figeac is about 3 km east of Libourne on the left-hand side of the D17e to St Emilion.

Figeac is one of the oldest and certainly largest wine estates of St Emilion. It owes it name to the Roman proprietors in the third and fourth centuries, a family by the name of Figeacus. From the 14th century to the middle of the 17th, the estate belonged to a noble family called de Cazes. Until 1590 there was a medieval castle on the site, but this was sacked by Henri de Navarre. In 1595 one of the de Cazes built a renaissance-style château, of which some parts – a turret, the pillars at the courtyard gate and the right-hand wall of the courtyard – still form part of the present building.

In 1654 Marie de Cazes married François de Carle, and the estate passed into his family, in whose ownership it remained until 1838. The present château was built by one of the de Carles in about 1780, in a style and proportion befitting the large country estate that it then was. During the next fifty years Figeac changed hands no less than seven times, and many small parcels on the boundaries had been sold off by the time Henri de Chevremont, great-grandfather of the present owner, bought Figeac in 1892. The vineyard in the north-eastern corner of the estate that was to become Cheval-Blanc had already been acquired by the Ducasse family in the latter part of the 18th century. It is indicative of the high quality and reputation of Figeac's wine in the 18th and 19th centuries that the wine of Cheval-Blanc was sold in 1832 as 'Vin de Figeac', and that all the small plots that were later sold off retained Figeac as part of their name.

The three generations of his family that preceded Thierry Manoncourt at Château Figeac used the house only as a holiday home, and, although the wine continued to be well and correctly made, contact with the Bordeaux wine trade was inevitably sporadic, and Figeac became something of a forgotten wine, a situation that has now been remedied by this remarkable man.

Château Figeac is Thierry Manoncourt's passion. A gentleman and a charmer is Monsieur Manoncourt, but behind that urbane and attractive façade there is an inexhaustible well-spring of knowledge, historical, geological and oenological. He loves an interested audience, and like the Ancient Mariner, he holds you with his glittering eye, and you cannot choose but hear! Probably the most important thread in the fascinating tapesty Monsieur Manoncourt weaves with his words is a geological one. In the Ice Age the rivers Isle and Dronne carried a mass of volcanic, gravelly soil from the Massif Central into this south-western corner of France, and deposited half a dozen *croupes*, or banks of crystal-quartz gravel, rounded and smoothed by their long journey, forming the plateau on which the vineyards of Figeac and Cheval-Blanc are sited. As Manoncourt rightly points out, every Premier Cru in the Médoc, as well as Haut-Brion in the Graves, has identical deep beds of the self-same gravel, and it is this highly unpromising terrain that is the *sine qua non* for the production of top-quality claret.

Until quite recently, all the St Emilion properties on the sandy plain between Figeac and the 'Côtes' vineyards of St Emilion itself were described as Graves de St Emilion. This was basically inaccurate, since only the two vineyards of Figeac and Cheval-Blanc possess a significant proportion of the precious pebbles, with only a few of their immediate neighbours having an almost negligible quantity. After a lot of tireless campaigning by Manoncourt, this blanket nomenclature of Graves St Emilion was dropped.

The intrinsic quality of the wine of Château Figeac is clearly demonstrated by the maintenance of its reputation during a period of over a hundred years of quasi-neglect between 1838 and 1947, the year Thierry Manoncourt came to live here and took over the running of the property. I qualify the word 'neglect', since the first 50 years of this period were marked by incessant changes of ownership, and the second by the physical absence of the owners, rather than by any actual falling off in standards of viticulture or vinification. Since 1947 the captain has very definitely been at the helm of his own ship, and, in spite of a stormy passage through and following the disastrous spring frosts of 1956, the voyage is proving ever more fruitful.

In 1953 Thierry Manoncourt made the first of a series of experiments, vinifying and ageing the

different grape varieties grown on the estate in separate casks, to determine the contribution made to the whole by each part. It was as a result of these trials that he decided to concentrate on the Cabernets, both Sauvignon and Franc, giving Figeac an encépagement that is essentially Médocain rather than the normally Merlot-dominated blend of St Emilion and Pomerol. He has also done much to improve the vineyard, and has enlarged and modernised the chais and vathouse; although fermentation still takes place in the old oak cuves, he has installed a range of stainless-steel vats, which are used for assemblage and malolactic fermentation, and can also be brought into service

305

in abundant vintages or when critical temperature control is called for at fermentation time.

All the new building work, including a splendid underground cellar, has been carried out with taste and style, and blends beautifully with the architecture of the château. This care for the quality of life is evident everywhere at Figeac; the house itself is surrounded by a fine park, and there is a lovely garden on the southern side of the château. This is in marked contrast to most St Emilion properties, where vines are usually planted right up to the walls of the houses; Figeac remains what it has been for centuries, a real country estate, now run and cared for by a loving owner.

Figeac's wine is certainly one of the very best St Emilions; it is quite Médocain in character, especially in its youth, when it is fairly hard and tannic; Thierry Manoncourt was not surprised or displeased when I guessed the 1970 which he gave me at lunch to be a 1975; a not unreasonable assumption, he said, bearing in mind that the wine was a St Emilion. With age, Château Figeac develops into a rounded, velvety claret with great charm and finesse that puts it in a class of its own. There is also a second wine produced, sold under the name of Château Grangeneuve.

TECHNICAL INFORMATION

General

Appellation:	St Emilion, Premier Grand Cru
Area under vines:	40 hectares
Average production:	12,500 cases
Distribution of vines:	One block
Owner:	M. Thierry Manoncourt
Maître de Chai:	M. Clément Brochard
Director/Oenologist:	M. Thierry Manoncourt, who is a qualified Ingénieur Agronome of the Institut National Agronomique de Paris

Viticulture

Geology:	$\frac{2}{3}$ gravel (see text), $\frac{1}{3}$ sand
Grape varieties:	35% Cabernet Sauvignon, 35% Cabernet Franc, 30% Merlot
Pruning:	Guyot Simple
Rootstock:	Various, as best suited to different soils of the vineyard
Vines per hectare:	6,000
Yield per hectare:	27 to 35 hectolitres
Replanting:	Average $\frac{1}{2}$ hectare per annum

Vinification

Added yeasts:	None
Length of maceration:	7 days
Temperature of fermentation:	30°C
Control of fermentation:	Cooling by cold water on stainless-steel vats when necessary
Type of vat:	Oak and stainless steel
Vin de presse:	Proportion incorporated according to vintage
Age of casks:	100% new each vintage
Time in cask:	18–20 months
Fining:	Egg whites
Type of bottle:	Bordelaise

Commercial

Vente Directe:	No
Exclusivities:	None
Sales:	Through the négociants
Visits:	Yes, by appointment Telephone: 57 24 72 26 office hours

THE TASTING AT CHATEAU FIGEAC, AND LATER AT CHATEAU MALESCASSE, 23 October 1984
J.S., M. Thierry Manoncourt, M. de St. Exupéry

1980 Lovely medium dark red. Bouquet open, with good, blackcurrant fruit. Already a very pleasing wine, with lots of open fruit flavour, but enough spine and tannin to keep it going for some time.

1976 Good, dense red, only just beginning to show brown at edges. Bouquet ripe and shows some finesse. This is now ready for drinking, but has none of the overripeness shown by some St Emilions of this year. Not particularly long, but has style and character.

1975 Deep, lovely red. Nose quite closed, but beginning to show well. Fruit and tannins starting to harmonise; will be a great bottle in four or five years. Lovely long aftertaste.

1970 Fine dense red, with only a little brown. Nose rich and aromatic, with slight earthy quality. I was given this blind, and identified it wrongly as 1975, to which it was far closer when compared with other St Emilions of that vintage. In the mouth it was still very concentrated, with great length and finesse, and a rich, long aftertaste.

1953 Lovely brilliant scarlet colour, with an open bouquet of ripe fruit. This was a half-bottle, but the flavour was still lively and delicious; most of the tannins have gone, leaving a perfect, mature Château Figeac. Superb.

CHATEAU
Fonplegade
ST EMILION

Leave Libourne on the Bergerac road, and take the left turn at the crossroads after the village of Bigaroux. After about half a kilometre, turn to your left, and Château Fonplegade is ½ km along this road on your right.

The elegant château was built in 1885 by a négociant from Libourne called Boisard. He must have been successful in his business, because the château is very fine, and rather out of proportion to the size of the vineyard.

Fonplegade has belonged in its time to the Duc de Morny and also to Mme. la Comtesse de Galard. In 1953 it was bought by M. Armand Moueix,

who has lived there since he was married in 1961.

It is for sure that this has been a vineyard for centuries, there is evidence that the Romans cultivated vines on the plateau. More recently it was cited among the 29 principal crus of St Emilion to be represented at the Universal Exposition in Paris in 1859, where it won a gold medal.

Other properties belonging to Monsieur Moueix, who is a cousin of Christian Moueix, owner of Château Pétrus, include Châteaux Moulinet and la Tour du Pin Figeac in St Emilion, Château Taillefer in Pomerol and Château La Croix Bellevue in Lalande Pomerol. It is at Taillefer that M.

307

Moueix's thriving négociant business is based, and where the administrative work for the wine properties is conducted.

The vineyard of Fonplegade is beautifully situated on the south-facing slopes of St Emilion; it occupies a sort of dent in the hillside, giving it protection from the wind, and maximum exposure to sunlight.

The soil is of three types, roughly equally divided: the upper part is the limestone of the plateau, the middle of the slope is clay/chalk and the lower part is silico-chalk.

The wine is consistently well made and reliable, and I noticed a remarkable continuity of depth of colour, even in the lesser of the last ten vintages that I tasted. Bernard Moueix, nephew of Armand, thinks this probably comes from the recirculation system that is employed during fermentation.

TECHNICAL INFORMATION

General

Appellation:	St Emilion, Grand Cru Classé
Area under vines:	18 hectares
Production:	9,000 cases
Distribution of vines:	In one piece – ⅓ third plateau, ⅓ côtes and ⅓ lower ground
Proprietor:	M. Armand Moueix
Oenologist:	M. Crebassa

Viticulture

Geology:	Limestone on plateau, clay/chalk on mid-slope, silico-chalk on lower ground
Grape varieties:	⅔ Merlot, ⅓ Cabernet Franc
Pruning:	Guyot Simple
Rootstock:	41B, 161/49, 420A
Vines per hectare:	5,400
Yield per hectare:	45 hectolitres
Replanting:	Regular replanting among the older vines to maintain average age of 25 years.

Vinification

Added yeasts:	Sometimes, in difficult years
Length of maceration:	15 days to three weeks
Temperature of fermentation:	25–30°C
Control of fermentation:	Water-cooled circulation
Type of cuves;	Cement
Vin de presse:	Generally used in declassified wine
Age of casks:	⅓ new, ⅓ one year old, ⅓ two years old
Time in cask:	12–15 months
Fining:	Egg-whites
Filtration:	Sur plaque, before bottling
Type of bottle:	Bordelaise

Commercial

Vente Directe:	No
Sales:	Handled solely by S.A. A. Moueix et Fils Château Taillefer, 33500 Libourne
Visits:	By appointment only Telephone: 57 51 50 63 (English spoken) Hours: Mon–Fri 0800 to 1200, 1400–1800

THE TASTING AT CHATEAU TAILLEFER,
14 September 1984
J.S., MM. Bernard and Armand Moueix

1983 Very dense colour. Good oaky bouquet. Hard, with backbone. Plenty of fruit and tannins and new wood. A wine for long keeping.

1982 Again very dense, dark red, almost black. Powerful, full fruity nose. In spite of being in bottle only three weeks, good balance and flavour showing. Will be a good bottle.

1981 Lovely deep colour. A little closed, but an attractive perfumed fragrance. Quite a tough mouthful, plenty of backbone with tannins evident. Good in a couple of years.

1980 Lighter, but still lively colour. Rounded, fruity fragrance. Well-made balanced wine. Good to drink now, but will last a while.

1979 Bluey red. Good blackcurrant fruit on nose. Well-balanced wine, will develop well. Good structure.

1978 Browny tinged, brilliant scarlet colour. Refined fragrance, quite closed. Good 1978 with finesse and complexity of flavours: a wine with fruit and depth. Will keep and improve.

1977 Good colour for 1977. Definite, attractive bouquet. Quite an agreeable wine with fruit and a touch of astringency, nice to drink now.

1976 Colour browning a little. Ripe, rounded nose. Soft fruity flavour-balance just right for drinking now, but will be OK for a year or two.

1975 Good garnet red. Gently perfumed, with fruit and flowers. Well made, balanced wine, more ready than most 1975 wines of St Emilion I have tasted.

1974 Quite good colour for '74, with a pleasant fruity bouquet. A bit short, but not at all a bad claret to drink now.

CHATEAU
La Gaffelière
ST EMILION

Approaching St Emilion from Libourne on the road to Bergerac, turn left at the crossroads after the village of Bigaroux. Go over the level crossing, and 400 metres further on, Château la Gaffelière is on your right, with its chai, storage and bottling rooms on the other side of the road.

The de Malet Roqueforts have been here for over 400 years, and la Gaffelière has been in the ownership of the same family longer than any other property in St Emilion. One of the oldest French families, the de Malets, Normans of Viking extraction, were ennobled by William the Conqueror for valour in the field of battle at Hastings. The first Comte de Malet, Roland, was accompanied by three sons during the English campaign; one of them stayed behind and founded an English branch of the family.

Although the château has been extended and refurbished several times, parts date back to the 12th century, notably the vaulted stone kitchen. The overall impression, however, is neo-Gothic, resulting from some extensive work during the 19th century. The garden is very beautiful, dominated by a magnificent cedar of Lebanon, 8 metres in circumference, planted by the first de Malet to live here some 400 years ago. 'Gaffelière' is an old French word for a leper colony, and it is quite possible that a hospital for these incurables existed here in times past, a prudent distance from the settlement of St Emilion.

In recent years a magnificent Gallo-Roman villa was discovered under part of the vineyard called le Palat (Latin – *Palatium*). The mosaics are quite magnificent, full of life and colour, depicting hunting scenes with lions and tigers. There is also a splendid centrepiece to the floor of what must have been the main room, showing a vine in full fruit, evidence, possibly, that wine was made here in the 4th century. Not unreasonably, Leo de Malet Roquefort suggests that this may well have been the site of Ausonius' palace.

One of the largest of the St Emilion vineyards, 22 hectares are planted with 65% Merlot, 20% Cabernet and 15% Cabernet Sauvignon grapes, on a limestone/chalk soil. Fermentation is in the gleaming array of stainless-steel vats, which were installed in 1974 in a building on the château side of the road. The wine of la Gaffeliére is then aged in oak casks, most of which are new each vintage, but the oldest of which is only two years. After use at la Gaffelière, the casks are passed on to Château Tertre Daugay, another property of the de Malet Roqueforts. Leo de Malet Roquefort plans to introduce two new labels for his properties, under which the wine from young vines, and any wine not suitable for inclusion in the Grand Vin, can be sold; the labels will be Clos la Gaffelière for Château la Gaffelière, and Château de Roquefort for Tertre Daugay.

The owner believes in a very long fermentation, and in replanting only when absolutely necessary to maintain a good average of old vines; these two factors, combined with the high proportion of new oak barriques, gives a firmness and body to the wine, and a tendency to slower maturing in bottle than some St Emilions.

TECHNICAL INFORMATION

General

Appellation:	St Emilion, Grand Cru
Area under vines:	22 hectares
Production:	8,000 to 10,000 cases
Distribution of vines:	In one piece
Proprietor:	Comte Leo de Malet Roquefort
Maître de Chai:	Alexandre Thienpont
Consultant Oenologist:	M. Chaine

Viticulture

Geology:	Limestone/clay
Grape varieties:	65% Merlot, 20% Cabernet Franc, 15% Cabernet Sauvignon
Pruning:	Guyot Simple
Rootstock:	Various
Density of vines per hectare:	5,800
Average yield per hectare:	38 hectolitres
Replanting:	As infrequently as possible, when necessary

Vinification

Length of maceration:	Three weeks
Temperature of fermentation:	Maximum 30°C
Control of fermentation:	Water-cooled stainless-steel cuves
Type of vat:	Stainless steel
Vin de presse:	Part vinified
Age of casks:	Maximum two years
Time in cask:	20–22 months
Fining:	Fresh egg-whites
Filtration:	Never
Type of bottle:	Bordelaise, Union des Grands Crus, personalised from 1983

Commercial

Exclusivities:	No
Sales:	Through Bordeaux wine trade
Visits:	Yes, by appointment Telephone: 57 24 72 15 Hours: Weekdays 0800–1200, 1400–1800

THE TASTING AT CHATEAU LA GAFFELIERE, 18 September 1984
J.S., Mlle. Berangère de Malet Roquefort

1983 Deep red, bluey tinges. Good nose with lots of fruit, not much oak. Quite approachable, plenty of fruit and tannin, but will, I feel, be ready sooner than some '83s I have seen.

1982 Good, deep red. Open, rounded, fruity bouquet. Flavour a bit muted, but this may be because this sample had only been in bottle for two weeks.

1981 Intense, brilliant colour. Powerful blackcurrant fragrance. Well structured wine, with some way to go.

1980 Lighter red, browning a little. Soft pleasant bouquet. Light wine, a bit on the short side, but agreeable claret for drinking now.

1979 Clear, rather tawny colour. Pleasing ripe nose. Well-made wine, with good, long aftertaste. Approaching readiness, but will keep.

1978 Colour brilliant red, shading towards russet. Very attractive, ripe nose – cedarwood? Complex flavour with backbone. To start drinking soon and for years to come.

1977 Browning red. Soft, fading fragrance. Light wine with fruit and charm. Good now.

1971 Pale orangey red. Soft, ripe and pleasant bouquet, a little burnt. Delicious flavour, *à point*. Not to keep for too long.

310

CHATEAU

Larcis-Ducasse

ST EMILION

Approaching St Emilion by the Libourne-Ber-gerac road, take the left turning at the crossroads immediately after the village of Bigaroux, go over the level-crossing, past the chais of Château la Gaffelière, and turn right along the D245. Château Larcis-Ducasse is about 1 km along this road on your left, next to Château Pavie.

Not much early history is known about this property, but it was certainly among the best vineyards of St Emilion as long ago as 1867, since it won a Gold Medal in the Universal Exposition in that year.

About 100 years ago, Larcis-Ducasse was purchased by Mr Henry Raba, a member of an ancient Bordeaux family. His granddaughter, Mme. Gratiot-Alphandéry, and her children are the present owners. For more than forty years Mme. Gratiot-Alphandéry has dealt with the whole management of the business. As a Professor of Psychology at the Sorbonne she mainly lives in Paris in winter, but she comes almost every week to Saint-Emilion and lives there permanently from June to the end of the grape harvest. A member of the Académie du Vin de Bordeaux since 1955, she attends many wine-tasting sessions in France as well as in other European countries while following closely the vinification and marketing of her own wines.

Philippe Dubois, the régisseur, was born at the château, and looks after the viticulture and vinification.

The vines, 65% Merlot, 25% Cabernet Sauvignon and the rest a mixture of Cabernet Franc and Malbec, cling tenaciously to a very steep, south-facing slope of chalky clay soil. It is a very difficult vineyard to work, since the steepest parts of the slope cannot even be reached with a caterpillar tractor, and heavy rain can wash away the topsoil from the highest levels. Making wine here is a real labour of love. However, the extreme height and the aspect of the vines give them optimum exposure to the sun.

Philippe Dubois, the present régisseur, is the successor to a régisseur who had been in charge for 36 years at Larcis-Ducasse. M. Dubois, although young and dynamic, remains quite faithful to the traditions and methods of vinification

which established the reputation of the great wines of Bordeaux. In the cellar of Larcis-Ducasse, after a short period of fermentation in cement vats, the wine ages on in oak vats and casks.

The wines are good, sound, and have plenty of fragrance and fruit, if a bit short on finesse. They stay well, and, at their best are really good St Emilion.

311

TECHNICAL INFORMATION

General

Appellation:	St Emilion, Grand Cru Classé
Area under vines:	11 hectares
Production;	5,000 cases
Distribution of vines:	In one piece, all sloping and facing south
Proprietor:	Mme. Hélène Gratiot-Alphandéry
Régisseur:	M. Philippe Dubois
Consultant Oenologist:	M. Chaise

Viticulture

Geology:	Limestone/clay
Grape varieties:	65% Merlot, 25% Cabernet Sauvignon, 10% Cabernet Franc and Malbec
Pruning:	Guyot Simple
Rootstock:	41B + 3309
Vines per hectare:	5,600
Average yield per hectare:	35 hectolitres
Replanting:	As necessary to maintain average vine age of 30 years

Vinification

Length of maceration:	As long as possible
Temperature of fermentation:	30°C
Control of fermentation:	Air circulation
Type of vat:	Concrete and wood for ageing
Vin de presse:	Mixed in on tasting if necessary
Age of casks:	4 years
Time in cask:	By rotation, average 6 months
Fining:	Egg whites
Filtration:	Yes
Type of bottle:	Bordelaise

Commercial

Vente Directe:	Yes
Direct ordering:	Yes
Exclusive agents:	No
Visits:	Yes, by appointement
	Telephone: 57 24 70 84
	Hours: 0800–1200, 1400–1800

THE TASTING AT CHATEAU LARCIS-DUCASSE, 13 September 1984
J.S., Christian Seely, Mr and Mrs David Nutting

The 1983 was tasted from a cask at the Château, but M. Dubois kindly gave me the other vintages to take away, as he thinks wine is so much better tasted with a meal, and I heartily concur.

1983 Colour brilliant, but much paler than most St Emilion 1983s I have tasted so far. Soft bouquet, closed, but fruit there, perfumed. Good balance, tannins there, but not at all aggressive.

1981 Good deep red. Pretty and open bouquet. Good fruit taste, with the right balance of tannins. Has some length and finesse – needs a couple of years.

1979 Deep bluey red. Nose good, with strong cassis. Rounded wine, well made, with good tannins – no great subtlety. A straightforward St Emilion to drink now.

1971 Very pale colour, showing age, quite a lot of brown. Beautiful fragrant bouquet. A really enjoyable glass of mature claret, absolutely ready, soft and full of fruit. Slight taste of strawberries. A good example of 1971 St Emilion.

1970 Dense colour, no browning. Open, ripe bouquet. Good, well structured wine, with good fruit and concentration of flavour. A ripe St Emilion, ready now.

CHATEAU
Larmande
ST EMILION

Take the D122 north from St Emilion towards Montagne, turn to your right at the crossroads after 1 km, and follow the small twisting road down into a valley and the entrance to Château Larmande is on your left after another half kilometre.

Larmande is one of St Emilion's oldest recorded winemaking properties. In the archives of the ton, there was a document showing that there were vines at Larmande in 1565, but, in spite of this evidence having been destroyed by a recent fire, the date 1640 is clearly carved in stone above the door of the chai.

According to M. Meneret-Capdemourlin, the present owner, Larmande was the joint property of both his paternal and maternal grandparents, who bought it from a M. Saint Genis. M. Meneret is closely tied to the Capdemourlin family, his mother being Alice Capdemourlin, sister of Jean and Roger.

Since he started to run Larmande in 1961, when there were only 11 hectares under vine, M. Meneret has gradually bought back bits here and

there, finally restoring the vineyard to its present, and original size of 23 hectares.

J.F. Meneret-Capdemourlin is President of the Association des Propriétaires des Grands Crus Classés de St Emilion, and is a member of a family that goes back 500 years in the history of wine-making in St Emilion.

He lives in a beautifully restored 14th-century house in the main street of St Emilion, beneath which is an extensive 13th-century cellar where the older wines of Larmande are kept.

The vines, a mixture of Merlot, Cabernet Franc, and Cabernet Sauvignon, grow in the 23-hectare vineyard on a soil that is a mixture of sand, gravel and clay on a chalky, stony subsoil. Many of the vines are extremely old – up to 100 years – giving an average age of 30 years. The combination of these well-aspected ancient vines, the typically 'difficult' soil, and the painstaking care which is given to every stage of the winemaking process, result in a wine that is well-structured, having power, elegance and longevity.

At a tasting organised by the Paris Chamber of

313

Commerce, mainly for the sommeliers of the top Paris restaurants, Château Larmande 1978 gained second place among the Premiers Grands Crus Classés B of St Emilion.

There is no château as such on the property, but the ancient creeper-clad buildings, though pictur-esque and full of rustic charm, are a model of cleanliness and efficiency within.

Professor Emile Peynaud has been consultant here since 1955, and Larmande was the first St Emilion property to avail itself of his services.

TECHNICAL INFORMATION

General

Appellation:	St Emilion, Grand Cru Classé
Area under vines:	18 hectares
Production:	6,700 cases
Distribution of vines:	All in one piece
Owner:	J.F. Meneret-Capdemourlin
Maître de Chai:	Roland Dudilot
Consultant Oenologists:	Professor Emile Peynaud and Guy Guimberteau

Viticulture

Geology:	Clay/limestone, clay/silica and ancient sand
Grape varieties:	65% Merlot, 30% Bouchet (Cabernet Franc), 5% Cabernet Sauvignon
Pruning:	Guyot-Simple
Rootstock:	3309, 420A
Vines per hectare:	From 5,400 to 7,000
Average yield per hectare:	Around 30 hectolitres
Replanting:	In very small parcels when necessary

Vinification

Length of maceration:	Three weeks and more
Temperature of fermentation:	30°–32°C
Control of fermentation:	Water cooling
Type of vat:	Stainless steel
Vin de presse:	Rarely included
Age of casks:	$\frac{1}{3}$ new, $\frac{1}{3}$ one year old, $\frac{1}{3}$ two years old
Time in cask:	12–18 months, depending on vintage
Type of bottle:	Bordelaise

Commercial

Vente Directe:	Very little
Exclusivities:	Yes, in Germany, Switzerland and Holland
Visits:	Yes, by appointment Telephone: 57 24 71 41

THE TASTING IN THE CUVIER AT CHATEAU LARMANDE, 7 September 1984
J.S., M. Meneret-Capdemourlin

1983 (Out of interest, we tasted firstly a wine from a new barrel, secondly a sample from a two-year-old cask.)
(a) New barrel. Good clear medium red. Strong vanilla nose, redolent of new wood. Long perfumed flavour, filling the mouth with long aftertaste. Tannin strongly predominant, but not aggressive.
(b) Two-year barrel. Definitely less tannin, and more fruit both on nose and palate.

1982 (M. Meneret did not plan to show this vintage, as it had been recently bottled, but at my request we tried a half-bottle.) The colour was a dense deep, ruby red. Nose closed at first, but opening into an explosion of vanilla and overpowering fruit, with strong perfume of blackcurrant. Fantastic, mouthfilling wine, full of fruit and tannin. Will become a fabulous bottle.

1981 Good dense, colour, with bluey tinges at the edge. Young, powerful bouquet. Well made wine with some oak still evident. To drink in two years.

1980 Very good colour for 1980. Bouquet still lively. A good bottle now with nice balance, but no hurry.

1979 Good red. Soft, blackcurrant perfume. Already rounded and charming, but will last and improve.

1978 Brilliant red. Lovely soft bouquet; complexity of fruit, vanilla and newly planed wood. Delicious, harmonious wine, with great concentration of flavour with long aftertaste.

1977 Palish red. Nose not assertive, but pleasant enough. Light luncheon wine, good for 1977 and could last a while yet.

1976 Good colour, showing a little brown. Nose quite undeveloped for '76. Well structured wine, ripe, but still plenty of life.

1975 Colour fairly light for the year. Elegant, per-fumed bouquet. Still a bit closed. A wine of elegance and finesse with masses of fruit, but tannins still predominant. Both the nose and the flavour begin to expand after a little time in the glass.

CHATEAU
Pavie
ST EMILION

From the D670 from Libourne to Bergerac, take the left turning to St Emilion after Les Bigaroux. Cross the level crossing, and watch for a small turning to your right just after Château la Gaffelière. Château Pavie is to be found about 1 km along this road on your left.

It is generally agreed that vines were widely planted throughout the St Emilion area from the fourth century during the Roman occupation, and Pavie's slopes were almost certainly among these early vineyards. It was not until as late as the mid-

19th century that individual vineyard names began to be generally known from St Emilion and Pomerol; the land was mostly owned by peasant farmers, and wine was made for home consumption and local sale. It should also be remembered that before the bridges over the Dordogne and the Garonne were built, St Emilion was very remote from the busy market of Bordeaux.

The first owners of this land I have been able to trace were a family called Fayard-Tallemon, who were proprietors in the first half of last century.

315

The first mention of Pavie in any work of reference is in the 1868 edition of Cocks et Feret, where the main proprietor is given as M. Pigasse, though he appears to have owned the vines that now form Pavie-Decesse at the top of the hill. There are also two smaller proprietors mentioned, with outputs of around nine and five tonneaux each, while Pigasse was producing up to thirty tonneaux. Good wine was certainly being made here at this time, attested by the Médaille d'Or awarded to the wine of Pavie in the Paris Exhibition of 1867.

The man who really put Château Pavie among the best St Emilions was Ferdinand Bouffard, who bought the property in 1885, extending the area under vines by adding the vineyards of several smaller crus, la Sable, which was already his, Larcis-Bergey and Pimpinelle, giving him a total of some 50 hectares under vines. Bouffard was also a Bordeaux merchant, assuring him of a ready market for the wine. He concentrated on the culture of the 'noble' varieties, and was evidently a most capable and scientific vigneron, since he won a special medal from the regional Agricultural Society for his work on the successful treatment of his vines against the phylloxera beetle. The quality of the wine made by Bouffard can be judged by the price achieved for the 1890 vintage, which was on a par with and above most of the Deuxième Crus Classés of the Médoc for the same year.

At the end of the First World War, Pavie was acquired by one Albert Porte, who remained in possession until 1943, when it was bought by Alexandre Valette, grandfather of Jean-Paul, who now runs the property. Valette was also a wine-merchant, but his business was based near Paris, and administration of his vineyards was directed from his office in Saint-Ouen-sur-Seine. He was also owner of Château Troplong-Mondot, whose vines run up to those of Pavie and Pavie-Decesse at the top of the hill. The Pigasse section of the property had been vinified separately since

Bouffard's day, and was sold as Château Pavie-Decesse. This was not part of Valette's 1943 purchase, and did not come into the family's possession until 1971.

On the death of Alexandre Valette in 1957, Château Troplong-Mondot passed to one branch of the family, while Pavie passed to the side of the family now represented by Jean-Paul, his grandson. Jean-Paul is a much-travelled man, with a wealth of widely diversified agricultural experience gained in the Dutch provinces and latterly ranching in Chile, where he met his wife. He took over responsibility for Château Pavie in 1967.

The vines of Pavie grow on a very steep slope, rising from 30 metres above sea-level to 90 metres, and are serviced by a zig-zagging track along which I was driven by Jean-Paul Valette at breakneck speed. The offices and cuvier are at the foot of the hill, the château half-way up, and the vast cellar where the casks lie is carved out of the limestone, nearly at the summit. It is possible that the name of Pavie may derive from this cellar, since *pavé* is the French for paving stone and *pavière* is a quarry, and it is from cellars such as this and those of Clos Fourtet and other properties that much of the stone used in the houses of the area must have been hacked in past centuries. Ideally suited for the ageing of wine as such cellars undoubtedly are, I was very much aware of the inherent danger in this underground cavern. The torrential rains that coincided with my visit were very much apparent in the cellar, and water streamed everywhere. Such rains eat away at the soil that binds the rock formations, and two major collapses have occurred in recent years. The last, in 1974, crushed some 50 casks of wine, though providentially the fall occurred during lunchtime, and nobody was injured. In the Pavie cask-cellar one can also see at first-hand the astonishing penetrative power of the vine, as the roots of the noble vines have found their way through the rock of the roof from the vineyards of Pavie-Decesse, some ten metres above.

The Pavie vines grow mainly on the light soil, covering brittle limestone rock, that comprises the 22 hectares of slopes; there are also 7 hectares of sandy clay on the lower ground, and 8 hectares of deep clay on the plateau. The whole vineyard is well aspected to the south. I find the wines of Château Pavie particularly charming; they tend towards an early readiness, but that is not to say that they do not age extremely gracefully. In youth they are less harshly tannic than many of their St Emilion peers, and as they evolve they develop a silky elegance, with an attractive summery fruitiness.

TECHNICAL INFORMATION

General

Appellation:	St Emilion
Area under vines:	35.5 hectares productive, total 37 hectares
Average production:	12,000 cases
Distribution of vines:	In one block
Owner:	Consorts Valette SCA
General Manager/ Director:	M. Jean-Paul Valette
Consultant Oenologist:	Since 1982 M. Pascal Ribereau-Gayon

Viticulture

Geology:	7 hectares low ground, sandy clay; 22 hectares slopes, light soil on limestone; 8 hectares plateau, heavy clay
Grape varieties:	25% Cabernet Franc (Bouchet), 20% Cabernet Sauvignon, 55% Merlot
Pruning:	Guyot Simple
Rootstock:	41B, 420A, 3320
Vines per hectare:	5,000 to 5,700
Average yield per hectare:	35 hectolitres (taken from 10 years figures)
Replanting:	As necessary to maintain average vine age of 45 years

Vinification

Added yeasts:	No
Length of maceration:	20–22 days
Temperature of fermentation:	28°–30°C
Control of fermentation:	Tubular cooling system
Type of vat:	Cement, glass- and resin-lined
Vin de presse:	Incorporated according to vintage
Age of casks:	⅓ new each vintage
Time in cask:	18–20 months
Fining:	Fresh egg-whites in the March before bottling
Filtration:	None
Type of bottle:	Bordelaise lourde

Commercial

Vente Directe:	No
Sales:	Through the Bordeaux négociants
Visits:	Yes, by appointment Telephone: 57 24 72 02 Hours: 0900–1200, 1400–1800

THE TASTING

M. Valette kindly gave me the following vintages to take away, and I tasted them at the home of my good friend Hugues Lawton on the Quai des Chartrons on 25 October 1984, which was followed by a delightful dinner, provided by Hugues's wife Micheline.
J.S., Hugues Lawton, Daniel Lawton, Pierre Lawton, Rupert Patrick

1981 Deep, bluey red. Bouquet quite evolved, with good fruit. Well-balanced wine, with good fruit and rounded tannins. Will be lovely.

1980 Medium deep red. Nose not yet pronounced, but has some fruitiness. Flavour good, but a little on the short side. All right to drink now.

1979 Good medium red. Bouquet good, but quite shy. A pleasing wine, good for drinking, a little light.

1978 Lovely ruby colour. Delicious bouquet of crushed strawberries. A mouthful of summer fruit, already very good. No great future, but superb for three or four years.

1976 Colour beginning to show a little brown. Very ripe nose. Good fruit in the mouth, with again that ripe, strawberry flavour. Delicious now, but short. To drink with enjoyment, but not for keeping.

1975 Brilliant medium red. Muted bouquet, good fruit present. Lots of fruit here, but also still very closed and tannic. Will be excellent in a year or two.

1973 Good scarlet colour. Attractive bouquet, soft and ripe. A wine of charm and elegance, with lovely flavour and aftertaste. Absolutely right for drinking now.

1971 Still has lovely colour. Open, ripe and ready bouquet. Tannins and fruit harmonising beautifully, with plenty of flesh left. Lovely now, but will stay a while yet.

1970 Dense red. Excellent, powerful nose. Concentrated, ripe flavour; still firm and rich with plenty of life. Very good.

1967 Lovely colour for such an old wine, only trace of brown. Very ripe full nose, with definite blackcurrant tones. Perfectly in balance now, very good and mouth-filling with a lingering aftertaste. Super.

CHATEAU
Pavie-Decesse
ST EMILION

Leave the Libourne-Bergerac road by the small road to the left just after Les Bigaroux, signposted to St Emilion. Cross the level crossing, and 500 metres further on turn right on the small road just past Château la Gaffelière. The entrance to Château Pavie is about 1 km along on your left, and Pavie-Decesse, with its vineyard, château and buildings, is at the top of the zig-zag track through Pavie's vines.

The history is closely tied in with that of Château Pavie, which I have already described in the chapter on that château. Separated from Pavie in the late 19th century, the two properties became re-united under the same ownership, when the Valette family bought the plateau vineyards of Pavie-Decesse in 1971.

There are eight of the total nine-and-a-half hectares currently in production, and the soil is a deep, chalky clay on a limestone base. The dominant grape here is the Merlot, with 60% of the vineyard planted with this variety. Vinification and ageing are similar to those applied by Jean-Paul Valette for Château Pavie, except that the vats at Pavie-Decesse are of stainless steel, with individual thermostatic temperature control.

The château itself, painted white and built in about 1890, is unoccupied, though Jean-Paul Valette's son may move in there shortly. It has a slightly Alpine atmosphere, and certainly commands an impressive view from its lofty – for the area – altitude of some 90 metres above sea-level.

I find the wine of Pavie-Decesse to have less

318

immediate appeal than that of Pavie, and it is perhaps slightly less typical of St Emilion in that respect, holding its charms in reserve until it has spent some time in bottle. This difference in character doubtless stems from the variation in soil type, for Pavie has only a small proportion of the limestone of the plateau which makes up the entirety of the Pavie-Decesse vineyard. After nearly ten years, the 1975 was opening up, and was developing into pleasing maturity. The 1980 I found to be more successful than at Pavie, which also indicates more 'backbone' in the style of the wine.

TECHNICAL INFORMATION

General

Appellation:	St Emilion
Area under vines:	8 hectares productive, 9.5 total
Average production:	4,500 cases
Distribution of vines:	In one block
Owner:	SCA du Château Pavie-Decesse (Valette family)
General Manager/ Director:	M. Jean-Paul Valette
Consultant Oenologist:	M. Pascal Ribereau-Gayon

Viticulture

Geology:	Deep clay on limestone
Grape varieties:	60% Merlot, 25% Cabernet Franc (Bouchet), 15% Cabernet Sauvignon
Pruning:	Guyot Simple
Rootstock:	41B, 420A
Vines per hectare:	5,400–5,700
Average yield per hectare:	40 hectolitres
Replanting:	As necessary to maintain vine age of 40 years

Vinification

Added yeasts:	No
Length of maceration:	20–22 days
Temperature of fermentation:	28–30°C
Control of fermentation:	By thermostatically controlled system
Type of vat:	Stainless steel and epoxy resin-lined cement
Vin de presse:	Included according to vintage
Age of casks:	⅓ new each vintage
Time in cask:	18–20 months
Fining:	Fresh egg-whites in the March before bottling
Filtration:	None
Type of bottle:	Bordelaise lourde

Commercial

Vente Directe:	No
Sales:	Through the Bordeaux négociants
Visits:	Yes: telephone: 57 24 71 81 Hours: Weekdays 0900–1200, 1400–1800

THE TASTING

Tasted at the home of my good friend Hugues Lawton on the Quai des Chartrons 25 October 1984
J.S., Hugues Lawton, Daniel Lawton, Pierre Lawton, Rupert Patrick

1981 Deep, bluey red. Nose has good fruit and some new wood. Harmonious and long, with fruit and tannins in balance. A wine of some finesse and elegance that will turn into a fine bottle with the passage of time.
1980 Fine, dark colour for this vintage. Nose soft and pleasing with good fruit. Straightforward, well-made 1980 with nice fruit flavour and no complications; finishes a bit dry.
1979 Purplish red. Fine bouquet of good fruit, hint of pepper. Very pleasing and rounded, but perhaps not up to the promise of the nose.
1978 Good, brilliant red, almost scarlet. Soft, ripe fruit bouquet. Lovely, soft and well rounded, perhaps lacking depth of some '78s.
1975 Lovely deep ruby, no browning. Good evolved aroma of ripe grapes. Mouthfilling, with excellent fruit, perhaps a shade less tannic than Pavie of the same year.

CHATEAU

La Tour Figeac

ST EMILION

Take the Libourne road from St Emilion; after about three kilometres turn right, signposted to Pomerol Centre. About 1½ km further on, having passed Château Figeac on your left, you will come to a left turn, and La Tour Figeac is about 500 metres along this road on your right-hand side.

As the name indicates, this property once formed part of the estate of Château Figeac itself, but was sold off in 1879. The tower which gave the vineyard the other part of its name stood until the end of the 18th century, and was rebuilt in 1960 at the same time as the château, a neat reconstruction of a Chartreuse hunting lodge.

La Tour Figeac now belongs to a German-owned company, and is run by Michel Boutet of Château Peyreau. The cellarmaster, a picturebook Bordeaux vigneron, is justly proud of the wine he makes, and of his fifty-odd years of work amongst the vines.

The 13.6-hectare vineyard is bounded by Château Figeac on the south side and Cheval-Blanc to the east, while the land to the west is in the commune of Pomerol. The soil is mainly sand, but there is a good outcrop of gravel on the higher ground. I was especially impressed with the improved quality of the later vintages I tasted, which I suspect may be put down to the introduction of a good proportion of new casks in the last two or three years.

TECHNICAL INFORMATION

General

Appellation:	St Emilion, Grand Cru Classé
Area under vines:	13.63 hectares
Average Production:	6,000 cases
Owner:	Société Civile du Château la Tour Figeac
Administrator:	M. Michel Boutet
Maître de Chai:	M. Beyly
Consultant Oenologist:	M. Cassignart

Viticulture

Geology:	Ancient sand, plus a good proportion of gravel
Grape varieties:	60% Merlot, 40% Cabernet Franc
Pruning:	Guyot Simple
Rootstock:	Various
Vines per hectare:	6,500
Average yield per hectare:	40 hectolitres
Replanting:	Average 5% per annum, maintaining average vine age of 35 years

Vinification

Added yeasts:	Yes, in difficult years
Length of maceration:	15–21 days
Temperature of fermentation:	28–32°C
Control of fermentation:	Running water on exterior of vats
Type of vat:	Lined cement and stainless steel
Vine de presse:	Proportion incorporated according to needs of vintage
Age of casks:	⅓ new each vintage
Time in cask:	18 months
Fining:	Albumen of egg in vat
Filtration:	Light, sur plaques, before bottling

Commercial

Vente Directe:	Yes, to callers
General sales:	Through the Bordeaux négociants
Visits:	Yes, for appointment telephone: 57 24 70 86

THE TASTING AT CHATEAU LA TOUR FIGEAC, 28 September 1984

1983 Very deep, dark red. Nose good, with fruit and new wood. Big wine with elegance and backbone. Will make a very good, well-structured St Emilion but it will take some time.

1982 Even darker colour. Nose closed, but fruit there in plenty. Big fat mouthful with backbone. Long aftertaste. Preferred it to the '83 and thought it might take longer to mature.

1981 Slightly lighter colour. Nose closed, but fragrance beginning to come through. Well made wine with good balance. Ready in eighteen months to two years.

1980 Lightish colour, but good for 1980. Fragrant blackcurrant nose, very pleasant. Round, easy wine with lots of fruit and some finesse. Good now, but no great hurry.

1979 Deep red. Good fruity nose, vigorous. Fruit to the fore, rounded and easy, long in the mouth. Tannins muted.

1978 Lighter colour than '79. Riper on nose. Ripe also to taste, with some tannin. I was not certain if there was enough fruit to keep this wine going overlong.

1977 Browning a little. Slightly overripe smell, but not unpleasant. Fruity, light but all right to drink now. Lacks the acidity of the '77s.

1976 Browny red. Nice ripe nose. Ready now, possibly beginning to fade.

1975 Tawny red. Still closed on nose, but showing promise. Plenty of everything it takes to make a really good bottle, but needs a year or two yet.

1974 Brown. Overripe bouquet. A bit maderised, but still has some fruit.

CHATEAU
Troplong-Mondot
ST EMILION GRAND CRU CLASSE

Take the D243 from St Emilion in the direction of St Christophe des Bardes. After half a kilometre, take the right fork, and Troplong-Mondot can be seen after another kilometre on the right. The gateposts are marked 'Mondot' and the château can be seen at the top of a plateau surrounded and backed by trees, with a huge water-tower, luckily mainly hidden by the trees, behind it.

The name of Mondot is a very old one. In 1746 the property belonged to the Sèze family, one of whom, Raymond, defended Louis XVI at his trial. It was acquired after the Revolution by M. Troplong, an eminent jurist. In the late 19th century, it came into the hands of a nephew of the family, who may have applied too many stringent economies, since the legend has it that the vendangeurs were so disgusted with the quality of the cuisine that they entered the château in a rebellious body and tipped their plates all over the carpets. The nephew was so annoyed with this display of ingratitude that he put the property on the market instantly. It was then bought by the Belgian Thienpont family; they ran it until the late 1920s, when they sold out to Claude Valette's great-grandfather, and moved to Vieux Château Certan in Pomerol, where they still live and make an excellent wine.

Troplong-Mondot is owned by a family com-

pany, and is now run by Christine Fabre, Claude Valette's very charming daughter. She lives in the château with her husband, who works with a sand and gravel company in Bordeaux. When they married, he was not interested in wine, but the life of St Emilion has worked its magic, and he is now converted.

Christine has now been in charge for three years, and, with the help of their oenologue, M. Roland of the Laboratoire Chevrier in Libourne, she is gradually making some small changes to try and improve the wine.

She was expecting a baby *après la vendange*, and hopes that he, or she, will grow up as involved with and devoted to the making of wine as she is herself.

Troplong-Mondot is beautifully situated on the highest piece of ground around St Emilion. The pretty ivy-covered house, surrounded on two sides and at the back by mature trees, has a lovely view over the vineyards to the rooftops and spire of St Emilion. Two thirds of the vineyard is overlooked by the château, and stretches to the slopes of Pavie to the south, owned by Jean-Paul Valette, cousin of Claude. The rest of the vineyard, together with the cuvier and chai, is to the rear of the house.

In all, 29 hectares are under vines, of which 65%

are Merlot, 25% Cabernet Franc, and 10% Cabernet Sauvignon. There is a high percentage of old vines, some over 100 years old, giving an average of 35 years.

The changes Christine Fabre has made include new varieties of rootstock, more use of new casks, a lower yield and later picking. It is this last change which has the most effect on the character of the wines, which was certainly noticeable in the tasting of the wines of 1981, 1982 and 1983. The use of riper grapes has produced a wine that is noticeably rounder and more open in bouquet and flavour.

TECHNICAL INFORMATION

General

Appellation:	St Emilion, Grand Cru Classé
Area under vines:	29 hectares
Production:	Around 12,000 cases
Distribution of vines:	In one piece
Proprietor:	Château Troplong-Mondot SA – Claude Valette
Régisseur/Manager:	Mme. Christine Fabre
Oenological Consultant:	M. Roland of Laboratoire Chevrier, Libourne

Viticulture

Geology:	Clay/Chalk
Grape varieties:	65% Merlot, 25% Cabernet Franc, 10% Cabernet Sauvignon
Pruning:	Guyot Simple
Rootstock:	420A, Gloire de Montpellier, SO4, etc
Vines per hectare;	6,000
Yield per hectare:	Around 40 hectolitres
Replanting:	None at present, but as necessary

Vinification

Added yeasts:	Rarely, in case of problematic fermentation
Length of maceration:	About 15–20 days
Temperature of fermentation:	About 28°C
Control of fermentation:	Water cooling and warm air circulation
Type of vat:	Stainless steel
Vin de presse:	Sometimes used in final assemblage if needed
Age of casks:	$\frac{1}{3}$ new, $\frac{1}{3}$ 1 year old, $\frac{1}{3}$ in vat
Time in cask:	12–16 months, according to vintage
Fining:	White of egg before bottling
Filtration:	Light, before bottling
Type of bottle:	Traditional bordelaise

Commercial

Vente Directe:	Yes
Direct ordering:	Yes, for French sales only
Agents in foreign countries:	Yes, in London
Visits:	Yes, telephone for appointment, Mme. Fabre 57 24 70 72 Hours: 0800–1200, 1400–1800

THE TASTING AT CHATEAU TROPLONG-MONDOT, 12 September 1984
J.S. Mme. Christine Fabre

1983 Good, medium red. Strong fruit and vanilla – new oak – on bouquet. Surprisingly approachable; loads of tannin and fruit, but tannin not overwhelming.

1982 Brilliant scarlet colour. Nose closed, and not too pleasant, but this is certainly due to sickness from bottling. This must be tasted again after it has had a month or two to recover.

1981 Light, clear red. Nose open, rounded and full of fruit. Very concentrated flavour with much tannin. A bottle to keep for a few years.

1980 Good deep colour for 1980. Soft, pleasant, Merlot bouquet. Nice, well made balanced wine. Excellent now, but will keep a while.

1979 Good, deep, bluey red. Good fruit on nose, but not very pronounced. Tannin predominates; a good round 1979 with plenty of life and depth.

1978 Lighter than 1979, but brilliantly clear. Nose surprisingly closed. Flavour a little short, but will develop.

1977 Pale colour, showing brown at edges. A bit tired on bouquet. A light wine, lacking fruit a little. To be drunk now.

1976 Lightish red, turning a bit brown. Ripe open nose. Delicious, mouthfilling with good fruit, and a long aftertaste. Perfect now.

1975 Deep, intense colour. Perfumed and full of fruit. Well structured wine with keeping qualities. One of the more open 75s of St Emilion.

1974 (Mme. Fabre was apprehensive about this vintage, and it was certainly not the best on show.) Medium browny-red. Strange, slightly antiseptic smell. Lacked fruit, perhaps not a good bottle.

1973 Light red. Slight cabbagey nose. Good flavour, ripe, well-made wine. Light and pleasant luncheon claret.

POMEROL

While Pomerol has an ancient history of viticulture, starting with the Romans and amplified by the Knights Templar of St John of Jerusalem, who founded a Hospital here in the 12th century, it is only since the middle of last century that it has been known for the production of high-quality red wine.

The wines of Pomerol have never been officially classified, although various experts have made listings of the properties of the commune based on price and quality. The 1850 edition of Charles Cocks makes no attempt to separate Pomerol from St Emilion, and it is not until the 1868 version of *Bordeaux et Ses Vins* that a number of named châteaux are mentioned. In the 1929 edition of this 'Bible of Bordeaux' some 120 crus are named; Château Petrus is given pride of place as a Premier Grand Cru, Vieux Château Certan and l'Evangile are listed as Grands Premiers Crus, followed by 52 Premiers Crus, 28 Deuxièmes Premiers Crus and 38 Deuxièmes Crus. The Bordeaux courtiers produced a list categorised solely by price in 1941; Alexis Lichine in his 1978 edition of *The Wines and Vineyards of France* lists about 40 properties, divided into five groups – Cru Hors Classe, Crus Exceptionnels, Grands Crus, Crus Supérieurs and Bons Crus. The most recent attempt was made by the late Henri Enjalbert in his scholarly work on the wines of St Emilion and Pomerol published in 1983; he lists 132 *marques* divided in four groupings, one Cru Hors Classe, 19 Très Grands Crus, 18 Grands Crus and 94 simply designated Autres Crus.

All these listings are in accord over the placing of Château Petrus in a class of its own above the rest, and are also more or less consistent in their rating of the top twenty or thirty châteaux.

The area entitled to the appellation is roughly diamond-shaped, with its southerly point some five kilometres north-east of the town of Libourne; the majority of the better vineyards are on the lower side of this diamond, that runs north-east from the village of Catusseau to Château Gazin, along the boundary between Pomerol and St Emilion. This proximity with the gravel vineyards of Cheval-Blanc and Figeac is noticeable in the style of such fine Pomerols as La Conseillante, l'Evangile and Petit Village.

The properties and the general atmosphere of Pomerol are in marked contrast to the seigneurial grandeur of the Crus Classés of the Médoc; most of the vineyards are far smaller – about 15 hectares

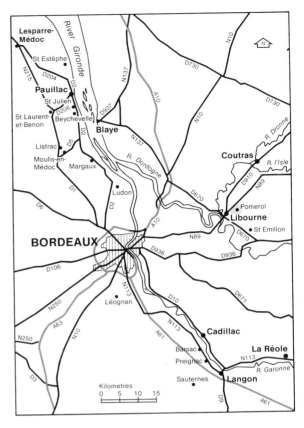

is the average – and the houses are mostly modest for the term 'château'. The properties are often 'owner-driven', and many of them share the services of a cellar-master with two or three other vineyards. The exception to this generality is the handful of properties owned by Jean-Pierre Moueix's Libourne-based company, with the fabled Petrus as the jewel in the crown. This remarkable Corrézien has probably done more for the world renown of the wine of Pomerol than any other single man, and his vineyards are models of cleanliness and order.

Pomerol wine, made principally from Merlot and Cabernet Franc grapes, is big, fat and gutsy. It matures relatively quickly, and is characterised by a beautiful depth of colour, said to stem from the ubiquitous ironstone subsoil or *crasse de fer*. It is also a supple wine with some finesse, and in the case of Petrus and the better châteaux on the St Emilion side, is capable of long and graceful ageing.

CHATEAU
Beauregard
POMEROL

From the village of Pomerol Catusseau, take the road for Montagne St Emilion, and Château Beauregard is the first property you will come to on your right.

During the 12th century, the knights of St John of Jerusalem, based in Malta, were landowners in Pomerol. They built a hospital here, a resting-place for weary pilgrims on their way to the shrine of St Jacques de Compostelle; in the garden of the château there is a stone bearing a Maltese cross, one of several found in the Pomerol area, doubtless serving as milestones or signposts for the pilgrims.

It was on the site of this ancient settlement that the de Beauregard family built a fine manor during the 17th century, which was totally destroyed by fire in the early 1700s. In 1775 M. de Chaussade de Chandos, who had married into the de Beauregard family and had become the owner of the estate, built the present château, engaging the services of a pupil of the great Victor Louis as architect.

The resulting château is one of the purest and most elegant examples of this period in the whole region, so much so that the English Georgian Society, which is devoted to the architecture and furniture of this period, recently made a special visit to Beauregard. So impressed was a wounded American soldier, who found himself in the region during the First World War, by the beauty and purity of the architecture of Beauregard, that he made detailed drawings of the château and took them back to the States. He was an architect in civilian life, and the drawings were to stand him in good stead in later years. In 1932 the widow of the

multimillionaire Harry Guggenheim, finding the vast mock-Tudor mansion she lived in too big and oppressive, commissioned our wandering architect to construct an exact replica of Château Beauregard on Long Island. This he did, and there it still stands. Beauregard in all but name and choice of building material, 'Mille Fleurs' is built of brick, slightly lacking the warmth of the sandstone original.

Just after the French Revolution, Beauregard passed into the hands of one Berthomieu de Barry from St Emilion: the wine trade was slack in the post-revolutionary years, especially due to the blockade of French ports by the English navy. De Barry was clearly an opportunist, for he grubbed up the vines and planted the land with garance, or madder, whose flowers were much in demand for the manufacture of red dye for military uniforms. The owner of nearby Château Figeac was also heavily involved in this operation, and actually built a factory for processing the plant. Berthomieu de Barry eventually sold to the Durand-Desgrange family, who re-established Beauregard's reputation as a wine property.

It was in 1920 that Château Beauregard came into the present owner's family, when it was inherited by Paul Clauzel's mother from her godfather. Clauzel is a name one encounters time and again in the course of research in the Bordeaux area. The family originates from the Médoc, where they have owned several properties in the past, and indeed there are today cousins of Paul Clauzel who make an excellent wine at Château la Tour de Mons in the commune of Margaux.

Traditions are maintained at Beauregard; at vintage time the grapes are gathered by hand, and loaded by the pickers into large wooden hods, carried on a fore-and-aft yoke by two men and emptied into wooden containers on the waiting trailer. Fermentation is in cement vats, and the wine is transferred to the usual oak casks, which are kept with wooden bungs to the side instead of on top. Clauzel is convinced this is better for the wine, since less evaporation takes place, therefore less topping-up is necessary and the wine consequently rests for longer periods, allowing for better precipitation of any matter suspended in the wine. As soon as Paul Clauzel judges that the correct marriage of tannins from the cask and from the wine has been arrived at, the wine is finally racked, and transferred to the vats where fining takes place with egg albumen. It is then transferred to glass-lined underground tanks, where it recovers from the fining and remains until bottling two or three months later.

Paul Clauzel is a friendly, likeable man, and an enthusiastic and talented winemaker. Château Beauregard is one of my favourite Pomerols, sturdy and well rounded, with a complementary element of finesse and backbone, which is doubtless due to the unusually high percentage of Cabernet Franc in the encépagement for this area; it has a good, bright colour that is always consistent, and in lesser years like 1980 and 1977 is always above average.

TECHNICAL INFORMATION

General

Appellation:	Pomerol
Area under vines:	13 hectares
Average production:	5,500 cases
Distribution of vines:	In one piece
Owner:	Héritiers Clauzel
Director:	M. Paul Clauzel
Maître de Chai:	M. Zucchi

Viticulture

Geology:	Gravel and sandy gravel with ironstone
Grape varieties:	48% Merlot, 44% Cabernet Franc, 6% Cabernet Sauvignon, 2% Malbec
Pruning:	Guyot Simple
Rootstock:	3309
Vines per hectare:	6,000
Yield per hectare:	35–40 hectolitres
Replanting:	As necessary

Vinification

Added yeasts:	No
Length of maceration:	3 weeks
Temperature of fermentation:	29°C
Control of fermentation:	Cooling apparatus
Type of vat:	Cement with silicate lining
Vin de presse:	Incorporated according to tasting
Age of casks:	$\frac{1}{3}$ new, $\frac{1}{3}$ casks of 1 vintage, $\frac{1}{3}$ casks of 2 vintages
Time in cask:	18–20 months
Type of bottle:	Bordelaise

Commercial

Vente Directe:	Yes
Direct ordering:	Only for French clients
Exclusivities:	None
Visits:	Yes, telephone: 57 51 13 36 Hours: 1000–1200, 1600–1800 Monday to Friday

THE TASTING AT CHATEAU BEAUREGARD, 18 October 1984
J.S., M. Paul Clauzel

1983 (In cask.) Very dense blackish red. Powerful nose of fruit – cassis and oak. Huge mouthful. All components there for a great bottle, oak, tannin plus fruit, very long.

1982 Beautiful deep clear red with bluey edges. Nose quite closed, but good fruit there. A big mouthfilling wine. Fruit and non-aggressive tannins in plenty. A great Pomerol.

1981 Medium-density bluey red. Nose quite closed, but beginning to come forward. Well-made wine, with fruit, tannin, backbone, and supple elegance. Will take a few years, and be very good.

1980 Good medium red, bright colour. Full rich bouquet. A good mouthful with fruit and tannin. Agreeable to drink now but no hurry. A good 1980.

1979 Middle red. Open nose with very good fruit. Flavour excellent, lots of fruit, tannins quite muted. Nearly ready.

1978 Bright scarlet, lovely colour. Lovely fragrant bouquet with fruit. A well-structured wine with fruit, tannin and backbone. Very long and perfumed in the mouth. To keep for quite some time.

1977 Colour only just beginning to brown. Very agreeable, ripe fruit on nose. Good flavour, finishing quite dry. All in all a good '77.

1976 Good medium deep red, slight brown. Ripe fruit on nose. Fruit and tannin harmonious, long and perfumed in mouth. Ready now, on plateau.

CHATEAU
La Cabanne
POMEROL

Leave Libourne on the RN89 in the direction of Perigueux; once clear of the built-up area, take the second turning on the right, and Château la Cabanne is about 500 metres along on your left, just before you come to Château Trotanoy on the opposite side.

Château la Cabanne is the property of Jean-Pierre Estager, who also owns Domaine de Gachet in Lalande de Pomerol and Château la Papeterie in Montagne St Emilion, as well as making the wine at Châteaux Haut-Maillet and Plincette in Pomerol and Domaine des Gourdins in St Emilion. La Cabanne is at the exact geographical centre of the Pomerol appellation, and the vines are well situated on the Haute Terrasse, bordering those of Château Trotanoy to the west.

There have been vines cultivated here since Gallo-Roman times, but the name of la Cabanne probably dates from the 14th century, when the area was dotted with isolated 'cabanes', or shanties in which the serfs lived. At that date, la Cabanne, like Clinet and Trotanoy, was part of the Bourgneuf estate.

In the 15th century it appears that the vineyard belonged to the Mays of Certan, who were the first to obtain a royal warrant authorising the culture of the vine on a large scale in Pomerol. Following them, the present proprietors have traced several owners, starting with Claude Louis de Gombaud, squire; around 1750 the property belonged to Monsieur Leonard Bulle, an advocate at court, Lieutenant-General and Mayor of

329

Libourne. The Berthomieux de Meynots, and the Destrilhe family also figure among past owners, the latter being ancestors of the well-known Libourne historian, Monsieur Guinodie.

Jean-Pierre Estager succeeded his father, François Estager, in 1966. The property is a model of cleanliness and good husbandry, and the wine is one of the best value for money Pomerols I have come across; rich, rounded and long, la Cabanne has excellent ageing qualities, and at the same time shows itself well while still relatively young. Made from a typically Merlot-dominated encépagement, the wine is fermented in epoxy-lined vats, and undergoes a three-week maceration period, followed by a long maturation in oak casks, of which half are new every vintage. Some 25% of the production is sold in France, and the rest is exported to many countries, finding specially good markets in the USA, Belgium and Switzerland. Sales are handled by Monsieur Estager's office in the Rue Montaudon in Libourne.

The château is a compact and attractive building; it is not inhabited, but has undergone recent refurbishment to provide a tasteful and atmospheric ambience for the reception of visitors and tastings.

TECHNICAL INFORMATION

General

Appellation:	Pomerol
Area under vines:	10 hectares
Average production:	5,000 cases
Distribution of vines:	Mainly in a block round the chateau, with a couple of small plots nearer to the D89
Owner:	M. Jean-Pierre Estager
Director and Administator:	M. Jean-Pierre Estager
Consultant Oenologist:	Laboratoire Pauquet, Libourne

Viticulture

Geology:	Clay/gravel on subsoil of clinker
Grape varieties:	80% Merlot, 20% Cabernet Franc
Pruning:	Guyot Simple
Rootstock:	Riparia, 420A, 60–34
Vines per hectare:	5,800
Average yield per hectare:	40–45 hectolitres
Replanting:	By rotation, in parcels of 1 to 1½ hectares

Vinification

Added yeasts:	No
Length of maceration:	3 weeks
Temperature of fermentation:	28–30°C
Control of fermentation:	By Alfa-Laval heat-exchange apparatus
Type of vat:	Epoxy-resin-lined cement
Vin de presse:	Proportion included according to needs of vintage
Age of casks:	30–40% new each vintage
Time in cask:	15 months
Fining:	Egg albumen, in vat
Filtration:	Light, sur terre
Type of bottle:	Bordelaise lourde

Commercial

Sales:	Enquiries to: J.-P. Estager, 35 rue de Montaudon, 33500 Libourne
Visits:	Yes, by appointment Telephone: 57 51 04 09

THE TASTING AT CHATEAU LA CABANNE, 9 May 1985
J.S., M. and Mme. J.-P. Estager

1984 Good deep colour. Nice bouquet, with soft fruit. Fruit and non-aggressive tannins there, with a long aftertaste.

1983 Same good deep red. Good bouquet, with some oak. Fruit good, with plenty of backbone, strong overtones of new oak.

1982 Darker than '83. Powerful and charming Merlot nose. A big, fat mouthful of wine; lots of fruit, backbone and ripe tannins. Excellent.

1981 Deep, bluish red. Fine bouquet with pleasing fruit. Quite closed still – fruit good, tannins slightly harsher than 1982, more finesse; will be a lovely bottle in a year or two.

1980 Excellent deep red for 1980. Open, attractive bouquet. A very pleasing flavour with good, almost sweet fruitiness. Perfect to drink now.

1979 Very deep, purplish red. Good nose, still quite closed. In flavour, firm, hard and closed, but all the elements are there if you wait a year or two.

1978 Good, intense red. Open, seductive nose. Ripe, well-balanced, with some complexity and long aftertaste. Ready but will also keep.

1966 (M. Estager gave me this blind, and I guessed it wrongly to be 67!) Colour still very good, only just starting to brown. Soft, lovely bouquet. Ripe and velvety in the mouth, fruit excellent, just right for drinking.

330

CHATEAU
La Conseillante
POMEROL

La Conseillante lies on the border of St Emilion and Pomerol. Take the road from the village of Pomerol-Catusseau in the St Emilion direction; pass Petit Village on your left, and you come to a crossroads. Château La Conseillante is the next property on your left.

The name of La Conseillante derives from an early owner of the property, one Mademoiselle Conseillante. The owners prior to the first Nicolas were a family called Leperche Princeteau, who were connected with the Toulouse-Lautrecs. Louis Nicolas, great-grandfather of Bernard and Francis, who now run the vineyard, bought La Conseillante in 1874, and four generations of Nicolas have built this into one of the best Pomerol vineyards with love and pride. Certainly they made wine of excellent quality, as is clearly indicated by the price fetched for the wine in the 1890s, which equalled and in many cases exceeded that realised by the better Second and Third Growths of the Médoc.

The property is currently owned by a family company, the Société Civile des Héritiers Nicolas and administered by Bernard and Francis with the same consuming passion as the preceding generations of Nicolas. Bernard does not live at the château; the only time he occupies the pretty, two-storeyed stone house is during the vintage, when nothing will tear him away from his beloved vineyard, day or night. On my visit to La Conseillante in 1984, M. Bernard Nicolas gave me much of his valuable time, and a most informative tasting. I should like to thank him for his Samaritan kindness to a traveller in a foreign country.

The 12 hectares of vines, 60% Merlot, 35% Cabernet Franc and 5% Malbec, are grown on a mixture of soils – gravel, sandy gravel, and clay with a subsoil of ironstone. This is one of the few properties in the area which can boast a good proportion of the character-giving 'graves' or gravel. Cheval-Blanc and Figeac across the road in St Emilion, and L'Evangile along the road also have their share. On the advice of Emile Peynaud, Bernard and Francis installed a battery of stainless-steel cuves in 1971; they were the first proprietors in Pomerol to do so. The vinification and ageing process is traditional, the wine spending 20

months in casks, half of which are new every year, and the rest only one vintage old. The dedication and care given at every stage of growing and vinification, as well as the variety of soil types and the high average age of the vines, enable the Nicolas family to produce a classic, elegant Pomerol with a superb colour even in the 'petites années'. This is one of my personal favourites.

TECHNICAL INFORMATION

General

Appellation:	Pomerol
Area under vines:	12 hectares
Production:	Average 45 tonneaux
Distribution of vines:	One piece
Proprietor;	Société Civile des Héritiers Nicolas
Directors:	MM. Bernard and Francis Nicolas
Oenological Consultant:	Professor Ribereau-Gayon

Viticulture

Geology:	Various; gravel, sandy gravel, and clay on an ironstone subsoil
Grape varieties:	60% Merlot, 35% Cabernet Franc, 5% Malbec
Pruning:	Guyot Simple
Rootstock:	SO4 and a 'father' of Riparia Gloire
Density of vines:	5,200 per hectare
Yield per hectare:	40–45 hectolitres
Replanting:	As little as possible, consistent with quality and maintenance of average vine age of 40 years

Vinification

Length of maceration:	18–20 days
Temperature of fermentation:	30–31°C – as high as possible, while keeping the yeasts alive
Regulation of fermentation:	Human!
Type of vat:	Stainless steel
Vin de presse:	Generally included
Age of casks:	50% new every year, 50% casks of one vintage
Time in cask:	20 months
Fining:	Four fresh egg-whites per cask
Filtration:	None
Type of bottle:	Bordelaise

Commercial

Vente Directe:	Very little
Exclusivities:	Absolutely none
Agents in foreign countries:	As arranged by the négociants with whom the château works
Visits:	Yes, by appointment Telephone: 57 51 15 32

THE TASTING AT CHATEAU LA CONSEILLANTE, 17 September 1984
J.S., M. Bernard Nicolas

1983 Good, brilliant ruby. Powerful bouquet of fruit and new oak. A big tannic wine, with all the ingredients of a promising stayer.

1982 Good colour, not especially deep. Nose agreeable, but closed. (Only bottled in July.) Soft, non-aggressive tannins, a bit unforthcoming, but this again probably due to recent bottling.

1981 Deeper red than 1982. Harmonious, perfumed fragrance – blackcurrant. Well-structured wine, excellent balance. Will drink quite well early.

1980 Excellent, dark colour, not at all typical of 1980. Fragrant, fruity nose of blackcurrants. Well-made, balanced wine, a technical success of which Bernard and Francis have cause to be proud. It will keep and improve.

1979 Good deep red. Soft fragrant nose. Lovely perfumed mouthful, with good aftertaste and an abundance of fruit and tannins to keep it going for years.

1978 Intense, deep colour. Bouquet closed, but promising, with fruit developing. A big, complex wine with balance, lots of tannin, but fruit there to balance; a wine to put away.

1977 Lighter red, with hardly a trace of brown. Open bouquet, with lots of fruit – fraises des bois? Balanced, ready to drink, without the acidity associated with '77.

1976 Pale garnet. Ripe nose. Harmonious and elegant. Perfect for drinking now, but will keep. Slightly burnt aftertaste.

1975 Brilliant, fairly light colour. Perfumed, if a bit muted nose. Delicious combination of fruit and tannin. A forward 1975.

1971 Pale russet, brilliant colour. Soft elegant fruit on nose. A very successful vintage – the first at La Conseillante with stainless-steel cuves. Perfect, elegant, balanced, ready now.

1967 Very lively red. Delicious fragrance, summer fruits and a hint of beeswax. Big and mouthfilling, excellent now, but with plenty of life.

CHATEAU
La Croix De Gay
POMEROL

La Croix de Gay is very near to the middle of Pomerol Centre. Driving along the small road that bisects the village on an east-west axis, you pass the impressive church set back from the road on your left. 200 metres further you come to a T-junction; turn left and the house and buildings of La Croix de Gay are on your right.

La Croix de Gay is very much a family concern. The good-humoured Noël Raynaud represents the fifth generation of his family to run this property. His daughter, married to a doctor, and his son, coincidentally also a doctor, are both very much involved and in love with the business. The doors of La Croix de Gay are virtually always open to visitors, so long as there is a member of the family around. They run an active 'vente directe' business, and have built a reception room next to the château, where, as well as the wine, the visitor may also buy delicious honey from the

hives of M. Raynaud's son-in-law.

When I asked if they had a special family recipe to go with their wine, I discovered that M. Raynaud had, by accident, become a snail farmer! In the spring of 1982 there was a plague of snails which started to defoliate the vines. The only way of dealing with this problem was simply to go out in the vineyard and collect them off the vines. There then arose the question, what to do with all those bucketsful of escargots? If they were thrown away, they would surely find their way back to the vines, and, being French and practical, it would have been a crime to destroy so much good food. As luck would have it, M. Raynaud had just taken delivery of a large circular, free-standing swimming pool for his children and grandchildren. The family, it appears, preferred swimming in the sea at Arcachon, so here was an ideal home for the snails, and in they went. It is now a veritable snail paradise, although would-be escapees are deterred by an electrified perimeter wire along the rim of the pool. M. Raynaud religiously feeds and waters his ever-increasing stock, and has even tried introducing the fatter, more juicy strain from Burgundy. The traditional enmity between the two great wine regions extends into the snail world, however, and mixed marriages have not occurred.

Although the Raynauds insist that La Croix de Gay is really too big and robust a wine to drink with their 'escargots Bordelaise', I have nevertheless included the recipe in the 'Gastronomie Bordelaise' section in memory of my visit.

The twelve hectares of vines are scattered around Pomerol Centre in parcels of three and four hectares, with a high percentage of Merlot. The soil is varied on a subsoil of part sandy gravel, part clay-gravel. There are some very old vines, dating back to 1920 and before. These are always harvested by hand, although machines have been used for the main part of the crop for three years. M. Raynaud regrets the passing of the old spirit of the vendange which he remembers as a time of 'fête', with the pickers enjoying a gay, holiday atmosphere in spite of the hard work, sitting down, sixty or seventy of them, to jolly lunches. The wine is invariably good, reliable and typical Pomerol – firm and muscular with a tendency to early maturity.

Vinification is pretty traditional; a combination of stainless-steel and cement vats are used for the cuvaison, but M. Raynaud prefers the cement for the malolactic fermentation, since the temperature after the first fermentation drops slowly and naturally, allowing a more even malolactic. The wine then spends 18 months ageing in oak casks, about 30% of which are renewed each year.

TECHNICAL INFORMATION

General

Appellation:	Pomerol
Area under vines:	12 hectares
Production:	6,000 to 7,500 cases
Distribution of vines:	Split up in parcels of three and four hectares
Proprietor:	M. Noël Raynaud
Oenological Consultant:	M. Rolland, Libourne

Viticulture

Geology:	Varied soil, on subsoil of part sandy gravel and part clay gravel
Grape varieties:	80% Merlot, 20% Cabernet Franc
Pruning:	Guyot Simple
Rootstock:	420A, 101–14, 3309, 504
Vines per hectare:	5,000 to 6,000
Average yield per hectare:	42 hectolitres

Vinification

Length of maceration:	Three weeks to one month
Temperature of fermentation:	32°C max.
Control of fermentation:	By water-cooled circulation
Type of vat:	Enamelled cement and stainless steel
Vin de presse:	Only very rarely incorporated
Age of casks:	25–30% new each year
Time in cask:	18 months
Fining:	Fresh egg-whites
Filtration:	Yes, sur terre before going into cask and sur plaque before bottling
Type of bottle:	Bordelaise

Commercial

Vente Directe:	Yes
Direct Ordering:	Yes
Agents in foreign countries:	Yes – England, USA, Belgium, Switzerland and Canada
Visits:	Yes: for appointment telephone 57 51 19 05 Hours: When anyone is at home!

THE TASTING AT LA CROIX DE GAY,
17 September 1984
J.S., M. Noël Raynaud

1983 Very deep intense red. Good, if reserved bouquet. Good fruit/tannin balance. Will be an excellent bottle.

1982 Dark, clear red. Open and attractive, round fruit on nose. A little bit 'bottle sick', although bottling was done in the spring.

1981 Deep, bluey red. Rich evolving blackcurrant fragrance. Still closed, with high tannin, but plenty of fruit. Will be a very good bottle in a year or so.

CHATEAU
L'Evangile
POMEROL

Follow the D21e from Libourne through Catus-seau in the direction of Montagne St Emilion. Just after Château la Conseillante there is a left fork, and Château l'Evangile is the first château on the left about 100 yards along this road.

The property has remained in the same family since 1862. During the Revolution, all the archives of the property were burnt, so any earlier history was lost for ever. The Ducasse name had long associations with the area; it was a Mlle. Henriette Ducasse from l'Evangile who, in 1852, married Jean Laussac-Fourcaud, and brought to the union an unknown vineyard known then, as now, under the name Cheval-Blanc. The family name is also perpetuated in that of Château Larcis-Ducasse, another St Emilion Grand Cru, which at one time was a family property.

Madame Ducasse, a dignified but very alert and charming old lady, now lives in the light, airy château; like her husband, Louis Ducasse, who died in 1982, she is fiercely proud of l'Evangile and its wines. Madame Ducasse speaks with obvious love of her late husband and of all he did for l'Evangile in the twenty-eight years during which he lived and worked at the property. It was, I feel, typical of the lady that she did not wish to be photographed, saying that with a tradition as long as the Ducasse/l'Evangile story, individuals really didn't count.

There is no doubt that the wine of l'Evangile is among the best of Pomerols. In good years it is superb, while the variety of soils in the vineyard give it the opportunity to turn out respectable wine in off-vintages. There are three distinctly different soils, sand, clay and some gravel, and the grapes grown are a typical Pomerol mixture of 65% Merlot and 35% Cabernet Franc, or Bou-chet, as it is sometimes called on this side of the Dordogne. The wine has a deep, rich colour and an unusually flowery and fragrant bouquet; in taste it is rounded and velvety in the best Pomerol tradition, yet in good years it has a marked feminine elegance which one does not always find in the wines of this region. There is never enough l'Evangile made to satisfy the huge demand. The three young vintages which Madame Ducasse gave me to taste were all excellent examples, the

1978 being especially to my taste, and, I am pleased to say, to that of the owner. Since leaving Bordeaux, Madame Ducasse has written me a charming letter, in which she curses herself roundly for having forgotten to give me a bottle of the great 1961 to taste, which she had specially prepared from her private cellar, and inviting me to call in when I am next passing. I think this will be very soon.

TECHNICAL INFORMATION

General

Appellation:	Pomerol
Area under vines:	13.67 hectares
Average production:	5,500 cases
Distribution of vines:	In several pieces
Owner:	Société Civile du Château l'Evangile – les Héritiers Ducasse
Director:	Mme. Louis Ducasse
Maître de Chai:	M. Toni Zucchi

Viticulture

Geology:	Gravel, clay and sand
Grape varieties:	65% Merlot, 35% Cabernet Franc (Bouchet)
Pruning:	Guyot Simple, severe
Rootstock:	420A, 110 Richter, 3309
Vines per hectare:	5,500
Yield per hectare:	Voluntarily kept down to 30–40 hectolitres
Replanting:	Small areas, every 2 years

Vinification

Added yeasts:	No
Length of maceration:	20–30 days
Temperature of fermentation:	30°C average
Control of fermentation:	Cooling by water-spray on cuves
Type of vat:	Cement
Vin de presse:	Part vinified, and incorporated depending on vintage
Age of casks:	⅓ new each vintage
Time in cask:	Average 15 months
Fining:	Fresh egg-white in cask
Filtration:	None
Type of bottle:	Bordelaise lourde

Commercial

Vente Directe:	No
Sales:	Through the Bordeaux négociants
Visits:	Yes, by appointment only Telephone: 57 51 15 30

THE TASTING AT CHATEAU L'EVANGILE, 11 September 1984
J.S., Madame Louis Ducasse, M. Toni Zucchi

1983 Very dense, almost black red. Powerful, aromatic nose. Big, mouthfilling wine with power, fruit and tannins. Also has structure and elegance, but one to keep a long, long time.

1982 Again lovely dark purple. Rich, rounded and floral bouquet, with a mass of fruit. A big tannic wine with lots of grip, but huge with fruit and beautifully lingering aftertaste.

1978 Good, clear dark red. Excellent perfumed grapey nose. Lovely ample wine, with backbone and distinctly feminine charm. Long, perfumed aftertaste that accompanied me all the way to lunch in St Emilion.

CHATEAU

Gazin

POMEROL

337

Take the D21e from Libourne, through the village of Pomerol-Catusseau, pass Châteaux Petit Village and la Conseillante on your left and you come to a left fork in the road; immediately on your left is Château l'Evangile. Continue along this road for about 1 km, with the vineyards of Gazin on both sides, until you arrive at a crossroads. Turn left, and the château is about 500 metres along on your right.

From the road, the long, low, stone-built château appears to be hiding in the vines, as it lies at the foot of a slope. The largest Pomerol vineyard of note, Gazin used to be a farm belonging to the knights of St John of Jerusalem, and indeed was formerly called the Domaine des Templiers. For several generations Gazin has been in the family of the present proprietors, the de Baillencourts.

The present owner, M. Etienne de Baillencourt, is a jolly, sporting gentleman of the old school; tweed-clad with a permanent Gauloise in his mouth, usually unlit and often the wrong way round, de Baillencourt owns a successful wine business based in the Oise department. He visits Gazin about once a month, but the vineyard is ably looked after in his absence by his chef de

culture M. Vallade and the maître de chai, M. Forest.

Château Gazin produces a round, gutsy Pomerol, tending towards early maturity, though the wine ages very well. Fermentation takes place in cement vats, curiously disguised to look like oak, and ageing is in traditional oak casks, some one-third of which are replaced annually.

TECHNICAL INFORMATION

General

Appellation:	Pomerol
Area under vines:	22.5 hectares
Production:	9,000 cases
Distribution of vines:	In one piece
Proprietor:	M. Etienne de Baillencourt, also known as M. de Courcal
Maître de Chai:	M. Forest
Régisseur/Chef de Culture:	M. Vallade
Consultant Oenologist:	C.B.C., Libourne

Viticulture

Geology:	Clay/gravel on an ironstone subsoil
Grape varieties:	$\frac{2}{3}$ Merlot, $\frac{1}{6}$ Cabernet Franc, $\frac{1}{6}$ Cabernet Sauvignon
Pruning:	Guyot Simple
Rootstock:	Various
Density of planting:	6,000 vines per hectare
Yield per hectare:	35–40 hectolitres
Replanting:	As necessary to maintain average vine age of 25 years

Vinification

Added yeasts:	None
Length of maceration:	About 10 days
Temperature of fermentation:	25–30°C
Control of fermentation:	Cold/heat exchange apparatus
Type of vat:	Cement
Vin de presse:	Incorporated according to vintage
Age of casks:	$\frac{1}{4}$ to $\frac{1}{3}$ renewed annually
Time in cask:	18 months
Fining:	Fresh egg-whites
Filtration:	None
Type of bottle:	Bordelaise

Commercial

Vente Directe:	Yes, to visitors
Commercialisation:	Via Bordeaux négocients
Visits:	Yes, by appointment Telephone: 57 51 07 05 or 57 51 88 66 (M. Vallade) Hours: Office hours, not weekends

THE TASTING AT CHATEAU GAZIN,
26 October 1984
J.S., Etienne de Baillencourt, M. Vallade

1983 (In cask.) Good medium red, bluey at edges. Oak and fruit good on nose. Plenty of fruit and tannin in mouth, very oaky. M. de Baillencourt reckoned it would drink in 5 years. I should be surprised. (The owner tells me that, on later tasting, it has become very close to the 1982 in style.)

1975 Good red, beginning to brown a shade, but still very dense. Nose open for 1975, full of ripe fruit. Lovely mouthfilling wine with a definite strawberry fragrance in the mouth. Finishes a little dry.

CHATEAU
Nénin
POMEROL

Leaving Libourne on the D21e towards the hamlet of Pomerol-Catusseau, you will find the gateway to Château Nénin on your right just before you enter Catusseau, with the vineyard on the left of the road.

The Despujol family have owned Nénin for five generations; when they first acquired the property 150 years ago there were only 20 hectares of vines, but the family gradually bought parcels of land and increased the vineyard to a total of 51 hectares just after the Second World War. Since then some land has been sold, reducing the area under vines to the present size of 28 hectares, which is still one of the largest Pomerol properties.

François Despujol is a very capable businessman with many other irons in the fire, including the Citroën agencies in two departments, a farm elsewhere, a bloodstock business and another property in the Médoc. He has a great love for Nénin, and a strong feeling for family continuity, and under his careful and skilful direction Nénin is enjoying a successful period. No corners are cut in vinification and viticulture; a range of new stainless-steel cuves have been installed, and at least 100 new casks are used for each vintage.

There is a high proportion of gravel in the soil of Château Nénin's vineyard, which, allied to the – for Pomerol – large amount of Cabernet Franc and Cabernet Sauvignon vines, gives a rather tannic wine which requires a little more ageing than other wines of this appellation. It is this slightly Médocain character, perhaps, which accounts for the wine's popularity in England, where it sells extremely well.

There is a second label, Château St Roch, under which the produce of young vines and much of the wine of lesser vintages is sold.

The attactive Chartreuse house, set in a wooded park, is lived in by François Despujol's sister, though he maintains an apartment in the château.

TECHNICAL INFORMATION

General

Appellation:	Pomerol
Area under vines:	28 hectares
Production;	12,000 cases
Distribution of vines:	In one block
Owner:	Société Civile Agricole du Château Nénin
Director:	M. François Despujol
Régisseur:	M. Pierre Esben
Maître de Chai:	M. Chambaud
Oenological Consultant;	Professor Roland (formerly Professor Peynaud)

Viticulture

Geology:	80% gravel, 20% sand
Grape varieties:	50% Merlot, 30% Bouchet (Cabernet Franc), 20% Cabernet Sauvignon
Pruning:	Guyot Simple
Rootstock:	Riparia Gloire, SO4
Density of planting:	6,000 vines per hectare
Replanting:	Average 1 hectare per annum

Vinification

Added yeasts:	None
Length of maceration:	15–28 days, depending on vintage
Temperature of fermentation:	25–26°C
Control of fermentation:	Refrigeration
Type of vat:	Cement and stainless steel
Vin de presse:	Added in some vintages
Age of casks:	100 new casks per annum (25%)
Time in cask:	18 months
Fining:	Fresh egg-whites, in cask
Filtration:	In some years before bottling
Type of bottle:	Bordelaise

Commercial

Vente Directe:	Yes, for Château St Roch
Exclusivities;	None
Agents abroad;	None
Visits:	Yes, telephone 57 51 00 01 Hours: 0800–1200, 1400–1800

THE TASTING AT CHATEAU NENIN,
20 September 1984
J.S., François Despujol

1983   Good, deep, purply red. Nose muted. Big, oaky wine, with lots of fruit and tannins. One to wait for.
1981   Again a good, dense colour, with bluey edges. Soft, fruity and fragrant. Good, well-made wine, supple, with fruit and tannin in harmony. Not aggressive.
1980   Exceptionally good colour for 1980. Attractive bouquet, slightly reminded me of nougat. Round, balanced and well-made, with plenty of life. A very good 1980.

CHATEAU

Petit-Village

POMEROL

Leave Libourne on the small D21e towards Montagne-St Emilion, drive through the village of Pomerol-Catusseau, and you will pass Château Beauregard on your right. Château Petit-Village, which is well signposted, is the next vineyard on the left.

The name of Petit-Village may owe its origin to an early settlement on this site, which could well have been the actual village of Pomerol. The history of individual properties in Pomerol is all very recent, since the suitability of the soil for the growing of the Merlot grape and the making of fine red wine was not discovered until the 19th century. Wine has certainly been made here since the Middle Ages, but it was predominantly white, and of no great quality. Doubtless this white wine was much appreciated by parched and weary pilgrims, on their way to the shrine of St Jacques-de-Compostelle, for the knights of St John of Jerusalem had a Hospital, or resting-house for these travellers here in Pomerol. Large stones have been found in the area, bearing a Maltese cross, which probably served as signposts for the devout travellers, pointing the way to rest and nourishment!

Château Petit-Village was bought in 1919 by Fernand Ginestet from Monsieur J.P. Heron. It now belongs to Domaines Prats, whose share-holders are three brothers, grandsons of Fernand Ginestet, Jean-Marie, Yves and Bruno Prats. They also own the fine Second Growth Château Cos d'Estournel in St Estèphe; the two properties are administered by Bruno Prats, a skilled wine-maker, and an active promoter at home and overseas of his own wines, and the Bordeaux region as a whole.

The vineyard is an 11-hectare triangle, surrounded by other Pomerol properties of high repute – Beauregard to the south, la Conseillante in the east and Vieux Château Certan to the north. It is situated on an elevated outcrop of gravel from the Isle river, and is planted with 80% Merlot grapes, with an above average 20% of Cabernets. The wine is one of the best Pomerols, gutsy and powerful, showing well in its early stages with bags of bouquet and round, ripe fruit flavour, but also ageing well, becoming more refined and less assertive as the years pass.

The château is a simple farmhouse, like many so-called châteaux in Pomerol and St Emilion. There is a large reception room at first-floor level, and the chai and cuvier bear the Prats' stamp of immaculate and functional cleanliness. It is a pity that Petit-Village is so 'petit', for a fine wine is made here, and demand invariably exceeds supply.

341

TECHNICAL INFORMATION

General

Appellation:	Pomerol
Area under vines:	11 hectares
Average production:	5,000 cases
Distribution of vines:	In one block around château
Owner:	Domaines Prats
Régisseur and Maître de Chai:	M. Gilbert Xans
Consultant Oenologist:	Professor Pascal Ribereau-Gayon

Viticulture

Geology:	Isle gravel on ironstone sub-soil
Grape varieties:	80% Merlot, 10% Cabernet Sauvignon, 10% Cabernet Franc
Pruning:	Guyot Simple
Rootstock:	101–14
Vines per hectare:	6,000
Yield per hectare:	40 hectolitres
Replanting:	As necessary, maintaining average vine age of 25 years

Vinification

Added yeasts:	Own and selected cultures
Length of maceration:	20–28 days, according to vintage
Temperature of fermentation:	Varied, according to vintage
Control of fermentation:	By heat-exchange pump
Type of vat:	Lined steel
Vin de presse:	Incorporated in Grand Vin
Age of casks:	100% new for big years, 70% new for average years, casks of one vintage for light years
Time in cask:	Varied, according to vintage
Fining:	Egg whites
Filtration:	Before going in cask, and before bottling
Type of bottle:	Traditional

Commercial

Vente Directe:	In France only
Sales:	Enquiries to Domaines Prats, 84 rue Turenne, 33000 Bordeaux
Visits:	Yes, by appointment Telephone: 56 44 11 37 Hours: 0900–1200, 1430–1730 Monday to Friday

THE TASTING AT CHATEAU PETIT-VILLAGE, 22 November 1984
J.S., M. Hallay (of Domaines Prats)

1983 Very dark red, almost black. Nose has lots of fruit and strong scent of new oak. Very big, tannic mouthful, loads of new wood and fruit. A fine Pomerol that will repay keeping.

1982 Deep colour. Nose beginning to evolve, lots of fruit and new wood. Very big, rounded wine, with tremendous power and long aftertaste. Tremendous ripeness, will be drinkable quite soon, but will also keep.

1981 Excellent medium dark red. Slightly smells of wet animal fur. A very well-balanced wine, promising well. An adolescent, but a well-bred one!

1980 Deep blackish red. Nose still closed, but good fruit coming through. Concentrated, mouthfilling flavour, with good tannins. Not typical of the vintage. Will keep and get better.

1976 Colour shading to orange. Nose lovely and very ripe. Approaching the peak. Very good now, finishing dry and a little short.

CHATEAU

Petrus

POMEROL

Take the road from Libourne through the village of Pomerol-Catusseau; after about 1 km pass Château Petit-Village on your left and you come to a crossroads. Turn left towards Pomerol Centre, then turn right at the next crossroads, leaving Vieux Château Certan on your right. Petrus is on your right just the other side of the next crossroads.

Château Petrus is really the shooting star of the Bordeaux region. Unknown until the mid-19th century, I found the first mention of the vineyard in Cocks et Feret's 1868 edition, when it was rated third of the then just emerging Pomerol wines. Although really good Pomerol was made here in the late 19th and early 20th centuries it was not until the fabulous 1945 vintage that the world's wine-lovers began to sit up and take note of this tiny property.

Madame Loubat, an intriguing lady of great character, owned Petrus from 1925 until her death in 1961. There is a glamorous painting of the lady in her heyday in the reception room downstairs at the château, as well as a photograph taken in later years and a dashing caricature by the artist SEM. Although she started buying shares in Petrus in 1925, she did not become sole owner until 1945. Her husband, Edmond, founded and owned the Hôtel Loubat in Libourne, and Madame Loubat was a popular patronne, especially with the young officers from the regiment garrisoned in Libourne. The stories about this grand old lady of Pomerol are legion. On the occasion of the engagement of Queen Elizabeth II of England, then Princess Elizabeth, to Prince Philip, Madame Loubat despatched a magnum of Château Petrus as a wedding-present, and as a result received an invitation to the royal wedding. On the trip to England, Madame Loubat, having never visited the country before, decided to take some of her own wine with her in the car 'just in case'. Duly installed in her hotel in London, she enquired if there was a good French restaurant at which she might dine, and was directed to the Mirabelle. Expecting a bistro type of establishment with a commensurate bill, the lady found herself short of cash when the account was placed before her. Not a whit discomfited, she sent her companion out to the car,

who returned with the case of Château Petrus, and an amicable exchange was effected. History does not record the vintage, but if it was the 1945 the restaurant got the better part of the deal, even at their prices!

Jean-Pierre Moueix, the human asteroid in the Pomerol galaxy, has been the other factor in the meteoric rise of Petrus. He has been sole distributor of its wine since 1945. When Madame Loubat died, Petrus was inherited by a niece, Madame Lily Lacoste, and a nephew; the latter's shares were bought by Moueix in 1964. He has been in charge of the property ever since, and his first and most important step was to appoint a very able régisseur in Michel Gillet. Moueix also employs a full-time oenologist, Jean-Claude Berrouet, a gentle and retiring man whose knowledge of wine and vinification is encylopedic. The Moueix business is gigantic; they own or manage sixteen important properties in Pomerol and St Emilion, and their négociant business, based in Libourne, is one of the biggest in the Bordeaux region. As well as dealing in wines from the Grands Crus, of which an astonishing stock is held in their 'Cathedral of Wine', as the warehouse on the Quai du Priourat is known, they do a thriving business by buying the wines of smaller properties, ageing them in cask in their capacious chais and marketing them all over the world.

Back to Petrus. Day-to-day running and administration are the direct responsibility of Jean-Pierre Moueix's tall, bearded and courteous son Christian. The tasting which he organised for my son, another Christian, and myself was unique. Never before have the owners given a vertical tasting of so many vintages of Château Petrus, even for themselves. It was a fascinating and privileged morning, and I was delighted that Michel Gillet, Jean-Claude Berrouet and Christian Moueix were obviously as pleased and interested as we were. The tasting, and the lunch which followed at Château Trotanoy, hosted by Christian's cousin Jean-Jacques Moueix, were high spots in my life in the world of wine, and I thank the Moueix family for their kindness.

The wine of Petrus beggars my powers of description. It has the most extraordinary power, rich-

ness and concentration of flavour of any wine I know, and cannot readily be compared with any other. It is this totally unique style, coupled with the fanatical care and love that the Moueix team give to its making, that have made Petrus the ultimate collector's dream. It now fetches prices above Lafite, and above the red wines of the fabled Romanée-Conti of Burgundy.

The vineyard and consequently the production of Château Petrus are very small. Some 4,000 cases are all that are available in an average vintage to slake an unquenchable world thirst for this remarkable wine. The 11.5-hectare vineyard, planted with virtually 100% Merlot, is harvested at exactly the optimum moment of ripeness in a matter of two or three days. This is done by

concentrating a labour-force of some 180 pickers on the vineyard, who only pick in the afternoons to ensure that the grapes are perfectly dry. The soil is a bluey clay with a subsoil of sandy gravel on a bed of 'crasse de fer', almost impenetrable iron-stone; there is a small amount of gravel on the edge of the vineyard. Vinification is traditional and meticulous; the wine ferments in concrete vats, the first press is always included from the start, and 100% new barrels are used every vintage. The whites of four or five fresh eggs are used for the fining, and bottling is done by hand after an average ageing of 21 months in cask.

Sadly, but understandably because of the diminutive production, visits and tastings are rarely permitted.

344

TECHNICAL INFORMATION

General

Appellation:	Pomerol
Area under vines:	11.5 hectares
Average production:	4,000 cases
Distribution of vines:	One block
Owner:	Société Civile du Château Petrus – two co-owners Mme Lily Lacoste, M. Jean-Pierre Moueix
Director:	M. Christian Moueix
Maître de Chai:	M. Veyssiere
Régisseur:	M. Michel Gillet
Oenologist:	M. Jean-Claude Berrouet

Viticulture

Geology:	90% clay, 10% gravel on the border
Grape varieties:	95% Merlot, 5% Cabernet Franc
Pruning:	Guyot Simple
Rootstock:	3309 – 101/14
Vines per hectare:	6,269
Yield per hectare:	35 hectolitres
Replanting:	One hectare every 8 years, average vine age of 40 years

Vinification

Added yeasts:	No
Length of maceration:	18–25 days
Temperature of fermentation:	30–32°C
Control of fermentation:	With cooler (and heater) by water circulation
Type of vat:	Concrete
Age of casks:	100% new every year
Time in cask:	18–22 months
Vin de presse:	Included from the beginning
Fining:	4–5 egg-whites per cask
Filtration:	None
Type of bottle:	Bordelaise normale

Commercial

Vente Directe:	No
Direct Ordering:	No
Exclusivities:	Ets. J.P. Moueix, Libourne
Agents overseas:	Corney and Barrow in England
Visits:	No

THE TASTING AT ETS. JEAN PIERRE MOUEIX IN LIBOURNE AND AT CHATEAU TROTANOY, 23 January 1985

J.S., Christian Seely, Christian Moueix, M. Veyssiere, Jean-Jacques Moueix, Jean-Claude Berrouet

1983 (From cask.) Very deep intense red. Nose quite closed. Palate rich, fat, lots of Merlot. Tannins quite aggressive. New oak evident.

1982 Colour almost black. Nose much more open than '83, giving lots of fruit – cassis. Very fat, concentration of flavour. Superb rich flavour, very long, but already very approachable.

1981 Deep red, almost as black as 1982. Nose quite evolved, more finesse, more supple than 1983, beginning to harmonise. Will be superb. Long aftertaste.

1980 Colour astonishing for vintage, only a shade less dark than '81. Nose open and rich in fruit. Excellent – already very open with attractive rich flavour. Quite long, can be kept for years, but giving lots of charm now.

1979 Again super colour. Nose big and voluptuous. Huge mouthful – tannic – with enormous concentrated flavour. Will take a long while.

1978 Colour a shade lighter. Nose open and attractive with plenty of fruit. Relatively open flavour. Elegant, and beginning to give of its favours. Not aggressive in tannins. Already superb.

1977 Excellent, bright medium red for 1977. Nose good and ripe for year. Flavour good and generous with none of the unpleasant acidity associated with '77. Ready now, but enough body and power to continue for many years.

1976 Dense, black in colour. Nose powerful, ripe fruit. Big, fat mouthful, very long. Ripe but no hurry at all for this '76.

1975 Colour beautiful and deep. Nose complex and beginning to give off heady aromas. Flavour incredibly concentrated and complex, closed at first, but astounding explosion of all things wonderful follows. Will be a real classic marathon runner.

1970 Deep blacky red. Bouquet heady with powerful ripe fruit aromas. Huge, round concentrated wine. Still astoundingly young, with lots more hidden treasure. Will keep for ever. Wonderful.

1967 Colour very dark, shading to deep brown. Rich, ripe nose. Lovely, mouthfilling and luscious. Perfectly ripe, but with tremendous length and power to keep it going for years.

CHATEAU
La Pointe
POMEROL

La Pointe is situated just outside Libourne, off the D21e just before you reach Catusseau. 500 metres before the village there is a left fork, take this road, and you will find the entrance soon on your right. Château la Pointe is one of the few Pomerol properties to merit a mention in Cocks et Feret of 1868, indeed there is even an illustration. At this time the château belonged to a family called Grandet; the wine must have been of good quality, since its price level at the time was on a par with the lesser Crus Classés of the Médoc, a standard infrequently reached by the little-known wines of Pomerol in the mid-19th century.

It was Monsieur Grandet who built the château; it is a nicely proportioned Directoire-style house,

flanked by two ivy-clad wings, constructed in the early 19th century from 18th-century plans.

In 1941 M. Delahoutre, a Lille négociant, bought La Pointe; it is his son-in-law, Bernard d'Arfeuille, who now owns and lives at la Pointe, though responsibility for day-to-day running of the wine properties and the Libourne-based négociant business falls largely on his two sons, Stéphane and Luc, who lives at Château la Serre (Grand Cru Classé St Emilion). The family also own a property in the Canon-Fronsac, Château Toumalin.

Since the war the vineyard has been totally replanted and the almost derelict chais and cuvier had to be virtually rebuilt. More recently twelve

346

stainless-steel vats have been installed, and a large, ultra-modern reception room has been added.

I was only able to taste the 1983 and the very new 1984 vintages. The '83 had a good colour, a rounded bouquet with fruit and new oak, and a robust style with lots of fruit and good tannin, which I felt would develop fairly quickly. The 1984 was hardly a fair yardstick by which to judge a property with such a normally high proportion of Merlot vines, since this variety almost entirely failed due to an attack of coulure in the spring; however, the young wine had a vigorous colour, smelt good, and had a long tannic flavour.

I have included below the tasting notes of Monsieur Rolland, consultant oenologist to the property, on the previous four vintages.

TECHNICAL INFORMATION

General

Appellation:	Pomerol
Area under vines:	20 hectares
Average production:	8,500 cases
Distribution of vines:	In one piece
Owner:	M. Bernard d'Arfeuille
Director:	M. Stéphane d'Arfeuille
Maître de Chai:	M. David
Consultant Oenologist:	M. Rolland

Viticulture

Geology:	Sandy gravel on clay subsoil
Grape varieties:	75% Merlot, 20% Cabernet Franc, 5% Malbec
Pruning:	Guyot Simple
Rootstock:	101.14, 3309
Vines per hectare:	6,000
Yield per hectare:	38.25 hectolitres average
Replanting:	As necessary to preserve average vine age of 35 years

Vinification

Added yeasts:	No
Length of maceration:	3 weeks
Temperature of fermentation:	28–32°C
Control of fermentation:	By heat-exchange apparatus
Type of vat:	12 stainless steel, the rest epoxy-resin lined steel
Vin de presse:	1st pressing only included, according to vintage
Age of casks:	35% new each vintage
Time in cask:	18–20 months
Fining:	Egg whites
Filtration:	None
Type of bottle:	Bordelaise lourde

Commercial

Vente Directe:	Yes
General Sales:	Contact M. d'Arfeuille, Quai du Priourat, 33500 Libourne
Visits:	Yes, for appointment telephone 57 51 17 57 (office) 57 51 02 11 (château) Office hours.

TASTING NOTES OF M. ROLLAND, OENOLOGIST

1982 Beautiful ruby colour. Nose flowery and new wood. Good fruit in mouth, strong, elegant finish, without excess tannin.
1981 Brilliant ruby. Fine nose, floral, round and long. Rich and elegant with good tannins. Good balance, supple, evolving rapidly – good Pomerol style.
1980 Brilliant cherry red. Fine bouquet, flowery and slightly gamey. Harmonious, supple wine with interesting and charming finish. Good evolution for the vintage, good for four years.
1979 Lovely intense colour. Nose well developed, meaty. Round, balanced, with some tannin still in reserve. A wine with charm and a future. Already showing ripe characteristics.

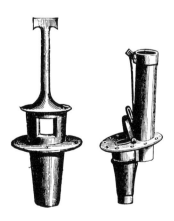

Vieux Chateau Certan

POMEROL

Leave Libourne on the road towards Montagne St Emilion. After passing through Pomerol-Catusseau, leave Château Petit-Village on your left, and turn left at the next crossroads, signposted Pomerol Centre. Vieux Château Certan is the property on your right at the next crossroads.

Before the French Revolution this property belonged to a family called de May, who were forced to sell parts of their estate following the emigration of a member of the family. It is due to this enforced sale that we now have Château Certan Demay, Château Certan-Giraud and this, the original Vieux Château Certan. 'Sertan', as the property is named in Belleyme's late-18th century maps, derives from an old French word for poor land, not suitable for general agriculture. Before the potential of Pomerol's soil for the cultivation of noble vines was understood, such land was exempted from local taxes.

It was not until the middle of last century that the wines of Pomerol were generally recognised for their quality, and this vineyard is one of the first to be mentioned in reference books of the period. In the 1853 edition of Wilhelm Franck Château de 'Curtan' is the only Pomerol vineyard to be named, and in Cocks et Feret of 1868 Vieux Certan is rated the top of a list of seventeen growths, followed by Trotanoy and Petrus.

In 1858 a Parisian named Charles de Bousquet bought the property. He was an absentee owner, but started to enlarge the pretty, 18th-century Chartreuse-style house, adding a taller tower (now out of proportion) at one end; his money ran out, however, probably due to the outbreak of phylloxera, and he fortunately never completed the Victorianisation of what is possibly one of the nicest houses in Pomerol.

The father of the present generation of Thienponts bought Vieux Château Certan in 1924, being already proprietor of Château Troplong-Mondot in St Emilion. The Thienponts are Belgian wine-merchants, and the wine of Vieux Château Certan is naturally well known and much sought after in that country; Troplong-Mondot, incidentally, still finds Belgium to be one of its most important export customers. It is interesting to note that Thienpont was not too enthusiastic about his acquisition of Troplong-Mondot in 1921, but nevertheless was able to pay back the borrowed purchase price in only five years; due to general economic difficulties, however, this fine St Emilion property was sold in 1935.

Georges Thienpont, père, died in 1962. His eldest son runs the Belgian wine-business, and Léon, who is the youngest son, lived at and ran Vieux Château Certan until his untimely death in 1985. Apart from Belgium, Gilbey de Loudenne were the exclusive distributors of this wine in 1971 and 1972, but it is now generally available through the Bordeaux négociants.

The vathouse and first-year cask chai are very traditional in appearance, in spite of having been built only a dozen years ago. The cuves are oak, and a full third of the casks are new every vintage. Vieux Château Certan is perhaps one of the more Médocain Pomerols in style, having a good depth of gravel and a comparatively high percentage of Cabernets in its 13-hectare vineyard. The wine certainly has style, finesse and backbone to complement the powerful robustness of its birthplace. It ages well, and I am sad to say that I have just drunk the last of the superb 1966 in my cellar – it was far from ready to die!

TECHNICAL INFORMATION

General

Appellation:	Pomerol
Area under vines:	13 hectares
Average production:	5,800 cases
Distribution of vines:	In one piece
Owner:	Société Civile du Vieux Château Certan–Héritiers Thienpont
Director:	M. Thienpont
Maître de Chai:	M. Zucchi
Consultant Oenologist:	M. Cazenave

Viticulture

Geology:	Gravel, and lighter gravel/clay
Grape varieties:	50% Merlot, 25% Cabernet Franc, 20% Cabernet Sauvignon, 5% Malbec
Pruning:	Guyot Simple
Rootstock:	420A, 3309 for new vines
Vines per hectare:	5,500
Yield per hectare:	35–40 hectolitres
Replanting:	By rotation

Vinification

Added yeasts:	No
Length of maceration:	20 days average
Temperature of fermentation:	28–30°C
Control of fermentation:	Serpentine water-cooled
Type of vat:	Oak for alcoholic fermentation and maceration Stainless steel used for assemblage, malolactic fermentation and bottling
Vin de presse:	Proportion included, according to vintage
Age of casks:	⅓ new each vintage
Time in cask:	20–22 months
Fining:	Fresh egg-whites
Filtration:	None
Type of bottle:	Bordelaise lourde

Commercial

Vente Directe:	No
Sales:	Through Bordeaux négociants
Exclusive agents:	No
Visits:	Yes: telephone 57 51 17 33 for appointment Hours: 0900–1200, 1400–1700 Monday to Friday

THE TASTING AT VIEUX CHATEAU CERTAN, 31 January 1985
J.S., Christian Seely, Léon Thienpont

1983 Dense, blackish red. Powerful nose with strong blackcurrant fruit. Big, fat mouthful of fruit and strong tannins. A stayer.

1982 Same very deep colour. Nose rounded and elegant with soft fruit. Long in the mouth, excellent and will mature quicker than 1983.

1981 Colour also deep, but a shade lighter than two later vintages. Has more finesse and sinew than 1982 or 1983. Classic Pomerol of considerable elegance. Will make a lovely bottle.

1966 (From own cellar.) Superb colour for a wine nearly 20 years old. Bouquet powerful, evolved, giving off heady fruit scents. Ripe, rich and rounded with a beautiful, lingering cassis aftertaste. Alas! this was my last bottle.

Gastronomie Bordelaise

The Département of the Gironde is, surprisingly, a gastronomic desert; there is, of course, one large oasis, and that is the city of Bordeaux, which has its share of good restaurants, though none boast a rating higher than a single rosette in the Guide Michelin. In a circle with a radius of some 40 km around the city, within which some of the world's finest wines are made, there are amazingly few good watering-holes for the hungry and thirsty pilgrims, and I have listed my personal favourites in the introductory section to each wine-growing region.

The reason given by the Bordelais for this curious anomaly is that most entertaining is done 'in house'. It is certainly true that important customers and favoured visitors are royally fed and wined at the tables of the châteaux, and I, for one, have no complaints about the quality and warmth of Girondin hospitality. This is no comfort, however, to the vast numbers of wine lovers who flood the area every year and are not fortunate enough to have the entrée to the tables of the châtelains. Surely great opportunities exist for enterprising restaurateurs?

Generally speaking the essence of the regional cuisine is simplicity; good basic ingredients such as fresh local fish, meat and vegetables are prepared with the minimum of fuss and serve best to complement the fine, delicate flavours of the great Bordeaux wines. Rich sauces are better suited to the full, voluptuous wines of Burgundy, and the delicate shallot is preferred to the strength and piquancy of garlic or onions. What better marriage could there be than the delicious langoustines of the Gironde estuary partnered by a bottle of Domaine de Chevalier White, or a plain Entrecôte Bordelaise, cooked over an open fire of vine twigs, served with chopped shallots and a noble Margaux, St Julien or Pauillac? The luscious, sweet whites of Sauternes or Barsac are sublime when drunk with fresh foie-gras, Roquefort cheese or, at the end of a meal, with fresh peaches, raspberries or other soft fruits; it is almost always a waste to drink them with rich, complicated puddings, and chocolate is death to a fine Sauternes.

I have collected a few recipes from various châteaux, and list them below.

From Susan Vinding-Diers at Château Rahoul in the Graves

Stuffed Oysters

For 3 people:
1½ dozen oysters
1 small shallot, finely chopped
20 grams butter
¼ pt double cream
1 dessertspoon finely grated Gruyère or Vieux Gouda cheese
Golden breadcrumbs
Freshly gound black pepper
Salt

Fry the shallot in the butter until pale. Add the cream, allow to boil for a minute; add the cheese and thicken with a teaspoon or more of the breadcrumbs. Season with pepper and a little salt.

Open the oysters, arrange them on a flat, ovenproof dish. Cover each oyster with the prepared sauce. Sprinkle lightly with more of the breadcrumbs and place under a hot grill for approximately 2 minutes, allowing the sauce to turn golden.

Serve immediately.

Susan's Stew

1 kilo stewing steak	Butter
30 grams flour	Oil
Salt and pepper	1 teaspoon redcurrant
Bouquet garni	jelly
200 grams carrots	Bread ⎫ For croûtons
200 grams leeks	Garlic ⎭
Red wine	Parsley

Brown the shallots in half butter and half oil (not olive). Cube the meat, flour it and add to saucepan; stir until brown, seasoning with salt and pepper.

Add enough red wine to cover meat, adding the teaspoon of redcurrant jelly.

Cut carrots and leeks into thick pieces and add to the saucepan. Simmer slowly until meat is tender (approx 3 hours). If sauce thickens too much, add stock or water.

Before serving, fry some croûtons in olive oil with a crushed clove of garlic. Garnish the stew with the croûtons, allowing them time to absorb moisture from the stew. Sprinkle with chopped parsley and serve.

Tastes like venison, and, so Susan says, converts all stew-haters!

From Monsieur Noël Raynaud at Château La Croix de Gay in Pomerol

Cuissot de Chevreuil aux cèpes

1 haunch of venison
15 grams butter
10 shallots
Tablespoon bilberry jam
Salt and pepper
For the marinade:

2 onions	1 bottle Pomerol, 2 or 3 years
2 carrots	old
2 tablespoons oil	Bouquet garni (parsley,
1 glass vinegar	thyme, bay leaf, juniper
	berries)

Leave the haunch to marinate in a cool place for 48 hours; turn the meat over twice a day to prevent blackening.

One hour before the meal, drain the vegetables and spices from the marinade. Wipe the haunch, and place it in an oiled oven-dish. Salt and pepper the meat and roast it in a hot oven (200° centigrade) for about 40 minutes for a haunch weighing 1 kilogram.

20 minutes before the roast is done, prepare the sauce as follows:

Melt the butter and fry gently with the shallots, add the drained marinade, leave it on a low heat to reduce slowly, adding the tablespoon of bilberry jam at the last moment.

Serve with cèpes, the delicious boletus mushrooms so loved by the Bordelais, fried in oil and sprinkled with chopped parsley and garlic.

The Raynauds recommend a bottle of ten-year-old Pomerol, preferably la Croix de Gay!

Escargots à la Bordelaise

Serves 8 to 10 people
150 to 200 'petits gris' snails
Rock salt
Vinegar

Thyme, bay leaves, salt and pepper
For the stuffing:
250 grams sausage meat
1 glass cognac
1 small tin tomato concentrate
1 onion
Oil
Tablespoon flour
Salt, pepper and cayenne pepper
Wash your snails thoroughly with rock or sea-salt and vinegar; repeat the operation several times till all the slime has disappeared.
Cook them in stock with thyme, bay leaf, salt and pepper for one hour.
Drain them.
In a saucepan fry the onion in a little oil, add the snails and the sausage-meat. Pour the brandy into the pan and light it. Sprinkle on the flour, cover with water, add the tomato concentrate and leave to cook for a further hour, seasoning to taste with salt, pepper and cayenne.
(Petits Gris are the small snails the Bordelais gather after the Spring showers).

The following four recipes come from Mme François-Xavier Borie of Château Grand-Puy-Lacoste in Pauillac.

Blanquette D'Agneau

A blanquette is a white ragoût bound with a liaison of yolks of egg and cream and accompanied with a garnish of small onions cooked in a *court bouillon* with mushrooms.
A breast of lamb, boned and diced
or 1 kilo of shoulder, cubed evenly
60 gr carrots
½ pt white wine
60 gr small onions
parsley
3 cloves garlic
Salt and pepper
60 gr butter ⎫
60 gr flour ⎭ for the sauce
In a saucepan cover the diced meat with water, add white wine, the carrots, cut, and the onions left whole, add parsley, garlic, salt and pepper. Leave to boil for 5 minutes; skim, and then leave it to simmer for an hour or more if necessary.
Drain the meat, keeping the stock.
Now make a roux with 60 gr of butter, slowly adding flour and stir until pale gold; at that moment add the stock, leave it to cook for 10 minutes and when it is ready to serve, thicken the mixture with an egg yolk.

Matelote D'Anguilles

A matelote is French for fish stew made with red or white wine.

1 kg eel
30 gr flour
60 gr chopped onions
125 gr fatty bacon, diced
125 gr mushrooms
Parsley, thyme, salt and pepper
2 litres red wine, ½ pint water or stock
For the roux 40 gr flour, 40 gr butter

Fry the onions and bacon with flour; when golden brown, put them aside; make a roux with flour and butter; add red wine and water or stock, and the fried onions and bacon; also add the mushrooms, parsley, 1 or 2 pieces of thyme, salt, pepper. Add the eel cut in pieces of around 5 cm in length, and simmer for 35 to 40 minutes.

Place the pieces of eel on a serving dish, cover the fish with the sauce, and serve very hot with a garnish of croûtons or bread fried in butter.

Veau en cocotte à la Bordelaise

1 kg shoulder of veal
200 gr onions
200 gr carrots
20 gr butter
Salt and pepper

Melt the butter in a heavy saucepan, add the meat and brown it slowly. Add salt and pepper and chopped onions and carrots. When the vegetables begin to brown, add a little water.

Cover and let it simmer slowly for 45 minutes to an hour.

To check whether the meat is ready, use a sharp knife to make a cut into the meat; it is cooked if you see a drop of clear liquid right next to the cut.

Slice the meat, place it on a dish and garnish with cèpes fried in butter.

Rognons de veau à la Bordelaise

2 veal kidneys ⎫
1 medium-sized onion ⎪
1 clove garlic ⎪
1 shallot ⎪
2 tablespoons olive oil ⎬ for the sauce
50 gr butter ⎪
1 tablespoon flour ⎪
1 cèpe ⎪
1 glass claret ⎪
1 cup meat juice ⎭

Lightly brown in butter the finely chopped onions, garlic, shallot and cèpe; add pepper, salt,

thyme, then flour: stir until flour browns a little, add claret and meat juice, boil for a few seconds.
Slice the kidneys in two, flour them.
Fry the kidneys in very hot butter; the cooking time is very short as the kidneys should remain a little pink inside. Pour the sauce over the kidneys and sprinkle with chopped parsley.

The following three recipes are staples of the Bordeaux gastonomic scene. Unfortunately nobody in the region volunteered recipes for these dishes, and I am indebted for them to Michèle Gibson, who is not only an inspired cook, but also undertook the daunting task of typing the manuscript of this book.

Lamproie à la Bordelaise

1 medium-sized lamprey
500 gr carrots
1 kg leeks
2 onions
1 clove garlic
Red wine
A knob of butter
30 gr flour ⎫
30 gr butter ⎬ for the roux

The lamprey should be bled, and the blood kept for the sauce.
Scald the fish and remove the skin.
Cut the fish into slices of about 5 cm in thickness.
Melt a knob of butter in a saucepan and add onions, carrots, garlic and fish. Season with salt and pepper, and add enough red wine to cover the lamprey. Boil for 15 minutes.
Drain the fish.
Steam the leeks, and arrange in a dish, alternating with the slices of fish. Keep warm.
Make a roux with the butter and flour, and stir in the drained cooking stock; simmer for 15 minutes.
Pour the sauce over the fish and leeks having mixed in the blood.
Garnish with croûtons.

Entrecôte Bordelaise

1 rib steak weighing 150 grams
4 beef marrow bones sawn in 5 cm lengths
1 chopped shallot
Parsley
Salt and pepper

The steak should be grilled over a charcoal fire (in Bordeaux vine twigs are used).
The marrow bones should be brought to the boil and then simmered for 20 minutes.

353

Fry the shallot in a little butter, add the marrow scooped out of the bone, sprinkle with parsley; spread this mixture over the grilled steak, and serve.

Cèpes à la Bordelaise

500 gr cèpes
4 cloves chopped shallots or garlic
Olive oil for frying
Chopped parsley
Salt and pepper
Wipe the cèpes' heads, chop the stalks.
Fry the heads in olive oil, and when they are browned add the chopped stalks with garlic or shallots and chopped parsley; let them cook in the saucepan 3 or 4 minutes.

The following are suggestions rather than recipes, but I think worthy of inclusion.

From Tom Heeter at Château Nairac in Barsac.
For the enjoyment of Château Nairac in particular, and the vins liquoreux of Sauternes and Barsac in general, he proposes three categories of pleasure:
i) *Simple*
    On melon
    With melon and prosciutto or Jambon de Bayonne
    Roquefort croûtons
    Vichysoisse
    Velouté of mushrooms
    Blanquette de veau
    Quenelles de Brochet
    Chicken à la crème
    Chicken livers
    Mussel soup and mushrooms in cream
ii) *Marvellous*
    Foie gras
    Duck liver with grapes
    Turbot Sauce Mousseline
    Calves' kidneys
    Bourrée à la Reine aux moules
    Mushroom pancakes
    All kinds of feuilletés
    Blanquette de Coquilles St Jacques
    Salmon terrine
    Sole au foie gras
    Sweetbreads – Ris de Veau
    Loup au Sauternes
    Turkey stuffed with chestnuts
and with selected desserts such as
    Tarte aux Amandes
    Sabayon au Sauternes
    Compotes
    Fresh fruit salad
    Sorbets
    Also as a perfect apéritif
iii) *Astonishing, but seductive*
    With Roquefort or genuine Pyrenean sheep's cheese
    Lamproie à la Bordelaise
    Boudin (Black pudding) aux pommes
    Quiches

From Brigitte Lurton at Château Bouscaut in the Graves; Red Graves stand up better to highly flavoured dishes than many Médocs; e.g. Game, certain cooked fish, strong cheese. White Graves, especially those aged in cask and containing a preponderance of Sémillon grapes, are best with five to ten years bottle age; they then go well with all fish – except smoked varieties – in sauces, the richer fish grilled, white meats like poultry, pork and veal, cheese and smooth pâtés.

The Comte Alexandre de Lur Saluces particularly favours Turbot with Sauce Mousseline with Château d'Yquem.

Hamilton Narby at Château Guiraud recommends drinking his fine Sauternes as an apéritif, with foie gras, Roquefort, poultry and lobster.

Glossary

Ampelology The science of viticulture

Appellation Controlée The legislation under which the wines of France are strictly controlled as to their nomenclature. The law is administered by the Institut National des Appellations d'Origine, or INAO, and defines the area of production, permissible grape varieties, viticultural and vinification methods, maximum yield and minimum alcoholic contents.

Assemblage The blending of the wine that will be bottled under a property's label. The constituent parts will be of wines from different grape varieties, various parts of the vineyard and from varying stages of the harvest. Rejected wines are either bottled under a château's second label, or will be sold off to be marketed as generic wine of a commune, labelled simply 'Margaux', 'St Julien', 'Pomerol' etc. This can be the produce of young vines, or may just not reach the exacting standards set by a proprietor for inclusion in his 'Grand Vin'.

Barrique The standard oak cask used for the first twelve to thirty months of ageing, of 225 litres capacity.

Bentonite A colloidal agent used for fining white wine.

Botrytis Cinerea The all-important fungoid growth, which forms on the skins of the grapes in Barsac and Sauternes, shrivelling the berries and concentrating the sugars and flavours of the juice which results in these wonderful *vins liquoreux*. Microclimatic conditions which allow its development obtain only here, in parts of the Rhine and Moselle valleys and in the Hungarian Tokay vineyards. Also known as *pourriture noble*, or the Noble Rot.

Bottle sickness A temporary state of 'tiredness'; a wine can experience this malady after the shock of bottling, but it will pass after some months in bottle.

Bouillie Bordelaise Bordeaux Mixture, a compound solution of copper sulphate and slaked lime, sprayed on the vines against mildew.

Cabernet Franc Red grape variety, used throughout the Bordeaux vineyards, more in St Emilion and Pomerol than the Médoc, where it is also called the 'Bouchet'.

Cabernet Sauvignon Principal grape variety of the Médoc and the Graves red wines. The aristocrat of the Bordeaux red varieties, it gives colour, tannin, breeding and longevity; also used in lesser proportions in St Emilion and Pomerol.

Cépage French word for 'grape variety'; e.g.: Cabernet Sauvignon, Sémillon etc.

Chai Above-ground cellars in which the wine matures in cask.

Chapeau The thick layer of pulp and skins that forms on top of the must during fermentation.

Chaptalisation The addition of sugar to the must before fermentation; only rarely authorised in Bordeaux in difficult years like 1965 and 1968.

Chef de Culture The vineyard foreman.

Classification The first official, and most famous classification of the wines of Bordeaux was in 1855, when the Chamber of Commerce were required to produce a graded list of all the great wines of Bordeaux for the Great Exhibition in Paris in that year. Only the wines of the Médoc and Sauternes were categorised, but Château Haut-Brion in the Graves was included in the Premiers Crus for its consistent outstanding quality. Apart from the elevation of Mouton-Rothschild to Premier Cru status in 1973, the 1855 classification remains in force today, and is, by and large, still a fair yardstick. The wines of the Graves were first classified in 1953, and this listing was revised in 1959. The wines of St Emilion were not classified until 1955 and the neighbouring Pomerol vineyards have never been the subject of any classification.

Coulure The dropping-off of the tiny buds at flowering time in June, caused by adverse weather conditions. The Merlot, flowering earlier than other varieties, is particularly susceptible, as in 1984.

Courtier Wine broker, a term peculiar to Bordeaux. The *courtiers* introduce sellers to buyers, acting on a strictly defined commission rate; they do not buy or sell wine themselves. They also act as intermediaries in the buying and selling of wine properties.

Cru French for growth. Denotes a vineyard of high quality–thus Grand Cru means a 'great wine', Cru Classé, a classified vineyard, Cru Bourgeois, a good, medium-quality property etc.

Cru Bourgeois Wine property rated just below the Crus Exceptionnels in the 1855 classification.

Cru Exceptionnel Wine property classified immediatly below the Crus Classés, and above the Crus Bourgeois.

Cuve The French for vat, the vessels used for fermentations, assemblage and storing the wine. These may be of varying sizes from 25 to 200 hectolitres, and are made of oak, cement, steel or stainless steel.

Cuvier or **Cuverie** The building which houses the fermenting vats.

Dégustation Tasting.

Double Magnum Bottle containing the equivalent of 4 standard bottles.

Dumb A tasting expression, used to denote a wine which remains hard and difficult to taste for a long time, usually due to excessive tannin.

Egrappage The process of separating the berries from the stalks. Egrappoir is the machine used for this purpose.

Fermé A tasting term; 'closed', or shut in, hard, still developing.

Finesse Elegance or breeding of a wine.

Fining This operation, called 'collage' in French, is the clarification of the wine by the addition of colloidal matter such as beaten fresh egg-whites in cask, the traditional method for Grand Cru red wines; gelatine or powdered egg albumen are also used in vat as an alternative. For white wines, fining is usually carried out with bentonite, either in cask or vat.

Floraison The flowering of the vine, which takes place in June in Bordeaux.

Foudre Large oak cask, used sometimes in Bordeaux for storing and maturing wine.

Generic wine Wine that is sold under the commune name of an Appellation, such as 'Sauternes', 'Médoc', 'St Emilion', etc.

Hogshead The English term for a *barrique* or cask, equivalent to 25 cases of twelve 75 cl bottles.

Impériale Large bottle, containing the equivalent of 8 standard bottles.

Jeroboam Bottle containing the equivalent of 6 standard bottles.

Levure Yeast; *levurage* means the introduction of non-natural yeast strains in order to start the fermentation.

Magnum Bottle containing 1.5 litres, double the size of a standard bottle.

Maître de Chai The cellar-master.

Malbec A red grape used in small proportions throughout the region.

Malolactic fermentation Secondary fermentation that takes place after the first, alcoholic fermentation, in which the malic acid converts to lactic acid. The beneficial effects of this process have only been understood and deliberately encouraged relatively recently.

Merlot The principal red grape of St Emilion and Pomerol, it also appears in lesser proportions in Médoc and Graves vineyards; maturing a week to ten days before the Cabernets, it is also susceptible to *coulure* at flowering time in June.

Mildew A wine disease which is treated by spraying with a solution of copper sulphate and slaked lime.

Muscadelle A white grape used in very small proportions, mainly in the Sauternes vineyards. Often confused with the Muscat, it gives a somewhat similar rich, dessert-grapey flavour.

Must Grape pulp and juice before it is fermented.

Négociant Wine merchant.

Oenology The science of wine; an oenologist is therefore a wine scientist.

Oidium Also known as 'powdery mildew'; a fungus disease of the vine which attacks the leaves and splits the berries, and eventually kills the vine if untreated. Originating from America, it first appeared in Europe in 1854, where it caused widespread devastation. The effective treatment, spraying with a solution of copper-sulphate and lime known as Bouillie Bordelaise was discovered in Bordeaux at Château Dauzac in 1855.

Ouillage The topping-up of the casks of wine, performed twice weekly, to replace wine lost by evaporation and prevent harmful contact with the air.

Palus Lower-lying marshy land, producing wines of inferior quality.

Petit Verdot A late-maturing red grape, mostly seen in small quantities in the Médoc. It gives a wine of deep colour, strong tannins and great concentration. It has its devotees, but it is difficult to grow, and has been abandoned by many properties.

Phylloxera The *Phylloxera vastatrix* is an aphid, a burrowing louse which attacks the vine roots and kills the vine. It virtually wiped out the vineyards of Europe at the end of the last century, until it was discovered that the only effective remedy was to graft the European varieties on to American rootstocks, which are resistant to the pest.

Pourriture Noble See Botrytis Cinerea.

Racking The 'running-off' of a wine from its lees in cask, and transfer to a clean cask; this is usually carried out every three months during the period that the wine stays in cask. The French term is soutirage.

Régisseur The general manager of a wine property.

Sauvignon A white grape, dominant in the white-wine vineyards of the Graves, but also used in lesser proportions in the making of Sauternes. It gives a fresh, crisp wine with great clarity of style.

Sémillon The principal grape of Sauternes, most readily affected by the all-important *pourriture noble*; it is also used in lesser quantities in the dry white wine of the Graves. It gives suppleness and a rich fullness to the wine.

Sur plaque The filtration method usually adopted before bottling, using cellulose filters.

Sur terre A filtration system, employed when the wine is transferred from vat to cask; the wine is passed through a screen of powdered shells, or fine earth, to remove impurities.

Soutirage See Racking.

Tannin One of the most important components in Bordeaux red wine. It is an astringent substance drawn from the skins, pips and stems, and gives character and longevity to the wine.

Tonneau Literally a 'large barrel'; although no such container exists, it is the standard measure in which wine is sold in Bordeaux. One tonneau of wine equals 100 cases of 12 × 75 cl bottles, or four casks or hogsheads.

Tri Literally 'sorting out'. Expression used for the successive passages made through the vineyards of Barsac and Sauternes, selecting only the grapes at their optimum state of 'noble rot'. The pickers may pass through the vines from three to as many as twelve times.

Ullage The air-space between the surface of the wine and the cork. Too great an ullage in a bottle of wine, usually caused by a bad cork or bad storage, usually means the wine will have suffered.

Veraison Term used to describe the turning of the grape from green to red, usually starting in August.

Vigneron Winemaker, winegrower, skilled vineyard-worker.

Vin de presse Wine made from the pressings of the residues, after the natural 'free run' wine has been made. It is very harsh and tannic, and is used in small amounts to bolster tannin levels in the assemblage of the Grand Vin.

Volatile acidity The state in a wine caused by the presence of acetic acid; it gives a vinegary flavour, and is often caused by insufficient attention to ouillage, or topping up of the wine in cask during its first year.

Index

The sections devoted to individual châteaux are indicated by page references in **bold** type.
References in *italic* type indicate people present at tasting sessions.